PAST TO PRESENT:
Ideas That Changed Our World

Stuart Hirschberg
Rutgers University
Terry Hirschberg

Prentice
Hall

Upper Saddle River, New Jersey 07458

Library of Congress Cataloging-in-Publication Data

HIRSCHBERG, STUART.
    Past to present : ideas that changed our world / Stuart Hirschberg, Terry Hirschberg.
        p. ; cm.
    Includes index.
    ISBN 0-13-097948-1
        1. College readers.   2. English language—Rhetoric—Problems, exercises, etc.   3.
Interdisciplinary approach in education—Problems, exercises, etc.   4. Report
writing—Problems, exercises, etc.   I. Hirschberg, Terry.   II. Title.

    PE1417.H535 2002
    808′ .0427—dc21

                                                                    2002019742

VP, Editor in Chief: Leah Jewell
Senior Acquisitions Editor: Corey Good
Production Editor: Maureen Benicasa
Production Assistant: Elizabeth Best
Prepress and Manufacturing Buyer: Mary Ann Gloriande
Manager, Prod/Formatting and Art: Guy Ruggiero
Marketing Manager: Rachel Falk
Marketing Assistant: Christine Moodie
Text Permissions Specialist: Frederick T. Courtright
Image Permissions Coordinator: Debbie Latronica
Cover Director: Jayne Conte
Cover Art: Jan Vermeer (1632–1675), *Head of a Girl (Girl with a Pearl Earring)*,
1665–1666. Oil on canvas. 44.5 × 39 cm ($17\frac{1}{2}$ × $15\frac{3}{8}$ in.) Royal Cabinet of Paintings
Mauritins, The Hague, The Netherlands.

This book was set in 10/12 ITC Bookman Light by DM Cradle Associates
and was printed and bound by Courier Companies, Inc.
The cover was printed by Phoenix Color Corp.

For permission to use copyrighted material, grateful
acknowledgment is made to the copyright holders
on pages 745–747, which are considered an extension
of this copyright page.

© 2003 by Pearson Education, Inc.
Upper Saddle River, New Jersey 07458

Printed in the United States of America
10 9 8 7 6 5 4 3 2 1

ISBN 0-13-097948-1

Pearson Education LTD., London
Pearson Education Australia PTY, Limited, Sydney
Pearson Education Singapore, Pte. Ltd
Pearson Education North Asia Ltd, Hong Kong
Pearson Education Canada, Ltd., Toronto
Pearson Educación de Mexico, S.A. de C.V.
Pearson Education—Japan, Tokyo
Pearson Education Malaysia, Pte. Ltd
Pearson Education, Upper Saddle River, New Jersey

CONTENTS

2   THE COLLECTIVE EXPERIENCE:
The Human Condition   121

6   THE MIND AND THE SPIRIT:
Understanding the Unknown — 511

RHETORICAL CONTENTS

IRONY, HUMOR, SATIRE

JOURNALS, DIARIES, LETTERS

SPEECHES

INTERVIEWS

PREFACE

Past to Present: Ideas That Changed Our World is intended for freshman composition, advanced and honors composition, history of ideas courses, and for courses that emphasize writing across the disciplines.

This book provides insight into the sources of the ideas that have shaped entire fields of study within the college curriculum, using the words of either those pioneers who have had great influence in these fields or those scholars who investigate the evolution of these important ideas.

The text is divided into seven thematic chapters, each tracing the history of important ideas that have, in many cases, defined the way we think about basic aspects of nature, culture, and the world. In the 74 selections included in this text, we can follow the evolution of important concepts from their origins through their articulation by the most creative artists and thinkers of every era, from the past to the present. The selections are arranged to illustrate the past-to-the-present adaption and/or reaction to important ideas that have shaped modern culture.

The readings are drawn equally from the humanities, social and political sciences, and the natural and physical sciences, and are designed to widen the students' field of vision to include the major ideas and "idea makers" who have shaped the disciplines that comprise the college curriculum. This text broadens the students' perspectives to include disciplines outside their majors and personal interests.

The wide range of rhetorical patterns used by these writers offers an unparalleled opportunity to study the techniques and strategies used by great writers in presenting the ideas that have shaped our world. We give extensive consideration to these rhetorical techniques, especially argumentation, and provide guidance in critical reading and in writing analytical essays.

CHAPTER DESCRIPTIONS

The readings in *Past to Present: Ideas That Changed Our World* are organized to highlight connections between past ideas and present applications and to move outward from the personal to the public, from the individual to the universal, and from the microcosm of the self to the macrocosm of the universe. To make these great ideas relevant for modern generations of readers we emphasize the issues of culture, race, social class, and technology. The seven chapters move from the individual experience (featuring letters, diaries, and essays by important figures) and the collective experience (that shapes entire societies) to consider the historical dimension and the natural and physical worlds. We cover profound reflections on the mind and the spirit and can appreciate the way the arts of civilization (art, music, drama, literature, architecture, cinema, dance, and language) have enhanced human existence.

Chapter 1, "The Individual Experience: Private Lives, Public Voices," introduces a range of autobiographical writing by personalities whose experiences have touched the lives of many people and whose works have had a profound impact in diverse cultures across the centuries.

Chapter 2, "The Collective Experience: The Human Condition," introduces authors who confront fundamental problems that have challenged the human species—overpopulation and the availability of food, the conflict between political equity and racism, the damaging effects of colonialism, and power inequities between men and women throughout history.

Chapter 3, "The Historical Dimension: The Importance of the Past," attests to the value of studying how the present has been shaped by events of the past, including an examination of why some civilizations flourish while others fail, whether history makes men or men make history, the causes and effects of war in the nineteenth and twentieth centuries, and the immigrant experience.

Chapter 4, "The Natural World: Instinct and Survival," looks at the impact of Darwin's theories and investigates migration and aggression in animals, the role of genes in the acquisition of language, the age-old question of nature versus nurture, and ethical issues arising from vivisection and cloning.

Chapter 5, "The Physical Universe: Knowledge of Animate and Inanimate Worlds," explores the impact of the oceans on every aspect of human life from biblical times to the present. It looks at changing conceptions of physicists and philosophers about the Earth and its place in the universe and touches on the world-altering implications of technology.

Chapter 6, "The Mind and the Spirit: Understanding the Unknown," presents the compelling ideas that have guided the search for the meaning of human existence, as framed by philosophers, psychologists, artists, the world's major religions, and modern-day skeptics.

Chapter 7, "The Arts of Civilization: The Human Element," examines the profound role that the arts—painting, sculpture, architecture, literature, drama, cinema, music, and dance—have played in enriching human existence. The readings encompass the Greek tragedies, Renaissance paintings and sculpture and the great cathedrals and mosques, through the evolution of English, realism in literature, and abstract art, to the invention of movies, and the pervasive effects of advertising on contemporary society.

EDITORIAL APPARATUS

The introduction, including sections on Critical Reading, Using Rhetorical Patterns to Develop Ideas, Purposes for Writing, Solving a Problem, and Arguing and Persuading, discusses the critical skills of reading for ideas and organization, marking and annotating as you read, keeping a journal, writing summaries, and generating topics for writing. We also explore the way authors, scholars, and scientists have adapted traditional rhetorical patterns (particularly argumentation) to support generalizations, assemble evidence, convey meaning, provide coherence, and persuade audiences to accept their interpretations. This introduction is intended to help students understand how writers develop and support their opinions.

Chapter introductions present the rationale for the organization of the selections in that chapter, and a short overview of how the readings relate to the central theme and illustrate its evolution from the past to the present.

Biographical sketches preceding each selection provide background information on the writer, and a subsequent discussion ("Approaching . . .") provides a context in which to understand the ideas being presented and analyzes salient rhetorical and stylistic features unique to that writer.

End-of-selection questions are of three kinds: (1) "Reading Critically for Ideas, Structure, and Style" asks students to think critically about the content, meaning, and purpose of the selections and to evaluate the author's underlying assumptions and rhetorical strategies; (2) "Extending Insights Through Writing" affords opportunities for readers to extend their thinking beyond the particular text, in expository and persuasive modes, and by drawing on sources discovered through research in the library and on the Internet; and (3) "Connecting Perspectives" on the theme of the chapter (for example, "Individual Experience") focuses on the relationships between readings within each chapter in ways that illuminate different perspectives on the same idea.

A separate set of "Book Connections" at the end of each chapter link readings between chapters to emphasize the evolution of important ideas across disciplines.

An appendix, "Writing About Great Ideas," discusses the important skills students need in order to write analytical essays that argue for an interpretation (illustrated by a sample comparative essay). Key points include formulating a thesis, drafting an essay, supporting opinions with evidence, paraphrasing, quoting, revising, and documenting sources.

INSTRUCTOR'S MANUAL

An accompanying instructor's manual provides: (1) sample syllabi and suggestions for organizing courses with different emphasis (argumentation, cultural studies, writing across the curriculum, history of ideas); (2) additional background on the selections; (3) illustrative responses to end-of-selection questions; (4) additional suggestions for writing assignments; (5) sentence outlines for some of the more challenging selections; and (6) bibliographies on the authors and the ideas for students who wish to explore these in greater detail.

ACKNOWLEDGMENTS

A particular debt of gratitude is owed to those teachers of composition who offered thoughtful comments and have given this book the benefit of their collective scholarship, judgment, and teaching experience. We would very much like to thank all the instructors who reviewed various stages of the manuscript, including Roy Stamper, North Carolina State Univ.; Richard Rupple, Viterbo Univ.; Raymond Duda, Univ. of Mich.; MeKonnen Haile, San Antonio College; Annabel Servat, Southeastern Louisiana Univ.; and Nancy Bara-Smith, Slippery Rock Univ. We owe much to the able staff at Prentice Hall, especially production editor Maureen Benicasa and to Fred T. Courtright for obtaining permissions. No expression of thanks can adequately convey our appreciation to our editor, Corey Good, for his enthusiasm and encouragement and to Leah Jewell for her support.

Stuart Hirschberg
Terry Hirschberg

INTRODUCTION

CRITICAL READING

The reading you do in an academic context introduces you to important ideas embodied in the texts that are at the core of every field of study. For example, you might read Aristotle, Frederick Douglass, Thomas Paine, Simone de Beauvoir, Charles Darwin, Plato, Sigmund Freud, or writers of equal stature throughout your college career. In your courses, you will encounter many profound ideas for the first time. When you read these texts you will respond to and interact with them in ways that are unique to your experiences. When you critically read you locate and analyze the important ideas the writer communicates and, at the same time, compare these ideas with your own values and create your own sense of what the text means to you. Critical reading also involves comparing what one writer says to the observations and claims of other writers.

The process of critically reading academic texts differs from ordinary reading (for example, of a newspaper or popular magazine article) in an important way. You need to read selections a second and even a third time in order to look beyond the immediately observable features (the topic of the essay, its length, or the author's stance) to a deeper understanding of the subordinate, but related, ideas and the underlying organization of the entire essay.

Critical thinking, and the closely related skills of critical reading and writing, might be new terms and concepts for you, but they form the basis for the way in which you become a successful reader and writer. Each skill depends on the others since much of what you write in college is based on your response to what others have written. During the writing process you learn how to explore the ideas of others and to form and support your own opinions. Some of the works you read may serve as models for your own writing, but first you must be able to identify the organizational strategies the writers use to present their thoughts.

The process of learning to read critically begins with becoming sensitive to what the writers are saying about the issues and comparing their assessments to your own experiences and knowledge. The most interesting texts are often the ones that challenge you the most since they offer new information and insights and present different perspectives on an issue. The process of reacting to what you read will prompt you to ask questions about your own experiences; this helps you create and support your opinions and ideas. Critical reading involves being able to evaluate the relative strengths and weaknesses of the author's presentation. When you read critically, you also develop the ability to distinguish statements that are facts (and can be verified) from those that are simply opinions. This process will prevent you from passively accepting information and uncritically accepting other people's beliefs without questioning them.

The writing you do in your college courses requires you to enter a conversation with the authors whose works you read. While we don't mean conversation in a literal sense, we do ask you to open a dialogue between yourself and the text. As in a real conversation, imagine that you are free to pose questions, ask for clarification of a point or start your own line of reasoning in response to what you have read. You can agree or disagree, defend your point of view, and even argue as long as you interact with the text. In this sense, you are the latest arrival at an ongoing conversation between the writer and all previous sources to which his or her essay is responding. You might think of it as being invited to a party where you can participate in many fascinating discussions that have started before you arrived.

Reading for Ideas and Organization

One of the most important skills you will need to develop is the ability to survey unfamiliar articles, essays, or excerpts and come away with an accurate understanding of what the author wanted to communicate and how the material is presented. On the first, and in subsequent readings of any of the selections in this text, especially the longer ones, pay particular attention to the title, look for the introductory and concluding paragraphs (that emphasize the author's initial statement or summary of key ideas), identify headings and subheadings (and determine the relationship between these and the title), and locate any unusual terms necessary to fully understand the author's concepts.

Finding a Thesis

As you read through an essay, look for cues to enable you to recognize the main parts or help you to perceive its overall organization. If possible, locate the author's thesis (whether stated specifically or implied) and underline it or state it in your own words. Then work your way through fairly rapidly, identifying the main ideas and the sequence in which they are presented. As you identify an important idea, ask yourself how this idea relates to the thesis statement you identified or to the idea expressed in the title.

Finding a thesis involves discovering the idea that serves as the focus of the essay. The thesis is often stated in the form of a single sentence that asserts the author's response to an issue that others might respond to in different ways. For example, in "Something About English" (Chapter 7), Paul Roberts expresses his opinion that historical events have shaped the evolution of the English language:

> *No understanding of the English language can be very satisfactory without a notion of the history of the language.* But we shall have to make due with just a notion. The history of English is long and complicated, and we can only hit the high spots.

The thesis (in italics) represents the writer's view of the subject from a certain perspective. Writers often place the thesis in the first paragraph, or group of paragraphs, so that the readers will be able to perceive the relationship between the supporting evidence and the main idea.

As you read, you might wish to underline the topic sentence or main idea of each paragraph or section (since key ideas are often developed over the course of several paragraphs). Jot it down in your own words in the margins, identify supporting statements and evidence (such as examples, statistics, and the testimony of authorities), and try to discover how the author organizes the material to support the development of these important ideas. Supporting material, in whatever form it appears, is always more specific than the main idea that it clarifies, illustrates, or develops.

TRANSITIONS AND LOGICAL CONNECTIONS In order to better see the relationships among major sections in the essay, pay particular attention to important transitional words, phrases, or short paragraphs used to connect long sections. Noticing how certain words or phrases act as transitions to link paragraphs or sections together will dramatically improve your reading comprehension. Also, look for section summaries, where the author draws together several preceding ideas.

Writers use certain words to signal the starting point of a chain of reasoning or series of statements that are designed to support the main idea. If you detect any of the following terms, look for the main idea they introduce:

since	as shown by	for the reason that
because	in as much as	may be inferred from
for	otherwise	may be derived from
as	as indicated by	may be deduced from
follows from	the reason is that	in view of the fact that

An especially important category of words is that which includes signals that the author will be stating a conclusion. Words to look for are:

therefore	in summary
hence	which shows that
thus	which means that
so	and which entails
accordingly	consequently
in consequence	proves that
it follows that	as a result
we may infer	which implies that
I conclude that	which allows us to infer
in conclusion	points to the conclusion that

As important as (if not more important than) such linear connections (because, therefore) are words that signal a shift in focus:

yet
however
on the other hand
surprisingly
in contrast
paradoxically
but

You may find it helpful to create a running dialogue with the author in the margins, posing and then trying to answer the basic questions as to *who, what, where, when,* and *why,* and to note observations on how the main idea of the article is related to the title. These notes can later be used to evaluate how effectively any specific section contributes to the overall line of thought.

Evaluating Tone

An important skill to develop in critical reading is the ability to make inferences about the writer from clues in the text. Looking beyond the facts (to see what they imply) requires readers to look carefully at the writer's word choices, level of knowledge about the subject, use of personal experience, and the skill with which the writer arranges various elements of the essay. Inferences about the writer's background, attitude towards the subject, purpose in writing the essay, and values go beyond what is on the page, but can help you get a sense of what the writer is like as a person.

Tone or "voice" plays a crucial element in establishing a writer's credibility. Tone is produced by the combined effect of word choice, sentence structure, and the writer's success in adapting his or her particular "voice" to suit the subject, the audience, and the occasion. When we try to identify and analyze the tone of a work, we are seeking to hear the actual "voice" of the author in order to understand how he or she intended the work to be perceived. It is important for writers to know what image of themselves they project. Writers should consciously decide on the particular style and tone that best suits the audience, the occasion, and their purpose in writing about a particular subject.

IRONY, HUMOR, AND SATIRE   A particular kind of tone encountered in many essays is called irony. Writers adopt this rhetorical strategy to express a discrepancy between the ideal and the real, the literal and the implied, and (most frequently) between the way things are and the way the writer thinks things ought to be.

Sometimes it is difficult to tell that not everything the writer says is intended to be taken literally. Authors will occasionally say the opposite of what they mean to catch the reader's attention. If your first response is "Can the writer really be serious?" look for signals that the writer really means the opposite of what is being said. One clear signal that the author is being ironic is a noticeable disparity between the tone and the subject. For example, George Bernard Shaw, in "She Would Have Enjoyed It," (Chapter 1) observes: "Why does a funeral always sharpen one's sense of humor and rouse one's spirits?" The clash between the subject (Shaw's mother's funeral) and Shaw's iconoclastic comment regarding funerals in general alerts the reader that Shaw is being satiric.

Irony is especially important in satire, an enduring form of argument that uses parody and caricature to poke fun at a subject, idea, or person. The satirist can create a "mask" or *persona* that is very different from the author's real self in order to shock the audience into a new awareness about an established institution or custom. Folly, greed, corruption, pride, self-righteous complacency, cultural pretensions, and hypocrisy, are frequent targets of the satirist's pen.

ANNOTATING AS YOU READ

The most effective way to think about what you read is to make notes and ask questions as you go along. Making notes as you read encourages you to think carefully about the meaning of each sentence.

This process, called annotating the text, only requires a pen or a pencil. There are as many styles of annotating as there are readers, and you will discover your own preferred method once you have done it a few times. Some readers underline major points or statements and jot down their reactions in the margins. Others prefer to summarize each paragraph or section to help them follow the author's line of thought. Still others circle key words or phrases that help them understand the main ideas. Your notes are a kind of conversation with the text in which you can ask questions and make observations. Be sure to mark unfamiliar words or phrases to look up later. Try to distinguish the main ideas from supporting points and examples and use the following guidelines to evaluate whether the author makes a credible case for the conclusions reached.

GUIDELINES FOR EVALUATING WHAT YOU READ

- When evaluating an essay, consider what the author's *purpose* is in writing it. Was it to inform, explain, solve a problem, make a recommendation, amuse, enlighten, or achieve some combination of these goals? How is the tone, or voice, the author projects related to the purpose in writing the essay?

- Closely related to the author's purpose are the *assumptions* or beliefs the writer expects the audience to share. Are these assumptions commonly held? Compare them with your own beliefs about the subject and evaluate whether the author provides sound reasons and supporting evidence to persuade you to agree.

- How effectively does the writer use authorities, statistics, or examples as *evidence* to support the claim? For example, do the *authorities* the author cites display any obvious biases, and are they really experts in that particular field. (Watch for experts described as "often quoted" or "highly placed reliable sources" without accompanying names, credentials, or appropriate documentation.) Is the author fair-minded in presenting authorities who hold opposing views?

- If *statistics* are cited to support a point, try to evaluate whether they come from verifiable and trustworthy sources and whether the author has interpreted them in ways that are slanted to support his or her interpretation. For example, are they current and generated from a representative sample and not just selected to support a pre-existing agenda?

- If real-life *examples* are used to support the author's opinions, evaluate whether they are truly representative, or are too atypical to serve as evidence. If the author relies on hypothetical examples or analogies evaluate whether they are too farfetched to support the author's claims.

- Look closely at how *key terms* are defined. Can they be defined in different ways? If so, has the author provided clear reasons to explain why one definition rather than another is preferable?

- One last point—take a close look at the idea expressed in the *title* before and after you read the essay to see how it relates to the main idea.

KEEPING A READING JOURNAL

The most effective way to keep track of your thoughts and impressions and to review what you have learned is to keep a reading journal. The comments you record in your journal may express your reflections, observations, questions, and reactions to the essays you read. You can write down questions that occur to you as you read, copy interesting or memorable phrases or sentences from the selection, give your opinion, and agree or disagree with the author's points. A reading journal will allow you to record your insights, keep track of questions you have, and unfamiliar words you intend to look up. Although there is no set form for what a journal should look like, reading journals are most useful for expanding your brief annotations into more complete entries that explore in depth your reactions to what you have read.

Summarizing

Reading journals may also be used to record summaries of the essays you read. The value of summarizing is that it requires you to pay close attention to the reading in order to distinguish the main points from the supporting details. Summarizing tests your understanding of the material by requiring you to restate concisely the author's main ideas in your own words. First, create a list composed of sentences that express the essential idea of each paragraph or of each group of related paragraphs. Your previous underlining of topic sentences, main ideas, and key terms (as part of the process of critical reading) will help you follow the author's line of thought. Next, whittle down this list still further by eliminating repetitive ideas. Then formulate a thesis statement that expresses the main idea in the article. Start your summary with the thesis statement and combine your notes so that the summary flows together and reads easily.

For example, here is a summary of Matt Ridley's essay, "Genome," in Chapter 4:

> In "Genome," Matt Ridley argues that a gene on chromosome 7, discovered by researchers in the Human Genome Project, guides our acquisition of language. This discovery is significant since it governs an aspect of human behavior hitherto believed to be solely a product of learning and culture. Previously, Noam Chomsky had theorized that there was a biological basis for a "language instinct" that allows us to acquire, use, and understand language. Chomsky's theory was validated by Derek Bickerton, who discovered that the children of migrant workers (who spoke different languages) evolved a fully formed Creole language within a generation. A recent study by Myrna Gopnick points to the existence of a genetic basis for certain kinds of language impairment (such as the inability to form plurals, observable in a family over three generations). Ridley concludes that the existence of a genetic basis for language does not conflict with Darwin's theory of natural selection since the evolution of even a slightly greater capacity to communicate would have conferred an enormous survival advantage for our ancestors.

Remember that summaries should be much shorter (usually no longer than half a page) than the original text (whether the original is one page or twenty pages long) and should accurately reflect the central ideas of the article in as few words as possible. Try not to intrude your own opinions or critical evaluations into the summary. Besides requiring you to read the original piece more closely, summaries are necessary first steps in developing papers that draw on materials from different sources. The test for a good summary, of course, is whether a person reading it without having read the original article would get an accurate, balanced, and complete account of the original material.

Using Your Reading Journal to Generate Ideas for Writing

You can use all the material in your reading journal (annotations converted to journal entries, reflections, observations, questions, rough and final summaries) to relate your own ideas to the ideas of the person who wrote the essay. Here are several different kinds of strategies you can use as you analyze an essay in order to generate material for your own:

1. What is missing in the essay? Information that is not mentioned is often just as significant as information the writer

chose to include. First, you must already have summarized the main points in the article. Then, make up another list of points that are not discussed, that is, missing information that you expected an article of this kind to cover or touch on. Write down the possible reasons why this missing material has been omitted, censored, or downplayed. What possible purpose could the author have had? Look for vested interests or biases that could explain why information of a certain kind is missing.

2. You might analyze an essay in terms of what you already know and what you didn't know about the issue. To do this, simply make a list of what concepts were already familiar to you and a second list of information or concepts that were new to you. Then write down three to five questions you would like answered about this new information and make a list of possible sources you might consult for answers.

3. Do you see any problems with the solutions the author presents? List the short-term and long-term effects or consequences of the action the writer recommends. Evaluate whether any positive short-term benefits would be offset by possible negative long-term consequences not mentioned by the author. This evaluation might provide you with a starting point for your own essay.

4. Clearly state what the author's position is on the subject and then imagine what other people in his or her society would say about the same issue, but from a different perspective. Now try to imagine that you are an arbitrator negotiating an agreement and formulate a viewpoint that would satisfy both the author and someone holding a different point of view.

USING RHETORICAL PATTERNS TO DEVELOP IDEAS

To achieve clear, accurate and effective communication, many authors, scholars, and scientists have adapted a variety of traditional writing strategies to meet the demands of style, format, and methodology within their particular fields of study. These rhetorical strategies are used by writers as a means to assemble evidence, support generalizations, convey meaning, give coherence to their writing, and most importantly, communicate what they have discovered to different audiences. An important part of becoming an effective writer depends on the ability to identify and evaluate how writers use these common patterns or techniques of thinking to develop their ideas. Thus, writers might describe how something looks, narrate an experience, analyze how something works, provide examples, define important terms, establish a classification, compare and contrast, create an analogy, explore the causes of something, diagnose a problem, or argue for an interpretation. What follows is an explanation of each pattern with examples from readings in this book.

Describing

Writers use descriptions for a variety of purposes, ranging from portraying the appearance of people, objects, or events to revealing the writer's feelings and reactions to these people, objects, or events.

A skillful writer will often arrange a description around a central impression in much the same way as a good photographer will locate a focal point for a picture. For example, in "Steerage" (Chapter 3), Oscar Handlin organizes the details of his description to give his readers insight into the cramped quarters and hardship that hundreds of thousands had to endure in order to immigrate to the United States on ships in the last century:

> Below decks is the place, its usual dimensions seventy-five feet long, twenty-five wide, five and a half high. Descend. In the fitful light your eye will discover a middle aisle five feet wide. It will be a while before you can make out the separate shapes within it, the water closets at either end (for the women; the men must go above deck), one or several cooking stoves, the tables. The aisle itself, you will see, is formed by two rows of bunks that run to the side of the ship.

Observe how Handlin arranges his description so that his readers "follow him" below decks and gradually discover what it must have been like to be an immigrant, living in cramped darkness, without enough food or water, on a 40-day journey.

Another effective way of organizing a description is to select and present details in order to create a feeling of suspense. The archeologist Howard Carter uses this technique in "Finding the Tomb" (Chapter 3) to recreate the tension he and his crew felt at the actual moment when, after many years of research and excavation, the long sought-after tomb of Tutankhamen was finally unearthed:

> At first I could see nothing, the hot air escaping from the chamber causing the candle flame to flicker, but presently, as my eyes grew accustomed to the light, details of the room within emerged slowly from the mist, strange animals, statues, and gold—everywhere the glint of gold. For the moment—an eternity it must have seemed to the others standing by—I was struck dumb with amazement, and when Lord Carnarvon, unable to stand the suspense any longer, inquired anxiously, "Can you see anything?" it was all I could do to get out the words. "Yes, wonderful things."...

Carter introduces one detail after another to heighten suspense as to whether the tomb was still intact or had been previously ransacked by robbers. The description is arranged to transport the readers into the scene so that they see what Carter saw on that day—concealed treasures gradually emerging out of the darkness.

Thus, description, as it is used by writers across many disciplines, is an indispensable tool for conveying the external appearance of persons, places, and things, and is also a means by which writers can relate their emotional reaction toward the subjects they describe.

Narrating

Narration is also an essential technique used by writers across a wide range of disciplines. The events related through narrative can entertain, inform, and dramatize an important moment or clarify a complex idea. Effective narration focuses on a single significant action that dramatically changes the relationship of the writer to his or her family, friends, or environment. A significant experience may be defined as a situation in which something important to the writer, or to the people he or she is writing about, is at stake. For example, George Orwell, in "Shooting an Elephant" (Chapter 2), relates how being forced to shoot an elephant was the decisive turning-point that disillusioned him with his life as a British official in Burma:

> And suddenly I realized that I should have to shoot the elephant after all. The people expected it of me and I had got to do it; I could feel their two thousand wills pressing me forward irresistibly. And it was at this moment, as I stood there with the rifle in my hands, that I first grasped the hollowness, the futility of the white man's domination in the East.

In more personal autobiographical narratives, the need to clarify and interpret one's past requires the writer to reconstruct the meaning and significance of experiences whose importance may not have been appreciated at the time they occurred.

Just as Orwell discovered the meaning of a past experience through the process of writing about it, other writers have used narration to focus on important moments of collective self-revelation. Walt Whitman employs a full spectrum of narrative techniques in "Death of Abraham Lincoln" (Chapter 3) to recreate the moment when Lincoln was assassinated:

> A moment's hush—a scream—the cry of "murder"—Mrs. Lincoln leaning out of the box, with ashy cheeks and lips, with involuntary

cry, pointing to the retreating figure, "He has kill'd the President."
And still a moment's strange, incredulous suspense—and then the
deluge!

Whitman draws on records and eyewitness accounts from this
moment in 1865 for specific details important in recreating the scene
for his readers and summarizes the necessary background information in order to set the stage for this dramatic, historic moment.
Whitman is faithful to the actual facts, yet his account is compelling
and memorable because of his extraordinary skill as a writer.

Illustrating With Examples

Writers also use a wide variety of evidence, including examples
drawn from personal experience, the testimony of experts, statistical
data, and case histories, to clarify and support the principle assertion or thesis. Of these perhaps the most important is the need to
provide good examples. A single well-chosen example or range of illustrations, introduced by "for example" or "for instance," can provide clear cases that document, substantiate, or illustrate a writer's
thesis. Eyewitness reports or a personal narrative of a memorable incident are important ways that examples can be used to clarify, develop, or illustrate the writer's ideas.

Case histories offer evidence of a particularly persuasive kind. A
case history is an in-depth account of the experiences of one person that
typifies the experiences of many people in the same situation. (For example, Margaret Sanger [in "The Turbid Ebb and Flow of Misery"] in
Chapter 2 describes the desperation of one of her patients, a Mrs.
Sachs, to typify the experiences of many poor women at the turn of the
twentieth century who did not have access to birth control information).

Defining

Another rhetorical pattern, definition, is a useful way of specify-
ing the basic nature of any phenomenon, idea, or thing. Frequently, we
arrive at the meaning of a concept by giving synonyms to clarify the
meaning of the term or phrase in question. By contrast, dictionaries
use a more formal method for establishing exact meanings. Dictionaries place the subject to be defined in the context of the general class of
things to which it belongs, and then give distinguishing features that
differentiate the term from all other subjects in its class with which it
might be confused. Definition can also clarify the meaning of key
terms either in the thesis or elsewhere in the essay. For example, in
his analysis of the methods historians use, R. G. Collingwood in "What
Is History?" (Chapter 3) writes:

The definition of history. Every historian would agree, I think, that history is a kind of research or inquiry. What kind of inquiry it is I do not yet ask. The point is that generically it belongs to what we call the sciences: that is, the forms of thought whereby we ask questions and try to answer them.

In some cases, writers may need to develop an entire essay to challenge preconceptions attached to a familiar term (as Collingwood does in "What Is History?") or to explore the connotations and meanings of an unfamiliar or unusual term, as Sergei Eisenstein does in "The Cinematographic Principle and the Ideogram" (Chapter 7), in order to explain the unfamiliar concept of "montage:"

By what, then, is montage characterized ... By collision. By the conflict of two pieces in opposition to each other.

Besides eliminating ambiguity, or defining a term important to the development of the essay, definitions can be used persuasively to influence the perceptions (or stir the emotions) of the reader about a particular issue. The definition of a controversial term not only characterizes it, but is designed to shape how people will perceive the subject. For example, Thomas Carlyle, in "On Heroes and Hero-Worship" (Chapter 3), broadens the definition of "hero-worship" so that it comes to include all that is best and noble in a society:

And what therefore is loyalty proper, the life-breath of all society, but an effluence of Hero-worship, submissive admiration for the truly great? Society is founded on Hero-worship.

The range of methods available to writers for the definition of technical terms, concepts, and processes goes well beyond the abbreviated formula type found in dictionaries. Writers can draw on any of the important rhetorical strategies (description, narration, exemplification, comparison and contrast, process analysis, classification, analogy, and cause and effect) to clarify and define the basic nature of any idea, term, condition, or phenomena.

Dividing and Classifying

Writers also divide and classify subjects (as Stendhal does in "The Crystallization of Love" in Chapter 1) on the basis of important similarities or criteria important to the author. These criteria are features that members of a group or category all possess. The purposes of the classifier determines which features are thought to be crucial. For example, Aristotle in "Poetics" (in Chapter 7) identifies the distinguishing features of tragedy and systematically classifies them in terms of their importance:

> Every Tragedy, therefore, must have six parts, which parts determine its quality—namely, Plot, Character, Diction, Thought, Spectacle, Song. Two of the parts constitute the medium of imitation, one of the manner, and three the objects of imitation.

Effective classifications shed light on the nature of what is being classified by identifying significant features, using these features as criteria in a systematic way, dividing phenomena into at least two different classes on the basis of these criteria, and presenting the results in a logical and consistent manner. For example, Sigmund Freud in "Typical Dreams" (Chapter 6) presents several types of dreams as examples of the way subconscious processes are symbolically represented during sleep:

> Another series of dreams which may be called typical are those whose content is that a beloved relative, a parent, brother, sister, child, or the like, has died. We must at once distinguish two classes of such dreams: those in which the dreamer remains unmoved, and those in which he feels profoundly grieved by the death of the beloved person, even expressing this grief by shedding tears in his sleep.

Comparing and Contrasting

Another way of arranging a discussion of similarities and differences relies on the rhetorical method of comparison and contrast. Using this method, the writer compares and contrasts relevant points about one subject with corresponding aspects of another. Blaise Pascal, in "The Two Infinites" (in Chapter 5), uses this technique to compel his audience to confront fundamental philosophical questions about the nature of existence:

> For in fact what is man in nature? A Nothing in comparison with the Infinite, and All in comparison with the Nothing, a mean between nothing and everything. Since he is infinitely removed from comprehending the extremes, the end of things and their beginning are hopelessly hidden from him in an impenetrable secret; he is equally incapable of seeing the Nothing from which he was made, and the Infinite in which he was swallowed up.

Comparisons may be arranged structurally in one of two ways. In one method, the writer discusses all the relevant points of one subject and then covers the same ground for the second. Writers may use transitional words like "although," "however," "but," "on the other hand," "instead of," "different from," and "as opposed to" to indicate contrast. Words used to show comparison include "similarly," "likewise," and "in the same way." Comparisons may also be arranged on a point-by-point basis to create a continual contrast between relevant aspects of two subjects. For example, Herodotus, in "Concerning Egypt" (in Chapter 3), compares unfamiliar Egyptian customs to the corresponding, but different customs, of his countrymen:

> In other countries the priests have long hair, in Egypt their heads are shaven; elsewhere it is customary, in mourning, for near relations to cut their hair close: the Egyptians, who wear no hair at any other time, when they lose a relative, let their beards and the hair of their heads grow long. All other men pass their lives separate from animals, the Egyptians have animals always living with them; others make barley and wheat their food; it is a disgrace to do so in Egypt, where the grain they live on is spelt, which some call *zea*. Dough they kneed with their feet; but they mix mud, and even take up dirt, with their hands.

Figurative Comparisons

The ability to create compelling images in picturesque language is an important element in communicating a writer's thoughts, feelings, and experiences. Imagery works by evoking a vivid picture in the audience's imagination through metaphors, similes, and other figures of speech. A simile compares one object or experience to another using "like" or "as." A metaphor applies a word or phrase to an object it does not literally denote in order to suggest the comparison. To be effective, metaphors must look at things in a fresh light to let the reader see a familiar subject in a new way.

Figurative comparisons often reveal the writer's feelings about the subject. For example, James Baldwin, in "Letter to My Nephew" (in Chapter 2), creates an intriguing metaphor by equating racial discord (in the United States) to an atmospheric disturbance:

> Please try to be clear, dear James, through the storm which rages about your youthful head today, about the reality which lies behind the words *acceptance* and *integration*.

Figurative language can also take the form of similes that use the words "as" or "like" to connect two seemingly unrelated logical categories. For example, George Bernard Shaw, in "She Would Have Enjoyed It" (in Chapter 1), describes his mother's cremation using a strikingly unsentimental simile:

The feet burst miraculously into streaming ribbons of garnet
coloured lovely flame, smokeless and eager, **like** pentecostal
tongues ...

ANALOGIES   Analogy, which is a comparison between two basical-
ly different things that have some points in common, is an extraordinarily useful tool that writers use to clarify subjects that otherwise
might prove too difficult to understand, too unfamiliar, or too
hard—to—visualize. The greater the numbers of similarities that the
writer is able to draw between what the audience finds familiar and
the newer complex idea the writer is trying to clarify, the more successful the analogy.

Scientists will often use analogies to explain concepts that by
their nature involve immense distances, speeds, or minute dimensions. In "The Continuous Creation of the Universe" in Chapter 5,
Fred Hoyle uses a surprisingly mundane object, a balloon, to convey
the size and placement of galaxies in respect to each other amidst an
expanding universe whose immense distances exceed the grasp of
our senses:

> Galaxies are rushing away from each other at enormous speeds,
> which for the most distant galaxies that we can see with the biggest
> telescopes become comparable with the speed of light itself.
>   My nonmathematical friends often tell me that they find it
> difficult to picture this expansion. Short of using a lot of mathe-
> matics I cannot do better than use the analogy of a balloon with a
> large number of dots marked on its surface. If the balloon is blown
> up, the distances between the dots increase in the same way as
> the distances between the galaxies....

The analogy is structured to bring out a number of convincing
similarities between the principles governing an expanding universe
and the appearance of increasing space between dots on an expanding balloon. Although Hoyle's analogy between an expanding universe and an inflated balloon is extremely useful, the analogy is
incorrect in several literal respects, as Hoyle himself is quick to
admit:

> The dots on the surface of a balloon would themselves increase in
> size as the balloon was being blown up. This is not the case for
> galaxies, for their internal gravitational fields are sufficiently strong
> to prevent any such expansion.

As this example shows, analogies, as long as they do not overstep logical boundaries or focus on similarities that are irrelevant,

are an unparalleled means of clarifying innovative but hard-to-visualize scientific theories.

In addition to explaining technical ideas, analogies are an extraordinarily useful rhetorical technique to explain abstract concepts in the social sciences. For example, in "Challenge and Response" (in Chapter 3), Arnold J. Toynbee employs an unusual analogy to illuminate the crucial differences he discovered between societies that fail to evolve and those that respond creatively to challenges:

> Primitive societies, as we know them by direct observation, may be likened to people lying torpid upon a ledge on a mountainside, with a precipice below and a precipice above; civilizations may be likened to companions of these sleepers who have just risen to their feet and have started to climb up the face of the cliff above....We can observe that, for every single one now strenuously climbing, twice that number...have fallen back onto the ledge defeated....

Toynbee's analogy between "ledge sitters" and primitive societies, and "cliff-climbers" and active civilizations, allows his audience to grasp the contrast between cultures that remain stagnant and those that are dynamic.

Effective analogies provide a way to shed new light on hidden, difficult, or complex ideas by relating them to everyday human experience. One of the most famous analogies ever conceived, Plato's "The Allegory of the Cave" (in Chapter 6), uses a series of comparisons to explore how lifelong conditioning deludes man into mistaking illusions for reality:

> Behold! Human beings living in an underground den, which had a mouth open towards the light and reaching all along the den; here they have been from their childhood, and have their legs and necks chained so that they cannot move, and can only see before them, being prevented by the chains from turning around their heads. Above and behind them is a fire blazing at a distance....

Plato explains that in this den, the prisoners, who have never seen anything outside the cave, mistake shadows cast on the wall by reflected firelight for reality. It is ironic, says Plato, that if they escaped from the cave, beheld the sunlight, and returned to the cave, they would be unable to see as well as the others. Moreover, if they persisted in trying to lead their fellow prisoners out of the cave into the light, the others would find their claim of greater light outside the cave to be ridiculous. Each element in the analogy—the fire, the prisoners, the shadows, the dazzling light—offers an unparalleled means for grasping the Platonic ideal of truth as a greater reality beyond the illusory shadows of what we mistake as the "real" world.

Thus, analogies are extraordinarily useful to natural and social scientists, as well as to poets and philosophers as an intellectual strategy and rhetorical technique for clarifying difficult subjects, explaining unfamiliar terms and processes, transmitting religious truths through parables, and spurring creativity in problem-solving by opening the mind to new ways of looking at things.

Process Analysis

One of the most effective ways to clarify the nature of something is to explain how it works. Writers divide a complex procedure into separate and easy-to-understand steps in order to explain how something works, how something happened, or how an action should be performed. To be effective, this rhetorical pattern should emphasize the significance of each step in the overall sequence and help the reader understand how each step emerges from the preceding stage and flows into the next. For example, Kenneth M. Stampp, in "To Make Them Stand in Fear" (in Chapter 3), uses process analysis to investigate a past era in our country's history, when blacks were brought to America as slaves. Stampp analyzes the instructions in manuals slaveowners relied on to condition newly transported blacks in order to break their spirits and transform them into "proper" slaves:

> Here, then, was the way to produce the perfect slave: accustom him to rigid discipline, demand from him unconditional submission, impress upon him his innate inferiority, develop in him a paralyzing fear of white men, train him to adopt the master's code of good behavior, and instill in him a sense of complete dependence. This, at least, was the goal.

Stampp's analysis of these documents reveals that the conditioning process began with measures designed to enforce external discipline and then shifted to emphasize psychological conditioning. In theory, a slave would become "respectful" and "docile" because he had internalized perceptions of his inferiority.

Whereas historians like Stampp use process analysis to show the inner workings of an historical or cultural event or phenomena, a creative writer, Marcel Proust, finds the same pattern useful in "The Bodily Memory" (in Chapter 6), to depict how a sequence of past memories can be triggered by a seemingly inconsequential event in the present ("I decide to attempt to make it reappear. I retrace my thoughts to the moment at which I drank the first spoonful of tea").

Causal Analysis

Whereas process analysis explains *how* something works, causal analysis seeks to discover *why* something happened or why it will happen, by dividing an ongoing stream of events into causes and effects. Writers may proceed from a given effect and attempt to discover what cause could have produced the observed effect or show how further effects will flow from a known cause. Causal analysis can produce erroneous conclusions when writers confuse sequence or coincidence with causation. Simply because A preceded B does not necessarily mean that A caused B. Perhaps A and B might both have been caused by some as yet unknown event, C. This is called the *post hoc* fallacy (from the Latin *post hoc, ergo propter hoc*—literally, "after this, therefore, because of this"). Writers are obligated to show how the specific causes they identify could have produced the effects in question. For example, Paul Roberts in "Something About English" (in Chapter 7), reveals how English has been shaped by historical events at almost every stage in its evolution:

> There were several other developments that had an effect upon the language. One was the invention of printing, an invention introduced into England by William Caxton in the year 1475. Where before books had been rare and costly, they suddenly became cheap and common. More and more people learned to read and write.

Causal analysis is an invaluable analytical technique used in many fields of study. Because of the complexity of causal relationships, writers try to identify as precisely as possible, both indirect causes that set the stage for an event and the direct causes that serve as a trigger. Causal analysis is an indispensable analytical method in the physical and biological sciences as well. Determining with any degree of certainty that X caused Y is more complicated in situations where one cause may have produced multiple effects or the same effect could have been produced by multiple causes. For example, Peter D. Ward and Donald Brownlee, in "Rare Earth" (in Chapter 5), present a startling causal analysis as to the improbable combination of factors that permit life on Earth to exist:

> Our planet received a volume of water sufficient to cover most—but not all—of the planetary surface. Asteroids and comets hit us but not so excessively so, thanks to the presence of giant gas planets such as Jupiter beyond us.... Alone among terrestrial planets we have a large moon, and this single fact which sets us apart from Mercury, Venus and Mars may have been crucial to the rise and continued existence of animal life on earth.

Another type of causal analysis investigates connecting sequences of causes and effects in a "chain of causation," in which an
effect acts as a cause of a further effect, and so on. Bill Gates's analysis in "The Road Ahead" (in Chapter 5) of the cascading effects of
e-business takes this form:

> As more business is transacted using the highway and the
> amount of information stored there accrues, governments will
> consciously set policies regarding privacy and access to infor-
> mation. The potential problem is abuse, not the mere existence
> of information.

PURPOSES FOR WRITING

Solving a Problem

Although not a recognized rhetorical mode, as such, writers in
many different fields use problem-solving techniques in various
ways. Writers identify the existence of a problem, define its nature,
search for and test various solutions, and communicate the results
of their inquiries to particular audiences. They are obligated to spell
out the history of the problem, describe the success or failure of previous attempts to solve it, and provide other relevant information.

The first step in solving a problem is recognizing that one exists.
Often the magnitude of the problem can be inferred from serious effects that the problem causes. For example, Thor Heyerdahl, in "How
to Kill an Ocean" (in Chapter 5), described how the mid-ocean conditions he encountered during his *Kon Tiki* and *Ra* expeditions alerted
him to the long-term effects of pollution:

> We treat the ocean as if we believed that it is not part of our own
> planet—as if the blue waters curved into space somewhere beyond
> the horizon where our pollutants would fall off the edge as ships
> were believed to do before the days of Christopher Columbus.

When the problem has been clearly perceived, it is often helpful
to present it as a single, clear-cut example, or to represent it in a
simplified form, as does Dava Sobel in "The Prize" (in Chapter 5):

> Since one degree of longitude spans sixty nautical miles (the equiv-
> alent of sixty-eight geographical miles) over the surface of the globe
> at the equator, even a fraction of a degree translates into a large
> distance—and consequently a great margin of error when trying to
> determine the whereabouts of a ship vis-a-vis its destination.

The definition of a problem is often the most crucial aspect of this kind of analysis since it suggests what can and cannot be done and how one should assess potential solutions. Since each discipline has different ways of defining what it considers to be a problem or an issue worth addressing, the methods used to find solutions vary widely. For example, the humanities and liberal arts address interpretative issues while the social sciences focus on the meaning of human behavior in social contexts, and the natural and physical sciences design experiments to test hypotheses about the fundamental forces in the world around us.

When a tentative solution has been discovered, it must take into account pertinent data uncovered during the search, withstand competing explanations, and conform to the methodology practiced within that discipline. For example, in "The Flood" (in Chapter 5), Sir Leonard Woolley describes how he tested his hypothesis as to the true nature of the flood described in Genesis, and interpreted the evidence turned up by his excavations:

> And then came the clean, water-laid mud, eleven feet of it, mud which on analysis proved to be the silt brought down by the River Euphrates from its upper reaches hundreds of miles away; and under the silt, based on what really was virgin soil, the ruin of the houses that had been overwhelmed by the flood and buried deep beneath the mud carried by its waters.
>
> This was the evidence we needed; a flood of a magnitude unparalleled in any later phase of Mesopotamian history; and since, as the pottery proved, it had taken place some little while before the time of the Erech dynasty, this was the Flood of the Sumerian king-lists and that of the Sumerian legend and that of Genesis.

The use of empirical evidence, or carefully designed scenarios to test hypotheses and solve problems, is characteristic of all the disciplines, although researchers rely on their own distinctive theoretical models. In fact, many of the "great ideas" represented in this text fundamentally altered the way people perceived issues within a discipline, or introduced new theoretical paradigms that created new fields of study. The works of Thomas Robert Malthus, Arnold J. Toynbee, Thomas Paine, Charles Darwin, Sigmund Freud, and Aristotle among others, have had this effect.

ARGUING AND PERSUADING

Some of the most interesting and effective writing takes the form of arguments that seek to persuade a specific audience (colleagues, fellow researchers, or the general public) of the validity of a proposition or claim through logical reasoning supported by facts, examples, data, or other kinds of evidence. Writers and researchers in all academic disciplines often are compelled to convince others of the validity of their ideas and discoveries. Discussion and debate accompany the development of central ideas, concepts, and theorems in all fields of study. Writers in the liberal arts, the political and social sciences, and the sciences rely on strategies of argument to support new interpretations of known facts, or to establish plausible cases for new hypotheses.

The purpose of an argument is to persuade an audience to accept the validity or probability of an idea, proposition, or claim. Essentially, a claim is an assertion that would be met with skepticism if it were not supported with sound evidence and persuasive reasoning. Argument plays a key role for writers who use the forums provided by literary and scientific journals to persuade colleagues of the accuracy of their experiments and investigations, and of the validity of their conclusions. Formal arguments differ from assertions based on likes and dislikes or personal opinion. Unlike questions of personal taste, arguments rest on evidence, whether in the form of facts, examples, the testimony of experts, or statistics, which can be brought forward to objectively prove or disprove the thesis in question.

Argumentation also differs from persuasion, although the two are frequently confused. Whereas argument presents reasons and evidence to gain an audience's intellectual agreement with the validity of a proposition, persuasion uses additional emotional appeals to motivate an audience to act in accordance with the writer's recommendations.

There is no hard and fast division between argumentation and persuasion, that is, between attempts to elicit the audience's intellectual agreement with the validity of a proposition, and the writer's or speaker's use of emotional appeals to connect to the needs and values of the audience. Originally, the field of study known as rhetoric referred to the process of seeking out the best arguments, arranging them in the most effective way, and presenting them in the manner best calculated to win agreement from a particular audience. Aristotle, whose "Poetics" is presented in Chapter 7, also formulated some basic rules persuaders could use, in his *Rhetoric*. He identified three elements that are present to some degree in every successful instance of persuasion. He defined these as: (1) an appeal to *logos*, or to the audience's reasoning capacity; (2) an appeal to *pathos*, or to the audience's emotions, and their needs and values; and (3) an appeal to *ethos*, based on the audience's confidence in the speaker's character, as a person of good sense, good judgment, who could be trusted to speak fairly. The appeal to the audience's reasoning capacity is demonstrated if the speaker follows the rules of logic and cites pertinent facts and evidence (in the form of statistics, case histories, surveys, polls, and precedents). The appeal to the audience's emotions was more problematic since skillful arguers might bypass a well-constructed logical case and appeal directly to the audience's baser emotions, prejudices, and fears. The third means, the appeal based on the audience's confidence in the character of the speaker, could amplify the effects of the other two approaches. Collectively, these three elements constituted effective oral arguments in Aristotle's time.

Logical Fallacies

Today, as we read and evaluate written arguments, we expect the evidence cited to substantiate or refute assertions that are sound, accurate, and relevant. Readers also expect that conclusions drawn from this evidence will follow the rules of logic and that the writer will acknowledge and answer objections of the opposition. Aristotle's concern that arguers might subvert the rules of logic to persuade an audience through illegitimate means has produced a study of different kinds of logical fallacies, of which the following three categories are the most common:

WHEN THE EVIDENCE OFFERED IS NOT RELEVANT TO THE CLAIM

- A *red herring* is irrelevant evidence intended to divert attention from the real issue at hand. For example: "Children will be harmed by witnessing violence on television because of the low-level radiation from television screens."
- A *non sequitur* is a statement that does not logically follow from a preceding one. For example: "We won't have universal health care unless all communities recycle."
- *Ad hominem* (Latin for "to the man") fallacies attack a person rather than address the issues. For example: "That marriage counselor has never been married so why should any couple follow her advice?"

WHEN THE EVIDENCE IS INSUFFICIENT TO SUPPORT THE CLAIM

- A hasty (or sweeping) generalization is a conclusion based on too little evidence or too few examples. For instance:

"Southpaws make better pitchers because two pitchers on our Little League team have higher ERAs." *Stereotyping* is a type of hasty generalization that occurs when someone makes prejudiced, sweeping claims about all members of a particular religious, ethnic, racial, or political group. For example: "All Asian kids are math geniuses."

WHEN THE CONCLUSION IS BASED ON UNWARRANTED ASSUMPTIONS

- *Begging the question* means that part of the conclusion is already assumed to be true and does not need to be proved. For example: "Everyone knows that American-made automobiles are not as good as foreign cars."

- An *either-or fallacy* that assumes that there are only two solutions or alternatives to a problem. For example: "If we do not create a Star Wars defense program, we will have to build up our stockpile of nuclear weapons as a deterrent to war."

- A *false cause fallacy* (also known as *post hoc, ergo propter hoc* from the Latin "after this, therefore because of this") is a mistaken assumption that when one event happens after another, the earlier event must have caused the later one. For example: "There are fewer pairs of breeding storks spotted in our part of the country, no wonder the birth rate has declined."

- A *slippery slope* is the false assumption that if one event is allowed to happen, a series of ever more undesirable events will follow. For example: In 1901 Henry T. Fink, writing in *The Independent*, forecast dire consequences if women were given the vote: "Woman's participation in political life...would involve the domestic calamity of a deserted home... Doctors tell us too, that thousands of children would be harmed or killed before birth by the injurious effect of untimely political excitement on their mothers."

- A *false analogy* is based on the assumption that two things that are similar in one way must be similar in many ways. For example: If you said that writing an essay required the writer to move through stages of prewriting, writing, and revising in ways that were comparable to that of an auto mechanic who changed the oil in a car, you would be equating two processes that are different in almost every important respect. A better analogy would be to equate the process of writing with a chef who plans a meal, cooks it, and serves it in an appetizing way.

Although arguments explore important issues and espouse specific theories, the forms in which arguments appear vary according to the style and format of the individual discipline. Evidence in different disciplines can appear in a variety of formats, including the interpretation of statistics, laws, precedents, or the citation of authorities. The means used in constructing arguments depend on the nature of the thesis, the accepted procedures for that particular discipline, and the needs, values, and expectations of the audience being addressed.

Different kinds of arguments seek to accomplish different objectives or goals. Generally speaking, four kinds of goals can be identified. People can disagree about the essential nature of the subject under discussion, what it is similar to or dissimilar to, how it should be defined. These are called arguments of *fact*. Even if people agree about the essential nature of X, they may disagree about what caused it or what effects it will cause, in turn. These are arguments of *causation*. By the same token, even if all the parties concerned agree what the nature of X is, what caused it, and what its effects may be, they may disagree over whether it is good or bad, or whether its effects are harmful or beneficial. These are arguments about *value*. The most complex form of argument—what should be done about X—is known as a *policy* argument. Policy arguments are complex because they may contain each of the three preceding forms of argument. For convenience, we will examine each of these four types of claims separately (the claim, expressed in the thesis, is a proposition we wish our audience to agree with or act upon).

Arguments That Define Key Terms or Concepts

All arguments generated in the context of any discipline require the writer to clearly formulate a position, explain why the issue is important, define ambiguous terms, and discover reasons and evidence that support the claim or thesis. An entire argument can often hinge on the definition of a key term or concept.

For example, in the field of medicine, new methods for prolonging life make it necessary to agree on what the terms "life" and "death" actually mean. Traditionally, "death" was defined as occurring when respiration ceased and the heart stopped beating. Since the advent of machines capable of sustaining respiration, "death" has now been redefined as synonymous with "brain death" (an important distinction, when decisions as to whether to terminate life support have to be made).

Court cases also turn on points of definition. In a specific case, sentencing may be determined by the nature of the charge. For example, a reduction of "intentional homicide" to the lesser charge of "voluntary manslaughter" depends on the defense attorney's ability to "define" the death of the victim as being the result of self-defense.

The central requirement of a definition argument is that the idea or term being defined must be clearly distinguished from anything else with which it might be mistaken. For example, Edward Said's essay "Reflections on Exile" (in Chapter 3) turns on the question of how exile ought to be defined:

> Although it is true that anyone prevented from returning home is an exile, some distinctions can be made between exiles, refugees, expatriates and emigres.

Said distinguishes between "exile" and other conditions with which it might be confused, and defines it in a way that supports his claim that "exile" is "the unhealable rift forced between a human being and a native place, between the self and its true home: its essential sadness can never be surmounted."

Arguments can also arise between disciplines over the lack of consensus of what commonly used terms mean. Thus, in the liberal arts, different fields of study might bring very different perspectives to bear on defining "Impressionism." A writer wishing to contend that there are certain qualities that characterize "Impressionism"—whether in the paintings of Monet and Pissarro, the sculpture of Rodin, the music of Debussy, the poetry of Carl Sandburg, or the short stories of Sherwood Anderson—would have to show that the term "Impressionism" alluded to certain stipulated qualities in the quite different contexts of art, music, and literature.

Most importantly, arguments that define and draw distinctions must identify the most important feature or crucial aspect of any phenomenon, event, or idea and provide good reasons why the definition should be accepted.

Arguments That Establish Causes or Predict Effects or Consequences

Claims about causation assert that one event is caused by another or will cause another to occur. The writer must demonstrate the means by which the effect could have been produced. Causal arguments are necessary when an audience might doubt that something could have caused the effect in question and needs to be shown how it was possible for X to have caused Y. For example, a writer who claimed that "cancer is caused by industrial chemicals" would be obligated to show the means (called the "agency") by which specific industrial chemicals could produce certain kinds of cancer. Causal arguments also offer plausible explanations as to the cause(s) of a series of events, or a trend. A trend is a prevailing tendency or general direction of a phenomenon that takes an irregular course, like the upward or downward trend of the stock market or the growing tendency to ban smoking in parks and other public areas.

Events that merely follow each other in sequence should not be confused with true cause and effect. Writers should also be wary of attempting to oversimplify—as in the statement "Violence portrayed on television causes aggression in children." The burden is on the writer to demonstrate clearly the existence of a plausible means by which a specific cause (violence on television) could have produced a particular effect (aggression in children).

INDUCTIVE REASONING In these cases, the argument moves from specific facts to the elaboration of a general causal hypothesis. This process of reasoning, which proceeds from the particular to the general, is called *inductive reasoning* (from the Latin phrase meaning "to lead towards"). Inductive arguments depend on drawing inferences from particular cases to support a generalization or claim about what is true about all these kinds of cases (including those that have not been observed). Many inferences we draw everyday follow this pattern. For example, if three friends tell you independently of each other that a particular movie is worth seeing, you might infer that the movie is probably a good one. Drawing inferences about a movie you have not yet seen involves what is called an "inductive leap." Thus, inductive reasoning strives to achieve a high degree of probability rather than absolute certainty.

Writers making inductive arguments must always guard against making hasty or sweeping generalizations or generalizations based on atypical or sparse examples. Because inductive reasoning generalizes from specific cases, the conclusion will be stronger in proportion to the number of relevant examples the writer can cite to support it. The validity of an inductive argument is strengthened by sufficient numbers of relevant examples or case histories.

Sigmund Freud uses an inductive argument in his classic essay, "Typical Dreams" (in Chapter 6) when he cites examples of the dreams of children that display a common element—the death or disappearance of brothers or sisters. For example, one of his patients recalled a dream she first had at the age of four ("when she was the youngest child, and had since dreamed repeatedly"):

> A number of children, all her brothers and sisters with her boy and girl cousins, were romping about in a meadow. Suddenly they all grew wings, flew up, and were gone.

Based on numerous case histories such as this, Freud uses inductive reasoning to generalize that childrens' dreams often contain repressed wishes (that is, the desire to be the only child upon whom parents lavish attention) in a disguised form. To make his case, Freud must demonstrate a plausible connection between the cause (a phenomenon he called "sibling rivalry") and the effect (dreams of the death or disappearance of siblings).

Charles Darwin, in "from The Origin of Species" (in Chapter 4), also uses inductive reasoning to draw inferences and make generalizations based on examples drawn from his research. Darwin's tactic is to emphasize the merits of his own position by pointing out the disadvantages of his opponents' views:

> Why, may it be asked, until recently did nearly all the most eminent living naturalists and geologists disbelieve in the mutability of species? It cannot be asserted that organic beings in a state of nature are subject to no variation; it cannot be proved that the amount of variation in the course of long ages is a limited quantity; no clear distinction has been, or can be, drawn between species and well-marked varieties.

Darwin's observations led him to postulate the existence of an evolutionary process based on "natural selection," which was capable of explaining why there are many varieties of the same species and why new varieties continue to develop. His opponents, by contrast, are put in the untenable position of proving that nothing in nature has ever changed or ever could change.

As persuasive as these instances are, we should remember that conclusions reached by inductive reasoning can only be stated in terms of relative certainty, since new observations may require the formulation of new hypotheses.

DEDUCTIVE REASONING   In contrast to inductive reasoning, which proceeds from specific facts, examples, and cases to a general hypothesis, *deductive reasoning* (from the Latin phrase meaning "to draw from") applies a set of given principles to specific cases and draws logical conclusions. The statements on which deductive reasoning is based appear as categorical propositions, or "laws."

If the original statements or premises are true, inferences drawn according to the rules of logic—applying the general "law" to specific cases—can produce deductions that must be valid. The term validity here refers only to the way in which the conclusion is drawn. If the premise on which the argument is based is faulty, then the conclusion will be invalid. The connection between inductive and deductive reasoning is an interesting one and often overlooked. The self-evident truths taken as premises in deductive reasoning are precisely those generalizations that have been previously established by inductive reasoning based on empirical evidence and observation.

For example, Thomas Robert Malthus, in "The Principle of Population" (in Chapter 2), unlike Freud, does not cite multiple examples of known instances and draw inferences from them, but begins with self-evident observations that lead to an inexorable conclusion:

> Population, when unchecked, increases in a geometric ratio. Subsistence increases only in an arithmetical ratio. A slight acquaintance with numbers will shew [show] the immensity of the first power in comparison of [with] the second.
>
> By that law of our nature which makes food necessary to the life of man, the effects of these two unequal powers must be kept equal.

Malthus points out that population increases geometrically (two parents have two children who each have two children, producing eight people) whereas the food supply can only increase arithmetically (same plot of land cannot increase its capacity eightfold to match the population increase). He deduces from these facts that given this permanent inequity between population and food supply, the hopes for social betterment must remain unrealized. If either or both of these premises were proved incorrect then his conclusion, although logically valid, would not be true.

Deductive reasoning is useful as an argumentative strategy in situations when an audience might reject a conclusion if it were stated at the outset (as Malthus's contemporaries most likely would have). A writer who can get an audience to agree with the assumptions upon which the argument is based stands a better chance of getting them to agree with the conclusion if he can show how the conclusion follows logically from the premises.

Arguments That Make Value Judgments

Arguments that make value judgments often use deductive reasoning, since in these arguments the underlying premise takes the form of an assumed moral or ethical truth that the writer applies to a specific instance. These value arguments apply ethical, moral, aesthetic, or utilitarian criteria to produce judgments that measure a subject against an ideal standard. For example, a writer who contends that "bilingual education" is or is not worthwhile or that "euthanasia" is or is not immoral would be obligated to clearly present the ideal standard against which the subject was being evaluated. Value arguments seek to answer the question as to whether something is good or bad, right or wrong, moral or immoral, practical or impractical.

For Hans Ruesch, in "Slaughter of the Innocent" (in Chapter 4), the crucial issue is whether experimentation on live animals is morally justified and whether it produces the supposed benefits for human beings that its defenders claim. Writers of value arguments do not merely express a personal opinion but are making a reasoned judgment based on identifiable standards of value. They must demonstrate that the standard being used is an appropriate one and must provide a convincing argument with reasons and evidence to influence the reader's judgment. Ruesch applies both ethical and utilitarian criteria and cites evidence that the results obtained from these kinds of experiments cannot be generalized onto humans. He then concludes that vivisection is a form of pseudoscience that plays on public fears:

> The anguish and sufferings of the animals deprived of their natural habitat or habitual surroundings, terrorized by what they see in the laboratories and the brutalities they are subjected to, alter their mental balance and organic reactions to such an extent that *any* result is *a priori* valueless. The laboratory animal is a monster, made so by the experimenters. Physically and mentally it has very little in common with a normal animal, and much less with man.

Value arguments are never made in a vacuum. It is important for the writer to assess what beliefs or attitudes (whether receptive, neutral, or hostile) the audience holds in relationship to the argument. The use of emotional appeals is perfectly legitimate as long as these appeals do not replace logic. Since readers bring very different value systems to what they perceive and can understand the same events in radically different ways, writers of these kinds of arguments should try to be aware of the extent to which their own assumptions shape their perceptions.

Arguments About Policy

In addition to arguments that make factual claims or define key terms or concepts, or those that seek to establish causes or consequences or make value judgments, there are arguments that recommend policy changes. Many arguments in law and politics are of this kind, but policy arguments also are made in the humanities, political and social sciences, and the natural and physical sciences.

For example, when investment advisory services issue buy or sell recommendations to their clients, when representatives of governments make the case that their country should host the next Olympic games, when an engineering firm recommends that ceramics would be better than steel for a particular project, when a director argues that a play of Shakespeare's ought to be staged in modern dress, or when a candidate for a job argues that he or she should be hired—it is important to demonstrate that the recommended action would be worthwhile, necessary, and useful.

Ideally, a policy argument should demonstrate that the way things are currently done is producing negative consequences and that the recommended action or policy change would be capable of producing better results. A policy argument must first establish that a problem exists that is serious enough to need solving. The writer then analyzes the problem to discover its causes, proposes a solution, and creates an argument that demonstrates that the proposed solution is feasible, effective, and attractive to the audience to whom it is proposed. Since policy arguments require not merely agreement, but action on the part of the audience, it is crucial for writers to anticipate how readers might react to the proposed solution. The best method is to put yourself into the position of those you wish to persuade, generate a list of possible objections, and then try to overcome them by showing how the benefits to be achieved will outweigh any disadvantages.

For example, Neil Postman, in "Information" (in Chapter 5), argues that modern society is drowning in a flood of useless information devoid of purpose and meaning ("without organized information, we may know something *of* the world, but very little *about* it"). He enlists his readers' support by appealing to commonly held beliefs (for example, that information should be useful and improve our lives). The solution he recommends is paradoxically to return to the values of the Enlightenment when information held an entirely different meaning than it does today. Postman presents reasons and evidence to support his analysis and uses a variety of persuasive techniques (including a controversial characterization of Bill Gates) to enlist his audience's support.

A policy argument also can take the form of strengthening an audience's resolve to accept a proposed course of action. John F. Kennedy does this in his "Inaugural Address 1961" (Chapter 3) when he concluded with the ringing summons "And so, my fellow Americans: ask not what your country can do for you—ask what you can do for your country." Kennedy was speaking in the context of an increasingly threatening arms race and sought to enlist public support for his policies involving the Soviet Union. This speech exemplifies how a skilled orator can interweave emotional appeals into a logical argument and reinforce these with the audience's existing perception of him as a confident and able leader.

CHAPTER 1

THE INDIVIDUAL
EXPERIENCE:
Private Lives, Public Voices

INTRODUCTION

The authors in this chapter are all public personalities whose thoughts and actions have had a profound effect on others. The forms of writing in which they express themselves—including memoirs, diaries, letters, autobiographical essays, and personal observations—are uncommonly candid, honest, and insightful. The idea that one's life is an appropriate object of examination is the defining feature of many of these works. Many readings also reflect important turning points in the authors' lives and illustrate how autobiographical writing can serve many purposes. The voices we hear in them establish an immediate connection with the reader and allow us to observe how gifted writers interpret personal experiences and articulate a meaningful and coherent account of their worlds.

We begin with Gayatri Devi's foray into the colorful and mysterious world of her childhood, glimpse the fabulous life she led, and gain a greater respect for her distinguished career as a member of the Indian parliament. Devi's life encompasses the history of modern India in the twentieth century, from its days under British rule through its independence in 1947 and into modern times.

In Anne Frank's confidences, poured out to a diary that she addresses as a friend, we can understand why she has been heralded as the voice of a generation and became a symbol of the indestructible nature of the human spirit, during World War II, when Holland was occupied by Nazi forces.

A particularly important kind of personal narrative is illustrated by the mixture of eyewitness reports and historical accounts that testify to Joan of Arc's undisputed role as the Patron Saint of France. She is credited with solidifying the French resistance against the English in the early 1400s. In this account, we can hear her words and those of her examiners as if we were present at her trial for heresy.

Autobiographical writing, because of its confidentiality, intimacy, and candor is also well-suited for revealing the thoughts, memories, and desires that underlie questions of sexual identity. In Paul Monette's memoir, we can see the difficulties he had coping with society's prejudice against homosexuals and his own ambivalence about being gay in the pre-AIDS 1960s in America. Monette, who later became a spokesman for the gay community, shows that courage can take many different forms, including the courage to face the past.

The need to clarify, interpret, and discover how one feels about the events in one's life is an important motive underlying personal narratives of the kind Monette has written. When we turn to Lord Chesterfield's letter to his son laying out a program for success in eighteenth-century English society, we encounter many close and detailed observations of the manners and mores of this era. Both in the form of the letter and in his emphasis on courtesy, gentility, deportment, and the control over one's actions, Chesterfield remains the quintessential eighteenth-century gentleman.

Few subjects are more intrinsically personal than romantic love. But Stendhal, in his analysis of the subject, reveals how being in love may serve a very public function in the form of self-advertisment. His opinions may strike some readers as cynical, but these classic observations (that Stendhal developed after an unhappy love affair) on the psychology of love have been enormously influential on later thinkers such as Sigmund Freud. In striking contrast to Stendhal's acerbic tone is John Keats's wildly effusive, heartfelt love letters to Fanny Brawne. In letters, as distinct from journal or diary entries, writers are normally restrained by knowing that what they write will be read by others. However, Keats's letters are filled with expressions of feelings that some readers have found too personal and revealing, but add a depth of insight that enhances our appreciation of Keats as the archetypal Romantic poet.

Upon final analysis, nothing is more powerful in stripping away the mask of everyday preoccupations than the prospect of death. We conclude this chapter with an essay by Joseph Addison and a letter by George Bernard Shaw that move beyond the most intensely personal considerations on the end of life to confront the most universal questions about the meaning and value of existence. Both writers are keen observers of the social forms civilizations use to come to terms with mortality. Addison takes a macabre delight in the baroque expressions of self-commemoration on the plaques and tombstones in Westminster Abbey. Shaw describes his mother's funeral, and subsequent cremation, in a letter that displays sublime detachment, and compassion for her, and for our need to make an exhibition out of death.

The experiences related in these readings may be harrowing, as in those of Anne Frank and Joan of Arc; witty and sardonic, as those of Stendhal, Addison, and Shaw; ironic and self-mocking, as in Monette; or give us a glimpse into the human heart (as Keats does) or into an unfamiliar time and culture (as do Chesterfield and Devi). All these writers transform personal experiences in ways that have touched many readers through the ages.

GAYATRI DEVI
(WITH SANTHA RAMA RAU)

A Princess Remembers

BACKGROUND

Gayatri Devi was born in 1919 in London and raised in West Bengal, India, as the daughter of the Maharaja of Cooch Behar and the Princess of Baroda. She married the Maharaja of Jaipur in 1940 and has had a distinguished, if somewhat turbulent career as a member of the Indian parliament. In 1962, she was elected as a representative from her district with a majority so large that it was recorded in the *Guinness Book of Records*. She won the seat again in both 1967 and 1971 and served until 1977. But because she ran against the ruling Congress Party of Indira Gandhi, Gandhi retaliated by abolishing the privy purses, that is, revenues delivered to royalty, and subsequently imprisoned Devi for five months.

As the Maharani of Jaipur, she is the founder of the Gayatri Devi Girl's Public School in Rajasthan (a region in Northwest India). Devi was the subject of a 1997 film, *Memoirs of a Hindu Princess*, directed by Francois Levie, and was listed by *Vogue* magazine as one of the world's most beautiful women of her era.

The following chapter is drawn from her autobiography *A Princess Remembers: The Memoirs of the Maharani of Jaipur* (1976), written with Santha Rama Rau, who is herself the author of eleven books, including *Home to India* (1945) and numerous magazine articles that have appeared in *The New Yorker, The Sunday New York Times Magazine*, and *Reader's Digest*. In this account, Devi re-creates the palatial splendor of her childhood home and reveals the close ties she had with her mother.

APPROACHING DEVI'S ESSAY

As a child, Devi enjoyed the excitement of traveling by train across India from Cooch Behar in the northeast corner (just between Bhutan and Bangladesh) to the state of Baroda (on the seacoast) 2,000 miles away. We learn that the palace for her was a mysterious realm with many opportunities for sports of all kinds, including cheetah hunts and elephant safaris. She was given a comprehensive education by resident tutors and brought up to assume her station as one of the ruling class whose life would be devoted to governing the state of Baroda. Devi describes many people in her family in ways that bring them to life for the reader. Her grandmother is a "somewhat terrifying woman" because of her imperious and dignified manner. By contrast, her grandfather was a kindly person who was the virtual ruler of Baroda: He was fluent in four languages, was a sports fanatic, and worked to reduce inequities produced by the caste system. Devi's mother elicits her most unqualified superlatives. Without doubt, she was the figure that Devi most idolized and sought to emulate. We also learn about the function of many customs such as *purdah* (which prohibited women from appearing in public without being veiled) that reflect important values in Indian life.

A Princess Remembers

During our childhood, our family often journeyed the two thousand miles from our home, the palace in Cooch Behar State, tucked into the north-east corner of India, right across the country to my grandparents' palace in the state of Baroda, on the shores of the Arabian Sea. All five of us children had watched with excited anticipation the packing of mountains of luggage. We seemed to be preparing for the most unlikely extremes of heat and cold, not to mention more predictable occasions such as a state visit or a horse show. On the day of our departure the station was a bedlam, what with all the luggage and staff that accompanied us wherever we went. But by the time we arrived everything was checked and on board, thanks to the efforts of our well-trained staff.

Nonetheless, my mother invariably had a deluge of instructions and questions as soon as we arrived. Where was the dressing-case that she wanted in her compartment? she would ask, in her slightly husky, appealing voice. Well, then, unload the baggage and find it. What about her *puja* box, which contained the incenses and powders necessary for the performance of her morning prayers? Ah, there it was. Fortunately, that meant that no one need hurry back to the palace to fetch it.

When she did actually leave, telegrams were sent in all directions: PLEASE SEND MY GOLD TONGUE-SCRAPER, or, HAVE LEFT MY SPOON AND LITTLE ONYX BELL BEHIND, or, IN THE LEFT-HAND CUPBOARD IN THE THIRD DRAWER DOWN YOU'LL FIND MY GREEN SILK DRESSING-GOWN. Then came the supplementaries: NOT THE DARK GREEN, THE LIGHT GREEN, or, IN THAT CASE LOOK IN THE DRESSING-ROOM.

Anyway, once we got started, those week-long journeys were among the most cherished memories of my childhood. As a child it seemed to me that we occupied the whole train. We had at least three four-berth first-class compartments. My mother, elder sister, and a friend or relation occupied one; my younger sister, a governess, and myself were in another; my two brothers and their companion with an aide in another. Then the aides and secretaries would have a couple of second-class compartments, while the maids, valets, and butlers travelled third class.

In the twenties, a train trip by even the most plain-living Indian was reminiscent of a Bedouin migration, for everything in the way of bedding, food, and eating utensils had to be taken along. In those days most Indian trains had no dining-cars and did not provide sheets, blankets, pillows, or towels, although there were proper bathrooms where you could take a shower. We always travelled with our personal servants to cope with the daily necessities of living on the long journey to Baroda.

First there was the overnight trip from Cooch Behar to Calcutta, and we broke our journey for a couple of days in our house there. Then we set off again for the longest part of the trip. The cooks prepared "tiffin-carriers," a number of pans, each holding different curries, rice, lentils, curds, and sweets. The pans fitted into each other, and a metal brace held them all together so that you could carry in one hand a metal tower filled with food. But those tiffin-carriers were intended to supply us with only our first meal on the train. From then on we were in the hands of a chain of railway caterers. You could give your order to the railway man at one stop and know that instructions would be wired ahead to the next stop and that your meal would be served, on the thick railway crockery, as soon as the train came into the station. More often than not we hadn't finished before the train left the station—but that didn't matter. Another waiter would be ready to pick up empty containers, glasses, cutlery, and plates at any further stop that the train made.

For us children the excitement of travelling across India by train was not so much in the ingenious arrangements for meals and service as in the atmosphere of the station platforms themselves. As soon as the train pulled in to any station, our carriage windows were immediately besieged by vendors of sweets, fruit, hot tea, and—my favourites—by men selling the charming, funny, painted wooden toys that I have seen nowhere except on Indian station platforms: elephants with their trunks raised to trumpet, lacquered in grey and scarlet, caparisoned in gold with floral designs picked out in contrasting colours; horses decked out as though for a bridegroom; camels, cheetahs, tigers, and dozens of others, all stiff and delightful, with wide, painted eyes and endearing, coquettish smiles. I wanted them all, but my mother said, "Nonsense, nonsense! You children have too many toys as it is." But she could never resist bargaining, so she had a lovely time with the fruit-, flower-, and sweets-vendors, and afterwards our compartment was filled with clinging tropical scents from all her purchases. I don't really know whether she was as good a bargainer as she thought—she was, by nature, very generous—and the vendors always went away looking appropriately bereaved, although with a secret air of satisfaction.

In any case, it didn't matter. All of us had the fun of chasing each other about the platforms, and when the train stayed in a station for an hour or more, we ate in the railway dining-room, ordering what we used to call "railway curry," designed to offend no palate—no beef, forbidden to Hindus;

no pork, forbidden to Muslims; so, inevitably, lamb or chicken curries and vegetables. Railway curry therefore pleased nobody. Long before the train was due to leave we were summoned by our aides or governess or tutor, telling us to hurry, not to dawdle over our meal in the station restaurant; the train was leaving in five minutes. Of course it didn't, and we soon learned to trust the railway personnel, who let us loiter till the last possible moment before bustling us back to our compartments.

Finally we would arrive in Baroda to be met at the station by a fleet of Baroda State cars and driven to Laxmi Vilas, the Baroda Palace and my mother's girlhood home. It is an enormous building, the work of the same architect who built our own palace in Cooch Behar in the mid-nineteenth century. In Baroda, he had adopted what I believe architects describe as the "Indo-Saracenic" style. Whatever one calls it, it is certainly imposing. Marble verandas with scalloped arches supported by groups of slender pillars bordered the building. Impressive façades were topped by onion-shaped domes. Outside the main entrance were palm trees standing like sentries along the edges of perfectly kept lawns that were watered daily. Tall and rather municipal-looking street lights with spherical bulbs illuminated the grand approach. And always on duty were the splendid household guards, dressed in white breeches with dark blue jackets and black top-boots. Because we were the grandchildren of the Maharaja, the ruler of the state, every time we went in or out of the front gate they played the Baroda anthem.

Inside, the palace was a strange blend of styles, partly Victorian, partly traditional Indian, with here and there a touch of antique English or French. There were courtyards with little pools surrounded by ferns and palms. Persian carpets flowed down interminable corridors. The halls were filled with displays of shields, swords, and armouries of spears. The sitting-rooms overflowed with French furniture, with photographs in silver frames, with ornaments and knickknacks on occasional tables. The palace also contained a gymnasium and a dispensary. Two doctors were permanently in residence, and one of them used to travel with my grandfather wherever he went.

Throughout the palace silent formality reigned, and there always seemed to be a number of anonymous, mysterious figures around—two or three sitting in every room. They must have had some proper place in the design of things, but we children never found out who they were or what they were doing. Waiting for an audience with our grandfather? Visiting from some other princely state? Guarding the many precious objects that were scattered throughout the palace? True to our training, we knew that we must pay our respects to our elders, so we may well have folded our hands in a *namaskar,* the traditional Indian greeting, or obeisance, to maidservants and companions as well as to distinguished guests.

In sharp contrast to our own decorous behaviour and the general standard of proper courtesy in the palace were the huge longtailed monkeys which roamed everywhere. They were easily aroused to anger and would often follow us down the passages, chattering and baring their teeth in a most terrifying manner.

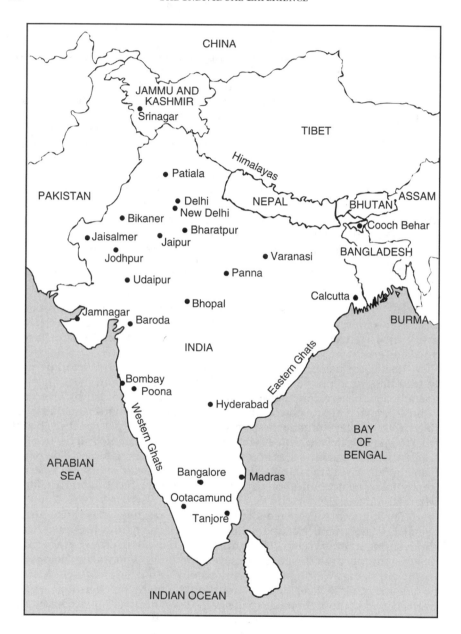

As with all old Indian palaces and family residences, our grandparents' home was divided into two parts, and each of them had its separate entrance. This tradition of special zenana quarters for the women, and their keeping of purdah, literally "a curtain," to shield them from the eyes of any men other than their husband or the male members of their immediate family, was introduced into India at the time of the Muslim invasions during the twelfth century. At first only Muslims kept these customs, but later, during the rule of the Mogul emperors of India, which lasted from the sixteenth century until the Indian Mutiny of 1857 when the British took over sovereign command, most of the princely states of India as well as the families of the nobles and the upper classes adopted a number of Muslim customs ranging from styles of architecture to a rich and varied cuisine. Among these borrowings was the tradition of keeping their womenfolk carefully segregated from the view of outside eyes.

In Baroda the full tradition of purdah no longer existed; both my grandparents were too liberal to allow it. Strict purdah would have required the women to stay entirely within the zenana quarters and, if they had any occasion to venture outside, to travel well chaperoned, only in curtained or shaded vehicles. But my grandparents treated the custom relatively loosely—women could go about fairly freely as long as they were chaperoned and had nothing to do with men outside their family circle. If, for instance, there was a cheetah hunt or a polo match, the ladies would all go together, separately from the men. They didn't have to be veiled; they just stayed on their side of the grounds and the men stayed on the opposite side. For us children, there were no restrictions at all. We wandered freely all over the palace, even to the billiard-room, which in Edwardian days was considered forbidden territory to any female.

My grandmother, a formidable lady, had grown up totally accepting   15
the idea of purdah. Following the custom of her time and the tradition of her family, she had, through her early years, observed the strictest purdah, never appearing in public, and in private only before women, close male relatives, and her husband. When she was only fourteen, a marriage was arranged for her to the ruler of Baroda. Her family, like his, was Maratha, members of the Kshatriya caste, which included many warriors and rulers. Like other Indian communities, Marathas traditionally married among themselves. She was, besides, of the right noble background, and he, after the untimely death of his first wife, the Princess of Tanjore, wanted to marry again.

My grandfather, well ahead of his time in many of his attitudes and actions, hired tutors for my grandmother, first to teach her to read and write (she was illiterate when she was married), then to expand her education. Later still, he encouraged her to free herself from suffocating Indian traditions and to pursue a role in public life. It was owing to his liberal views that my grandmother emerged as an important leader in the women's movement in India. She became the president of the All India Women's Conference, the largest women's organization in the world and one which concerns itself with women's rights as well as with the spread of education and the loosening of the constricting ties of orthodox Indian society on its women. She was not just a figure-head in this important office but a very effective spokeswoman for the emancipation of Indian women. Eventually she even wrote a book, now a standard reference work, on the position of Indian women in their society. After all, she could draw amply on her own experience, first as a sheltered, obedient daughter of a conservative family and later as a free and progressive wife.

But it wasn't for her—or for any of us, her three granddaughters or our mother—a total transformation. Within the family in the Baroda Palace she still retained much of the conventional manners and the severe sense of propriety of all upper-class Indian households. All of us always touched her feet as a sign of respect when we first arrived in Baroda, again before we left, and also on all ceremonial occasions. (This custom, still observed in most Hindu families, applied not only to our grandmother but to all close relatives who were our seniors, even brothers, sisters, and cousins who might be just a few months older.)

It was at public functions that my grandparents made it most clear that they had more or less dispensed with the rules of purdah, for they always appeared together. Although they still maintained separate kitchens and separate household staffs, my grandfather came to take his meals with the rest of us, and with whatever visitors happened to be staying in Baroda, in my grandmother's dining-room. There she served the most marvellous food in the Indian way, on *thals,* round silver trays loaded with small matching silver bowls containing quantities of rice pilau, meat, fish and vegetable curries, lentils, pickles, chutneys, and sweets. She was a great gourmet and the food from her kitchen was delicious, whether it was the Indian chef who was presiding or, when she was unsure of the tastes of foreign visitors, the cook for English food who was in charge. She spent endless time and trouble consulting with her cooks, planning menus to suit the different guests she invited. It was dangerous to be even faintly appreciative of any dish, for if you took a second helping, she noticed and thrust a third and a fourth upon you, saying, "Come on, come on, you know you like this." Her kitchen was particularly well known for the marvellous pickles it produced and for the huge, succulent prawns from the estuary. Only when there were a large number of outside guests, and on ceremonial occasions like my grandfather's Diamond Jubilee, were meals served from his kitchen and in the banqueting hall on his side of the palace.

On religious and ceremonial occasions, durbars were held in his great audience hall. These were very elaborate affairs, something like holding court. The nobility and other important families came formally to offer their allegiance to their rulers—usually a token of a single gold coin.

20   Often we went duck shooting, sometimes we watched the falconing, and then there were the special thrills of elephant fights and, better yet, the tense and gripping cheetah hunts, a speciality of Baroda, when carefully trained cheetahs hooded and chained, were taken out in the scrub land in shooting-brakes. There they were unhooded and let loose into a herd of black buck. With foot full down on the accelerator, one could just manage to keep pace with the astonishing speed of the animals during the chase.

My own favourite entertainment as a child came from the relatively tame performances of my grandfather's trained parrots. They used to ride tiny silver bicycles, drive little silver cars, walk tightropes, and enact a variety of dramatic scenes. I remember one in particular in which a parrot was run over by a car, examined by a parrot doctor, and finally carried off on a stretcher by parrot bearers. The grand climax of their performance was always a salute fired on a tiny silver cannon. It made the most amazing noise for a miniature weapon, and the parrots were the only ones to remain unperturbed.

While my grandmother approved of all these innocent diversions for the children, she wanted us to retain the traditional skills of Indian girls. She wanted us, for instance, to learn how to cook proper Maratha food. My sisters, Ila and Menaka, showed talent and profited by the lessons, while I never seemed able to grasp even the rudiments of cooking.

Because almost every princely Indian family put strong emphasis on sports—and also because we ourselves were sports-mad—we used to get up at daybreak and go riding. By the time we returned, my grandmother's side of the palace was already bustling with activity, with maids preparing for the day, women waiting for an audience, and countless arrangements being made. We used to go in to say our required "Good morning" to her before we went to our rooms to settle down to lessons with our tutors. The floors of her apartments were covered, in the traditional Indian fashion, with vast white cloths. We had to take off our shoes before entering, and everyone except my grandmother sat on the floor.

I remember her from those days as an admirable, remarkable, and somewhat terrifying woman. She must have been beautiful when she was young. Even to my childish eyes, at that time, she was still handsome and immensely dignified. She wasn't tall, though she gave the impression of height partly because her manner was so very regal. But she had a sour sense of humour.

My grandfather was an impressive though kindly figure in our lives, and I remember how his eyes were always laughing. We often took our morning ride with him on the four-mile bridle-path around the Baroda Palace grounds. It was difficult to keep up with him because he liked strenuous exercise and had his favourite horse specially trained to trot very fast.

When we returned to the palace he would leave us and spend the rest of the morning dealing with work that he lumped under the comprehensive heading of "matters of state." Though I didn't know the details at the time, the ruler of an Indian princely state had important functions to fulfil and was a real sovereign to his people. The British, as they gradually took over the major role in India during the nineteenth century, made varying agreements with the different princes defining the division of responsibilities, although much was also left to evolving custom. One major point of all the agreements was that the princes could have relations with foreign powers only through the British. Each of the more important states—and Baroda was one of the most important—had a British Resident who was the voice of the British Government of India. But the states had their own laws, their own courts of justice, their own taxes, and in many cases their own military forces, so that the people of each state looked towards the prince, and not towards anyone else, as the real governmental authority in their lives. My grandfather had, therefore, to confer with his ministers (who were responsible only to him) and to decide many things that affected the lives of millions of people.

I knew him, however, not as a statesman but as a man and a grandfather. One conversation with him lives clearly in my memory. I had gone to say good night to him. He was, as always at that time of day, at the billiard table. He stopped his game and said, in a friendly way, "Ah, I see you're off to bed. I hope you have a good sleep."

I explained to him that there was no question of sleep for some time to come as I had to think about all that had happened during the day.

"No, no," he said, gently but emphatically. "If you go to bed, you should sleep. If you are reading, you should read. If you are eating, you should eat. And if you are thinking, then you should think. Never mix the different activities. No good ever comes of it, and what's more, you can't enjoy—neither can you profit from—any of them."

30 Then, because he was playing billiards, he turned back to the table and gave the game his undivided attention once more. He lived by the clock all his life and did everything in strict order: up at sunrise, walk or ride, work until lunch, brief rest, work until tea, recreation, evening work, supper, reading. It had been the same for fifty years.

My grandfather was known as the Gaekwar of Baroda, Gaekwar being both a family name and a title. Most of the Indian princes had the hereditary titles of Maharaja ("Great King") or Raja (simply, "Ruler," or "King"), depending on the size, importance, and history of their states. I always knew that my grandfather was a special person but it was only years later, when I knew the full range of his background and accomplishments, that I realized what an extraordinary man he was.

He had spent the first twelve years of his life in a village about two hundred miles south of Baroda City. His father, a distant relative of the ruling family, was village headman and earned only a modest living from farming. However, when the previous ruler of Baroda was deposed by the British for misrule, someone from the family had to be chosen as a successor. My grandfather, along with one of his brothers and a cousin, was brought to the capital of the state and presented to the Dowager Maharani of Baroda, the widow of the deposed ruler's father. She was asked by the British to select one of the boys to be the new ruler, and her choice fell upon my grandfather.

Since he had been brought up in a village where a sound practical grasp of farming was considered the only necessary knowledge, he could neither read nor write, so the six years following his arrival at the palace were devoted exclusively to his education, and habits were instilled that lasted all his life. He always rose at six o'clock and went to bed at ten, and with the exception of two hours' riding (considered an essential princely skill), one hour of games of various kinds suitable to his rank, and breaks for meals, the entire day was devoted to work. He learned to read and write in four languages: Marathi, the language of his princely ancestors; Gujarati, the language of the bulk of the population in Baroda; Urdu, the language of his Muslim subjects, employing the Arabic script; and, of course, English. India was still the "brightest jewel" in the British imperial crown, so he had to study English history as well as Indian; beyond that, he received intensive tuition in arithmetic, geography, chemistry, political economy, philosophy, Sanskrit, and something that his tutor called "conversations on given subjects," which was, I suppose, designed to fill any gaps in the small-talk of royal social life.

It is astonishing, when I think back on it, that these two people, brought up in such a tradition-ridden atmosphere, married in the customary way by an arrangement between their elders, should have become leaders of change and reform, encouraging new and more liberal ideas in an orthodox society. My grandfather devoted his life to modernizing the state of Baroda, building schools, colleges, libraries, and an outstanding museum and providing an admirable and just administration. He took an enthusiastic interest in everything from commissioning a special translation of *Alice in Wonderland* into Marathi to working for Hindu women's emancipation, even to the point of introducing the revolutionary concept of divorce in Baroda. (My mother used to tease my grandmother, undaunted by her rectitude, about having a husband who was so warm an advocate of divorce. My grandmother tried to be dignified and huffy but was soon overcome by that wonderful silent laugh of hers, her face contorted, her body shaking like a jelly, and not a sound out of her mouth.)

My grandfather felt particularly strongly about the inequalities and abuses that had evolved in Indian society and were protected by the caste system. Hindus are born into one of four castes, which are, in descending order, the Brahmins (originally the scholars and priests), the Kshatriyas (warriors and often, as a result of skill in conquest or a reward for success, rulers and large landowners), Vaisyas (usually businessmen, traders, artisans), and Sudras (usually the peasants, though all peasants are not Sudras). In a separate group were those Hindus who were excluded from the ordinary social and religious privileges of Hinduism and were known as Untouchables. They performed the most menial tasks—sweeping streets, cleaning latrines—and thus were thought to carry pollution to caste Hindus.

Mahatma Gandhi, in the emotional battle for the acceptance of the Untouchables by Hindu society, acted as their champion, changing their name to Harijans (Loved Ones of God) and insisting that they be allowed access to temples from which they had always been excluded. Their legal battles were fought for them by one of the most brilliant men in Indian politics, Dr. Bhimrao Ramji Ambedkar, himself a Harijan. Dr. Ambedkar was one of my grandfather's special protégés, encouraged and educated by him when he was a penniless boy. After his long crusade for the advancement of his community, Dr. Ambedkar was appointed chairman of the committee that drafted the Constitution of free India.

My grandmother played a strong though less conspicuous part in the life of Baroda State. I can see her so plainly in the mornings, coping with

35

her personal affairs—choosing saris, making up her mind about lengths of silk or cloth of gold that her maids held up, listening attentively to the cooks with menus for the day, giving orders to the tailor, asking about domestic details; in short, supervising the running of an enormous household—and still giving her alert attention to the grievances and complaints of any of her women subjects, whether it was the illness of a child or a dispute in a family about the inheritance of land.

This was all part of a maharani's duty, and so were the more ceremonial occasions, as when she presided over formal durbars in the women's apartments of the Baroda Palace. I especially remember the first one I saw, her birthday durbar. All the wives and womenfolk of the nobility and the great landowners were assembled in their richest clothes and jewellery to pay homage to my grandmother. She was seated on a *gaddi,* a cushioned throne, and wore a sari made of rose-pink cloth of gold, draped in the Maratha way with a pleated train between the legs.

Along with her dazzling sari, my grandmother wore all the traditional jewellery for this occasion, including heavy diamond anklets and a wealth of diamond rings on her fingers and toes. The noble ladies paid their respects to her with a formal folding of hands in a *namaskar* and offered her the traditional gold coin to signify their allegiance. At the end of the hall was a troupe of musicians and dancers from Tanjore in south India. Like many Indian princes, my grandfather maintained the troupe as palace retainers, and they always gave a performance of the classical south Indian dancing called *bharata natyam* at any important palace occasion. At such festive times, the family all ate off gold *thals,* while everyone else ate off silver. (This distinction always used to embarrass me.)

40   My mother, Princess Indira Gaekwar of Baroda, was the only daughter of these two extraordinary people. Because of their advanced views on education, she was one of the first Indian princesses to go to school and to graduate from Baroda College. She also accompanied her parents on their trips to England. One of the earliest stories I know about her tells how she and her four brothers, all quite small and dressed identically in white pyjama trousers and brocade jackets, with gold-embroidered caps, were taken to Buckingham Palace to be presented to Queen Victoria. As they stood before her, the elderly Queen-Empress asked which one was the little girl. Five pairs of dark brown eyes stared back at her, and then, because they all enjoyed fooling grown-ups, one of the boys stepped forward. But they underestimated Queen Victoria, who, sensing that something was wrong, walked around to the back of the row of solemn children, and there a long black pigtail betrayed my mother.

It is difficult to describe my mother without slipping into unconvincing superlatives. She was, quite simply, the most beautiful and exciting woman any of us knew. Even now, when I have travelled widely and have met many famous beauties from all levels of society, she remains in my memory as an unparalleled combination of wit, warmth, and exquisite looks. She was photographed and painted many times, but while those pictures show the physical charm—the enormous eyes, the lovely modelling of her face, the slightly drooping mouth that made you want to make her smile, the tiny fragile figure—none of them captures the electric vitality that made her the focus of attention wherever she went. Her own passionate interest and concern for others made her both special and accessible to anybody. She was always called "Ma," not only by us but by friends and even by the peasants of Cooch Behar. As a child I was fascinated by her—what she said, what she did, what she wore. With her, nothing was ever dull and one felt that at any moment anything might happen.

She herself was oddly unaware of the impression she created, and this, I suppose, was due to her mother's fear, during her childhood, that she might become spoiled—an only daughter, adored by her father, loved and cherished by her brothers. If anyone commented favourably on my mother's looks, my grandmother would immediately counter the admiration with some deprecating comment like, "Her nose is too lumpy at the end—just look," or, "Her hair hasn't a trace of a curl to it."

My mother once told me that she had no idea that she was even passably good-looking until one day when her brothers were discussing some attractive girl they had met. Seeing their sister looking a bit dejected, one of them said, with true brotherly enthusiasm, "You know, you're not all that bad yourself."

For the first time she really *looked* at herself in the mirror and thought, Well, he may be right. I'm *not* all that bad.

READING CRITICALLY FOR IDEAS, STRUCTURE, AND STYLE

1. What features of Devi's account give you the clearest idea of what her life was like in the privileged surroundings in which she was raised? What kinds of activities did she enjoy the most?

2. What impressions do you get of her grandparents and mother and their influence on her life?

3. How was Devi educated and made aware of the special responsibilities she would have to assume as a member of royalty?

4. What role do the different cultural customs reflected in Devi's account play in her life at the palace?

EXTENDING INSIGHTS THROUGH WRITING

1. Contained in the panoramic sweep of Devi's descriptions are innumerable fascinating aspects of her everyday life, which she touches on but does not explore in depth. Choose one of these and, after doing some research, write a short essay that explains

its function in Indian culture. You might wish to visit her Web site @ <http://www.umiacs.umd.edu/users/sawweb/sawnet/people/gayatri_devi.html> to gather more information.

2. What is the most exciting, colorful, foreign place you have ever visited or can imagine visiting? Describe the architecture, everyday rituals, and customs that will bring your reader into this world.

CONNECTING PERSPECTIVES
ON THE INDIVIDUAL EXPERIENCE

1. Compare the values involved in the affluent life of Devi as a member of royalty, in India, during the mid-twentieth-century with the social values that Lord Chesterfield, wished his son, Philip, to acquire in the early eighteenth-century in England.

2. What insight does Devi's account offer into why those born into positions of wealth and power would choose to devote their lives to the welfare of their countrymen? Compare her experiences and motives with those of Joan of Arc's.

ANNE FRANK

The Diary of Anne Frank

BACKGROUND

Anne Frank (1929–1945) was born in Frankfurt, Germany, of Jewish parents. Her family moved to Amsterdam in 1934, and for her thirteenth birthday, she received a small red-orange checkered diary that has become an international treasure. That same year, her sister Margo received a notice to report to the Nazis, and the family went into hiding. With the Nazi occupation of Holland during World War II, Jewish residents were severely restricted in almost every conceivable way, from entering into business, attending school, going to parks, beaches, movies, libraries, or any other public places. By 1942, they had to wear yellow Stars of David stitched to their clothes and were eventually deported to concentration camps where millions were sytematically exterminated. Anne and her family, along with four others, spent twenty-four months in an annex of rooms (concealed by a bookcase that swung away from an opening where the steps led up to a hidden door) above Otto Frank's office in Amsterdam. After being betrayed to the Nazis in 1944, all eight were arrested and sent to concentration camps. Nine months later Anne died of typhus at the Bergen-Belsen death camp at the age of fifteen. Her diary was saved by one of the family's helpers, Miep Gies, who gave it to Anne's father, Otto (who was the sole survivor). It was first published in 1947 and has been translated into sixty-seven languages; next to the Bible, Anne's diary is one of the most widely read books in the world. In 1955 it was adapted as a stage play and has been the source of countless films, biographies, documentaries, and television specials. The following excerpts are drawn from this; the last entry was made on August 4, 1944, when the German police raided the building where the family was hiding.

APPROACHING FRANK'S DIARY

A tragedy as monumental as the Holocaust can only be approached and understood through the stories of individuals. The first impression one gets of Anne is that she is unusually thoughtful and insightful, with a clear gift for writing, who remains a typical teenager. Lines of hers such as "I still believe, in spite of everything, that people are still truly good at heart" have come to define her own goodness and innocence. But, as the letters show, she had the same concerns of self-doubt, awakening sexual feelings, and misunderstandings with her parents that teenagers all over the world have experienced, although within the harrowing circumstances of leading a life in hiding and confinement. The letters to her diary put into focus the extreme courage and pathos of a self-aware individual fighting to retain her humanity and hope for the future, in the midst of the most destructive, overwhelming darkness that could befall a civilization.

The Secret Annexe

SUNDAY MORNING, JUST BEFORE ELEVEN O'CLOCK,
16 APRIL, 1944

Darlingest Kitty,[1]

Remember yesterday's date, for it is a very important day in my life. Surely it is a great day for every girl when she receives her first kiss? Well, then, it is just as important for me too! Bram's kiss on my right cheek doesn't count any more, likewise the one from Mr. Walker on my right hand.

How did I suddenly come by this kiss? Well, I will tell you.

Yesterday evening at eight o'clock I was sitting with Peter on his divan, it wasn't long before his arm went round me. "Let's move up a bit," I said, "then I don't bump my head against the cupboard." He moved up, almost into the corner, I laid my arm under his and across his back, and he just about buried me, because his arm was hanging on my shoulder.

[1]An imaginary friend to whom Anne addressed her diary.

Now we've sat like this on other occasions, but never so close together as yesterday. He held me firmly against him, my left shoulder against his chest; already my heart began to beat faster, but we had not finished yet. He didn't rest until my head was on his shoulder and his against it. When I sat upright again after about five minutes, he soon took my head in his hands and laid it against him once more. Oh, it was so lovely, I couldn't talk much, the joy was too great. He stroked my cheek and arm a bit awkwardly, played with my curls and our heads touching most of the time. I can't tell you, Kitty, the feeling that ran through me all the while. I was too happy for words, and I believe he was as well.

We got up at half past eight. Peter put on his gym shoes, so that when he toured the house he wouldn't make a noise, and I stood beside him. How it came about so suddenly, I don't know, but before we went downstairs he kissed me, through my hair, half on my left cheek, half on my ear; I tore downstairs without looking round, and am simply longing for today!

Yours, Anne

MONDAY, 17 APRIL, 1944

Dear Kitty,

Do you think that Daddy and Mummy would approve of my sitting and kissing a boy on a divan—a boy of seventeen and a half and a girl of just under fifteen? I don't really think they would, but I must rely on myself over this. It is so quiet and peaceful to lie in his arms and to dream, it is so thrilling to feel his cheek against mine, it is so lovely to know that there is someone waiting for me. But there is indeed a big "but," because will Peter be content to leave it at this? I haven't forgotten his promise already, but ... he *is* a boy!

I know myself that I'm starting very soon, not even fifteen, and so independent already! It's certainly hard for other people to understand, I know almost for certain that Margot would never kiss a boy unless there had been some talk of an engagement or marriage, but neither Peter nor I have anything like that in mind. I'm sure too that Mummy never touched a man before Daddy. What would my girl friends say about it if they knew that I lay in Peter's arms, my heart against his chest, my head on his shoulder and with his head against mine!

Oh, Anne, how scandalous! But honestly, I don't think it is; we are shut up here, shut away from the world, in fear and anxiety, especially just lately. Why, then, should we who love each other remain apart? Why should we wait until we've reached a suitable age? Why should we bother?

I have taken it upon myself to look after myself; he would never want to cause me sorrow or pain. Why shouldn't I follow the way my heart leads me, if it makes us both happy? All the same, Kitty, I believe you can sense that I'm in doubt, I think it must be my honesty which rebels against doing anything on the sly! Do you think it's my duty to tell Daddy what I'm doing? Do you think we should share our secret with a third person? A lot of the beauty would be lost, but would my conscience feel happier? I will discuss it with "him."

Oh, yes, there's still so much I want to talk to him about, for I don't see the use of only just cuddling each other. To exchange our thoughts, that shows confidence and faith in each other, we would both be sure to profit by it!

Yours, Anne

Friday, 28 April, 1944

Dear Kitty,

I have never forgotten my dream about Peter Wessel (see beginning of January). If I think of it, I can still feel his cheek against mine now, and recall that lovely feeling that made everything good.

Sometimes I have had the same feeling here with Peter, but never to such an extent, until yesterday, when we were, as usual, sitting on the divan, our arms around each other's waists. Then suddenly the ordinary Anne slipped away and a second Anne took her place, a second Anne who is not reckless and jocular, but one who just wants to love and be gentle.

I sat pressed closely against him and felt a wave of emotion come over me, tears sprang into my eyes, the left one trickled onto his dungarees, the right one ran down my nose and also fell onto his dungarees. Did he notice? He made no move or sign to show that he did. I wonder if he feels the same as I do? He hardly said a word. Does he know that he has two Annes before him? These questions must remain unanswered.

At half past eight I stood up and went to the window, where we always say good-by. I was still trembling, I was still Anne number two. He came towards me, I flung my arms around his neck and gave him a kiss on his left cheek, and was about to kiss the other cheek, when my lips met his and we pressed them together. In a whirl we were clasped in each other's arms, again and again, never to leave off. Oh, Peter does so need tenderness. For the first time in his life he has discovered a girl, has seen for the first time that even the most irritating girls have another side to them, that they have hearts and can be different when you are alone with them. For the first time in his life he has given of himself and, having never had a boy or girl friend in his life before, shown his real self. Now we have found each other. For that matter, I didn't know him either, like him having never had a trusted friend, and this is what it has come to....

Once more there is a question which gives me no peace: "Is it right? Is it right that I should have yielded so soon, that I am so ardent, just as ardent and eager as Peter himself? May I, a girl, let myself go to this extent?" There is but *one* answer: "I have longed so much and for so long—I am so lonely—and now I have found consolation."

In the mornings we just behave in an ordinary way, in the afternoons more or less so (except just occasionally); but in the evenings the suppressed longings of the whole day, the happiness and the blissful memories of all the previous occasions come to the surface and we only think of each other. Every evening, after the last kiss, I would like to dash away, not to look into his eyes any more—away, away alone in the darkness.

And what do I have to face, when I reach the bottom of the staircase? Bright lights, questions, and laughter; I have to swallow it all and not show a thing. My heart still feels too much; I can't get over a shock such as I received yesterday all at once. The Anne who is gentle shows herself too little anyway and, therefore, will not allow herself to be suddenly driven into the background. Peter has touched my emotions more deeply than anyone has ever done before—except in my dreams. Peter has taken possession of me and turned me inside out; surely it goes without saying that anyone would require a rest and a little while to recover from such an upheaval?

Oh Peter, what have you done to me? What do you want of me? Where will this lead us? Oh, now I understand Elli; now, now that I am going through this myself, now I understand her doubt; if I were older and he should ask me to marry him, what should I answer? Anne, be honest! You would not be able to marry him, but yet, it would be hard to let him go. Peter hasn't enough character yet, not enough will power, too little courage and strength. He is still a child in his heart of hearts, he is no older than I am; he is only searching for tranquillity and happiness.

Am I only fourteen? Am I really still a silly little school-girl? Am I really so inexperienced about everything? I have more experience than most; I have been through things that hardly anyone my age has undergone. I am afraid of myself, I am afraid that in my longing I am giving myself too quickly. How,

later on, can it ever go right with other boys? Oh, it is so difficult, always battling with one's heart and reason; in its own
time, each will speak, but do I know for certain that I have
chosen the right time?

Yours, Anne

WEDNESDAY, 3 MAY, 1944

Dear Kitty,

20　　First, just the news of the week. We're having a holiday
from politics; there is nothing, absolutely nothing to announce. I too am gradually beginning to believe that the invasion will come. After all, they can't let the Russians clear up
everything; for that matter, they're not doing anything either
at the moment.

Mr. Koophuis comes to the office every morning again
now. He's got a new spring for Peter's divan, so Peter will have
to do some upholstering, about which, quite understandably,
he doesn't feel a bit happy.

Have I told you that Boche has disappeared? Simply vanished—we haven't seen a sign of her since Thursday of last
week. I expect she's already in the cats' heaven, while some
animal lover is enjoying a succulent meal from her. Perhaps
some little girl will be given a fur cap out of her skin. Peter is
very sad about it.

Since Saturday we've changed over, and have lunch at
half past eleven in the mornings, so we have to last out with
one cupful of porridge; this saves us a meal. Vegetables are
still very difficult to obtain: we had rotten boiled lettuce this
afternoon. Ordinary lettuce, spinach and boiled lettuce,
there's nothing else. With these we eat rotten potatoes, so it's
a delicious combination!

As you can easily imagine we often ask ourselves here de-
spairingly: "What, oh, what is the use of the war? Why can't
people live peacefully together? Why all this destruction?"

25　　The question is very understandable, but no one has
found a satisfactory answer to it so far. Yes, why do they
make still more gigantic planes, still heavier bombs and, at
the same time, prefabricated houses for reconstruction? Why
should millions be spent daily on the war and yet there's not
a penny available for medical services, artists, or for poor
people?

Why do some people have to starve, while there are sur-
pluses rotting in other parts of the world? Oh, why are people
so crazy?

I don't believe that the big men, the politicians and the capitalists alone, are guilty of the war. Oh no, the little man is just as guilty, otherwise the peoples of the world would have risen in revolt long ago! There's in people simply an urge to destroy, an urge to kill, to murder and rage, and until all mankind, without exception, undergoes a great change, wars will be waged, everything that has been built up, cultivated, and grown will be destroyed and disfigured, after which mankind will have to begin all over again.

I have often been downcast, but never in despair; I regard our hiding as a dangerous adventure, romantic and interesting at the same time. In my diary I treat all the privations as amusing. I have made up my mind now to lead a different life from other girls and, later on, different from ordinary housewives. My start has been so very full of interest, and that is the sole reason why I have to laugh at the humorous side of the most dangerous moments.

I am young and I possess many buried qualities; I am young and strong and am living a great adventure; I am still in the midst of it and can't grumble the whole day long. I have been given a lot, a happy nature, a great deal of cheerfulness and strength. Every day I feel that I am developing inwardly, that the liberation is drawing nearer and how beautiful nature is, how good the people are about me, how interesting this adventure is! Why, then should I be in despair?

Yours, Anne

THURSDAY, 11 MAY, 1944

Dear Kitty,

I'm frightfully busy at the moment, and although it sounds mad, I haven't time to get through my pile of work. Shall I tell you briefly what I have got to do? Well, then, by tomorrow I must finish reading the first part of *Galileo Galilei*, as it has to be returned to the library. I only started it yesterday, but I shall manage it.

Next week I have got to read *Palestine at the Crossroads* and the second part of *Galilei*. Next I finished reading the first part of the biography of *The Emperor Charles V* yesterday, and it's essential that I work out all the diagrams and family trees that I have collected from it. After that I have three pages of foreign words gathered from various books, which have all got to be recited, written down, and learned. Number four is that my film stars are all mixed up together and are simply gasping to be tidied up; however, as such a clearance would take several days,

30

and since Professor Anne, as she's already said, is choked with work, the chaos will have to remain a chaos.

Next Theseus, Oedipus, Peleus, Orpheus, Jason, and Hercules[2] are all awaiting their turn to be arranged, as their different deeds lie crisscross in my mind like fancy threads in a dress; it's also high time Myron and Phidias[3] had some treatment, if they wish to remain at all coherent. Likewise it's the same with the seven and nine years' war; I'm mixing everything up together at this rate. Yes, but what can one do with such a memory! Think how forgetful I shall be when I'm eighty!

Oh, something else, the Bible; how long is it still going to take before I meet the bathing Suzanna? And what do they mean by the guilt of Sodom and Gomorrah? Oh, there is still such a terrible lot to find out and to learn. And in the meantime I've left Lisolette of the Pfalz completely in the lurch.

Kitty, can you see that I'm just about bursting?

Now, about something else: you've known for a long time that my greatest wish is to become a journalist someday and later on a famous writer. Whether these leanings towards greatness (or insanity?) will ever materialize remains to be seen, but I certainly have the subject in my mind. In any case, I want to publish a book entitled *Het Achterhuis*[4] after the war. Whether I shall succeed or not, I cannot say, but my diary will be a great help. I have other ideas as well, besides *Het Achterhuis*. But I will write more fully about them some other time, when they have taken a clearer form in my mind.

Yours, Anne

THURSDAY, 25 MAY, 1944

Dear Kitty,

There's something fresh every day. This morning our vegetable man was picked up for having two Jews in his house. It's a great blow to us, not only that those poor Jews are balancing on the edge of an abyss, but it's terrible for the man himself.

The world has turned topsy-turvy, respectable people are being sent off to concentration camps, prisons, and lonely cells, and the dregs that remain govern young and old, rich and poor. One person walks into the trap through the black market, a second through helping the Jews or other people

---

[2]Greek mythological heroes.
[3]Ancient Greek sculptors.
[4]The "Secret Annexe" where Anne's family lived in hiding.

who've had to go "underground;" anyone who isn't a member of the N.S.B.[5] doesn't know what may happen to him from one day to another.

This man is a great loss to us too. The girls can't and aren't allowed to haul along our share of potatoes, so the only thing to do is to eat less. I will tell you how we shall do that; it's certainly not going to make things any pleasanter. Mummy says we shall cut out breakfast altogether, have porridge and bread for lunch, and for supper fried potatoes and possibly once or twice per week vegetables or lettuce, nothing more. We're going to be hungry, but anything is better than being discovered.

Yours, Anne

SATURDAY, 15 JULY, 1944

Dear Kitty,

We have had a book from the library with the challenging title of: *What Do You Think of the Modern Young Girl?* I want to talk about this subject today.

The author of this book criticizes "the youth of today" from top to toe, without, however, condemning the whole of the young brigade as "incapable of anything good." On the contrary, she is rather of the opinion that if young people wished, they have it in their hands to make a bigger, more beautiful and better world, but that they occupy themselves with superficial things, without giving a thought to real beauty.

In some passages the writer gave me very much the feeling she was directing her criticisms at me, and that's why I want to lay myself completely bare to you for once and defend myself against this attack.

I have one outstanding trait in my character, which must strike anyone who knows me for any length of time, and that is my knowledge of myself. I can watch myself and my actions, just like an outsider. The Anne of every day I can face entirely without prejudice, without making excuses for her, and watch what's good and what's bad about her. This "self-conscious-ness" haunts me, and every time I open my mouth I know as soon as I've spoken whether "that ought to have been different" or "that was right as it was." There are so many things about myself that I condemn; I couldn't begin to name them all. I understand more and more how true Daddy's words were

[5]NSB = Nationaal Socialistische Beweging: a radical right-wing movement in Holland that manifested anti-Semitism.

when he said: "All children must look after their own upbringing." Parents can only give good advice or put them on the right paths, but the final forming of a person's character lies in their own hands.

In addition to this, I have lots of courage, I always feel so strong and as if I can bear a great deal, I feel so free and so young! I was glad when I first realized it, because I don't think I shall easily bow down before the blows that inevitably come to everyone.

But I've talked about these things so often before. Now I want to come to the chapter of "Daddy and Mummy don't understand me." Daddy and Mummy have always thoroughly spoiled me, were sweet to me, defended me, and have done all that parents could do. And yet I've felt so terribly lonely for a long time, so left out, neglected, and misunderstood. Daddy tried all he could to check my rebellious spirit, but it was no use, I have cured myself, by seeing for myself what was wrong in my behavior and keeping it before my eyes.

45 How is it that Daddy was never any support to me in my struggle, why did he completely miss the mark when he wanted to offer me a helping hand? Daddy tried the wrong methods, he always talked to me as a child who was going through difficult phases. It sounds crazy, because Daddy's the only one who has always taken me into his confidence, and no one but Daddy has given me the feeling that I'm sensible. But there's one thing he's omitted: you see, he hasn't realized that for me the fight to get on top was more important than all else. I didn't want to hear about "symptoms of your age," or "other girls," or "it wears off by itself;" I didn't want to be treated as a girl-like-all-others, but as Anne-on-her-own-merits. Pim[6] didn't understand that. For that matter, I can't confide in anyone, unless they tell me a lot about themselves, and as I know very little about Pim, I don't feel that I can tread upon more intimate ground with him. Pim always takes up the older, fatherly attitude, tells me that he too has had similar passing tendencies. But still he's not able to feel with me like a friend, however hard he tries. These things have made me never mention my views on life nor my well-considered theories to anyone but my diary and, occasionally, to Margot. I concealed from Daddy everything that perturbed me; I never shared my ideals with him. I was aware of the fact that I was pushing him away from me.

I couldn't do anything else. I have acted entirely according to my feelings, but I have acted in the way that was best for my peace of mind. Because I should completely lose my repose and self-confidence, which I have built up so shakily, if, at this stage, I were to accept criticisms of my half-completed task.

---

[6]Anne's nickname for her brother.

And I can't do that even from Pim, although it sounds very hard, for not only have I not shared my secret thoughts with Pim but I have often pushed him even further from me, by my irritability.

This is a point that I think a lot about: why is it that Pim annoys me? So much so that I can hardly bear him teaching me, that his affectionate ways strike me as being put on, that I want to be left in peace and would really prefer it if he dropped me a bit, until I felt more certain in my attitude towards him? Because I still have a gnawing feeling of guilt over that horrible letter that I dared to write him when I was so wound up. Oh, how hard it is to be really strong and brave in every way!

Yet this was not my greatest disappointment; no, I ponder far more over Peter than Daddy. I know very well that I conquered him instead of he conquering me. I created an image of him in my mind, pictured him as a quiet, sensitive, lovable boy, who needed affection and friendship. I needed a living person to whom I could pour out my heart; I wanted a friend who'd help to put me on the right road. I achieved what I wanted, and, slowly but surely, I drew him towards me. Finally, when I had made him feel friendly, it automatically developed into an intimacy which, on second thought, I don't think I ought to have allowed.

We talked about the most private things, and yet up till now we have never touched on those things that filled, and still fill, my heart and soul. I still don't know quite what to make of Peter, is he superficial, or does he still feel shy, even of me? But dropping that, I committed one error in my desire to make a real friendship: I switched over and tried to get at him by developing it into a more intimate relation, whereas I should have explored all other possibilities. He longs to be loved and I can see that he's beginning to be more and more in love with me. He gets satisfaction out of our meetings, whereas they just have the effect of making me want to try it out with him again. And yet I don't seem able to touch on the subjects that I'm so longing to bring out into the daylight. I drew Peter towards me, far more than he realizes. Now he clings to me, and for the time being, I don't see any way of shaking him off and putting him on his own feet. When I realized that he could not be a friend for my understanding, I thought I would at least try to lift him up out of his narrow-mindedness and make him do something with his youth.

"For in its innermost depths youth is lonelier than old age." I read this saying in some book and I've always remembered it, and found it to be true. Is it true then that grownups have a more difficult time here than we do? No. I know it isn't. Older people have formed their opinions about everything, and don't waver before they act. It's twice as hard for us young ones to hold our ground, and maintain our opinions, in a time when all ideals are being shattered and destroyed, when people are showing their worst side, and do not know whether to believe in truth and right and God.

Anyone who claims that the older ones have a more difficult time here certainly doesn't realize to what extent our problems weigh down on us, problems for which we are probably much too young, but which thrust themselves upon us continually, until, after a long time, we think we've found a solution, but the solution doesn't seem able to resist the facts which reduce it to nothing again. That's the difficulty in these times: ideals, dreams, and cherished hopes rise within us, only to meet the horrible truth and be shattered.

It's really a wonder that I haven't dropped all my ideals, because they seem so absurd and impossible to carry out. Yet I keep them, because in spite of everything I still believe that people are really good at heart. I simply can't build up my hopes on a foundation consisting of confusion, misery, and death. I see the world gradually being turned into a wilderness, I hear the ever approaching thunder, which will destroy us too, I can feel the sufferings of millions and yet, if I look up into the heavens, I think that it will all come right, that this cruelty too will end, and that peace and tranquillity will return again.

In the meantime, I must uphold my ideals, for perhaps the time will come when I shall be able to carry them out.

Yours, Anne

EPILOGUE

Anne's diary ends here. On August 4, 1944, the Grüne Polizei made a raid on the "Secret Annexe." All the occupants, together with Kraler and Koophuis, were arrested and sent to German and Dutch concentration camps.

The "Secret Annexe" was plundered by the Gestapo. Among a pile of old books, magazines, and newspapers which were left lying on the floor, Miep and Elli found Anne's diary. Apart from a very few passages, which are of little interest to the reader, the original text has been printed.

Of all the occupants of the "Secret Annexe," Anne's father alone returned. Kraler and Koophuis, who withstood the hardships of the Dutch camp, were able to go home to their families.

In March, 1945, two months before the liberation of Holland, Anne died in the concentration camp at Bergen-Belsen.

READING CRITICALLY FOR IDEAS, STRUCTURE AND STYLE

1. Anne addresses her diary as "Kitty" as if she were talking to a friend. In what different ways is this illusion of the diary being another person maintained? What are the psychological benefits for Anne in doing so?

2. On what specific occasions does Anne discuss herself as if she were two people; what are the different psychological characteristics of the two Annes? Does her sense of having a dual personality seem psychologically normal? Why or why not?

3. What kind of a crisis with her father does Anne's relationship with Peter provoke? How does this episode reveal the emotional awakening of a 14 year-old girl (a universal experience), albeit in the harrowing circumstances of hiding from the Nazis?

4. Anne tells her diary that she wants to become a writer. Does the way she uses dialogue to describe her relationship with Peter and the crisis with her father that it provokes suggest that she has the potential to be a good writer? Why or why not?

EXTENDING INSIGHTS THROUGH WRITING

1. Anne Frank's diary has become known throughout the world in a variety of cinematic and dramatic forms. In your opinion, is this due primarily to its role as a historical document or because of its sensitive portrait of the universal experiences of adolescents—or both? Explain your answer in a few paragraphs.

2. Writing a diary can be psychologically helpful and give you insight into how writers use observations of themselves and others for material. Keep a detailed diary for a few days. Try to describe events and discuss the meaning of those events in such a way that you would be able to "relive" these days six months from now.

CONNECTING PERSPECTIVES ON THE INDIVIDUAL EXPERIENCE

1. Paul Monette's experiences (see "Becoming a Man") would seem to be a world away from Anne Frank's. Yet, the underlying emotions both experience reveal some surprising similarities. How do both accounts illuminate the confusing and tumultuous experience of adolescence, complicated by their awareness of being cast into the role of the "other" or scapegoat by society?

2. It requires great insight to be aware of one's role as an actor in a great historical event. Joan of Arc, (see "I Have Nothing More to Say") who at 17 led an army to fight against the English on behalf of the French, reveals a unique self-awareness. Despite the vastly different circumstances and eras in which Anne Frank and Joan of Arc lived, both display unusual courage in confronting challenges. In a short essay, discuss the larger-than-life symbolic role each projects.

JOAN OF ARC

I Have Nothing More to Say

BACKGROUND

Joan of Arc (1412–1431), the French saint and national heroine—called the maid of Orlean(s)—was born in Domremy, which was part of the Burgundian domain that was distinct, at that time, from France. The events in her life took place during the Hundred Years' War (which lasted from 1337 to 1453). During this period, England lost most of its possessions in France (which at the time consisted of little more than independent principalities). France, because of Joan's actions and influence, became a unified nation under Charles VII.

As a farm girl and the youngest of five children, Joan never learned to read or write, but was skilled in sewing and spinning. At 13, she heard her first angelic "voices" (of St. Michael, St. Catherine, and St. Margaret) and at seventeen she went, at their bidding, to the French commander, Robert de Baudricourt, at Vaucouleurs, and persuaded him to grant her an escort to the Dauphin (later, Charles VII of France) who had been kept from the throne by the English during the Hundred Years' War. Under her leadership, the French won noteworthy victories: In May 1429 she raised the seige of Orléans and in June she defeated the English at Patay. She witnessed the achievement of the mission given to her by the "voices" when she saw Charles crowned as King of France at Rheims. In September of the same year, she besieged Paris and in the following spring at the seige of Compiegne she was isolated from her troops and captured by the Burgundians, who sold her to the English. To escape blame, the English turned her over to the ecclesiastical court of Rouen, where she was tried for sorcery by the Bishop of Beauvais, who was assisted by members of the faculty of the University of Paris, which was under English control. Her main crime was the claim of direct inspiration from God and the refusal to accept the church hierarchy. After a 14-month interrogation, at the age of nineteen, on May 30, 1431 she was burned at the stake in the Rouen marketplace, and her ashes were thrown into the Seine River.

"I Have Nothing More to Say" is drawn from *Joan of Arc, a Self Portrait,* translated by Willard Trask in 1936.

APPROACHING JOAN OF ARC'S ESSAY

Joan's life has been the subject of innumerable works of art, plays, novels, and in the twentieth and twenty-first centuries, several films.

What follows is an account drawn from the records of Joan's trial. We hear her own words in the description of her early life. The interviews with Robert de Baudricourt and the Dauphin, as well as her actions in battle, are reported as they were at the trial, either in Joan's words or by witnesses. We also can hear the questions of her examiners and Joan's answers as they were reflected in the actual court records.

The conditions under which she was held during the extensive period of interrogation were severe in that she was at first kept in an iron cage, chained by neck, hands, and feet. She was not allowed an advocate (defense attorney) nor was she permitted to attend mass since she was accused of being a heretic. We can observe her qualities of good sense, piety, and fortitude as well as her shrewd attempts to avoid falling into the traps that her inquisitors set for her. This record provides an unparalleled sense of her strength and character.

Without the inspired courageous role that she played, it is doubtful whether the English would have been expelled and France unified. The proceedings of her trial were annulled in 1456 and she was formally announced innocent. She was beatified in 1909 and canonized as a saint in 1920 by Pope Benedict XV.

I Have Nothing More to Say

I was born in the village of Domremy. My father's name is Jacques d'Arc, my mother's Isabelle.

As long as I lived at home, I worked at common tasks about the house, going but seldom afield with our sheep and other cattle. I learned to sew and spin: I fear no woman in Rouen at sewing and spinning.

As to my schooling, I learned my faith, and was rightly and duly taught to do as a good child should.

From my mother I learned "Our Father," "Hail Mary," and "I believe." And my teaching in my faith I had from her and from no one else.

5   Once a year I confessed my sins to our parish-priest, or, when he was unable, to another with his permission. And I received the sacrament of the Eucharist at Easter time.

Not far from Domremy there is a tree called the Ladies' Tree, and others call it the Fairies' Tree,[1] and near it there is a fountain. And I have heard that those who are sick with fever drink at the fountain or fetch water from it, to be made well. Indeed, I have seen them do so, but I do not know whether it makes them well or not. I have heard, too, that the sick, when they can get up, go walking under the tree. It is a great tree, a beech, and from it our fair May-branches come; and it was in the lands of Monseigneur Pierre de Bourlemont. Sometimes I went walking there with the other girls, and I have made garlands under the tree for the statue of the Blessed Virgin of Domremy.

I have often heard it said by old people (they were not of my own elders) that the fairies met there. My godmother even told me that she had seen fairies there, but I do not know whether it was true or not. I never saw any fairies under the tree to my knowledge. I have seen girls hang wreaths on the branches; I have sometimes hung my own with the others, and sometimes we took them away with us and sometimes we left them behind.

I do not know whether, after I reached years of discretion, I ever danced at the foot of the tree; I may have danced there sometimes with the children; but I sang there more than I danced....

When I was thirteen, I had a voice from God to help me to govern myself. The first time, I was terrified. The voice came to me about noon: it was summer, and I was in my father's garden. I had not fasted the day before. I heard the voice on my right hand, towards the church. There was a great light all about.

I vowed then to keep my virginity for as long as it should please God. 10

I saw it many times before I knew that it was Saint Michael. Afterwards he taught me and showed me such things that I knew that it was he.

He was not alone, but duly attended by heavenly angels. I saw them with the eyes of my body as well as I see you. And when they left me, I wept, and I wished that they might have taken me with them. And I kissed the ground where they had stood, to do them reverence.

Above all, Saint Michael told me that I must be a good child, and that God would help me. He taught me to behave rightly and to go often to church. He said that I would have to go into France.

He told me that Saint Catherine and Saint Margaret would come to me, and that I must follow their counsel; that they were appointed to guide and counsel me in what I had to do, and that I must believe what they would tell me, for it was at our Lord's command.

He told me the pitiful state of the Kingdom of France. 15

And he told me that I must go to succour the King of France.

---

[1]Throughout the trial, Joan's examiners were trying to get her to confess to witch-craft. Here, evidently, they have laid a trap for her by asking whether, as a child, she shared the common peasant belief that certain trees, springs, wells, and so on, were sacred to the "fairies"—that is, to ancient pagan gods who had, in the course of time, become reduced to "fairies." Dancing round the Maypole and the giving of May baskets are—like the May branches and May dancing Joan speaks of—residua of such beliefs.

Saint Catherine and Saint Margaret had rich crowns upon their heads. They spoke well and fairly, and their voices are beautiful—sweet and soft.

The name by which they often named me was *Jehanne the Maid, child of God.*

They told me that my King would be restored to his Kingdom, despite his enemies. They promised to lead me to Paradise, for that was what I asked of them.

20   Twice and thrice a week the voice told me that I must depart and go into France.

And the voice said that I would raise the siege before Orléans. And it told me to go to Vaucouleurs, to Robert de Baudricourt, captain of the town, who would give me men to go with me.

And I answered the voice that I was a poor girl who knew nothing of riding and warfare....

My mother had told me that my father often dreamed that I would run away with a band of soldiers. That was more than two years after I first heard the voices. She told me that he had said to my brothers, "If I believed that the thing I have dreamed about her would come to pass, I would want you to drown her; and if you would not, I would drown her myself." On account of these dreams, my father and mother watched me closely and kept me in great subjection. And I was obedient in everything.

But since God had commanded me to go, I must do it. And since God had commanded it, had I had a hundred fathers and a hundred mothers, and had I been a king's daughter, I would have gone.

25   It pleased God thus to act through a simple maid in order to turn back the King's enemies.

I went to my uncle and told him that I would visit him for a time. I was in his house for about a week; then I told him that I must go to Vaucouleurs. And my uncle took me there.

When I came to Vaucouleurs I knew Robert de Baudricourt, though I had never seen him before. The voice told me that it was he.

30   And I told him that I must go into France.

HER WORDS TO ROBERT DE BAUDRICOURT

The Kingdom of France is not the Dauphin's but my Lord's. But my Lord wills that the Dauphin shall be made King and have the Kingdom in custody. The Dauphin shall be King despite his enemies, and I shall lead him to his anointing.

Twice he refused and rejected me.

AT HER LODGING TO JEAN DE METZ

I am come to this town, which is the King's, to ask Robert de Baudricourt to take me or send me to the King. And he heeds neither me nor my words. Nevertheless, I must be with the King before mid-Lent, though I wear my legs to the knees on the road. For there is none in this world—neither kings, nor dukes, nor the King of Scotland's daughter, nor any other—who can restore the Kingdom of France. Nor is there any succour for it but from me.

Far rather would I sit and sew beside my poor mother, for this thing is not of my condition. But I must go, and I must do this thing, because my Lord will have it so.

Rather now than tomorrow, and tomorrow than the day after!   35

And the third time he received me and gave me men. The voice had told me that so it would come to pass....

I set out from Vaucouleurs in men's clothing. I carried a sword that Robert de Baudricourt had given me, but no other arms. With me there were a knight, a squire, and four serving-men.

Robert de Baudricourt made those who went with me swear that they would guide me well and safely. To me at parting he said: "Go, and, whatever may come of it, let it come!"....

I came to Chinon about noon and put up at an inn, and, after dinner, I went to the King in his castle. And when I entered the King's chamber, I knew him among the rest, for the voice counselled me and revealed it to me. And I told the King that I would go to make war on the English.

HER WORDS TO CHARLES

I bring you news from God, that our Lord will give you back your kingdom, bringing you to be crowned at Reims, and driving out your enemies. In this I am God's messenger. Do you set me bravely to work, and I will raise the siege of Orléans.

For three weeks I was examined by learned men in Chinon and Poitiers, and the King received a sign concerning what I had done before he would believe in me....

HER ANSWERS TO HER EXAMINERS

I do not know A from B.[2]   40

I am come from the King of Heaven to raise the siege of Orléans and to lead the Dauphin to Reims to be crowned and anointed...

HER WORDS TO CHARLES

I shall last a year, and but little longer: we must think to do good work in that year. Four things are laid upon me: to drive out the English; to bring you to be crowned and anointed at Reims; to rescue the Duke of Orléans from the hands of the English; and to raise the siege of Orléans.

And the King set me to work, giving me ten or twelve thousand men, and I went to Orléans.

---

[2]Joan could not read or write. The letter to the King of England that follows was dictated.

Letter, March 22, 1429

Jhesus Maria

King of England, and you, Duke of Bedford, who call yourself Regent of the Kingdom of France; you, William de la Pole, Earl of Suffolk; John, Lord Talbot; and you, Thomas, Lord Scales, who call yourselves lieutenants of the said Duke of Bedford: Do justice to the King of Heaven; surrender to the Maid, who is sent here from God, King of Heaven, the keys of all the good towns you have taken and violated in France. She is come from God to uphold the blood royal. She is ready to make peace if you will do justice, relinquishing France and paying for what you have withheld.

45 As to you, you archers and men-at-arms, gentle[3] and others, who are before the town of Orléans, go hence into your own country in God's name; and if you do not so, expect to hear news of the Maid, who will shortly come to see you, to your very great damage.

King of England, if you do not so, I am a commander, and in whatever place in France I come upon your men, I will make them leave it, will they or nill they; and if they will not yield obedience, I will have them all slain. I am sent here from God, King of Heaven, to put you, hand to hand, out of all France. Yet if they will yield obedience, I will grant them mercy.

And think not otherwise: for you shall not hold the Kingdom of France from God, King of Heaven, Saint Mary's son, but King Charles shall hold it, the true heir. For so God, King of Heaven, wills it; and so it has been revealed to him by the Maid, and he shall enter Paris with a fair company.

If you will not believe this news from God and the Maid, wherever we find you, there we shall strike; and we shall raise such a battle-cry as there has not been in France in a thousand years, if you will not do justice. And know surely that the King of Heaven will send more strength to the Maid than you can bring against her and her good soldiers in any assault. And when the blows begin, it shall be seen whose right is the better before the God of Heaven.

You, Duke of Bedford: The Maid prays and beseeches you not to bring on your own destruction. If you will do her justice, you may yet come in her company there where the French shall do the fairest deed that ever was done for Christendom. So answer if you will make peace in the city of Orléans. And if you do not so, consider your great danger speedily.

Written this Tuesday in Holy Week.

Orléans: Capture of The English Fortress of Saint-Loup, May 4

50 *To Her Page*

Ha! wretched boy! you did not tell me that French blood was flowing! Where are those who should arm me? To horse! To horse!

---

[3]Noble, of high birth.

Orléans: Capture of the Bridge, May 7

I was the first to set a ladder against the fortress on the bridge, and, as I raised it, I was wounded in the throat by a cross-bow bolt. But Saint Catherine comforted me greatly. And I did not cease to ride and do my work.

To Her Soldiers
Courage! Do not fall back: in a little the place will be yours. Watch! when you see the wind blow my banner against your bulwark, you shall take it!
In, in, the place is yours!

To the English Captain   55
Glasdale, Glasdale, yield, yield to the King of Heaven. You have called me "whore": I pity your soul and the souls of your men.

To Those Who Offered to Charm Her Wound
I would rather die than do what I know to be sin.

Orléans: The English Raise the Siege, May 8

To Her Soldiers
In God's name! they go. Let them depart. And go we to give thanks to God. We shall not follow them farther, for it is Sunday. Seek not to harm them. It suffices me that they go.

Melun, Week of April 16

Last Easter week,—I was standing near the moat at Melun,—my voices told me that I would be taken prisoner before Saint John's Day, and that it must be so, and that I must not be frightened but accept it willingly, and God would help me.
And I begged of my voices that, when I should be taken, I might die straightway, without long travail in prison.

Near Crépy-En-Valois, August 10 or 11

To the Archbishop of Reims   60
This is a good people. I have seen no other people so joyful at the coming of our most noble King. And would that I might be so happy, when I shall end my days, as to be buried in the earth of this place!
(He answers, "O Jehanne, where do you expect to die?" Then Jehanne:)
Wherever it may please God, for I am no more sure of the hour or the season or the place than you. And would that it were pleasing to God my maker that I might now turn back, laying off my arms, and go to serve my father and my mother, keeping their sheep with my sister and my brothers; they would be very glad to see me!

Compiègne, May 23

I came to Compiègne at a secret hour in the morning, and entered the town, I think, without our enemies knowing it. And the same day, towards evening, I made the sally in which I was taken.

I had a sword which had been taken from a Burgundian. I got it at Lagny, and I carried it from Lagny to Compiègne because it was a good war-sword, good to give good buffets and good thrusts. I was riding a half-courser.

I did not know that I would be taken that day.

65   I crossed the bridge and the bulwark, and went with a company of our soldiers against Monseigneur de Luxembourg's men. I drove them back twice, as far as the Burgundian camp, and a third time half-way. Then the English who were there cut us off, both me and my men, coming between me and the bulwark. And so my men fell back. And as I fell back flankwise into the fields towards Picardie, near the bulwark, I was taken.

HER FIRST APPEARANCE BEFORE HER JUDGES IN THE CHAPEL ROYAL, ROUEN CASTLE, WEDNESDAY, FEBRUARY 21

Concerning my father and mother and what I have done since I took the road to France I will willingly swear to tell the truth. But the revelations which have come to me from God I have never told or revealed to anyone, except to Charles, my King. Nor would I reveal them if I were to be beheaded. A week from today I shall have learned whether I may reveal them....

I protest against being kept in chains and irons.

It is true that I have wished, and that I still wish, what is permissible for any captive: to escape!

Tuesday, February 27

"How have you fared since Saturday?"[4]

70   You can see very well how I have fared. I have fared as well as I could.

"Have you heard the voice that comes to you, since Saturday?"

Yes indeed. I have heard it many times.

"Did you hear it in this room on Saturday?"

That has nothing to do with your trial! I did hear it here.

75   I did not understand it well. I did not understand anything that I could repeat to you until I had returned to my room.

It told me to answer you bravely.

I asked the voice for counsel on the things about which I was questioned. On some points I have had counsel. Concerning others that I may be asked to answer I will not answer without leave. If I were to answer without leave, perhaps I should not have the voices for protection. But when I

---

[4]The italicized questions are those put to her at the trial.

shall have leave from our Lord I shall not be afraid to speak, for then I shall have good protection.

The voice is Saint Catherine's voice and Saint Margaret's. And their heads are crowned with a fair crown, most richly and most preciously. Concerning that, I have leave from our Lord. And if you doubt it, send to Poiters where I was questioned before.

I know very well that it is they, and I can very well tell them apart!

"Which of them appeared to you first?" 80

I did not recognize them as soon as that. I knew once, but I have forgotten. If I can have leave, I will tell you willingly; it is set down in the register at Poitiers. And I had comfort from Saint Michael.

"Is it long since you first had the voice of Saint Michael?"

I am not saying "the voice of Saint Michael"; I am telling you of great comfort.

I have told you often enough that they are Saint Catherine and Saint Margaret. Believe me if you like!

"Are you forbidden to tell what sign you have that they are Saint 85 *Catherine and Saint Margaret?"*

I have not yet clearly understood whether that is forbidden me or not.

"Did God command you to put on men's clothing?"[5]

My clothing is a small matter, one of the least. But I did not put on men's clothing by the counsel of any man on earth. I did not put on this clothing, nor do anything else, except at the bidding of God and the angels.

All that I have done is by our Lord's bidding. And if he had bid me put on other clothing I should have put it on because it was at his bidding.

All that I have done at our Lord's bidding I believe that I have done 90 rightly. And I expect good protection for it and good succour.

"When you saw the voice coming to you, was there any light?"

There was light all about, and so there should be! All light does not come to you.

"Was there an angel over your King's head when you saw him for the first time?"

By Blessed Mary! If there was, I know nothing about it. I did not see one.

"Was there any light?" 95

There were more than three hundred knights and fifty torches—without counting the spiritual light!

"How did it happen that your King had faith in what you said?"

He had good tokens; and because of his learned men.

"What revelations did your King have?"

You shall not get that from me yet, nor this year! 100

"Did you ever offer prayers to the end that your sword should be more fortunate?"

It is a good thing to know that I would want my arms to be fortunate.

---

[5]That Joan dressed like a soldier seems to have bothered her examiners greatly. Clearly, living and fighting with men, she had to.

Thursday, March 1

About what I know which concerns this trial I will freely tell the truth, and I will tell you just as much as I should tell if I were before the Pope of Rome.

"What have you to say as to our lord the Pope, and as to whom you believe is the true Pope?"

105 Are there two?

"Have you talked with Saint Catherine and Saint Margaret since Tuesday?"

Yes, but I do not know the hour.

"What day was it?"

Yesterday and today. There is no day that I do not hear them.

110 *"Do you always see them in the same dress?"*

I always see them in the same form. I know nothing of their garments.

"What form do you see?"

I see the face.

"Have the saints who appear to you hair?"

115 It is a good thing to know!

"Was their hair long and hanging?"

I do not know. And I do not know if there was any semblance of arms or of other members. They spoke well and fairly, and I understood them well.

"How do they speak if they do not have members?"

I leave that to God. They speak the French tongue.

120 *"Does not Saint Margaret speak English?"*

Why should she speak English when she is not of the English party?

"In what form was Saint Michael when he appeared to you?"

I saw no crown upon him. I know nothing of his garments.

"Was he naked?"

125 Do you think that God has not wherewith to clothe him?

"Had he hair?"

Why should it have been cut off? I have not seen Blessed Michael since I left the castle of Crotoy; I do not see him very often.

Monday, March 12

"Was the angel who brought the sign the angel who first appeared to you, or was it another?"

It is always one and the same. And he has never failed me.

130 *"Has not the angel failed you in worldly things in allowing you to be taken prisoner?"*

I believe, since it pleases our Lord, that it is best that I am a prisoner.

"Has he not failed you in the things of grace?"[6]

How can he have failed me, when he comforts me every day? I mean by the comfort from Saint Catherine and Saint Margaret.

---

[6]Divine favor and mercy, spiritual well-being.

"Do you call them, or do they come without your calling?"

They often come without my calling. And sometimes, if they did not   135
come quickly, I prayed our Lord to send them.

"Did you ever call them, and they did not come?"

I have never had need of them and not had them.

"When you promised our Lord to keep your virginity, was it to him that you spoke?"

It ought to be enough to promise it to those who were sent by him, that is, Saint Catherine and Saint Margaret.

"When you saw Saint Michael and the angels, did you show them   140
reverence?"

Yes.

"Were they with you long?"

They often come among Christian people and are not seen. I have seen them many times among Christians.

Saturday, March 17

"Will you submit yourself to the determination of our mother, holy Church, in respect to all your words and deeds, whether good or evil?"

As for the Church, I love it and I would wish to support it with all my   145
might for the sake of our Christian faith: it is not I who should be prevented from going to church and hearing mass! [7] As for the good work I have done and my first coming, I must needs leave that with the King of Heaven, who sent me to Charles, son of Charles King of France, who shall be King. And you shall see that the French will very soon achieve a great task which God will send to the French, and such that almost the whole Kingdom of France will tremble. And I say it, so that when it comes to pass it will be remembered that I said it.

"Answer whether you will refer yourself to the determination of the Church?"

I refer myself to our Lord who sent me, to Our Lady, and to all the blessed saints in Paradise. It seems to me that our Lord and the Church are one and the same, and that no one should make difficulties about that. Why do you make difficulties about it not being one and the same?

RE-EXAMINATION

In the Room Off the Hall of State, Tuesday, March 27

First, for your admonishing me for my good and in our faith, I thank you and all this company. As for the counsellor that you offer me, I thank you too: but I do not intend to forsake the counsel of our Lord.

---

[7]In prison she was not allowed to hear mass or take the sacraments—one form of the pressure that was put upon her to confess witchcraft.

I believe that our holy father the Pope of Rome and the bishops and other churchmen are there to guard the Christian faith and to punish those who are faulty. But as for me I will not submit myself in respect to my deeds, save to the church in Heaven alone—that is, to God, the Virgin Mary and the saints in Paradise. And I firmly believe that I have not been faulty in our Christian faith. Nor would I wish to be.

150   I do not do wrong to serve God!

If the judges refuse to let me hear mass, it certainly lies in our Lord to let me hear it, when he shall please to, without them.

At Arras and at Beaurevoir I was many times admonished to wear women's clothing: I refused, and I still refuse. As to other womanly duties, there are enough other women to perform them.

As to the Duke of Burgundy, I begged him, by letters and through his ambassadors, that there might be peace. As to the English, the peace that is needed with them is that they should go back to their homes in England.

There was neither sorcery nor any other evil art in anything that I have done.

155   If the English had believed my letter they would have done wisely. And before seven years are ended, they shall be well aware of the things that I wrote to them.

I did not send it out of pride or presumption, but at the bidding of our Lord.

First I asked them to make peace. And in case they would not make peace, I was all ready to fight.

Wednesday, March 28

... It lies with our Lord to make revelations to whom he pleases.

As for signs, if those who ask for one are not worthy of it, I am not accountable for that!

160   I believe, as firmly as I believe that our Lord Jesus Christ suffered death to redeem us from the pains of Hell, that they are Saint Michael and Saint Gabriel and Saint Catherine and Saint Margaret, whom our Lord sends to comfort and counsel me.

I shall call them to help me as long as I live.

I ask in this manner:

"Most sweet God, in honor of your holy passion I beg you, if you love me, to reveal to me what I am to answer to these churchmen. As to this clothing I well know by what commandment I began to wear it. But I do not know the manner in which I am to quit it. Therefore, may it please you to teach me."
And immediately they come.

That Jesus has failed me I deny.

As to the Church militant,[8] I wish to show it all the honor and reverence that I can. As for referring my deeds to the Church militant, I must needs refer them to our Lord, who caused me to do what I have done.

I am a good Christian.

165

The offenses that you bring against me I have not committed: as for the rest, I refer it to our Lord.

SHE IS THREATENED WITH TORTURE IN THE PRESENCE OF THE INSTRUMENTS[9]

Donjon of the Castle, Wednesday, May 9

Truly, if you were to have me torn limb from limb and send my soul out of my body, I would say nothing else. And if I did say anything, afterwards I should always say that you had made me say it by force.

I have asked my voices to counsel me whether I should submit to the Church, because the churchmen were pressing me to submit to the Church. And my voices have told me that, if I want our Lord to help me, I must lay all my deeds before him.

LAST SESSION: SHE IS AGAIN ADMONISHED

Wednesday, May 23

If I were at the place of execution, and I saw the fire lighted, and the faggots catching and the executioner ready to build up the fire, and if I were in the fire, even so I would say nothing else, and I would maintain what I have said at this trial until death.

I have nothing more to say.

READING CRITICALLY FOR IDEAS, STRUCTURE, AND STYLE

1. What was Joan's life like before and after she heard the "voices"?

2. Joan's remarkable presence of mind and her steadfast beliefs are extraordinary in one who is only 19. How do these character

---

[8]The Church on earth, thought of as in warfare against evil—as distinguished from "the Church triumphant."
[9]The instruments of torture.

traits reveal themselves in the way she handles the questions put to her? For example, when her interrogators try to trick her or get her to contradict herself or recant, how does she answer them?

3. In your opinion, does Joan display a sense of irony, or even humor, in what might be described as tragic circumstances? Explain your answer.

EXTENDING INSIGHTS THROUGH WRITING

1. How would the modern world be likely to interpret Joan's visions and voices? What does this difference suggest about the psychological climate in which we live and our capacity to understand someone like Joan?

2. Joan of Arc has been a source of fascination for writers through the ages. How has she been depicted in works such as Verdi's 1845 opera, *Giovanna d' Arco*, George Bernard Shaw's play *Saint Joan*, Mark Twain's essay "Personal Recollections of Joan of Arc," in biographies by Anatole France and V. Sackville-West, or more recently in the 1999 film, *The Messenger: The Story of Joan of Arc*. Compare any of these works with "I Have Nothing More to Say" in terms of how she is portrayed.

CONNECTING PERSPECTIVES ON THE INDIVIDUAL EXPERIENCE

1. Compare Joan of Arc to Paul Monette (see "Becoming a Man") in terms of society's attitude toward those who are different and even ostracized because of this difference, in cultures as diverse as medieval France and contemporary America.

2. In what respects might Joan of Arc's love for France illustrate a more universal application of what Stendhal describes as passion-love?

PAUL MONETTE

Becoming a Man

BACKGROUND

Paul Monette is a distinguished writer of poetry, novels, and autobiographical volumes. He was born in 1945, attended Yale University, and first received critical attention in 1975 with the publication of his poetry collection *The Carpenter at the Asylum*. His novels include *Taking Care of Mrs. Carroll* (1978), *The Gold Diggers* (1979), *The Long Shot* (1981), *Lightfall* (1982), *Afterlife* (1990), and *Halfway Home* (1991). He also adapted Oliver Stone's screenplay for *Scarface* as a novel, in 1983. Following the death from AIDS of his longtime lover, Roger Horwitz, Monette addressed the tragedy in a collection of poems *Love Alone: Eighteen Elegies for Rog* (1988) and wrote an acclaimed prose account, *Borrowed Time: An AIDS Memoir* for which he received a National Book Critics Circle Award nomination for the best autobiography in 1988. At this time, Monette was diagnosed as being HIV-positive. Monette has also written *Becoming a Man: Half a Life Story* (1992), from which the following selection is taken, in which he recounts the difficulties he experienced coming to terms with his homosexuality. This memoir won the prestigious National Book Award for Nonfiction. His final published work was *Last Watch of the Night: Essays Too Personal and Otherwise* (1995), the same year Monette died from AIDS.

APPROACHING MONETTE'S ESSAY

This account relates experiences from Monette's life before he openly declared that he was gay. In the time period Monette describes, the early 1960s, openly revealing oneself to be gay was a traumatic experience, not only because of societal condemnation, but because of inner guilt and self-recrimination. Monette has a keen eye for the comedy of manners aspect of miscommunication when he describes his sexual attraction to, and admiration for, his two macho roommates from California and his pathetic attempts to ingratiate himself and enter their world. Before going to college, his role model and openly gay friend, Alex, may have set off Paul's desire to defy society's rules (in a shoplifting misadventure that could have jeopardized his admission to Yale). Monette's style is engaging, thoroughly honest, and carries us back to a more innocent time, before AIDS, when sexual preference was a very private matter and those outside the norm knew they would be ostracized.

Becoming a Man

Audieris in quo, Flacce, balneo plausum,
Maronis illic esse mentulam scito.

—*Martial (circa A.D. 40–104)*

Lux et Veritas

You ask at the Baths why all this sudden
    applause?
It's their habit, Cabot.
Another Yale type has stepped out of his drawers.

—*Translated by Dudley Fitts*

Assuming the judge's threat was real, I was lucky to get to Yale at all. That final summer before leaving home I worked at Nick's for the last time. I knew in my bones I was bound for a one-way trip, that as soon as I hung up my apron in the closet by the ice-cream maker, I would forfeit the inside track on life in a small town. That strange amalgam of Norman Rockwell folksiness and the quiet desperation of *Winesburg, Ohio.* Vinnie O'Connor, having dropped out of Andover High at sixteen, was already picking up garbage door-to-door in his own truck, his bully days behind him. And I knew every bachelor and old maid on sight—the sensible shoes and the rubbers for rain, that wincing sense of apology for their very being. Going no place, the end of the line.

But if I was about to engineer my flight from same, I was more overwhelmed than I'd freely admit, especially to myself. I spent most of my working days with Alex, and after work as well, a ritual stack of records on the turntable, *Oklahoma* to *Candide.* Alex, whose high school C's were making it unlikely that he could take the college route of escape, was already talking cosmetology and hair. But not at the local level, please. His sights were on Madison Avenue and Beverly Hills, centers of style and chic, and not "this Ann Taylor woolen bullshit."

For all his queenly dish, or maybe because of it, Alex had a much more confident feel than I of a world out there to conquer. He had been noisily defying for so long his father's Greek ideal of manhood. "My son is a girl!" Nick would bellow as if accursed, Alex shaking his pom-poms in retort.

I can't say I actually envied him, but his raw, confrontive style had a certain antic charm about it. He was a drag queen without the dress and makeup, a caricature of a sissy, over the top in a town that had never seen gender-fuck at all. Consequently the bullies gave him a sort of theatrical clearance.

In a way I couldn't begin to explain, Alex was defining himself more truly than I with all my school credentials. He said whatever came into his head, nothing to lose, go screw yourself if you didn't like it. Two months later I would have been mortified if any of my Yale friends had seen us laughing together, so desperate was I to pass. But in that summer of finishing life in the provinces I took a curious refuge in the camp of Alex Anestos, who might say absolutely anything and usually did.

"Good morning, sir," he'd greet a bleary customer. "You look like you   5 need a little Ex-Lax, or is it a Kotex?" And they didn't quite hear it, because they couldn't believe it. There was something about these manic sendups, murmured just under his breath, that suggested a marvelous anarchy. Pinning a KICK ME sign on the seat of pompous WASP and shanty Irish alike.

Alex went with me to the mall one day, a half-hour's drive to Peabody. I was meant to buy clothes for school, but I'd been fretting that my summer savings weren't enough to steer me through the unchartered waters of starting college. We wandered around looking for sales, I wistfully passing up sweaters and jackets I couldn't afford. Without any premeditation I can recall, I found myself at the underwear counter at Kresge's, surreptitiously stuffing a package of Jockey shorts into my shopping bag. I think the idea was to rip off the little stuff so I could buy a sexy sweater. Unless I was simply out to prove that Paul was no longer perfect.

With scant experience at thievery, I was blithely unaware of mall security. In the next store I took my time picking a nice pair of flannel pajamas, then dropped them into my bag. (From that day on I never wore p.j.'s again.) Suddenly a hand grabbed my elbow, and I was dragged unceremoniously to the store's office, matrons gaping at me from every aisle. I broke into a cold sweat, half fainted. The plainclothesman, who reminded me of my father, summoned a cop who formally arrested me. Both stores were pressing charges, and I was to appear the following morning at the Salem courthouse.

All the way home, Alex tried gently to laugh it off as an adventure, but I was profoundly rattled. I told my mother with shamefaced tears. Though she was pained, she hugged me and promised we'd get through it. When Dad got home, he looked like he'd taken a punch in the gut, but as usual he was unbearably decent. The hardest thing was to drive to Salem at seven A.M., just he and I, the feeling I had of his sidelong looks, as if he didn't know what to make of me anymore.

The judge saw us in chambers. After hearing the cop's testimony and a halting plea from Dad, he turned to me and said, "You realize, don't you, if Yale finds out about this, you're out." Now it was my turn to squirm and plead, how I understood the advantages I'd been given and would hereafter be a model citizen—a speech of Ciceronian clarity. He listened with pursed lips, a moment's silence as he toyed with my fate. Then gruffly dismissed the case, with a warning that I was *persona non grata* at the Northshore Mall forever.

We drove back to Andover wilted with relief. And yet I remember being   10 struck by the most perverse thought: *If Yale found out about this, I wouldn't have to go.* Unthinkable really, that I should seek a way to derail my glorious rise to privilege. I buried it rather than face it. But the incident shows how conflicted I was about sailing into the future, as well as an instinct for sabotage. Something in me didn't want more schooling, dreaded the claustrophobia of being one of the guys. Alex's life by contrast was utterly free to happen, changeable as the color of his hair.

But as I say, I buried all that along with my police record. Yale was the next step, period. My mother and Nana dutifully sewed the nametags into my clothes, Nana's dignity much offended by the artificial leg and cane that had lately become her cross. She might have been going to Yale herself, so passionate was the vicarious thrill, for I was the first on the English side to ever get to college. The night before we left for New Haven, my Uncle Dan, with eight kids to feed, tucked ten bucks he couldn't afford into my shirt pocket. "Go buy a round of beers at Mory's," he said with a fond wink, sending the family hero off to claim his knighthood.

The next day, driving down, we stopped at a Hojo's just out of Hartford. ("Is that New York?" my brother asked in an awestruck voice as we swung by Hartford's three tall buildings. "No," we all laughed, though scarcely more worldly than he.) My father and I had a moment alone as he paid the bill, Bobby and Mother off to find the washroom. With an unsettling depth of feeling Dad put his arm around me and said, "Now remember, don't get involved with the wrong kind of girl. Okay?"

I nodded dumbly, seized by a rush of sorrow. Sad that my secrets kept us eternally out of phase, and hopeless of ever changing things.

The homesick blues were intolerable that first fall semester of '63, especially because I denied them. My life in 1068 Bingham Hall was a full-time job, chameleon and ventriloquist, so there wasn't a lot of time left over to feel how lonely I was. A two-bedroom suite, with bunk beds in each. The powers that be had paired me up with a studious lad from Andover, though we had barely been on nodding terms at school. This Russell (never Russ) had already decided on Chinese Studies, arriving at Yale with several thousand vocabulary cards and a placid air that was positively Confucian. He took the upper, I the lower.

15   Our two California roommates arrived in tandem: Sean and Jake, respectively a rock climber from Marin and a tennis jock from Santa Barbara. Outsize figures from the moment they walked through the door. They'd been buddies at the Trimble School—best of the West, old California gold, where every boy was required to keep a horse because it built character. Jake was third generation Trimble himself, grandson of the founding gentleman cowboy. He and Sean were smart as anybody from Andover, but not so polished, and proud of that. As to the mores and climate of Yale, everything struck them as being so *Eastern*, which only fortified their free-range superiority.

I was smitten by them both inside of twenty minutes. Not sexually, exactly—sexually was the least of it. Though they were strapping good athletes and frontier rugged, they never occupied a slot in the Olympian frieze of my fantasies. I needed them both to be more real than that, or else how would they ever transform my doggy life? For I quickly came to see them as my salvation, the pals I never had among the Apollo and Dionysus ranks of Andover. I'd never been on the inside before, shooting the breeze in a bull session. Never been anyone's confidant about women.

I took to the role with near-demented enthusiasm. To curry the favor of Sean and Jake I underwent a personality change—voluble where I'd been tongue-tied before, flattering them at every turn, adopting their sneering distaste for the East, I who'd never been west of the Hudson. I dressed like they did, took every meal I could with them. *Courtier* is far too pretty a term for my servile hero worship; *sycophant* is closer. Yet it wasn't at all unconscious: I saw my new friends as a last chance to leave behind the nothing I was in high school.

Thus I stopped answering Francis's letter from Georgetown, sealing the tomb on our old playful style, because it felt tainted with faggotry. Till the first snowfall I'd get up with Sean on Sunday mornings and pile in a van with the Mountaineering Club, to spend hair-raising afternoons climbing the sheer faces of northern Connecticut's bony hills. Graceless and panting, biting the tongue of my acrophobia, I clambered up the gorse till my knuckles bled, all for a macho nod from Sean at the summit. Back at the dorm, I laughed myself hoarse at Jake's razor wit, becoming his personal buffoon and comic foil. He wanted to be a writer, and therefore so did I. Prose was his meat and potatoes, and therefore I took poetry.

It amazes me now, that I made life choices for no other reason than to get in Sean and Jake's good graces. Today I haven't a clue where they live or what they've done since Yale. I realize college provides a classic ground for reinvention of self, but self had nothing to do with this. The very opposite: all I wanted to be was the two of them, burying every trace of Paul Monette.

Bury especially the hungry voyeur with the secrets. Jake had what amounted to a knee-jerk loathing of queers, every third remark a withering bash of anybody who seemed the least bit eccentric. He'd pout his lips and affect a nancy lisp and a wobbly wrist, dismissing whatever felt effete or even intellectual. Since there were so many closeted teachers about, Yale was fertile territory for his HUAC-style snipery, every bachelor guilty till proven innocent. And I was the first to go along, frantic to hide my own fellow-traveling. Eagerly I learned how to mock my brothers behind their backs—anything to make Jake laugh.

But more was required to prove one's manhood than just the putting down of queers. In those pre-coed days, Yale men hardly talked of anything except getting laid, unless it was getting drunk. The best of all worlds therefore was scoring in both at once: a dream Saturday night where you'd be shitfaced from the rotgut punch at a mixer and mauling some poor townie girl. Jake and Sean were more than eager to get in on the action, pestering me to set them up with dates since I was the one with the East Coast connections. I could no more admit I'd never dated than I could my heterosexual virginity. So I invented my own modest tales of carnal prowess, cobbling details here and there from other men's boasting.

For Dartmouth weekend I invited a girl I knew from Rosemary Hall, who arrived with a blushing pair of her classmates. I hated attending the football game, having no idea what was going down on the field, but the worst was the mixer that night. Guys throwing up in the bushes outside and a general air of male entitlement, showing off their women and making their moves in the shadows to the tawdry strains of *Louie Louie*. I was engaged in the upstream battle of *not* scoring, avoiding sex at all costs. Here my four-year schizophrenic pattern laid itself out: the requisite girl on my arm, the looking good, the frenzied round of sports and museums and parties, anything to avoid too much time *à deux*, the compulsory makeout.

I wasn't unaware even at the time what a grim sham I was putting the girls through. Oh, I made up for my carnal detachment with frantic charm and witticisms, and for a while at least found dates who seemed relieved not to be mauled. But I would almost never see a girl twice, for fear of the expectations. The girl from Rosemary Hall kept writing till Christmas, and I was too frozen to answer. Every minute of a date felt like a lie, but if you didn't date, you couldn't be one of the guys. My guys anyway, whose opinion I cared about more than my own.

For Harvard weekend I invited Missy Cabot to come down from Middlebury, spending my self-imposed month's allowance just on tickets for The Game. As Missy wasn't due in till six on Friday, I spent the afternoon out at the soccer field, timing the freshman match between Harvard and Yale. I hadn't suddenly developed a fondness for the sport that gave me chilblains all through four rotten autumns at Andover. It was because Sean and Jake were playing for Yale, and I their constant companion could get no closer than sitting on the bench with a stopwatch.

25   In the middle of the third quarter a campus policeman came up to huddle with the coach. From where I sat, the cop looked like he was crying. When he turned away, the coach walked over to me, who till now was as insignificant to him as a cockroach. "The President's been shot," he said, and at first I thought he meant the president of Yale. "He's still alive. I don't want the players told. We'll finish the game."

I don't think I could have been less political in those days. Because of my endless self-absorption and twenty-four-hour vigilance at the closet door, I never read the papers except for the theater page. The Cuban missile crisis had passed without causing a ripple in my pond. I'd only worn a Kennedy button in '60 because everyone in my family was voting for Nixon. I had no personal investment, in other words, and yet the coach's cavalier priorities offended me for the President's sake. Would he have stopped the game if the news had come in the *first* quarter?

By the time I bleated the horn at the end—a 3–3 tie—Kennedy was dead. Too late to stop Missy from coming. So the weekend proceeded, in New Haven as elsewhere, to the sound of muffled drums. We spent most of our time in front of the one snowy TV in the dorm, the world reduced to black and white. And yet what I remember most is the over-riding sense of relief, as Missy cradled her head on my shoulder and cried softly into a handkerchief. Relief that I wouldn't have to make any carnal moves, wouldn't have to prove my hormonal mettle. A chaste goodnight kiss was more in keeping with national tragedy.

A grotesque perspective, to put it mildly. The self-obsession that fears exposure will grab at almost anything to keep the closet door shut. When I bundled Missy off on the bus on Sunday afternoon—just after Ruby shot Oswald—the psychic pain had bonded us, travelers thrown together by a crash. I wouldn't be inviting her again, of course, though I basked for a few days after in Sean and Jake's praise of her winsome beauty and Mayflower cheekbones. I had turned Missy into a "beard" without knowing the term, like the artificial dates those closeted powers of Hollywood take in their limos to all the openings and awards. Except in L.A., the starlets line up around the block for such an honor.

READING CRITICALLY FOR IDEAS, STRUCTURE, AND STYLE

1. Describe the circumstances in which Monette's career at Yale was jeapordized. To what extent do you think Monette's shoplifting represented his attempt to emulate his friend Alex and/or to forestall having to attend Yale? Explain your answer.

2. Consider the subterfuges to which Monette had to resort in order to conceal his homosexuality. How did these subterfuges make him feel about himself?

3. What qualities in Monette's account suggest that he is uncompromisingly honest in seeing through personal and social facades, including his own? How would you characterize the tone of this essay—jaded, ironic? Explain your answer.

4. What insight does his account give you into the values of American society at that time?

EXTENDING INSIGHTS THROUGH WRITING

1. When you started attending college, were there aspects of your personality you had to hide in order to gain acceptance? Compare your experiences with those of Monette's in a 300–500 word essay.

2. In what ways have social attitudes towards homosexuality changed since Monette attended college and since he wrote this in 1992?

CONNECTING PERSPECTIVES ON THE INDIVIDUAL EXPERIENCE

1. Both Monette and Joseph Addison possess very distinctive literary styles. Write a few paragraphs comparing and contrasting these styles, in terms of wit, understatement, and irony.

2. Does Monette's infatuation with Sean and Jake follow Stendhal's analysis of what he calls "the crystallization of love"? Why or why not?

LORD CHESTERFIELD

Letter to His Son

BACKGROUND

Philip Dormer Stanhope (1694–1773), the fourth Earl of Chesterfield, was one of the most influential English statesmen of his age. He was born in London and rose to prominent public positions. He was twice ambassador to The Hague, Secretary of State, negotiator of the second treaty of Vienna in 1731, and an amazingly successful Lord Lieutenant of Ireland in 1746, during a particularly dangerous time, when his goverance elicited the appreciation of both England and Ireland for more than a century. His book on courtesy, deportment, and manners in the form of letters written to his illegitimate son, Philip, embodied the urbane pragmatism of the eighteenth century. In 1755, Lord Chesterfield quarreled with Dr. Samuel Johnson who was so angry at Chesterfield's refusal to patronize his famous dictionary that he condemned the *Letters* for "teach [ing] the morals of a whore, and the manners of a dancing master," but conceded that it might prove useful, "take out the immorality, and it should be put into the hands of every young gentleman." A model of courtly elegance, Lord Chesterfield also gave his name to a style of overcoat (single or double breasted with a narrow velvet collar) and a kind of couch (a large overstuffed sofa or divan with a back and upholstered arms).

APPROACHING CHESTERFIELD'S LETTER

These letters, begun when Philip was quite young and continuing for many years, were designed to shrewdly appraise the conduct of his peers and to advise Philip on the ways in which he might move easily through the treacherous shoals of eighteenth-century society. Ironically, these worldy and to some, cynical, observations failed in their intent: Philip married a woman of low social position, never achieved the rank his father had sought to prepare him for, and predeceased Lord Chesterfield by five years. After Philip's death, Chesterfield, who had not known of the existence of his daughter-in-law and grandsons, showed a very human side when he befriended them. Although Philip did not benefit from Chesterfield's wit and wisdom, we, almost 300 years later, can appreciate his studied eloquence, engaging style, and often quite sound advice.

Letter to His Son

BATH, OCTOBER 19, 1748.

Dear Boy,

Having, in my last, *pointed out* what sort of company you should keep, I will now give you some rules for your conduct in it; rules which my own EXPERIENCE and OBSERVATION ENABLE me to lay down and communicate to you with some degree of confidence. I have often given you hints of this kind before, but then it has been by snatches; I will now be more regular and methodical. I shall say nothing with regard to your bodily carriage and address, but leave them to the care of your dancing-master, and to your own attention to the best models: remember, however, that they are of consequence.

Talk often, but never long; in that case, if you do not please, at least you are sure not to tire your hearers. Pay your own reckoning, but do not treat the whole company; this being one of the very few cases in which people do not care to be treated, every one being fully convinced that he has wherewithal to pay.

Tell stories very seldom, and absolutely never but where they are very apt, and very short. Omit every circumstance that is not material, and beware of digressions. To have frequent recourse to narrative betrays great want of imagination.

Never hold anybody by the button, or the hand, in order to be heard out; for, if people are not willing to hear you, you had much better hold your tongue than them.

5   Most long talkers single out some one unfortunate man in company (commonly him whom they observe to be the most silent, or their next neighbour) to whisper, or at least, in a half voice, to convey a continuity of words to. This is excessively ill-bred, and, in some degree, a fraud; conversation-stock being a joint and common property. But, on the other hand, if one of these unmerciful talkers lays hold on you, hear him with patience, and at least seeming attention, if he is worth obliging; for nothing will oblige him more than a patient hearing, as nothing would hurt him more than either to leave him in the midst of his discourse, or to discover your impatience under your affliction.

Take, rather than give, the tone of the company you are in. If you have parts,[1] you will show them, more or less, upon every subject; and, if you have not, you had better talk sillily upon a subject of other people's than of your own choosing.

Avoid as much as you can, in mixed companies, argumentative polemical conversations; which, though they should not, yet certainly do, indispose, for a time, the contending parties towards each other; and, if the controversy grows warm and noisy, endeavour to put an end to it by some genteel levity or joke. I quieted such a conversation hubbub once, by representing to them that, though I was persuaded none there present would repeat, out of company, what passed in it, yet I could not answer for the discretion of the passengers in the street, who must necessarily hear all that was said.

Above all things, and upon all occasions, avoid speaking of yourself, if it be possible. Such is the natural pride and vanity of our hearts, that it perpetually breaks out, even in people of the best parts, in all the various modes and figures of the egotism.

Some abruptly speak advantageously of themselves, without either pretence or provocation. They are impudent. Others proceed more artfully, as they imagine, and forge accusations against themselves, complain of calumnies which they never heard, in order to justify themselves, by exhibiting a catalogue of their many virtues. "They acknowledge it may, indeed, seem odd, that they should talk in that manner of themselves; it is what they do not like, and what they never would have done; no, no torture should ever have forced it from them, if they had not been thus unjustly and monstrously accused. But, in these cases, justice is surely due to one's self, as well as to others; and, when our character is attacked, we may say, in our own justification, what otherwise

---

[1]If you are intelligent.

we never would have said." This thin veil of modesty drawn before vanity, is much too transparent to conceal it, even from very moderate discernment.

Others go more modestly and more slyly still (as they think) to work; but, in my mind, still more ridiculously. They confess themselves (not without some degree of shame and confusion) into all the cardinal virtues; by first degrading them into weaknesses, and then owning their misfortune, in being made up of those weaknesses. "They cannot see people suffer, without sympathizing with, and endeavouring to help them. They cannot see people want, without relieving them; though, truly, their own circumstances cannot very well afford it. They cannot help speaking truth, though they know all the imprudence of it. In short, they know that, with all these weaknesses, they are not fit to live in the world, much less to thrive in it. But they are now too old to change, and must rub on as well as they can." This sounds too ridiculous and *outré*, almost for the stage; and yet, take my word for it, you will frequently meet with it upon the common stage of the world. And here I will observe, by the bye, that you will often meet with characters in nature so extravagant, that a discreet poet would not venture to set them upon the stage in their true and high colouring.

This principle of vanity and pride is so strong in human nature, that it descends even to the lowest objects; and one often sees people angling for praise, where, admitting all they say to be true (which, by the way, it seldom is), no just praise is to be caught. One man affirms that he had rode post[2] an hundred miles in six hours: probably it is a lie; but supposing it to be true, what then? Why, he is a very good postboy, that is all. Another asserts, and probably not without oaths, that he has drank six or eight bottles of wine at a sitting; out of charity, I will believe him a liar; for, if I do not, I must think him a beast.

Such, and a thousand more, are the follies and extravagancies, which *vanity* draws people into, and which always defeat their own purpose, and, as Waller says upon another subject:

> Make the wretch the most despised,
> Where most he wishes to be prized.[*]

The only sure way of avoiding these evils is never to speak of yourself at all. But when historically you are obliged

---

[2]Rode fast, like a mail (post) carrier.
[*]These lines are adapted from Waller's *On Love*. The couplet is:
> Postures which render him despised,
> Where he endeavors to be prized.

to mention yourself, take care not to drop one single word, that can directly or indirectly be construed as fishing for applause. Be your character what it will, it will be known; and nobody will take it upon your own word. Never imagine that anything you can say yourself will varnish your defects, or add lustre to your perfections; but, on the contrary, it may, and nine times in ten will, make the former more glaring, and the latter obscure. If you are silent upon your own subject, neither envy, indignation, nor ridicule will obstruct or allay the applause which you may really deserve; but if you publish your own panegyric, upon any occasion, or in any shape whatsoever, and however artfully dressed or disguised, they will all conspire against you, and you will be disappointed of the very end you aim at.

Take care never to seem dark and mysterious; which is not only a very unamiable character, but a very suspicious one too; if you seem mysterious with others, they will be really so with you, and you will know nothing. The height of abilities is, to have *volto sciolto* and *pensieri stretti*;[3] that is, a frank, open, and ingenuous exterior, with a prudent and reserved interior; to be upon your own guard, and yet, by a seeming natural openness, to put people off theirs. Depend upon it, nine in ten of every company you are in will avail themselves of every indiscreet and unguarded expression of yours, if they can turn it to their own advantage. A prudent reserve is therefore as necessary as a seeming openness is prudent. Always look people in the face when you speak to them; the not doing it is thought to imply conscious guilt; besides that, you lose the advantage of observing by their countenances what impression your discourse makes upon them. In order to know people's real sentiments, I trust much more to my eyes than to my ears; for they can say whatever they have a mind I should hear; but they can seldom help looking what they have no intention that I should know.

15   Neither retail nor receive scandal willingly; for though the defamation of others may for the present gratify the malignity of the pride of our hearts, cool reflection will draw very disadvantageous conclusions from such a disposition; and in the case of scandal, as in that of robbery, the receiver is always thought as bad as the thief.

Mimicry, which is the common and favourite amusement of little low minds, is in the utmost contempt with great ones. It is the lowest and most illiberal of all buffoonery. Pray, neither practise it yourself, nor applaud it in others. Besides that,

---

[3]A candid appearance and reserved thoughts.

the person mimicked is insulted; and, as I have often observed to you before, an insult is never forgiven.

I need not, I believe, advise you to adapt your conversation to the people you are conversing with; for I suppose you would not, without this caution, have talked upon the same subject and in the same manner to a Minister of state, a Bishop, a philosopher, a Captain, and a woman. A man of the world must, like the chameleon, be able to take every different hue, which is by no means a criminal or abject, but a necessary complaisance, for it relates only to manners, and not to morals.

One word only as to swearing; and that I hope and believe is more than is necessary. You may sometimes hear some people in good company interlard their discourse with oaths, by way of embellishment, as they think; but you must observe, too, that those who do so are never those who contribute in any degree to give that company the denomination of good company. They are always subalterns, or people of low education; for that practice, besides that it has no one temptation to plead, is as silly and as illiberal as it is wicked.

Loud laughter is the mirth of the mob, who are only pleased with silly things; for true wit or good sense never excited a laugh since the creation of the world. A man of parts and fashion is therefore only seen to smile, but never heard to laugh.

But, to conclude this long letter; all the above-mentioned rules, however carefully you may observe them, will lose half their effect if unaccompanied by the Graces. Whatever you say, if you say it with a supercilious, cynical face, or an embarrassed countenance, or a silly, disconcerted grin, will be ill received. If, into the bargain, *you mutter it, or utter it indistinctly and ungracefully,* it will be still worse received. If your air and address are vulgar, awkward, and *gauche,* you may be esteemed indeed if you have great intrinsic merit; but you will never please, and without pleasing you will rise but heavily. Venus, among the ancients, was synonymous with the Graces, who were always supposed to accompany her; and Horace tells us, that even youth, and Mercury, the god of arts and eloquence, would not do without her.

20

> —*Parum comis* sine te Juventas
> Mercuriusque.[4]

They are not inexorable ladies, and may be had if properly and diligently pursued. Adieu!

---

[4]*Odes* I. 30: "Without thee, youth and even Mercury himself have no charm."

READING CRITICALLY FOR IDEAS, STRUCTURE, AND STYLE

1. What do Chesterfield's precepts suggest about the nature of eighteenth-century English society and the qualities that would be necessary to gain advancement?

2. What can you infer about Lord Chesterfield's personality from the voice that you hear in this letter? What clues tell you that he is worldly and sophisticated?

3. Analyze some of the unique stylistic features of Lord Chesterfield's letter (for example, look at the first sentence in the second paragraph and the last sentence in the fifth paragraph) in terms of how well-suited they are to the subject. What values guide Lord Chesterfield in giving this advice?

4. Is he concerned primarily about taking actions that are morally correct, prudent, or simply expedient? Cite instances in "Letter to His Son" to support your opinion?

EXTENDING INSIGHTS THROUGH WRITING

1. Are the same qualities required for success in the modern world as were required when Lord Chesterfield wrote this letter? Can you imagine a father today writing a letter containing advice on manners to a son, or daughter, in college? Why or why not?

2. Rewrite two or three paragraphs of Lord Chesterfield's letter updating it so that it applies to today's society. Try to emulate his pithy epigrammatic style.

CONNECTING PERSPECTIVES ON THE INDIVIDUAL EXPERIENCE

1. In what ways do both Stendhal (in his analysis of the different forms of love) and Lord Chesterfield (in his advice to his son) emphasize the overwhelming role that pride and vanity play in human nature?

2. Write a short letter as if you were Lord Chesterfield advising Paul Monette on how to cope with the crisis he confronts in "Becoming a Man." Avoid simplistic responses such as "stay in the closet" and try to give really useful advice of the kind Chesterfield might have given.

STENDHAL

The Crystallization of Love

BACKGROUND

Stendhal (the pseudonym of Marie Henri Beyle, 1783–1842), the French novelist, essayist, and critic, was born and educated in Grenoble, France. In 1806, he served with Napoleon in Germany and Austria, and witnessed the climactic battle at Moscow. He left the army in 1813 and traveled to Italy, where he lived for seven years, immersing himself in music, literature, art, and high society. While in Italy, he wrote his first work, *Rome, Naples, and Florence* (1817), under the name Stendhal. An unhappy love affair during this period awakened his interest in the psychology of love, the results of which appear in his well-known work *On Love* (1822), which Freud praised as "a manifestation of psychological genius." The novels on which Stendhal's fame rests, *The Red and the Black* (1831) and *The Charterhouse of Parma* (1839), display an intimate understanding of human nature, expressed with an irony that springs from Stendhal's awareness of his own capacity for self-deception in matters of the heart. As Stendhal himself predicted, his work was appreciated only after his death. In "The Crystallization of Love," from *On Love,* Stendhal expresses his belief that behavior is governed by passions and self-interest and presents a classification of four different types of love.

APPROACHING STENDHAL'S ESSAY

The meaning of romantic love has engaged thinkers and philosophers from Plato and Ovid to Montaigne and Freud, to Fromm and Sartre. Views on it range from St. Augustine's comment that "there is no such thing as romantic love. It is a myth which is intended to confuse the human soul from his quest for true and honest love for God" to Voltaire's witty appraisal that "love is the triumph of stupidity over reason." In the early nineteenth century, Stendhal developed an intriguing theory using the word "crystallization" to describe how we overlook the flaws, imperfections, and inconsistencies in people we love. The psychological process is comparable to the way a twig of a tree that is pushed into a mound of salt gathers crystals and hence sparkles, giving the appearance of something beautiful. Stendhal explained this phenomenon of "crystallization" in his book *On Love* as a natural "mental process which draws from everything that happens new proofs of the perfection of the loved one." In this state, the lover perceives the beloved as perfect and endows the beloved with "a thousand perfections."

Stendhal believed that four types of love exist: (1) "passion-love" (which he sees as a profound form of love between kindred souls); (2) "sympathy-love" (a masochistic form of love in which the lover takes pleasure in wallowing in his misery); (3) "sensual-love" (based on indulgence of the senses and satisfaction of basic sex drives as an end in itself); and (4) "vanity-love" (which Stendhal characterizes as egotism and a desire to possess, "as one might own or possess a fine horse"). In "vanity love," the lover's objective is enhancement of his own self-esteem. Stendhal's classification of "love" into four different types—although he admits "one could easily adopt eight or ten shades" (para. 15)—is well-suited to clarify a complex, subjective psychological phenomena.

The division of his essay into short chapters makes it easier for the reader to perceive the very real differences between different kinds of love and the different stages through which love evolves. By classifying "love" into these four different kinds, Stendhal made it easier for his readers to recognize each type, evaluate one kind against the others, and ultimately avoid self-deception.

The Crystallization of Love

CHAPTER I

ON LOVE

I am trying to account for that passion all of whose developments are inherently beautiful.

There are four different kinds of love:

1. Passion-love, that of the Portuguese Nun, of Héloïse for Abélard, of Captain de Vésel, of the Cento man-at-arms.[1]

---

[1]The *Letters of a Portuguese Nun*, unfolding the true story of a woman seduced, abandoned, and still passionately in love, went into many French and English editions in the seventeenth and eighteenth centuries. As for the captain and the man-at-arms mentioned here, Stendhal, when asked about them, said he had forgotten their story.

2. Sympathy-love, such as was prevalent in Paris in 1760, and is found in the memoirs and romances of that period, in Crébillon, Lauzun, Duclos, Marmontel, Chamfort, Madame d'Epinay, etc., etc.

It is a picture in which everything, even to the shadows, must be rose coloured, and into which nothing unpleasant must intrude under any pretext whatever, at the risk of infringing custom, fashion, refinement, etc. A well-bred man knows in advance everything that he must do and expect in the various stages of this kind of love; as there is nothing passionate or unexpected about it, it is often more refined than real love, for it is always sprightly; it is like a cold and pretty miniature compared with a picture by the Caracci; and, whereas passion-love carries us away against all our interests, sympathy-love always knows how to adjust itself to them. It is true that if you strip this poor form of love of its vanity, very little remains; without its vanity, it is like a feeble convalescent who is scarcely able to drag himself along.

3. Sensual love.

Whilst out shooting, to meet a fresh, pretty country girl who darts away into a wood. Every one knows the love founded on pleasures of this kind; however unromantic and wretched one's character, it is there that one starts at the age of sixteen.

4. Vanity-love.

The great majority of men, especially in France, desire and possess a fashionable woman as they would possess a fine horse, as a necessary luxury for a young man. Their vanity, more or less flattered and more or less stimulated, gives rise to rapture. Sometimes sensual love is present also, but not always; often there is not even sensual pleasure. The Duchesse de Chaulnes used to say that a duchess is never more than thirty years old to a snob; and people who frequented the Court of that upright man, King Louis of Holland, still recall with amusement a pretty woman at the Hague who could never bring herself to think a man anything but charming if he was a Duke or a Prince. But, faithful to the monarchic principle, as soon as a Prince arrived at Court she dropped the Duke. She was a kind of insignia of the Corps Diplomatique.

The most agreeable form of this rather insipid relationship is the one in which sensual pleasure is increased by habit. In that case past memories make it seem something like real love; there is piqued vanity and sadness on being abandoned; and, becoming seized by romantic ideas, you begin to think you are in love and melancholy, for your vanity always aspires to have a great passion to its credit. The one thing certain is that to whatever kind of love one owes one's pleasures, so long as they are accompanied by mental exhilaration, they are very keen and their memory is entrancing; and in this passion, contrary to most others, the memory of what we have lost always seems sweeter than anything that we can hope for in the future.

Sometimes, in vanity-love, habit and the despair of finding anything better produces a kind of friendship, the least agreeable of all its kinds; it prides itself on its *security*, etc.

Sensual pleasure, being part of our nature, is within the grasp of every one, but it only holds a very low place in the eyes of tender and passionate beings. Although they may be ridiculous in drawing-rooms, although worldly people may often make them unhappy by their intrigues, on the other hand they taste pleasures utterly inaccessible to those hearts who only thrill to vanity or to gold.

Some virtuous and affectionate women have almost no idea at all of sensual pleasure; they have only very rarely laid themselves open to it, if I may put it so, and even then the raptures of passion-love have almost made them forget the pleasures of the body.

Some men are the victims and instruments of a satanic pride, a sort of Alfieri pride. These people, who are perhaps cruel because, like Nero, they live in constant fear, judging every one by their own heart, these people, I say, cannot obtain any sensual pleasure unless it is accompanied by circumstances which flatter their pride abnormally, that is to say, unless they can perpetrate some cruelty on the companion of their pleasures.... These men cannot feel the emotion of security with anything less.

However, instead of distinguishing four different kinds of love, one could easily adopt eight or ten shades. There are perhaps as many different ways of feeling as of seeing amongst men; but these differences in terms do not affect the reasoning that follows. Every kind of love that one meets here below is born, lives, dies or becomes immortal, according to the same laws.

CHAPTER II

THE BIRTH OF LOVE

This is what goes on in the mind:
1. Admiration.
2. One says to one's self: "How delightful to kiss her, to be kissed in return," etc.
3. Hope.

One studies her perfections. It is at this moment that a woman should surrender herself, to get the greatest possible sensual pleasure. The eyes of even the most modest women light up the moment hope is born; passion is so strong and pleasure is so acute that they betray themselves in the most obvious manner.

4. Love is born.

To love is to derive pleasure from seeing, touching and feeling through all one's senses and as closely as possible, a lovable person who loves us.

5. The first crystallization begins.

We take a joy in attributing a thousand perfections to a woman of whose love we are sure; we analyze all our happiness with intense satisfaction. This reduces itself to giving ourselves an exaggerated idea of a magnificent possession which has just fallen to us from Heaven in some way we do not understand, and the continued possession of which is assured to us.

This is what you will find if you let a lover turn things over in his mind for twenty-four hours.

In the salt mines of Salzburg a bough stripped of its leaves by winter is thrown into the depths of the disused workings; two or three months later it is pulled out again, covered with brilliant crystals: even the tiniest twigs, no bigger than a tomtit's claw, are spangled with a vast number of shimmering, glittering diamonds, so that the original bough is no longer recognizable.

I call crystallization that process of the mind which discovers fresh perfections in its beloved at every turn of events.[2]

For instance, should a traveller speak of the coolness of Genoese orange groves by the seashore on a scorching summer day, you immediately think how delightful it would be to enjoy this coolness in her company!

One of your friends breaks his arm out hunting: how sweet, you think, to be nursed by a woman you love! To be with her always and to revel in her constant love would almost make your pain blessèd; and you leave your friend's broken arm still more firmly convinced of the angelic sweetness of your mistress. In short, it is sufficient to think of a perfection in order to see it in the person you love.

This phenomenon which I have allowed myself to call *crystallization,* arises from the promptings of Nature which urge us to enjoy ourselves and drive the blood to our brains, from the feeling that our delight increases with the perfections of the beloved, and from the thought: "She is mine." The savage has no time to get beyond the first step. He grasps his pleasures, but his brain is concentrated on following the buck fleeing from him through the forest, and with whose flesh he must repair his own strength as quickly as possible, at the risk of falling beneath the hatchet of his enemy.

At the other extreme of civilization, I have no doubt that a sensitive woman arrives at the point of experiencing no sensual pleasure except with the man she loves. This is in direct opposition to the savage. But, amongst civilized communities woman has plenty of leisure, whilst the savage lives so close to essentials that he is obliged to treat his female as a beast of burden. If the females of many animals have an easier lot, it is only because the subsistence of the males is more assured.

But let us leave the forests and return to Paris. A passionate man sees nothing but perfection in the woman he loves; and yet his affections may still wander, for the spirit wearies of monotony, even in the case of the most perfect happiness.

So what happens to rivet his attention is this:

6. Doubt is born.

When his hopes have first of all been raised and then confirmed by ten or a dozen glances, or a whole series of other actions which may be com-

---

[2]What Stendhal calls "crystallization" we would probably call "projection." The lover projects upon the beloved qualities which exist only in his imagination and which have little or no relation to the actual person.

pressed into a moment or spread over several days, the lover, recovering from his first amazement and growing used to his happiness, or perhaps merely guided by theory which, based always on his most frequent experiences, is really only correct in the case of light women, the lover, I say, demands more positive proofs of love and wants to advance the moment of his happiness.

If he takes too much for granted he will be met with indifference, coldness or even anger: in France there will be a suggestion of irony which seems to say: "You think you have made more progress than you really have." A woman behaves in this way either because she is recovering from a moment of intoxication and obeys the behests of modesty, which she is alarmed at having transgressed, or merely from prudence or coquettishness.

The lover begins to be less sure of the happiness which he has promised himself; he begins to criticize the reasons he gave himself for hoping.

He tries to fall back on the other pleasures of life. *He finds they no longer exist.* He is seized with a dread of appalling misery, and his attention becomes concentrated.

7. Second crystallization.

Now begins the second crystallization, producing as its diamonds various confirmations of the following idea:

"She loves me."

Every quarter of an hour, during the night following the birth of doubt, after a moment of terrible misery, the lover says to himself: "Yes, she loves me"; and crystallization sets to work to discover fresh charms; then gaunt-eyed doubt grips him again and pulls him up with a jerk. His heart misses a beat; he says to himself: "But does she love me?" Through all these harrowing and delicious alternations the poor lover feels acutely: "With her I would experience joys which she alone in the world could give me."

It is the clearness of this truth and the path he treads between an appalling abyss and the most perfect happiness, that make the second crystallization appear to be so very much more important than the first.

The lover hovers incessantly amongst these three ideas:

1. She is perfect in every way.
2. She loves me.
3. How can I get the strongest possible proof of her love for me?

The most heart-rending moment in love that is still young is when it finds that it has been wrong in its chain of reasoning and must destroy a whole agglomeration of crystals.

Even the fact of crystallization itself begins to appear doubtful.

CHAPTER III

... The thing that ensures the duration of love is the second crystallization, during which at every moment one realizes that one must either be loved or perish. How, with this conviction ever present in one's mind, and grown into a habit by several months of love, can one bear even the thought of ceasing to love? The more determined a man's character, the less liable is he to be inconstant.

This second crystallization is practically non-existent in love inspired by women who surrender themselves too quickly.

As soon as the crystallizations have taken place, especially the second one, which is much the stronger, indifferent eyes no longer recognize the bough:
1. For, It is adorned by perfections or diamonds which they do not see;
2. It is adorned by perfections which are not perfections in their sight....

CHAPTER IV

IN the mind of a completely unbiased person, that, for instance, of a young girl living in a country house in an isolated part of the country—the most insignificant unexpected event may lead to a little admiration, and if this is followed by the slightest ray of hope, it causes the birth of love and crystallization.

In a case of this kind, the first attraction of love is that it is a distraction.

Surprise and hope are powerfully assisted by the need of love and the melancholy which one has at the age of sixteen. It is fairly clear that the main anxiety of that age is a thirst for love, and it is characteristic of that thirst not to be unreasonably particular about the kind of draught that chance may offer to slake it....

CHAPTER V

MAN is not free to refuse to do the thing which gives him more pleasure than any other conceivable action.

Love is like a fever; it comes and goes without the will having any part in the process. That is one of the principal differences between sympathy-love and passion-love, and one can only congratulate one's self on the fine qualities of the person one loves as on a lucky chance.

Love, indeed, belongs to every age: take, for instance, the passion of Madame du Deffand for the unattractive Horace Walpole.

CHAPTER VI

THE SALZBURG BOUGH

DURING love, crystallization hardly ever stops. This is its history: so long as you are on a distant footing with the person you love, crystallization takes place from an *imaginary solution*; it is only in your imagination that you are certain of the existence of any particular perfection in the woman you love. After you have arrived at terms of intimacy, constantly renewed fears are calmed by more real solutions. In this way, happiness is never uniform except in its source. Every day has a different flower.

If the loved woman surrenders to the passion she feels and falls into the grievous error of killing fear by the ardour of her transports, crystallization stops for a moment; but, when love loses its ardour, that is to say, its fears, it acquires the charm of complete unconstraint, of boundless confidence, and

a sweet familiarity comes to deaden all the sorrows of life and bring fresh interest into one's pleasures.

If you are deserted, crystallization starts again; and the thought of every
act of admiration and each delight which she can bestow on you and of which
you had ceased to think, ends in this harrowing reflection: "That rapturous
joy will *never* be mine again! And it is through my own fault that I have lost
it!" If you try to find happiness in emotions of a different kind your heart
refuses to react to them....

CHAPTER VII

DIFFERENCES BETWEEN THE BIRTH OF LOVE IN THE TWO SEXES

WOMEN attach themselves by their favours. As nineteen-twentieths of their
ordinary day-dreams are connected with love, these day-dreams are all concentrated on one person after intimacy; they endeavour to justify such an
extraordinary proceeding, so decisive and so contrary to all the habits of modesty. Men have no task of this kind to perform; later, a woman's imagination
pictures minutely and at her leisure such moments of delight.

Since love makes one doubt even the most clearly proven things, the
woman who before intimacy was so sure that her lover was a man above the
common herd, is terrified lest he has only been trying to add another woman
to his list of conquests, as soon as she thinks she has nothing more to refuse
him.

That is the moment for the appearance of the second crystallization
which, because of the fear that accompanies it, is much the stronger.

A woman thinks that from being a queen she has made herself a slave.
This state of mind and soul is encouraged by the nervous intoxication which
is the result of indulgence in pleasures which are all the more emotional in
proportion to the rarity of their occurrence. Again, a woman seated before her
embroidery frame, a dull form of work which only occupies her hands, dreams
of her lover, whereas he, galloping across the plains with his squadron, is in
a position where the slightest miscalculation may lead to his being placed
under arrest.

I should imagine, therefore, that the second crystallization is much
stronger in the case of women, because they have more to fear, their vanity
and honour are at stake, and they have less to distract them from it....

READING CRITICALLY FOR IDEAS, STRUCTURE, AND STYLE

1. What Stendhal calls "crystallization" might be understood as an
   analysis of the psychological projections lovers confer upon
   each other. How does this process operate and what forms does
   it take?

2. Stendhal's classification of four kinds of love draws some interesting distinctions. For example, he does not equate "passion-love" with "sensual love." According to Stendhal, what are the differences between the two? Do you agree with his assessment? Why or why not?

3. What features of Stendhal's essay suggest that it was intended for both the edification and amusement of his eighteenth-century readers?

4. Discuss the evidence that suggests that Stendhal's unhappy experiences with unrequited love underlie the sardonic wit of this treatise.

EXTENDING INSIGHTS THROUGH WRITING

1. This is not an essay of the kind to which we are accustomed. How is the unusual form of Stendhal's writing designed to communicate the way his thoughts develop on the subject?

2. Everyone can see some aspect of past or present love relationships in the finely drawn portraits of character types sketched by Stendhal. What parallels in contemporary life do Stendhal's four kinds of love have? Draw on examples either from your own experiences or what you have observed in fiction or film.

CONNECTING PERSPECTIVES ON THE INDIVIDUAL EXPERIENCE

1. In what respects do John Keats's "Letters to Fanny Brawne" illustrate what Stendhal calls "passion-love"? Would you agree this is a profound form of love between kindred souls or is it simply an example of Keats's self-deception?

2. In what respects is Stendhal's analysis of the process by which love develops (in the "Birth of Love") an accurate description of Anne Frank's romantic feelings towards Peter, as expressed in *The Diary of Anne Frank*?

JOHN KEATS

Letters to Fanny Brawne

BACKGROUND

John Keats (1795–1821), one of the greatest English poets, was born in Moorfields, London, where his father managed a livery stable. He was the eldest of four children and intitially apprenticed to a surgeon in 1811 (although he was already translating classic works, such as Virgil's *The Aeneid*). He passed his medical examinations, but was more interested in writing poetry and his verses (such as "On First Looking Into Chapman's Homer" [1815]) came to the attention of Leigh Hunt, who published many of Keats's first poems. At the age of 22 he traveled to the Isle of Wight and began work on his 4,000-line allegorical romance, *Endymion* (whose famous first line is "a thing of beauty is a joy forever"). It was published in 1818, the year that Keats fell in love with Fanny Brawne, a pretty 17-year old girl who lived nearby. Fanny's mother did not want her attractive daughter to marry a poor poet. Yet, when Keats was stricken with tuberculosis, both Fanny and her mother cared for him in their home. Shortly after the publication of Keats's last volume, *Lamia, Isabella, The Eve of St. Agnes, and Other Poems*, in July, 1820, Keats went to Italy for his health and died there at the age of 25. The quality of Keats's poems (including "Ode to a Nightingale," "To Autumn," and "Ode on a Grecian Urn") intertwine unequalled melody, rich imagery, and a romantic medievalism that define the romantic imagination at its finest. He is able to empathetically join himself to whatever he observes (which he referred to as "negative capability") and transcend the limits of his ordinary self—a trait fully evident in the following letters, first published in 1878.

APPROACHING KEATS'S LETTERS

When Keats's "Letters to Fanny Brawne" were first published, Victorian readers were horrified by the uncompromisingly honest picture of Keats they displayed. Fanny had married in 1833, had three children, and her son,

Herbert Lindon, sold these letters at auction. Fanny's letters to Keats had already been destroyed in September 1820 by mutual agreement, before Keats left for Italy, so that later her reputation would not be harmed. The impression of Keats that we get from these letters reveal a complex and contradictory struggle within the young poet. He yearns for a completely consuming relationship with Fanny, yet he is committed to his freedom as an artist to write poetry in whatever time still remained to him. The letters display a degree of emotional abandonment that some readers found unsettling, since they show Keats as almost insanely jealous and possessive, and Fanny as flighty, flirtatious, and even heartless. Throughout, his expressions of love are darkened by the shadow of pain from his tuberculosis and the prospect of an early death.

Letters to Fanny Brawne

1 July 1819.

My dearest Lady,

    I am glad I had not an opportunity of sending off a Letter which I wrote for you on Tuesday night—'twas too much like one out of Ro⟨u⟩s-seau's Heloise.[1] I am more reasonable this morning. The morning is the only proper time for me to write to a beautiful Girl whom I love so much: for at night, when the lonely day has closed, and the lonely, silent, unmusical Chamber is waiting to receive me as into a Sepulchre, then believe me my passion gets entirely the sway, then I would not have you see those R⟨h⟩apsodies which I once thought it impossible I should ever give way to, and which I have often laughed at in another, for fear you should ⟨think me⟩ either too unhappy or perhaps a little mad. I am now at a very pleasant Cottage window, looking onto a beautiful hilly country, with a glimpse of the sea; the morning is very fine. I do not know how elastic my spirit might be, what pleasure I might have in living here and

---

[1] *La Nouvelle Héloïse*, a novel by Jean Jacques Rousseau, had set a fashion in romantic sentiment.

breathing and wandering as free as a stag about this beautiful Coast if the remembrance of you did not weigh so upon me. I have never known any unalloy'd Happiness for many days together: the death or sickness of some one has always spoilt my hours—and now when none such troubles oppress me, it is you must confess very hard that another sort of pain should haunt me. Ask yourself my love whether you are not very cruel to have so entrammelled me, so destroyed my freedom. Will you confess this in the Letter you must write immediately and do all you can to console me in it—make it rich as a draught of poppies to intoxicate me—write the softest words and kiss them that I may at least touch my lips where yours have been. For myself I know not how to express my devotion to so fair a form: I want a brighter word than bright, a fairer word than fair. I almost wish we were butterflies and liv'd but three summer days—three such days with you I could fill with more delight than fifty common years could ever contain. But however selfish I may feel, I am sure I could never act selfishly: as I told you a day or two before I left Hampstead, I will never return to London if my Fate does not turn up Pam[2] or at least a Court-card. Though I could centre my Happiness in you, I cannot expect to engross your heart so entirely—indeed if I thought you felt as much for me as I do for you at this moment I do not think I could restrain myself from seeing you again tomorrow for the delight of one embrace. But no—I must live upon hope and Chance. In case of the worst that can happen, I shall still love you—but what hatred shall I have for another! Some lines I read the other day are continually ringing a peal in my ears:

> To see those eyes I prize above mine own
> Dart favors on another—
> And those sweet lips (yielding immortal nectar)
> Be gently press'd by any but myself—
> Think, think Francesca, what a cursed thing
> It were beyond expression!

Do write immediately. There is no Post from this Place, so you must address Post Office, Newport, Isle of Wight. I know before night I shall curse myself for having sent you so cold a Letter; yet it is better to do it as much in my senses as possible. Be as kind as the distance will permit to your

J. Keats.

---

[2]The knave of clubs in the game of loo. Around 1800 loo was England's most popular card game. The Jack of Clubs is "Pam" (short for *Pamphilus* that means "beloved of all") that beats all other cards.

8 July 1819.

My sweet Girl,

Your Letter gave me more delight, than any thing in the world but yourself could do; indeed I am almost astonished that any absent one should have that luxurious power over my senses which I feel. Even when I am not thinking of you I receive your influence and a tenderer nature steeling upon me. All my thoughts, my unhappiest days and nights have I find not at all cured me of my love of Beauty, but made it so intense that I am miserable that you are not with me: or rather breathe in that dull sort of patience that cannot be called Life. I never knew before, what such a love as you have made me feel, was; I did not believe in it; my Fancy was affraid of it, lest it should burn me up. But if you will fully love me, though there may be some fire, 'twill not be more than we can bear when moistened and bedewed with Pleasures. You mention 'horrid people' and ask me whether it depend upon them, whether I see you again. Do understand me, my love, in this. I have so much of you in my heart that I must turn Mentor when I see a chance of harm befalling you. I would never see any thing but Pleasure in your eyes, love on your lips, and Happiness in your steps. I would wish to see you among those amusements suitable to your inclinations and spirits; so that our loves might be a delight in the midst of Pleasures agreeable enough, rather than a resource from vexations and cares. But I doubt much, in case of the worst, whether I shall be philosopher enough to follow my own Lessons: if I saw my resolution give you a pain I could not. Why may I not speak of your Beauty, since without that I could never have lov'd you. I cannot conceive any beginning of such love as I have for you but Beauty. There may be a sort of love for which, without the least sneer at it, I have the highest respect and can admire it in others: but it has not the richness, the bloom, the full form, the enchantment of love after my own heart. So let me speak of you⟨r⟩ Beauty, though to my own endangering; if you could be so cruel to me as to try elsewhere its Power. You say you are affraid I shall think you do not love me—in saying this you make me ache the more to be near you. I am at the diligent use of my faculties here, I do not pass a day without sprawling some blank verse or tagging some rhymes; and here I must confess, that, (since I am on that subject,) I love you the more in that I believe you have liked me for my own sake and for nothing else. I have met with women whom I really think would like to be married to a Poem and to be given away by a Novel. I have seen your Comet, and only wish it was a sign that poor Rice would get well whose illness makes him rather a melancholy companion: and the more so as so to conquer his feelings and hide them from me, with a forc'd Pun. I kiss'd your writing over in the hope you had indulg'd me by leaving a trace of honey—What was your dream? Tell it me and I will tell you the interpretation thereof.

Ever yours, my love!
John Keats.

Do not accuse me of delay—we have not here an opportunity of sending letters every day. Write speedily.

25 July 1819.

My sweet Girl,

I hope you did not blame me much for not obeying your request of a Letter on Saturday: we have had four in our small room playing at cards night and morning leaving me no undisturb'd opportunity to write. Now Rice and Martin are gone I am at liberty. Brown to my sorrow confirms the account you give of your ill health. You cannot conceive how I ache to be with you: how I would die for one hour—for what is in the world? I say you cannot conceive; it is impossible you should look with such eyes upon me as I have upon you: it cannot be. Forgive me if I wander a little this evening, for I have been all day employ'd in a very abstr⟨a⟩ct Poem and I am in deep love with you—two things which must excuse me. I have, believe me, not been an age in letting you take possession of me; the very first week I knew you I wrote myself your vassal; but burnt the Letter as the very next time I saw you I thought you manifested some dislike to me. If you should ever feel for Man at the first sight what I did for you, I am lost. Yet I should not quarrel with you, but hate myself if such a thing were to happen—only I should burst if the thing were not as fine as a Man as you are as a Woman. Perhaps I am too vehement, then fancy me on my knees, especially when I mention a part of your Letter which hurt me; you say speaking of Mr Severn 'but you must be satisfied in knowing that I admired you much more than your friend'. My dear love, I cannot believe there ever was or ever could be any thing to admire in me especially as far as sight goes—I cannot be admired, I am not a thing to be admired. You are, I love you; all I can bring you is a swooning admiration of your Beauty. I hold that place among Men which snubnos'd brunettes with meeting eyebrows do among women—they are trash to me—unless I should find one among them with a fire in her heart like the one that burns in mine. You absorb me in spite of myself—you alone: for I look not forward with any pleasure to what is call'd being settled in the world; I tremble at domestic cares—yet for you I would meet them, though if it would leave you the happier I would rather die than do so. I have two luxuries to brood over in my walks, your Loveliness and the hour of my death. O that I could have possession of them both in the same minute. I hate the world: it batters too much the wings of my self-will, and would I could take a sweet poison from your lips to send me out of it. From no others would I take it. I am indeed astonish'd to find myself so careless of all cha⟨r⟩ms but yours—rememb⟨e⟩ring as I do the time when even a bit of ribband was a matter of interest with me. What softer words can I find for you after this—what it is I will not read. Nor will I say more here, but in a Postscript answer anything else you may have mentioned in your Letter in so many words—for I am distracted with a thousand thoughts. I will imagine you Venus to-night and pray, pray, pray to your star like a He⟨a⟩then.

> *Your's ever, fair Star,*
> *John Keats.*

13 Oct. 1819.

My dearest Girl,

　　This moment I have set myself to copy some verses out fair. I cannot proceed with any degree of content. I must write you a line or two and see if that will assist in dismissing you from my Mind for ever so short a time. Upon my Soul I can think of nothing else. The time is passed when I had power to advise and warn you against the unpromising morning of my Life. My love has made me selfish. I cannot exist without you. I am forgetful of every thing but seeing you again—my Life seems to stop there—I see no further. You have absorb'd me. I have a sensation at the present moment as though I was dissolving—I should be exquisitely miserable without the hope of soon seeing you. I should be affraid to separate myself far from you. My sweet Fanny, will your heart never change? My love, will it? I have no limit now to my love—You⟨r⟩ note came in just here—I cannot be happier away from you. 'Tis richer than an Argosy of Pearles. Do not threat me even in jest. I have been astonished that Men could die Martyrs for religion—I have shudder'd at it. I shudder no more—I could be martyr'd for my Religion—Love is my religion—I could die for that. I could die for you. My Creed is Love and you are its only tenet. You have ravish'd me away by a Power I cannot resist; and yet I could resist till I saw you; and even since I have seen you I have endeavoured often 'to reason against the reasons of my Love'. I can do that no more—the pain would be too great. My love is selfish. I cannot breathe without you.

> *Yours for ever*
> *John Keats.*

⟨May 1820.⟩

My dearest Girl,

I wrote a Letter for you yesterday expecting to have seen your mother. I shall be selfish enough to send it though I know it may give you a little pain, because I wish you to see how unhappy I am for love of you, and endeavour as much as I can to entice you to give up your whole heart to me whose whole existence hangs upon you. You could not step or move an eyelid but it would shoot to my heart—I am greedy of you. Do not think of any thing but me. Do not live as if I was not existing—Do not forget me—But have I any right to say you forget me? Perhaps you think of me all day. Have I any right to wish you to be unhappy for me? You would forgive me for wishing it, if you knew the extreme passion I have that you should love me—and for you to love me as I do you, you must think of no one but me, much less write that sentence. Yesterday and this morning I have been haunted with a sweet vision—I have seen you the whole time in your shepherdess dress. How my senses have ached at it! How my heart has been devoted to it! How my eyes have been full of Tears at it! I⟨n⟩deed I think a real Love is enough to occupy the widest heart—Your going to town alone, when I heard of it was a shock to me—yet I expected it—*promise me you will not for some time, till I get better.* Promise me this and fill the paper full of the most endearing names. If you cannot do so with good will, do my Love tell me—say what you think—confess if your heart is too much fasten'd on the world. Perhaps then I may see you at a greater distance, I may not be able to appropriate you so closely to myself. Were you to loose a favorite bird from the cage, how would your eyes ache after it as long as it was in sight; when out of sight you would recover a little. Perhaps if you would, if so it is, confess to me how many things are necessary to you besides me, I might be happier, by being less tantaliz'd. Well may you exclaim, how selfish, how cruel, not to let me enjoy my youth! to wish me to be unhappy! You must be so if you love me—upon my Soul I can be contented with nothing else. If you could really what is call'd enjoy yourself at a Party—if you can smile in peoples faces, and wish them to admire you *now,* you never have nor ever will love me. I see *life* in nothing but the certainty of your Love—convince me of it my sweetest. If I am not somehow convinc'd I shall die of agony. If we love we must not live as other men and women do—I cannot brook the wolfsbane of fashion and foppery and tattle. You must be mine to die upon the rack if I want you. I do not pretend to say I have more feeling than my fellows—but I wish you seriously to look over my letters kind and unkind and consider whether the Person who wrote them can be able to endure much longer the agonies and uncertainties which you are so peculiarly made to create—My recovery of bodily hea⟨l⟩th will be of no benefit to me if you are not all mine when I am well. For God's sake save me—or tell me my passion is of too awful a nature for you. Again God bless you.

J. K.

No—my sweet Fanny—I am wrong. I do not want you to be unhappy—and yet I do, I must while there is so sweet a Beauty—my loveliest my darling! Good bye! I Kiss you—O the torments!

⟨*5 July?*⟩ *1820.*

My dearest Girl,

I have been a walk this morning with a book in my hand, but as usual I have been occupied with nothing but you: I wish I could say in an agreeable manner. I am tormented day and night. They talk of my going to Italy.[3] 'Tis certain I shall never recover if I am to be so long separate from you: yet with all this devotion to you I cannot persuade myself into any confidence of you. Past experience connected with the fact of my long separation from you gives me agonies which are scarcely to be talked of. When your mother comes I shall be very sudden and expert in asking her whether you have been to Mrs Dilke's, for she might say no to make me easy. I am literally worn to death, which seems my only recourse. I cannot forget what has pass'd. What? nothing with a man of the world, but to me dreadful. I will get rid of this as much as possible. When you were in the habit of flirting with Brown you would have left off, could your own heart have felt one half of one pang mine did. Brown is a good sort of Man—he did not know he was doing me to death by inches. I feel the effect of every one of those hours in my side now; and for that cause, though he has done me many services, though I know his love and friendship for me, though at this moment I should be without pence were it not for his assistance, I will never see or speak to him until we are both old men, if we are to be. I *will* resent my heart having been made a football. You will call this madness. I have heard you say that it was not unpleasant to wait a few years— you have amusements—your mind is away—you have not brooded over one idea as I have, and how should you? You are to me an object intensely desireable—the air I breathe in a room empty of you is unhealthy. I am not the same to you—no—you

---

[3]Keats had suffered his first hemorrhage from tuberculosis in February 1820. He left for Italy in September and died in Rome six months later.

can wait—you have a thousand activities—you can be happy without me. Any party, any thing to fill up the day has been enough. How have you pass'd this month? Who have you smil'd with? All this may seem savage in me. You do not feel as I do—you do not know what it is to love—one day you may—your time is not come. Ask yourself how many unhappy hours Keats has caused you in Loneliness. For myself I have been a Martyr the whole time, and for this reason I speak; the confession is forc'd from me by the torture. I appeal to you by the blood of that Christ you believe in: Do not write to me if you have done anything this month which it would have pained me to have seen. You may have altered—if you have not—if you still behave in dancing rooms and other societies as I have seen you—I do not want to live—if you have done so I wish this coming night may be my last. I cannot live without you, and not only you but *chaste you; virtuous you.* The Sun rises and sets, the day passes, and you follow the bent of your inclination to a certain extent—you have no conception of the quantity of miserable feeling that passes through me in a day.—Be serious! Love is not a plaything—and again do not write unless you can do it with a crystal conscience. I would sooner die for want of you than—

Yours for ever
J. Keats.

READING CRITICALLY FOR IDEAS, STRUCTURE, AND STYLE

1. Keats's love for Fanny Brawne (when she was eighteen and he was twenty-three) displays an increasingly tortured and fervent tone. In what specific instances can you see this obsession taking over his personality? Would you characterize his feelings for her as pathological? Why or why not?

2. What is there about these letters in terms of style and use of imagery that demonstrates Keats had the sensibility of a great poet?

3. Does Keats seem to be conscious of how his obsession with Fanny was taking over his life? Explain your answer.

EXTENDING INSIGHTS THROUGH WRITING

1. These letters (whose publication elicited much controversy) present a side of Keats with which most people are not familiar, who know him through such poems as "Ode to a Grecian Urn" and "Ode to a Nightingale." How did reading these letters enhance or in any way alter your impression of Keats as a poet?

2. An interesting research project might be to interpret poems thought by scholars to reveal Keats's relationship with Fanny Brawne. These include the sonnet whose first line is "bright star, would I were stedfast as thou art—" and the eerie ballad "La Belle Dame sans Merci."

CONNECTING PERSPECTIVES ON THE INDIVIDUAL EXPERIENCE

1. In a short essay, discuss Keats's letters and Joan of Arc's essay "I Have Nothing More to Say" in terms of their individual obsessions and the fine line between religious and secular passion they display.

2. The differences between the Age of Reason and Romanticism are well illustrated in the contrasting styles and values of Lord Chesterfield and Keats. Draw on these two works to write a comparative analysis of the defining characteristics of each era.

JOSEPH ADDISON

Reflections in Westminster Abbey

BACKGROUND

English essayist and journalist Joseph Addison (1672–1719) had a distinguished career as a diplomat, member of Parliament, and secretary of state. But he is best known for his collaboration with Richard Steele on the periodicals *The Tatler* (1709–1710) and *The Spectator* (1711–1712, 1714). His sparkling and perceptive observations on different aspects of society are well worth revisiting. In the following essay from *The Spectator* (Number 26, dated March 30, 1711) Addison takes us through the famous gothic cathedral in London where all English monarchs have been crowned since William I (1027–1087) and where kings, statesmen, poets, and others of distinction are buried, including Addison himself.

APPROACHING ADDISON'S ESSAY

For many generations of composition students, Addison was required reading as a model of literary style. Merely reading Addison was actually supposed to enhance one's ability to express oneself in an elegant manner. Students dutifully studied—and sought to emulate—the effortless construction of his sentences and his splendid use of figurative language. We should remember that the titles of his essays, including the following, were not chosen by Addison, but were later supplied by editors.

Changes in public taste from the eighteenth century to the present have made it less likely that students today will read his essays; but, in his time, he was considered one of the most brilliant literary figures of the age (Dr. Samuel Johnson referred to his writings as "humorous, urbane, and decorous"). "Reflections in Westminster Abbey" illustrates the play of a cultivated intelligence on a potentially morbid subject.

110

Reflections in Westminster Abbey

WHEN I am in a serious humour, I very often walk by myself in Westminster-abbey; where the gloominess of the place, and the use to which it is applied, with the solemnity of the building, and the condition of the people who lie in it, are apt to fill the mind with a kind of melancholy, or rather thoughtfulness, that is not disagreeable. I yesterday passed a whole afternoon in the churchyard, the cloisters, and the church, amusing myself with the tomb-stones and inscriptions that I met with in those several regions of the dead. Most of them recorded nothing else of the buried person, but that he was born upon one day, and died upon another; the whole history of his life being comprehended in those two circumstances that are common to all mankind. I could not but look upon these registers of existence, whether of brass or marble, as a kind of satire upon the departed persons; who had left no other memorial of them, but that they were born, and that they died. They put me in mind of several persons mentioned in the battles of heroic poems, who have sounding names given them, for no other reason but that they may be killed, and are celebrated for nothing but being knocked on the head....

The life of these men is finely described in holy writ by 'the path of an arrow,' which is immediately closed up and lost.

Upon my going into the church, I entertained myself with the digging of a grave; and saw in every shovel-full of it that was thrown up, the fragment of a bone or skull intermixed with a kind of fresh mouldering earth that some time or other had a place in the composition of a human body. Upon this I began to consider with myself, what innumerable multitudes of people lay confused together under the pavement of that ancient cathedral; how men and women, friends and enemies, priests and soldiers, monks and prebendaries, were crumbled amongst one another, and blended together in the same common mass; how beauty, strength, and youth, with old age, weakness, and deformity, lay undistinguished, in the same promiscuous heap of matter.

After having thus surveyed this great magazine of mortality, as it were in the lump, I examined it more particularly by the accounts which I found on several of the monuments which are raised in every quarter of that ancient fabric. Some of them were covered with such extravagant epitaphs, that if it were possible for the dead person to be acquainted with them, he would blush at the praises which his friends have bestowed upon him. There are others so excessively modest, that they deliver the character of the person departed in Greek or Hebrew, and by that means are not understood once in a twelvemonth. In the poetical quarter, I found there were poets who had no monuments, and monuments which had no poets. I observed, indeed, that the present war had filled the church with many of these uninhabited monuments, which had been erected to the memory of persons whose bodies were perhaps buried in the plains of Blenheim,[1] or in the bosom of the ocean.

I could not but be very much delighted with several modern epitaphs, which are written with great elegance of expression and justness of thought, and therefore do honour to the living as well as the dead. As a foreigner is very apt to conceive an idea of the ignorance or politeness of a nation from the turn of their public monuments and inscriptions, they should be submitted to the perusal of men of learning and genius before they are put in execution. Sir Cloudesley Shovel's monument has very often given me great offence. Instead of the brave rough English admiral, which was the distinguishing character of that plain gallant man, he is represented on his tomb by the figure of a beau, dressed in a long periwig, and reposing himself upon velvet cushions, under a canopy of state. The inscription is answerable to the monument; for instead of celebrating the many remarkable actions he had performed in the service of his country, it acquaints us only with the manner of his death, in which it was impossible for him to reap any honour. The Dutch, whom we are apt to despise for want of genius, show an infinitely greater taste of antiquity and politeness in their buildings and works of this nature, than what we meet with in those of our own country. The monuments of their admirals, which have been erected at the public expense, represent them like themselves, and are adorned with rostral crowns and naval ornaments, with beautiful festoons of sea-weed, shells, and coral.

But to return to our subject. I have left the repository of our English kings for the contemplation of another day, when I shall find my mind disposed for so serious an amusement. I know that entertainments of this nature are apt to raise dark and dismal thoughts in timorous minds, and gloomy imaginations; but for my own part, though I am always serious, I do not know what it is to be melancholy; and can therefore take a view of nature, in her deep and solemn scenes, with the same pleasure as in her most gay and delightful ones. By this means I can improve myself with those objects, which others consider with terror. When I look upon the tombs of the great, every emotion of envy dies in me; when I read the epitaphs of the beautiful, every inordinate desire goes out; when I meet with the grief of parents upon a tombstone, my heart melts with compassion; when I see the tomb of the parents themselves, I consider the vanity of grieving for those whom we must quickly follow. When I see kings lying by those who deposed them, when I consider rival wits placed side by side, or the holy men that divided the world with their contests and disputes, I reflect with sorrow and astonishment on the little competitions, factions, and debates of mankind. When I read the several dates of the tombs, of some that died yesterday, and some six hundred years ago, I consider that great day when we shall all of us be contemporaries, and make our appearance together.

---

[1]In Bavaria, where the Duke of Marlborough, in 1704, defeated the French, in the War of the Spanish Succession.

READING CRITICALLY FOR IDEAS, STRUCTURE, AND STYLE

1. Addison's attitude and behavior may seem unusual or even bizarre, but he has a serious point to make: What is it?

2. Addison's reputation as a stylist worthy of emulation is clearly visible in the syntax and structure in this essay. For example, how is his handling of parallelism in the third paragraph well-suited to convey his views?

3. Addison values certain qualities in epitaphs and monuments, which we can infer from his criticisms of those who do not meet with his approval. Do you agree with these values? Why or why not?

EXTENDING INSIGHTS THROUGH WRITING

1. Addison's ability to find humor in such a macabre environment might be off-putting to some. Is it out of place, considering the circumstances? Explain your answer.

2. Pay a visit to a public monument in your town or community, or visit a Web site dedicated to a famous memorial, such as the Vietnam wall of names in Washington, D. C. Then, compose your own short "reflection," in which you emulate some of the distinctive features of Addison's style. Imagine that you are buried in Westminster Abbey. What do you think your epitaph should say?

CONNECTING PERSPECTIVES ON THE INDIVIDUAL EXPERIENCE

1. Compare and contrast the perspectives of Addison and George Bernard Shaw (in "She Would Have Enjoyed It") in terms of the authors' curiosity about the manners and customs that surround epitaphs and funerals.

2. Examine Addison's and Stendhal's analytical dissection of attitudes towards love (in France) and death (in England). Discuss how some of the same themes emerge in both accounts.

GEORGE BERNARD SHAW

She Would Have Enjoyed It

BACKGROUND

George Bernard Shaw (1856–1950) was born in Dublin into an impoverished family. He attended local schools from 1867–1869 and at age fifteen started working as a clerk in a real estate office, which he continued for the next four years. After early unsuccessful attempts to have his five novels published, Shaw was inspired by a lecture in 1882 by the American political theorist, Henry George. Shaw helped found the Fabian Society in 1884 and began a lifelong committment to social issues. He wrote his first play, *Widower's House*, in 1882 in an effort to use the theater as a vehicle for his ideas. This was followed in 1893 by *Mrs. Warren's Profession*, which censors banned because it dealt with prostitution. The driving force behind Shaw's prolific output, as well as his political and public speaking, is a satirical assault on social conventions and inequities. Among his many plays are *Man and Superman* (1903), on men, women and marriage; *Major Barbara* (1905), arguing poverty as the root of all evil; *Pygmalion* (1913), a satire on English class attitudes, which was made into the 1956 musical, *My Fair Lady*; and *Saint Joan* (1924), a dramatization of Joan of Arc as the quintessential Shavian heroine.

He was awarded the Nobel Prize for Literature in 1925 and gave away the money to start the Anglo-Swedish Literary Society. This letter first appeared in *The Shaw-Campbell Letters* (1952) from Shaw's correspondence with Mrs. Patrick Campbell, an actress, with whom Shaw was linked romantically and for whom he wrote several plays (she played the part of Liza in *Pygmalion*).

APPROACHING SHAW'S ESSAY

This letter, written on the occasion of his mother's funeral service and cremation, illustrates two important aspects of Shaw's personality: his love for his mother, from whom he inherited a lifelong passion for music, and his devilish sense of fun and "superficial blasphemy," which Shaw said he had inherited from his unsuccessful father and a "wicked uncle." This letter also demonstrates how Shaw presents serious ideas in a provocative and entertaining manner. Many of Shaw's plays reveal his quest to discover an essential religious faith, detached from particular systems of morality or established religions. In *Back to Methuselah* (1921), Shaw formulated his doctrine of Creative Evolution and the Life Force, a belief that blended his socialistic and mystical yearnings for a better world and a better self. By contrast, his attitude towards the rituals of bourgeois morality and the customs of traditional religions (such as funerals and cremations) becomes more iconoclastic, as is reflected in the title of this letter, "She Would Have Enjoyed It."

She Would Have Enjoyed It

The Mitre, Oxford.
22nd February 1913

WHAT a day! I must write to you about it, because there is no one else who didn't hate her mother, and even who doesn't hate her children. Whether you are an Italian peasant or a Superwoman I cannot yet find out; but anyhow your mother was not the Enemy.

Why does a funeral always sharpen one's sense of humor and rouse one's spirits? This one was a complete success. No burial horrors. No mourners in black, snivelling and wallowing in induced grief. Nobody knew except myself, Barker and the undertaker. Since I could not have a splendid procession with lovely colors and flashing life and triumphant music, it was best with us three. I particularly mention the undertaker because the humor of the occasion began with him. I went down in the tube to Golders Green with Barker, and walked to the Crematorium; and there came also the undertaker presently with his hearse, which had walked (the horse did) conscientiously at a funeral pace through the cold; though my mother would have preferred an invigorating trot. The undertaker approached me in the character of a man shattered with grief; and I, hard as nails and in loyally high spirits (rejoicing irrepressibly in my mother's memory), tried to convey to him that this professional chicanery, as I took it to be, was quite unnecessary. And lo! it wasn't professional chicanery at all. He had done all sorts of work for her for years, and was actually and really in a state about losing her, not merely as a customer, but as a person he liked and was accustomed to. And the coffin was covered with violet cloth—not black.

I must rewrite that burial service; for there are things in it that are deader than anyone it has ever been read over; but I had it read not only because the parson must live by his fees, but because with all its drawbacks it is the most beautiful thing than can be read as yet. And the parson did not gabble and hurry in the horrible manner common on such occasions. With Barker and myself for his congregation (and Mamma) he did it with his utmost feeling and sincerity. We could have made him perfect technically in two rehearsals; but he was excellent as it was; and I shook his hand with unaffected gratitude in my best manner.

At the passage "earth to earth, ashes to ashes, dust to dust" there was a little alteration of the words to suit the process. A door opened in the wall; and the violet coffin mysteriously passed out through it and vanished as it closed. People think that door the door of the furnace; but it isn't. I went behind the scenes at the end of the service and saw the real thing. People are afraid to see it; but it is wonderful. I found there the violet coffin opposite another door, a real unmistakable furnace door. When it lifted there was a plain little chamber of cement and firebrick. No heat. No noise. No roaring draught. No flame. No fuel. It looked cool, clean, sunny, though no sun could get there. You would have walked in or put your hand in without misgiving. Then the violet coffin moved again and went in feet first. And behold! The feet burst miraculously into streaming ribbons of garnet coloured lovely flame, smokeless and eager, like pentecostal tongues, and as the whole coffin passed in it sprang into flame all over; and my mother became that beautiful fire.

The door fell; and they said that if we wanted to see it all through, we should come back in an hour and a half. I remembered the wasted little figure with the wonderful face, and said "Too long" to myself; but we went off and looked at the Hampstead Garden Suburb (in which I have shares), and telephoned messages to the theatre, and bought books, and enjoyed ourselves generally.

By the way I forgot one incident. Hayden Coffin[1] suddenly appeared in the chapel. *His* mother also. The end was wildly funny, she would have enjoyed it enormously. When we returned we looked down through an opening in the floor to a lower floor close below. There we saw a roomy kitchen, with a big cement table and two cooks busy at it. They had little tongs in their hands, and they were deftly and busily picking nails and scraps of coffin handles out of Mamma's dainty little

---

[1] Comedian and light-opera singer.

heap of ashes and samples of bone. Mamma herself being at that moment leaning over beside me, shaking with laughter. Then they swept her up into a sieve, and shook her out; so that there was a heap of dust and a heap of calcined bone scraps. And Mamma said in my ear, "Which of the two heaps is me, I wonder!"

And that merry episode was the end, except for making dust of the bone scraps and scattering them on a flower bed.

O grave, where is thy victory?

In the afternoon I drove down to Oxford, where I write this. The car was in a merry mood, and in Notting Hill Gate accomplished a most amazing skid, swivelling right round across the road one way and then back the other, but fortunately not hitting anything.

The Philanderer, which I came down to see (Mona Limerick as Julia) went with a roar from beginning to end. Tomorrow I drive to Reading and thence across Surrey into Kent to the Barkers. The deferred lunch at the German Embassy will take place on Monday. Unless I find at Adelphi Terrace before 1.15 a telegram forbidding me ever to see you again, I *know* I shall go straight from the Embassy to your bedside. I must see you again after all these years.

Barrie is in bed ill (caught cold in Oxford a week ago) and ought to be petted by somebody.

I have many other things of extreme importance to say, but must leave them until Monday. By the way you first said you were leaving Hinde St on the 23rd; but you said last time to Lady Jekyll "Another ten days." If you are gone when I call I shall hurl myself into the area and perish.

And so goodnight, friend who understands about one's mother, and other things.

G.B.S.

READING CRITICALLY FOR IDEAS, STRUCTURE, AND STYLE

1. What picture do you get of Shaw's mother from what is implied in this letter? Does it help explain his seemingly irreverent attitude?

2. What can you infer about Shaw's relationship with Mrs. Patrick Campbell?

3. What sense do you get of Shaw's personality from the voice you hear in this letter with its unusual curiosity about the mechanics of cremation? Does Shaw's attitude seem to reflect any religious belief? Why or why not?

4. Shaw's style depends on his ability to create vividly descriptive sentences and phrases. Choose a few examples and discuss what makes them so effective.

EXTENDING INSIGHTS THROUGH WRITING

1. If you have ever attended a funeral, describe it the way Shaw might, in a letter or e-mail to a friend.

2. For a research project, write an essay about Shaw's theory of Creative Evolution and the Life Force as he developed it in plays such as *Man and Superman* (1903), *Androcles and the Lion* (1916), *Back to Methuslah* (1921), and *Saint Joan* (1924).

CONNECTING PERSPECTIVES ON THE INDIVIDUAL EXPERIENCE

1. Few letters could offer a more striking contrast in philosophy, style, and tone than Shaw's account of his mother's funeral and John Keats's "Letters to Fanny Brawne." How do they demonstrate the contrast between the Romantic and Modern temperament?

2. How do the intents, methods, and objectives of cremation differ from those of internment displayed on monuments, as described by Joseph Addison in "Reflections in Westminster Abbey?" Which do you think is more appropriate in today's world? Explain your answer.

BOOK CONNECTIONS FOR CHAPTER 1

1. In what ways is the opulent lifestyle of Gayatri Devi, as a Maharani, also visible in the elaborate splendor of the Taj Mahal as described by P. D. Ouspensky in "The Taj Mahal" (Chapter 7)?

2. Discuss the elements of tragedy in Anne Frank's life drawing on Aristotle's discussion of the defining features of tragedy in Greek theater (see "Poetics" in Chapter 7).

3. Draw on Thomas Carlyle's analysis in "On Heroes and Hero-Worship" in Chapter 3 and discuss Joan of Arc's role as a divinely-inspired catalyst of historical events.

4. Broaden Edward Said's definition of the condition of exile (see "Reflections on Exile" in Chapter 2) to include people who become society's scapegoats as Paul Monette thought likely would happen to him were he to declare his homosexuality.

5. Discuss how Lord Chesterfield and G. E. Moore (see "The Indefinability of Good" in Chapter 7) are pragmatists, but might define what is "good" in very different ways.

6. In what respects does Marcel Proust (see "The Bodily Memory" in Chapter 6) illustrate Stendhal's psychological theory of "crystallization" where the lover is not so much in love with the love object but rather with his or her own "crystallizations," or projections, that surround the object?

7. In his letter, Gustav Flaubert (see "Letters to Louise Colete" in Chapter 7) says that "passion does not make poetry, and the more personal you are, the weaker." Discuss his conception of poetry and the poetic temperament in relationship to John Keats as the archetypal poet. Does Keats refute Flaubert? Why or why not?

8. Compare the tombs Joseph Addison describes with that described by Howard Carter (see "Finding the Tomb" in Chapter 3) in terms of the different cultural attitudes towards memorializing the great that they display.

9. Discuss the importance of rituals in ancient Egypt as described by Herodotus, (see "Concerning Egypt" in Chapter 3) and in twentieth-century England, as discussed by George Bernard Shaw in "She Would Have Enjoyed It."

CHAPTER 2

THE COLLECTIVE EXPERIENCE:
The Human Condition

INTRODUCTION

The authors in this chapter address the fundamental challenges that confront the human species. The availability of food and the relationship between growing populations and the resources necessary to support them are basic. The eighteenth-century economist Thomas Robert Malthus presents the classic formulation of the ratio between population and food supply as a cautionary note to philosophical speculations about the perfectability of society. Yet, the cultural meanings of food go beyond mere subsistence, and—as Diane Ackerman explores by examining a variety of societies through the ages—they include the extremes of indulgence and denial.

The next cluster of readings, by Thomas Paine, Kenneth M. Stampp, Frederick Douglass, and James Baldwin, present a striking contrast between one of the most fundamental human aspirations—the right to form a collective union of like-minded citizens under the protection of a government—with an equally powerful, albeit twisted version of this dream: the belief that one race is intrinsically superior, and therefore, has the right to enslave and exploit the other. In the United States, the call for a free society based on inalienable "natural" and "civil" rights was eloquently proposed by Thomas Paine at the dawn of America's independence. But within a hundred years the institution of slavery had become an entrenched feature of life in the southern United States. Kenneth M. Stampp has studied the peculiar rationale that was used to justify slavery and describes the methods by which blacks who were transported from Africa and sold into slavery were conditioned to accept their servitude. Frederick Douglass then reveals how, as a slave in Maryland preceding the Civil War, he had to outwit all attempts to keep him illiterate and learned how to read and write. With James Baldwin's account, we move to mid-twentieth-century America, when racism was less of a legal condition (since segregation had been outlawed), but was still so endemic that Baldwin feared his fifteen-year-old nephew would become psychologically scarred (as he himself had been).

Colonialism, the subject of the essays by Ngũgĩ wa Thiong'o and George Orwell, reveal another aspect of nationhood and race: The policies of nations that seek to extend their authority over other territories are always supported by assumptions of cultural superiority of the colonizer over the colonized. Thiong'o describes the destructive effects on Kenyan society by the British (who first came as traders in the late 1800s and made it a Crown Colony in 1920) prohibition on school children from speaking their native languages. Thiong'o discusses the debilitating consequences when a white imperial power undermines the cultural integrity of a black nation using language as an instrument for political domination. George Orwell, too, was well aware of the impact of British colonialism on the everyday lives of people in Burma when he was stationed there in the police force. These selections offer complementary perspectives on colonialism in both Kenya and Burma and demonstrate that racism in the service of national expansion corrupts the oppressor and undermines the culture of those who are oppressed.

In the last three readings, we consider how women, as half of humanity, have witnessed tremendous changes in their power to make decisions that affect their lives in more profound ways than any other time in history. Margaret Sanger describes the origins of the movement for reproductive freedom, an unheard of concept, especially for the poor, at the turn of the twentieth century. Thirty years later, Simone de Beauvoir almost single-handedly changed prevailing cultural perceptions about the subservient role women played as the "second sex" and, by implication, emphasized their need to lead independent lives. In the present, Marilyn Yalom updates the ongoing struggle of women to free themselves from the traditional power inequities that have existed in the past. The different social realities described by Sanger, de Beauvoir, and Yalom are so extensive that we must recognize that the collective experiences of women (at least in Western societies) have undergone a profound transformation.

THOMAS ROBERT MALTHUS

The Principle of Population

BACKGROUND

Thomas Robert Malthus (1766–1834), considered the father of social demography, was born in Surrey, England, and was trained as a mathematician, graduating in 1788 from Cambridge University. He became curate of Albury in Surrey in 1798, compassionately ministering to the poor. Malthus's first essay, "The Crisis," written in response to Pitt's Poor Law Bill of 1796, showed his concern about society's ability to cope with drastic increases in population. In 1799, Malthus and William Otter traveled throughout Scandinavia and Russia. He based his later arguments on evidence from the diaries he kept. His major work, *An Essay On the Principle of Population* (1798; rev.ed. 1803), from which the following excerpt is taken, stated the "Malthusian principle" that geometrical growth of population would always outstrip the available food supply (which can only increase arithmetically). Malthus wrote his essay in response to Pitts's proposed legislation and works by William Godwin and Condorcet, which envisioned a perfectable society. Malthus—as a demographer, economist, and pastor—spoke of the realities brought about by the Industrial Revolution: burgeoning city population, high infant mortality, epidemics, and periodic famines. Charles Darwin declared that because of Malthus's essay, he began to think in terms of a "struggle for existence" where successful adaptations would result in the evolutionary formation of new species. "The Principle of Population" is set up as a deductive argument whose consequences follow from postulates that Malthus takes as self-evident.

APPROACHING MALTHUS'S ESSAY

In 1998, the year of Malthus's bicentennial, the world was infinitely more congested than even he could have imagined: Today, 250,000 more people are added to the Earth's population, and 1 billion people go to bed hungry.

Malthus observes that the inequality between the world's population and the available food supply will always make the hope for social betterment an elusive dream. Malthus structures his essay as a deductive argument: If his premises are valid, then his conclusion, however depressing, inevitably follows. The factors cited by Malthus that limit population are war, pestilence, famine, and plague. Since its publication, Malthus's argument has aroused a great deal of criticism. In 1807, the essayist William Hazlitt (1778–1830) wrote an extensive "Reply to the Essay on Population" in which he argued that Malthus was wrong because he confused the potential of a population to increase at a geometric rate with its actual observed tendencies: As a result his ratios are incorrect and his conclusions misleading. Modern theorists also have noted that developments in agricultural science have permitted farmers to make much more efficient use of their land than Malthus could have imagined. However, population has exploded in underdeveloped nations to the extent that Malthus's theories may be relevant after all. Thus, the seesaw battle between Malthus and his critics continues into the twenty-first century.

The Principle of Population

The great and unlooked for discoveries that have taken place of late years in natural philosophy, the increasing diffusion of general knowledge from the extension of the art of printing, the ardent and unshackled spirit of inquiry that prevails throughout the lettered and even unlettered world, the new and extraordinary lights that have been thrown on political subjects which dazzle and astonish the understanding, and particularly that tremendous phenomenon in the political horizon, the French revolution, which, like a blazing comet, seems destined either to inspire with fresh life and vigour, or to scorch up and destroy the shrinking inhabitants of the earth, have all concurred to lead able men into the opinion that we were touching on a period big with the most important changes, changes that would in some measure be decisive of the future fate of mankind.

It has been said that the great question is now at issue, whether man shall henceforth start forwards with accelerated velocity towards illimitable, and hitherto unconceived improvement, or be condemned to a perpetual oscillation between happiness and misery, and after every effort remain still at an immeasurable distance from the wished-for goal . . . .

I have read some of the speculations of the perfectibility of man and society with great pleasure. I have been warmed and delighted with the enchanting picture which they hold forth. I ardently wish for such happy improvements. But I see great, and, to my understanding, unconquerable difficulties in the way to them. These difficulties it is my present purpose to state, declaring, at the same time, that so far from exulting in them, as a cause of triumph over the friends of innovation, nothing would give me greater pleasure than to see them completely removed.

The most important argument that I shall adduce is certainly not new. The principles on which it depends have been explained in part by Hume, and more at large by Dr. Adam Smith. It has been advanced and applied to the present subject, though not with its proper weight, or in the most forcible point of view, by Mr. Wallace, and it may probably have been stated by many writers that I have never met with. I should certainly therefore not think of advancing it again, though I mean to place it in a point of view in some degree different from any that I have hitherto seen, if it had ever been fairly and satisfactorily answered.

The cause of this neglect on the part of the advocates for the per-   5 fectibility of mankind is not easily accounted for. I cannot doubt the talents of such men as Godwin and Condorcet. I am unwilling to doubt their candour. To my understanding, and probably to that of most others, the difficulty appears insurmountable. Yet these men of acknowledged ability and penetration, scarcely deign to notice it, and hold on their course in such speculations, with unabated ardour and undiminished confidence. I have certainly no right to say that they purposely shut their eyes to such arguments. I ought rather to doubt the validity of them, when neglected by such men, however forcibly their truth may strike my own mind. Yet in this respect it must be acknowledged that we are all of us too prone to err. If I saw a glass of wine repeatedly presented to a man, and he took no notice of it, I should be apt to think that he was blind or uncivil. A juster philosophy might teach me rather to think that my eyes deceived me and that the offer was not really what I conceived it to be.

In entering upon the argument I must premise that I put out of the question, at present, all mere conjectures, that is, all suppositions, the probable realization of which cannot be inferred upon any just philosophical grounds. A writer may tell me that he thinks man will ultimately become an ostrich. I cannot properly contradict him. But before he can expect to bring any reasonable person over to his opinion, he ought to shew, that the necks of mankind have been gradually elongating, that the lips have grown harder and more prominent, that the legs and feet are daily altering their shape, and that the hair is beginning to change into stubs of feathers. And till the probability of so wonderful a conversion can be shewn, it is surely lost time and lost eloquence to expatiate on the happiness of man in such a state; to describe his powers, both of running and flying, to paint him in a condition where all narrow luxuries would be contemned, where he would be employed only in collecting the necessaries of life, and where, consequently, each man's share of labour would be light, and his portion of leisure ample.

I think I may fairly make two postulata.

First, That food is necessary to the existence of man.

Secondly, That the passion between the sexes is necessary and will remain nearly in its present state.

These two laws, ever since we have had any knowledge of mankind,   10 appear to have been fixed laws of our nature, and, as we have not hitherto seen any alteration in them, we have no right to conclude that they will ever cease to be what they now are, without an immediate act of power in that Being who first arranged the system of the universe, and for the advantage of his creatures, still executes, according to fixed laws, all its various operations.

I do not know that any writer has supposed that on this earth man will ultimately be able to live without food. But Mr. Godwin has conjectured that the passion between the sexes may in time be extinguished. As, however, he calls this part of his work a deviation into the land of conjecture, I will not dwell longer upon it at present than to say that the best arguments for the perfectibility of man are drawn from a contemplation of the great progress that [man] has already made from the savage state and the difficulty of saying where he is to stop. But towards the extinction of the passion between the sexes, no progress whatever has hitherto been made. It appears to exist in as much force at present as it did two thousand or four thousand years ago. There are individual exceptions now as there always have been. But, as these exceptions do not appear to increase in number, it would surely be a very unphilosophical mode of arguing, to infer merely from the existence of an exception, that the exception would, in time, become the rule, and the rule the exception.

Assuming then, my postulata as granted, I say, that the power of population is indefinitely greater than the power in the earth to produce subsistence for man.

Population, when unchecked, increases in a geometrical ratio. Subsistence increases only in an arithmetical ratio. A slight acquaintance with numbers will shew the immensity of the first power in comparison of the second.

By that law of our nature which makes food necessary to the life of man, the effects of these two unequal powers must be kept equal.

15

This implies a strong and constantly operating check on population from the difficulty of subsistence. This difficulty must fall some where and must necessarily be severely felt by a large portion of mankind.

Through the animal and vegetable kingdoms, nature has scattered the seeds of life abroad with the most profuse and liberal hand. She has been comparatively sparing in the room and the nourishment necessary to rear them. The germs of existence contained in this spot of earth, with ample food, and ample room to expand in, would fill millions of worlds in the course of a few thousand years. Necessity, that imperious all pervading law of nature, restrains them within the prescribed bounds. The race of plants, and the race of animals shrink under this great restrictive law. And the race of man cannot, by any efforts of reason, escape from it. Among plants and animals its effects are waste of seed, sickness, and premature death. Among mankind, misery and vice. The former, misery, is an absolutely necessary consequence of it. Vice is a highly probable consequence, and we therefore see it abundantly prevail, but it ought not, perhaps, to be called an absolutely necessary consequence. The ordeal of virtue is to resist all temptation to evil.

This natural inequality of the two powers of population and of production in the earth and that great law of our nature which must constantly keep their effects equal form the great difficulty that to me appears insurmountable in the way to the perfectibility of society. All other arguments are of slight and subordinate consideration in comparison of this. I see no way by which man can escape from the weight of this law which pervades all animated nature. No fancied equality, no agrarian regulations in their utmost extent, could remove the pressure of it even for a single century. And it appears, therefore, to be decisive against the possible existence of a society, all the members of which should live in ease, happiness, and comparative leisure; and feel no anxiety about providing the means of subsistence for themselves and families.

Consequently, if the premises are just, the argument is conclusive against the perfectibility of the mass of mankind . . . .

READING CRITICALLY FOR IDEAS, STRUCTURE AND STYLE

1. Explain Malthus's theory of the "geometrical" increase in population as compared with the "arithmetical" increase in the food supply. According to Malthus, what factors will inevitably defeat plans for social betterment?

2. What rhetorical means does Malthus use to undercut arguments of those who believe in human "perfectibility" and a society free from want? Did you find his ostrich analogy effective? Why or why not?

3. Examine the syntactical structure of the first sentence in the essay, which occupies an entire paragraph, and break it down into several shorter sentences. Is the original more effective than your rewritten version? Why or why not?

EXTENDING INSIGHTS THROUGH WRITING

1. Implicit in Malthus's argument is a critique of population overload. Should the United States change its current immigration levels (now about 1 million per year) to offset this alarming scenario? Why or why not? What relevance does Malthus's message, if any, still have today?

2. How do different societies cope with the dual problem of overpopulation and the need to ensure a safe abundant food supply? Do some research on China's one-child policy and discuss the consequences of social engineering to ensure population control.

CONNECTING PERSPECTIVES ON THE COLLECTIVE EXPERIENCE

1. Compare Malthus's argument based on quantity of available food with Diane Ackerman's analysis (in "The Social Sense") of the qualitative constraints that determine what different cultures consider edible or inedible.

2. Why was Malthus less hopeful about the ability of birth control to keep the population in check than was Margaret Sanger, who as a nurse, was faced with the real social consequences of overpopulation?

DIANE ACKERMAN

The Social Sense

BACKGROUND

Diane Ackerman was born in 1948 in Waukegan, Illinois, received a B.A. from Pennsylvania State University in 1970 and a Ph. D. from Cornell University in 1978. She has taught at the University of Pittsburgh and Washington University. She was a staff writer for *The New Yorker* and is an accomplished poet and essayist whose works include *A Natural History of Love* (1994), *The Rarest of the Rare* (1995), *A Slender Thread* (1996), *I Praise My Destroyer* (1998), *Deep Play* (1999), and *Cultivating Delight: A Natural History of My Garden* (2001). "The Social Sense" is drawn from *A Natural History of the Senses* (1990), which later became a PBS television series titled *Mystery of the Senses*.

APPROACHING ACKERMAN'S ESSAY

Although we might not realize that what we like to eat is culturally determined, Ackerman shows us this is indeed the case by revealing that what is considered tasty or repulsive, edible or inedible, varies from culture to culture down through the ages. She begins by exploring the central role corn plays in the Native American culture of the Hopi Indians. Innumerable rituals in many cultures commemorate food on which that society depends as a gift from the gods. In ancient times rituals took the form of fertility rites designed to celebrate the fecundity of nature. She extends this analysis by discussing the religious basis of food taboos and draws on a variety of sources, including medicine, physiology, history, and mythology. Her lively and provocative writing style reveals that food plays a vital role in reflecting important themes within a culture: For example, she makes us aware that the food preferences of early Christians may well have been a reaction to the extravagance of the Romans. Ackerman believes that the decadence of Roman society can be deduced from the elaborate and perverse concoctions served at their banquets, along with the accompanying grotesque entertainments and spectacles. Romans competed with each other as to who could stage the most elaborate dinner party, and indulging in the senses was the hallmark of the empire. In this context it is plausible that the "denial of the senses became part of a Christian creed of salvation" as a reaction to such perversions. Food and sensuality has always been closely intertwined (as Ackerman discusses in the section "Food and Sex") and these two extremes of indulgence and denial have been evident in many civilizations. The overall effect is to show how thoroughly integrated attitudes towards food are in every conceivable aspect of human society in ways that run the gamut from the profane to the sacred.

The Social Sense

The other senses may be enjoyed in all their beauty when one is alone, but taste is largely social. Humans rarely choose to dine in solitude, and food has a powerful social component. The Bantu feel that exchanging food makes a contract between two people who then have a "clanship of porridge." We usually eat with our families, so it's easy to see how "breaking bread" together would symbolically link an outsider to a family group. Throughout the world, the stratagems of business take place over meals; weddings end with a feast; friends reunite at celebratory dinners; children herald their birthdays with ice cream and cake; religious ceremonies offer food in fear, homage, and sacrifice; wayfarers are welcomed with a meal. As Brillat-Savarin says, "every . . . sociability . . . can be found assembled around the same table: love, friendship, business, speculation, power, importunity, patronage, ambition, intrigue . . ." If an event is meant to matter emotionally, symbolically, or mystically, food will be close at hand to sanctify and bind it. Every culture uses food as a sign of approval or commemoration, and some foods are even credited with supernatural powers, others eaten symbolically, still others eaten ritualistically, with ill fortune befalling dullards or skeptics who forget the recipe or get the order of events wrong. Jews attending a Seder eat a horseradish dish to symbolize the tears shed by their ancestors when they were slaves in Egypt. Malays celebrate important events with rice, the inspirational center of their lives. Catholics and Anglicans take a communion of wine and wafer. The ancient Egyptians thought onions symbolized the many-layered universe, and swore oaths on an onion as we might on a Bible. Most cultures embellish eating with fancy plates and glasses, accompany it with parties, music, dinner theater, open-air barbecues, or other forms of revelry. Taste *is* an intimate sense. We can't taste things at a distance. And how we taste things, as well as the exact makeup of our saliva, may be as individual as our fingerprints.

Food gods have ruled the hearts and lives of many peoples. Hopi Indians, who revere corn, eat blue corn for strength, but all Americans might be worshiping corn if they knew how much of their daily lives depended on it. Margaret Visser, in *Much Depends on Dinner*, gives us a fine history of corn and its uses: livestock and poultry eat corn; the liquid in canned foods contains corn; corn is used in most paper products, plastics, and adhesives; candy, ice cream, and other goodies contain corn syrup; dehydrated and instant foods contain cornstarch; many familiar objects are made from corn products, brooms and corncob pipes to name only two. For the Hopis, eating corn is itself a form of reverence. I'm holding in my hand a beautifully carved Hopi corn kachina doll made from cottonwood; it represents one of the many spiritual essences of their world. Its cob-shaped body is painted ocher, yellow, black, and white, with dozens of squares drawn in a cross-section-of-a-kernel design, and abstract green leaves spearing up from below. The face has a long, black, rootlike nose, rectangular black eyes, a black ruff made of rabbit fur, white string corn-silk-like ears, brown bird-feather bangs, and two green, yellow, and ocher striped horns topped by rawhide tassels. A fine, soulful kachina, the ancient god Maïs stares back at me, tastefully imagined.

Throughout history, and in many cultures, *taste* has always had a double meaning. The word comes from the Middle English *tasten*, to examine by touch, test, or sample, and continues back to the Latin *taxare*, to touch sharply. So a taste was always a trial or test. People who have taste are those who have appraised life in an intensely personal way and found some of it sublime, the rest of it lacking. Something in bad taste tends to be obscene or vulgar. And we defer to professional critics of wine, food, art, and so forth, whom we trust to taste things for us because we think their taste more refined or educated than ours. A companion is "one who eats bread with another," and people sharing food as a gesture of peace or hospitality like to sit around and chew the fat.

The first thing we taste is milk from our mother's breast,* accompanied by love and affection, stroking, a sense of security, warmth, and well-being, our first intense feelings of pleasure. Later on she will feed us solid food from her hands, or even chew food first and press it into our mouths, partially digested. Such powerful associations do not fade easily, if at all. We say "food" as if it were a simple thing, an absolute like rock or rain to take for granted. But it is a big source of pleasure in most lives, a complex realm of satisfaction both physiological and emotional, much of which involves memories of childhood. Food must taste good, must reward us, or we would not stoke the furnace in each of our cells. We must eat to live, as we must breathe. But breathing is involuntary, finding food is not; it takes energy and planning, so it must tantalize us out of our natural torpor. It must decoy us out of bed in the morning and prompt us to put on constricting clothes, go to work, and perform tasks we may not enjoy for eight hours a day, five days a week, just to "earn our daily bread," or be "worth our salt," if you like, where the word *salary* comes from. And, because we are omnivores, many tastes must appeal to us, so that we'll try new foods. As children grow, they meet regularly throughout the day—at mealtimes—to hear grown-up talk, ask questions, learn about customs, language, and

---

*This special milk, called colostrum, is rich in antibodies, the record of the mother's epidemiologic experience.

the world. If language didn't arise at mealtimes, it certainly evolved and became more fluent there, as it did during group hunts.

We tend to see our distant past through a reverse telescope that compresses it: a short time as hunter-gatherers, a long time as "civilized" people. But civilization is a recent stage of human life, and, for all we know, it may not be any great achievement. It may not even be the final stage. We have been alive on this planet as recognizable humans for about two million years, and for all but the last two or three thousand we've been hunter-gatherers. We may sing in choirs and park our rages behind a desk, but we patrol the world with many of a hunter-gatherer's drives, motives, and skills. These aren't knowable truths. Should an alien civilization ever contact us, the greatest gift they could give us would be a set of home movies: films of our species at each stage in our evolution. Consciousness, the great poem of matter, seems so unlikely, so impossible, and yet here we are with our loneliness and our giant dreams. Speaking into the perforations of a telephone receiver as if through the screen of a confessional, we do sometimes share our emotions with a friend, but usually this is too disembodied, too much like yelling into the wind. We prefer to talk *in person*, as if we could temporarily slide into their feelings. Our friend first offers us food, drink. It is a symbolic act, a gesture that says: *This food will nourish your body as I will nourish your soul.* In hard times, or in the wild, it also says *I will endanger my own life by parting with some of what I must consume to survive.* Those desperate times may be ancient history, but the part of us forged in such trials accepts the token drink and piece of cheese and is grateful.

FOOD AND SEX

What would the flutterings of courtship be without a meal? As the deliciously sensuous and ribald tavern scene in Fielding's *Tom Jones* reminds us, a meal can be the perfect arena for foreplay. Why is food so sexy? Why does a woman refer to a handsome man as a real dish? Or a French girl call her lover *mon petit chou* (my little cabbage)? Or an American man call his girlfriend cookie? Or a British man describe a sexy woman as a bit of crumpet (a flat, toasted griddlecake well lubricated with butter)? Or a tart? Sexual hunger and physical hunger have always been allies. Rapacious needs, they have coaxed and driven us through famine and war, to bloodshed and serenity, since our earliest days.

Looked at in the right light, any food might be thought aphrodisiac. Phallic-shaped foods such as carrots, leeks, cucumbers, pickles, sea cucumbers (which become tumescent when soaked), eels, bananas, and asparagus all have been prized as aphrodisiacs at one time or another, as were oysters and figs because they reminded people of female genitalia; caviar because it was a female's eggs; rhinoceros horn, hyena eyes, hippopotamus snout, alligator tail, camel hump, swan genitals, dove brains, and goose tongues, on the principle that anything so rare and exotic must have magical powers; prunes (which were offered free in Elizabethan brothels);

peaches (because of their callipygous rumps?); tomatoes, called "love apples," and thought to be Eve's temptation in the Garden of Eden; onions and potatoes, which look testicular, as well as "prairie oysters," the cooked testicles of a bull; and mandrake root, which looks like a man's thighs and penis. Spanish fly, the preferred aphrodisiac of the Marquis de Sade, with which he laced the bonbons he fed prostitutes and friends, is made by crushing a southern European beetle. It contains a gastrointestinal irritant and also produces a better blood flow, the combination of which brings on a powerful erection of either the penis or the clitoris, but also damages the kidneys; it can even be fatal. Musk, chocolate, and truffles also have been considered aphrodisiacs and, for all we know, they might well be. But, as sages have long said, the sexiest part of the body and the best aphrodisiac in the world is the imagination.

Primitive peoples saw creation as a process both personal and universal, the earth's yielding food, humans (often molded from clay or dust) burgeoning with children. Rain falls from the sky and impregnates the ground, which brings forth fruit and grain from the tawny flesh of the earth—an earth whose mountains look like reclining women, and whose springs spurt like healthy men. Fertility rituals, if elaborate and frenzied enough, could encourage Nature's bounty. Cooks baked meats and breads in the shape of genitals, especially penises, and male and female statues with their sexual organs exaggerated presided over orgiastic festivities where sacred couples copulated in public. A mythic Gaia poured milk from her breasts and they became the galaxies. The ancient Venus figures with global breasts, swollen bellies, and huge buttocks and thighs symbolized the female life-force, mother to crops and humans. The earth itself was a goddess, curvy and ripe, radiant with fertility, aspill with riches. People have thought the Venus figures imaginative exaggerations, but women of that time may indeed have resembled them; all breasts, belly, and rump: When pregnant, they would have bulged into quite an array of shapes.

Food is created by the sex of plants or of animals; and we find it sexy. When we eat an apple or peach, we are eating the fruit's placenta. But, even if that weren't so, and we didn't subconsciously associate food with sex, we would still find it sexy for strictly physical reasons. We use the mouth for many things—to talk and kiss, as well as to eat. The lips, tongue, and genitals all have the same neural receptors, called Krause's end bulbs, which make them ultrasensitive, highly charged. There's a similarity of response.

A man and woman sit across from one another in a dimly lit restaurant. A small bouquet of red-and-white spider lilies sweetens the air with a cinnamonlike tingle. A waiter passes with a plate of rabbit sausage in molé sauce. At the next table, a blueberry soufflé oozes scent. Oysters on the half shell, arranged on a large platter of shaved ice, one by one polish the woman's tongue with silken saltiness. A fennel-scented steam rises from thick crabcakes on the man's plate. Small loaves of fresh bread breathe sweetly. Their hands brush as they both reach for the bread. He stares into her eyes, as if filling them with molten lead. They both know where this delicious prelude will lead. "*I'm so hungry,*" she whispers.

THE OMNIVORE'S PICNIC

You have been invited to dinner at the home of extraterrestrials, and asked to bring friends. Being considerate hosts, they first inquire if you have any dietary allergies or prohibitions, and then what sort of food would taste good to you. What do humans eat? they ask. Images cascade through your mind, a cornucopia of plants, animals, minerals, liquids, and solids, in a vast array of cuisines. The Masai enjoy drinking cow's blood. Orientals eat stir-fried puppy. Germans eat rancid cabbage (sauerkraut), Americans eat decaying cucumbers (pickles). Italians eat whole deep-fried songbirds, Vietnamese eat fermented fish dosed with chili peppers, Japanese and others eat fungus (mushrooms). French eat garlic-soaked snails. Upper-class Aztecs ate roasted dog (a hairless variety named *xquintli*, which is still bred in Mexico). Chinese of the Chou dynasty liked rats, which they called "household deer,"* and many people still do eat rodents, as well as grasshoppers, snakes, flightless birds, kangaroos, lobsters, snails, and bats. Unlike most other animals, which fill a small yet ample niche in the large web of life on earth, humans are omnivorous. The Earth offers perhaps 20,000 edible plants alone. A poor season for eucalyptus will wipe out a population of koala bears, which have no other food source. But human beings are Nature's great ad libbers and revisers. Diversity is our delight. In time of drought, we can ankle off to a new locale, or break open a cactus, or dig a well. When plagues of locusts destroy our crops, we can forage on wild plants and roots. If our herds die, we find protein in insects, beans, and nuts. Not that being an omnivore is easy. A koala bear doesn't have to worry about whether or not its next mouthful will be toxic. In fact, eucalyptus is highly poisonous, but a koala has an elaborately protective gut, so it just eats eucalyptus, exactly as its parents did. Cows graze without fear on grass and grain. But omnivores are anxious eaters. They must continually test new foods to see if they're palatable and nutritious, running the risk of inadvertently poisoning themselves. They must take chances on new flavors, and, doing so, they frequently acquire a taste for something offbeat that, though nutritious, isn't the sort of thing that might normally appeal to them—chili peppers (which Columbus introduced to Europe), tobacco, alcohol, coffee, artichokes, or mustard, for instance. When we were hunter-gatherers, we ate a great variety of foods. Some of us still do, but more often we add spices to what we know, or find at hand, *for variety*, as we like to say. Monotony isn't our code. It's safe, in some ways, but in others it's more dangerous. Most of us prefer our foods cooked to the steaminess of freshly killed prey. We don't have ultrasharp carnivore's teeth, but we don't need them. We've created sharp tools. We do have incisor teeth for slicing fruits, and molars for crushing seeds and nuts, as well as canines for ripping flesh. At times, we eat nasturtiums and pea pods and even, the effluvia from the

---

*It was the food-obsessed Chinese who started the first serious restaurants during the time of the T'ang dynasty (A.D. 618–907). By the time the Sung dynasty replaced the T'ang, they were all-purpose buildings, with many private dining rooms, where one went for food, sex, and barroom gab.

mammary glands of cows, churned until it curdles, or frozen into a solid and attached to pieces of wood.

Our hosts propose a picnic, since their backyard is a meadow lit by two suns, and they welcome us and our friends. Our Japanese friend chooses the appetizer: sushi, including shrimp still alive and wriggling. Our French friend suggests a baguette, or better still croissants, which have an unlikely history, which he insists on telling everyone: To celebrate Austria's victory against the invading Ottoman Turks, bakers created pastry in the shape of the crescent on the Turkish flag, so that the Viennese could devour their enemies at table as they had on the battlefield. Croissants soon spread to France and, during the 1920s, traveled with other French ways to the United States. Our Amazonian friend chooses the main course—nuptial kings and queens of leaf-cutter ants, which taste like walnut butter, followed by roasted turtle and sweet-fleshed piranha. Our German friend insists that we include some spaetzle and a loaf of darkest pumpernickel bread, which gets its name from the verb *pumpern*, "to break wind," and *Nickel*, "the devil," because it was thought to be so hard to digest that even the devil would fart if he ate it. Our Tasaday friend wants some natek, a starchy paste his people make from the insides of caryota palm trees. The English cousin asks for a small platter of potted ox tongues, very aged blue cheese, and, for dessert, trifle—whipped cream and slivered almonds on top of a jam-and-custard pudding thick with sherry-soaked ladyfingers.

To finish our picnic lunch, our Turkish friend proposes coffee in the Turkish style—using a mortar and pestle to break up the beans, rather than milling them. To be helpful, he prepares it for us all, pouring boiling water over coffee grounds through a silver sieve into a pot. He brings this to a light boil, pours it through the sieve again, and offers us some of the clearest, brightest coffee we've ever tasted. According to legend, he explains; coffee was discovered by a ninth-century shepherd, who one day realized that his goats were becoming agitated whenever they browsed on the berries of certain bushes. For four hundred years, people thought only to chew the berries. Raw coffee doesn't brew into anything special, but in the thirteenth century someone decided to roast the berries, which releases a pungent oil and the mossy-bitter aroma now so familiar to us. Our Indian friend passes round cubes of sugar, which we are instructed to let melt on the tongue as we sip our coffee, and our minds roam back to the first recorded instance of sugar, in the Atharvaveda, a sacred Hindu text from 800 B.C., which describes a royal crown made of glittering sugar crystals. Then he circulates a small dish of coriander seeds, and we pinch a few in our fingers, set them on our tongues, and feel our mouths freshen from the aromatic tang. A perfect picnic. We thank our hosts for laying on such a splendid feast, and invite them to our house for dinner next. "What do jujubarians eat?" we ask.

OF CANNIBALISM AND SACRED COWS

Even though grass soup was the main food in the Russian gulags, according to Solzhenitsyn's *One Day in the Life of Ivan Denisovich*, humans don't prefer wood, or leaves, or grass—the cellulose is impossible to digest.

We also can't manage well eating excrement, although some animals adore it, or chalk or petroleum. On the other hand, cultural taboos make us spurn many foods that are wholesome and nourishing. Jews don't eat pork, Hindus don't eat beef, and Americans in general won't eat dog, rat, horse, grasshopper, grubs, or many other palatable foods prized by peoples elsewhere in the world. Anthropologist Claude Lévi-Strauss found that primitive tribes designated foods "good to think" or "bad to think." Necessity, the mother of invention, fathers many codes of conduct. Consider the "sacred cow," an idea so shocking it has passed into our vocabulary as a thing, event, or person considered sacrosanct. Though India has a population of around 700 million and a constant need for protein, over two hundred million cattle are allowed to roam the streets as deities while many people go hungry. The cow plays a central role in Hinduism. As Marvin Harris explains in *The Sacred Cow and the Abominable Pig:*

> Cow protection and cow worship also symbolize the protection and adoration of human motherhood. I have a collection of colorful Indian pin-up calendars depicting jewel-bedecked cows with swollen udders and the faces of beautiful human madonnas. Hindu cow worshippers say: "The cow is our mother. She gives us milk and butter. Her male calves till the land and give us food." To critics who oppose the custom of feeding cows that are too old to have calves and give milk, Hindus reply: "Will you then send your mother to a slaughter house when she gets old?"

15   Not only is the cow sacred in India, even the dust in its hoofprints is sacred. And, according to Hindu theology, 330 million gods live inside each cow. There are many reasons why this national tantalism has come about; one factor may be that an overcrowded land such as India can't support the raising of livestock for food, a system that is extremely inefficient. When people eat animals that have been fed grains, "nine out of ten calories and four out of five grams of protein are lost for human consumption." The animal uses up most of the nutrients. So vegetarianism may have evolved as a remedy, and been ritualized through religion. "I feel confident that the rise of Buddhism was related to mass suffering and environmental depletions," Harris writes, "because several similar nonkilling religions . . . arose in India at the same time." Including Jainism, whose priests not only tend stray cats and dogs, but keep a separate room in their shelters just for insects. When they walk down the street, an assistant walks ahead of them to brush away any insects lest they get stepped on, and they wear gauze masks so they don't accidentally inhale a wayward midge or other insect.

One taboo stands out as the most fantastic and forbidden. "What's eating you?" a man may ask an annoyed friend. Even though his friend just got fired by a tyrannical boss with a mind as small as a noose, he would never think to say "*Who's* eating you?" The idea of cannibalism is so far from our ordinary lives that we can safely use the euphemism *eat* in a sexual context, say, and no one will think we mean literally consume. But omnivores can eat anything, even each other,* and human flesh is one of the finest sources of protein. Primitive peoples all over the world have indulged in cannibalism, always ritualistically, but sometimes as a key source of protein missing from their diets. For many it's a question of head-hunting, displaying the enemy's head with much magic and flourish; and then, so as not to be wasteful, eating the body. In Britain's Iron Age, the Celts consumed large quantities of human flesh. Some American Indian tribes tortured and ate their captives, and the details (reported by Christian missionaries who observed the rites) are hair-raising. During one four-night celebration in 1487, the Aztecs were reported to have sacrificed about eighty thousand prisoners, whose flesh was shared with the gods, but mainly eaten by a huge meat-hungry population. In *The Power of Myth*, the late Joseph Campbell, a wise observer of the beliefs and customs of many cultures, tells of a New Guinea cannibalism ritual that "enacts the planting-society myth of death, resurrection and *cannibalistic* consumption." The tribe enters a sacred field, where they chant and beat drums for four or five days, and break all the rules by engaging in a sexual orgy. In this rite of manhood, young boys are introduced to sex for the first time:

> There is a great shed of enormous logs supported by two uprights. A young woman comes in ornamented as a deity, and she is brought to lie down in this place beneath the great roof. The boys, six or so, with the drums going and chanting going, one after another, have their first experience of intercourse with the girl. And when the last boy is with her in full embrace, the supports are withdrawn, the logs drop, and the couple is killed. There is the union of male and female . . . as they were in the beginning. . . . There is the union of begetting and death. They are both the same thing.

> Then the couple is pulled out and roasted and eaten that very evening. The ritual is the repetition of the original act of the killing of a god followed by the coming of food from the dead savior.

When the explorer Dr. Livingstone died in Africa, his organs were apparently eaten by two of his native followers as a way to absorb his strength and courage. Taking communion in the Catholic Church enacts a symbolic eating of the body and blood of Christ. Some forms of cannibalism were more bloodthirsty than others. According to Philippa Pullar, Druid priests "attempted divination by stabbing a man above his midriff, foretelling the future by the convulsions of his limbs and the pouring of his blood. . . . Then . . . they devoured him." Cannibalism doesn't horrify us because we find human life sacred, but because our social taboos happen to forbid it, or, as Harris says: "the real conundrum is why we who live in

---

*In German, humans eat (*essen*), but animals devour or feed (*fressen*). Cannibals are called *Menschenfresser*—humans who become animals when they eat.

a society which is constantly perfecting the art of mass-producing human bodies on the battlefield find humans good to kill but bad to eat."*

THE ULTIMATE DINNER PARTY

Romans adored the voluptuous feel of food: the sting of pepper, the pleasure-pain of sweet-and-sour dishes, the smoldery sexiness of curries, the piquancy of delicate and rare animals, whose exotic lives they could contemplate as they devoured them, sauces that reminded them of the smells and tastes of lovemaking. It was a time of fabulous, fattening wealth and dangerous, killing poverty. The poor served the wealthy, and could be beaten for a careless word, destroyed for amusement. Among the wealthy, boredom visited like an impossible in-law, whom they devoted most of their lives to entertaining. Orgies and dinner parties were the main diversions, and the Romans amused themselves with the lavishness of a people completely untainted by annoying notions of guilt. In their culture, pleasure glistened as a good in itself; a positive achievement, nothing to repent. Epicurus spoke for a whole society when he asked:

> Is man then meant to spurn the gifts of Nature? Has he been born but to pluck the bitterest fruits? For whom do those flowers grow, that the gods make flourish at mere mortals' feet? . . . It is a way of pleasing Providence to give ourselves up to the various delights which she suggests to us; our very needs spring from her laws, and our desires from her inspirations.

Fighting the enemy, boredom, Romans staged all-night dinner parties and vied with one another in the creation of unusual and ingenious dishes. At one dinner a host served progressively smaller members of the food chain stuffed inside each another: Inside a calf, there was a pig, inside the pig a lamb, inside the lamb a chicken, inside the chicken a rabbit, inside the rabbit a dormouse, and so on. Another host served a variety of dishes that looked different but were all made from the same ingredient. Theme parties were popular, and might include a sort of treasure hunt, where guests who located the peacock brains or flamingo tongues received a prize. Mechanical devices might lower acrobats from the ceiling along with the next course, or send in a plate of lamprey milt on an eel-shaped trolley. Slaves brought garlands of flowers to drape over the diners, and rubbed their bodies with perfumed ungents to relax them. The floor might be knee-deep in rose petals. Course after course would appear, some with peppery

---

*For an excellent discussion of cannibalism and the nutritional fiats that have prompted it in a variety of cultures (Aztecs, Fijians, New Guineans, American Indians, and many others), including truly horrible and graphic accounts by eyewitnesses, see Harris's chapter on "People Eating." Marvin Harris, *The Sacred Cow and the Abominable Pig: Riddles of Food and Culture* (New York: Simon & Schuster/Touchstone Books, 1987).

sauces to spark the taste buds, others in velvety sauces to soothe them. Slaves blew exotic scents through pipes into the room, and sprinkled the diners with heavy, musky animal perfumes like civet and ambergris. Sometimes the food itself squirted saffron or rose water or some other delicacy into the diner's face, or birds flew out of it, or it turned out to be inedible (because it was pure gold). The Romans were devotees of what the Germans call *Schadenfreude*, taking exquisite pleasure in the misfortune of someone else. They loved to surround themselves with midgets, and handicapped and deformed people, who were made to perform sexually or cabaret-style at the parties. Caligula used to have gladiators get right up on the dinner table to fight, splashing the diners with blood and gore. Not all Romans were sadists, but numbers of the wealthy class and many of the emperors were, and they could own, torture, maltreat, or murder their slaves as much as they wished. At least one high-society Roman is recorded to have fattened his eels on the flesh of his slaves. Small wonder Christianity arose as a slave-class movement, emphasizing self-denial, restraint, the poor inheriting the earth, a rich and free life after death, and the ultimate punishment of the luxury-loving rich in the eternal tortures of hell. As Philippa Pullar observes in *Consuming Passions*, it was from this "class-consciousness and a pride in poverty and simplicity the hatred of the body was born. . . ." All agreeable sensations were damned, all harmonies of taste and smell, sound, sight and feel, the candidate for heaven must resist them all. Pleasure was synonymous with guilt, it was synonymous with Hell. . . . "Let your companions be women pale and thin with fasting, instructed Jerome." Or, as Gibbon put it, "every sensation that is offensive to man was thought acceptable to God." So the denial of the senses became part of a Christian creed of salvation. The Shakers would later create their stark wooden benches, chairs, and simple boxes in such a mood, but what would they make now of the voluptuousness with which people enjoy Shaker pieces, not as a simple necessity but extravagantly, as art, as an expensive excess bought for the foyer or country house? The word "vicarious" hinges on "vicar," God's consul in the outlands, who lived like an island in life's racy current, delicate, exempt, and unflappable, while babies grew out of wedlock and bulls died, crops shriveled up like pokers or were flooded, and local duennas held musicales for vicar, matrons, and spicy young women (riper than the saintliest mettle could bear). No wonder they lived vicariously, giving pause, giving aid, and, sometimes, giving in to embolisms, dietary manias, and sin. Puritanism denounced spices as too sexually arousing; then the Quakers entered the scene, making all luxury taboo, and soon enough there were revolts against these revolts. Food has always been associated with cycles of sexuality, moral abandon, moral restraint, and a return to sexuality once again—but no one did so with as much flagrant gusto as the ancient Romans.

Quite possibly the Roman empire fell because of lead poisoning, which can cause miscarriages, infertility, a host of illnesses, and insanity. Lead suffused the Romans' lives—not only did their water pipes, cooking pots, and jars contain it, but also their cosmetics. But before it did poison them, they staged some of the wildest and most extravagant dinner parties ever 20 known, where people dined lying down, two, three, or more to a couch. While saucy Roman poets like Catullus wrote rigorously sexy poems about affairs with either sex, Ovid wrote charming ones about his robust love of women, how they tormented his soul, and about the roller coaster of flirtation he observed at dinner parties. "Offered a sexless heaven," he wrote, "I'd say *no thank you*, women are such sweet hell." In one of his poems, he cautions his mistress that, since they've both been invited to the same dinner, he's bound to see her there with her husband. *Don't let him kiss you on the neck*, Ovid tells her, *it will drive me crazy.*

READING CRITICALLY FOR IDEAS, STRUCTURE, AND STYLE

1. In what ways do the rituals involving food help create a culture's sense of its own identity? For example, what role does corn play in the life of the Hopi Indians?

2. What examples cited by Ackerman most clearly illustrate the role cultural values play in determining what people consider edible or inedible? How does she use sources drawn from a variety of fields to support her analysis?

3. According to Ackerman, in what way might Christian values have been a reaction to Roman food practices? Evaluate her assumption that you can draw inferences about a society based on its food preferences.

EXTENDING INSIGHTS THROUGH WRITING

1. Which of the five sections in Ackerman's analysis was most interesting to you? Extend her analysis for that section on the basis of some independent research in the library or using the Internet. A relevant Web site is *Food and Culture @* <http://lilt.ilstu.edu/rtdirks/TABOO.html>.

2. After watching one of the many popular television shows devoted to food preparation (*Julia and Jacques, Emeril Live, The Iron Chef, Cooking Live*) discuss the cultural significance of these kinds of shows in a society that seems all but addicted to fast food.

**CONNECTING PERSPECTIVES ON THE COLLECTIVE
EXPERIENCE**

1. Compare the different perspectives on the social meaning of
   food preparation as discussed by Ackerman with Simone de
   Beauvoir's analysis of the domestic duties of women in different
   cultures in "The Married Woman."

2. How does Marilyn Yalom's article, "The Wife Today," suggest
   that convenience foods, fast foods, and the disappearance of the
   family dinner reveal new trends when compared with Ackerman's discussion of the traditional role food has played in various cultures?

THOMAS PAINE

The Rights of Man

BACKGROUND

Thomas Paine (1737–1809), following Benjamin Franklin's advice, left England and came to America in 1774, served in the Revolutionary Army, and supported the cause of the colonies through his influential pamphlets *Common Sense*, 1776 and *The Crisis* (1776–1783). He also supported the French Revolution and wrote *The Rights of Man* (1792) and *The Age of Reason* (1793). *The Rights of Man* was written in reply to Edmund Burke's *Reflections upon the Revolution in France* and proved so popular that it sold hundreds of thousands of copies in France and England. In it Paine disputes Burke's doctrine that one generation can compel succeeding ones to follow a particular form of government. Paine defines the inalienable "natural" and "civil" rights of mankind and expounds on society's obligation to protect these rights.

APPROACHING PAINE'S ESSAY

The purpose of government, according to Paine, is to secure for people rights that they cannot secure for themselves. He called for many features (a constitution with a bill of rights, the outlawing of privilege by birthright, a right to vote) that are now in effect in democratic societies throughout the world.

In *The Rights of Man* Paine asserts that all men possess certain natural rights because all come from the Maker of man. As a Deist, Paine stated "I believe in one God, and no more; and I hope for happiness beyond this life." He states that each generation is equal in rights to the generation that preceded it, and every individual is born equal in rights with his contemporaries. Every child, he contends, born into the world must be considered as deriving his or her existence from God. Since these natural rights are God-given, they may not be abridged. Paine's argument is designed to show that the American colonists were simply reasserting those "natural" rights that had been infringed upon by England.

Paine's writing reflects the philosophical assumptions of the American Revolution and many of his words and phrases (for example, "inalienable rights") echo Thomas Jefferson's draft of the *Declaration of Independence*. Paine's style is simple, down-to-earth, and concise. He makes the case by drawing conclusions from premises stated as self-evident truths. The few examples of poetic imagery he uses display a blend of biblical cadence and colonial plain-speaking (for example, "the duty of man is not a wilderness of turnpike gates, through which he is to pass by tickets by one to the other").

The Rights of Man

If any generation of men ever possessed the right of dictating the mode by which the world should be governed for ever, it was the first generation that existed; and if that generation did it not, no succeeding generation can show any authority for doing it, nor can set any up. The illuminating and divine principle of the equal rights of man, (for it has its origin from the Maker of man) relates, not only to the living individuals, but to generations of men succeeding each other. Every generation is equal in rights to the generations which preceded it, by the same rule that every individual is born equal in rights with his contemporary.

Every history of the creation, and every traditionary account, whether from the lettered or unlettered world, however they may vary in their opinion or belief of certain particulars, all agree in establishing one point, *the unity of man*; by which I mean, that men are all of *one degree*, and consequently that all men are born equal, and with equal natural right, in the same manner as if posterity had been continued by *creation* instead of *generation*, the latter being only the mode by which the former is carried forward; and consequently, every child born into the world must be considered as deriving its existence from God. The world is as new to him as it was to the first man that existed, and his natural right in it is of the same kind.

The Mosaic account of the creation, whether taken as divine authority, or merely historical, is full to this point, *the unity or equality of man*. The expressions admit of no controversy. "And God said, Let us make man in our own image. In the image of God created he him; male and female created he them." The distinction of sexes is pointed out, but no other distinction is even implied. If this be not divine authority, it is at least historical authority, and shows that the equality of man, so far from being a modern doctrine, is the oldest upon record.

It is also to be observed, that all the religions known in the world are founded, so far as they relate to man, on the *unity of man*, as being all of one degree. Whether in heaven or in hell, or in whatever state man may be supposed to exist hereafter, the good and the bad are the only distinctions. Nay, even the laws of governments are obliged to slide into this principle, by making degrees to consist in crimes, and not in persons.

5   It is one of the greatest of all truths, and of the highest advantage to cultivate. By considering man in this light, and by instructing him to consider himself in this light, it places him in a close connexion with all his duties, whether to his Creator, or to the creation, of which his is a part; and it is only when he forgets his origin, or, to use a more fashionable phrase, his *birth and family*; that he becomes dissolute. It is not among the least of the evils of the present existing governments in all parts of Europe, that man, considered as man, is thrown back to a vast distance from his Maker, and the artificial chasm filled up by a succession of barriers, or sort of turnpike gates, through which he has to pass. I will quote Mr. Burke's[1] catalogue of barriers that he has set up between man and his Maker. Putting himself in the character of a herald, he says—"We fear God—we look with *awe* to kings—with affection to parliaments—with duty to magistrates—with reverence to priests, and with respect to nobility." Mr. Burke has forgotten to put in "*chivalry*." He has also forgotten to put in Peter.

The duty of man is not a wilderness of turnpike gates, through which he is to pass by tickets from one to the other. It is plain and simple, and consists but of two points. His duty to God, which every man must feel; and with respect to his neighbour, to do as he would be done by. If those to whom power is delegated do well, they will be respected; if not, they will be despised: and with regard to those to whom no power is delegated, but who assume it, the rational world can know nothing of them.

Hitherto we have spoken only (and that but in part) of the natural rights of man. We have now to consider the civil rights of man, and to show how the one originates from the other. Man did not enter into society to become *worse* than he was before, nor to have fewer rights than he had before, but to have those rights better secured. His natural rights are the foundation of all his civil rights. But in order to pursue this distinction with more precision, it will be necessary to mark the different qualities of natural and civil rights.

A few words will explain this. Natural rights are those which appear to man in right of his existence. Of this kind are all the intellectual rights, or rights of the mind, and also all those rights of acting as an individual for his own comfort and happiness, which are not injurious to the natural rights of others.—Civil rights are those which appertain to man in right of his being a member of society. Every civil right has for its foundation, some natural right pre-existing in the individual, but to the enjoyment of which his individual power is not, in all cases, sufficiently competent. Of this kind are all those which relate to security and protection.

From this short review, it will be easy to distinguish between that class of natural rights which man retains after entering into society, and those which he throws into the common stock as a member of society.

10   The natural rights which he retains, are all those in which the *power* to execute is as perfect in the individual as the right itself. Among this class,

---

[1] *Edmund Burke (1729–1797)*: Irish statesman, orator, and writer who sympathized with the American Revolution but opposed the French Revolution on the grounds that it was a completely unjustified break with tradition.

as is before mentioned, are all the intellectual rights, or rights of the mind: consequently, religion is one of those rights. The natural rights which are not retained, are all those in which, though the right is perfect in the individual, the power to execute them is defective. They answer not his purpose. A man, by natural right, has a right to judge in his own cause; and so far as the right of mind is concerned; he never surrenders it: But what availeth it him to judge, if he has not power to redress? He therefore deposits this right in the common stock of society, and takes the arm of society, of which he is a part, in preference and in addition to his own. Society *grants* him nothing. Every man is a proprietor in society, and draws on the capital as a matter of right.

From these premises, two or three certain conclusions will follow.

First, That every civil right grows out of a natural right; or, in other words, is a natural right exchanged.

Secondly, that civil power, properly considered as such, is made up of the aggregate of that class of the natural rights of man, which becomes defective in the individual in point of power, and answers not his purpose; but when collected to a focus, becomes competent to the purpose of every one.

Thirdly, That the power produced from the aggregate of natural rights, imperfect in power in the individual, cannot be applied to invade the natural rights, which are retained in the individual, and in which the power to execute is as perfect as the right itself.

We have now, in a few words, traced man from a natural individual 15 to a member of society, and shown, or endeavoured to show, the quality of the natural rights retained, and of those which are exchanged for civil rights. Let us now apply these principles to governments.

In casting our eyes over the world, it is extremely easy to distinguish the governments which have arisen out of society, or out of the social compact, from those which have not: but to place this in a clearer light than what a single glance may afford, it will be proper to take a review of the several sources from which governments have arisen, and on which they have been founded.

They may be all comprehended under three heads. First, Superstition. Secondly, Power. Thirdly, the common interest of society, and the common rights of man.

READING CRITICALLY FOR IDEAS, STRUCTURE, AND STYLE

1. Why does Paine believe that everyone possesses certain natural rights? Where did these rights originate?

2. What is the relationship between these "natural" rights and corresponding sets of "civil" rights?

3. What justifies the existence of the state and why must it never overstep the boundaries of any person's "natural inalienable" rights? How does Paine use this idea as a rationale to justify rejecting British rule over the American colonies?

EXTENDING INSIGHTS THROUGH WRITING

1. Paine's argument that Americans are free to withdraw their allegiance from Great Britain and create their own government reflects ideas found in the *Declaration of Independence*. In a short paper discuss Paine's essay in terms of the ideas and actual words and phrases that also appear in the more famous document.

2. What fundamentally different assumptions about human nature and the function of the state separate Paine's political theories from Communist theorists such as Karl Marx and Vladimir Lenin? Do some research and write a short essay contrasting these two political systems on the key issue of what function the state is to serve.

CONNECTING PERSPECTIVES ON THE COLLECTIVE EXPERIENCE

1. Paine's idealism for the newly emerging country is seemingly negated when read against Frederick Douglass's account of being a slave. Write a critique of Paine's argument from Frederick Douglass's viewpoint.

2. What parallels can you discover in Paine's rejection of British rule in the eighteenth century and in Ngũgĩ wa Thiong'o's analysis of the effects of British rule in Kenya in the twentieth century?

KENNETH M. STAMPP

To Make Them Stand in Fear

BACKGROUND

Kenneth M. Stampp was born in 1912 in Milwaukee, Wisconsin, and earned his Ph.D. from the University of Wisconsin in 1942. Stampp is the Morrison Professor Emeritus of American History at the University of California at Berkeley and has served as president of the Organization of American Historians. He has been Harmsworth Professor of American History at Oxford University, a Fulbright lecturer at the University of Munich, and has received a Guggenheim fellowship. In addition to editing *The Causes of the Civil War* (1974), Stampp is the author of many distinguished studies, including *And the War Came* (1950), *The Imperiled Union: Essays on the Background of the Civil War* (1980), and *America in 1857: A Nation on the Brink* (1990). "To Make Them Stand in Fear" is reprinted from his 1956 book, *The Peculiar Institution: Slavery in the Anti-Bellum South.* In this essay, Stampp describes the step-by-step process by which slavemasters in the South sought to break the spirits of newly arrived blacks.

APPROACHING STAMPP'S ESSAY

In order to appreciate the nature and impact of Stampp's analysis we have to understand that it was originally published in 1956, two years after the Supreme Court's *Brown* v. *Board of Education* decision outlawing segregation in public schools. Before this time, historians had been heavily influenced by the works of U.B. Phillips who, writing in 1918, had characterized slavery as an institution designed to maintain social stability in the antebellum South. Stampp's critique of Phillips's thesis in *The Peculiar Institution* was so well documented that it not only challenged Phillips's contentions, but destroyed the myths about master-slave relationships and revealed the fundamental economic basis of racial exploitation. Coming as it did at the beginning of the civil rights revolution in the United States, Stampp's book not only impressed historians, but achieved a wider audience and played a part in changing basic perceptions about race for the next generation.

Stampp's analysis is organized to show how the most important goal, which the various techniques of behavioral control were designed to achieve, ultimately depended on the bondsman himself internalizing the belief that he was, in fact and in spirit, a slave.

Stampp uses a variety of source documents, including recorded testimony of slave owners in Mississippi, South Carolina, North Carolina, and Virginia, as well as the actual manuals written to advise plantation owners on the management of slaves. He gives us an invaluable portrait of what was called the "peculiar institution."

To Make Them Stand in Fear

A wise master did not take seriously the belief that Negroes were natural-born slaves. He knew better. He knew that Negroes freshly imported from Africa had to be broken to bondage; that each succeeding generation had to be carefully trained. This was no easy task, for the bondsman rarely submitted willingly. Moreover, he rarely submitted completely. In most cases there was no end to the need for control—at least not until old age reduced the slave to a condition of helplessness.

Masters revealed the qualities they sought to develop in slaves when they singled out certain ones for special commendation. A small Mississippi planter mourned the death of his "faithful and dearly beloved servant" Jack: "Since I have owned him he has been true to me in all respects. He was an obedient trusty servant. . . . I never knew him to steal nor lie and he ever set a moral and industrious example to those around him. . . . I shall ever cherish his memory." A Louisiana sugar planter lost a "very valuable Boy" through an accident: "His life was a very great one. I have always found him willing and obedient and never knew him to fail to do anything he was put to do." These were "ideal" slaves, the models slaveholders had in mind as they trained and governed their workers.

How might this ideal be approached? The first step, advised those who wrote discourses on the management of slaves, was to establish and maintain strict discipline. An Arkansas master suggested the adoption of the "Army Regulations as to the discipline in Forts." "They must obey at all times, and under all circumstances, cheerfully and with alacrity," affirmed a Virginia slaveholder. "It greatly impairs the happiness of a negro, to be allowed to cultivate an insubordinate temper. Unconditional submission is the only footing upon which slavery should be placed. It is precisely similar to the attitude of a minor to his parent, or a soldier to his general." A South Carolinian limned a perfect relationship between a slave and his master: "that the slave should know that his master is to govern absolutely, and he is to obey implicitly. That he is never for a moment to exercise either his will or judgment in opposition to a positive order."

The second step was to implant in the bondsmen themselves a consciousness of personal inferiority. They had "to know and keep their places," to "feel the difference between master and slave," to understand that bondage was their natural status. They had to feel that African ancestry tainted them, that their color was a badge of degradation. In the country they were to show respect for even their master's nonslave-holding neighbors; in the towns they were to give way on the streets to the most wretched white man. The line between the races must never be crossed, for familiarity caused slaves to forget their lowly station and to become "impudent."

Frederick Douglass explained that a slave might commit the offense   5
of impudence in various ways: "in the tone of an answer; in answering at all; in not answering; in the expression of countenance; in the motion of the head; in the gait, manner and bearing of the slave." Any of these acts, in some subtle way, might indicate the absence of proper subordination. "In a well regulated community," wrote a Texan, "a negro takes off his hat in addressing a white man. . . . Where this is not enforced, we may always look for impudent and rebellious negroes."

The third step in the training of slaves was to awe them with a sense of their master's enormous power. The only principle upon which slavery could be maintained, reported a group of Charlestonians, was the "principle of fear." In his defense of slavery James H. Hammond admitted that this, unfortunately, was true but put the responsibility upon the abolitionists. Antislavery agitation had forced masters to strengthen their authority: "We have to rely more and more on the power of fear. . . . We are determined to continue masters, and to do so we have to draw the reign tighter and tighter day by day to be assured that we hold them in complete check." A North Carolina mistress, after subduing a troublesome domestic, realized that it was essential "to make them stand in fear"!

In this the slaveholders had considerable success. Frederick Douglass believed that most slaves stood "in awe" of white men; few could free themselves altogether from the notion that their masters were "invested with a sort of sacredness." Olmsted saw a small white girl stop a slave on the road and boldly order him to return to his plantation. The slave fearfully obeyed her command. A visitor in Mississippi claimed that a master, armed only with a whip or cane, could throw himself among a score of bondsmen and cause them to "flee with terror." He accomplished this by the "peculiar tone of authority" with which he spoke. "Fear, awe, and obedience . . . are interwoven into the very nature of the slave."

The fourth step was to persuade the bondsmen to take an interest in the master's enterprise and to accept his standards of good conduct. A South Carolina planter explained: "The master should make it his business to show his slaves, that the advancement of his individual interest, is at the same time an advancement of theirs. Once they feel this, it will require but little compulsion to make them act as it becomes them." Though slaveholders induced only a few chattels to respond to this appeal, these few were useful examples for others.

The final step was to impress Negroes with their helplessness, to create in them "a habit of perfect dependence" upon their masters. Many believed it dangerous to train slaves to be skilled artisans in the towns, because they tended to become self-reliant. Some thought it equally dangerous to hire them to factory owners. In the Richmond tobacco factories they were alarmingly independent and "insolvent." A Virginian was dismayed to find that his bondsmen, while working at an iron furnace, "got a habit of roaming about and *taking care of themselves*." Permitting them to hire their own time produced even worse results. "No higher evidence can be furnished of its baneful effects," wrote a Charlestonian, "than the unwillingness it produces in the slave, to return to the regular life and domestic control of the master."

A spirit of independence was less likely to develop among slaves kept on the land, where most of them became accustomed to having their master provide their basic needs, and where they might be taught that they were unfit to look out for themselves. Slaves then directed their energies to the attainment of mere "temporary ease and enjoyment." "Their masters," Olmsted believed, "calculated on it in them—do not wish to cure it—and by constant practice encourage it."

Here, then, was the way to produce the perfect slave: accustom him to rigid discipline, demand from him unconditional submission, impress upon him his innate inferiority, develop in him a paralyzing fear of white men, train him to adopt the master's code of good behavior, and instill in him a sense of complete dependence. This, at least, was the goal.

But the goal was seldom reached. Every master knew that the average slave was only an imperfect copy of the model. He knew that some bondsmen yielded only to superior power—and yielded reluctantly. This complicated his problem of control.

READING CRITICALLY FOR IDEAS, STRUCTURE, AND STYLE

1. Stampp demonstrates that the process of conditioning newly arrived blacks depended on instilling a set of psychological controls. What are these, and what were they designed to achieve?

2. How does Stampp's division of the conditioning process into a number of distinct steps help his readers to grasp his thesis and understand his analysis?

3. Stampp's discussion takes the form of an analysis of the process slavemasters used. Why is this form well-suited to Stampp's purpose?

EXTENDING INSIGHTS THROUGH WRITING

1. The manuals Stampp uses to illustrate his analysis describe the goal to be achieved and the methods for achieving it as an ideal. Is it plausible that the methods described here could have produced the required results? Why or why not?

2. As Stampp describes it, slaveholders showed some apprehension about allowing slaves to be trained as artisans. In a paragraph or two, discuss the reasons for this.

CONNECTING PERSPECTIVES ON THE COLLECTIVE EXPERIENCE

1. In what respects does Frederick Douglass (see "Learning to Read and Write") illustrate precisely the kind of reaction to slavery that the slaveholders most feared?

2. The roots of racism in the United States are well-illustrated in Stampp's essay. Draw on Stampp's analysis and James Baldwin's "Letter to My Nephew" and write an essay that explores this issue and its social and psychological effects, then and now.

FREDERICK DOUGLASS

Learning to Read and Write

BACKGROUND

Frederick Douglass (1817–1895) was born into slavery in Maryland, where he worked as a field hand and servant. In 1838, after previous failed attempts to escape, for which he was beaten and tortured, he successfully made his way to New York using the identity papers of a freed black sailor. There he adopted the last name of Douglass (his given name was Bailey) and subsequently settled in New Bedford, Massachusetts. The first black American to rise to prominence as a national figure, Douglass gained renown as a speaker for the Massachusetts Anti-Slavery League and was an editor for the *North Star*, an abolitionist newspaper, from 1847–1860. He was a friend to John Brown, helped convince President Lincoln to issue the Emancipation Proclamation, and became ambassador to several foreign countries. *The Narrative of the Life of Frederick Douglass, an American Slave* (1845) is one of the most illuminating of the many slave narratives written during the nineteenth century. "Learning to Read and Write," drawn from this autobiography, reveals his ingenuity in manipulating circumstances so as to become literate.

APPROACHING DOUGLASS'S ESSAY

The circumstances that Douglass describes occurred when he was sent from Lloyd plantation in Talbot County, Maryland, where his mother, Harriet Bailey, was a slave, to Fell Point in Baltimore where he lived in the house of Hugh Auld (the "Master Hugh," in Douglass's account). Auld's wife, Sophia, initially wanted to help Douglass to learn to read and write, but soon became aware of the threat that his newfound literacy would pose. She not only ceased all further attempts to instruct him, but prevented him from being taught by anyone else. Douglass is not unsympathetic toward Mrs. Auld, who was originally a Northerner who moved to Maryland when she married. Despite her natural liberal inclinations, being a slaveholder transformed her into as tyrannical a mistress as those who were raised in slaveowning families. Douglass's observations about the advantages to slaveholders in denying an education to their slaves contain powerful insights as to the way education is a key to freedom. Douglass structures his narrative by identifying important milestones in his struggle to learn to read and write, which involved learning letters by observing the markings on pieces of timber used in the shipyard where he worked.

Learning to Read and Write

I lived in Master Hugh's family about seven years. During this time, I succeeded in learning to read and write. In accomplishing this, I was compelled to resort to various stratagems. I had no regular teacher. My mistress, who had kindly commenced to instruct me, had, in compliance with the advice and direction of her husband, not only ceased to instruct, but had set her face against my being instructed by any one else. It is due, however, to my mistress to say of her, that she did not adopt this course of treatment immediately. She at first lacked the depravity indispensable to shutting me up in mental darkness. It was at least necessary for her to have some training in the exercise of irresponsible power, to make her equal to the task of treating me as though I were a brute.

My mistress was, as I have said, a kind and tender-hearted woman; and in the simplicity of her soul she commenced, when I first went to live with her, to treat me as she supposed one human being ought to treat another. In entering upon the duties of a slaveholder, she did not seem to perceive that I sustained to her the relation of a mere chattel, and that for her to treat me as a human being was not only wrong, but dangerously so. Slavery proved as injurious to her as it did to me. When I went there, she was a pious, warm, and tender-hearted woman. There was no sorrow or suffering for which she had not a tear. She had bread for the hungry, clothes for the naked, and comfort for every mourner that came within her reach. Slavery soon proved its ability to divest her of these heavenly qualities. Under its influence, the tender heart became stone, and the lamb-like disposition gave way to one of tiger-like fierceness. The first step in her downward course was in her ceasing to instruct me. She now commenced to practice her husband's precepts. She finally became even more violent in her opposition than her husband himself. She was not satisfied with simply doing as well as he had commanded; she seemed anxious to do better. Nothing seemed to make her more angry than to see me with a newspaper. She seemed to think that here lay the danger. I have had her rush at me with a face made all up of fury, and snatch from me a newspaper, in a manner that fully revealed her apprehension. She was an apt woman; and a little experience soon demonstrated, to her satisfaction, that education and slavery were incompatible with each other.

From this time I was most narrowly watched. If I was in a separate room any considerable length of time, I was sure to be suspected of having a book, and was at once called to give an account of myself. All this, however, was too late. The first step had been taken. Mistress, in teaching me the alphabet, had given me the *inch*, and no precaution could prevent me from taking the *ell*.[1]

The plan which I adopted, and the one by which I was most successful, was that of making friends of all the little white boys whom I met in the street. As many of these as I could, I converted into teachers. With their kindly aid, obtained at different times and in different places, I finally succeeded in learning to read. When I was sent on errands, I always took my book with me, and by going one part of my errand quickly, I found time to get a lesson before my return. I used also to carry bread with me, enough of which was always in the house, and to which I was always welcome; for I was much better off in this regard than many of the poor white children in our neighborhood. This bread I used to bestow upon the hungry little urchins, who, in return, would give me that more valuable bread of knowledge. I am strongly tempted to give the names of two or three of those little boys, as a testimonial of the gratitude and affection I bear them; but prudence forbids;—not that it would injure me, but it might embarrass them; for it is almost an unpardonable offence to teach slaves to read in this Christian country. It is enough to say of the dear little fellows, that they lived on Philpot Street, very near Durgin and Bailey's ship-yard. I used to talk this matter of slavery over with them. I would sometimes say to them, I wished I could be as free as they would be when they got to be men. "You will be free as soon as you are twenty-one, *but I am a slave for life!* Have not I as good a right to be free as you have?" These words used to trouble them; they would express for me the liveliest sympathy, and console me with the hope that something would occur by which I might be free.

I was now about twelve years old, and the thought of being *a slave for life* began to bear heavily upon my heart. Just about this time, I got hold of a book entitled "The Columbian Orator."[2] Every opportunity I got, I used to read this book. Among much of other interesting matter, I found in it a dialogue between a master and his slave. The slave was represented as having run away from his master three times. The dialogue represented the conversation which took place between them, when the slave was retaken the third time. In this dialogue, the whole argument in behalf of slavery was brought forward by the master, all of which was disposed of by the slave. The slave was made to say some very smart as well as impressive things in reply to his master—things which had the desired though unexpected effect; for the conversation resulted in the voluntary emancipation of the slave on the part of the master.

In the same book, I met with one of Sheridan's mighty speeches on and in behalf of Catholic emancipation. These were choice documents to

---

[1]An ell is equal to 1.14 meters.
[2]*The Columbian Orator* (1797): Written by Caleb Bingham; it was one of the first readers used in New England schools.

me. I read them over and over again with unabated interest. They gave tongue to interesting thoughts of my own soul, which had frequently flashed through my mind, and died away for want of utterance. The moral which I gained from the dialogue was the power of truth over the conscience of even a slaveholder. What I got from Sheridan was a bold denunciation of slavery, and a powerful vindication of human rights. The reading of these documents enabled me to utter my thoughts, and to meet the arguments brought forward to sustain slavery; but while they relieved me of one difficulty, they brought on another even more painful than the one of which I was relieved. The more I read, the more I was led to abhor and detest my enslavers. I could regard them in no other light than a band of successful robbers, who had left their homes, and gone to Africa, and stolen us from our homes, and in a strange land reduced us to slavery. I loathed them as being the meanest as well as the most wicked of men. As I read and contemplated the subject, behold! that very discontentment which Master Hugh had predicted would follow my learning to read had already come, to torment and sting my soul to unutterable anguish. As I writhed under it, I would at times feel that learning to read had been a curse rather than a blessing. It had given me a view of my wretched condition, without the remedy. It opened my eyes to the horrible pit, but to no ladder upon which to get out. In moments of agony, I envied my fellow-slaves for their stupidity. I have often wished myself a beast. I preferred the condition of the meanest reptile to my own. Any thing, no matter what, to get rid of thinking! It was this everlasting thinking of my condition that tormented me. There was no getting rid of it. It was pressed upon me by every object within sight or hearing, animate or inanimate. The silver trump of freedom had roused my soul to eternal wakefulness. Freedom now appeared, to disappear no more forever. It was heard in every sound, and seen in every thing. It was ever present to torment me with a sense of my wretched condition. I saw nothing without seeing it, I heard nothing without hearing it, and felt nothing without feeling it. It looked from every star, it smiled in every calm, breathed in every wind, and moved in every storm.

I often found myself regretting my own existence, and wishing myself dead; and but for the hope of being free, I have no doubt but that I should have killed myself, or done something for which I should have been killed. While in this state of mind, I was eager to hear any one speak of slavery. I was a ready listener. Every little while, I could hear something about the abolitionists. It was some time before I found what the word meant. It was always used in such connections as to make it an interesting word to me. If a slave ran away and succeeded in getting clear, or if a slave killed his master, set fire to a barn, or did any thing very wrong in the mind of a slaveholder, it was spoken of as the fruit of *abolition.* Hearing the word in this connection very often, I set about learning what it meant. The dictionary afforded me little or no help. I found it was "the act of abolishing," but then I did not know what was to be abolished. Here I was perplexed. I did not dare to ask any one about its meaning, for I was satisfied that it was something they wanted me to know very little about. After a patient waiting, I got one of our city papers, containing an account of the number of petitions from the north, praying for the abolition of slavery in the District of Columbia, and of the slave trade between the States. From this time I understood the words *abolition* and *abolitionist*, and always drew near when that word was spoken, expecting to hear something of importance to myself and fellow-slaves. The light broke in upon me by degrees. I went one day down on the wharf of Mr. Waters; and seeing two Irishmen unloading a scow of stone, I went, unasked, and helped them. When we had finished, one of them came to me and asked me if I were a slave. I told him I was. He asked, "Are ye a slave for life?" I told him that I was. The good Irishman seemed to be deeply affected by the statement. He said to the other that it was a pity so fine a little fellow as myself should be a slave for life. He said it was a shame to hold me. They both advised me to run away to the north; that I should find friends there, and that I should be free. I pretended not to be interested in what they said, and treated them as if I did not understand them; for I feared they might be treacherous. White men have been known to encourage slaves to escape, and then, to get the reward, catch them and return them to their masters. I was afraid that these seemingly good men might use me so; but I nevertheless remembered their advice, and from that time I resolved to run away. I looked forward to a time at which it would be safe for me to escape. I was too young to think of doing so immediately; besides, I wished to learn how to write, as I might have occasion to write my own pass. I consoled myself with the hope that I should one day find a good chance. Meanwhile, I would learn to write.

The idea as to how I might learn to write was suggested to me by being in Durgin and Bailey's ship-yard, and frequently seeing the ship carpenters, after hewing, and getting a piece of timber ready for use, write on the timber the name of that part of the ship for which it was intended. When a piece of timber was intended for the larboard side, it would be marked thus—"L." When a piece was for the starboard side, it would be marked thus—"S." A piece for the larboard side forward, would be marked thus— "L. F." When a piece was for starboard side forward, it would be marked thus—"S. F." For larboard aft, it would be marked thus—"L. A." For starboard aft, it would be marked thus—"S. A." I soon learned the names of these letters, and for what they were intended when placed upon a piece of timber in the ship-yard. I immediately commenced copying them, and in a short time was able to make the four letters named. After that, when I met with any boy who I knew could write, I would tell him I could write as well as he. The next word would be, "I don't believe you. Let me see you try it." I would then make the letters which I had been so fortunate as to learn, and ask him to beat that. In this way I got a good many lessons in writing, which it is quite possible I should never have gotten in any other way. During this time, my copy-book was the board fence, brick wall, and pavement; my pen and ink was a lump of chalk. With these, I learned mainly how to write. I then commenced and continued copying the Italics in Webster's Spelling Book, until I could make them all without looking on the book. By this time, my little Master Thomas had gone to school, and learned how to write, and had written over a number of copy-books. These had been brought home, and shown to some of our near neighbors, and then laid aside. My mistress used to go to class meeting at the Wilk Street meetinghouse every Monday afternoon, and leave me to take care of the house. When left thus, I used to spend the time in writing in the spaces left in Master Thomas's copy-book, copying what he had written. I continued to do this until I could write a hand very similar to that of Master Thomas. Thus, after a long, tedious effort for years, I finally succeeded in learning how to write.

READING CRITICALLY FOR IDEAS, STRUCTURE, AND STYLE

1. Why was Douglass' relationship with the mistress of the household, Sophia Auld, made more difficult when she became aware of how earnestly he wished to learn to read and write?

2. In what context did Douglass become acquainted with the concept of "abolition," and how did it influence his quest to become literate?

3. What ingenious methods did Douglass use to learn how to read and write? What insight do you get into his motivations for wanting to do so?

EXTENDING INSIGHTS THROUGH WRITING

1. Douglass observes that "education and slavery were incompatible with each other." In a 300–500 word essay, discuss the significance of his observation.

2. Imagine that you are illiterate and describe, using specific examples, what a typical day would be like for you.

CONNECTING PERSPECTIVES ON THE COLLECTIVE EXPERIENCE

1. James Baldwin's letter is especially poignant when viewed in connection with Douglass' narrative. What common themes emerge, although these accounts were written over 100 years apart?

2. In what respects was the cultural brainwashing in twentieth-century Kenya, which Ngũgĩ wa Thiong'o describes in "Decolonising the Mind," similar to the restrictions placed on Douglass as a slave in nineteenth-century America?

JAMES BALDWIN

Letter to My Nephew

BACKGROUND

James Baldwin (1924–1987) was born and raised in Harlem where his stepfather was an evangelical minister. Alienated by racism in the United States, he moved to Paris in 1948. When he returned to America nine years later, he became involved in the civil rights movement and devoted himself to the exploration of the quest for personal identity in the lives of African-Americans. His first novel, *Go Tell It On the Mountain* (1953), explores the problems of racial and sexual identity, as do *Giovanni's Room* (1956) and *Another Country* (1962). Baldwin's most important essays and social commentaries appear in *Notes of a Native Son* (1955), *Nobody Knows My Name* (1961), and *The Fire Next Time* (1963), in which "Letter to My Nephew" was first published. His last works include a book of essays, *The Price of the Ticket* (1985), a novel, *Harlem Quartet* (1987), and a play, *The Welcome Table* (1987).

APPROACHING BALDWIN'S LETTER

As the grandson of slaves, whose career as a writer began when segregation was still legal, Baldwin was well aware of the tragic consequences of racism that would await his nephew if he became embittered. This is the central warning expressed in this letter to his fifteen-year-old nephew, James. Baldwin does not side-step the damage done by racism, and acquaints his nephew with the integral role that black people have played in the cultural history of the nation.

The voice we hear in this letter is eloquent and evokes the rhythms and phrasing of a sermon (in his youth Baldwin aspired to become a preacher). Baldwin's strengths as a psychologist of race relations are well illustrated; he was one of the few writers who explored the hitherto unexpressed meanings of racism in its actual impact on people's everyday lives. This was especially important since one of the most destructive aspects of racism was that it denied the basic humanity of blacks (a process begun by slavery, which Kenneth M. Stampp describes earlier in this chapter).

Letter to My Nephew

Dear James:

I have begun this letter five times and torn it up five times. I keep seeing your face, which is also the face of your father and my brother. Like him, you are tough, dark, vulnerable, moody—with a very definite tendency to sound truculent because you want no one to think you are soft. You may be like your grandfather in this, I don't know, but certainly both you and your father resemble him very much physically. Well, he is dead, he never saw you, and he had a terrible life; he was defeated long before he died because, at the bottom of his heart, he really believed what white people said about him. This is one of the reasons that he became so holy. I am sure that your father has told you something about all that. Neither you nor your father exhibit any tendency towards holiness: you really *are* of another era, part of what happened when the Negro left the land and came into what the late E. Franklin Frazier called "the cities of destruction." You can only be destroyed by believing that you really are what the white world calls a *nigger*. I tell you this because I love you, and please don't you ever forget it.

I have known both of you all your lives, have carried your Daddy in my arms and on my shoulders, kissed and spanked him and watched him learn to walk. I don't know if you've known anybody from that far back; if you've loved anybody that long, first as an infant, then as a child, then as a man, you gain a strange perspective on time and human pain and effort. Other people cannot see what I see whenever I look into your father's face as it is today are all those other faces which were his. Let him laugh and I see a cellar your father does not remember and a house he does not remember and I hear in his present laughter his laughter as a child. Let him curse and I remember him falling down the cellar steps, and howling, and I remember, with pain, his tears, which my hand or your grandmother's so easily wiped away. But no one's hand can wipe away those tears he sheds invisibly today, which one hears in his laughter and in his speech and in his songs. I know what the world has done to my brother and how narrowly he has survived it. And I know, which is much worse, and this is the crime of which I accuse my country and my countrymen, and for which neither I nor time nor history will ever forgive them, that they have destroyed and are destroying hundreds of thousands of lives and do not know it and do not want to know it. One can be, indeed one must strive to become, tough and philosophical concerning destruction and death, for this is what most of mankind has been best at since we have heard of man. (But remember: *most* of mankind is not *all* of mankind.) But it is not permissible that the authors of devastation should also be innocent. It is the innocence which constitutes the crime.

Now, my dear namesake, these innocent and well-meaning people, your countrymen, have caused you to be born under conditions not very far removed from those described for us by Charles Dickens in the London of more than a hundred years ago. (I hear the chorus of the innocents screaming, "No! This is not true! How *bitter* you are"—but I am writing this letter to *you*, to try to tell you something about how to handle *them*, for most of them do not yet really know that you exist. I *know* the conditions under which you were born, for I was there. Your countrymen were *not* there, and haven't made it yet. Your grandmother was also there, and no one has ever accused her of being bitter. I suggest that the innocents check with her. She isn't hard to find. Your countrymen don't know that *she* exists, either, though she has been working for them all their lives.)

Well, you were born, here you came, something like fifteen years ago; and though your father and mother and grandmother, looking about the streets through which they were carrying you, staring at the walls into which they brought you, had every reason to be heavyhearted, yet they were not. For here you were, Big James, named for me—you were a big baby, I was not—here you were: to be loved. To be loved, baby, hard, at once, and forever, to strengthen you against the loveless world. Remember that: I know how black it looks today, for you. It looked bad that day, too, yes, we were trembling. We have not stopped trembling yet, but if we had not loved each other none of us would have survived. And now you must survive because we love you, and for the sake of your children and your children's children.

5   This innocent country set you down in a ghetto in which, in fact, it intended that you should perish. Let me spell out precisely what I mean by that, for the heart of the matter is here, and the root of my dispute with my country. You were born where you were born and faced the future that you faced because you were black and *for no other reason*. The limits of your ambition were, thus, expected to be set forever. You were born into a society which spelled out with brutal clarity, and in as many ways as possible, that you were a worthless human being. You were not expected to aspire to excellence: you were expected to make peace with mediocrity. Wherever you have turned, James, in your short time on this earth, you

have been told where you could go and what you could do (and *how* you could do it) and where you could live and whom you could marry. I know your countrymen do not agree with me about this, and I hear them saying, "You exaggerate." They do not know Harlem, and I do. So do you. Take no one's word for anything, including mine—but trust your experience. Know whence you came. If you know whence you came, there is really no limit to where you can go. The details and symbols of your life have been deliberately constructed to make you believe what white people say about you. Please try to remember that what they believe, as well as what they do and cause you to endure, does not testify to your inferiority but to their inhumanity and fear. Please try to be clear, dear James, through the storm which rages about your youthful head today, about the reality which lies behind the words *acceptance* and *integration*. There is no reason for you to try to become like white people and there is no basis whatever for their impertinent assumption that *they* must accept *you*. The really terrible thing, old buddy, is that *you* must accept *them*. And I mean that very seriously. You must accept them and accept them with love. For these innocent people have no other hope. They are, in effect, still trapped in a history which they do not understand; and until they understand it, they cannot be released from it. They have had to believe for many years, and for innumerable reasons, that black men are inferior to white men. Many of them, indeed, know better, but, as you will discover, people find it very difficult to act on what they know. To act is to be committed, and to be committed is to be in danger. In this case, the danger, in the minds of most white Americans, is the loss of their identity. Try to imagine how you would feel if you woke up one morning to find the sun shining and all the stars aflame. You would be frightened because it is out of the order of nature. Any upheaval in the universe is terrifying because it so profoundly attacks one's sense of one's own reality. Well, the black man has functioned in the white man's world as a fixed star, as an immovable pillar: and as he moves out of his place, heaven and earth are shaken to their foundations. You, don't be afraid. I said that it was intended that you should perish in the ghetto, perish by never being allowed to go behind the white man's definitions, by never being allowed to spell your proper name. You have, and many of us have, defeated this intention; and, by a terrible law, a terrible paradox, those innocents who believed that your imprisonment made them safe are losing their grasp of reality. But these men are your brothers—your lost, younger brothers. And if the word *integration* means anything, this is what it means: that we, with love, shall force our brothers to see themselves as they are, to cease fleeing from reality and begin to change it. For this is your home, my friend, do not be driven from it; great men have done great things here, and will again, and we can make America what America must become. It will be hard, James, but you come from sturdy, peasant stock, men who picked cotton and dammed rivers and built railroads, and, in the teeth of the most terrifying odds, achieved an unassailable and monumental dignity. You come from a long line of great poets, some of the greatest poets since Homer. One of them said, *The very time I thought I was lost, My dungeon shook and my chains fell off.*

You know, and I know, that the country is celebrating one hundred years of freedom one hundred years too soon. We cannot be free until they are free. God bless you, James, and Godspeed.

Your uncle,
James

READING CRITICALLY FOR IDEAS, STRUCTURE, AND STYLE

1. What attitude is it vitally important for Baldwin to instill in his nephew? Why is it important for his nephew to understand that he must not reenact the bitterness and sadness that blighted the lives of his ancestors?
2. What does Baldwin mean by the "cities of destruction"? How does Baldwin's letter seek to foster a love that transcends the personal relationship of uncle and nephew and acts as a constructive force to solve a pressing social problem?
3. What stylistic qualities in this account (diction, imagery, sentence structure) demonstrate that Baldwin has written a letter to his fifteen-year-old nephew rather than a formal essay to express his social concerns?

EXTENDING INSIGHTS THROUGH WRITING

1. Write a short letter to a younger person, that expresses your concerns about a real social issue that includes any advice you would wish to pass on.
2. Baldwin's letter provides an invaluable perspective on his works of fiction. Read one of these, such as the short story "Sonny's Blues" (1957) or the novel *Go Tell It On the Mountain* (1953) and analyze the relationship between this letter and the fictional work in terms of characters, incidents, and themes.

CONNECTING PERSPECTIVES ON THE COLLECTIVE EXPERIENCE

1. The degrading effects of racism in America correspond in many ways to the oppressive way the British treated native Kenyans as described by Ngũgĩ wa Thiong'o. What differences separate the two authors in terms of their attitudes towards the oppressors?

2. Both Baldwin and Frederick Douglass (see "Learning to Read and Write") are remarkably objective in viewing racism as a system that degrades both oppressors and victims. Compare their insights.

NGŨGĨ WA THIONG'O

Decolonising the Mind

BACKGROUND

Ngũgĩ wa Thiong'o is regarded as one of the most important contemporary writers from the African continent. He wrote his first novels, *Weep, Not, Child* (1964) and *The River Between* (1965), in English, and *Caitaani Mutharava-Ini* (translated as *Devil on the Cross*, 1982) in his native language, Gĩkũyũ. He was chairman of the Department of Literature at the University of Nairobi until his detention, without trial, by the Kenyan authorities in 1976, an account of which appeared under the title *Detained: A Writer's Prison Diary* (1981). The international outcry over his imprisonment eventually brought about his release two years later, after which he left Kenya. The following selection comes from *Decolonising the Mind: The Politics of Language in African Literature* (1986), a work that constitutes, says Thiong'o, "my farewell to English as a vehicle for any of my writings." Subsequently, he has written novels and plays in Gĩkũyũ. Thiong'o currently is a Professor of Comparative Literature at New York University.

APPROACHING THIONG'O'S ESSAY

From Thiong'o's essay, we gain a clearer picture of how the British sought to achieve complete economic, political, and cultural control over the Kenyans. This East African nation became a British protectorate in 1890 and a Crown Colony in 1920 and only gained independence in 1963. Under British colonial rule, Kenyans were compelled to view themselves only from the British point-of-view, a form of cultural programming reinforced by teaching children only in English and exposing them to "images of his world as mirrored in the written languages of his colonizer." Since language, in Thiong'o's view, serves as a vehicle for the values of the culture, changing the language people are allowed to speak must inevitably change the way they perceive themselves.

164

Thiong'o tells us that punishments were meted out for the speaking of Gĩkũyũ: The speaking of English was rewarded and became the single most important factor that determined one's advancement in school and in society. In order to stress what was lost, Thiong'o describes the integral role Gĩkũyũ had played in tribal, village, and family life in Kenya before the British colonized the country. Gĩkũyũ was not only the language of communication within the village, but it provided an important cohesive element underlying all relationships between people and within families. While Gĩkũyũ conferred a positive self-image, the picture Kenyans had of themselves under the British was designed to instill a sense of low self-esteem and to foster a desire to adopt the values as well as the language of British culture. The situation described by Thiong'o has changed so that children are now taught in their native languages for the first three years of school, after which instruction is exclusively in English.

Decolonising the Mind

I was born into a large peasant family: father, four wives and about twenty-eight children. I also belonged, as we all did in those days, to a wider extended family and to the community as a whole.

We spoke Gĩkũyũ as we worked in the fields. We spoke Gĩkũyũ in and outside the home. I can vividly recall those evenings of story-telling around the fireside. It was mostly the grown-ups telling the children but everybody was interested and involved. We children would re-tell the stories the following day to other children who worked in the fields picking the pyrethrum flowers, tea-leaves or coffee beans of our European and African landlords.

The stories, with mostly animals as the main characters, were all told in Gĩkũyũ. Hare, being small, weak but full of innovative wit and cunning, was our hero. We identified with him as he struggled against the brutes of prey like lion, leopard, hyena. His victories were our victories and we learnt that the apparently weak can outwit the strong. We followed the animals in their struggle against hostile nature—drought, rain, sun, wind—a confrontation often forcing them to search for forms of co-operation. But we were also interested in their struggles amongst themselves, and particularly between the beasts and the victims of prey. These twin struggles, against nature and other animals, reflected real-life struggles in the human world.

Not that we neglected stories with human beings as the main characters. There were two types of characters in such human-centred narratives: the species of truly human beings with qualities of courage, kindness, mercy, hatred of evil, concern for others; and a man-eat-man two-mouthed species with qualities of greed, selfishness, individualism and hatred of what was good for the larger co-operative community. Co-operation as the ultimate good in a community was a constant theme. It could unite human beings with animals against ogres and beasts of prey, as in the story of how dove, after being fed with castor-oil seeds, was sent to fetch a smith work-ing far away from home and whose pregnant wife was being threatened by these man-eating two-mouthed ogres.

5   There were good and bad story-tellers. A good one could tell the same story over and over again, and it would always be fresh to us, the listen-ers. He or she could tell a story told by someone else and make it more alive and dramatic. The differences really were in the use of words and images and the inflexion of voices to effect different tones.

We therefore learnt to value words for their meaning and nuances. Language was not a mere string of words. It had a suggestive power well beyond the immediate and lexical meaning. Our appreciation of the suggestive mag-ical power of language was reinforced by the games we played with words through riddles, proverbs, transpositions of syllables, or through nonsensical but musically arranged words.[1] So we learnt the music of our language on top of the content. The language, through images and symbols, gave us a view of the world, but it had a beauty of its own. The home and the field were then our pre-primary school but what is important, for this discussion, is that the language of our evening teach-ins, and the language of our immediate and wider community, and the language of our work in the fields were one.

And then I went to school, a colonial school, and this harmony was broken. The language of my education was no longer the language of my culture. I first went to Kamaandura, missionary run, and then to another called Maanguuũ run by nationalists grouped around the Gĩkũyũ Independent and Karinga Schools Association. Our language of education was still Gĩkũyũ. The very first time I was ever given an ovation for my writ-ing was over a composition in Gĩkũyũ. So for my first four years there was still harmony between the language of my formal education and that of the Limuru peasant community.

It was after the declaration of a state of emergency over Kenya in 1952 that all the schools run by patriotic nationalists were taken over by the colonial regime and were placed under District Education Boards chaired by Englishmen. English became the language of my formal education. In Kenya, English became more than a language: it was *the* language, and all the others had to bow before it in deference.

Thus one of the most humiliating experiences was to be caught speak-ing Gĩkũyũ in the vicinity of the school. The culprit was given corporal pun-ishment—three to five strokes of the cane on bare buttocks—or was made to carry a metal plate around the neck with inscriptions such as I AM STU-PID or I AM A DONKEY. Sometimes the culprits were fined money they could hardly afford. And how did the teachers catch the culprits? A button was initially given to one pupil who was supposed to hand it over to whoever

---

[1]Example from a tongue twister: 'Kaana ka Nikoora koona koora koora: na ko koora koona kaana ka Nikoora koora koora.' I'm indebted to Wangui wa Goro for this exam-ple. "Nichola's child saw a baby frog and ran away: and when the baby frog saw Nichola's child it also ran away.' A Gĩkũyũ speaking child has to get the correct tone and length of vowel and pauses to get it right. Otherwise it becomes a jumble of *k*'s and *r*'s and *na*'s [author's note].

was caught speaking his mother tongue. Whoever had the button at the end of the day would sing who had given it to him and the ensuing process would bring out all the culprits of the day. Thus children were turned into witch-hunters and in the process were being taught the lucrative value of being a traitor to one's immediate community.

The attitude to English was the exact opposite: any achievement in   10
spoken or written English was highly rewarded; prizes, prestige, applause; the ticket to higher realms. English became the measure of intelligence and ability in the arts, the sciences, and all the other branches of learning. English became *the* main determinant of a child's progress up the ladder of formal education.

As you may know, the colonial system of education in addition to its apartheid racial demarcation had the structure of a pyramid: a broad primary base, a narrowing secondary middle, and an even narrower university apex. Selections from primary into secondary were through an examination, in my time called Kenya African Preliminary Examination, in which one had to pass six subjects ranging from Maths to Nature Study and Kiswahili. All the papers were written in English. Nobody could pass the exam who failed the English language paper no matter how brilliantly he had done in the other subjects. I remember one boy in my class off 1954 who had distinctions in all subjects except English, which he had failed. He was made to fail the entire exam. He went on to become a turn boy in a bus company. I who had only passes but a credit in English got a place at the Alliance High School, one of the most elitist institutions for Africans in colonial Kenya. The requirements for a place at the University, Makerere University College, were broadly the same: nobody could go on to wear the undergraduate red gown, no matter how brilliantly they had performed in all the other subjects unless they had a credit—not even a simple pass!—in English. Thus the most coveted place in the pyramid and in the system was only available to the holder of an English language credit card. English was the official vehicle and the magic formula to colonial elitedom.

Literary education was now determined by the dominant language while also reinforcing that dominance. Orature (oral literature) in Kenyan languages stopped. In primary school I now read simplified Dickens and Stevenson alongside Rider Haggard. Jim Hawkins, Oliver Twist, Tom Brown—not Hare, Leopard and Lion—were now my daily companions in the world of imagination. In secondary school, Scott and G. B. Shaw vied with more Rider Haggard, John Buchan, Alan Paton, Captain W. E. Johns. At Makerere I read English: from Chaucer to T. S. Eliot with a touch of Graham Greene.

Thus language and literature were taking us further and further from ourselves to other selves, from our world to other worlds.

What was the colonial system doing to us Kenyan children? What were the consequences of, on the one hand, this systematic suppression of our languages and the literature they carried, and on the other the elevation of English and the literature it carried? To answer those questions, let me first examine the relationship of language to human experience, human culture, and the human perception of reality.

15   Language, any language, has a dual character: it is both a means of communication and a carrier of culture. Take English. It is spoken in Britain and in Sweden and Denmark. But for Swedish and Danish people English is only a means of communication with non-Scandinavians. It is not a carrier of their culture. For the British, and particularly the English, it is additionally, and inseparably from its use as a tool of communication, a carrier of their culture and history. Or take Swahili in East and Central Africa. It is widely used as a means of communication across many nationalities. But it is not the carrier of a culture and history of many of those nationalities. However in parts of Kenya and Tanzania, and particularly in Zanzibar, Swahili is inseparably both a means of communication and a carrier of the culture of those people to whom it is a mother-tongue.

Culture transmits or imparts those images of the world and reality through the spoken and the written language, that is through a specific language. In other words, the capacity to speak, the capacity to order sounds in a manner that makes for mutual comprehension between human beings is universal. This is the universality of language, a quality specific to human beings. It corresponds to the universality of the struggle against nature and that between human beings. But the particularity of the sounds, the words, the word order into phrases and sentences, and the specific manner, or laws, of their ordering is what distinguishes one language from another. Thus a specific culture is not transmitted through language in its universality but in its particularity as the language of a specific community with a specific history. Written literature and orature are the main means by which a particular language transmits the images of the world contained in the culture it carries.

Language as communication and as culture are then products of each other. Communication creates culture: culture is a means of communication. Language carries culture, and culture carries, particularly through orature and literature, the entire body of values by which we come to perceive ourselves and our place in the world. How people perceive themselves affects how they look at their culture, at their politics and at the social production of wealth, at their entire relationship to nature and to other beings. Language is thus inseparable from ourselves as a community of human beings with a specific form and character, a specific history, a specific relationship to the world.

So what was the colonialist imposition of a foreign language doing to us children?

The real aim of colonialism was to control the people's wealth: what they produced, how they produced it, and how it was distributed; to control, in other words, the entire realm of the language of real life. Colonialism imposed its control of the social production of wealth through military conquest and subsequent political dictatorship. But its most important area of domination was the mental universe of the colonised, the control, through culture, of how people perceived themselves and their relationship to the world. Economic and political control can never be complete or effective without mental control. To control a people's culture is to control their tools of self-definition in relationship to others.

20   For colonialism this involved two aspects of the same process: the destruction or the deliberate undervaluing of a people's culture, their art,

dances, religions, history, geography, education, orature and literature, and the conscious elevation of the language of the coloniser. The domination of a people's language by the languages of the colonising nations was crucial to the domination of the mental universe of the colonised.

Take language as communication. Imposing a foreign language, and suppressing the native languages as spoken and written, were already breaking the harmony previously existing between the African child and the three aspects of language. Since the new language as a means of communication was a product of and was reflecting the 'real language of life' elsewhere, it could never as spoken or written properly reflect or imitate the real life of that community. This may in part explain why technology always appears to us as slightly external, *their* product and not *ours*. The word 'missile' used to hold an alien far-away sound until I recently learnt its equivalent in Gĩkũyũ, *ngurukuhĩ*, and it made me apprehend it differently. Learning, for a colonial child, became a cerebral activity and not an emotionally felt experience.

But since the new, imposed languages could never completely break the native languages as spoken, their most effective area of domination was the third aspect of language as communication, the written. The language of an African child's formal education was foreign. The language of the books he read was foreign. The language of his conceptualisation was foreign. Thought, in him, took the visible form of a foreign language. So the written language of a child's upbringing in the school (even his spoken language within the school compound) became divorced from his spoken language at home. There was often not the slightest relationship between the child's written world, which was also the language of his schooling, and the world of his immediate environment in the family and the community. For a colonial child, the harmony existing between the three aspects of language as communication was irrevocably broken. This resulted in the disassociation of the sensibility of that child from his natural and social environment, what we might call colonial alienation. The alienation became reinforced in the teaching of history, geography, music, where bourgeois Europe was always the centre of the universe.

This disassociation, divorce, or alienation from the immediate environment becomes clearer when you look at colonial language as a carrier of culture.

Since culture is a product of the history of a people which it in turn reflects, the child was now being exposed exclusively to a culture that was a product of a world external to himself. He was being made to stand outside himself to look at himself. *Catching Them Young* is the title of a book on racism, class, sex, and politics in children's literature by Bob Dixon. 'Catching them young' as an aim was even more true of a colonial child. The images of this world and his place in it implanted in a child take years to eradicate, if they ever can be.

Since culture does not just reflect the world in images but actually, through those very images, conditions a child to see that world in a certain way, the colonial child was made to see the world and where he stands in it as seen and defined by or reflected in the culture of the language of imposition.

And since those images are mostly passed on through orature and literature it meant the child would now only see the world as seen in the literature of his language of adoption. From the point of view of alienation, that is of seeing oneself from outside oneself as if one was another self, it does not matter that the imported literature carried the great humanist tradition of the best in Shakespeare, Goethe, Balzac, Tolstoy, Gorky, Brecht, Sholokhov, Dickens. The location of this great mirror of imagination was necessarily Europe and its history and culture and the rest of the universe was seen from that centre.

But obviously it was worse when the colonial child was exposed to images of his world as mirrored in the written languages of his coloniser. Where his own native languages were associated in his impressionable mind with low status, humiliation, corporal punishment, slow-footed intelligence and ability or downright stupidity, non-intelligibility and barbarism, this was reinforced by the world he met in the works of such geniuses of racism as a Rider Haggard or a Nicholas Monsarrat; not to mention the pronouncement of some of the giants of western intellectual and political establishment, such as Hume ('. . . the negro is naturally inferior to the whites . . .'),[2] Thomas Jefferson ('. . . the blacks . . . are inferior to the whites on the endowments of both body and mind . . . '),[3] or Hegel with his Africa comparable to a land of childhood still enveloped in the dark mantle of the night as far as the development of self-conscious history was concerned. Hegel's statement that there was nothing harmonious with humanity to be found in the African character is representative of the racist images of Africans and Africa such a colonial child was bound to encounter in the literature of the colonial languages.[4] The results could be disastrous.

In her paper read to the conference on the teaching of African literature in schools held in Nairobi in 1973, entitled 'Written Literature and Black Images'[5] the Kenyan writer and scholar Professor Mĩcere Mũgo related how a reading of the description of Gagool as an old African woman in Rider Haggard's *King Solomon's Mines* had for a long time made her feel mortal terror whenever she encountered old African women. In his autobiography *This Life* Sydney Poitier describes how, as a result of the literature he had read, he had come to associate Africa with snakes. So on arrival in Africa and being put up in a modern hotel in a modern city, he could not

---

[2]Quoted in Eric Williams, *A History of the People of Trinidad and Tobago*, London 1964, p. 32 [Author's note].

[3]Eric Williams, ibid, p. 31 [Author's note].

[4]In references to Africa in the introduction to his lectures in *The Philosophy of History*, Hegel gives historical, philosophical, rational expression and legitimacy to every conceivable European racist myth about Africa. Africa is even denied her own geography where it does not correspond to the myth. Thus Egypt is not part of Africa; and North Africa is part of Europe. Africa proper is the especial home of ravenous beasts, snakes of all kinds. The African is not part of humanity. Only slavery to Europe can raise him, possibly, to the lower ranks of humanity. Slavery is good for the African. 'Slavery is in and for itself *injustice*, for the essence of humanity is *freedom*; but for this man must be matured. The gradual abolition of slavery is therefore wiser and more equitable than its sudden removal.' (Hegel, *The Philosophy of History*, Dover edition, New York: 1956, pp. 91–9.) Hegel clearly reveals himself as the nineteenth-century Hitler of the intellect [Author's note].

[5]The paper is now in Akivaga and Gachukiah's *The Teaching of African Literature in Schools*, published by Kenya Literature Bureau [Author's note].

sleep because he kept on looking for snakes everywhere, even under the bed. These two have been able to pinpoint the origins of their fears. But for most others the negative image becomes internalised and it affects their cultural and even political choices in ordinary living.

READING CRITICALLY FOR IDEAS, STRUCTURE, AND STYLE

1. How do the stories told to children in Gĩkũyũ stress the kind of cultural values that would be important as they grew up in Kenyan society?

2. In addition to transmitting cultural values, how did hearing these stories along with riddles and proverbs imbue children with a love of the language of Gĩkũyũ and enhance their responsiveness to features of narrative, imagery, inflection, and tone?

3. Describe the disruption Thiong'o experienced when he first attended a colonial school. How did the kind of punishments meted out for speaking Gĩkũyũ give you insight into the psychologically damaging effects of such an experience on a child?

4. In what way were the methods employed by British rulers in Kenya designed to encourage diminished self-esteem in blacks, coupled with an inflated view of British superiority?

EXTENDING INSIGHTS THROUGH WRITING

1. In what way does changing the language people are allowed to speak change how they perceive themselves? In a few paragraphs discuss the reasons why the British tried to make it impossible for the Kenyans to draw on the cultural values embodied in their native language.

2. Do the stories and fairy tales told to children in our culture serve the same function as those Thiong'o discusses? Why or why not?

CONNECTING PERSPECTIVES ON THE COLLECTIVE EXPERIENCE

1. What aspects of Thiong'o's essay and James Baldwin's "Letter to My Nephew" are concerned with the damaging effects on children who may internalize a negative self image?

2. In what way can this account by Thiong'o and Thomas Paine's essay *The Rights of Man* be understood as documents of resistance to colonial powers (the British in the colonies in the eighteenth century and in Kenya in the twentieth century)?

GEORGE ORWELL

Shooting an Elephant

BACKGROUND

George Orwell was the pen name taken by Eric Blair (1903–1950), who was born in Bengal, India. Educated on a scholarship at Eton, he served as a British official in the police in Burma and became disillusioned with the aims and methods of colonialism. He describes the next few years in his first book *Down and Out in Paris and London* (1933), a gripping account of life on the fringe. In 1936, Orwell went to Spain to report on the Civil War and joined the Communist P.O.U.M. militia to fight against the Fascists. His account of this experience, in which he was severely wounded, titled *Homage to Catalonia* (1938) is an unflinching account of the bleak and comic aspects of trench warfare. In *Animal Farm* (1945), he satirized the Russian Revolution and the machinations of the Soviet bureacracy. In his acclaimed novel, *Nineteen Eighty-Four* (1949), his distrust of totalitarianism emerged as a grim prophecy of a bureacratic, regimented England of the future whose citizens are constantly watched by "big brother." Five collections of his essays have been published, including *Shooting an Elephant and Other Essays* (1946) where this selection first appeared.

APPROACHING ORWELL'S ESSAY

Between 1922 and 1927 Orwell served as a British police official in Burma and became disillusioned with the aims and methods of colonialism. The conflict between his position as an official and his disenchantment with the bureacracy obviously colors his account of shooting an elephant that had run wild and had trampled a villager. Although the elephant had returned to normalcy, Orwell, as a policeman, must kill it or forfeit his authority with the local Burmese. Orwell's essay opens with his comment that, for the only time in his life, he "was hated by large numbers of people" because of his position as a British official in the police, a position he had come, ironically, to despise. The final paragraph of Orwell's account summarizes both the political and circumstantial situations that seem to motivate the shooting of the elephant, but Orwell's honest assessment of himself makes clear his more powerful personal motivation: "I often wonder whether any of the others grasped that I had done it solely to avoid looking a fool." Orwell faces a decisive turning point the moment he realizes he will have to shoot the elephant; it is that same moment that he perceives that "when the white man turns tyrant it is his own freedom that he destroys." In this essay as well as in other works, Orwell points out that tyranny tends to enslave not only the oppressed but the tyrants themselves. Orwell's style exemplifies the same qualities of candor, freedom from self-deception, and plainspeaking that he espoused in his influential 1946 essay, *Politics and the English Language.*

Shooting an Elephant

In Moulmein, in Lower Burma, I was hated by large numbers of people—the only time in my life that I have been important enough for this to happen to me. I was sub-divisional police officer of the town, and in an aimless, petty kind of way anti-European feeling was very bitter. No one had the guts to raise a riot, but if a European woman went through the bazaars alone somebody would probably spit betel juice over her dress. As a police officer I was an obvious target and was baited whenever it seemed safe to do so. When a nimble Burman tripped me up on the football field and the referee (another Burman) looked the other way, the crowd yelled with hideous laughter. This happened more than once. In the end the sneering yellow faces of young men that met me everywhere, the insults hooted after me when I was at a safe distance, got badly on my nerves. The young Buddhist priests were the worst of all. There were several thousands of them in the town and none of them seemed to have anything to do except stand on street corners and jeer at Europeans.

All this was perplexing and upsetting. For at that time I had already made up my mind that imperialism was an evil thing and the sooner I chucked up my job and got out of it the better. Theoretically—and secretly, of course—I was all for the Burmese and all against their oppressors, the British. As for the job I was doing, I hated it more bitterly than I can perhaps make clear. In a job like that you see the dirty work of Empire at close quarters. The wretched prisoners huddling in the stinking cages of the lock-ups, the grey, cowed faces of the long-term convicts, the scarred buttocks of the men who had been flogged with bamboos—all these oppressed me with an intolerable sense of guilt. But I could get nothing into perspective. I was young and ill-educated and I had had to think out my problems in the utter silence that is imposed on every Englishman in the East. I did not even know that the British Empire is dying, still less did I know that it is a great deal better than the younger empires that are going to supplant it. All I knew was that I was stuck between my hatred of the empire I served and my rage against the evil-spirited little beasts who tried to make my job impossible. With one part of my mind I thought of the British Raj[1] as an unbreakable tyranny, as something clamped down, in *saecula saeculorum,*[2] upon the will of prostrate peoples; with another part I thought that the greatest joy in the world would be to drive a bayonet into a Buddhist priest's guts. Feelings like these are the normal by-products of imperialism; ask any Anglo-Indian official, if you can catch him off duty.

One day something happened which in a roundabout way was enlightening. It was a tiny incident in itself, but it gave me a better glimpse than I had had before of the real nature of imperialism—the real motives for which despotic governments act. Early one morning the sub-inspector at a police station the other end of the town rang me up on the 'phone and said that an elephant was ravaging the bazaar. Would I please come and do something about it? I did not know what I could do, but I wanted to see what was happening and I got on to a pony and started out. I took my rifle, an old .44 Winchester and much too small to kill an elephant, but I thought the noise might be useful *in terrorem.* Various Burmans stopped me on the way and told me about the elephant's doings. It was not, of course, a wild elephant, but a tame one which had gone "must."[3] It had been chained up, as tame elephants always are when their attack of "must" is due, but on the previous night it had broken its chain and escaped. Its mahout, the only person who could manage it when it was in that state, had set out in pursuit, but had taken the wrong direction and was now twelve hours' journey away, and in the morning the elephant had suddenly reappeared in the town. The Burmese population had no weapons and were quite helpless against it. It had already destroyed somebody's bamboo hut, killed a cow and raided some fruit-stalls and devoured the stock; also it had met the municipal rubbish van and, when the driver jumped out and took to his heels, had turned the van over and inflicted violences upon it.

The Burmese sub-inspector and some Indian constables were waiting for me in the quarter where the elephant had been seen. It was a very poor quarter, a labyrinth of squalid bamboo huts, thatched with palm-leaf, winding all over a steep hillside. I remember that it was a cloudy, stuffy morning at the beginning of the rains. We began questioning the people as to where the elephant had gone and, as usual, failed to get any definite information. That is invariably the case in the East; a story always sounds clear enough at a distance, but the nearer you get to the scene of events the vaguer it becomes. Some of the people said that the elephant had gone in one direction, some said that he had gone in another, some professed not even to have heard of any elephant. I had almost made up my mind that the whole story was a pack of lies, when we heard yells a little distance away. There was a loud, scandalized cry of "Go away, child! Go away this

---

[1]The imperial government of British India and Burma.
[2]Forever and ever.
[3]Gone into sexual heat.

instant!" and an old woman with a switch in her hand came round the corner of a hut, violently shooing away a crowd of naked children. Some more women followed, clicking their tongues and exclaiming; evidently there was something that the children ought not to have seen. I rounded the hut and saw a man's dead body sprawling in the mud. He was an Indian, a black Dravidian coolie, almost naked, and he could not have been dead many minutes. The people said that the elephant had come suddenly upon him round the corner of the hut, caught him with its trunk, put its foot on his back and ground him into the earth. This was the rainy season and the ground was soft, and his face had scored a trench a foot deep and a couple of yards long. He was lying on his belly with arms crucified and head sharply twisted to one side. His face was coated with mud, the eyes wide open, the teeth bared and grinning with an expression of unendurable agony. (Never tell me, by the way, that the dead look peaceful. Most of the corpses I have seen looked devilish.) The friction of the great beast's foot had stripped the skin from his back as neatly as one skins a rabbit. As soon as I saw the dead man I sent an orderly to a friend's house nearby to borrow an elephant rifle. I had already sent back the pony, not wanting it to go mad with fright and throw me if it smelt the elephant.

5   The orderly came back in a few minutes with a rifle and five cartridges, and meanwhile some Burmans had arrived and told us that the elephant was in the paddy fields below, only a few hundred yards away. As I started forward practically the whole population of the quarter flocked out of the houses and followed me. They had seen the rifle and were all shouting excitedly that I was going to shoot the elephant. They had not shown much interest in the elephant when he was merely ravaging their homes, but it was different now that he was going to be shot. It was a bit of fun to them, as it would be to an English crowd; besides they wanted the meat. It made me vaguely uneasy. I had no intention of shooting the elephant—I had merely sent for the rifle to defend myself if necessary—and it is always unnerving to have a crowd following you. I marched down the hill, looking and feeling a fool, with the rifle over my shoulder and an evergrowing army of people jostling at my heels. At the bottom, when you got away from the huts, there was a metalled road and beyond that a miry waste of paddy fields a thousand yards across, not yet ploughed but soggy from the first rains and dotted with coarse grass. The elephant was standing eight yards from the road, his left side towards us. He took not the slightest notice of the crowd's approach. He was tearing up bunches of grass, beating them against his knees to clean them and stuffing them into his mouth.

I had halted on the road. As soon as I saw the elephant I knew with perfect certainty that I ought not to shoot him. It is a serious matter to shoot a working elephant—it is comparable to destroying a huge and costly piece of machinery—and obviously one ought not to do it if it can possibly be avoided. And at that distance, peacefully eating, the elephant looked no more dangerous than a cow. I thought then and I think now that his attack of "must" was already passing off; in which case he would merely wander harmlessly about until the mahout came back and caught him. Moreover, I did not in the least want to shoot him. I decided that I would watch him for a little while to make sure that he did not turn savage again, and then go home.

But at that moment I glanced round at the crowd that had followed me. It was an immense crowd, two thousand at the least and growing every minute. It blocked the road for a long distance on either side. I looked at the sea of yellow faces above the garish clothes—faces all happy and excited over this bit of fun, all certain that the elephant was going to be shot. They were watching me as they would watch a conjurer about to perform a trick. They did not like me, but with the magical rifle in my hands I was momentarily worth watching. And suddenly I realized that I should have to shoot the elephant after all. The people expected it of me and I had got to do it; I could feel their two thousand wills pressing me forward, irresistibly. And it was at this moment, as I stood there with the rifle in my hands, that I first grasped the hollowness, the futility of the white man's dominion in the East. Here was I, the white man with his gun, standing in front of the unarmed native crowd—seemingly the leading actor of the piece; but in reality I was only an absurd puppet pushed to and fro by the will of those yellow faces behind. I perceived in this moment that when the white man turns tyrant it is his own freedom that he destroys. He becomes a sort of hollow, posing dummy, the conventionalized figure of a sahib. For it is the condition of his rule that he shall spend his life in trying to impress the "natives," and so in every crisis he has got to do what the "natives" expect of him. He wears a mask, and his face grows to fit it. I had got to shoot the elephant. I had committed myself to doing it when I sent for the rifle. A sahib has got to act like a sahib; he has got to appear resolute, to know his own mind and do definite things. To come all that way, rifle in hand, with two thousand people marching at my heels, and then to trail feebly away, having done nothing—no, that was impossible. The crowd would laugh at me. And my whole life, every white man's life in the East, was one long struggle not to be laughed at.

But I did not want to shoot the elephant. I watched him beating his bunch of grass against his knees, with that preoccupied grandmotherly air that elephants have. It seemed to me that it would be murder to shoot him. At that age I was not squeamish about killing animals, but I had never shot an elephant and never wanted to. (Somehow it always seems worse to kill a *large* animal.) Besides, there was the beast's owner to be considered. Alive, the elephant was worth at least a hundred pounds; dead, he would only be worth the value of his tusks, five pounds, possibly. But I had got to act quickly. I turned to some experienced-looking Burmans who had been there when we arrived, and asked them how the elephant had been behaving. They all said the same thing; he took no notice of you if you left him alone, but he might charge if you went too close to him.

It was perfectly clear to me what I ought to do. I ought to walk up to within, say, twenty-five yards of the elephant and test his behavior. If he charged, I could shoot; if he took no notice of me, it would be safe to leave him until the mahout came back. But also I knew that I was going to do no such thing. I was a poor shot with a rifle and the ground was soft mud into which one would sink at every step. If the elephant charged and I missed him, I should have about as much chance as a toad under a steam-roller. But even then I was not thinking particularly of my own skin, only of the watchful yellow faces behind. For at that moment, with the crowd watching me, I was not afraid in the ordinary sense, as I would have been if I had been alone. A white man mustn't be frightened in front of "natives"; and so, in general, he isn't frightened. The sole thought in my mind was that if anything went wrong those two thousand Burmans would see me pursued, caught, trampled on and reduced to a grinning corpse like that Indian up the hill. And if that happened it was quite probable that some of them would laugh. That would never do. There was only one alternative. I shoved the cartridges into the magazine and lay down on the road to get a better aim.

10   The crowd grew very still, and a deep, low, happy sigh, as of people who see the theatre curtain go up at last, breathed from innumerable throats. They were going to have their bit of fun after all. The rifle was a beautiful German thing with cross-hair sights. I did not then know that in shooting an elephant one would shoot to cut an imaginary bar running from ear-hole to ear-hole. I ought, therefore, as the elephant was sideways on, to have aimed straight at his ear-hole; actually I aimed several inches in front of this, thinking the brain would be further forward.

When I pulled the trigger I did not hear the bang or feel the kick—one never does when a shot goes home—but I heard the devilish roar of glee that went up from the crowd. In that instant, in too short a time, one would have thought, even for the bullet to get there, a mysterious, terrible change had come over the elephant. He neither stirred nor fell, but every line of his body had altered. He looked suddenly stricken, shrunken, immensely old, as though the frightful impact of the bullet had paralysed him without knocking him down. At last, after what seemed a long time—it might have been five seconds, I dare say—he sagged flabbily to his knees. His mouth slobbered. An enormous senility seemed to have settled upon him. One could have imagined him thousands of years old. I fired again into the same spot. At the second shot he did not collapse but climbed with desperate slowness to his feet and stood weakly upright, with legs sagging and head drooping. I fired a third time. That was the shot that did for him. You could see the agony of it jolt his whole body and knock the last remnant of strength from his legs. But in falling he seemed for a moment to rise, for as his hind legs collapsed beneath him he seemed to tower upward like a huge rock toppling, his trunk reaching skywards like a tree. He trumpeted, for the first and only time. And then down he came, his belly towards me, with a crash that seemed to shake the ground even where I lay.

I got up. The Burmans were already racing past me across the mud. It was obvious that the elephant would never rise again, but he was not dead. He was breathing very rhythmically with long rattling gasps, his great mound of a side painfully rising and falling. His mouth was wide open—I could see far down into caverns of pale pink throat. I waited a long time for him to die, but his breathing did not weaken. Finally I fired my two remaining shots into the spot where I thought his heart must be. The thick blood welled out of him like red velvet, but still he did not die. His body did not even jerk when the shots hit him, the tortured breathing continued without a pause. He was dying, very slowly and in great agony, but in some world remote from me where not even a bullet could damage him further. I felt that I had got to put an end to that dreadful noise. It seemed dreadful to see the great beast lying there, powerless to move and yet powerless to die, and not even to be able to finish him. I sent back for my small rifle and poured shot after shot into his heart and down his throat. They seemed to make no impression. The tortured gasps continued as steadily as the ticking of a clock.

In the end I could not stand it any longer and went away. I heard later that it took him half an hour to die. Burmans were bringing dahs[4] and baskets even before I left, and I was told they had stripped his body almost to the bones by the afternoon.

Afterwards, of course, there were endless discussions about the shooting of the elephant. The owner was furious, but he was only an Indian and could do nothing. Besides, legally I had done the right thing, for a mad elephant has to be killed, like a mad dog, if its owner fails to control it. Among the Europeans opinion was divided. The older men said I was right, the younger men said it was a damn shame to shoot an elephant for killing a coolie, because an elephant was worth more than any damn Coringhee coolie. And afterwards I was very glad that the coolie had been killed; it put me legally in the right and it gave me a sufficient pretext for shooting the elephant. I often wondered whether any of the others grasped that I had done it solely to avoid looking a fool.

READING CRITICALLY FOR IDEAS, STRUCTURE, AND STYLE

1. How is the untenable position in which Orwell finds himself, as an officer, a direct result of the British occupation of Burma? How does he react to the task he is required to perform?

2. Analyze the different kinds of motivations that prompted Orwell to shoot the elephant. In your view, which of these motives—personal, political, circumstantial—played the most decisive role?

3. Select a paragraph from the essay that you find especially effective in communicating Orwell's views. Analyze it in terms of the literary techniques and rhetorical devices he uses. Evaluate the means Orwell uses to evoke this incident so that the reader feels he or she is present.

[4]Butcher knives.

EXTENDING INSIGHTS THROUGH WRITING

1. At the heart of this account is Orwell's analysis of the insidious effects of social pressures. Have you ever experienced something akin to this that fundamentally changed your outlook? Describe this incident in such a way that your readers will feel they understand both what happened and your reaction to the event.

2. This essay provides an important clue as to why Orwell frequently found himself disillusioned with political systems he had willingly joined. For example, you might wish to read about his experiences fighting fascism in Spain, in his acclaimed *Homage to Catalonia* (1938). Compare "Shooting an Elephant" to this book in terms of Orwell's insights into political processes.

CONNECTING PERSPECTIVES ON THE COLLECTIVE EXPERIENCE

1. Compare the effects of British colonial rule on everyday life in the accounts by Orwell and Ngũgĩ wa Thiong'o (see "Decolonising the Mind") from their very opposite perspectives.

2. Contrast Orwell's unusual insights into what it meant to be a white figurehead in a system constructed by colonialism with Baldwin's insights into how racism determines the roles both blacks and whites must play in America.

MARGARET SANGER

The Turbid Ebb and Flow of Misery

BACKGROUND

Margaret Sanger (1879–1966) was born in Corning, New York, and was an early, and tenacious, advocate for the dissemination of birth control information in America. Initially, she worked as a maternity nurse in the Lower East Side of New York City, but was so appalled by what she saw—poverty-stricken pregnant women who often died in childbirth or from botched abortions—that she left nursing and began a lifelong struggle against the mores of the time to bring contraceptive literature and devices to the public. Doubtless, a factor in Sanger's committment was the memory of her mother, a working-class Irish immigrant, who bore eleven children and died of consumption in 1899. In 1914, she founded the National Birth Control League and published the *Women Rebel* magazine. Sanger was repeatedly arrested for her activities and, while in prison in 1916, founded and edited Birth Control Review. She wrote numerous books and articles on the subject of birth control and sex education, including *Woman and the New Race*, with an introduction by Havelock Ellis (1920), and *The Pivot of Civilization*, with an introduction by H. G. Wells (1922). In the 1920s these two books sold more than half a million copies and were enormously influential in leading to the Planned Parenthood Federation of America. In "The Turbid Ebb and Flow of Misery," from *Margaret Sanger: An Autobiography* (1938), she describes how her social conscience was awakened by the plight of poor women whose lives were destroyed because they lacked access to birth control information and contraceptive devices.

APPROACHING SANGER'S ESSAAY

Sanger found that pregnancy was a chronic condition of poor women on the Lower East Side of New York. For Sanger, these women were not statistics: They were, instead, living human beings with hopes and aspirations, yet they were destined to be "thrown on the scrap heap" before they reached the age of thirty-five. Her encounter with Sadie Sachs (a symbol of all the poor immigrant women), who had become a friend and who later died from an infection following a self-induced abortion, changed Sanger's life. After this happened, Sanger left nursing and began a lifelong crusade to establish family planning clinics. Sanger confronted much opposition because, in 1912, it was illegal to distribute information on contraception. There has been a continuing national debate about whether or not federally funded family planning agencies (whose existence are a result of Sanger's forty-year struggle) should be permitted to suggest abortion (which is legal) as an option for pregnant women.

The title of Sanger's essay is drawn from Victorian poet Matthew Arnold's poem "Dover Beach," which Sanger adapts to comment on the misery and helplessness of lower class women. The essay's epigraph also refers to the theme of the blighted lives of unwanted children with its lines from a poem by William Blake.

The Turbid Ebb and Flow of Misery

> Every night and every morn
> Some to misery are born.
> Every morn and every night
> Some are born to sweet delight.
> Some are born to sweet delight,
> Some are born to endless night.
> —William Blake

During these years [about 1912] in New York trained nurses were in great demand. Few people wanted to enter hospitals; they were afraid they might be "practiced" upon, and consented to go only in desperate emergencies. Sentiment was especially vehement in the matter of having babies. A woman's own bedroom, no matter how inconveniently arranged, was the usual place for her lying-in. I was not sufficiently free from domestic duties to be a general nurse, but I could ordinarily manage obstetrical cases because I was notified far enough ahead to plan my schedule. And after serving my two weeks I could get home again.

Sometimes I was summoned to small apartments occupied by young clerks, insurance salesmen, or lawyers, just starting out, most of them under thirty and whose wives were having their first or second baby. They were always eager to know the best and latest method in infant care and feeding. In particular, Jewish patients, whose lives centered around the family, welcomed advice and followed it implicitly.

Chapter 7 of *An Autobiography* (1938). Sanger has taken her chapter title from a line in Matthew Arnold's poem "Dover Beach" [Editor's note].

But more and more my calls began to come from the Lower East Side, as though I were being magnetically drawn there by some force outside my control. I hated the wretchedness and hopelessness of the poor, and never experienced that satisfaction in working among them that so many noble women have found. My concern for my patients was now quite different from my earlier hospital attitude. I could see that much was wrong with them which did not appear in the physiological or medical diagnosis. A woman in childbirth was not merely a woman in childbirth. My expanded outlook included a view of her background, her potentialities as a human being, the kind of children she was bearing, and what was going to happen to them.

The wives of small shopkeepers were my most frequent cases, but I had carpenters, truck drivers, dishwashers, and pushcart vendors. I admired intensely the consideration most of these people had for their own. Money to pay doctor and nurse had been carefully saved months in advance—parents-in-law, grandfathers, grandmothers, all contributing.

As soon as the neighbors learned that a nurse was in the building they came in a friendly way to visit, often carrying fruit, jellies, or gefüllter fish made after a cherished recipe. It was infinitely pathetic to me that they, so poor themselves, should bring me food. Later they drifted in again with the excuse of getting the plate, and sat down for a nice talk; there was no hurry. Always back of the little gift was the question, "I am pregnant (or my daughter, or my sister is). Tell me something to keep from having another baby. We cannot afford another yet." 5

I tried to explain the only two methods I had ever heard of among the middle classes, both of which were invariably brushed aside as unacceptable. They were of no certain avail to the wife because they placed the burden of responsibility solely upon the husband—a burden which he seldom assumed. What she was seeking was self-protection she could herself use, and there was none.

Below this stratum of society was one in truly desperate circumstances. The men were sullen and unskilled, picking up odd jobs now and then, but more often unemployed, lounging in and out of the house at all hours of the day and night. The women seemed to slink on their way to market and were without neighborliness.

These submerged, untouched classes were beyond the scope of organized charity or religion. No labor union, no church, not even the Salvation Army reached them. They were apprehensive of everyone and rejected help of any kind, ordering all intruders to keep out; both birth and death they considered their own business. Social agents, who were just beginning to appear, were profoundly mistrusted because they pried into homes and lives, asking questions about wages, how many were in the family, had any of them ever been in jail. Often two or three had been there or were now under suspicion of prostitution, shoplifting, purse snatching, petty thievery, and, in consequence, passed furtively by the big blue uniforms on the corner.

The utmost depression came over me as I approached this surreptitious region. Below Fourteenth Street I seemed to be breathing a different air, to be in another world and country where the people had habits and customs alien to anything I had ever heard about.

10　　　　There were then approximately ten thousand apartments in New York into which no sun ray penetrated directly; such windows as they had opened only on a narrow court from which rose fetid odors. It was seldom cleaned, though garbage and refuse often went down into it. All these dwellings were pervaded by the foul breath of poverty, that moldy, indefinable, indescribable smell which cannot be fumigated out, sickening to me but apparently unnoticed by those who lived there. When I set to work with antiseptics, their pungent sting, at least temporarily, obscured the stench.

I remember one confinement case to which I was called by the doctor of an insurance company. I climbed up the five flights and entered the airless rooms, but the baby had come with too great speed. A boy of ten had been the only assistant. Five flights was a long way; he had wrapped the placenta in a piece of newspaper and dropped it out the window into the court.

Many families took in "boarders," as they were termed, whose small contributions paid the rent. These derelicts, wanderers, alternately working and drinking, were crowded in with the children; a single room sometimes held as many as six sleepers. Little girls were accustomed to dressing and undressing in front of the men, and were often violated, occasionally by their own fathers or brothers, before they reached the age of puberty.

Pregnancy was a chronic condition among the women of this class. Suggestions as to what to do for a girl who was "in trouble" or a married woman who was "caught" passed from mouth to mouth—herb teas, turpentine, steaming, rolling downstairs, inserting slippery elm, knitting needles, shoe-hooks. When they had word of a new remedy they hurried to the drugstore, and if the clerk were inclined to be friendly he might say, "Oh, that won't help you, but here's something that may." The younger druggists usually refused to give advice because, if it were to be known, they would come under the law; midwives were even more fearful. The doomed women implored me to reveal the "secret" rich people had, offering to pay me extra to tell them; many really believed I was holding back information for money. They asked everybody and tried anything, but nothing did them any good. On Saturday nights I have seen groups of from fifty to one hundred with their shawls over their heads waiting outside the office of a five-dollar abortionist.

Each time I returned to this district, which was becoming a recurrent nightmare, I used to hear that Mrs. Cohen "had been carried to a hospital, but had never come back," or that Mrs. Kelly "had sent the children to a neighbor and had put her head into the gas oven." Day after day such tales were poured into my ears—a baby born dead, great relief—the death of an older child, sorrow but again relief of a sort—the story told a thousand times of death from abortion and children going into institutions. I shuddered with horror as I listened to the details and studied the reasons back of them—destitution linked with excessive childbearing. The waste of life seemed utterly senseless. One by one worried, sad, pensive, and aging faces marshaled themselves before me in my dreams, sometimes appealingly, sometimes accusingly.

15　　　　These were not merely "unfortunate conditions among the poor" such as we read about. I knew the women personally. They were living, breathing, human beings, with hopes, fears, and aspirations like my own, yet their weary, misshapen bodies, "always ailing, never failing," were destined to be thrown on the scrap heap before they were thirty-five. I could not escape from the facts of their wretchedness; neither was I able to see any way out. My own cozy and comfortable family existence was becoming a reproach to me.

Then one stifling mid-July day of 1912 I was summoned to a Grand Street tenement. My patient was a small, slight Russian Jewess, about twenty-eight years old, of the special cast of feature to which suffering lends a madonna-like expression. The cramped three-room apartment was in a sorry state of turmoil. Jake Sachs, a truck driver scarcely older than his wife, had come home to find the three children crying and her unconscious from the effects of a self-induced abortion. He had called the nearest doctor, who in turn had sent for me. Jake's earnings were trifling, and most of them had gone to keep the none-too-strong children clean and properly fed. But his wife's ingenuity had helped them to save a little, and this he was glad to spend on a nurse rather than have her go to a hospital.

The doctor and I settled ourselves to the task of fighting the septicemia. Never had I worked so fast, never so concentratedly. The sultry days and nights were melted into a torpid inferno. It did not seem possible there could be such heat, and every bit of food, ice, and drugs had to be carried up three flights of stairs.

Jake was more kind and thoughtful than many of the husbands I had encountered. He loved his children, and had always helped his wife wash and dress them. He had brought water up and carried garbage down before he left in the morning, and did as much as he could for me while he anxiously watched her progress.

After a fortnight Mrs. Sachs' recovery was in sight. Neighbors, ordinarily fatalistic as to the results of abortion, were genuinely pleased that she had survived. She smiled wanly at all who came to see her and thanked them gently, but she could not respond to their hearty congratulations. She appeared to be more despondent and anxious than she should have been, and spent too much time in meditation.

At the end of three weeks, as I was preparing to leave the fragile patient   20 to take up her difficult life once more, she finally voiced her fears, "Another baby will finish me, I suppose?"

"It's too early to talk about that," I temporized.

But when the doctor came to make his last call, I drew him aside. "Mrs. Sachs is terribly worried about having another baby."

"She well may be," replied the doctor, and then he stood before her and said, "Any more such capers, young woman, and there'll be no need to send for me."

"I know, doctor," she replied timidly, "but," and she hesitated as though it took all her courage to say it, "what can I do to prevent it?"

The doctor was a kindly man, and he had worked hard to save her, but such incidents had become so familiar to him that he had long since lost whatever delicacy he might once have had. He laughed good-naturedly. "You want to have your cake and eat it too, do you? Well, it can't be done."

Then picking up his hat and bag to depart he said, "Tell Jake to sleep on the roof."

25   I glanced quickly at Mrs. Sachs. Even through my sudden tears I could see stamped on her face an expression of absolute despair. We simply looked at each other, saying no word until the door had closed behind the doctor. Then she lifted her thin, blue-veined hands and clasped them beseechingly. "He can't understand. He's only a man. But you do, don't you? Please tell me the secret, and I'll never breathe it to a soul. *Please!*"

What was I to do? I could not speak the conventionally comforting phrases which would be of no comfort. Instead, I made her as physically easy as I could and promised to come back in a few days to talk with her again. A little later, when she slept, I tiptoed away.

Night after night the wistful image of Mrs. Sachs appeared before me. I made all sorts of excuses to myself for not going back. I was busy on other cases; I really did not know what to say to her or how to convince her of my own ignorance; I was helpless to avert such monstrous atrocities. Time rolled by and I did nothing.

The telephone rang one evening three months later, and Jake Sachs' agitated voice begged me to come at once; his wife was sick again and from the same cause. For a wild moment I thought of sending someone else, but actually, of course, I hurried into my uniform, caught up my bag, and started out. All the way I longed for a subway wreck, an explosion, anything to keep me from having to enter that home again. But nothing happened, even to delay me. I turned into the dingy doorway and climbed the familiar stairs once more. The children were there, young little things.

Mrs. Sachs was in a coma and died within ten minutes. I folded her still hands across her breast, remembering how they had pleaded with me, begging so humbly for the knowledge which was her right. I drew a sheet over her pallid face. Jake was sobbing, running his hands through his hair and pulling it out like an insane person. Over and over again he wailed, "My God! My God! My God!"

30   I left him pacing desperately back and forth, and for hours I myself walked and walked and walked through the hushed streets. When I finally arrived home and let myself quietly in, all the household was sleeping. I looked out my window and down upon the dimly lighted city. Its pains and griefs crowded in upon me, a moving picture rolled before my eyes with photographic clearness: women writhing in travail to bring forth little babies; the babies themselves naked and hungry, wrapped in newspapers to keep them from the cold; six-year-old children with pinched, pale, wrinkled faces, old in concentrated wretchedness, pushed into gray and fetid cellars, crouching on stone floors, their small scrawny hands scuttling through rags, making lamp shades, artificial flowers; white coffins, black coffins, coffins, coffins interminably passing in never-ending succession. The scenes piled one upon another on another. I could bear it no longer.

As I stood there the darkness faded. The sun came up and threw its reflection over the house tops. It was the dawn of a new day in my life also. The doubt and questioning, the experimenting and trying, were now to be put behind me. I knew I could not go back merely to keeping people alive.

I went to bed, knowing that no matter what it might cost, I was finished with palliatives and superficial cures; I was resolved to seek out the root of evil, to do something to change the destiny of mothers whose miseries were vast as the sky.

READING CRITICALLY FOR IDEAS, STRUCTURE, AND STYLE

1. How did her experiences as a nurse change the path Sanger's life followed?

2. What insight does Sanger offer into the vast differences in experiences of women in different social classes at that time?

3. In what ways does the experience of Sadie Sachs epitomize the social evils that Sanger resolved to combat?

EXTENDING INSIGHTS THROUGH WRITING

1. What current social issues, in your opinion, are mainly caused by the lack of information in much the same way as what Sanger observed in 1912? Write a short argument on the remedial measures you would propose?

2. What does Sanger's use of lines from poems, with which she assumes her audience would be familiar, suggest about the education and social class of her readers?

CONNECTING PERSPECTIVES ON THE COLLECTIVE EXPERIENCE

1. Can Sanger be considered an early feminist in the same tradition as Simone de Beauvoir (see "The Married Woman")?

2. In what ways is access to information the theme that connects Sanger's essay with Frederick Douglass's memoir "Learning to Read and Write"?

SIMONE DE BEAUVOIR

The Married Woman

BACKGROUND

Simone de Beauvoir (1908–1986), a prominent French novelist, essayist, and pioneer of the women's movement, was born in Paris and studied philosophy at the Sorbonne, where she later taught from 1941 through 1943. De Beauvoir's literary career is intertwined with that of Jean Paul Sartre's and the French Existentialist Movement. Her many illuminating works include *All Men Are Mortal* (1946; trans. 1947); *The Second Sex* (1949; trans. 1956), her most influential book; *The Mandarins* (1954; trans. 1957), winner of the Prix Goncourt (1954); *A Very Easy Death* (trans. 1966), a touching account of the death of Francoise de Beauvoir, the author's mother; and *All Said and Done* (trans. 1974), one of several brilliant autobiographical memoirs. In "The Married Woman," from *The Second Sex*, de Beauvoir defines, with eloquence and profound insight, the life of servitude and frustration that is the fate of "the married woman."

APPROACHING DE BEAUVOIR'S ESSAY

When *The Second Sex* appeared in 1949, readers were astounded by de Beauvoir's frank opening statement—"one is not born a woman, one becomes one"—and her advice that women should avoid becoming the "relative beings" implied in the title. She has been credited by such writers as Gloria Steinem, Kate Millet, and Betty Friedan with being the single most influential person responsible for the international women's movement.

In "The Married Woman," drawn from this work, we can observe a searching inquiry into the everyday lives of women from an existentialist, philosophical perspective. According to de Beauvoir, the nature of housework reinforces the housekeeper's passivity because this type of work makes a woman totally dependent on her family, produces nothing, has no bearing on the future, and is not directly useful to society. Much of the "married woman's" life is defined by a fruitless struggle against dirt, dust, and disorder. In de Beauvoir's view, the contrast between the nature of the "married woman's" work with work that men do outside of the home could not be clearer. Women do all the behind-the-scenes work without getting paid, while men get paid and do work that they feel is important to society. Although men may do some tasks around the house, by and large they are able to escape daily chores, and seek novelty, risk, and challenge through work. A man's work brings him into contact with companions and friends, which take him away from solitude. Unlike women's work, his work leads to a final result (in contrast to chores, which must be repeated endlessly), which gives his life meaning, autonomy, and identity as a productive citizen.

The Married Woman

Few tasks are more like the torture of Sisyphus than housework, with its endless repetition: the clean becomes soiled, the soiled is made clean, over and over, day after day. The housewife wears herself out marking time, she makes nothing, simply perpetuates the present. She never senses conquest of a positive Good, but rather indefinite struggle against negative Evil. A young pupil writes in her essay: "I shall never have house-cleaning day"; she thinks of the future as constant progress toward some unknown summit; but one day, as her mother washes the dishes, it comes over her that both of them will be bound to such rites until death. Eating, sleeping, cleaning—the years no longer rise up toward heaven, they lie spread out ahead, gray and identical. The battle against dust and dirt is never won.

Washing, ironing, sweeping, ferreting out rolls of lint from under wardrobes—all this halting of decay is also the denial of life; for time simultaneously creates and destroys, and only its negative aspect concerns the housekeeper. Hers is the position of the Manichaeist, regarded philosophically. The essence of Manichaeism is not solely to recognize two principles, the one good, the other evil; it is also to hold that the good is attained through the abolition of evil and not by positive action. In this sense Christianity is hardly Manichaeist in spite of the existence of the devil, for one fights the demon best by devoting oneself to God and not by endeavoring to conquer the evil one directly. Any doctrine of transcendence and liberty subordinates the defeat of evil to progress toward the good. But woman is not called upon to build a better world: her domain is fixed and she has only to keep up the never ending struggle against the evil principles that creep into it; in her war against dust, stains, mud, and dirt she is fighting sin, wrestling with Satan.

But it is a sad fate to be required without respite to repel an enemy instead of working toward positive ends, and very often the housekeeper submits to it in a kind of madness that may verge on perversion, a kind of sado-masochism. The maniac housekeeper wages her furious war against dirt, blaming life itself for the rubbish all living growth entails. When any living being enters her house, her eye gleams with a wicked light: "Wipe your feet, don't tear the place apart, leave that alone!" She wishes those of her household would hardly breathe; everything means more thankless work for her. Severe, preoccupied, always on the watch, she loses *joie de vivre*, she becomes overprudent and avaricious. She shuts out the sunlight, for along with that come insects, germs, and dust, and besides, the sun ruins silk hangings and fades upholstery; she scatters naphthalene, which scents the air. She becomes bitter and disagreeable and hostile to all that lives: the end is sometimes murder.

The healthy young woman will hardly be attracted by so gloomy a vice. Such nervousness and spitefulness are more suited to frigid and frustrated women, old maids, deceived wives, and those whom surly and dictatorial husbands condemn to a solitary and empty existence. I knew an old beldame, once gay and coquettish, who got up at five each morning to go over her closets; married to a man who neglected her, and isolated on a lonely estate, with but one child, she took to orderly housekeeping as others take to drink. In this insanity the house becomes so neat and clean that one hardly dares live in it; the woman is so busy she forgets her own existence. A household, in fact, with its meticulous and limitless tasks, permits to woman a sado-masochistic flight from herself as she contends madly with the things around her and with herself in a state of distraction and mental vacancy. And this flight may often have a sexual tinge. It is noteworthy that the rage for cleanliness is highest in Holland, where the women are cold, and in puritanical civilizations, which oppose an ideal of neatness and purity to the joys of the flesh. If the Mediterranean Midi lives in a state of joyous filth, it is not only because water is scarce there: love of the flesh and its animality is conducive to toleration of human odor, dirt, and even vermin.

5   The preparation of food, getting meals, is work more positive in nature and often more agreeable than cleaning. First of all it means marketing, often the bright spot of the day. And gossip on doorsteps, while peeling vegetables, is a gay relief for solitude; to go for water is a great adventure for half-cloistered Mohammedan women; women in markets and stores talk about domestic affairs, with a common interest, feeling themselves members of a group that—for an instant—is opposed to the group of men as the essential to the inessential. Buying is a profound pleasure, a discovery, almost an invention. As Gide says in his *Journal*, the Mohammedans, not knowing gambling, have in its place the discovery of hidden treasure; that is the poetry and the adventure of mercantile civilizations. The housewife knows little of winning in games, but a solid cabbage, a ripe Camembert, are treasures that must be cleverly won from the unwilling storekeeper; the game is to get the best for the least money; economy means not so much helping the budget as winning the game. She is pleased with her passing triumph as she contemplates her well-filled larder.

Gas and electricity have killed the magic of fire, but in the country many women still know the joy of kindling live flames from inert wood. With her fire going, woman becomes a sorceress; by a simple movement, as in beating eggs, or through the magic of fire, she effects the transmutation of substances: matter becomes food. There is enchantment in these alchemies, there is poetry in making preserves; the housewife has caught duration in the snare of sugar, she has enclosed life in jars. Cooking is revolution and creation; and a woman can find special satisfaction in a successful cake or a flaky pastry, for not everyone can do it: one must have the gift.

Here again the little girl is naturally fond of imitating her elders, making mud pies and the like, and helping roll real dough in the kitchen. But as with other housework, repetition soon spoils these pleasures. The magic of the oven can hardly appeal to Mexican Indian women who spend half their lives preparing tortillas, identical from day to day, from century to century. And it is impossible to go on day after day making a treasure-hunt of the marketing or ecstatically viewing one's highly polished faucets. The male and female writers who lyrically exalt such triumphs are persons who are seldom or never engaged in actual housework. It is tiresome, empty, monotonous, as a career. If, however, the individual who does such work is also a producer, a creative worker, it is as naturally integrated in life as are the organic functions; for this reason housework done by men seems much less dismal; it represents for them merely a negative and inconsequential moment from which they quickly escape. What makes the lot of the wife-servant ungrateful is the division of labor which dooms her completely to the general and the inessential. Dwelling-place and food are useful for life but give it no significance: the immediate goals of the housekeeper are only means, not true ends. She endeavors, naturally, to give some individuality to her work and to make it seem essential. No one else, she thinks, could do her work as well; she has her rites, superstitions, and ways of doing things. But too often her "personal note" is but a vague and meaningless rearrangement of disorder.

Woman wastes a great deal of time and effort in such striving for originality and unique perfection; this gives her task its meticulous, disorganized, and endless character and makes it difficult to estimate the true load of domestic work. Recent studies show that for married women housework averages about thirty hours per week, or three fourths of a working week in employment. This is enormous if done in addition to a paid occupation, little if the woman has nothing else to do. The care of several children will naturally add a good deal to woman's work: a poor mother is often working all the time. Middle-class women who employ help, on the other hand, are almost idle; and they pay for their leisure with ennui. If they lack outside interests, they often multiply and complicate their domestic duties to excess, just to have something to do.

The worst of it all is that this labor does not even tend toward the creation of anything durable. Woman is tempted—and the more so the greater pains she takes—to regard her work as an end in itself. She sighs as she contemplates the perfect cake just out of the oven: "it's a shame to eat it!" It is really too bad to have husband and children tramping with their muddy feet all over her waxed hardwood floors! When things are used they are soiled or destroyed—we have seen how she is tempted to save them from being used; she keeps preserves until they get moldy; she locks up the parlor. But times passes inexorably; provisions attract rats; they become wormy; moths attack blankets and clothing. The world is not a dream carved in stone, it is made of dubious stuff subject to rot; edible material is as equivocal as Dali's fleshy watches: it seems inert, inorganic, but hidden larvae may have changed it into a cadaver. The housewife who loses herself in things becomes dependent, like the things, upon the whole world: linen is scorched, the roast burns, chinaware gets broken; these are absolute disasters, for when things are destroyed, they are gone forever. Permanence and security cannot possibly be obtained through them. The pillage and bombs of war threaten one's wardrobes, one's house.

10   The products of domestic work, then, must necessarily be consumed; a continual renunciation is required of the woman whose operations are completed only in their destruction. For her to acquiesce without regret, these minor holocausts must at least be reflected in someone's joy or pleasure. But since the housekeeper's labor is expended to maintain the *status quo*, the husband, coming into the house, may notice disorder or negligence, but it seems to him that order and neatness come of their own accord. He has a more positive interest in a good meal. The cook's moment of triumph arrives when she puts a successful dish on the table: husband and children receive it with warm approval, not only in words, but by consuming it gleefully. The culinary alchemy then pursues its course, food becomes chyle and blood.

Thus, to maintain living bodies is of more concrete, vital interest than to keep a fine floor in proper condition; the cook's effort is evidently transcended toward the future. If, however, it is better to share in another's free transcendence than to lose oneself in things, it is not less dangerous. The validity of the cook's work is to be found only in the mouths of those around her table; she needs their approbation, demands that they appreciate her dishes and call for second helpings; she is upset if they are not hungry, to the point that one wonders whether the fried potatoes are for her husband or her husband for the fried potatoes. This ambiguity is evident in the general attitude of the housekeeping wife: she takes care of the house for her husband; but she also wants him to spend all he earns for furnishings and an electric refrigerator. She desires to make him happy; but she approves of his activities only in so far as they fall within the frame of happiness she has set up.

There have been times when these claims have in general found satisfaction: times when such felicity was also man's ideal, when he was attached above all to his home, to his family, and when even the children chose to be characterized by their parents, their traditions, and their past. At such times she who ruled the home, who presided at the dinner table, was recognized as supreme; and she still plays this resplendent role among certain landed proprietors and wealthy peasants who here and there perpetuate the patriachal civilization.

But on the whole marriage is today a surviving relic of dead ways of life, and the situation of the wife is more ungrateful than formerly, because she still has the same duties but they no longer confer the same rights, privileges, and honors. Man marries today to obtain an anchorage in immanence, but not to be himself confined therein; he wants to have hearth and home while being free to escape therefrom; he settles down but often remains a vagabond at heart; he is not contemptuous of domestic felicity, but he does not make of it an end in itself; repetition bores him; he seeks after novelty, risk, opposition to overcome, companions and friends who take him away from solitude *à deux*. The children, even more than their father, want to escape beyond family limits: life for them lies elsewhere, it is before them; the child always seeks what is different. Woman tries to set up a universe of permanence and continuity; husband and children wish to transcend the situation she creates, which for them is only a given environment. This is why, even if she is loath to admit the precarious nature of the activities to which her whole life is devoted, she is nevertheless led to impose her services by force: she changes from mother and housewife into harsh stepmother and shrew.

Thus woman's work within the home gives her no autonomy; it is not directly useful to society, it does not open out on the future, it produces nothing. It takes on meaning and dignity only as it is linked with existent beings who reach out beyond themselves, transcend themselves, toward society in production and action. That is, far from freeing the matron, her occupation makes her dependent upon husband and children; she is justified through them; but in their lives she is only an inessential intermediary. That "obedience" is legally no longer one of her duties in no way changes her situation; for this depends not on the will of the couple but on the very structure of the conjugal group. Woman is not allowed to *do* something positive in her work and in consequence win recognition as a complete person. However respected she may be, she is subordinate, secondary, parasitic. The heavy curse that weighs upon her consists in this: the very meaning of her life is not in her hands. That is why the successes and the failures of her conjugal life are much more gravely important for her than for her husband; he is first a citizen, a producer, secondly a husband; she is before all, and often exclusively, a wife; her work does not take her out of her situation; it is from the latter on the contrary, that her work takes its value, high or low. Loving, generously devoted, she will perform her tasks joyously; but they will seem to her mere dull drudgery if she performs them with resentment. In her destiny they will never play more than an inessential role; they will not be a help in the ups and downs of conjugal life. We must go on to see, then, how woman's condition is concretely experienced in life—this condition which is characterized essentially by the "service" of the bed and the "service" of the housekeeping and in which woman finds her place of dignity only in accepting her vassalage.

READING CRITICALLY FOR IDEAS, STRUCTURE, AND STYLE

1. How is de Beauvoir's characterization of the tasks performed by the married woman designed to change her readers' perception about what they may take for granted? Why does she use the myth of Sisyphus to describe the nature of these tasks?
2. Why is preparing food a more desirable kind of task for the married woman than cleaning the house?

3. How does de Beauvoir draw into her analysis anecdotal evidence from a wide variety of cultures in order to contrast why the married woman's life is so different in character from that of the married man?

EXTENDING INSIGHTS THROUGH WRITING

1. What, if any, are the positive features, attributes, and qualities that de Beauvoir omits from her negative appraisal of the life of the married woman?

2. To what extent are de Beauvoir's observations still relevant, or have changes in society since she wrote this in 1949 made her analysis obsolete? Explain your answer.

CONNECTING PERSPECTIVES ON THE COLLECTIVE EXPERIENCE

1. Is de Beauvoir's characterization of the married woman still valid in light of Marilyn Yalom's analysis of "The Wife Today"? Why or why not?

2. In what respects can both de Beauvoir and Ngũgĩ wa Thiong'o be understood as documents of resistance to domination in the spheres of government and the institution of marriage?

MARILYN YALOM

The Wife Today

BACKGROUND

Marilyn Yalom was born in 1932 in Chicago and was educated at Wellesley College, received a master's degree from Harvard in 1956, and a Ph.D. from Johns Hopkins in 1963. She is currently a senior scholar at the Institute for Research on Women and Gender at Stanford University. Yalom was a professor of French at Stanford when she became motivated by the women's movement in the mid-1970s to broaden her focus to include feminist scholarship. Evidence of this new focus appear in such works as *A History of the Breast* (1997); *Maternity, Mortality and the Literature of Madness* (1985); *Blood Sisters: The French Revolution in Women's Memory* (1993); and *The History of the Wife* (2001), from which the following excerpt is drawn.

APPROACHING YALOM'S ESSAY

In the Introduction to *The History of the Wife*, Yalom observes "at this particular moment of history, when the word 'wife' has become problematic and could become obsolete, it makes sense to take stock of her inheritance. Where did Western ideas about the wife begin?" Thus begins Yalom's chronicle of the turning points in the history of the wife. We learn that in ancient Greece, daughters were given by fathers to husbands to create legitimate offspring, that marriage was considered a religious duty in medieval Europe, and that the notion of romantic love, so important today, was considered a novelty in the Middle Ages. The modern ideal of marriage as companionship came to the fore during the Reformation and the Age of Enlightenment, and in twentieth-century America, a "new model of spousal relationships" emerged that Yalom describes in "The Wife Today."

Yalom's research shows that about 90 percent of Americans marry at least once in their lives, and those who divorce marry again in three out of four cases. Some states, such as Vermont, have taken steps to legalize same-sex partnerships: Canada and many Western European countries (for example, Denmark, Sweden, Switzerland, Belgium, and France) have erased virtually all legal distinctions between heterosexual marriages and same-sex unions. But perhaps the most important development is the expectation that both men and women will earn a living (although the hourly wages for women range from 70 percent to 90 percent of their male counterparts).

The Wife Today

American wives and mothers, most of whom work inside and outside the home, are constantly improvising and juggling to provide adequate day care and schooling for their children, comfortable housing, wholesome meals, decent clothing, weekly entertainment, and summertime vacations. Little wonder that they complain and that some return, when economically feasible, to full-time homemaking.

Yet, as Stephanie Coontz argues in *The Way We Really Are*, wives and mothers will continue to work outside the home for more than financial reasons. Most women enjoy the satisfactions offered by their jobs. "They consistently tell interviewers they like the social respect, self-esteem, and friendship networks they gain from the job, despite the stress they may face finding acceptable childcare and negotiating household chores with their husbands." In support of this position, Coontz points to a 1995 Harris survey reporting that less than a third of working women would stay at home, if money were no object.[1]

There are several reasons married women like to work. In the first place, they do not want to be economically dependent on their husbands. They have absorbed the lessons of early feminists—Charlotte Perkins Gilman and Simone de Beauvoir, among others—arguing that women will always be the second sex as long as they depend on men for support. Some remember their own mothers asking their husbands for allowances and having little say in how the family income was spent. Many feel that earning an income puts them on an equal footing with their husbands, as expressed by one dual-career wife in the following manner: "I'm in the relationship because I want to be, not because somebody's taking care of me. . . . I feel like I don't have to say, 'Well, you're bringing in the money that's putting food on the table, that's keeping me alive.' I'm putting in money, too."[2]

Most women understand intuitively the theory of "bargaining power" outlined by gender theorists Strober and Chan. Put succinctly, "the more resources, particularly economic resources, a spouse brings to a marriage, the greater is his or her bargaining power."[3] Bargaining power affects the

[1]Stephanie Coontz, *The Way We Really Are* (New York: Basic Books, 1997), p. 58.
[2]Rosanna Hertz, *More Equal than Others: Women and Men in Dual-Career Marriages* (Berkeley, Los Angeles, London: University of California Press, 1986), p. 101.
[3]Myra H. Strober and Agnes Miling Keneko Chan, *The Road Winds Uphill All the Way: Gender, Work and Family in the United States and Japan* (Cambridge, MA, and London: MIT Press, 1999), p. 87.

decisions couples make about almost everything, from the advancement of one partner's career over the other's to the division of household tasks. This hard-nosed, economic view of spousal relations is by no means the exclusive purview of academic theory. Even women's magazines have become more forthright about the clout a wife commands when she, too, brings home a paycheck. Clinicial psychologist Judith Sills, writing in that bastion of domesticity *Family Circle* (March 7, 2000), states bluntly, "The power balance in a marriage changes when one person either stops or starts earning money. . . . Power automatically accrues to the one who earns the money."

Some wives and husbands keep their income in separate accounts. With divorce an eventuality for half of all marriages, both parties feel they must be cautious in money matters, just in case. Even women in secure marriages, who would like to take time off when they have young children, are afraid of losing both salary and seniority, because, if they divorced, they would find themselves in dire financial straits.[4]

Social Security also penalizes the person who takes time off from work. One CPA wife and mother, who stayed at home when her children were little, accurately observed: "For every quarter a mother stays home to take care of her kids, she gets zero on her Social Security. And all those zeros will be averaged into her final payment. . . . I froth at the mouth every time I get my statement from Social Security. Every zero year is factored in."[5]

A second, and in my opinion, equally important reason why married women choose to work is that they do not want to be confined to the perimeters of the home. They do not want to operate within the cagelike frame of traditional domesticity. Greater education for women has meant that their horizons extend far beyond the kitchen, the parlor, and the garden. Once again, we must remember that higher education for women is a relatively recent phenomenon. The American women's colleges and most coed universities were a late-nineteenth-century creation admitting only a very small percentage of females, mostly from the upper and middle classes. As late as 1950, there were three male students granted a BA for every female college graduate.[6] Today, females receive educations comparable to males— 55 percent of BAs, over 50 percent of law and medical degrees, and 45 percent of PhDs. Like the men in their college courses, they expect to use their minds for the rest of their lives. Paid employment can present a challenge to one's intelligence, as well as to one's interpersonal skills. It allows a person the opportunity to interact with others in the workplace, and sometimes even to make a difference in their lives.

I have no illusions about the nature of work in general. It does not always challenge the intellect, and rarely allows for innovation and imagination. It can produce stress and pain and damage to private life. Yet I cannot imagine the world of the immediate future without it. Wives, like husbands, look to the work world for satisfactions that few can find within

[4]David Elkind, *Ties That Stress: The New Family Imbalance* (Cambridge, MA, and London: Cambridge University Press, 1994), p. 51.
[5]*Wellesley*, Winter 2000, p. 25.
[6]Cynthia Fuchs Epstein, *Woman's Place: Options and Limits in Professional Careers* (Berkeley, Los Angeles, London: University of California Press, 1971), p. 57.

themselves or within the four walls of their houses. Most husbands today assume that their wives will have a commitment outside the home, and many husbands are credited with being their wives' "strongest supporters." In addition, many husbands count on their wives to share the economic burdens of supporting a family.

Of course, there are some women who refuse this scenario, some wives who prefer to be the domestic anchor for their husbands and children. They find satisfaction in caring for their children, driving them to and from school, attending their soccer and baseball games, cooking, cleaning, washing and ironing, gardening, sewing, shopping, and taking care of a parent or sick relative. Theoretically, housewives, especially those with the means to pay for a maid or a team of housecleaners, should have more time than employed women to read, answer E-mail, surf the Internet, look at television, play tennis, do yoga, go to the gym, take hikes, practice the piano, listen to music, paint, entertain, write letters or creative literature, do volunteer work, meet with friends, and follow their own rhythms. But few full-time homemakers, especially those with children, think of their lives as leisurely. Obligations to home, family, and the community always seem to expand into the hours one tries to sequester for oneself, perhaps because homemaking is, by nature, always open to the unpredictable—a sick child, a broken washing machine, storm damage to the roof. Moreover, without the extra income of a second wage earner, housewives often have to sacrifice material rewards in order to stay at home. For some women, being available to their children when they are small is reward enough. The life of a housewife (or house husband) can be fulfilling if it is freely chosen, if the other spouse's income is adequate, or if the wife has sufficient assets of her own. A relatively small percentage of married women today are economically able to choose this life.

10   With the increased longevity of women, the child-raising period takes up a relatively short part of the life span. If a woman waits until her late twenties to have a child, as many do, and lives until she is eighty, as statistics say she will, she will spend only a third of her life in the active phase of mothering. Before and after her child-rearing years, there are long stretches of time for paid employment or sustained volunteer work. Most wives, even those who take time off when their children are young, work for economic reasons, and many wives, even those who do not have to, work because they want to.

Every societal revolution has a conservative reaction that eventually forces it to retreat partially, if not wholly, from acquired ground. The backlash symbolized by the election of President Ronald Reagan in 1980 and invoked in the battle cry "family values" undid some of the victories claimed by the sexual and feminist revolutions. During the eighties, abortion rights began to be curtailed. ERA was all but buried. Androgyny gave way to a renewed femininity featuring sexy underwear, breast implants, and push-up bras. Expensive weddings with brides in elaborate white gowns came back into fashion. Women's paid employment came under attack, with wives accused of undermining their husbands, and mothers indicted for sacrificing their children on the altar of professional success. The popular press remained skeptical over women's ability to have both a successful marriage and a successful career, and castigated the working woman who wanted to "have it all."[7]

Documenting the backlash in 1992, author Susan Faludi exploded some of the antifeminist myths that had proliferated during the eighties.[8] Magazines and newspapers eager to discredit women's gains exploited questionable research, such as the 1986 Harvard-Yale marriage study announcing that unwed women over thirty had very little likelihood of ever marrying at all, or sociologist Lenore Weitzman's 1985 finding that divorced women had a 73 percent drop in their standard of living a year after divorce. Subsequent research proved both of these findings to be greatly exaggerated. The gloom-and-doom picture of liberated women promulgated by the media and the glowing pictures of mothers who had chosen to give up demanding careers in favor of domesticity were clearly intended to stop the clock and send women scurrying back to the safety of home.

Yet, according to historian Ruth Rosen's assessment, "By the end of the 20th century, feminist ideas had burrowed too deeply into our culture for any resistance or politics to root them out.[9] Even those who lamented the excesses of the sexual and feminist revolutions were not about to ask their daughters or sweethearts to remain virgins until marriage or to retreat full-time to the kitchen once they had become wives. Increasingly, men sizing up prospective spouses expected them to carry their weight in both the bedroom and the boardroom.

One sign of the times is that the old jokes about nagging, frigid, dumb, unattractive wives have run their course. Remember comedian Henny Youngman's repertoire of wife jokes? "Take my wife, please!" "My wife has a black belt in shopping." "She got a mudpack and looked great for two days. Then the mud fell off." "I've been in love with the same woman for forty-nine years. If my wife ever finds out, she'll kill me." Wives are no longer the targets of such easy ridicule coming from husbands confident of their superiority. If anything, jokes about husbands have become more numerous, as in the following examples currently circulating on E-mail:

"I think—therefore I'm single." Attributed to Lizz Winstead.

"I never married because there was no need. I have three pets at home which answer the same purpose as a husband. I have a dog which growls every morning, a parrot which swears all afternoon and a cat that comes home late at night." Attributed to Marie Corelli.

"Behind every successful man is a surprised woman." Attributed to Maryon Pearson.

[7]Dana Vannoy-Hiller and William W. Philliber, *Equal Partners: Successful Women in Marriage* (Newbury Park, CA: Sage Publications, 1989), pp. 16–17.
[8]Susan Faludi, *Backlash: The Undeclared War Against American Women* (New York: Crown Publishers, Inc. 1992).
[9]Ruth Rosen, *The World Split Open: How the Modern Women's Movement Changed America* (New York: Viking, 2000), p. xv.

15   In the vein of the last witticism, here is a joke that was frequently repeated in 1999. "Hillary and Bill Clinton drive into a gas station. The man at the pump is particularly warm toward the First Lady, and when they drive away, she tells her husband that he had been one of her first boyfriends. Bill says smugly: 'Aren't you glad you married me instead of a gas station attendant?' To which she replies, 'If I had married him, he'd be the president.' "

INTIMATIONS OF THE NEW WIFE

The story of Hillary and Bill Clinton played out on the national stage some of the ambiguities inherent in the role of the new wife. Like 1990s soap operas, theirs was a dramatic saga of dual-career ambitions, marriage, infidelity, forgiveness, and love. In 1992, America was not ready for Hillary Rodham Clinton. After Nancy Reagan and Barbara Bush, women who had incarnated the traditional wife par excellence, a lawyer first lady on a par with her husband was just too threatening for much of the American public. They viewed her political activities with suspicion and felt vindicated when her health care plan went down to defeat. During Clinton's first term in office, Hillary was constantly changing her tactics and her hairdo so as to meet public approval. But whatever she did, there were numerous Americans who made no secret of the revulsion they felt for her.

All of this changed, of course, when she became an injured wife. As the gross details of President Clinton's marital infidelity with Monica Lewinsky became daily pap for the media, and Hillary maintained her dignity in spite of everything, her popularity with the American people soared. She became the woman who "stood by her man," a wife with whom other American women could identify. The damage to Clinton's reputation did not spill over similarly to his spouse. She emerged from their sensational story with a determination to pursue her own career, even at the expense of abandoning the role of first lady during her husband's last year in office. As I write these pages, she has just been elected to the United States Senate. Is the American public now ready for wives who are as well educated, assertive, and as ambitious as Hillary Rodham Clinton?

Fundamental aspects of the new wife can be observed in those reliable standards, the women's magazines. At the start of the new millennium, they focus on homemaking, recipes, diet, health, work, children, love, and sex. The most venerable of these magazines known as "the seven sisters" (*Ladies' Home Journal, Redbook, McCall's, Good Housekeeping, Family Circle, Woman's Day,* and *Better Homes and Gardens*), originally oriented toward traditional wives with children, have been obliged to move with the times. Today, they are claiming the sexually explicit content that used to be the exclusive purview of magazines intended for single women (e.g., *Glamour, Cosmopolitan,* and *Mademoiselle*).

"101 Ways to Sex Up Your Marriage," in the January 2000 *Ladies' Home Journal,* assumes that spouses occasionally need to bring "more sizzle" into the bedroom, and that it's the wife's responsibility to make this happen. The February *Redbook* presents "Your 39 Most Embarrassing Sex

Questions" in graphic detail, as well as an insightful piece titled "What Happy Couples Know about Marriages That Last." *More*, the magazine for older women put out by *Ladies' Home Journal*, offers a surprisingly frank and relatively guilt-free article titled "I Am the Other Woman," confessing the trials and tribulations of an anonymous woman in love with a married man.

Even financial matters have to be sexy. An article titled "Creating Financial Intimacy: A Couple's Guide to Getting Rich" (January 2000 *Good Housekeeping*) insinuates sex into the process of buying stock. It reads:

> Consider buying a stock for your beloved. It's surprising how sexy (yes, sexy) such a gift can be. . . . Sneak off to a financial seminar together one evening instead of to a movie; sit in the back, dress up, and wear your best perfume. Scan the newstand for a financial magazine that features an article reflecting your family's situation, and share it during a quiet moment alone. All powerful and positive acts, acts that will help you and your money grow, and you and your husband grow closer.

While the sexed-up prose is downright silly, the article does point to the central nexus of sex and money in the maintenance of a marriage. It argues convincingly that shared responsibility for money matters makes for a powerful bond between spouses. Whereas men once had total control over families finances, today, in more egalitarian marriages, both sex and money are often considered joint ventures capable of drawing spouses more closely together—that is, if they don't drive them further apart. It's not surprising that the year 2000 began with paeans in the popular press to both sources of empowerment for wives, with sexual performance hyped far beyond any other wifely virtue. Kinsey's midcentury belief that good sex is indispensable to enduring unions has by now become an American cliché, and, like most clichés, one that tends to obscure competing truths. While sexual satisfaction is generally recognized as a sensitive index of marital happiness, especially in the early years, there are undoubtedly some good marriages with bad or minimal sex, and some bad marriages with great sex.[10]

And what of love, that romantic feeling that gained primacy in the early nineteenth century and that has been claiming special status ever since? In the past, at least among middle- and upper-class couples, love was supposed to precede sex, indeed, to make sex possible. Today it is usually the other way around. Young people engage in sex with several partners, then "fall in love" with one of them. Subsequently some combination of sexual desire and romantic love impels the couple to vow to stay together forever. But sex and romance do not, in and of themselves, cement a relationship, at least not for a lifetime. Common interests, values, and goals, mutual respect and moral commitment, may, in the long run, prove as valuable as sex, love, and money in the preservation of a union.

[10]See, for example, Mirra Komarovsky (with the collaboration of Jane H. Philips), *Blue-Collar Marriage*, 2nd ed. (New Haven, CT: Yale University Press, 1987), pp. 94–111.

Young women today, marrying on average around twenty-five, often have at least some college education and work experience behind them when they become wives. They enter into marriage on a relatively equal footing with their husbands, and expect to maintain this parity for the rest of their lives. The old ideal of companionate marriage has been reformulated under such new labels as egalitarian marriage, equal partnership, and marital equality.

Unfortunately, married life today is not yet truly equal. According to a 1997 research study, which follows the lead of sociologist Jessie Bernard in *The Future of Marriage* (1972), "his" marriage continues to be better than "hers."[11] The data on marital satisfaction, garnered from surveys, interviews, and personal assessments, indicate that husbands have a more positive view of marriage than their wives, and that wives fall behind husbands on numerous measures of marital satisfaction. One consistent finding is that single men do *worse* than married men on almost all measures of mental health (e.g., suicide, depression, nervous breakdown), whereas single women do *better* than married women on these same measures.[12] All agree that wives experience greater stress than husbands from their career/family obligations, and that women put more time into caring for children, aged parents, and sick relatives.

25   When couples divorce, it is almost always the ex-wife who loses out financially. According to the latest statistics, divorce produces a 27 percent decline in women's standard of living and 10 percent increase in that of men.[13] This represents an almost 40 percent gap between what ex-wives and what ex-husbands experience financially in the aftermath of a divorce. Part of this difference is attributable to the fact that mothers, in the great majority of cases, are granted custody of the children. Even when the mother is awarded child support, it is frequently insufficient and not always forthcoming. Another factor is the lower earning power of women on the whole—75 percent of what men earn. Many women are still segregated in low-paying jobs and hindered in advancement by home and childcare responsibilities, as well as by the sacrifices they have made promoting their husbands' careers rather than their own.

In addition to the disadvantageous financial consequences of divorce for many women and their children, the emotional distress is often deep and long-lasting. While no-fault divorce, first instituted in California in 1970 and subsequently adopted in most of the United States, was intended to remove the blame and acrimony from prolonged adversarial litigation, today's divorces are still often as bitter as those of the past. Divorce continues to be a major family disruption with prolonged consequences for the spouses, their offspring, and extended kin.

Here is how Susan Straight, an articulate ex-wife and mother of three school-aged children, described the devastation that divorce

---

[11]Janice M. Steil, *Marital Equality: Its Relationship to the Well-Being of Husbands and Wives* (Thousand Oaks, London, New Delhi: Sage Publications, 1997), p. xix. See also differences in his and her appraisals of marriage in Alford-Cooper, *For Keeps*, p. 107.
[12]Faludi, *Backlash*, pp. 17, 36–37.
[13]Richard R. Peterson, "A Re-Evaluation of the Economic Consequences of Divorce," *American Sociological Review*, Vol. 61, No. 3, June 1996, pp. 528–536.

brought into her life, a devastation she shared with her best friend, who had been widowed.

> My best friend on the street, Jeannine, whose four kids had baby-sat mine and played with them, lost her husband, too. He was killed in a car accident. Jeannine and I were both thirty-five that year. We couldn't believe we had to do this alone. Seven kids. Old houses with flickering electrical wires and flooding basements and overgrown hedges and missing shingles. Jeannine was in her last year of nursing school. I was working. We were stunned.
>
> . . . Some nights we were both mad. She'd met her husband at fourteen, like me. After we talked, I would lie in bed, my body aching, my hands raw from dishes and floors and branches and baby shampoo, thinking that when I got married, I always assumed I'd work hard, have kids and a house and some fun. . . .
>
> And when my husband first left, I thought, So I work a little harder. But now, the realization has set in, piled high and crackling as the mulberry leaves falling from those spear straight branches one more year; I have to do all of this forever. Fix the vacuum cleaner, kill the spiders, correct the spelling and make the math flash cards and pay for pre-school and trim the tree. Trim the tree.
>
> Now, sometimes, I feel like a burro. A small frame, feet hard as hooves, back sagging a little. Now the edges of my life are a bit ragged, and things don't always get done as they should.[14]

Susan Straight's story is, unfortunately, writ over and over again in the lives of myriad American mothers whose husbands have left them, or who have themselves chosen to leave an unhappy marriage, or who never had a husband in the first place. In her words, she and the other ex-wives have no "backup," and backup is "what marriage is really about." So if she and her children look "slightly askew," she asks us not to blame her. "When you see us, don't shake your heads and think, How irresponsible. Responsible is all I'm good at anymore."

In serial marriages, the husband often "marries down" in terms of age and is far more likely to start a new family. The ex-wife who remarries has a selection of males usually her own age or older, but fewer candidates to choose from, since there are more older women than older men. For the same reasons, widows remarry less frequently than widowers. Another difference between older men and older women lies in the ability to reproduce. After menopause, a woman is unable to become pregnant (without technological intervention), in contrast to men, who usually can go on reproduc-

[14]Susan Straight, "One Drip at a Time," in *Mothers who Think: Tales of Real-Live Parenthood*, ed. Camille Peri and Kate Moses (New York: Villard Books, 1999), pp. 50, 51, 55. For a sensitive appraisal of divorce in America, see Barbara Defoe Whitehead, *The Divorce Culture: Rethinking Our Committments to Marriage and Family* (New York: Vintage Books, 1998).

ing in their fifties, sixties, and beyond. Whether this is advisable, given the father's probable death when his children are still young, the ability to reproduce at any age does confer a fundamental existential advantage to men.

30   At the same time, females have certain advantages over males. They live approximately seven years longer. They have the amazing possibility of carrying babies within their bodies and of establishing a unique connection to their offspring through pregnancy and lactation. They are probably more flexible than men in terms of sexual orientation, moving more easily between heterosexual and same-sex relations (though not everyone will see this as an advantage). They more frequently establish close bonds of friendship with other women that are sources of deep pleasure and ongoing support, whereas men, in general, have fewer intimate friends.

One thing many women have learned during the past twenty to thirty years is that wifehood is not one's only option. With women no longer economically dependent on men, they do not have to marry for the mere sake of survival. Business and professional women tend to defer marriage during early adulthood and sometimes do not marry at all. Susan Faludi's assertion that "the more women are paid, the less eager they are to marry" should not surprise us.[15] And even more than marriage per se, motherhood has become problematic for working women, given the "mommy gap" in wages between mothers and non-mothers. While the hourly wages of women without children are roughly 90 percent of men's, the comparable figure for women with children is 70 percent.[16] Thus women concerned about their present and future economic well-being are obliged to consider the effects of both marriage and motherhood on their working lives.

In the case of black women, the "marriage-market" theory advanced by sociologist Henry Walker attributes their low incidence of marriage to their new earning power, which is now roughly the same as that of black men. Perhaps even more important, black women have a smaller pool of economically viable black men to choose from, as compared to white women in relation to white men, since black men are more likely to have been killed, more likely to be incarcerated, and more likely to be unemployed than white men.[17]

Not surprisingly, careers loom larger than ever for women of all races, with many companies and institutions providing a kind of ersatz "family." Many people now look to their jobs for close interpersonal relations and for a sense of meaning they have not found either in their families or in their communities. Indeed, this growing job orientation is beginning to cause concern to many societal observers, who believe the workplace is replacing the home as the center of American life.

Another issue of concern is the "merging" of home life and work life that often occurs when people work out of their homes. Now that computers have made it possible for both men and women to earn substantial incomes without leaving the house, there is the danger that paid work will cannibalize

---

[15]Faludi, *Backlash*, p. 16.

[16]*Boston Globe*, May 13, 2000, A19, citing the work of economist Jane Waldfogel of Columbia University.

[17]Henry A. Walker, "Black-White Differences in Marriage and Family Patterns," in *Feminism*, ed. Dornbusch and Strober, pp. 87–112.

the time needed for quality family life. While this may present a problem for some workaholics, it can also be a boon for parents needing flexible schedules for childcare. In some ways we may be returning to a preindustrial mode, when artisans, professionals, and shopkeepers did indeed work out of their homes, with children always in the wings or underfoot.

Alternatives to marriage come in numerous forms. The number of Americans living alone (a quarter of all households) has never been higher. The number of men and women living together without marrying has also reached a record high, with heterosexual couples often taking years to decide whether they will or will not become husband and wife. Same-sex couples cohabitate without the legal and economic benefits that a marriage license confers, although many are taking advantage of the "domestic partnerships" offered by numerous cities, states, and institutions. In the future, Vermont-style "civil unions" will probably serve the needs not only of gay couples, but also of heterosexuals opting for an intermediary step between cohabitation and marriage.

Similarly, childlessness is no longer seen as a curse for adult females. The proportion of childless women aged forty to forty-four was 19 percent in 1998 (up from 10 percent in 1980), and many of these women are childless by choice, according to some demographers.[18] At the same time, single parenting is on the ascendency, without the stigma of past eras. Unmarried girls and women who become pregnant accidentally often decide to bear and raise the child, rather than have an abortion or give the baby up for adoption. Some unmarried women, especially those around forty, are now choosing to be mothers without intending to marry the baby's father. All of these girls and women take on a formidable challenge when they raise a child on their own: at present, their children are much more likely to be brought up in poverty than children in two-parent families.

Some single mothers manage to extend the family network by living with relatives or friends. In black communities, where single mothers greatly outnumber married mothers, children often grow up in female households headed by a mother or grandmother. Private and government programs to bring fathers back into the picture may, in time, reverse this trend somewhat, but it is unlikely that the nuclear family consisting of a married couple and their children, which peaked numerically for blacks in 1950 and for whites in 1960, will return to its former hegemonic position in American society.[19]

What, then, can a woman today anticipate, or at at least hope, when she becomes a wife? Surely she hopes that her marriage will be among the 50 percent that adheres to a lifelong script. Despite the well-known statistics on divorce, people usually marry with the belief that *their* marriage is "for keeps"—86 percent, according to a survey conducted by the *New York Times Magazine* (May 7, 2000). And most women still hope to become mothers. In fact, motherhood has remained central to most women's core conception of self and may even have "supplanted marriage as a source of

[18]Margaret L. Usdansky, "Numbers Show Families Growing Closer as They Pull Apart," *The New York Times*, March 8, 2000, D10.
[19]Walker, "Black-White Differences," in *Feminism*, ed. Dornbusch and Strober, pp. 92–93.

romantic fantasy for many young single women," in the judgment of Peggy Orenstein, the astute author of *School Girls* and *Flux.*[20]

The new wife will not be able to count on children to keep the marriage intact, as in the past when people often did stay together "for the children." In fact, children are known to bring conflict into a marriage, especially when they are very young and again in adolescence. Those spouses who make it past the stress-filled child-rearing years are likely to experience a bonus in later life. Older couples often enjoy a special bond based on their shared history—a level of intimacy paid for in past tears and joys. In the words of Mark Twain: "No man or woman really knows what perfect love is until they have been married a quarter of a century."[21]

When one vows at the onset of a marriage to live together "for better, for worse," one anticipates little of the "for worse" scenario. Yet heartache, tragedy, sickness, and death are invariably a part of marriage, especially in the later years. Then one is particularly grateful for the support and love of a lifelong partner—someone who remembers you as you once were and who continues to care for you as you are now. To be the intimate witness of another person's life is a privilege one can fully appreciate only with time. To have weathered the storms of early and middle marriage—the turmoil of children, the unfaithfulness of one or both spouses, the death of one's parents, the adult struggles of one's own children—can create an irreplaceable attachment to the person who has shared that history with you.

What I have referred to as "unfaithfulness" can, of course, make it impossible for a couple to go on as before. Many marriages do come to an end when one of the spouses has an affair. But many don't. Many continue to think of their marital union as the "essential" relationship, even while they engage in an extramarital affair. Since young people today have the opportunity to make love to more than one potential partner before they marry and since they tend to marry at a supposedly mature age, they *should* be ready to settle down to a monogamous union when they exchange vows. Yet, as we know, the "shoulds" sometimes falter in the face of unexpected passion. Even when one is seriously committed to one's spouse, temptations do arise, and married women as well as married men are more likely today than in the past to give in to those temptations. This does not necessarily lead to divorce, or even permanent bitterness, though it often creates turmoil and suffering. When a husband or wife has an affair, it is usually for a cluster of reasons, of which sex per se is only a part. The affair can act as a catalyst that forces the spouses to look more closely at their own relationship, to renegotiate the terms of their union, and to rededicate themselves to one another.

The present statistics on lifelong marriages being what they are, I do not envy today's young women the pain that will come from divorce, the hardships

[20]Peggy Orenstein, *Flux: Women on Sex, Work, Kids, Love, and Life in a Half-Changed World* (New York: Doubleday, 2000), p. 39.

[21]This paragraph draws from Susan Turk Charles and Laura L. Carstensen, "Marriage in Old Age," in *Inside the American Couple,* ed. Marilyn Yalom and Laura Carstensen (Berkeley: University of California Press, forthcoming).

they will endure as single parents, the poverty in which many will live. But I do believe in their expanded possibilities, which are greater now than ever before and which contrast dramatically to the more circumscribed lives most married women accepted in the past and still experience today in many parts of the world. Above all, I wish them the courage to persevere toward that ideal of equality in marriage that has been in the making for several centuries.

Wives, spouses, partners, companions, and lovers all wish to be confirmed by their chosen mates and to share a profound, mutual connection. Such a union demands commitment and recommitment. Ironically, we may come to think of marriage as a vocation requiring the kind of devotion that was once expected only of celibate monks and nuns. To be a wife today when there are few prescriptions or proscriptions is a truly creative endeavor. It is no longer sufficient to "think back through our mothers," in the words of Virginia Woolf; we must project ahead into the future and ask ourselves what kind of marital legacy we want to leave for our daughters and sons.

While the traditional wife who submerged her identity into that of her husband may no longer represent a viable model for most women, Americans are not giving up on wifehood. Instead, they are straining to create more perfect unions on the basis of their new status as coearners and their husbands' fledgling status as co-homemakers. I suspect that the death of the "little woman" will not be grieved by the multitude, even if society must endure severe birth pangs in producing the new wife.

READING CRITICALLY FOR IDEAS, STRUCTURE, AND STYLE

1. What insight does Yalom offer into the dynamics of feminism and the backlash it produced for today's wife in American society?
2. How does Yalom use statistics, extended examples, and quotations from scholary and popular sources as well as personal narratives to support her analysis?
3. In Yalom's view, what are the new defining features of the wife today in terms of economic, legal, and social frameworks?

EXTENDING INSIGHTS THROUGH WRITING

1. Discuss one of the important factors that, in your view, distinguishes the married woman of today from her traditional counterpart.
2. How would you characterize the kind of marriage you would hope for in relationship to the realities that Yalom describes?

CONNECTING PERSPECTIVES ON THE COLLECTIVE EXPERIENCE

1. Simone de Beauvoir's description of the life of "The Married Woman" would be almost unrecognizable in Yalom's portrait of "The Wife Today," or would it? What pressures have translated old inequities into new forms?
2. Margaret Sanger's description of the horrendous lives of poor women at the turn of the twentieth century would seem to make present circumstances (women can make a living and choose whether or not to have children) seem ideal by comparison. Is this the case? Why or why not?

BOOK CONNECTIONS FOR CHAPTER 2

1. In what ways did Charles Darwin adapt the ideas of Thomas Robert Malthus in his *The Origin of Species* (Chapter 4)?
2. What insight does Herodotus in "Concerning Egypt" (Chapter 3) provide into the everyday food practices of the ancient Egyptians, and how do they compare with those of the Romans, as described by Diane Ackerman?
3. Thomas Paine criticizes Edmund Burke's adulation of the aristocracy and power brokers of all kinds. Take this criticism into account and write a short dialogue between Paine and Thomas Carlyle (see "Heroes and Hero-Worship" in Chapter 3).
4. How do the methods Kenneth M. Stampp uses exemplify what R. G. Collingwood recommends in "What Is History" (Chapter 3)?
5. How does Neil Postman's (see "Information" Chapter 5) analysis raise important questions as to the difference between being literate, that was Frederick Douglass's goal, and using it to improve one's life?
6. In what respects might James Baldwin be asking his nephew to release himself from hatred and illusions in much the same way as Hinduism preaches (see "Readings from the Scriptures in Hinduism" Chapter 6).
7. In what way does Ngũgĩ wa Thiong'o challenge Paul Roberts's analysis of the unequivocally beneficial effects of the spread of the English language (see "Something About English" Chapter 7)?
8. Discuss George Orwell's essay in relationship to Maurizio Chierici's interview, "The Man from Hiroshima," (Chapter 3) in terms of their insight into the psychology of guilt and remorse.
9. How does Margaret Sanger's essay provide a glimpse into the next chapter in the lives of the emigrants that Oscar Handlin describes in "Steerage" in Chapter 3?
10. How does Simone de Beauvoir apply the philosophical premises and methods of inquiry of existentialism as discussed by Jean Paul Sartre (see "Existentialism" in Chapter 6) to the domestic sphere?
11. Which of Stendhal's categories (see "Crystallization of Love" in Chapter 1) seem closest to the kind of relationship between husbands and wives in today's world that Marilyn Yalom envisages? Explain your answer.

CHAPTER 3

THE HISTORICAL DIMENSION:
The Importance of the Past

INTRODUCTION

The readings in the following chapter probe the question as to why we should study the past. By providing a clear account of the conditions in which people have lived in past eras, historians attempt to explain how the present has been shaped by the past. Historical research is capable of illuminating important military, social, economic, and political events from the past, and of bringing personalities to life within the context of history.

We start with R. G. Collingwood's thesis that the purpose of history is to enable us to gain collective self-knowledge. Collingwood emphasized that historians do not simply recreate events from available documents, but create a dialogue between the past and the present. We then present the observations of the Greek historian, Herodotus, who discusses Egypt from his own contemporary perspective. Herodotus was fascinated by the customs, rituals, and details of the daily life of Egyptians and traveled there to gather materials for his research. His method of first hand inquiry explains why he is considered to be one of the first historians. Howard Carter then reveals the incalculable effect of discovering the world of ancient Egypt through Tutenkhamen's tomb. Carter's excavations dramatized the splendors of an ancient culture and produced a sense of connection with the past that few archeological discoveries have achieved.

The next two readings, by Arnold J. Toynbee and Elaine Pagels, offer intriguing interpretations about why some cultures flourish while others fail and how the concept of Satan evolved within a very specific social and political context at one point in the early history of Christianity. Both authors shed light on the way cultures define and react to perceived threats to their existence by mythologizing evil.

The accounts by Thomas Carlyle and Walt Whitman seek to answer the classic question as to whether history makes men or men make history. Carlyle sees history as having been shaped by the efforts of great artists, writers, thinkers, and political leaders who served as catalysts to inspire the masses who, without them, would lapse into anarchy. Whitman's reverence for and appreciation of Lincoln suggests how a hero can possess significance for future generations.

If the purpose of history is to gain collective "self-knowledge" as Collingwood proposed, then the interview by Maurizio Chierici of Claude Eatherly (the American pilot who was part of the mission that dropped the atomic bomb on Hiroshima on August 6, 1945) confronts us with a terrifying picture of humanity in the twentieth century. This event shaped the lives of thousands of people at the time and quite literally of everyone on the planet since then. The continuing threat of nuclear annihilation is at the core of John F. Kennedy's "Inaugural Address in 1961" and when read this way, becomes a valuable historical document, not just an inspiring political speech.

The final two selections by Oscar Handlin and Edward Said provide unique complementary perspectives on the uprooted. Handlin describes what is considered the classic immigrant experience, the journey of millions in the 1800s and 1900s in steerage from Europe to the United States. Said brings the immigrant experience into the present moment through an insightful analysis of the condition of exile as a fact of life for millions and as a psychological state that defines much of the literature of the twentieth century.

R. G. COLLINGWOOD

What Is History?

BACKGROUND

R. G. (Robin George) Collingwood (1889–1943), the philosopher, historian, and archeologist, was born in Lancashire, England. He was trained in the classics and was awarded a scholarship to University College, Oxford, where he later became a professor of history and philosophy. He was also a distinguished archeologist whose research on Roman ruins in Great Britain was published in volumes including *The Archeology of Roman Britain* (1930). He is best known for works in which he examines how the idea of history has evolved from the time of Herodotus (484 B.C.– 425 B.C.). to the twentieth century. According to Collingwood, history is not just a series of events that occurred in the past but rather a re-creation of events in the mind of the historian living in the present. This concept underlies many of Collingwood's books, including *The Idea of Nature* (published posthumously in 1945), which studies nature in terms of changing human accounts, and *The Idea of History* (1946; reissued 1957) in which the following essay first appeared. Collingwood was the first to add a subjective, psychological, and interpretive dimension to the study of history. Collections of Collingwood's essays include *Essays in the Philosophy of History*, edited by William Debbins (1965), and *Essays in Political Philosophy*, edited by David Boucher (1989).

APPROACHING COLLINGWOOD'S ESSAY

In this essay, Collingwood leads us to understand that historians who perform their job correctly do not simply colate facts, figures, dates, and other data regarding an event or period. This would mean they were only studying the exterior aspects of an event or action. And, under the influence of the natural sciences, this is the way historians had traditionally tried to understand history. Instead, Collingwood urges historians to understand that history is written in the present and reflects the writer's thoughts, analyses, interpretations, and especially his or her own era and its understanding of the past. His highly original concept of what a historian does changed the discipline of history so that historians understood they were looking at past events through the perspective of the present. Because the historian recreates the events of the past in the here and now, Collingwood finds Herodotus an especially interesting figure to study.

Herodotus was the first to try to establish a narrative of events that tell a story and establish causation for these events. Collingwood is fully aware of both the strengths and limitations of Herodotus's method. Herodotus tried to learn as much as he could about earlier culture and history, but did not look too deeply into trying to discover meanings, movements, or trends in the way a modern historian would (or should). Collingwood's analysis reflects his training in both philosophy and history in that he requires historians to understand events in the context of the philosophical beliefs of the period of time in which they occurred. History, in essence, is actually the history of thought about events rather than a recreation of events themselves. Collingwood understood that historians, in the future, can always discover new information (or see the past in a new light) that will change the meaning of past events.

What Is History?

WHAT history is, what it is about, how it proceeds, and what it is for, are questions which to some extent different people would answer in different ways. But in spite of differences there is a large measure of agreement between the answers. And this agreement becomes closer if the answers are subjected to scrutiny with a view to discarding those which proceed from unqualified witnesses. History, like theology or natural science, is a special form of thought. If that is so, questions about the nature, object, method, and value of this form of thought must be answered by persons having two qualifications.

First, they must have experience of that form of thought. They must be historians. In a sense we are all historians nowadays. All educated persons have gone through a process of education which has included a certain amount of historical thinking. But this does not qualify them to give an opinion about the nature, object, method, and value of historical thinking. For in the first place, the experience of historical thinking which they have thus acquired is probably very superficial; and the opinions based on it are therefore no better grounded than a man's opinion of the French people based on a single week-end visit to Paris. In the second place, experience of anything whatever gained through the ordinary educational channels, as well as being superficial, is invariably out of date. Experience of historical thinking, so gained, is modelled on text-books, and text-books always describe not what is now being thought by real live historians, but what was thought by real live historians at some time in the past when the raw material was being created out of which the text-book has been put together. And it is not only the results of historical thought which are out of date by the time they get into the text-book. It is also the principles of historical thought: that is, the ideas as to the nature, object, method, and value of historical thinking. In the third place, and connected with this, there is a peculiar illusion incidental to all knowledge acquired in the way of education: the illusion of finality. When a student is *in statu pupillari*[1] with respect to any subject whatever, he has to believe that things are settled because the text-books and his teachers regard them as settled. When he emerges from that state and goes on studying the subject for himself he finds that nothing is settled. The dogmatism which is an invariable mark of immaturity drops away from him. He looks at so-called facts with a new eye. He says to himself: 'My teacher and text-books told me that such and such was true; but is it true? What reasons had they for thinking it true, and were these reasons adequate?' On the other hand, if he emerges from the status of pupil without continuing to pursue the subject he never rids himself of this dogmatic attitude. And this makes him a person peculiarly unfitted to answer the questions I have mentioned. No one, for example, is likely to answer them worse than an Oxford philosopher who, having read Greats[2] in his youth, was once a student of history and thinks that this youthful experience of historical thinking entitles him to say what history is, what it is about, how it proceeds, and what it is for.

The second qualification for answering these questions is that a man should not only have experience of historical thinking but should also have reflected upon that experience. He must be not only an historian but a philosopher; and in particular his philosophical thought must have included special attention to the problems of historical thought. Now it is possible to be a quite good historian (though not an historian of the highest order) without thus reflecting upon one's own historical thinking. It is even easier to be a quite good teacher of history (though not the very best kind of teacher) without such reflection. At the same time, it is important to remember that experience comes first, and reflection on that experience second. Even the least reflective historian has the first qualification. He possesses the experience on which to reflect; and when he is asked to reflect on it his reflections have a good chance of being to the point. An historian who has never worked much at philosophy will probably answer our four questions in a more intelligent and valuable way than a philosopher who has never worked much at history.

I shall therefore propound answers to my four questions such as I think any present-day historian would accept. Here they will be rough and ready answers, but they will serve for a provisional definition of our subject-matter and they will be defended and elaborated as the argument proceeds.

[1]Having pupil's status; under instruction.
[2]Having done the reading for the final examination for the bachelor's degree in classics at Oxford.

a. *The definition of history.* Every historian would agree, I think, that history is a kind of research or inquiry. What kind of inquiry it is I do not yet ask. The point is that generically it belongs to what we call the sciences: that is, the forms of thought whereby we ask questions and try to answer them. Science in general, it is important to realize, does not consist in collecting what we already know and arranging it in this or that kind of pattern. It consists in fastening upon something we do not know, and trying to discover it. Playing patience with things we already know may be a useful means towards this end, but it is not the end itself. It is at best only the means. It is scientifically valuable only in so far as the new arrangement gives us the answer to a question we have already decided to ask. That is why all science begins from the knowledge of our own ignorance: not our ignorance of everything, but our ignorance of some definite thing — the origin of parliament, the cause of cancer, the chemical composition of the sun, the way to make a pump work without muscular exertion on the part of a man or a horse or some other docile animal. Science is finding things out: and in that sense history is a science.

b. *The object of history.* One science differs from another in that it finds out things of a different kind. What kind of things does history find out? I answer, *res gestae*:[3] actions of human beings that have been done in the past. Although this answer raises all kinds of further questions many of which are controversial, still, however they may be answered, the answers do not discredit the proposition that history is the science of *res gestae*, the attempt to answer questions about human actions done in the past.

c. *How does history proceed?* History proceeds by the interpretation of evidence: where evidence is a collective name for things which singly are called documents, and a document is a thing existing here and now, of such a kind that the historian, by thinking about it, can get answers to the questions he asks about past events. Here again there are plenty of difficult questions to ask as to what the characteristics of evidence are and how it is interpreted. But there is no need for us to raise them at this stage. However they are answered, historians will agree that historical procedure, or method, consists essentially of interpreting evidence.

d. Lastly, *what is history for?* This is perhaps a harder question than the others; a man who answers it will have to reflect rather more widely than a man who answers the three we have answered already. He must reflect not only on historical thinking but on other things as well, because to say that something is 'for' something implies a distinction between A and B, where A is good for

---

[3]Literally, things done.

something and B is that for which something is good. But I will suggest an answer, and express the opinion that no historian would reject it, although the further questions to which it gives rise are numerous and difficult.

My answer is that history is 'for' human self-knowledge. It is gener-   5
ally thought to be of importance to man that he should know himself: where knowing himself means knowing not his merely personal peculiarities, the things that distinguish him from other men, but his nature as man. Knowing yourself means knowing, first, what it is to be a man; secondly, knowing what it is to be the kind of man you are; and thirdly, knowing what it is to be the man *you* are and nobody else is. Knowing yourself means knowing what you can do; and since nobody knows what he can do until he tries, the only clue to what man can do is what man has done. The value of history, then, is that it teaches us what man has done and thus what man is. . . .

THE CREATION OF SCIENTIFIC HISTORY BY HERODOTUS

. . . The Greeks quite clearly and consciously recognized both that history is, or can be, a science, and that it has to do with human actions. Greek history is not legend, it is research; it is an attempt to get answers to definite questions about matters of which one recognizes oneself as ignorant. It is not theocratic,[4] it is humanistic. . . . Moreover, it is not mythical. The events inquired into are not events in a dateless past, at the beginning of things: they are events in a dated past, a certain number of years ago.

This is not to say that legend, either in the form of theocratic history or in the form of myth, was a thing foreign to the Greek mind. The work of Homer is not research, it is legend; and to a great extent it is theocratic legend. The gods appear in Homer as intervening in human affairs in a way not very different from the way in which they appear in the theocratic histories of the Near East. Similarly, Hesiod[5] has given us an example of myth. Nor is it to say that these legendary elements, theocratic or mythical as the case may be, are entirely absent even from the classical works of the fifth-century historians. F. M. Cornford in his *Thucydides Mythistoricus* (London, 1907) drew attention to the existence of such elements even in the hard-headed and scientific Thucydides.[6] He was of course perfectly right; and similar legendary elements are notoriously frequent in Herodotus. But what is remarkable about the Greeks was not the fact that their historical thought contained a certain residue of elements which we should call non-historical, but the fact that, side by side with these, it contained elements of what we call history.

[4]Does not interpret the past as determined by acts of God.
[5]Greek poet of the eighth century B.C., who wrote in his *Theogony* of the origin of the universe and the dynasties of the gods.
[6]Fifth-century B.C. historian of the Peloponnesian War.

The four characteristics of history which I enumerated in the Introduction were (*a*) that it is scientific, or begins by asking questions, whereas the writer of legends begins by knowing something and tells what he knows; (*b*) that it is humanistic, or asks questions about things done by men at determinate times in the past; (*c*) that it is rational, or bases the answers which it gives to its questions on grounds, namely appeal to evidence; (*d*) that it is self-revelatory, or exists in order to tell man what man is by telling him what man has done. Now the first, second, and fourth of these characteristics clearly appear in Herodotus: (i) The fact that history as a science was a Greek invention is recorded to this day by its very name. History is a Greek word, meaning simply an investigation or inquiry. Herodotus, who uses it in the title of his work, thereby 'marks a literary revolution' (as Croiset, an historian of Greek literature, says). Previous writers had been . . . writers-down of current stories: 'the historian', say How and Wells,[7] sets out to "find" the truth.' It is the use of this word, and its implications, that make Herodotus the father of history. The conversion of legend-writing into the science of history was not native to the Greek mind, it was a fifth-century invention, and Herodotus was the man who invented it. (ii) It is equally clear that history for Herodotus is humanistic as distinct from either mythical or theocratic. As he says in his preface, his purpose is to describe the deeds of men. (iii) His end, as he describes it himself, is that these deeds shall not be forgotten by posterity. Here we have my fourth characteristic of history, namely that it ministers to man's knowledge of man. In particular, Herodotus points out, it reveals man as a rational agent: that is, its function is partly to discover what men have done and partly to discover why they have done it. . . . Herodotus does not confine his attention to bare events; he considers these events in a thoroughly humanistic manner as actions of human beings who had reasons for acting as they did: and the historian is concerned with these reasons.

These three points reappear in the preface of Thucydides, which was obviously written with an eye on that of Herodotus. . . . To make it clear that he is no logographer but a scientific student, asking questions instead of repeating legends, he defends his choice of subject by saying that events earlier than those of the Peloponnesian War cannot be accurately ascertained. . . . He emphasizes the humanistic purpose and the self-revelatory function of history, in words modelled on those of his predecessor. And in one way he improves on Herodotus, for Herodotus makes no mention of evidence (the third of the characteristics mentioned above), and one is left to gather from the body of his work what his idea of evidence was; but Thucydides does say explicitly that historical inquiry rests on evidence. . . .

ANTI-HISTORICAL TENDENCY OF GREEK THOUGHT

In the meantime, I should like to point out how remarkable a thing is this creation of scientific history by Herodotus, for he was an ancient Greek, and ancient Greek thought as a whole has a very definite prevailing

[7]Authors of a commentary on Herodotus.

tendency not only uncongenial to the growth of historical thought but actually based, one might say, on a rigorously anti-historical metaphysics. History is a science of human action: what the historian puts before himself is things that men have done in the past, and these belong to a world of change, a world where things come to be and cease to be. Such things, according to the prevalent Greek metaphysical view, ought not to be knowable, and therefore history ought to be impossible.

For the Greeks, the same difficulty arose with the world of nature since it too was a world of this kind. If everything in the world changes, they asked, what is there in such a world for the mind to grasp? They were quite sure that anything which can be an object of genuine knowledge must be permanent; for it must have some definite character of its own, and therefore cannot contain in itself the seeds of its own destruction. If it is to be knowable it must be determinate; if it is determinate, it must be so completely and exclusively what it is that no internal change and no external force can ever set about making it into something else. Greek thought achieved its first triumph when it discovered in the objects of mathematical knowledge something that satisfied these conditions. A straight bar of iron may be bent into a curve, a flat surface of water may be broken into waves, but the straight line and the plane surface, as the mathematician thinks of them, are eternal objects that cannot change their characteristics.

Following the line of argument thus opened up, Greek thought worked out a distinction between the two types of thought, knowledge proper . . . and what we translate by 'opinion.' . . .[8] Opinion is the empirical semi-knowledge we have of matters of fact, which are always changing. It is our fleeting acquaintance with the fleeting actualities of the world; it thus only holds good for its own proper duration, for the here and now; and it is immediate, ungrounded in reasons, incapable of demonstration. True knowledge, on the contrary, holds good not only here and now but everywhere and always, and it is based on demonstrative reasoning and thus capable of meeting and overthrowing error by the weapon of dialectical criticism.

Thus, for the Greeks, process could be known only so far as it was perceived, and the knowledge of it could never be demonstrative. An exaggerated statement of this view, as we get it in the Eleatics,[9] would misuse the weapon of dialectic, which is really valid only against error in the sphere of knowledge strictly so called, to prove that change does not exist and that the 'opinions' we have about the changing are really not even opinions but sheer illusions. Plato rejects that doctrine and sees in the world of change something not indeed intelligible but real to the extent of being perceptible, something intermediate between the nullity with which the Eleatics had identified it and the complete reality and intelligibility of the eternal. On such a theory, history ought to be impossible. For history must have

[8]This distinction is made in Plato's *Symposium.*
[9]Followers of Parmenides of Elea (5th century B.C.), who taught that true being is one and indivisible, that it cannot not-be, and therefore that change (coming into being or ceasing to be) is unreal.

these two characteristics: first it must be about what is transitory, and secondly it must be scientific or demonstrative. But on this theory what is transitory cannot be demonstratively known; it cannot be the object of science; it can only be a matter of . . . perception, whereby human sensibility catches the fleeting moment as it flies. And it is essential to the Greek point of view that this momentary sensuous perception of momentary changing things cannot be a science or the basis of a science.

GREEK CONCEPTION OF HISTORY'S NATURE AND VALUE

15   The ardour with which the Greeks pursued the ideal of an unchanging and eternal object of knowledge might easily mislead us as to their historical interests. It might, if we read them carelessly, make us think them uninterested in history, somewhat as Plato's attack on the poets[10] might make an unintelligent reader fancy that Plato cared little for poetry. In order to interpret such things correctly we must remember that no competent thinker or writer wastes his time attacking a man of straw. An intense polemic against a certain doctrine is an infallible sign that the doctrine in question figures largely in the writer's environment and even has a strong attraction for himself. The Greek pursuit of the eternal was as eager as it was, precisely because the Greeks themselves had an unusually vivid sense of the temporal. They lived in a time when history was moving with extraordinary rapidity, and in a country where earthquake and erosion change the face of the land with a violence hardly to be seen elsewhere. They saw all nature as a spectacle of incessant change, and human life as changing more violently than anything else. Unlike the Chinese, or the medieval civilization of Europe, whose conception of human society was anchored in the hope of retaining the chief features of its structure unchanged, they made it their first aim to face and reconcile themselves to the fact that such permanence is impossible. This recognition of the necessity of change in human affairs gave to the Greeks a peculiar sensitiveness to history.

Knowing that nothing in life can persist unchanged, they came habitually to ask themselves what exactly the changes had been which, they knew, must have come about in order to bring the present into existence. Their historical consciousness was thus not a consciousness of agelong tradition moulding the life of one generation after another into a uniform pattern; it was a consciousness of violent. . . catastrophic changes from one state of things to its opposite, from smallness to greatness, from pride to abasement, from happiness to misery. This was how they interpreted the general character of human life in their dramas, and this was how they narrated the particular parts of it in their history. The only thing that a

---

[10]In the *Republic* it is argued that poets should not be allowed in the ideal common wealth because they deal in fictions, composing "images" or "copies" of things at a third remove from true (eternal) "reality," and because their stories—like those of Homer and the tragic dramatists—show men in the blind excitement of passions. But elsewhere, as in the *Phaedrus*, Plato spoke very differently of poets.

shrewd and critical Greek like Herodotus would say about the divine power that ordains the course of history is that . . . it rejoices in upsetting and disturbing things. He was only repeating . . . what every Greek knew: that the power of Zeus is manifested in the thunderbolt, that of Poseidon in the earthquake, that of Apollo in the pestilence, and that of Aphrodite in the passion that destroyed at once the pride of Phaedra and the chastity of Hippolytus.[11]

It is true that these catastrophic changes in the condition of human life, which to the Greeks were the proper theme of history, were unintelligible. There could be . . . of them no demonstrative scientific knowledge.[12] But all the same history had for the Greeks a definite value. Plato himself laid it down that right opinion (which is the sort of pseudo-knowledge that perception gives us of what changes) was no less useful for the conduct of life than scientific knowledge, and the poets maintained their traditional place in Greek life as the teachers of sound principles by showing that in the general pattern of these changes certain antecedents normally led to certain consequents. Notably, an excess in any one direction led to a violent change into its own opposite. Why this was so they could not tell; but they thought it a matter of observation that it was so; that people who became extremely rich or extremely powerful were thereby brought into special danger of being reduced to a condition of extreme poverty or weakness. There is here no theory of causation; the thought does not resemble that of seventeenth-century inductive science with its metaphysical basis in the axiom of cause and effect; the riches of Croesus[13] are not the cause of his downfall, they are merely a symptom, to the intelligent observer, that something is happening in the rhythm of his life which is likely to lead to a downfall. Still less is the downfall a punishment for anything that, in an intelligible moral sense, could be called wrongdoing. When Amasis in Herodotus . . . broke off his alliance with Polycrates,[14] he did it simply on the ground that Polycrates was too prosperous: the pendulum had swung too far one way and was likely to swing as far in the other. Such examples have their value to the person who can make use of them; for he can use his own will to arrest these rhythms in his life before they reach the danger-point, and check the thirst for power and wealth instead of allowing it to drive him to excess. Thus history has a value; its teachings are useful for human life; simply because the rhythm of its changes is likely to repeat

---

[11]In the powers attributed to the great gods of the Greek pantheon there resides a profound wisdom of the opposing forces of creation and destruction that surge throughout all nature and life. It is the destructive attributes of the gods that are mentioned here: Zeus, the supreme god of the heavens, with his lightning; Poseidon, god of the sea, as the "earth-shaker"; Apollo, god of the sun, of prophecy, poetry, and music, as also the bringer of the plague; and Aphrodite, goddess of love, in her opposite aspect as destroyer. Euripides' *Hippolytus* tells of the lust of Phaedra, wife of Theseus, for her stepson Hippolytus, and of the horrible destruction sent upon them.

[12]See the distinction between "knowledge" and "opinion" in the preceding section of the essay.

[13]Immensely wealthy 6th-century B.C. king of Lydia in Asia Minor.

[14]Amasis was king of Egypt and Polycrates tyrant of Samos in the 6th century B.C.

itself, similar antecedents leading to similar consequents; the history of notable events is worth remembering in order to serve as a basis for prognostic judgements, not demonstrable but probable, laying down not what will happen but what is likely to happen, indicating the points of danger in rhythms now going on.

This conception of history was the very opposite of deterministic, because the Greeks regarded the course of history as flexible and open to salutary modification by the well-instructed human will. Nothing that happens is inevitable. The person who is about to be involved in a tragedy is actually overwhelmed by it only because he is too blind to see his danger. If he saw it, he could guard against it. Thus the Greeks had a lively and indeed a naïve sense of the power of man to control his own destiny, and thought of this power as limited only by the limitations of his knowledge. The fate that broods over human life is, from this Greek point of view, a destructive power only because man is blind to its workings. Granted that he cannot understand these workings, he can yet have right opinions about them, and in so far as he acquires such opinions he becomes able to put himself in a position where the blows of fate will miss him.

On the other hand, valuable as the teachings of history are, their value is limited by the unintelligibility of its subject-matter; and that is why Aristotle said that poetry is more scientific than history, for history is a mere collection of empirical facts, whereas poetry extracts from such facts a universal judgement.[15] History tells us that Croesus fell and that Polycrates fell; poetry, according to Aristotle's idea of it, makes not these singular judgements but the universal judgement that very rich men, as such, fall. Even this is, in Aristotle's view, only a partially scientific judgement, for no one can see why rich men should fall; the universal cannot be syllogistically demonstrated; but it approaches the status of a true universal because we can use it as the major premiss for a new syllogism applying this generalization to fresh cases. Thus poetry is for Aristotle the distilled essence of the teaching of history. In poetry the lessons of history do not become any more intelligible and they remain undemonstrated and therefore merely probable, but they become more compendious and therefore more useful.

20   Such was the way in which the Greeks conceived the nature and value of history. They could not, consistently with their general philosophical attitude, regard it as scientific. They had to consider it as, at bottom, not a science but a mere aggregate of perceptions. What, then, was their conception of historical evidence? The answer is that, conformably with this view, they identified historical evidence with the reports of facts given by eyewitnesses of those facts. Evidence consists of eyewitnesses' narratives, and historical method consists of eliciting these.

---

[15]The usual translation of the statement is that poetry is more philosophic than history, whereas Collingwood uses the word "scientific." "Poetry," as Aristotle speaks of it, has its ancient inclusive meaning, referring to all the arts that use rhythmical language, including drama.

GREEK HISTORICAL METHOD AND ITS LIMITATIONS

Quite clearly, it was in this way that Herodotus conceived of evidence and method. This does not mean that he uncritically believed whatever eyewitnesses told him. On the contrary, he is in practice highly critical of their narratives. And here again he is typically Greek. The Greeks as a whole were skilled in the practice of the law courts, and a Greek would find no difficulty in applying to historical testimony the same kind of criticism which he was accustomed to direct upon witnesses in court. The work of Herodotus or Thucydides depends in the main on the testimony of eyewitnesses with whom the historian had personal contact. And his skill as a researcher consisted in the fact that he must have crossquestioned an eyewitness of past events until he had called up in the informant's own mind an historical picture of those events far fuller and more coherent than any he could have volunteered for himself. The result of this process was to create in the informant's mind for the first time a genuine knowledge of the past events which he had perceived. . . .

This conception of the way in which a Greek historian collected his material makes it a very different thing from the way in which a modern historian may use printed memoirs. Instead of the easy-going belief on the informant's part that his prima facie[16] recollection was adequate to the facts, there could grow up in his mind a chastened and criticized recollection which had stood the fire of such questions as 'Are you quite sure that you remember it just like that? Have you not now contradicted what you were saying yesterday? How do you reconcile your account of that event with the very different account given by so-and-so?' This method of using the testimony of eyewitnesses is undoubtedly the method which underlies the extraordinary solidity and consistency of the narratives which Herodotus and Thucydides finally wrote about fifth-century Greece.

No other method deserving the name scientific was available to the fifth-century historians, but it had [certain] limitations:

First, it inevitably imposed on its users a shortness of historical perspective. The modern historian knows that if only he had the capacity he could become the interpreter of the whole past of mankind; but whatever Greek historians might have thought of Plato's description of the philosopher as the spectator of all time, they would never have ventured to claim Plato's words as a description of themselves. Their method tied them on a tether whose length was the length of living memory: the only source they could criticize was an eyewitness with whom they could converse face to face. It is true that they relate events from a remoter past, but as soon as Greek historical writing tries to go beyond its tether, it becomes a far weaker and more precarious thing. . . .

[16]On first view; unexamined.

25   Nevertheless, this contrast in Herodotus and Thucydides between the unreliability of everything farther back than living memory and the critical precision of what comes within living memory is a mark not of the failure of fifth-century historiography but of its success. The point about Herodotus and Thucydides is not that the remote past is for them still outside the scope of scientific history but that the recent past is within that scope. Scientific history has been invented. Its field is still narrow; but within that field it is secure. Moreover, this narrowness of field did not matter much to the Greeks, because the extreme rapidity with which their own civilization was developing and changing afforded plenty of first-class historical material within the confines set by their method, and for the same reason they could produce first-rate historical work without developing what in fact they never did develop, any lively curiosity concerning the remote past.

Secondly, the Greek historian's method precludes him from choosing his subject. He cannot, like Gibbon, begin by wishing to write a great historical work and go on to ask himself what he shall write about. The only thing he can write about is the events which have happened within living memory to people with whom he can have personal contact. Instead of the historian choosing the subject, the subject chooses the historian; I mean that history is written only because memorable things have happened which call for a chronicler among the contemporaries of the people who have seen them. One might almost say that in ancient Greece there were no historians in the sense in which there were artists and philosophers; there were no people who devoted their lives to the study of history; the historian was only the autobiographer of his generation and autobiography is not a profession. . . .

The greatness of Herodotus stands out in the sharpest relief when, as the father of history, he is set against a background consisting of the general tendencies of Greek thought. The most dominant of these was antihistorical, as I have argued, because it involved the position that only what is unchanging can be known. Therefore history is a forlorn hope, an attempt to know what, being transitory, is unknowable. But we have already seen that, by skilful questioning, Herodotus was able . . . to attain knowledge in a field where Greeks had thought it impossible.

His success must remind us of one of his contemporaries, a man who was not afraid, either in war or in philosophy, to embark on forlorn hopes. Socrates brought philosophy down from heaven to earth by insisting that he himself knew nothing, and inventing a technique whereby, through skilful questioning, knowledge could be generated in the minds of others as ignorant as himself. Knowledge of what? Knowledge of human affairs: in particular, of the moral ideas that guide human conduct.

The parallel between the work of the two men is so striking that I put Herodotus side by side with Socrates as one of the great innovating geniuses of the fifth century.

READING CRITICALLY FOR IDEAS, STRUCTURE, AND STYLE

1. Collingwood disagrees with the conventional definitions of "history" and offers his own definition. According to Collingwood, what distinctive approach should historians use?

2. What aspects of Collingwood's analysis underscore his view that history is not so much a record of past events but rather a recreation of those events in the mind of the historian? Why is it important to understand that the meaning we give to past events may put meanings into these events that were not originally there?

3. Collingwood delves into the work of early Greek historians, such as Herodotus. In what respects do they serve as precursors for the modern study of history? What were the limitations of the ancient historical method?

EXTENDING INSIGHTS THROUGH WRITING

1. In a short essay, discuss how Collingwood's definition of history serves as a basis for organizing and unifying his entire discussion. Draw on different sections as evidence to support your analysis.

2. Collingwood speaks about the "illusion of finality" or "dogmatism," as something historians should avoid. In your history classes, what methods did your teachers use—compared with what Collingwood recommends?

CONNECTING PERSPECTIVES ON THE HISTORICAL DIMENSION

1. Do you agree with Collingwood's evaluation of Herodotus's methods as they are presented in "Concerning Egypt"? Why or why not?

2. Compare Collingwood's approach to history with that of another eminent historian, Arnold J. Toynbee, in "Challenge and Response." What different assumptions guide their research?

HERODOTUS

Concerning Egypt

BACKGROUND

Herodotus (484 B.C.– 425 B.C.), whom Cicero called the "father of history" for his detailed account of the wars between the Greeks and the Persians (500 B.C. and 479 B.C.), was born at Halicarnassus, in Caria, a province bordering the Coast of Asia Minor. In order to gather materials for his monumental work, *History,* he traveled widely in Greece, Macedonia, and regions that are now Bulgaria, Turkey, Israel, Iran, and Egypt. His history of the Persian wars was the first comprehensive attempt at writing a secular narrative history. It not only tried to fix a chronology but also to establish the relationship between events and their causes. His works offer a wealth of information about the ancient world, written in an anecdotal style that is colorful and compelling. Herodotus was something of a moralist, who attempts to see the lessons inherent in the events he describes. His work was published in Latin in 1474, but it was not until 1502 that it was printed in the original Greek, by Aldus Manutius, whose edition is divided into nine books, each named after one of the Muses. The following essay is drawn from *History,* translated by George Rawlinson (1858 –1860). Rawlinson (1812 –1902), the English orientalist and historian, is known for his authoritative histories of the ancient world and his highly acclaimed translations.

APPROACHING HERODOTUS'S ESSAY

In "Concerning Egypt" we can observe that the expository principle Herodotus uses is that of comparison and contrast, which is well-suited for understanding the unfamiliar Egyptian customs in relationship to the corresponding but different customs of his Greek countrymen, the audience for whom he is writing. Herodotus always supports his observations with a wealth of concrete details. We learn about habits of diet, cooking, bathing, hairstyles, how parents are treated, shopping in the market, weaving practices, and a multitude of other customs that take the reader directly into the everyday lives of the ancient Egyptians. Herodotus began the modern study of history by asking questions about things of which people had little, if any, knowledge, and tried to answer these questions based on his own travels and investigations. He also changed the focus from writing about legendary figures, gods, or heroes, to real people. He also believed that history could offer moral lessons, especially those drawn from the comparison of cultures, that would be useful to his fellow Greeks. Herodotus sets a standard for later historians in his use of evidence and source material by indicating where his data comes from and distinguishing common beliefs from his own interpretations and conclusions. In this selection, he pays considerable attention to the religious customs of the Egyptians. This is not unusual, since Egypt was a theocratic society in which every action, such as the ritual sacrifice of animals, had special significance.

Concerning Egypt

CONCERNING Egypt itself I shall extend my remarks to a great length, because there is no country that possesses so many wonders, nor any that has such a number of works which defy description. Not only is the climate different from that of the rest of the world, and the rivers unlike any other rivers, but the people also, in most of their manners and customs, exactly reverse the common practice of mankind. The women attend the markets and trade, while the men sit at home at the loom; and here, while the rest of the world works the woof up the warp, the Egyptians work it down; the women likewise carry burthens upon their shoulders, while the men carry them upon their heads. They eat their food out of doors in the streets, but retire for private purposes to their houses, giving as a reason that what is unseemly, but necessary, ought to be done in secret, but what has nothing unseemly about it, should be done openly. A woman cannot serve the priestly office, either for god or goddess, but men are priests to both; sons need not support their parents unless they choose, but daughters must, whether they choose or no.

In other countries the priests have long hair, in Egypt their heads are shaven; elsewhere it is customary, in mourning, for near relations to cut their hair close: the Egyptians, who wear no hair at any other time, when they lose a relative, let their beards and the hair of their heads grow long. All other men pass their lives separate from animals, the Egyptians have animals always living with them; others make barley and wheat their food; it is a disgrace to do so in Egypt, where the grain they live on is spelt, which some call *zea*. Dough they knead with their feet; but they mix mud, and even take up dirt, with their hands. They are the only people in the world— they at least, and such as have learnt the practice from them—who use circumcision. Their men wear two garments apiece, their women but one.

They put on the rings and fasten the ropes to sails inside; others put them outside. When they write or calculate, instead of going, like the Greeks, from left to right, they move their hand from right to left; and they insist, notwithstanding, that it is they who go to the right, and the Greeks who go to the left. They have two quite different kinds of writing, one of which is called sacred, the other common.

They are religious to excess, far beyond any other race of men, and use the following ceremonies:—They drink out of brazen cups, which they scour every day: there is no exception to this practice. They wear linen garments, which they are specially careful to have always fresh washed. They practise circumcision for the sake of cleanliness, considering it better to be cleanly than comely. The priests shave their whole body every other day, that no lice or other impure thing may adhere to them when they are engaged in the service of the gods. Their dress is entirely of linen, and their shoes of the papyrus plant: it is not lawful for them to wear either dress or shoes of any other material. They bathe twice every day in cold water, and twice each night; besides which they observe, so to speak, thousands of ceremonies. They enjoy, however, not a few advantages. They consume none of their own property, and are at no expense for anything; but every day bread is baked for them of the sacred corn, and a plentiful supply of beef and of goose's flesh is assigned to each, and also a portion of wine made from the grape. Fish they are not allowed to eat; and beans,—which none of the Egyptians ever sow, or eat, if they come up of their own accord, either raw or boiled—the priests will not even endure to look on, since they consider it an unclean kind of pulse. Instead of a single priest, each god has the attendance of a college, at the head of which is a chief priest, when one of these dies, his son is appointed in his room.

Male kine are reckoned to belong to Epaphus,[1] and are therefore tested in the following manner:—One of the priests appointed for the purpose searches to see if there is a single black hair on the whole body, since in that case the beast is unclean. He examines him all over, standing on his legs, and again laid upon his back; after which he takes the tongue out of his mouth, to see if it be clean in respect to the prescribed marks (what they are I will mention elsewhere); he also inspects the hairs of the tail, to observe if they grow naturally. If the animal is pronounced clean in all these various points, the priest marks him by twisting a piece of papyrus round his horns, and attaching thereto some sealing clay, which he then stamps with his own signet-ring. After this the beast is led away; and it is forbidden, under the penalty of death, to sacrifice an animal which has not been marked in this way.

---

[1]Son of Zeus by Io. In a jealous fit, the goddess Hera had changed Io into a cow, who wandered finally to Egypt, where Epaphus was born and where he became king and father of a famous line of heroes. The myth has interest in relation to the religious reverence for the cow in Egypt, sacred to the goddess Isis, as Herodotus says. A goddess perhaps older than Isis, Hathor, was represented as a cow in ancient Egyptian engravings, shown as standing over the earth and giving suck to mankind from her great udders.

The following is their manner of sacrifice:—They lead the victim, marked with their signet, to the altar where they are about to offer it, and setting the wood alight, pour a libation of wine upon the altar in front of the victim, and at the same time invoke the god. Then they slay the animal, and cutting off his head, proceed to flay the body. Next they take the head, and heaping imprecations on it, if there is a market-place and a body of Greek traders in the city, they carry it there and sell it instantly; if, however, there are no Greeks among them, they throw the head into the river. The imprecation is to this effect:—They pray that if any evil is impending either over those who sacrifice, or over universal Egypt, it may be made to fall upon that head. These practices, the imprecations upon the heads, and the libations of wine, prevail all over Egypt, and extend to victims of all sorts; and hence the Egyptians will never eat the head of any animal.

The disembowelling and burning are, however, different in different sacrifices. I will mention the mode in use with respect to the goddess whom they regard as the greatest, and honour with the chiefest festival. When they have flayed their steer they pray, and when their prayer is ended they take the paunch of the animal out entire, leaving the intestines and the fat inside the body; they then cut off the legs, the ends of the loins, the shoulders, and the neck; and having so done, they fill the body of the steer with clean bread, honey, raisins, figs, frankincense, myrrh, and other aromatics. Thus filled, they burn the body, pouring over it great quantities of oil. Before offering the sacrifice they fast, and while the bodies of the victims are being consumed they beat themselves. Afterwards, when they have concluded this part of the ceremony, they have the other parts of the victim served up to them for a repast.

The male kine, therefore, if clean, and the male calves, are used for sacrifice by the Egyptians universally; but the females they are not allowed to sacrifice since they are sacred to Isis.[2] The statue of this goddess has the form of a woman but with horns like a cow, resembling thus the Greek representations of Io; and the Egyptians, one and all, venerate cows much more highly than any other animal. This is the reason why no native of Egypt, whether man or woman, will give a Greek a kiss, or use the knife of a Greek, or his spit, or his cauldron, or taste the flesh of an ox, known to be pure, if it has been cut with a Greek knife. When kine die, the following is the manner of their sepulture:—The females are thrown into the river; the males are buried in the suburbs of the towns, with one or both of their horns appearing above the surface of the ground to mark the place. When the bodies are decayed, a boat comes, at an appointed time, from the island called Prosôpitis—which is a portion of the Delta, nine schoenes[3] in circumference,—and calls at the several cities in turn to collect the bones of the oxen. Prosôpitis is a district containing several cities; the name of that from which the boats come is Atarbêchis. Venus has a temple there of much

---

[2]Great nature-goddess, worshiped with Osiris as his sister and wife. Hathor the cow-goddess. The worship blended into and became identified with that of Isis.
[3]A land measurement of several miles.

sanctity. Great numbers of men go forth from this city and proceed to the other towns, where they dig up the bones, which they take away with them and bury together in one place. The same practice prevails with respect to the interment of all other cattle—the law so determining; they do not slaughter any of them.

Such Egyptians as possess a temple of the Theban Jove, or live in the Thebaïc canton, offer no sheep in sacrifice, but only goats; for the Egyptians do not all worship the same gods, excepting Isis and Osiris,[4] the latter of whom they say is the Grecian Bacchus. Those, on the contrary, who possess a temple dedicated to Mendes, or belong to the Mendesian canton, abstain from offering goats, and sacrifice sheep instead. The Thebans, and such as imitate them in their practice, give the following account of the origin of the custom:—"Hercules," they say, "wished of all things to see Jove, but Jove did not choose to be seen of him. At length, when Hercules persisted, Jove hit on a device—to flay a ram, and, cutting off his head, hold the head before him, and cover himself with fleece. In this guise he showed himself to Hercules." Therefore the Egyptians give their statues of Jupiter the face of a ram: and from them the practice has passed to the Ammonians, who are a joint colony of Egyptians and Ethiopians, speaking a language between the two; hence also, in my opinion, the latter people took their name of Ammonians, since the Egyptian name for Jupiter is Amun. Such, then, is the reason why the Thebans do not sacrifice rams, but consider them sacred animals. Upon one day in the year, however, at the festival of Jupiter, they slay a single ram, and stripping off the fleece, cover with it the statue of that god, as he once covered himself, and then bring up to the statue of Jove an image of Hercules. When this has been done, the whole assembly beat their breasts in mourning for the ram, and afterwards bury him in a holy sepulchre. . . .

The pig is regarded among them as an unclean animal, so much so that if a man in passing accidentally touch a pig, he instantly hurries to the river, and plunges in with all his clothes on. Hence, too, the swineherds, notwithstanding that they are of pure Egyptian blood, are forbidden to enter into any of the temples, which are open to all other Egyptians; and further, no one will give his daughter in marriage to a swineherd, or take a wife from among them, so that the swineherds are forced to intermarry among themselves. They do not offer swine in sacrifice to any of their gods, excepting

---

[4]Osiris was a plant-god and fertility-god, actually a "Lord of Life" like Dionysus (Bacchus), Adonis, Atys (or Attis), Tammuz, and others. He was slain in youth by his brother Set, and the pieces of his body were scattered over the land. Isis, his sister-wife, wandered everywhere searching for him and grieving, until the fragments of his body were collected and put together. Then the god was resurrected into life. This fertility myth has many parallels originally symbolizing the cycle of winter and summer, the death of vegetation and its annual renewal. Later the myth came to symbolize the more mystical belief in human resurrection and immortality.

Bacchus and the Moon,[5] whom they honour in this way at the same time, sacrificing pigs to both of them at the same full moon, and afterwards eating of the flesh. There is a reason alleged by them for their detestation of swine at all other seasons, and their use of them at this festival, with which I am well acquainted, but which I do not think it proper to mention. The following is the mode in which they sacrifice the swine to the Moon:—As soon as the victim is slain, the tip of the tail, the spleen, and the caul are put together, and having been covered with all the fat that has been found in the animal's belly, are straightway burnt. The remainder of the flesh is eaten on the same day that the sacrifice is offered, which is the day of the full moon: at any other time they would not so much as taste it. The poorer sort, who cannot afford live pigs, form pigs of dough, which they bake and offer in sacrifice.

To Bacchus, on the eve of his feast, every Egyptian sacrifices a hog 10 before the door of his house, which is then given back to the swineherd by whom it was furnished, and by him carried away. In other respects the festival is celebrated almost exactly as Bacchic festivals are in Greece, excepting that the Egyptians have no choral dances. They also use instead of phalli[6] another invention, consisting of images a cubit high, pulled by strings, which the women carry round to the villages.

A piper goes in front, and the women follow, singing hymns in honour of Bacchus. They give a religious reason for the peculiarities of the image.

Melampus,[7] the son of Amytheon, cannot (I think) have been ignorant of this ceremony—nay, he must, I should conceive, have been well acquainted with it. He it was who introduced into Greece the name of Bacchus, the ceremonial of his worship, and the procession of the phallus. He did not, however, so completely apprehend the whole doctrine as to be able to communicate it entirely, but various sages since his time have carried out his teaching to greater perfection. Still it is certain that Melampus introduced the phallus, and that the Greeks learnt from him the ceremonies which they now practise. I therefore maintain that Melampus, who was a wise

---

[5]Osiris and Isis. Herodotus has previously suggested an identification between Osiris and the Greek Bacchus; and Isis was goddess of the moon as well as of the rest of nature (one of her emblems was the crescent moon). Pigs are one of the ancient animal symbols of reproductive fertility. In the custom Herodotus speaks of here, it is because of the fertility aspect of Osiris and Isis that pigs were sacrificed to them. The custom corresponds to that of the ancient Greeks, who threw slaughtered pigs into crevices of the earth as offerings to Persephone (daughter of Demeter, the corn-goddess). In Ireland, pigs carved out of bog oak are given as good-luck symbols. The normal Egyptian taboo on the eating of swine meat (except for the monthly sacrifice) was no doubt acquired by the Hebrews during their stay in Egypt, like the practice of circumcision.

[6]This religious fertility symbolism is universal. In the myth of the death and the scattering of the parts of Osiris' body, the phallus was the last to be found, and without it Osiris could not come back to life. It had fallen into the Nile, on which Egyptian agriculture depends.

[7]Mythological seer who understood the speech of all creatures.

man, and had acquired the art of divination, having become acquainted with the worship of Bacchus through knowledge derived from Egypt, introduced it into Greece, with a few slight changes, at the same time that he brought in various other practices. For I can by no means allow that it is by mere coincidence that the Bacchic ceremonies in Greece are so nearly the same as the Egyptian—they would then have been more Greek in their character, and less recent in their origin. Much less can I admit that the Egyptians borrowed these customs, or any other, from the Greeks. My belief is that Melampus got his knowledge of them from Cadmus the Tyrian, and the followers whom he brought from Phoenicia into the country which is now called Boeotia.[8]

Almost all the names of the gods came into Greece from Egypt. My inquiries prove that they were all derived from a foreign source, and my opinion is that Egypt furnished the greater number. For with the exception of Neptune and the Dioscûri, whom I mentioned above, and Juno, Vesta, Themis, the Graces, and the Nereids, the other gods have been known from time immemorial in Egypt. This I assert on the authority of the Egyptians themselves. The gods, with whose names they profess themselves unacquainted, the Greeks received, I believe, from the Pelasgi, except Neptune. Of him they got their knowledge from the Libyans, by whom he has been always honoured, and who were anciently the only people that had a god of the name. The Egyptians differ from the Greeks also in paying no divine honours to heroes.. . .[9]

Whence the gods severally sprang, whether or no they had all existed from eternity, what forms they bore—these are questions of which the Greeks knew nothing until the other day, so to speak. For Homer and Hesiod were the first to compose Theogonies, and give the gods their epithets, to allot them their several offices and occupations, and describe their forms; and they lived but four hundred years before my time, as I believe. As for the poets who are thought by some to be earlier than these, they are, in my judgment, decidedly later writers. In these matters I have the authority of the priestesses of Dodôna for the former portion of my statements; what I have said of Homer and Hesiod is my own opinion.. . .[10]

[8]Cadmus, legendary founder of Thebes, was said to have brought the alphabet from Tyre in Phoenicia (on the eastern Mediterranean coast) to Greece. Boeotia was the ancient name of the country north of the Gulf of Corinth, dominated by Thebes.

[9]The Dioscuri (dios-kuroi, god's sons) were Castor and Pollux, sons of Zeus and Leda, conceived when Zeus met Leda in the form of a swan, and brothers of Helen and Clytemnestra. They were patrons of horsemanship, boxing, and all the athletic skills of the Olympic Games. At their death they became the constellation Gemini, the Twins. Vesta was an ancient earth-goddess who became, in the Olympian pantheon, goddess of the home and hearth. Themis was another very ancient earth-goddess, a Titaness (the Titans were nature-gods who preceded the Olympians), mother of Prometheus. The oracle at Delphi spoke through her priestesses. The Pelasgi were, so far as is known, aboriginal inhabitants of Greece, whose immense rough stonework is found in various parts of Greece. The Nereids were daughters of an ancient sea-god, Nereus, who were represented as attending the later sea-god, Poseidon, riding sea horses; they are the original "mermaids."

[10]Modern scholars tend to accept Herodotus' date for Homer ("four hundred years before my time") as correct. Theogonies are genealogies of the gods. Dodona was a famous oracle of Zeus in northwestern Greece.

The Egyptians first made it a point of religion to have no converse 15
with women in the sacred places,[11] and not to enter them without washing, after such converse. Almost all other nations, except the Greeks and
the Egyptians, act differently, regarding man as in this matter under no
other law than the brutes. Many animals, they say, and various kinds of
birds, may be seen to couple in the temples and the sacred precincts,
which would certainly not happen if the gods were displeased at it. Such
are the arguments by which they defend their practice, but I nevertheless
can by no means approve of it. In these points the Egyptians are specially careful, as they are indeed in everything which concerns their sacred
edifices.

Egypt, though it borders upon Libya, is not a region abounding in
wild animals. The animals that do exist in the country, whether domesticated or otherwise, are all regarded as sacred. If I were to explain why they
are consecrated to the several gods, I should be led to speak of religious matters, which I particularly shrink from mentioning;[12] the points whereon I
have touched slightly hitherto have all been introduced from sheer necessity. Their custom with respect to animals is as follows:—For every kind
there are appointed certain guardians, some male, some female, whose
business it is to look after them; and this honour is made to descend from
father to son. The inhabitants of the various cities, when they have made
a vow to any god, pay it to his animals in the way which I will now explain.
At the time of making the vow they shave the head of the child, cutting off
all the hair, or else half, or sometimes a third part, which they then weigh
in a balance against a sum of silver; and whatever sum the hair weighs is
presented to the guardian of the animals, who thereupon cuts up some
fish, and gives it to them for food—such being the stuff whereon they fed.
When a man has killed one of the sacred animals, if he did it with malice
prepense,[13] he is punished with death; if unwittingly, he has to pay such
a fine as the priests choose to impose. When an ibis, however, or a hawk
is killed, whether it was done by accident or on purpose, the man must
needs die.

The number of domestic animals in Egypt is very great, and would be
still greater were it not for what befalls the cats. As the females, when they
have kittened, no longer seek the company of the males, these last, to obtain
once more their companionship, practise a curious artifice. They seize the
kittens, carry them off, and kill them, but do not eat them afterwards. Upon
this the females, being deprived of their young, and longing to supply their
place, seek the males once more, since they are particularly fond of their
offspring. On every occasion of a fire in Egypt the strangest prodigy occurs
with the cats. The inhabitants allow the fire to rage as it pleases, while they

[11]Ritual prostitution in temple precincts, setting a symbolic example to the earth to
renew its fertility, was common in ancient Greece.
[12]The sacred mysteries were not to be lightly spoken of or gossiped about, even by a historian. The famous mysteries of Eleusis (a few miles from Athens) apparently had
much in common with those of Isis and Osiris in Egypt.
[13]Malice aforethought.

stand about at intervals and watch these animals, which, slipping by the men or else leaping over them, rush headlong into the flames. When this happens, the Egyptians are in deep affliction. If a cat dies in a private house by a natural death, all the inmates of the house shave their eyebrows; on the death of a dog they shave the head and the whole of the body.

The cats on their decease are taken to the city of Bubastis, where they are embalmed, after which they are buried in certain sacred repositories. The dogs are interred in the cities to which they belong, also in sacred burial-places. The same practice obtains with respect to the ichneumons; the hawks and shrew-mice, on the contrary, are conveyed to the city of Buto for burial, and the ibises to Hermopolis. The bears, which are scarce in Egypt, and the wolves, which are not much bigger than foxes, they bury wherever they happen to find them lying. . . .

They have also another sacred bird called the phoenix, which I myself have never seen, except in pictures. Indeed it is a great rarity, even in Egypt, only coming there (according to the accounts of the people of Heliopolis) once in five hundred years, when the old phoenix dies. Its size and appearance, if it is like the pictures, are as follow:—The plumage is partly red, partly golden, while the general make and size are almost exactly that of the eagle. They tell a story of what this bird does, which does not seem to me to be credible: that he comes all the way from Arabia, and brings the parent bird, all plastered over with myrrh, to the temple of the Sun, and there buries the body. In order to bring him, they say, he first forms a ball of myrrh as big as he finds that he can carry; then he hollows out the ball, and puts his parent inside, after which he covers over the opening with fresh myrrh, and the ball is then of exactly the same weight as at first; so he brings it to Egypt, plastered over as I have said, and deposits it in the temple of the Sun. Such is the story they tell of the doings of this bird. . . .

20   With respect to the Egyptians themselves, it is to be remarked that those who live in the corn country, devoting themselves, as they do, far more than any other people in the world, to the preservation of the memory of past actions, are the best skilled in history of any men that I have ever met. The following is the mode of life habitual to them:—For three successive days in each month they purge the body by means of emetics and clysters, which is done out of a regard for their health, since they have a persuasion that every disease to which men are liable is occasioned by the substances whereon they feed. Apart from any such precautions, they are, I believe, next to the Libyans, the healthiest people in the world—an effect of their climate, in my opinion, which has no sudden changes. Diseases almost always attack men when they are exposed to a change, and never more than during changes of the weather. They live on bread made of spelt, which they form into loaves called in their own tongue *cyllêstis*. Their drink is a wine which they obtain from barley, as they have no vines in their country. Many kinds of fish they eat raw, either salted or dried in the sun. Quails also, and ducks and small birds, they eat uncooked, merely first salting them. All other birds and fishes, excepting those which are set apart as sacred, are eaten either roasted or boiled.

In social meetings among the rich, when the banquet is ended, a servant carries round to the several guests a coffin, in which there is a wooden image of a corpse, carved and painted to resemble nature as nearly as possible, about a cubit or two cubits in length. As he shows it to each guest in turn, the servant says, "Gaze here, and drink and be merry; for when you die, such will you be." . . .

The Egyptian likewise discovered to which of the gods each month and day is sacred; and found out from the day of a man's birth, what he will meet with in the course of his life, and how he will end his days, and what sort of man he will be—discoveries whereof the Greeks engaged in poetry have made a use. The Egyptians have also discovered more prognostics than all the rest of mankind besides. Whenever a prodigy takes place, they watch and record the result; then, if anything similar ever happens again, they expect the same consequences. . . .

The following is the way in which they conduct their mournings and their funerals:—On the death in any house of a man of consequence, forthwith the women of the family beplaster their heads, and sometimes even their faces, with mud; and then, leaving the body indoors, sally forth and wander through the city, with their dress fastened by a band, and their bosoms bare, beating themselves as they walk. All the female relations join them and do the same. The men too, similarly begirt, beat their breasts separately. When these ceremonies are over, the body is carried away to be embalmed.

There are a set of men in Egypt who practice the art of embalming, and make it their proper business. These persons, when a body is brought to them, show the bearers various models of corpses, made in wood, and painted so as to resemble nature. The most perfect is said to be after the manner of him whom I do not think it religious to name[14] in connection with such a matter; the second sort is inferior to the first, and less costly; the third is the cheapest of all. All this the embalmers explain, and then ask in which way it is wished that the corpse should be prepared. The bearers tell them, and having concluded their bargain, take their departure, while the embalmers left to themselves, proceed to their task. The mode of embalming, according to the most perfect process, is the following:—They take first a crooked piece of iron, and with it draw out the brain through the nostrils, thus getting rid of a portion, while the skull is cleared of the rest by rinsing with drugs; next they make a cut along the flank with a sharp Ethiopian stone, and take out the whole contents of the abdomen, which they then cleanse, washing it thoroughly with palm wine, and again frequently with an infusion of pounded aromatics. After this they fill the cavity with purest bruised myrrh, with cassia, and every other sort of spicery except frankincense, and sew up the opening. Then the body is placed in natrum[15] for

[14]Undoubtedly Osiris. Though he might feel free to name Osiris in other contexts, Herodotus speaks again here as one who was under the seal of mysteries corresponding with those of Egypt.

[15]Sodium carbonate.

seventy days, and covered entirely over. After the expiration of that space of time, which must not be exceeded, the body is washed, and wrapped round, from head to foot, with bandages of fine linen cloth, smeared over with gum, which is used generally by the Egyptians in the place of glue, and in this state it is given back to the relations, who enclose it in a wooden case which they have had made for the purpose, shaped into the figure of a man. Then fastening the case, they place it in a sepulchral chamber, upright against the wall. Such is the most costly way of embalming the dead.

25   If persons wish to avoid expense, and choose the second process, the following is the method pursued:—Syringes are filled with oil made from the cedar-tree, which is then, without any incision or disembowelling, injected into the abdomen. The passage by which it might be likely to return is stopped, and the body laid in natrum the prescribed number of days. At the end of the time the cedar-oil is allowed to make its escape; and such is its power that it brings with it the whole stomach and intestines in a liquid state. The natrum meanwhile has dissolved the flesh, and so nothing is left of the dead body but the skin and the bones. It is returned in this condition to the relatives, without any further trouble being bestowed upon it.

The third method of embalming, which is practised in the case of the poorer classes, is to clear out the intestines with a clyster, and let the body lie in natrum the seventy days, after which it is at once given to those who come to fetch it away.

The wives of men of rank are not given to be embalmed immediately after death, nor indeed are any of the more beautiful and valued women. It is not till they have been dead three or four days that they are carried to the embalmers. This is done to prevent indignities from being offered them. It is said that once a case of this kind occurred; the man was detected by the information of his fellow-workman. . . .

Thus far I have spoken of Egypt from my own observation, relating what I myself saw, the ideas that I formed, and the results of my own researches.

READING CRITICALLY FOR IDEAS, STRUCTURE, AND STYLE

1. How do the religious customs described by Herodotus suggest that Egypt was a theocratic civilization in which all actions had a religious significance?

2. Why is the method of comparison and contrast well-suited as a rhetorical technique to Herodotus's subject?

3. What principles guide the way Herodotus collected material for his observations? What standards does he apply in deciding which reports are credible?

EXTENDING INSIGHTS THROUGH WRITING

1. The religious rituals described by Herodotus were designed to ensure fertility of the land and the people and featured ceremonial sacrifices. How do modern ceremonial feasts (such as Thanksgiving) or customs (dying eggs different colors and Easter egg hunts) express some of the same themes? In a few paragraphs, discuss the significance of these modern customs.

2. Customs with which you are familiar might appear as strange to an observer as those of the Egyptians did to Herodotus. Describe a cultural custom (for example, fashion trend, tatooing, fast food, beauty salons, shopping malls, marriage rituals) to someone who might not be at all familiar with what it is and what it means.

CONNECTING PERSPECTIVES ON THE HISTORICAL DIMENSION

1. Compare the different perspectives on what, for Herodotus, were current observable customs of a thriving civilization with those of Howard Carter (see "Finding the Tomb") as an archeologist. In what ways do these two accounts complement each other?

2. Collingwood says that Herodotus innovated the modern study of history by being "scientific," "humanistic," and ministering to "man's knowledge of man." Now that you have read both essays, evaluate Collingwood's analysis of Herodotus's methods.

HOWARD CARTER

Finding the Tomb

BACKGROUND

Howard Carter (1873–1939), the English archeologist whose work resulted in the discovery of the tomb of Tutankhamen, the boy king of the eighteenth dynasty (fourteenth century B.C.), was born in London and first went to Egypt in 1891 as a draughtsman with the Archaeological Survey Department. Carter was convinced that there was at least one undiscovered tomb in the Valley of the Kings and persuaded Lord Carnarvon, a wealthy aristocrat, to be his backer. Although his first excavations began in 1902, it was not until November 1922 that he made his greatest discovery at Thebes, accompanied by Lord Carnarvon (who died in 1923, during the excavation of Tutankhamen's tomb, under mysterious circumstances). "Finding the Tomb," from Carter's three-volume account of the excavation, *The Tomb of Tutankhamen* (1933), describes the exciting story of one of the greatest archeological discoveries of all time.

APPROACHING CARTER'S ESSAY

In the nineteenth century, European archeologists began extensive excavations in hopes of discovering the tombs of pharoahs, whom the ancient Egyptians revered as gods. The bodies in these tombs were carefully preserved through elaborate embalming procedures. Unfortunately, most of these tombs had been discovered by grave robbers and the search for an unplundered tomb became Carter's obsession. He was convinced that the tomb of a boy king, whose name was Tutankhamen, murdered when he was only nineteen, remained to be discovered, along with the treasures that were buried with him.

On November 4, 1922, Carter's work crew discovered a step cut into a rock, which on further excavation revealed fifteen more steps leading to a sealed doorway. Carter assumed that the tomb might have been ransacked because he found that a part of the surface of the door had been opened twice

236

and resealed. Since Lord Carnarvon had supported Carter in his previous endeavors at considerable expense for many years, Carter felt it was only fair that he delay opening the tomb until he could be present to share in the excitement of the discovery.

In presenting his account, Carter heightens suspense by alternating phrases filled with excitement and hope with those filled with despair and doubt. Not until the very end of the piece is the reader certain as to whether or not the opening of the tomb would fulfill Carter's fantastic expectations.

The story of how Egyptian hieroglyphs (including those Carter found) were deciphered is as fascinating as the discovery of the tomb: As Napoleon was retreating from Egypt, he instructed his men to set up camp to hold off the advancing English and Turkish forces. On August 2, 1799, a soldier's pickaxe uncovered a stone with strange inscriptions near the town of Rosetta in the Nile delta. The so-called Rosetta Stone was covered with three scripts— that is three languages—of which only one, modern Greek, could be deciphered. The other two were the ancient Egyptian hieroglyphs, or "sacred signs," and an early Greek dialect. The different signs and hieroglyphs actually expressed the same meaning in three separate inscriptions. By a painstaking point-by-point comparison of ancient and modern Greek with the Egyptian hieroglyphic forms, Jean-Francois Champollion (1790–1832), the French linguist and Egyptologist, deciphered the royal "cartouche" containing the name of Cleopatra. After this astonishing feat of comparative translation, other hieroglyphs could be deciphered as well, and the history of a whole civilization, previously unknown, was suddenly revealed. Throughout Egypt, stones silent for thousands of years spoke to those who could now understand them.

Finding The Tomb

The history of the Valley, as I have endeavoured to show in former chapters, has never lacked the dramatic element, and in this, the latest episode, it has held to its traditions. For consider the circumstances. This was to be our final season in the Valley. Six full seasons we had excavated there, and season after season had drawn a blank; we had worked for months at a stretch and found nothing, and only an excavator knows how desperately depressing that can be; we had almost made up our minds that we were beaten, and were preparing to leave the Valley and try our luck elsewhere; and then—hardly had we sat hoe to ground in our last despairing effort than we made a discovery that far exceeded our wildest dreams. Surely, never before in the whole history of excavation has a full digging season been compressed within the space of five days.

Let me try and tell the story of it all. It will not be easy, for the dramatic suddenness of the initial discovery left me in a dazed condition, and the months that have followed have been so crowded with incident that I have hardly had time to think. Setting it down on paper will perhaps give me a chance to realize what has happened and all that it means.

I arrived in Luxor[1] on 28 October, and by 1 November I had enrolled my workmen and was ready to begin. Our former excavations had stopped short at the north-east corner of the tomb of Rameses VI, and from this point I started trenching southwards. It will be remembered that in this area there were a number of roughly constructed workmen's huts, used probably by the labourers in the tomb of Rameses. These huts, built about three feet above bed-rock, covered the whole area in front of the Ramesside tomb, and continued in a southerly direction to join up with a similar group of huts on the opposite side of the Valley, discovered by Davis in connexion with his work on the Akhenaton[2] cache. By the evening of 3 November we had laid bare a sufficient number of these huts for experimental purposes, so, after we had planned and noted them, they were removed, and we were ready to clear away the three feet of soil that lay beneath them.

Hardly had I arrived on the work next morning (4 November) than the unusual silence, due to the stoppage of the work, made me realize that something out of the ordinary had happened, and I was greeted by the announcement that a step cut in the rock had been discovered underneath the very first hut to be attacked. This seemed too good to be true, but a short amount of extra clearing revealed the fact that we were actually in the entrance of a steep cut in the rock, some thirteen feet below the entrance to the tomb of Rameses VI, and a similar depth from the present bed level of the Valley. The manner of cutting was that of the sunken stairway entrance so common in the Valley, and I almost dared to hope that we had found our tomb at last. Work continued feverishly throughout the whole of that day and the morning of the next, but it was not until the afternoon of 5 November that we succeeded in clearing away the masses of rubbish that overlay the cut, and were able to demarcate the upper edges of the stairway on all its four sides.

5   It was clear by now beyond any question that we actually had before us the entrance to a tomb, but doubts, born of previous disappointments, persisted in creeping in. There was always the horrible possibility, suggested by our experience in the Thothmes III Valley, that the tomb was an unfinished one, never completed and never used: if it had been finished there was the depressing probability that it had been completely plundered in ancient times. On the other hand, there was just the chance of an untouched or only partially plundered tomb, and it was with ill-suppressed excitement that I watched the descending steps of the staircase, as one by one they came to light. The cutting was excavated in the side of a small hillock, and, as the work progressed, its western edge receded under the slope of the rock until it was, first partially, and then completely, roofed in, and became a passage, ten feet high by six feet wide. Work progressed more rapidly now; step succeeded step, and at the level of the twelfth, towards

[1]*Luxor*: ancient city in central Egypt, on the Nile River, near the Valley of the Tombs of the Kings containing the temples and burial mounds of the pharoahs.
[2]*Akenaton*: Egyptian king (c. 372– 54 B.C.); a religious innovator who embraced solar monotheism, holding that he was the offspring of the sun.

sunset, there was disclosed the upper part of a doorway, blocked, plastered, and sealed.

A sealed doorway—it was actually true, then! Our years of patient labour were to be rewarded after all, and I think my first feeling was one of congratulation that my faith in the Valley had not been unjustified. With excitement growing to fever heat I searched the seal impressions on the door for evidence of the identity of the owner, but could find no name: the only decipherable ones were those of the well-known royal necropolis seal, the jackal and nine captives. Two facts, however, were clear: first, the employment of this royal seal was certain evidence that the tomb had been constructed for a person of very high standing; and second, that the sealed door was entirely screened from above by workmen's huts of the Twentieth Dynasty was sufficiently clear proof that at least from that date it had never been entered. With that for the moment I had to be content.

While examining the seals I noticed, at the top of the doorway, where some of the plaster had fallen away, a heavy wooden lintel. Under this, to assure myself of the method by which the doorway had been blocked, I made a small peephole, just large enough to insert an electric torch, and discovered that the passage beyond the door was filled completely from floor to ceiling with stones and rubble—additional proof this of the care with which the tomb had been protected.

It was a thrilling moment for an excavator. Alone, save for my native workmen, I found myself, after years of comparatively unproductive labour, on the threshold of what might prove to be a magnificent discovery. Anything, literally anything, might lie beyond that passage, and it needed all my self-control to keep from breaking down the doorway, and investigating then and there.

One thing puzzled me, and that was the smallness of the opening in comparison with the ordinary Valley tombs. The design was certainly of the Eighteenth Dynasty. Could it be the tomb of a noble buried here by royal consent? Was it a royal cache, a hiding-place to which a mummy and its equipment had been removed for safety? Or was it actually the tomb of the king for whom I had spent so many years in search.

Once more I examined the seal impressions for a clue, but on the part 10
of the door so far laid bare only those of the royal necropolis seal already mentioned were clear enough to read. Had I but known that a few inches lower down there was a perfectly clear and distinct impression of the seal of Tutankhamen, the king I most desired to find, I would have cleared on, had a much better night's rest in consequence, and saved myself nearly three weeks of uncertainty. It was late, however, and darkness was already upon us. With some reluctance I re-closed the small hole that I had made, filled in our excavation for protection during the night, selected the most trustworthy of my workmen—themselves almost as excited as I was—to watch all night above the tomb, and so home by moonlight, riding down the Valley.

Naturally my wish was to go straight ahead with our clearing to find out the full extent of the discovery, but Lord Carnarvon was in England, and in fairness to him I had to delay matters until he could come.

Accordingly, on the morning of 6 November I sent him the following cable: "At last have made wonderful discovery in Valley; a magnificent tomb with seals intact; re-covered same for your arrival; congratulations."

My next task was to secure the doorway against interference until such time as it could finally be reopened. This we did by filling our excavation up again to surface level, and rolling on top of it the large flint boulders of which the workmen's huts had been composed. By the evening of the same day, exactly forty-eight hours after we had discovered the first step of the staircase, this was accomplished. The tomb had vanished. So far as the appearance of the ground was concerned there never had been any tomb, and I found it hard to persuade myself at times that the whole episode had not been a dream.

I was soon to be reassured on this point. News travels fast in Egypt, and within two days of the discovery congratulations, inquiries, and offers of help descended upon me in a steady stream from all directions. It became clear, even at this early stage, that I was in for a job that could not be tackled single-handed, so I wired to Callender, who had helped me on various previous occasions, asking him if possible to join me without delay, and to my relief he arrived on the very next day. On the 8th I had received two messages from Lord Carnarvon in answer to my cable, the first of which read, "Possibly come soon," and the second, received a little later, "Propose arrive Alexandria 20th."

We had thus nearly a fortnight's grace, and we devoted it to making preparations of various kinds, so that when the time of reopening came, we should be able, with the least possible delay, to handle any situation that might arise. On the night of the 18th I went to Cairo for three days, to meet Lord Carnarvon and make a number of necessary purchases, returning to Luxor on the 21st. On the 23rd Lord Carnarvon arrived in Luxor with his daughter, Lady Evelyn Herbert, his devoted companion in all his Egyptian work, and everything was in hand for the beginning of the second chapter of the discovery of the tomb. Callender had been busy all day clearing away the upper layer of rubbish, so that by morning we should be able to get into the staircase without any delay.

15   By the afternoon of the 24th the whole staircase was clear, sixteen steps in all, and we were able to make a proper examination of the sealed doorway. On the lower part the seal impressions were much clearer, and we were able without any difficulty to make out on several of them the name of Tutankhamen. This added enormously to the interest of the discovery. If we had found, as seemed almost certain, the tomb of that shadowy monarch, whose tenure of the throne coincided with one of the most interesting periods in the whole of Egyptian history, we should indeed have reason to congratulate ourselves.

With heightened interest, if that were possible, we renewed our investigation of the doorway. Here for the first time a disquieting element made its appearance. Now that the whole door was exposed to light it was possible to discern a fact that had hitherto escaped notice—that there had been two successive openings and reclosings of a part of its surface: furthermore, that the sealing originally discovered, the jackal and nine captives, had been applied to the re-closed portions, whereas the sealings of Tutankhamen covered the untouched part of the doorway, and were therefore those with which the tomb had been originally secured. The tomb then was not absolutely intact, as we had hoped. Plunderers had entered it, and entered it more than once—from the evidence of the huts above, plunderers of a date not later than the reign of Rameses VI—but that they had not rifled it completely was evident from the fact that it had been re-sealed.

Then came another puzzle. In the lower strata of rubbish that filled the staircase we found masses of broken potsherds and boxes, the latter bearing the names of Akhenaten, Smenkhkare and Tutankhamen, and, what was much more upsetting, a scarab of Thothmes III and a fragment with the name of Amenhetep III. Why this mixture of names? The balance of evidence so far would seem to indicate a cache rather than a tomb, and at this stage in the proceedings we inclined more and more to the opinion that we were about to find a miscellaneous collection of objects of the Eighteenth Dynasty kings, brought from Tell el Amarna by Tutankhamen and deposited here for safety.

So matters stood on the evening of the 24th. On the following day the sealed doorway was to be removed, so Callender set carpenters to work making a heavy wooden grille to be set up in its place. Mr. Engelbach, Chief Inspector of the Antiquities Department, paid us a visit during the afternoon, and witnessed part of the final clearing of rubbish from the doorway.

On the morning of the 25th the seal impressions on the doorway were carefully noted and photographed, and then we removed the actual blocking of the door, consisting of rough stones carefully built from floor to lintel, and heavily plastered on their outer faces to take the seal impressions.

This disclosed the beginning of a descending passage (not a staircase), the same width as the entrance stairway, and nearly seven feet high. As I had already discovered from my hole in the doorway, it was filled completely with stone and rubble, probably the chip from its own excavation. This filling, like the doorway, showed distinct signs of more than one opening and re-closing of the tomb, the untouched part consisting of clean white chip, mingled with dust, whereas the disturbed part was composed mainly of dark flint. It was clear that an irregular tunnel had been cut through the original filling at the upper corner on the left side, a tunnel corresponding in position with that of the hole in the doorway. [20]

As we cleared the passage we found, mixed with the rubble of the lower levels, broken potsherds, jar sealings, alabaster jars, whole and broken, vases of painted pottery, numerous fragments of smaller articles, and water skins, these last having obviously been used to bring up the water needed for the plastering of the doorways. These were clear evidence of plundering, and we eyed them askance. By night we had cleared a considerable distance down the passage, but as yet saw no sign of second doorway or of chamber.

The day following (26 November) was the day of days, the most wonderful that I have ever lived through, and certainly one whose like I can never hope to see again. Throughout the morning the work of clearing continued, slowly perforce, on account of the delicate objects that were mixed with the filling. Then, in the middle of the afternoon, thirty feet down from the outer door, we came upon a second sealed doorway, almost an exact replica of the first. The seal impressions in this case were less distinct, but still recognizable as those of Tutankhamen and of the royal necropolis. Here again the signs of opening and reclosing were clearly marked upon the plaster. We were firmly convinced by this time that it was a cache that we were about to open, and not a tomb. The arrangement of stairway, entrance passage and doors reminded us very forcibly of the cache of Akhenaten and Tyi material found in the very near vicinity of the present excavation by Davis, and the fact that Tutankhamen's seals occurred there likewise seemed almost certain proof that we were right in our conjecture. We were soon to know. There lay the sealed doorway, and behind it was the answer to the question.

Slowly, desperately slowly it seemed to us as we watched, the remains of passage debris that encumbered the lower part of the doorway were removed, until at last we had the whole door clear before us. The decisive moment had arrived. With trembling hands I made a tiny breach in the upper left-hand corner. Darkness and blank space, as far as an iron testing-rod could reach, showed that whatever lay beyond was empty, and not filled like the passage we had just cleared. Candle tests were applied as a precaution against foul gases, and then, widening the hole a little, I inserted the candle and peered in, Lord Carnarvon, Lady Evelyn and Callender standing anxiously beside me to hear the verdict. At first I could see nothing, the hot air escaping from the chamber causing the candle flame to flicker, but presently, as my eyes grew accustomed to the light, details of the room within emerged slowly from the midst, strange animals, statues, and gold—everywhere the glint of gold. For the moment, an eternity it must have seemed to the others standing by—I was struck dumb with amazement, and when Lord Carnarvon, unable to stand the suspense any longer, inquired anxiously, "Can you see anything?" it was all I could do to get out the words. "Yes, wonderful things." Then, widening the hole a little further, so that we both could see, we inserted an electric torch.

READING CRITICALLY FOR IDEAS, STRUCTURE, AND STYLE

1. Carter's account of the excavation of the tomb of Tutankhamen emphasizes the many obstacles he had to overcome. How is his account organized to enable his readers to understand the demanding nature of the work that archeologists do?

2. What can you infer about the attitude of the ancient Egyptians towards their pharoahs and the elaborate means deployed (often unsuccessful) to prevent tombs from being plundered?

3. How does Carter organize his essay to heighten suspense as to whether the tomb was still intact or had been previously ransacked by robbers?

EXTENDING INSIGHTS THROUGH WRITING

1. Carter's excavation gave rise to legends connected with the so-called "Mummy's curse," the subject of many films. What recent incarnations has this story assumed, and why do you think it exercises such a hold on the popular imagination? For example, you might rent the 2001 film *Return of the Mummy* and analyze the mythic themes in it.

   Details on the historical basis for the "Mummy's curse," such as the untimely death of Lord Carnarvon (Carter's sponsor) and scores of people connected with the discovery of the tomb, can be found @ <http: //www.unmuseum.org/mummy.htm>.

2. Consult the archives of Carter's records at the Web site of the Ashmolean Museum in Oxford, England, which includes sketches, notes, photographs, diaries and maps, @ <http: //www.ashmol.ox.ac.uk/gri/4tut.html>. In a few paragraphs, discuss how these resources were blended into a coherent narrative by Carter.

CONNECTING PERSPECTIVES ON THE HISTORICAL DIMENSION

1. What insight does Thomas Carlyle's analysis in "On Heroes and Hero-Worship" of the larger-than-life meanings projected onto heroes give you into the role of the pharoahs in ancient Egypt, as described by Carter?

2. Arnold J. Toynbee's contrast of primitive societies (who worship dead ancestors) with forward-looking societies (who idolize creative living personalities) would seem to be at odds with Carter's findings. In a short paper, draw on both accounts and discuss this seeming paradox.

ARNOLD J. TOYNBEE

Challenge and Response

BACKGROUND

Arnold J. Toynbee (1889– 1975), perhaps the greatest modern historian, was educated at Winchester and Balliol College, Oxford. He was professor
of Byzantine and modern Greek language, literature, and history at King's
College, London (1919– 1924). From 1925 to 1955, when he retired, Toynbee
held the chair of research professor of international history at the University
of London and was also the director of studies at the Royal Institute of
International Affairs. His monumental comparison of the historical patterns
of twenty-six civilizations, in *A Study of History*, was published in ten volumes
between 1934 and 1954. Toynbee's research focused on questions of how civilizations were created and why some flourished while others failed. Toynbee
discovered that challenges (such as those of climate and foreign invasion) great
enough to cause extinction of culture but not so severe that the culture could
not respond creatively was the ideal condition in which great civilizations
developed. In "Challenge and Response," from *A Study of History*, Toynbee
uses analogy as his main expository principle to synthesize conclusions he
reached on the rise and decline of civilizations.

APPROACHING TOYNBEE'S ESSAY

Toynbee's essay gives new insights into the work of the historian: He
takes examples and theories from many disciplines, especially literature and
religion, and uses them to prove his thesis on the evolution of civilizations. He
does not merely present facts, but investigates, interprets, organizes, and presents a coherent analysis, using material from many other disciplines to give
weight, perspective, and focus to his argument.

The crucial difference Toynbee discovered between primitive cultures
and higher cultures is that primitive societies remain static whereas higher
cultures respond creatively to challenge. This outside challenge may present
itself in many forms—ranging from threat by invasion, unexpected natural

244

disasters, other cultures competing for the same resources and trade routes—but Toynbee underscores the fact that no civilization has ever evolved without successfully responding to a grave threat to its integrity—hence, the title of his concluding chapter: "Challenge and Response."

Toynbee uses a vivid analogy to make his thesis clearer and to enable his readers to more easily grasp the distinction between cultures that remain stagnant and those that undergo a dynamic change and become a flourishing civilization.

Challenge and Response

THE PROBLEM STATED

What is the essential difference between the primitive and the higher societies? It does not consist in the presence or absence of institutions for institutions are the vehicles of the impersonal relations between individuals in which all societies have their existence, because even the smallest of primitive societies is built on a wider basis than the narrow circle of an individual's direct personal ties. Institutions are attributes of the whole genus "societies" and therefore common properties of both its species. Primitive societies have their institutions—the religion of the annual agricultural cycle; totemism and exogamy; tabus, initiations and age-classes; segregations of the sexes, at certain stages of life, in separate communal establishments—and some of these institutions are certainly as elaborate and perhaps as subtle as those which are characteristic of civilizations.

Nor are civilizations distinguished from primitive societies by the division of labour, for we can discern at least the rudiments of the division of labour in the lives of primitive societies also. Kings, magicians, smiths and minstrels are all "specialists"—though the fact that Hephaestus,[1] the smith of Hellenic legend, is lame, and Homer, the poet of Hellenic legends, is blind, suggests that in primitive societies specialism is abnormal and apt to be confined to those who lack the capacity to be "all-round men" or "jacks of all trades."

An essential difference between civilizations and primitive societies *as we know them* (the *caveat*[2] will be found to be important) is the direction taken by mimesis or imitation. Mimesis is a generic feature of all social life. Its operation can be observed both in primitive societies and in civilizations, in every social activity from the imitation of the style of film-stars by their

---

[1]The Greek god of fire, metallurgy, and craftsmanship.
[2]Something important to remember, a significant reservation.

humbler sisters upwards. It operates, however, in different directions in the two species of society. In primitive societies, as we know them, mimesis is directed towards the older generation and towards dead ancestors who stand, unseen but not unfelt, at the back of the living elders, reinforcing their prestige. In a society where mimesis is thus directed backward towards the past, custom rules and society remains static. On the other hand, in societies in process of civilization, mimesis is directed towards creative personalities who commanded a following because they are pioneers. In such societies, "the cake of custom," as Walter Bagehot[3] called it in his *Physics and Politics*, is broken and society is in dynamic motion along a course of change and growth.

But if we ask ourselves whether this difference between primitive and higher societies is permanent and fundamental, we must answer in the negative; for, if we only know primitive societies in a static condition, that is because we know them from direct observation only in the last phases of their histories. Yet, though direct observation fails us, a train of reasoning informs us that there must have been earlier phases in the histories of primitive societies in which these were moving more dynamically than any 'civilized' society has moved yet. We have said that primitive societies are as old as the human race, but we should more properly have said that they are older. Social and institutional life of a kind is found among some of the higher mammals other than man, and it is clear that mankind could not have become human except in a social environment. This mutation of subman into man, which was accomplished, in circumstances of which we have no record, under the aegis of primitive societies, was a more profound change, a greater step in growth, than any progress which man has yet achieved under the aegis of civilization.

Primitive societies, as we know them by direct observation, may be likened to people lying torpid upon a ledge on a mountain-side, with a precipice below and a precipice above; civilizations may be likened to companions of these sleepers who have just risen to their feet and have started to climb up the face of the cliff above; while we for our part may liken ourselves to observers whose field of vision is limited to the ledge and to the lower slopes of the upper precipice and who have come upon the scene at the moment when the different members of the party happen to be in these respective postures and positions. At first sight we may be inclined to draw an absolute distinction between the two groups, acclaiming the climbers as athletes and dismissing the recumbent figures as paralytics; but on second thoughts we shall find it more prudent to suspend judgement.

After all the recumbent figures cannot be paralytics in reality; for they cannot have been born on the ledge, and no human muscles except their own can have hoisted them to this halting-place up the face of the precipice below. On the other hand, their companions who are climbing at the moment have only just left this same ledge and started to climb the precipice above; and, since the next ledge is out of sight, we do not know how high or how arduous the next pitch may be. We only know that it is impossible

[3]Nineteenth-century economist.

to halt and rest before the next ledge, wherever that may lie, is reached. Thus, even if we could estimate each present climber's strength and skill and nerve, we could not judge whether any of them have any prospect of gaining the ledge above, which is the goal of their present endeavours. We can, however, be sure that some of them will never attain it. And we can observe that, for every single one now strenuously climbing, twice that number (our extinct civilization) have fallen back onto the ledge, defeated. . . .

This alternating rhythm of static and dynamic, of movement and pause and movement, has been regarded by many observers in many different ages as something fundamental in the nature of the Universe. In their pregnant imagery the sages of the Sinic[4] Society described these alternations in terms of Yin and Yang—Yin the static and Yang the dynamic. The nucleus of the Sinic character which stands for Yin seems to represent dark coiling clouds overshadowing the Sun, while the nucleus of the character which stands for Yang seems to represent the unclouded sun-disk emitting its rays. In the Chinese formula Yin is always mentioned first, and within our field of vision, we can see that our breed, having reached the "ledge" of primitive human nature 300,000 years ago, has reposed there for ninety-eight per cent of that period before entering on the Yang-activity of civilization. We have now to seek for the positive factor, whatever it may be, which has set human life in motion again by its impetus. . . .

THE MYTHOLOGICAL CLUE

An encounter between two superhuman personalities is the plot of some of the greatest dramas that the human imagination has conceived. An encounter between Yahweh[5] and the Serpent is the plot of the story of the Fall of Man in the Book of Genesis; a second encounter between the same antagonists, transfigured by a progressive enlightenment of Syriac souls, is the plot of the New Testament which tells the story of the Redemption; an encounter between the Lord and Satan is the plot of the Book of Job; an encounter between the Lord and Mephistopheles is the plot of Goethe's *Faust*; an encounter between Gods and Demons is the plot of the Scandinavian *Voluspa*;[6] an encounter between Artemis and Aphrodite[7] is the plot of Euripides' *Hippolytus*.

We find another version of the same plot in that ubiquitous and ever-recurring myth—a "primordial image" if ever there was one—of the encounter between the Virgin and the Father of her Child. The characters in this myth have played their allotted parts on a thousand different stages under an infinite variety of names: Danae and the Shower of Gold; Europa and the Bull; Semele the Stricken Earth and Zeus the Sky that launches the thunderbolt; Creusa and Apollo in Euripides' *Ion*; Psyche and Cupid;

---

[4]"Sinic" refers to the Chinese.
[5]Jehovah.
[6]An ancient epic poem in Old Norse.
[7]The play by Euripides focuses on Aphrodite's (the goddess of love) revenge against Hippolytus, who was vowed to chastity as a follower of Artemis (Diana).

Gretchen and Faust. The theme recurs, transfigured, in the Annuniciation. In our own day in the West this protean myth has re-expressed itself as the last word of our astronomers on the genesis of the planetary system, as witness the following *credo*:

> "We believe . . . that some two thousand million years ago . . . a second star, wandering blindly through space, happened to come within hailing distance of the Sun. Just as the Sun and Moon raise tides on the Earth, this second star must have raised tides on the surface of the Sun. But they would be very different from the puny tides which the small mass of the Moon raises in our oceans; a huge tidal wave must have travelled over the surface of the Sun, ultimately forming a mountain of prodigious height, which would rise ever higher and higher as the cause of the disturbance came nearer and nearer. And, before the second star began to recede, its tidal pull had become so powerful that this mountain was torn to pieces and threw off small fragments of itself, much as the crest of a wave throws off spray. These small fragments have been circulating round their parent sun ever since. They are the planets, great and small, of which our Earth is one."[8]

10   Thus out of the mouth of the mathematical astronomer, when all his complex calculations are done, there comes forth, once again, the myth of the encounter between the Sun Goddess and her ravisher that is so familiar a tale in the mouths of the untutored children of nature.

The presence and potency of this duality in the causation of the civilizations whose geneses we are studying is admitted by a Modern Western archaeologist whose studies begin with a concentration on environment and end with an intuition of the mystery of life:

> "Environment . . . is not the total causation in culture-shaping. . . . It is, beyond doubt, the most conspicuous single factor. . . . But there is still an indefinable factor which may best be designated quite frankly as x, the unknown quantity, apparently psychological in kind. . . . If x be not the most conspicuous factor in the matter, it certainly is the most important, the most fate-laden."[9]

In our present study of history this insistent theme of the superhuman encounter has asserted itself already. At an early stage we observed that "a society . . . is confronted in the course of its life by a succession of problems" and that "the presentation of each problem is a challenge to undergo an ordeal."

[8]Sir James Jeans, *The Mysterious Universe* (Cambridge: Cambridge University Press, 1930), pp. 1–2.
[9]P. A. Means, *Ancient Civilizations of the Andes* (New York and London: Scribners, 1931), pp. 25–26.

Let us try to analyse the plot of this story or drama which repeats itself in such different contexts and in such various forms.

We may begin with two general features: the encounter is conceived of as a rare and sometimes as a unique event; and it has consequences which are vast in proportion to the vastness of the breach which it makes in the customary course of nature.

Even in the easy-going world of Hellenic mythology, where the gods saw the daughters of men that they were fair, and had their way with so many of them that their victims could be marshalled and paraded in poetic catalogues, such incidents never ceased to be sensational affairs and invariably resulted in the births of heroes. In the versions of the plot in which both parties to the encounter are superhuman, the rarity and momentousness of the event are thrown into stronger relief. In the Book of Job, "the day when the Sons of God came to present themselves before the Lord, and Satan came also among them," is evidently conceived of as an unusual occasion; and so is the encounter between the Lord and Mephistopheles in the "Prologue in Heaven" (suggested, of course, by the opening of the Book of Job) which starts the action of Goethe's *Faust*. In both these dramas the consequences on Earth of the encounter in Heaven are tremendous. The personal ordeals of Job and Faust represent, in the intuitive language of fiction, the infinitely multiple ordeal of mankind; and, in the language of theology, the same vast consequence is represented as following from the superhuman encounters that are portrayed in the Book of Genesis and in the New Testament. The expulsion of Adam and Eve from the Garden of Eden, which follows the encounter between Yahweh and the Serpent, is nothing less than the Fall of Man; the passion of Christ in the New Testament is nothing less than Man's Redemption. Even the birth of our planetary system from the encounter of two suns, as pictured by our modern astronomer, is declared by the same authority to be "an event of almost unimaginable rarity."

In every case the story opens with a perfect state of Yin. Faust is perfect in knowledge; Job is perfect in goodness and prosperity; Adam and Eve are perfect in innocence and ease; the Virgins—Gretchen, Danae and the rest—are perfect in purity and beauty. In the astronomer's universe the Sun, a perfect orb, travels on its course intact and whole. When Yin is thus complete, it is ready to pass over into Yang. But what is to make it pass? A change in a state which, by definition, is perfect after its kind can only be started by an impulse or motive which comes from outside. If we think of the state as one of physical equilibrium, we must bring in another star. If we think of it as one of psychic beatitude or *nirvana*,[10] we must bring another actor on to the stage: a critic to set the mind thinking again by suggesting doubts; an adversary to set the heart feeling again by instilling distress or discontent or fear or antipathy. This is the role of the Serpent in Genesis, of Satan in the Book of Job, or Mephistopheles in *Faust*, of Loki in the Scandinavian mythology, of the Divine Lovers in the Virgin myths.

---

[10]In Buddhism, a state of enlightenment free from passion and illusion.

In the language of science we may say that the function of the intruding factor is to supply that on which it intrudes with a stimulus of the kind best calculated to evoke the most potently creative variations. In the language of mythology and theology, the impulse or motive which makes a perfect Yin-state pass over into new Yang-activity comes from an intrusion of the Devil into the universe of God. The event can best be described in these mythological images because they are not embarrassed by the contradiction that arises when the statement is translated into logical terms. In logic, if God's universe is perfect, there cannot be a Devil outside it, while, if the Devil exists, the perfection which he comes to spoil must have been incomplete already through the very fact of his existence. This logical contradiction, which cannot be logically resolved, is intuitively transcended in the imagery of the poet and prophet, who give glory to an omnipotent God yet take it for granted that He is subject to two crucial limitations.

The first limitation is that, in the perfection of what He has created already, He cannot find an opportunity for further creative activity. If God is conceived of as transcendent, the works of creation are as glorious as ever they were but they cannot "be changed from glory into glory." The second limitation on God's power is that when the opportunity for fresh creation is offered to Him from outside He cannot but take it. When the Devil challenges Him He cannot refuse to take the challenge up. God is bound to accept the predicament because He can refuse only at the price of denying His own nature and ceasing to be God.

If God is thus not omnipotent in logical terms, is He still mythologically invincible? If He is bound to take up the Devil's challenge, is He also bound to win the ensuing battle? In Euripides' *Hippolytus*, where God's part is played by Artemis and the Devil's by Aphrodite, Artemis is not only unable to decline the combat but is foredoomed to defeat. The relations between the Olympians are anarchic and Artemis in the epilogue can console herself only by making up her mind that one day she will play the Devil's role herself at Aphrodite's expense. The result is not creation but destruction. In the Scandinavian version destruction is likewise the outcome in Ragnarök[11] —when "Gods and Demons slay and are slain"—though the unique genius of the author of *Voluspa* makes his Sibyl's vision pierce the gloom to behold the light of a new dawn beyond it. On the other hand, in another version of the plot, the combat which follows the compulsory acceptance of the challenge takes the form, not of an exchange of fire in which the Devil has the first shot and cannot fail to kill his man, but of a wager which the Devil is apparently bound to lose. The classic works in which this wager *motif* is worked out are the Book of Job and Goethe's *Faust*.

It is in Goethe's drama that the point is most clearly made. After the Lord has accepted the wager with Mephistopheles in Heaven, the terms are agreed on Earth, between Mephistopheles and Faust, as follows:

---

[11]In the *Volupsa*, a destructive battle between the gods and the powers of evil led by Loki, gives way to a vision (by the Sibyl, Voluspa) of a world resurrected through the efforts of the god Balder, where the sole surviving human beings, called "Life" and "Desiring Life" repopulate the earth.

Faust.   Comfort and quiet—no, no! none of these
           For me—I ask them not—I seek them not.
           If ever I upon the bed of sloth
           Lie down and rest, then be the hour in which
           I so lie down and rest my last of life.
           Canst thou by falsehood or by flattery
           Delude me into self-complacent smiles,
           Cheat me into tranquillity? Come then,
           And welcome, life's last day—be this our wager.
Meph.   Done.
Faust.   Done, say I: clench we at once the bargain.
    If ever time should flow so calmly on,
    Soothing my spirits in such oblivion
    That in the pleasnt trance I would arrest
    And hail the happy moment in its course,
    Bidding it linger with me. . . .
    Then willingly do I consent to perish.[12]

The bearing of this mythical compact upon our problem of the geneses of civilizations can be brought out by identifying Faust, at the moment when he makes his bet, with one of those "awakened sleepers" who have risen from the ledge on which they had been lying torpid and have started to climb on up the face of the cliff. In the language of our simile, Faust is saying: "I have made up my mind to leave this ledge and climb this precipice in search of the next ledge above. In attempting this I am aware that I am leaving safety behind me. Yet, for the sake of the possibility of achievement, I will take the risk of a fall and destruction."

In the story as told by Goethe the intrepid climber, after an ordeal of mortal dangers and desperate reverses, succeeds in the end in scaling the cliff triumphantly. In the New Testament the same ending is given, through the revelation of a second encounter between the same pair of antagonists, to the combat between Yahweh and the Serpent which, in the original version in Genesis, had ended rather in the manner of the combat between Artemis and Aphrodite in the *Hippolytus*.

In Job, *Faust* and the New Testament alike it is suggested, or even declared outright, that the wager cannot be won by the Devil; that the Devil, in meddling with God's work, cannot frustrate but can only serve the purpose of God, who remains master of the situation all the time and gives the Devil rope for the Devil to hang himself. Then has the Devil been created? Did God accept a wager which He knew He could not lose? That would be a hard saying; for if it were true the whole transaction would have been a sham. An encounter which was no encounter could not produce the consequences of an encounter—the vast cosmic consequence of causing Yin to pass over into Yang. Perhaps the explanation is that the wager which the Devil offers and which God accepts covers, and thereby puts in real jeopardy, a part of God's creation but not the whole of it. The part really is at

---

[12]*Faust*, 11. 1692–1706 (John Anster's translation).

stake; and, though the whole is not, the chances and changes to which the part is exposed cannot conceivably leave the whole unaffected. In the language of mythology, when one of God's creatures is tempted by the Devil, God Himself is thereby given the opportunity to re-create the World. The Devil's intervention, whether it succeeds or fails on the particular issue—and either result is possible—has accomplished that transition from Yin to Yang for which God has been yearning.

As for the human protagonist's part, suffering is the keynote of it in every presentation of the drama, whether the player of the part is Jesus or Job or Faust or Adam and Eve. The picture of Adam and Eve in the Garden of Eden is a reminiscence of the Yin-state to which primitive man attained in the food-gathering phase of economy, after he had established his ascendancy over the rest of the flora and fauna of the Earth. The Fall, in response to the temptation to eat of the Tree of the Knowledge of Good and Evil, symbolizes the acceptance of a challenge to abandon this achieved integration and to venture upon a fresh differentiation out of which a fresh integration may—or may not—arise. The expulsion from the Garden into an unfriendly world in which the Woman must bring forth children in sorrow and the Man must eat bread in the sweat of his face, is the ordeal which the acceptance of the Serpent's challenge has entailed. The sexual intercourse between Adam and Eve, which follows, is an act of social creation. It bears fruit in the birth of two sons who impersonate two nascent civilizations: Abel the keeper of sheep and Cain the tiller of the ground.

25   In our own generation, one of our most distinguished and original-minded students of the physical environment of human life tells the same story in his own way:

"Ages ago a band of naked, houseless, fireless savages started from their warm home in the torrid zone and pushed steadily northward from the beginning of spring to the end of summer. They never guessed that they had left the land of constant warmth until in September they began to feel an uncomfortable chill at night. Day by day it grew worse. Not knowing its cause, they travelled this way or that to escape. Some went southward, but only a handful returned to their former home. There they resumed the old life, and their descendants are untutored savages to this day. Of those who wandered in other directions, all perished except one small band. Finding that they could not escape the nipping air, the members of this band used the loftiest of human faculties, the power of conscious invention. Some tried to find shelter by digging in the ground, some gathered branches and leaves to make huts and warm beds, and some wrapped themselves in the skins of the beasts that they had slain. Soon these savages had taken some of the greatest steps towards civilization. The naked were clothed; the houseless sheltered; the improvident learnt to dry meat and store it, with nuts, for the winter; and at last the art of preparing fire was discovered as a means of keeping warm. Thus they subsisted where at first they thought that they were doomed. And in the process of adjusting themselves to a hard environment they advanced by enormous strides, leaving the tropical part of mankind far in the rear."[13]

A classical scholar likewise translates the story into the scientific terminology of our age:

"It is . . . a paradox of advancement that, if Necessity be the mother of Invention, the other parent is Obstinacy, the determination that you will go on living under adverse conditions rather than cut your losses and go where life is easier. It was no accident, that is, that civilization, as we know it, began in that ebb and flow of climate, flora and fauna which characterizes the fourfold Ice Age. Those primates who just 'got out' as arboreal conditions wilted retained their primacy among the servants of natural law, but they forewent the conquest of nature. Those others won through, and became men, who stood their ground when they were no more trees to sit in, who 'made do' with meat when fruit did not ripen, who made fires and clothes rather than follow the sunshine; who fortified their lairs and trained their young and vindicated the reasonableness of a world that seemed so reasonless."[14]

The first stage, then, of the human protagonist's ordeal is a transition from Yin to Yang through a dynamic act—performed by God's creature under temptation from the Adversary—which enables God Himself to resume His creative activity. But this progress has to be paid for; and it is not God but God's servant, the human sower, who pays the price. Finally, after many vicissitudes, the sufferer triumphant serves as the pioneer. The human protagonist in the divine drama not only serves God by enabling Him to renew His creation but also serves his fellow men by pointing the way for others to follow. . . .

THE MYTH APPLIED TO THE PROBLEM

The Unpredictable Factor

By the light of mythology we have gained some insight into the nature of challenges and responses. We have come to see that creation is the outcome of an encounter, that genesis is a product of interaction. . . . We shall no longer be surprised if, in the production of civilizations, the same race or the same environment appears to be fruitful in one instance and sterile in another. . . . We shall be prepared now to recognize that, even if we were exactly acquainted with all the racial, environmental, and other data that

---

[13]Ellsworth Huntington, *Civilization and Climate*, 3rd edition (New Haven: Yale University Press, 1924), pp. 405–406.

[14]J. L. Myres, *Who Were the Greeks?* (Berkeley: University of California Press, 1930), pp. 277–278.

are capable of being formulated scientifically, we should not be able to predict the outcome of the interaction between the forces which these data represent, any more than a military expert can predict the outcome of a battle or campaign from an "inside knowledge" of the dispositions and resources of both the opposing general staffs, or a bridge expert the outcome of a game from a similar knowledge of all the cards in every hand.

30   In both these analogies "inside knowledge" is not sufficient to enable its possessor to predict results with any exactness or assurance because it is not the same thing as complete knowledge. There is one thing which must remain an unknown quantity to the best-informed onlooker because it is beyond the knowledge of the combatants, or players, themselves; and it is the most important term in the equation which the would-be calculator has to solve. This unknown quantity is the reaction of the actors to the ordeal when it actually comes. These psychological momenta, which are inherently impossible to weigh and measure and therefore to estimate scientifically in advance, are the very forces which actually decide the issue when the encounter takes place. And that is why the very greatest military geniuses have admitted an incalculable element in their successes. If religious, they have attributed their victories to God, like Cromwell; if merely superstitious, to the ascendancy of their "star," like Napoleon.

READING CRITICALLY FOR IDEAS, STRUCTURE, AND STYLE

1. Toynbee's analysis of how civilizations are created, and why some flourish while others fail, begins by examining "mimesis," or imitation in societies at different levels. What does he mean by this?

2. How does Toynbee use the analogy of the "cliff-climbers" and the "ledge-sitters" to explain the difference between static and dynamic cultures?

3. According to Toynbee, how does mythology reflect his scenario of "challenge and response"?

EXTENDING INSIGHTS THROUGH WRITING

1. Draw on Toynbee's concept of "challenge and response" to analyze a current social, political, or even a personal situation. In your analysis, what form does the "adversary" take?

2. Write a short essay on the way "mimesis" functions in contemporary society in terms of who people choose to emulate (parents, peer group, politicians, artists, scientists, film stars) and whether our society is dynamic or static.

CONNECTING PERSPECTIVES ON THE HISTORICAL DIMENSION

1. How does Elaine Pagels's (see "The Social History of Satan") sociological explanation for the representation of evil as Satan contrast with Toynbee's "challenge and response" model of the "adversary"?

2. How is the rhetoric of John F. Kennedy's inaugural address designed to inspire Americans to become the kind of nation that Toynbee would see as dynamic and capable of responding to challenges creatively?

ELAINE PAGELS

The Social History of Satan

BACKGROUND

Elaine Pagels was born in 1943 in Palo Alto, California, and was educated at Stanford University and Harvard University, where she received her doctorate in 1970. Since 1982 she has been professor of religion at Princeton University. Pagel's highly original research and interpretations of historical documents centering on religions are grounded in her training as a scholar. She has received many awards, including the National Book Award in 1980 for *The Gnostic Gospels* (1979)—an investigation of fifty-two ancient scrolls, written in the Coptic language, that were discovered in 1945 by an Egyptian farmer. These have been likened in importance to the Dead Sea Scrolls and reveal the political battles within the early Christian church. Pagels's investigation of early Christianity continued in *Adam, Eve and the Serpent* (1988) and *The Origin of Satan: The New Testament Origins of Christianity's Demonization of Jews, Pagans, & Heretics* (1996), from which the following essay is drawn.

APPROACHING PAGELS'S ESSAY

Pagels has always been fascinated by the struggles within early Christianity to cope with their antagonists and with breakaway sects. In "The Social History of Satan," she explores how the concept of an evil entity served an enormously useful function in providing a common enemy, and a cosmic one at that, to unify the early Christians who were being persecuted. This process of demonization (whether they were Romans, pagans, Jews, or even their fellow Christians) reveals the psychodynamics of an embattled faith that needs to define itself in opposition to an arch fiend—Satan. Pagels examines the transformation of Satan from his depiction in the *Hebrew Bible* (where he is merely the adversary who tests the faithful) to the *Gospel's* vision of him as a Prince of Darkness who brings about the crucifixion of Jesus as part of the cosmic struggle between good and evil. Pagels illuminates her thesis with examples drawn from many sources, including biblical passages and commentaries by scholars and historians.

The Social History of Satan

At certain points in Israel's history, especially in times of crisis, war, and danger, a vociferous minority spoke out, not against the alien tribes and foreign armies ranged against Israel, but to blame Israel's misfortunes upon members of its own people. Such critics, sometimes accusing Israel as a whole, and sometimes accusing certain rulers, claimed that Israel's disobedience to God had brought down divine punishment.

The party that called for Israel's allegiance to "the Lord alone," including such prophets as Amos (c. 750 B.C.E.), Isaiah (c. 730 B.C.E.), and Jeremiah (c. 600 B.C.E.), indicted especially those Israelites who adopted foreign ways, particularly the worship of foreign gods.[1] Such prophets, along with their supporters, thought of Israel as a truly separate people, "holy to the Lord." The more radical prophets denounced those Israelites who tended toward assimilation as if they were as bad as the nations; only a remnant, they said, remained faithful to God.

Certain of these prophets, too, had called forth the monsters of Canaanite mythology to symbolize Israel's enemies.[2] Later (sixth century) material now included in the first part of the book of the prophet Isaiah proclaims that "the Lord is coming *to punish the inhabitants of the earth*; and the earth will disclose the blood shed upon her, and will no more cover the slain" (Isa. 26:21; emphasis added). The same author goes on, apparently in parallel imagery, to warn that "in that day, the Lord with his great hand will *punish the Leviathan, the twisting serpent, and he will slay the dragon that is in the sea*" (Isa. 27:1; emphasis added). The author of the second part of Isaiah also celebrates God's triumph over traditional mythological figures—over Rahab, "the dragon," and "the sea"—as he proclaims God's imminent triumph over Israel's enemies. Thereby, as the biblical scholar Jon Levenson observes, "the enemies cease to be merely earthly powers . . . and become, instead or in addition, cosmic forces of the utmost malignancy.[3]

---

[1]See Morton Smith, *Palestinian Parties and Politics That Shaped the Old Testament* (New York: Columbia University Press, 1971), especially 62–146; also Paul Hanson, *The Dawn of Apocalyptic* (Philadelphia: Fortress Press, 1975).

[2]Jon D. Levenson, *Creation and the Persistence of Evil: The Jewish Drama of Divine Omnipotence* (San Francisco: Harper and Row, 1988). I am grateful to John Collins for referring me to this work.

[3]*Ibid.*, 44.

Certain writers of the sixth century B.C.E. took a bold step further. They used mythological imagery to characterize their struggle against some of their fellow Israelites. But when Israelite writers excoriated their fellow Jews in mythological terms, the images they chose were usually not the animalistic or monstrous ones they regularly applied to their foreign enemies. Instead of Rahab, Leviathan, or "the dragon," most often they identified their Jewish enemies with an exalted, if treacherous, member of the divine court whom they called the *satan*. The *satan* is not an animal or monster but one of God's angels, a being of superior intelligence and status; apparently the Israelites saw their intimate enemies not as beasts and monsters but as *superhuman* beings whose superior qualities and insider status could make them more dangerous than the alien enemy.

In the Hebrew Bible, as in mainstream Judaism to this day, Satan never appears as Western Christendom has come to know him, as the leader of an "evil empire," an army of hostile spirits who make war on God and humankind alike.[4] As he first appears in the Hebrew Bible, Satan is not necessarily evil, much less opposed to God. On the contrary, he appears in the book of Numbers and in Job as one of God's obedient servants—a messenger, or *angel*, a word that translates the Hebrew term for messenger (*mal'āk*) into Greek (*angelos*). In Hebrew, the angels were often called "sons of God" (*benē'elōhim*), and were envisioned as the hierarchical ranks of a great army, or the staff of a royal court.

In biblical sources the Hebrew term the *satan* describes an adversarial role. It is not the name of a particular character.[5] Although Hebrew storytellers as early as the sixth century B.C.E. occasionally introduced a supernatural character whom they called the *satan*, what they meant was any one of the angels sent by God for the specific purpose of blocking or obstructing human activity. The root *śtn* means "one who opposes, obstructs, or acts as adversary." (The Greek term *diabolos*, later translated "devil," literally means "one who throws something across one's path.")

The *satan's* presence in a story could help account for unexpected obstacles or reversals of fortune. Hebrew storytellers often attribute misfortunes to human sin. Some, however, also invoke this supernatural character, the *satan*, who, by God's own order or permission, blocks or opposes human plans and desires. But this messenger is not necessarily malevolent. God sends him, like the angel of death, to perform a specific task,

---

[4]Many scholars have made this observation; for a recent discussion see Neil Forsyth, *The Old Enemy: Satan and the Combat Myth* (Princeton, NJ: Princeton University Press, 1987), 107: "In the collection of documents . . . known to Christians as the Old Testament, the word [Satan] never appears . . . as the name of the adversary. . . . rather, when the satan appears in the Old Testament, he is a member of the heavenly court, albeit with unusual tasks." See also the article on *démon*, in *La Dictionnaire de Spiritualité* 3 (Paris: Beauchesne, 1957), 142–46; H. A. Kelly, "Demonology and Diabolical Temptation," *Thought* 46 (1965): 165–70.

[5]M. Delcor, "Le Mythe de la chute des anges et l'origine des géants comme explication du mal dans le monde dans l'apocalyptique juive: Histoire des traditions," *Revue de l'histoire des religions* 190:5–12; P. Day, *An Adversary in Heaven: Satan in the Hebrew Bible* (Atlanta, GA.: Scholars Press, 1988).

although one that human beings may not appreciate; as the literary scholar Neil Forsyth says of the *satan*, "If the path is bad, an obstruction is good."[6] Thus the *satan* may simply have been sent by the Lord to protect a person from worse harm. The story of Balaam in the biblical book of Numbers, for example, tells of a man who decided to go where God had ordered him not to go. Balaam saddled his ass and set off, "but God's anger was kindled because he went; and the angel of the Lord took his stand in the road as his *satan*" [*le-śātān-lō*]—that is, as his adversary, or his obstructor. This supernatural messenger remained invisible to Balaam, but the ass saw him and stopped in her tracks:

> And the ass saw the angel of the Lord standing in the road, with a drawn sword in his hand; and the ass turned aside out of the road, and went into the field; and Balaam struck the ass, to turn her onto the road. Then the angel of the Lord stood in a narrow path between the vineyards, with a wall on each side. And when the ass saw the angel of the Lord, she pushed against the wall, so he struck her again (22:23–25).

The third time the ass saw the obstructing angel, she stopped and lay down under Balaam, "and Balaam's anger was kindled, and he struck the ass with his staff." Then, the story continues,

> the Lord opened the mouth of the ass, and she said to Balaam, "What have I done to you, that you have struck me three times?" And Balaam said to the ass, "Because you have made a fool of me. I wish I had a sword in my hand, for then I would kill you." And the ass said to Balaam, "Am I not your ass, that you have ridden all your life to this very day? Did I ever do such things to you?" And he said, "No" (22:28–30).

Then "the Lord opened the eyes of Balaam, and he saw the angel of the Lord standing in the way, with his drawn sword in his hand, and he bowed his head, and fell on his face." Then the *satan* rebukes Balaam, and speaks for his master, the Lord:

> "Why have you struck your ass three times? Behold, I came here to oppose you, because your way is evil in my eyes; and the ass saw me. . . . If she had not turned away from me, I would surely have killed you right then, and let her live" (22:31–33).

Chastened by this terrifying vision, Balaam agrees to do what God, [10] speaking through his *satan*, commands.

---

[6]Forsyth, *The Old Enemy*, 113.

The book of Job, too, describes the *satan* as a supernatural messenger, a member of God's royal court.[7] But while Balaam's *satan* protects him from harm, Job's *satan* takes a more adversarial role. Here the Lord himself admits that the *satan* incited him to act *against* Job (2:3). The story begins when the *satan* appears as an angel, a "son of God" (*ben'elōhīm*), a term that, in Hebrew idiom, often means "one of the divine beings." Here this angel, the *satan*, comes with the rest of the heavenly host on the day appointed for them to "present themselves before the Lord." When the Lord asks whence he comes, the *satan* answers, "From roaming on the earth, and walking up and down on it." Here the storyteller plays on the similarity between the sound of the Hebrew *satan* and *shūt*, the Hebrew word "to roam," suggesting that the *satan's* special role in the heavenly court is that of a kind of roving intelligence agent, like those whom many Jews of the time would have known—and detested—from the king of Persia's elaborate system of secret police and intelligence officers. Known as "the king's eye" or "the king's ear," these agents roamed the empire looking for signs of disloyalty among the people.[8]

God boasts to the *satan* about one of his most loyal subjects: "Have you considered my servant Job, that there is no one like him on earth, a blessed and upright man, who fears God and turns away from evil?" The *satan* then challenges the Lord to put Job to the test:

> "Does Job fear God for nothing? . . . You have blessed the work of his hands, and his possessions have increased. But put forth your hand now, and touch all that he has, and he will curse you to your face" (1:9–11).

The Lord agrees to test Job, authorizing the *satan* to afflict Job with devastating loss, but defining precisely how far he may go: "Behold, all that belongs to him is in your power; only do not touch the man himself." Job withstands the first deadly onslaught, the sudden loss of his sons and daughters in a single accident, the slaughter of his cattle, sheep, and camels, and the loss of all his wealth and property. When the *satan* appears again among the sons of God on the appointed day, the Lord points out that "Job still holds fast to his integrity, although you incited me against him, to harm him without cause." Then the *satan* asks that he increase the pressure:

> "Skin for skin. All that a man has he will give for his life. But put forth your hand now, and touch his flesh and his bone, and he will curse you to your face." And the Lord said to the *satan*, "Behold, he is in your power; only spare his life" (2:4–6).

According to the folktale, Job withstands the test, the *satan* retreats, and "the Lord restored the fortunes of Job . . . and he gave him twice as

[7]See discussion in Day, *An Adversary*, 69–106.
[8]Forsyth, *The Old Enemy*, 114.

much as he had before" (42:10). Here the *satan* terrifies and harms a person but, like the angel of death, remains an angel, a member of the heavenly court, God's obedient servant.

Around the time Job was written (c. 550 B.C.E.), however, other biblical writers invoked the *satan* to account for division within Israel.[9] One court historian slips the *satan* into an account concerning the origin of census taking, which King David introduced into Israel c. 1000 B.C.E. for the purpose of instituting taxation. David's introduction of taxation aroused vehement and immediate opposition—opposition that began among the very army commanders ordered to carry it out. Joab, David's chief officer, objected, and warned the king that what he was proposing to do was evil. The other army commanders at first refused to obey, nearly precipitating a revolt; but finding the king adamant, the officers finally obeyed and "numbered the people."

Why had David committed what one chronicler who recalls the story regards as an evil, aggressive act "against Israel"? Unable to deny that the offending order came from the king himself, but intent on condemning David's action without condemning the king directly, the author of 1 Chronicles suggests that a supernatural adversary within the divine court had managed to infiltrate the royal house and lead the king himself into sin: "The *satan* stood up against Israel, and incited David to number the people" (1 Chron. 21:1). But although an angelic power incited David to commit this otherwise inexplicable act, the chronicler insists that the king was nevertheless personally responsible—and guilty. "God was displeased with this thing, and he smote Israel." Even after David abased himself and confessed his sin, the angry Lord punished him by sending an avenging angel to destroy seventy thousand Israelites with a plague; and the Lord was barely restrained from destroying the city of Jerusalem itself.

Here the *satan* is invoked to account for the division and destruction that King David's order aroused within Israel.[10] Not long before the chronicler wrote, the prophet Zechariah had depicted the *satan* inciting factions among the people. Zechariah's account reflects conflicts that arose within Israel after thousands of Jews—many of them influential and educated—whom the Babylonians had captured in war (c. 687 B.C.E.) and exiled to Babylon, returned to Palestine from exile. Cyrus, king of Persia, having recently conquered Babylon, not only allowed these Jewish exiles to go home but intended to make them his allies. Thus he offered them funds to reconstruct Jerusalem's defensive city walls, and to rebuild the great Temple, which the Babylonians had destroyed. Those returning were eager to reestablish the worship of "the Lord alone" in their land, and they naturally expected to reestablish themselves as rulers of their people.

They were not warmly welcomed by those whom they had left behind. Many of those who had remained saw the former exiles not only as agents

---

[9]Note that 2 Samuel 24:1–17 tells a different version of the story, in which the Lord himself, not "the *satan*," incites David to take the census. For discussion, see Morton Smith, *Palestinian Parties and Politics That Shaped the Old Testament* (New York: Columbia University Press, 1971), 62–146; Forsyth, *The Old Enemy*, 119–120.

[10]Pagels, "The Social History of Satan, the 'Intimate Enemy': A Preliminary Sketch," *Harvard Theological Review* 84:2 (1991): 112–114.

of the Persian king but as determined to retrieve the power and land they had been forced to relinquish when they were deported. Many resented the returnees' plan to take charge of the priestly offices and to "purify" the Lord's worship.

As the biblical scholar Paul Hanson notes, the line that had once divided the Israelites from their enemies had separated them from foreigners. Now the line separated two groups *within Israel*:

> Now, according to the people who remained, their beloved land was controlled by the enemy, and although that enemy in fact comprised fellow Israelites, yet they regarded these brethren as essentially no different from Canaanites.[11]

The prophet Zechariah sides with the returning exiles in this heated conflict and recounts a vision in which the *satan* speaks for the rural inhabitants who accuse the returning high priest of being a worthless candidate:

> The Lord showed me Joshua, the high priest, standing before the angel of the Lord, and the *satan* standing at his right hand to accuse him. The Lord said to the *satan*, "The Lord rebuke you, O *satan*! The Lord who has chosen Jerusalem rebuke you" (Zech. 3:1–2).

Here the *satan* speaks for a disaffected—and unsuccessful—party against another party of fellow Israelites. In Zechariah's account of factions within Israel, the *satan* takes on a sinister quality, as he had done in the story of David's census, and his role begins to change from that of God's agent to that of his opponent. Although these biblical stories reflect divisions within Israel, they are not yet sectarian, for their authors still identify with Israel as a whole.

Some four centuries later in 168 B.C.E., when Jews regained their independence from their Seleucid rulers, descendents of Alexander the Great, internal conflicts became even more acute.[12] For centuries, Jews had been pressured to assimilate to the ways of the foreign nations that successively had ruled their land—the Babylonians, then the Persians, and, after 323 B.C.E., the Hellenistic dynasty established by Alexander. As the first book of Maccabees tells the story, these pressures reached a breaking point in 168 B.C.E., when the Seleucid ruler, the Syrian king Antiochus Epiphanes, suspecting resistance to his rule, decided to eradicate every trace of the Jews' peculiar and "barbaric" culture. First he outlawed circumcision, along with study and observance of Torah. Then he stormed the Jerusalem Temple and desecrated it by rededicating it to the Greek god Olympian Zeus. To enforce submission to his new regime, the king built and garrisoned a massive new fortress overlooking the Jerusalem Temple itself.

---

[11]Paul D. Hanson, *The Dawn of Apocalyptic* (Philadelphia: Fortress Press, 1975), 125.
[12]An excellent account of these events is to be found in Victor Tcherikover's *Hellenistic Civilization and the Jews* (New York: Atheneum, 1970).

Jewish resistance to these harsh decrees soon flared into a widespread revolt, which began, according to tradition, when a company of the king's troops descended upon the village of Modein to force the inhabitants to bow down to foreign gods. The old village priest Mattathias rose up and killed a Jew who was about to obey the Syrian king's command. Then he killed the king's commissioner and fled with his sons to the hills—an act of defiance that precipitated the revolt led by Mattathias's son Judas Maccabeus.[13]

As told in 1 Maccabees, this famous story shows how those Israelites determined to resist the foreign king's orders and retain their ancestral traditions battled on two fronts at once—not only against the foreign occupiers, but against those Jews who inclined toward accommodation with the foreigners, and toward assimilation. Recently the historian Victor Tcherikover and others have told a more complex version of that history. According to Tcherikover, many Jews, especially among the upper classes, actually favored Antiochus's "reform" and wanted to participate fully in the privileges of Hellenistic society available only to Greek citizens.[14] By giving up their tribal ways and gaining for Jerusalem the prerogatives of a Greek city, they would win the right to govern the city themselves, to strike their own coins, and to increase commerce with a worldwide network of other Greek cities. They could participate in such cultural projects as the Olympic games with allied cities and gain the advantages of mutual defense treaties. Many wanted their sons to have a Greek education. Besides reading Greek literature, from the *Iliad* and the *Odyssey* to Sophocles, Plato, and Aristotle, and participating in public athletic competitions, as Greeks did, they could advance themselves in the wider cosmopolitan world.

But many other Jews, perhaps the majority of the population of Jerusalem and the countryside—tradespeople, artisans, and farmers—detested these "Hellenizing Jews" as traitors to God and Israel alike. The revolt ignited by old Mattathias encouraged people to resist Antiochus's orders, even at the risk of death, and oust the foreign rulers. After intense fighting, the Jewish armies finally won a decisive victory. They celebrated by purifying and rededicating the Temple in a ceremony commemorated, ever since, at the annual festival of Hanukkah.

Jews resumed control of the Temple, the priesthood, and the government; but after the foreigners had retreated, internal conflicts remained, especially over who would control these institutions. These divisions now intensified, as the more rigorously separatist party dominated by the Maccabees opposed the Hellenizing party. The former, having won the war, had the upper hand.

Ten to twenty years after the revolt began, the influential Hasmonean family gained control of the high priesthood in what was now essentially a theocratic state. Although originally identified with their Maccabean ancestors, successive generations of the family abandoned the austere habits of their predecessors. Two generations after the Maccabean victory, the party of Pharisees, advocating increased religious rigor, challenged the Hasmo-

---

[13]1 Maccabees, 2.
[14]Tcherikóvér, *Hellenistic Civilization*, 132–174.

neans. According to Tcherikover's analysis, the Pharisees, backed by trades-people and farmers, despised the Hasmoneans as having become essentially secular rulers who had abandoned Israel's ancestral ways. The Pharisees demanded that the Hasmoneans relinquish the high priesthood to those who deserved it—people like themselves, who strove to live according to religious law.[15]

During the following decades, other, more radical dissident groups joined the Pharisees in denouncing the great high priestly family and its allies. Such groups were anything but uniform: they were fractious and diverse, and with the passage of time included various groups of Essenes, the monastic community at Kirbet Qûmran, as well as their allies in the towns, and the followers of Jesus of Nazareth. What these groups shared was their opposition to the high priest and his allies and to the Temple, which they controlled.

The majority of Jews, including the Pharisees, still defined themselves in traditional terms, as "Israel against 'the nations.' " But those who joined marginal or more extreme groups like the Essenes, bent on separating Israel radically from foreign influence, came to treat that traditional identifica-tion as a matter of secondary importance. What mattered primarily, these rigorists claimed, was not whether one was Jewish—this they took for grant-ed—but rather "which of us [Jews] really are on God's side" and which had "walked in the ways of the nations," that is, adopted foreign cultural and commercial practices. The separatists found ammunition in biblical pas-sages that invoke terrifying curses upon people who violate God's covenant, and in prophetic passages that warn that only a "righteous remnant" in Israel will remain faithful to God.

30   More radical than their predecessors, these dissidents began increas-ingly to invoke the *satan* to characterize their Jewish opponents; in the process they turned this rather unpleasant angel into a far grander—and far more malevolent—figure. No longer one of God's faithful servants, he begins to become what he is for Mark and for later Christianity—God's antagonist, his enemy, even his rival.[16] Such sectarians, contending less against "the nations" than against other Jews, denounce their opponents as apostate and accuse them of having been seduced by the power of evil, whom they call by many names—Satan, Beelzebub, Semihazah, Azazel, Belial, Prince of Darkness. These dissidents also borrowed stories, and

[15]*Ibid.*, 253–265.

[16]Such scholars as Knut Schäferdick, in his article "Satan in the Post Apostolic Fathers," s.v. "*satâs*," *Theological Dictionary of the New Testament 7* (1971): 163–65, attributes this development to Christians. Others, including Harold Kuhn, "The Angelology of the Non-Canonical Jewish Apocalypses," *Journal of Biblical Literature 67* (1948): 217; Claude Montefiore, *Lectures on the Origin and Growth of Religion as Illustrated by the Religion of the Ancient Hebrews* (London: Williams and Norgate, 1892), 429; and George Foote Moore, *Judaism in the First Centuries of the Christian Era*, vol. 1, *The Age of the Tannaim* (Cambridge, Harvard University Press, 1927), rightly locate the development of angelology and demonology in pre-Christian Jewish sources, and offer different interpretations of this, as noted in Pagels, "The Social History of Satan, the 'Intimate Enemy,' " 107.

wrote their own, telling how such angelic powers, swollen with lust or arrogance, fell from heaven into sin. Those who first elaborated such stories, as we shall see, most often used them to characterize what they charged was the "fall into sin" of human beings—which usually meant the dominant majority of their Jewish contemporaries.

As Satan became an increasingly important and personified figure, stories about his origin proliferated. One group tells how one of the angels, himself high in the heavenly hierarchy, proved insubordinate to his commander in chief and so was thrown out of heaven, demoted, and disgraced, an echo of Isaiah's account of the fall of a great prince:

> How are you fallen from heaven, day star, son of the dawn! How are you fallen to earth, conqueror of the nations! You said in your heart, "I will ascend to heaven, above the stars of God; I will set my throne on high . . . I will ascend upon the high clouds.. . ." But you are brought down to darkness [or: the underworld, *sheol*], to the depths of the pit (Isa. 14:12–15).

Nearly two and a half thousand years after Isaiah wrote, this luminous falling star, his name translated into Latin as Lucifer ("light-bearer") was transformed by Milton into the protagonist of *Paradise Lost.*

Far more influential in first-century Jewish and Christian circles, however, was a second group of apocryphal and pseudepigraphic stories, which tell how lust drew the angelic "sons of God" down to earth. These stories derive from a cryptic account in Genesis 6, which says:

> When men began to multiply on the earth, and daughters were born to them, the sons of God saw the daughters of men, that they were fair.

Some of these angels, transgressing the boundaries that the Lord had established between heaven and earth, mated with human women, and produced offspring who were half angel, half human. According to Genesis, these hybrids became "giants in the earth . . . the mighty men of renown" (Gen. 6:4). Other storytellers, probably writing later,[17] as we shall see, say that these monstrous offspring became demons, who took over the earth and polluted it.

Finally, an apocryphal version of the life of Adam and Eve gives a third account of angelic rebellion. In the beginning, God, having created Adam, called the angels together to admire his work and ordered them to bow

35

---

[17]Which account is earlier—that in Genesis 6 or in *1 Enoch* 6–11—remains a debatable issue. See, for example, J. T. Milik, *The Books of Enoch: Aramaic Fragments of Qûmran Caves* (Oxford: Clarendon, 1976); George W. E. Nickelsburg, "Apocalyptic and Myth in *1 Enoch* 6–11," *Journal of Biblical Literature* 96 (1977): 383–405; Margaret Barker, "Some Reflections on the Enoch Myth," *JSOT* 15 (1980): 7-29; Philip S. Alexander, "The Targumim and Early Exegesis of the 'Sons of God' in Genesis 6," *Journal of Jewish Studies* 23 (1972): 60–71.

down to their younger human sibling. Michael obeyed, but Satan refused, saying,

> "Why do you press me? I will not worship one who is younger than I am, and inferior. I am older than he is; he ought to worship me!" (*Vita Adae et Evae* 14:3).

Thus the problem of evil begins in sibling rivalry.[18]

At first glance these stories of Satan may seem to have little in common. Yet they all agree on one thing: that this greatest and most dangerous enemy did not originate, as one might expect, as an outsider, an alien, or a stranger. Satan is not the distant enemy but the intimate enemy—one's trusted colleague, close associate, brother. He is the kind of person on whose loyalty and goodwill the well-being of family and society depend—but one who turns unexpectedly jealous and hostile. Whichever version of his origin one chooses, then, and there are many, all depict Satan as an *intimate* enemy—the attribute that qualifies him so well to express conflict among Jewish groups. Those who asked, "How could God's own angel become his enemy?" were thus asking, in effect, "How could one of *us* become one of *them*?" Stories of Satan and other fallen angels proliferated in these troubled times, especially within those radical groups that had turned against the rest of the Jewish community and, consequently, concluded that others had turned against *them—or (as they put it) against God.*

READING CRITICALLY FOR IDEAS, STRUCTURE, AND STYLE

1. According to Pagels, in what ways did the concept of *satan* initially evolve as a way of denouncing troublesome elements —that only later acquired the theological status of an entity called the Devil?
2. What insight does Pagels offer into the dynamics by which groups stigmatize others and magnify these differences into a good versus evil cosmology?
3. How well does Pagels support her argument with citations and evidence, given her controversial thesis?

[18]For a survey of this theme of rivalry between angels and humans, see Peter Schäfer's fine work *Rivalität Zwischen Engeln und Menschen: Untersuchungen zur rabbinischen Engelvorstellung* (Berlin and New York: de Gruyter, 1975). For a discussion of one strand of Muslim tradition, see Peter Awn, *Satan's Tragedy and Redemption: Iblīs in Sufi Psychology* (Leiden: E. J. Brill, 1983).

EXTENDING INSIGHTS THROUGH WRITING

1. In Pagels's view, it was impossible for the early Church fathers to promote their beliefs without demonizing their opponents. Has this tendency to demonize others continued into the present? If so, what forms does it take? Write a short summary (not more than a page) that covers the main points of Pagels's analysis.

2. The same process that Pagels describes (in a religious context) can also be observed in dictatorships and totalitarian governments. For example, what form did this take in George Orwell's depiction of communism and Stalin in his futuristic novel, *1984* (1949) or in his fable, *Animal Farm* (1945)?

CONNECTING PERSPECTIVES ON THE HISTORICAL DIMENSION

1. In what respects does Walt Whitman's description of the assasination in "Death of Abraham Lincoln" mythologize real historical events into a cosmic drama of good and evil in ways comparable to those discussed by Pagels?

2. What insight does Maurizio Chierici's interview give you into how the psychology of demonization operates during times of war, as discussed by Pagels?

THOMAS CARLYLE

On Heroes and Hero-Worship

BACKGROUND

Thomas Carlyle (1795–1881) the Scottish philosopher, social critic, essayist and historian, was educated at Edinburgh University. His Calvinist parents intended for him to become a minister, but in 1870 he rejected this choice, although Calvinism as a faith, with its stern moral dictates, continued to shape the rest of his life. His spiritual crisis in the summer of 1822 is recorded in *Sartor Resartus* (1835). The title means "the tailor re-tailored" because of Carlyle's allegorical emphasis on social customs and mores as the "clothing" of ultimate truth, just as the body is the clothing of the soul. The book states many themes that become important in Carlyle's later writings, including his thesis that heroes are necessary to galvanize and inspire the masses.

Perhaps his most controversial work was *The French Revolution* (1837), which still stands as one of the most imaginative refigurings of the events that occurred during this tumultuous era. The existence of this work is something of a miracle since Carlyle had to rewrite the entire first volume. He had journeyed to London to gather materials for this work and lent the completed manuscript to his friend, John Stuart Mill, who unknown to Carlyle, had left it with a friend, a Mrs. Taylor, whose servant girl carelessly used it to light fires. Carlyle had no other copy and preserved no notes. The essay reprinted below is from *On Heroes, Hero-Worship, and the Heroic in History* (1841). In this, he elaborates his thesis that strong compelling leadership is required to avoid social anarchy, an idea also present in his biographical studies of Oliver Cromwell (1845) and Frederick the Great (1865).

APPROACHING CARLYLE'S ESSAY

The force of Carlyle's personality can be felt even in this short selection. His literary style is quite unusual when compared with the sonorous cadences of other prose written during the Victorian era. He invents unusual hybrid forms of words (for example, "light-fountain," "life-breath," and of course, "hero-worship"), creates striking metaphors, inverts syntax, uses typographical oddities, and structures English sentences as if he were writing in German, as in: "hero-worship, heartfelt prostrate admiration, submission, burning, boundless, for a noblest godlike Form of Man, —is not that the germ of Christianity itself?"

Between 1837 and 1841, Carlyle gave a series of annual lectures on the history of literature, culture, revolution, and the idea of the hero. These lectures were compiled and published as *On Heroes, Hero-Worship and the Heroic in History*. In this work, Carlyle discusses a wide range of personalities, both literary and historical, including Dante, Homer, Shakespeare, Rousseau, Luther, and Napoleon, among others. It becomes clear that Carlyle admires upstarts who make their own way in society, found empires, and place themselves above the crowd (much as Carlyle saw himself as having done). In fact, historians have observed that many of his biographies about great men are really as much about Carlyle himself as about his purported subjects.

As we see in this excerpt, Carlyle's criteria for the hero is that such a person is capable of inspiring others in their struggles in a moral and spiritual sense during very different periods of history and cultures. Carlyle's work can be understood as a reaction to what he perceived as the Victorian obsession with scientific progress and economic profit, a trend that would produce a soulless society.

On Heroes and Hero-Worship

We have undertaken to discourse here for a little on Great Men, their manner of appearance in our world's business, how they have shaped themselves in the world's history, what ideas men formed of them, what work they did;—on Heroes, namely, and on their reception and performance; what I call Hero-worship and the Heroic in human affairs. Too evidently this is a large topic; deserving quite other treatment than we can expect to give it at present. A large topic; indeed, an illimitable one; wide as Universal History itself. For, as I take it, Universal History, the history of what man has accomplished in this world, is at bottom the History of the Great Men who have worked here. They were the leaders of men, these great ones; the modellers, patterns, and in a wide sense creators, of whatsoever the general mass of men contrived to do or to attain; all things that we see standing accomplished in the world are properly the outer material result, the practical realisation and embodiment, of Thoughts that dwelt in the Great Men sent into the world: the soul of the whole world's history, it may justly be considered, were the history of these. Too clearly it is a topic we shall do no justice to in this place!

One comfort is, that Great Men, taken up in any way, are profitable company. We cannot look, however imperfectly, upon a great man, without gaining something by him. He is the living light-fountain, which it is good and pleasant to be near. The light which enlightens, which has enlightened the darkness of the world; and this not as a kindled lamp only, but rather as a natural luminary shining by the gift of Heaven; a flowing light-fountain, as I say, of native original insight, of manhood and heroic nobleness;— in whose radiance all souls feel that it is well with them. On any terms whatsoever, you will not grudge to wander in such neighbourhood for a while. These Six classes of Heroes, chosen out of widely-distant countries and epochs, and in mere external figure differing altogether, ought, if we look faithfully at them, to illustrate several things for us. Could we see *them* well, we should get some glimpses into the very marrow of the world's history. How happy, could I but, in any measure, in such times as these, make manifest to you the meanings of Heroism; the divine relation (for I may well call it such) which in all times unites a Great Man to other men; and thus, as it were, not exhaust my subject, but so much as break ground on it! At all events, I must make the attempt.. . .

Worship of a Hero is transcendent admiration of a Great Man. I say great men are still admirable; I say there is, at bottom, nothing else admirable! No nobler feeling than this of admiration for one higher than himself dwells in the breast of man. It is to this hour, and at all hours, the vivifying influence in man's life. Religion I find stand upon it; not Paganism only, but far higher and truer religions,—all religion hitherto known. Hero-worship, heartfelt prostrate admiration, submission, burning, boundless, for a noblest godlike Form of Man,—is not that the germ of Christianity itself? The greatest of all Heroes is One—whom we do not name here! Let sacred silence meditate that sacred matter; you will find it the ultimate perfection of a principle extant throughout man's whole history on earth.

Or coming into lower, less *un*speakable provinces, is not all Loyalty akin to religious Faith also? Faith is loyalty to some inspired Teacher, some spiritual Hero. And what therefore is loyalty proper, the life-breath of all society, but an effluence of Hero-worship, submissive admiration for the truly great? Society is founded on Hero-worship. All dignities of rank, on which human association rests, are what we may call a *Hero*archy (Government of Heroes),—or a Hierarchy, for it is 'sacred' enough withal! The Duke means *Dux*, Leader; King is *Kön-ning, Kan-ning*, Man that *knows* or *cans*. Society everywhere is some representation, not *in*supportably inaccurate, of a graduated Worship of Heroes;—reverence and obedience done to men really great and wise. Not *in*supportably inaccurate, I say! They are all as bank-notes, these social dignitaries, all representing gold;—and several of them, alas, always are *forged* notes. We can do with some forged false notes; with a good many even; but not with all, or the most of them forged! No: there have to come revolutions then; cries of Democracy, Liberty and Equality, and I know not what:—the notes being all false, and no gold to be had for *them*, people take to crying in their despair that there is no gold, that there never was any!—'Gold,' Hero-worship, *is* nevertheless, as it was always and everywhere, and cannot cease till man himself ceases.

5   I am well aware that in these days Hero-worship, the thing I call Hero-worship, professes to have gone out, and finally ceased. This, for reasons

which it will be worth while some time to inquire into, is an age that as it were denies the existence of great men; denies the desirableness of great men. Show our critics a great man, a Luther for example, they begin to what they call 'account' for him; not to worship him, but take the dimensions of him,—and bring him out to be a little kind of man! He was the 'creature of the Time,' they say; the Time called him forth, the Time did everything, he nothing—but what we the little critic could have done too! This seems to me but melancholy work. The Time call forth? Alas, we have known Times *call* loudly enough for their great man; but not find him when they called! He was not there Providence had not sent him; the Time, *calling* its loudest, had to go down to confusion and wreck because he would not come when called.

For if we will think of it, no Time need have gone to ruin, could it have *found* a man great enough, a man wise and good enough: wisdom to discern truly what the Time wanted, valour to lead it on the right road thither; these are the salvation of any Time. But I liken common languid Times, with their unbelief, distress, perplexity, with their languid doubting characters and embarrassed circumstances, impotently crumbling-down into ever worse distress towards final ruin;—all this I liken to dry dead fuel, waiting for the lightning out of Heaven that shall kindle it. The great man, with his free force direct out of God's own hand, is the lightning. His word is the wise healing word which all can believe in. All blazes round him now, when he has once struck on it, into fire like his own. The dry mouldering sticks are thought to have called him forth. They did want him greatly; but as to calling him forth—!—Those are critics of small vision, I think, who cry 'See, is it not the sticks that made the fire?' No sadder proof can be given by a man of his own littleness than disbelief in great men. There is no sadder symptom of a generation than such general blindness to the spiritual lightning, with faith only in the heap of barren dead fuel. It is the last consummation of unbelief. In all epochs of the world's history, we shall find the Great Man to have been the indispensable saviour of his epoch;—the lightning, without which the fuel never would have burnt. The History of the World, I said already, was the Biography of Great Men.

Such small critics do what they can to promote unbelief and universal spiritual paralysis: but happily they cannot always completely succeed. In all times it is possible for a man to arise great enough to feel that they and their doctrines are chimeras and cobwebs. And what is notable, in no time whatever can they entirely eradicate out of living men's hearts a certain altogether peculiar reverence for Great Men; genuine admiration, loyalty, adoration, however dim and perverted it may be. Hero-worship endures for ever while man endures. Boswell venerates his Johnson, right truly even in the Eighteenth century. The unbelieving French believe in their Voltaire; and burst-out round him into very curious Hero-worship, in that last act of his life when they 'stifle him under roses.' It has always seemed to me extremely curious this of Voltaire. Truly, if Christianity be the highest instance of Hero-worship, then we may find here in Voltaireism one of the lowest! He whose life was that of a kind of Antichrist, does again on this side exhibit a curious contrast. No people ever were so little prone to admire at all as those French of Voltaire. *Persiflage* was the character of their whole mind; adoration had nowhere a place in it. Yet see! The old man of Ferney comes up to Paris; an old, tottering, infirm man of eighty-four years. They feel that he too is a kind of Hero; that he has spent his life in opposing error and injustice, delivering Calases, unmasking hypocrites in high places; —in short that *he* too, though in a strange way, has fought like a valiant man. They feel withal that, if *persiflage* be the great thing, there never was such a *persifleur*. He is the realised ideal of every one of them; the thing they are all wanting to be; of all Frenchmen the most French. *He* is properly their god,—such god as they are fit for. Accordingly all persons, from the Queen Antoinette to the Douanier at the Porte St. Denis, do they not worship him? People of quality disguise themselves as tavern-waiters. The Maître de Poste, with a broad oath, orders his Postillion, '*Va bon train*; thou art driving M. de Voltaire.' At Paris his carriage is 'the nucleus of a comet, whose train fills whole streets.' The ladies pluck a hair or two from his fur, to keep it as a sacred relic. There was nothing highest, beautifulest, noblest in all France, that did not feel this man to be higher, beautifuler, nobler.

Yes, from Norse Odin to English Samuel Johnson, from the divine Founder of Christianity to the withered Pontiff of Encyclopedism, in all times and places, the Hero has been worshipped. It will ever be so. We all love great men; love, venerate and bow down submissive before great men: nay can we honestly bow down to anything else? Ah, does not every true man feel that he is himself made higher by doing reverence to what is really above him? No nobler or more blessed feeling dwells in man's heart. And to me it is very cheering to consider that no sceptical logic, or general triviality, insincerity and aridity of any Time and its influences can destroy this noble inborn loyalty and worship that is in man. In times of unbelief, which soon have to become times of revolution, much down-rushing, sorrowful decay and ruin is visible to everybody. For myself, in these days, I seem to see in this indestructibility of Hero-worship the everlasting adamant lower than which the confused wreck of revolutionary things cannot fall. The confused wreck of things crumbling and even crashing and tumbling all round us in these revolutionary ages, will get down so far; *no* farther. It is an eternal corner-stone, from which they can begin to build themselves up again. That man, in some sense or other, worships Heroes; that we all of us reverence and must ever reverence Great Men: this is, to me, the living rock amid all rushings-down whatsoever;—the one fixed point in modern revolutionary history, otherwise as if bottomless and shoreless.

READING CRITICALLY FOR IDEAS, STRUCTURE, AND STYLE

1. In what way is the concept of the "great man" or the divinely inspired hero a key to Carlyle's thinking? In his view, what transcendent function does the hero serve?

2. What unusual features distinguish Carlyle's literary style, and does it enhance or detract from the presentation of his argument?

3. In what sense is "the History of the World," in Carlyle's view, the "Biography of Great Men"? Write a short essay discussing whether men make history or are simply propelled into positions of importance by events.

EXTENDING INSIGHTS THROUGH WRITING

1. What effect have heroes and heroines had in your personal life? What qualities made them heroic to you even if they were not viewed that way by others?

2. Do you find Carlyle's choice of heroes eccentric? Why or why not? Who would you nominate as a hero of today in terms of Carlyle's criteria or in terms of your own standards? Explain your answer.

CONNECTING PERSPECTIVES ON THE HISTORICAL DIMENSION

1. Would Arnold J. Toynbee (in "Challenge and Response") subscribe to Carlyle's notion of the hero, or would he find it simplistic in light of his own complex myth of "challenge and response"? Why or why not?

2. In what respects does Walt Whitman's portrayal (see "Death of Abraham Lincoln") and characterization of Lincoln suggest the kind of hero-worship Carlyle discusses?

WALT WHITMAN

Death of Abraham Lincoln

BACKGROUND

Walt Whitman (1819–1892) was born in then-rural Huntington, Long Island, into a family of Quakers. The family then moved to Brooklyn, at that time a city of fewer than 10,000 inhabitants, where he worked as a carpenter. He attended school briefly and in 1830 went to work as an office boy, but he soon turned to printing and journalism and until the 1850s worked as a newspaperman. He was the editor of the *Brooklyn Eagle* from 1846 to 1848. In 1855, Whitman published the first of many editions of *Leaves of Grass*, a work that established Whitman as one of the most innovative figures of nineteenth-century poetry. In subsequent editions, he proved capable of writing long, intricately orchestrated poems that embrace the ideals of working-class democracy expressed in experimental free-verse rhythms and realistic imagery. When the Civil War broke out, Whitman was too old to enlist, but he went to the front in 1862 to be with his brother George who had been reported wounded. During the remainder of the war, Whitman served as a nurse tending wounded soldiers, Union and Confederate alike. "Death of Abraham Lincoln" was a set piece that Whitman delivered on many lecture tours.

APPROACHING WHITMAN'S ESSAY

This is an unusual prose work of Whitman's, given his greater fame as a poet. For Whitman, Lincoln embodied the virtues of American democracy, and his elegy on Lincoln's death "when lilacs last in the dooryard bloomed," is generally regarded as one of Whitman's greatest poems. It was one of four elegies titled "Memories of President Lincoln" added after Lincoln's death to Whitman's collection, *Drumtaps* (1865). Whitman first describes Lincoln on a silent stage: The hostile crowds watch him as he alights from his unprepossessing carriage in New York City, a place where, Whitman notes, Lincoln had no personal friends in the immense crowd. Whitman points out that doubtless there were many with weapons at the ready should a riot in protest against

Lincoln break out. In his description of the chaos immediately following the shooting of Lincoln by Booth, Whitman brings home to his readers the reality of the moment. Each detail is mentioned, each pause in the action minutely rendered. As soon as the deed is done, and the cry of "murder" is heard, all dissolves into the language of catastrophe. Mrs. Lincoln screams, and a deluge follows ("that mixture of horror, noises, uncertainty"), vividly described as if observed directly by the reader.

Death of Abraham Lincoln

I shall not easily forget the first time I ever saw Abraham Lincoln. It must have been about the 18th or 19th of February, 1861. It was rather a pleasant afternoon, in New York City, as he arrived there from the West, to remain a few hours, and then pass on to Washington, to prepare for his inauguration. I saw him in Broadway, near the site of the present Post-office. He came down, I think from Canal street, to stop at the Astor House. The broad spaces, sidewalks, and streets in the neighborhood, and for some distance, were crowded with solid masses of people, many thousands. The omnibuses and other vehicles had all been turn'd off, leaving an unusual hush in that busy part of the city. Presently two or three shabby hack barouches made their way with some difficulty through the crowd, and drew up at the Astor House entrance. A tall figure stepp'd out of the centre of these barouches, paus'd leisurely on the sidewalk, look'd up at the granite walls and looming architecture of the grand old hotel—then, after a relieving stretch of arms and legs, turn'd round for over a minute to slowly and good-humoredly scan the appearance of the vast and silent crowds. There were no speeches—no compliments—no welcome—as far as I could hear, not a word said. Still much anxiety was conceal'd in the quiet. Cautious persons had fear'd some mark'd insult or indignity to the President-elect—for he possess'd no personal popularity at all in New York City, and very little political. But it was evidently tacitly agreed that if the few political supporters of Mr. Lincoln present would entirely abstain from any demonstration on their side, the immense majority, who were anything but supporters, would abstain on their sides also. The result was a sulky, unbroken silence, such as certainly never before characterized so great a New York crowd.

Almost in the same neighborhood I distinctly remember'd seeing Lafayette on his visit to America in 1825. I had also personally seen and heard, various years afterward, how Andrew Jackson, Clay, Webster, Hungarian Kossuth, Filibuster Walker, the Prince of Wales on his visit, and other *célèbres*, native and foreign, had been welcom'd there—all that indescribable human roar and magnetism, unlike any other sound in the universe—the glad exulting thunder-shouts of countless unloos'd throats of men! But on this occasion, not a voice—not a sound. From the top of an omnibus, (driven up one side, close by, and block'd by the curbstone and the crowds), I had, I say, a capital view of it all, and especially of Mr. Lincoln, his look and gait—his perfect composure and coolness—his unusual and uncouth height, his dress of complete black, stovepipe hat push'd back on the head, dark-brown complexion, seam'd and wrinkled yet canny-looking face, black, bushy head of hair, disproportionately long neck, and his hands held behind as he stood observing the people. He look'd with curiosity upon that immense sea of faces, and the sea of faces return'd the look with similar curiosity. In both there was a dash of comedy, almost farce, such as Shakspere puts in his blackest tragedies. The crowd that hemm'd around consisted I should think of thirty to forty thousand men, not a single one his personal friend—while I have no doubt, (so frenzied were the ferments of the time,) many an assassin's knife and pistol lurk'd in hip or breast-pocket there, ready, soon as break and riot came.

But not break or riot came. The tall figure gave another relieving stretch or two of arms and legs; then with moderate pace, and accompanied by a few unknown-looking persons, ascended the portico-steps of the Astor House, disappear'd through its broad entrance—and the dumb-show ended.

I saw Abraham Lincoln often the four years following that date. He changed rapidly and much during his Presidency—but this scene, and him in it, are indelibly stamp'd upon my recollection. As I sat on the top of my omnibus, and had a good view of him, the thought, dim and inchoate then, has since come out clear enough, that four sorts of genius, four mighty and primal hands, will be needed to the complete limning of this man's future portrait—the eyes and brains and finger-touch of Plutarch and Eschylus and Michel Angelo, assisted now by Rabelais.

5   And now—(Mr. Lincoln passing on from this scene to Washington, where he was inaugurated, amid armed cavalry, and sharpshooters at every point—the first instance of the kind in our history—and I hope it will be the last)—now the rapid succession of well-known events, (too well-known—I believe, these days, we almost hate to hear them mention'd)— the national flag fired on at Sumter—the uprising of the North, in paroxysms of astonishment and rage—the chaos of divided councils—the call for troops—the first Bull Run—the stunning cast-down, shock, and dismay of the North—and so in full flood the Secession war. Four years of lurid, bleeding, murky, murderous war. Who paint those years, with all their scenes?—the hard-fought engagements—the defeats, plans, failures— the gloomy hours, days, when our Nationality seem'd hung in pall of doubt, perhaps death—the Mephistophelean sneers of foreign lands and attachés—the dreaded Scylla of European interference, and the Charybdis of the tremendously dangerous latent strata of secession sympathizers throughout the free States, (far more numerous than is supposed) —the long marches in summer—the hot sweat, and many a sunstroke, as on the rush to Gettysburg in '63—the night battles in the woods, as under Hooker at Chancellorsville—the camps in winter—the military prisons—the hospitals—(alas! alas! the hospitals).

The Secession war? Nay, let me call it the Union war. Though whatever call'd, it is even yet too near us—too vast and too closely overshadowing —its branches unform'd yet, (but certain,) shooting too far into the future—and the most indicative and mightiest of them yet ungrown. A great literature will yet arise out of the era of those four years, those scenes—era compressing centuries of native passion, first-class pictures, tempests of life and death—an inexhaustible mine for the histories, drama, romance, and even philosophy, of peoples to come—indeed the verteber[1] of poetry and art, (of personal character too,) for all future America—far more grand, in my opinion, to the hands capable of it, than Homer's siege of Troy, or the French wars to Shakspere.

But I must leave these speculations, and come to the theme I have assign'd and limited myself to. Of the actual murder of President Lincoln, though so much has been written, probably the facts are yet very indefinite in most persons' minds. I read from my memoranda, written at the time, and revised frequently and finally since.

The day, April 14, 1865, seems to have been a pleasant one throughout the whole land—the moral atmosphere pleasant too—the long storm, so dark, so fratricidal, full of blood and doubt and gloom, over and ended at last by the sunrise of such an absolute National victory, and utter breakdown of Secessionism—we almost doubted our own senses! Lee had capitulated beneath the apple-tree of Appomattox. The other armies, the flanges of the revolt, swiftly follow'd. And could it really be, then? Out of all the affairs of this world of woe and failure and disorder, was there really come the confirm'd, unerring sign of plan, like a shaft of pure light—of rightful rule—of God? So the day, as I say, was propitious. Early herbage, early flowers, were out. (I remember where I was stopping at the time, the season being advanced, there were many lilacs in full bloom. By one of those caprices that enter and give tinge to events without being at all a part of them, I find myself always reminded of the great tragedy of that day by the sight and odor of these blossoms.[2] It never fails.)

But I must not dwell on accessories. The deed hastens. The popular afternoon paper of Washington, the little *Evening Star*, has spatter'd all over its third page, divided among the advertisements in a sensational manner. In a hundred different places, "*The President and his Lady will be at the Theatre this evening. . . .*" (Lincoln was fond of the theatre. I have myself seen him there several times. I remember thinking how funny it was that he, in some respects the leading actor in the stormiest drama known to real history's stage through centuries, should sit there and be so completely interested and absorb'd in those human jackstraws, moving about with their silly little gestures, foreign spirit, and flatulent text.)

On this occasion the theatre was crowded, many ladies in rich and gay costumes, officers in their uniforms, many well-known citizens, young folks, the usual clusters of gas-lights, the usual magnetism of so many   10

---

[1]*Verteber*: vertebrae.
[2]Cf. Whitman's elegy on Lincoln, "When Lilacs Last in the Dooryard Bloom'd" (1865–1866).

people, cheerful, with perfumes, music of violins and flutes—(and over all, and saturating all, that vast, vague wonder, *Victory*, the nation's victory, the triumph of the Union, filling the air, the thought, the sense, with exhilaration more than all music and perfumes).

The President came betimes, and, with his wife, witness'd the play from the large stage-boxes of the second tier, two thrown into one, and profusely drap'd with the national flag. The acts and scenes of the piece—one of those singularly written compositions which have at least the merit of giving entire relief to an audience engaged in mental action or business excitements and cares during the day, as it makes not the slightest call on either the moral, emotional, esthetic, or spiritual nature—a piece, (*Our American Cousin*,) in which, among other characters so call'd, a Yankee, certainly such a one as was never seen, or the least like it ever seen, in North America, is introduced in England, with a varied fol-de-rol of talk, plot, scenery, and such phantasmagoria as goes to make up a modern popular drama—had progress'd through perhaps a couple of its acts, when in the midst of this comedy, or nonsuch, or whatever it is to be call'd, and to offset it, or finish it out, as if in Nature's and the great Muse's mockery of those poor mimes, came interpolated that scene, not really or exactly to be described at all, (for on the many hundreds who were there it seems to this hour to have left a passing blur, a dream, a blotch)—and yet partially to be described as I now proceed to give it. There is a scene in the play representing a modern parlor, in which two unprecedented English ladies are inform'd by the impossible Yankee that he is not a man of fortune, and therefore undesirable for marriage-catching purposes; after which, the comments being finish'd, the dramatic trio make exit, leaving the stage clear for a moment. At this period came the murder of Abraham Lincoln. Great as all its manifold train, circling round it, and stretching into the future for many a century, in the politics, history, art &c., of the New World, in point of fact the main thing, the actual murder, transpired with the quiet and simplicity of any commonest occurrence—the bursting of a bud or pod in the growth of vegetation, for instance. Through the general hum following the stage pause, with the change of positions, came the muffled sound of a pistol-shot, which not one-hundredth part of the audience heard at the time—and yet a moment's hush—somehow, surely, a vague startled thrill—and then, through the ornamented, draperied, starr'd and striped space-way of the President's box, a sudden figure, a man, raises himself with hands and feet, stands a moment on the railing, leaps below to the stage, (a distance of perhaps fourteen or fifteen feet), falls out of position, catching his boot-heel in the copious drapery, (the American flag,) falls on one knee, quickly recovers himself, rises as if nothing had happen'd, (he really sprains his ankle, but unfelt then)—and so the figure, Booth, the murderer, dress'd in plain black broadcloth, bare-headed, with full, glossy, raven hair, and his eyes like some mad animal's flashing with light and resolution, yet with a certain strange calmness, holds aloft in one hand a large knife—walks along not much back from the footlights—turns fully toward the audience his face of statuesque beauty, lit by those basilisk eyes, flashing with desperation, perhaps insanity—launches out in a firm and steady voice the words

Sic semper tyrannis[3]—and then walks with neither slow nor very rapid pace diagonally across to the back of the stage, and disappears. (Had not all this terrible scene—making the mimic ones preposterous—had it not all been rehears'd, in blank, by Booth, beforehand?)

A moment's hush—a scream—the cry of "*murder*"—Mrs. Lincoln leaning out of the box, with ashy cheeks and lips, with involuntary cry, pointing to the retreating figure, "*He has kill'd the President.*" And still a moment's strange, incredulous suspense—and then the deluge! Then that mixture of horror, noises, uncertainty—(the sound, somewhere back, of a horse's hoofs clattering with speed)—the people burst through chairs and railings, and break them up—there is inextricable confusion and terror —women faint— quite feeble persons fall, and are trampl'd on—many cries of agony are heard—the broad stage suddenly fills to suffocation with a dense and motley crowd, like some horrible carnival—the audience rush generally upon it, at least the strong men do—the actors and actresses are all there in their play-costumes and painted faces, with mortal fright showing through the rouge—the screams and calls, confused talk—redoubled, trebled—two or three manage to pass up water from the stage to the President's box—others try to clamber up—&c., &c.

In the midst of all this, the soldiers of the President's guard, with others, suddenly drawn to the scene, burst in—(some two hundred altogether) —they storm the house, through all the tiers, especially the upper ones, inflam'd with fury, literally charging the audience with fix'd bayonets, muskets, and pistols, shouting "*Clear out! clear out! you sons of* ———". . . . Such a wild scene, or a suggestion of it rather, inside the play-house that night.

Outside, too, in the atmosphere of shock and craze, crowds of people, fill'd with frenzy, ready to seize any outlet for it, come near committing murder several times on innocent individuals. One such case was especially exciting. The infuriated crowd, through some chance, got started against one man, either for words he utter'd, or perhaps without any cause at all, and were proceeding at once to actually hang him on a neighboring lamppost, when he was rescued by a few heroic policemen, who placed him in their midst, and fought their way slowly and amid great peril toward the station-house. It was a fitting episode of the whole affair. The crowd rushing and eddying to and fro—the night, the yells, the pale faces, many frighten'd people trying in vain to extricate themselves—the attack'd man, not yet freed from the jaws of death, looking like a corpse—the silent, resolute, half-dozen policemen, with no weapons but their little clubs, yet stern and steady through all those eddying swarms—made a fitting side-scene to the grand tragedy of the murder. They gain'd the station-house with the protected man, whom they placed in security for the night, and discharged him in the morning.

And in the midst of that pandemonium, infuriated soldiers, the audience and the crowd, the stage, and all its actors and actresses, its paint-pots, spangles, and gas-lights—the life blood from those veins, the best and

---

[3]*Sic semper tyrannis*: "Thus always to tyrants."

sweetest of the land, drips slowly down, and death's ooze already begins its little bubbles on the lips.

Thus the visible incidents and surroundings of Abraham Lincoln's murder, as they really occur'd. Thus ended the attempted secession of these States: thus the four years' war. But the main things come subtly and invisibly afterward, perhaps long afterward—neither military, political, nor (great as those are,) historical. I say, certain secondary and indirect results, out of the tragedy of this death, are, in my opinion, greatest. Not the event of the murder itself. Not that Mr. Lincoln strings the principal points and personages of the period, like beads, upon the single string of his career. Not that his idiosyncrasy, in its sudden appearance and disappearance, stamps this Republic with a stamp more mark'd and enduring than any yet given by any one man—(more even than Washington's;)—but, join'd with these, the immeasurable value and meaning of that whole tragedy lies, to me, in senses finally dearest to a nation, (and here all our own)—the imaginative and artistic senses—the literary and dramatic ones. Not in any common or low meaning of those terms, but a meaning precious to the race, and to every age. A long and varied series of contradictory events arrives at last at its highest poetic, single, central, pictorial dénouement. The whole involved, baffling, multiform whirl of the secession period comes to a head, and is gather'd in one brief flash of lightning-illumination—one simple, fierce deed. Its sharp culmination, and as it were solution, of so many bloody and angry problems, illustrates those climax-moments on the stage of universal Time, where the historic Muse at one entrance, and the tragic Muse at the other, suddenly ringing down the curtain, close an immense act in the long drama of creative thought, and give it radiation, tableau, stranger than fiction. Fit radiation—fit close! How the imagination—how the student loves these things! America, too, is to have them. For not in all great deaths, not far or near—not Caesar in the Roman senate-house, or Napoleon passing away in the wild night-storm at St. Helena—not Paleologus,[4] falling, desperately fighting, piled over dozens deep with Grecian corpses—not calm old Socrates, drinking the hemlock—out-vies that terminus of the secession war, in one man's life, here in our midst, in our time—that seal of the emancipation of three million slaves—that parturition and delivery of our at last really free Republic, born again, henceforth to commence its career of genuine homogenous Union, compact, consistent with itself.

Nor will ever future American Patriots and Unionists, indifferently over the whole land, or North or South, find a better moral to their lesson. The final use of the greatest men of a Nation is, after all, not with reference to their deeds in themselves, or their direct bearing on their times or lands. The final use of a heroic-eminent life—especially of a heroic-eminent death—is its indirect filtering into the nation and the race, and to give, often at many removes, but unerringly, age after age, color and fibre to the personalism of the youth and maturity of that age, and of mankind. Then, there is a cement to the whole people, subtler, more underlying, than any

---

[4]*Paleologus*: Emperor Constantine XI, who yielded Constantinople to the Turks in 1453.

thing in written constitution, or courts or armies—namely, the cement of a death identified thoroughly with that people, at its head, and for its sake. Strange, (is it not?) that battles, martyrs, agonies, blood, even assassination, should so condense—perhaps only really, lastingly condense—a Nationality.

I repeat it—the grand deaths of the race—the dramatic deaths of every nationality—are its most important inheritance-value—in some respects beyond its literature and art—(as the hero is beyond his finest portrait, and the battle itself beyond its choicest song or epic.) Is not here indeed the point underlying all tragedy? the famous pieces of the Grecian masters— and all masters? Why, if the old Greeks had had this man, what trilogies of plays—what epics—would have been made out of him! How the rhapsodies would have recited him! How quickly that quaint tall form would have enter'd into the region where men vitalize gods, and gods divinify men! But Lincoln, his times, his death—great as any, any age—belong altogether to our own, and are autochthonic.[5] (Sometimes indeed I think our American days, our own stage—the actors we know and have shaken hands, or talk'd with—more fateful than any thing in Eschylus[6]—more heroic than the fighters around Troy—afford kings of men for our Democracy prouder than Agamemnon—models of character acute and hardy as Ulysses—deaths more pitiful than Priam's.)

When centuries hence, (as it must, in my opinion, be centuries hence before the life of these States, or of Democracy, can be really written and illustrated,) the leading historians and dramatists seek for some personage, some special event, incisive enough to mark with deepest cut, and mnemonize, this turbulent nineteenth century of ours, (not only these States, but all over the political and social world)—something, perhaps, to close that gorgeous procession of European feudalism, with all its pomp and caste-prejudices, (of whose long train we in America are yet so inextricably the heirs)—something to identify with terrible identification, by far the greatest revolutionary step in the history of the United States, (perhaps the greatest of the world, our century)—the absolute extirpation and erasure of slavery from the States—those historians will seek in vain for any point to serve more thoroughly their purpose, than Abraham Lincoln's death.

Dear to the Muse—thrice dear to Nationality—to the whole human race—precious to this Union—precious to Democracy—unspeakably and forever precious—their first great Martyr Chief.   20

---

[5]*Autochthonic*: Aboriginal, indigenous.
[6]*Eschylus* (i.e., Aeschylus): Greek tragic dramatist (525– 456 B.C.) whose plays feature Agamemnon, commander of the Greek forces; Ulysses, the hero of Homer's *Odyssey*; and Priam, patriarch of Troy.

READING CRITICALLY FOR IDEAS, STRUCTURE, AND STYLE

1. What inferences about Lincoln's significance for his contemporaries can you derive from Whitman's account?

2. How is Whitman's training as a journalist evident in his use of an objective viewpoint, tight narrative, and details that convey a great deal of information?

3. Whitman's account invests Lincoln's assassination with great mythological, historical, and cosmic meaning. How does he accomplish this in terms of specific rhetorical techniques?

EXTENDING INSIGHTS THROUGH WRITING

1. What contemporary event, if any, would lend itself to the kind of grand treatment displayed in Whitman's essay? In a short paper, try to catch the tone of Whitman's style and cover an event in recent times of comparable magnitude.

2. Although written in prose, Whitman's essay suggests the free-flowing associative style that characterizes his poetry. Read a few poems from *Leaves of Grass* (1855) or *Drum Taps* (1865) that refer to Lincoln's assassination and compare them with this essay.

CONNECTING PERSPECTIVES ON THE HISTORICAL DIMENSION

1. John F. Kennedy's "Inaugural Address 1961," although shadowed by our awareness of his assassination, suggests what Americans look for in a leader. Compare Kennedy's speech with Whitman's account, in terms of political idealism, past and present.

2. How does Whitman portray the turbulent era of the Civil War as a period of "challenge and response," using Arnold J. Toynbee's view of how history works?

MAURIZIO CHIERICI

The Man from Hiroshima

BACKGROUND

Maurizio Chierici is an Italian journalist who worked as a special correspondent for the Milan newspaper *Corriere della Sera*. "The Man from
Hiroshima," translated from the Italian by Wallis Wilde-Menozzi, first appeared in *Granta* (Autumn, 1987). At the time Chierici interviewed him,
Claude Eatherly was the only American pilot still alive who could provide a
firsthand account, and some historical perspective, on the mission over Hiroshima that resulted in the dropping of the atomic bomb. Eatherly was the
lead pilot who had to decide if weather conditions permitted the bomb to be
dropped. Chierci discovered that Eatherly, who was a much decorated, well-
respected pilot, had been irrevocably changed by this event and was now tormented by guilt. Fourteen months after this interview, Eatherly committed
suicide. The following interview offers an unparalled insight into the meaning
of Hiroshima from the perspective of an American pilot who was part of the
crew responsible for dropping the atomic bomb.

APPROACHING CHIERICI'S INTERVIEW

To obtain this exclusive interview, Chierici flew from Italy to Texas.
Eatherly had been briefly interviewed before, but felt that the reporter had
abused his trust, and so was wary in granting Chierici the interview.

Chierici learned that Eatherly had originally enlisted in the Air Force
and that there was nothing in his psychological profile or past to suggest he
would react as he did. After the mission Eatherly was tormented by a sense
of responsibility and guilt. He felt betrayed by his fellow officers and the government who he blamed for using him in their quest to win the war with Japan
at any cost. Not surprisingly, military physicians who tried to persuade him

he had nothing to feel guilty about diagnosed him as being mentally unstable. Eatherly describes how he was plagued by nightmares in which he reexperiences the final moments of his mission and sees the rising yellow cloud produced by the atomic bomb.

As an interviewer, Chierci is discreet and refrains from steering the conversation for any predetermined purpose. He simply allows Eatherly to unburden himself and only asks questions necessary to keep the conversation going. We learn that one of Eatherly's most poignant and desperate gestures is his decision to give up his military pension to help Japanese war widows and survivors of Hiroshima. He even goes so far as to forge checks and rob convenience stores in order to raise money to help these victims and their families, actions that led his wife to divorce him and to his confinement in a mental hospital. This interview dramatizes in the most extreme way possible how moral codes are suspended during wartime and how society punishes what in other circumstances would be seen as righteous and moral behavior.

The Man from Hiroshima

The protagonists of Hiroshima have no nostalgia. Even those people only remotely connected with the event have had difficult lives. All except one: Colonel Paul Tibbets, pilot of the *Enola Gay*, the plane that carried the atom bomb. On TV, serene under his white locks, he was unrepentant: 'I did my duty; I would do it again.' Tibbets is the only one to have passed these years without so much as a shiver. One of the pilots in the formation which flew over Hiroshima that day was unable to participate in the victory celebrations; he took his life three days before the official ceremony.

I knew another pilot full of problems; it wasn't at all easy to arrange to meet him. Everyone said: 'You'll need patience. But if he gave you his word, you'll hear from him sooner or later.' For days I waited and no one came. Then the pilot called to apologize. There was fog at the airport: the plane couldn't take off. Or: he had no money and the banks were closed. He would buy the ticket tomorrow. Tomorrow came and went; there was always a different story. Eventually I made a proposal: 'Eatherly, in five days it will be Christmas. I want to be back home in Italy before then. So I'll come to see you. It's much warmer where you are than in New York, and I've never been to Texas. I'll leave this afternoon.'

'No, stay where you are,' Eatherly interrupted. 'It's hard to talk here. Being in Texas blocks me; the people inhibit me. They know me too well, and there's no love lost between us. I plan to spend the holidays in New Jersey with a friend—I'd go out of my mind staying in Waco for Christmas— so I'll come and see you.'

I waited. Hours and hours in the lobby of the Hotel St Moritz, Central Park south. Behind windows the city is grey. Great lighted clocks scan the seconds at the tops of skyscrapers. Soon it will start to snow. People rush past who have come to New York on business, and who are going home laden with presents in coloured packages, their ribbons fluttering to the ground. In this festive atmosphere I find it strange to be meeting a man who contributed to the deaths of 60,000 people and turned their city into a monument for all time.

Three hours later the man sits down on the other side of the table, a glass in his hands. He is thin; his eyes are deeply marked, making his glance look old. But his hands are calm. When we shook hands I could feel they were cold and dry. He speaks first.

'How do I look?'

'I couldn't say. I've only seen your photographs. In them you seem older. And more tired and down on your luck.'

'I'm not old, or tired; only tormented. But not all the time. They have taken care of my nightmares. Right there in Waco; a doctor by the name of Parker. Grey-haired man; thin. It was heavy treatment. I don't know if their methods have changed, but the one they used with me was useless. "Give it up, Claude," Parker said, "you're not guilty. It just fell to you to pilot a plane over Hiroshima. How many other Claudes were there in the air force who would have carried out an order as important as that one? The war finished; they went home. And what was the order anyway? Look at the sky and say: *Too many clouds here. Can't see Kokura and Nagasaki. Better do Hiroshima.*" Every day for fourteen months Doctor Parker gave me more or less the same speech. In the end I had to ask not to see him any more. I'd got worse.'

'There are a lot of stories, Mr. Eatherly. Some people say you're a fake. Why?'

He doesn't answer immediately. Instead he asks if he can take advantage of my hospitality: would I have another drink with him? I wouldn't like to give the impression that Eatherly was an alcoholic. He could hold a bottle of whisky without any trouble and his eyes never clouded over. They remained alert and cold, just as they had been when he entered, bringing in a little of the wind from the city.

'You mean what Will Bradfort Huie wrote? He's a journalist who spent two days with me and then wrote a book—a whole book—about my life. Who am I? I don't know. But no one can describe himself in a minute. If I asked you point blank: "Do you think of yourself as an honest person, or someone who works at giving others an impression to suit your own needs?" would you be able to demonstrate either in a minute? I doubt it. I didn't know how to answer him either.'

'Are you a pacifist as you've claimed for years?'

'I am, and sincerely so, as is any American of good will. If I were religious, I would say that pacifism springs from a Jewish or Christian consciousness, but I'm not religious, and I don't want to look a fool expounding my philosophy. I can't be religious after Hiroshima. When someone makes a trip like mine and returns alive, he either kills himself or he lives like a

Trappist monk. Cloistered; praying that the world changes and that the likes of Claude Eatherly and Paul Tibbets and the scientists who worked on the bomb are never born again.'

Claude grew up in Texas, where discourse is uninformed by Edwardian whispers from New England. Hearty laughter and loud voices; every sensation seems amplified. After the Japanese bombed Pearl Harbor, Texas offered more volunteers than any other state—the yellow devils had to be punished. Eatherly was among the volunteers. The youngest of six children, and a tackle on the Texas North College football team, he had a level head and a solid way of bringing them down. He didn't miss in the air either: he shot down thirty-three planes and his career took off. After three years he became a major, and a brilliant future seemed to await the handsome man with two bravery medals on his chest. The medals were what dug his grave. In the summer of 1945, he got orders to return home, but first he had to carry out one more mission. Just one.

15   You don't send a soldier home for the pleasure of giving him a little of the good life. In the letter he posted to his mother announcing his imminent return, Claude wrote, 'This will be the last cigarette they stick in this prisoner's mouth.' Nothing to get worried about. He went to New Mexico and joined a formation of supermen: the best, bravest, most famous pilots, all being trained in secret. They assigned him to a Boeing B-29 Superfortress that Claude christened *Straight Flush*.

The account of that morning some weeks later belongs to history. Three planes take off during the night of 6 August from Tinian in the Mariana Islands. Paul Tibbets is the group's commander. Eatherly opens the formation. There are no bombs in his plane; as for the others, no one suspects what a terrible device is hidden inside the *Enola Gay*. A bigger contrivance, they think, nothing more. Eatherly's job is to pinpoint the target with maximum accuracy. He must establish whether weather conditions allow for the centre to be Hiroshima, Kokura or Nagasaki, or whether they should continue towards secondary targets. He tells the story of that morning's events in a voice devoid of emotion which suggests that the recitation is the thousandth one.

'I had command of the lead plane, the *Straight Flush*. I flew over Hiroshima for fifteen minutes, studying the clouds covering the target—a bridge between the military zone and the city. Fifteen Japanese fighters were circling beneath me, but they're not made to fly above 29,000 feet where we were to be found. I looked up: cumulus clouds at 10,000, 12,000 metres. The wind was blowing them towards Hiroshima. Perfect weather. I could see the target clearly: the central span of the bridge. I laugh now when I think of the order: "I want only the central arch of the bridge, *only* that, you understand?" Even if I'd guessed that we were carrying something a bit special, the houses, the roads, the city still seemed very far away from our bomb. I said to myself: This morning's just a big scare for the Japanese.

'I transmitted the coded message, but the person who aimed the bomb made an error of 3,000 feet. Towards the city, naturally. But three thousand feet one way or the other wouldn't have made much difference: that's what I thought as I watched it drop. Then the explosion stunned me momentarily. Hiroshima disappeared under a yellow cloud. No one spoke after that. Usually when you return from a mission with everyone still alive, you exchange messages with each other, impressions, congratulations. This time the radios stayed silent; three planes close together and mute. Not for fear of the enemy, but for fear of our own words. Each one of us must have asked forgiveness for the bomb. I'm not religious and I didn't know who to ask forgiveness from, but in that moment I made a promise to myself to oppose all bombs and all wars. Never again that yellow cloud . . .'

Eatherly raises his voice. It is clear the yellow cloud accompanies him through his life.

'And what did Tibbets say?'   20

'Tibbets has nerves of steel, but the evening afterwards he explained how he spent those minutes. They had told him to be extremely careful: he was most at risk. So when the machine gunner yelled that the shock waves were on their way, he veered to take photographs; but the aeroplane just bounced like a ping-pong ball held up by a fountain. Calm returned and Tibbets felt tired; he asked to be relieved, and fell asleep. But he talked about it that evening when the number of victims was just beginning to be known. He kept on saying: "I'm sorry guys, I did my duty. I've no regrets." And I don't have his nerves. A year later I asked to be discharged.'

'What reason did you give?'

'Exhaustion. I was exhausted. And I wanted to get married. It's risky to bring matters of conscience into it when you're in the forces. They were astounded—how could I throw away such a promising future? The day of my discharge they waved a sheet of paper in front of me. It said I would receive 237 dollars a month pension. That was good money in those days, but I turned it down. And since the regulations didn't allow me to refuse, I put it in writing that the sum was to go to war widows. The end of my relationship with flying.'

He didn't tell the rest of the story willingly. He returns to Texas where his family doesn't recognize him: thin, nervous, irascible, 24 years old. He marries the Italian girl he met in New Mexico while he was training for the final mission. Concetta Margetti had tried Hollywood and finally been reduced to selling cigarettes in a local nightclub—not perhaps the ideal wife for someone in Claude's state. But they write to each other, they get married. A war story, yes; but the war had shredded Eatherly's nerves. In the middle of the night he wakes his wife, breathless and in tears: 'Hit the ground, the yellow cloud's coming!' It goes on like this for four years. His family finally convince him to enter the psychiatric hospital in Waco as a voluntary patient. He can take walks in the park any time of the day or night. He plays golf and receives visitors. Concetta keeps him company on Sunday. His brother brings him books and a pair of running shoes.

Then the problems start. Claude forges a cheque to send to the victims of Hiroshima. He enters a bank with a toy pistol; for a few minutes the employees are terrified until Eatherly bursts out laughing. One day his move succeeds; he threatens a department store clerk with a fake gun and makes her turn over the money, which he throws from a balcony before   25 escaping. They catch him and take him back to Waco. He's no longer a voluntary patient: now they lock him in. They accuse him of behaving in an antisocial way. (This euphemism is the last show of respect for his heroic war record.) He is confined to his room.

After fourteen months in the mental hospital he leaves, a ghost. His wife abandons him. His brother closes his bank account. Claude cannot look after himself or his money. And now the protest smoulders again. He enters a bar in Texas, armed. He threatens the people inside and gets them to put their money into the sack he is holding, just like he's seen in films. But it comes to nothing. He is handcuffed and taken to gaol in a police car. The sergeant accompanying him doesn't know who he is, only that he's an ex-pilot. I asked Eatherly how it felt to be facing a prison sentence for the first time.

'I should say terrible, but it wasn't. Nothing mattered to me. I'd been in prison all the time; the door was inside me. In the police car the sergeant was staring at me. He was curious. He was thinking about some famous criminal . . . It was a long trip. I was quiet, but his staring eyes bothered me. "Where do you come from, sergeant?" I asked him. "From Chicago." And I: "I knew you came from somewhere." I wanted to unfreeze the atmosphere, but he wasn't having it. He asked me: "It's not strictly legal, but can you talk, here in the car?" I made a yes sign.

' "Where are you from?"

' "From here."

30   ' "Where were you based during the war?"

' "In the Pacific."

' "I was in the Pacific too. Where did they land you?"

' "Tinian, in the Marianas, special group 509."

'He looked at me, stunned. "I know who you are. You're Major Eatherly! Good God, Major, how did you end up like this? You're sick, right? I read that somewhere. I'll give you a hand."

35   'Then they locked me up in the loony bin again.'

His torment went on: a poor soul, incapable of getting on with the business of life. No one understands his drama. People's aversion to him grows. Let's not forget that Eatherly lived out this difficult period in the America of Senator McCarthy—the Grand Inquisitor of frustrated nationalism. McCarthy fomented a type of suspicion which reflected the cold war: the witch hunt. Eatherly becomes a witch. His passionate, if slightly naïve, criticism of the mechanisms of war is considered a threat to national security. The judges disagree over his case. The biography confected by William Bradfort Huie from less than two days of interviews weakens his defence. For Bradfort, the Major 'never saw the ball of fire, nor was he aware of the yellow wave. By the time of the explosion, he and his gunner were 100 kilometres from the site.' Returning to base he was surprised by the journalists and photographers crowding the runway where the *Enola Gay* had landed. 'If Eatherly is mad,' writes Bradfort, 'then his madness was hatched on 6 August, 1945, not from horror but from jealousy.'

'When I knew him,' Bradfort Huie continues implacably, 'he was already a fraud. Right off he asked me for five hundred dollars. He had never once attempted suicide. I spent a long time with him, and I looked at his wrists: there were no scars.'

'Is that true Claude?'

'These are not the kind of things you want to brag about. Look at my arms.' He turns up the sleeves of his jacket and unbuttons his cuffs. Two purple scars, deep and unpleasant, run towards his hands. 'I don't want you to pity me. I'm happy to have been able to talk. Now I've got to go.'

He disappeared as he had appeared, with the same suddenness.   40
Before passing through the bar door and turning out into the hall he looked back, as if he had forgotten something. 'I want to apologize for being late. And thanks for these . . .' He gestured towards the row of glasses on the table.

'It was my pleasure to meet you. Merry Christmas.'

Fourteen months later Claude Eatherly took his life.

READING CRITICALLY FOR IDEAS, STRUCTURE, AND STYLE

1. How did Claude Eatherly's decision regarding the weather conditions over Japan, on the day the atomic bomb was dropped irrevocably alter his life?

2. What means does Chierici use, as an interviewer, to put Eatherly's story in a context that will allow the reader to understand how Eatherly was ultimately destroyed by this event?

3. How does Eatherly's personal guilt, despite what the military physicians tell him should be the case, take over his life?

EXTENDING INSIGHTS THROUGH WRITING

1. Conduct an interview with someone who was involved in a momentous event and write up your results in a way that will allow your readers to understand why the event was important (in a social, political, or historical context) and the effect it had on the person's life.

2. How does Eatherly's story illustrate society's attitude towards those who perform its "dirty work" in wartime?

CONNECTING PERSPECTIVES ON THE HISTORICAL DIMENSION

1. Eatherly, as the person who made the ultimate decision that weather permitted the dropping of the bomb on Hiroshima, clearly changed history. Would Thomas Carlyle's definition of the hero (as stated in "On Heroes and Hero-Worship") apply to Eatherly? Why or why not?

2. What insight does Eatherly's evolution into a scapegoat figure offer into the psychological process by which Satan came to represent evil, according to Elaine Pagels?

JOHN F. KENNEDY

Inaugural Address 1961

BACKGROUND

John Fitzgerald Kennedy (1917–1963) was the President of the United States from 1960–1963. He was born in Brookline, Massachusetts, graduated from Harvard University in 1940, and rose through the ranks of local and national politics, first serving as a congressman from the 11th congressional district in Massachusetts between 1946 and 1952 to a senator from 1952–1960 to become president in 1960. He was the youngest elected president in history and the country's first Roman Catholic head of state. The contrast between the young, handsome, personable Kennedy and Dwight Eisenhower, who was then seventy-years old, the oldest man to hold this office, suggested that a new day was indeed about to dawn. During World War II, Kennedy was a decorated PT boat commander in the Navy. In 1953, he married Jacqueline Lee Bouvier and had two children, Caroline and John, Jr. Kennedy's reign in office came to be known as Camelot because of the aura of glamour and sense of promise that it conveyed.

He is the author of a number of important works, including *While England Slept* (1940) and *Profiles in Courage* (1956), which won the Pulitzer Prize for that year. Kennedy's speeches, which were fashioned in collaboration with Ted Sorenson (who in 1954 became Kennedy's speech writer), are models of persuasive public rhetoric. The inaugural address that he delivered on January 20, 1961, defines both the Kennedy *persona* and his hopes for America in the forthcoming years. Kennedy was assassinated on November 22, 1963, in Dallas, Texas, and is buried in Arlington National Cemetery in Virginia.

APPROACHING KENNEDY'S SPEECH

The night before the inauguration, heavy snow had fallen and there was some discussion about canceling the inauguration ceremonies. It went forward as scheduled because Kennedy wanted to enlist public support for his program in view of the closeness of the election between him and the Republican candidate, Richard M. Nixon. Poet Robert Frost had composed a verse for the occasion but was unable to read it because of glare from the sun, and instead recited a poem from memory. Chief Justice Earl Warren administered the oath of office, and Kennedy delivered the following short address that he had been revising as early as that morning. Kennedy had decided the week before that the address should concentrate on international rather than just domestic issues and had suggested that Ted Sorenson study Lincoln's Gettysburg Address to discover why it proved so effective. The speech Sorenson and Kennedy fashioned was short and to the point, avoids polysyllabic words, and does not use clichéd or hackneyed expressions. The resulting text makes use of alliteration, balanced clauses, and memorable lines (for example, "Ask not what your country can do for you—ask what you can do for your country"). The address strikes just the correct balance between a willingness to negotiate with the Soviet Union and resolve the tensions of the Cold War and a readiness to defend the Americas from Soviet expansion.

Inaugural Address

Friday, January 20, 1961

Vice President Johnson, Mr. Speaker, Mr. Chief Justice, President Eisenhower, Vice President Nixon, President Truman, reverend clergy, fellow citizens, we observe today not a victory of party, but a celebration of freedom—symbolizing an end, as well as a beginning—signifying renewal, as well as change. For I have sworn before you and Almighty God the same solemn oath our forebears prescribed nearly a century and three quarters ago.

The world is very different now. For man holds in his mortal hands the power to abolish all forms of human poverty and all forms of human life. And yet the same revolutionary beliefs for which our forebears fought are still at issue around the globe—the belief that the rights of man come not from the generosity of the state, but from the hand of God.

We dare not forget today that we are the heirs of that first revolution. Let the word go forth from this time and place, to friend and foe alike, that the torch has been passed to a new generation of Americans—born in this century, tempered by war, disciplined by a hard and bitter peace, proud of our ancient heritage—and unwilling to witness or permit the slow undoing of those human rights to which this Nation has always been committed, and to which we are committed today at home and around the world.

Let every nation know, whether it wishes us well or ill, that we shall pay any price, bear any burden, meet any hardship, support any friend, oppose any foe, in order to assure the survival and the success of liberty.

This much we pledge—and more. 5

To those old allies whose cultural and spiritual origins we share, we pledge the loyalty of faithful friends. United, there is little we cannot do in a host of cooperative ventures. Divided, there is little we can do—for we dare not meet a powerful challenge at odds and split asunder.

To those new States whom we welcome to the ranks of the free, we pledge our word that one form of colonial control shall not have passed away merely to be replaced by a far more iron tyranny. We shall not always expect to find them supporting our view. But we shall always hope to find them strongly supporting their own freedom—and to remember that, in the past, those who foolishly sought power by riding the back of the tiger ended up inside.

To those peoples in the huts and villages across the globe struggling to break the bonds of mass misery, we pledge our best efforts to help them help themselves, for whatever period is required—not because the Communists may be doing it, not because we seek their votes, but because it is right. If a free society cannot help the many who are poor, it cannot save the few who are rich.

To our sister republics south of our border, we offer a special pledge— to convert our good words into good deeds—in a new alliance for progress— to assist free men and free governments in casting off the chains of poverty. But this peaceful revolution of hope cannot become the prey of hostile powers. Let all our neighbors know that we shall join with them to oppose aggression or subversion anywhere in the Americas. And let every other power know that this Hemisphere intends to remain the master of its own house.

To that world assembly of sovereign states, the United Nations, our 10 last best hope in an age where the instruments of war have far outpaced the instruments of peace, we renew our pledge of support—to prevent it from becoming merely a forum for invective—to strengthen its shield of the new and the weak—and to enlarge the area in which its writ may run.

Finally, to those nations who would make themselves our adversary, we offer not a pledge but a request: that both sides begin anew the quest for peace, before the dark powers of destruction unleashed by science engulf all humanity in planned or accidental self-destruction.

We dare not tempt them with weakness. For only when our arms are sufficient beyond doubt can we be certain beyond doubt that they will never be employed.

But neither can two great and powerful groups of nations take comfort from our present course—both sides overburdened by the cost of modern weapons, both rightly alarmed by the steady spread of the deadly atom, yet both racing to alter that uncertain balance of terror that stays the hand of mankind's final war.

So let us begin anew—remembering on both sides that civility is not a sign of weakness, and sincerity is always subject to proof. Let us never negotiate out of fear. But let us never fear to negotiate.

Let both sides explore what problems unite us instead of belaboring 15 those problems which divide us.

Let both sides, for the first time, formulate serious and precise proposals for the inspection and control of arms—and bring the absolute power to destroy other nations under the absolute control of all nations.

Let both sides seek to invoke the wonders of science instead of its terrors. Together let us explore the stars, conquer the deserts, eradicate disease, tap the ocean depths, and encourage the arts and commerce.

Let both sides unite to heed in all corners of the earth the command of Isaiah—to "undo the heavy burdens . . . and to let the oppressed go free."

And if a beachhead of cooperation may push back the jungle of suspicion, let both sides join in creating a new endeavor, not a new balance of power, but a new world of law, where the strong are just and the weak secure and the peace preserved.

20   All this will not be finished in the first 100 days. Nor will it be finished in the first 1,000 days, nor in the life of this Administration, nor even perhaps in our lifetime on this planet. But let us begin.

In your hands, my fellow citizens, more than in mine, will rest the final success or failure of our course. Since this country was founded, each generation of Americans has been summoned to give testimony to its national loyalty. The graves of young Americans who answered the call to service surround the globe.

Now the trumpet summons us again—not as a call to bear arms, though arms we need; not as a call to battle, though embattled we are—but a call to bear the burden of a long twilight struggle, year in and year out, "rejoicing in hope, patient in tribulation"—a struggle against the common enemies of man: tyranny, poverty, disease, and war itself.

Can we forge against these enemies a grand and global alliance, North and South, East and West, that can assure a more fruitful life for all mankind? Will you join in that historic effort?

In the long history of the world, only a few generations have been granted the role of defending freedom in its hour of maximum danger. I do not shrink from this responsibility—I welcome it. I do not believe that any of us would exchange places with any other people or any other generation. The energy, the faith, the devotion which we bring to this endeavor will light our country and all who serve it—and the glow from that fire can truly light the world.

25   And so, my fellow Americans: ask not what your country can do for you—ask what you can do for your country.

My fellow citizens of the world: ask not what America will do for you, but what together we can do for the freedom of man.

Finally, whether you are citizens of America or citizens of the world, ask of us the same high standards of strength and sacrifice which we ask of you. With a good conscience our only sure reward, with history the final judge of our deeds, let us go forth to lead the land we love, asking His blessing and His help, but knowing that here on earth God's work must truly be our own.

READING CRITICALLY FOR IDEAS, STRUCTURE, AND STYLE

1. Based on a careful reading of Kennedy's speech, what can you infer about the state of the world and the nature of the challenges the new government would face at the time he gave this Inaugural Address in 1961?

2. What elements in this address are rhetorically crafted to resonate at that moment and to be remembered in the future? How does Kennedy's style depend on balance, symmetry, and epigrammatic conciseness?

3. Kennedy's public _persona_ and image were greatly strengthened by this speech. Why do you think this was the case?

EXTENDING INSIGHTS THROUGH WRITING

1. Paraphrase one section of Kennedy's Inaugural Address and analyze what is gained or lost in terms of stylistic effects.

2. Imagine you are President Kennedy and write an Inaugural Address in the same style suitable for today.

CONNECTING PERSPECTIVES ON THE HISTORICAL DIMENSION

1. Do some research on Kennedy's life and presidency and discuss whether he fits Thomas Carlyle's definition of the hero.

2. Drawing on Arnold J. Toynbee's analysis, discuss how Kennedy's Inaugural Address was a response to the challenges that faced the United States at that time.

OSCAR HANDLIN

Steerage

BACKGROUND

Oscar Handlin, born in 1915 in New York City as the son of Jewish immigrants, received his Ph. D. from Harvard in 1935. A distinguished social
historian, Handlin is the author of many definitive works, including *The Uprooted* (1951), which received the Pulitzer Prize; *Immigration as a Factor in
American History* (1959); *Truth in History* (1979); and *The Distortion of America* (1981). He has also served as the editor of important works that interpret
the immigrant experience in America, which include *Children of the Uprooted*
(1966) and the *Harvard Encyclopedia of American Ethnic Groups* (1980). His
most recent works include *The Road to Gettysburg* (1986) and a multivolume
series (with Lillian Handlin), *Liberty in America, 1600 to the Present*, of which
the latest is *Liberty and Equality, 1920–1994* (1994). "Steerage," drawn from
the second chapter of *The Uprooted*, conveys Handlin's mastery in compressing
a wealth of detail on the immigrant experience into a few telling pages.

APPROACHING HANDLIN'S ESSAY

In his description of immigration as a defining experience for millions of
Americans, Handlin tells us that the forty-day journey in steerage from
Liverpool to New York was a hardship because the small ships were crammed
with 400 to 1,000 passengers. Each family received meager rations, which
had to last the entire journey. Because food and water supplies were limited,
many passengers starved to death. The average mortality figure for those making the crossing in the middle 1800s was between 10 percent and 20 percent.
Unscrupulous, merciless captains preyed on the immigrants by extorting every
last possession from them in return for food and drink. Disease was rampant,
the monotony was unbearable, petty thievery was common, and women were
considered fair game by the seamen.

Handlin skillfully weaves together a set of descriptive details to give his readers insight into the cramped quarters that hundreds of thousands had to endure in order to emigrate on ships to America in the twentieth century.

Steerage

The difficulty of residence in the ports complicated the problems of securing passage. The overpowering desire to get away as soon as possible took precedence over every other consideration. The temptation was to regard the ship quickest found, the best. Haste often led to unexpected and tragic consequences.

Until after the middle of the nineteenth century, the emigrants were carried in sailing vessels, few in number, irregular in the routes they followed, and uncertain as to their destination. Often the masters of these craft did not know for which port they would head until the sails were set; generally the cargo dictated the course. But there was no assurance, even after the ship was under way, that wind or weather would not induce a change. Only rarely could the passengers protest or, as on the *Mary Ann* in 1817, actually revolt. The generality did not expect to be able to choose a precise place of landing in the New World; if they reached shore somewhere in America that was enough.

Nor could they be overly fastidious about the character of their conveyance. Reckoning up the sum of guarded coins, the emigrants knew how little power they had to command favorable terms. The fare could, of course, be haggled over; there were no established rates and those who shared the same steerage would later discover that the charge varied from two to five pounds, depending upon the bargaining power of the various parties. But in the long run the shipmasters held the more favorable situation and could push the rate nearer the higher than the lower limit.

Indeed, as the volume of traffic mounted, the captains no longer had to trouble with these negotiations themselves. The business fell into the hands of middlemen. Enterprising brokers contracted for the steerage space of whole ships and then resold accommodations to prospective travelers. As might be expected, avarice magnified the fancied capacity of the vessels to an unbearable degree, in fact, to a degree that provoked government intervention. But even when the American and British governments began to regulate the number of passengers and, after 1850, even began to enforce those regulations, the emigrant was but poorly protected. The brokers continued to sell as many tickets as they could; and the purchasers above the legal limit, denied permission to board, could only hope to hunt up the swindler who had misled them and seek the return of their funds.

In time, at last, the day approached. On the morning the fortunate ones whose turn it was worriedly gathered their possessions, hastened from

5

lodginghouse to ship's side. The children dragged along the trusses of straw on which they would sleep while the men wrestled onward with the cumbrous barrels that would hold their water, with the battered chests crammed with belongings. Not into the ship yet, but into a thronging expectant crowd they pushed their way, shoving to keep sight of each other, deafened by their own impatient noises and by the cries of peddlers who thrust at them now nuts and taffy for the moment, now pots and provisions for the way.

Some, having waited so long, would wait no more and tried to clamber up the dangling ropes. The most stayed anxiously still and when the moment came jostled along until they stood then upon the ship. And when they stood then upon the ship, when the Old Land was no longer beneath them, they sensed the sea in uneasy motion and knew they were committed to a new destiny. As they lined up for the roll call, their curious gaze sought out the features of this their unfamiliar home—the rising masts, the great folds of sail, the web of rigging, and the bold, pointing bowsprit. Silenced and as if immobilized by the decisiveness of the moment, they remained for a while on deck; and some, raising their eyes from examination of the ship itself, noticed the shores of the Mersey or Weser move slowly by. There was time, before they passed through the estuary to the empty ocean, to reflect on the long way they had come, to mingle with the hope and gratitude of escape the sadness and resentment of flight.

In the early days there was leisure enough for reflection on these matters. The journey was long, the average from Liverpool to New York about forty days. Favorable weather might lower the figure to a month, unfavorable raise it to two or three. The span was uncertain, for the ship was at the mercy of the winds and tides, of the primitive navigation of its masters, and of the ignorance of its barely skilled sailors.

These unsubstantial craft sailed always at the edge of danger from the elements. Wrecks were disastrous and frequent. A single year in the 1830's saw seventeen vessels founder on the run from Liverpool to Quebec alone. Occasional mutinies put the fate of all in dubious hands. Fire, caused by the carelessness of passengers or crew, added another hazard to the trials of the journey. At a blow, such catastrophes swept away scores of lives, ended without further ado many minor histories in the peopling of the new continent.

Other perils too, less dramatic but more pervasive, insidiously made shipwreck of hopes. In the slow-elapsing crossing, the boat became a circumscribed universe of its own, with its own harsh little way of life determined by the absence of space. Down to midcentury the vessels were pitifully small; three hundred tons was a good size. Yet into these tiny craft were crammed anywhere from four hundred to a thousand passengers.

10   These numbers set the terms of shipboard life. If they talked of it later, the emigrants almost forgot that there had also been cabins for the other sort of men who could pay out twenty to forty pounds for passage. Their own world was the steerage.

Below decks is the place, its usual dimensions seventy-five feet long, twenty-five wide, five and a half high. Descend. In the fitful light your eye will discover a middle aisle five feet wide. It will be a while before you can make out the separate shapes within it, the water closets at either end (for the women; the men must go above deck), one or several cooking stoves, the tables. The aisle itself, you will see, is formed by two rows of bunks that run to the side of the ship.

Examine a bunk. One wooden partition reaches from floor to ceiling to divide it from the aisle, another stretches horizontally from wall to aisle to create two decks. Within the partitions are the boxlike spaces, ten feet wide, five long, less than three high. For the months of the voyage, each is home for six to ten beings.

This was the steerage setting. Here the emigrants lived their lives, day and night. The more generous masters gave them access to a portion of the deck at certain hours. But bad weather often deprived the passengers of that privilege, kept them below for days on end.

Life was hard here. Each family received its daily ration of water, adding to it larger and larger doses of vinegar to conceal the odor. From the limited hoard of provisions brought along, the mother struggled to eke out food for the whole journey. She knew that if the potatoes ran out there would be only the captain to turn to, who could be counted on mercilessly to extort every last possession in return; some masters, in fact, deliberately deceived the emigrants as to the length of the journey, to be able to profit from the sale of food and grog. Later, at midcentury, the government would specify the supplies that had to be taken for each passenger. But there remained ways of avoiding such regulations; tenders followed the ships out of the harbor and carried back the casks checked on for the inspector.

It was no surprise that disease should be a familiar visitor. The only   15
ventilation was through the hatches battened down in rough weather. When the close air was not stifling hot, it was bitter cold in the absence of fire. Rats were at home in the dirt and disorder. The result: cholera, dysentery, yellow fever, smallpox, measles, and the generic "ship fever" that might be anything. It was not always as bad as on the *April*, on which five hundred of eleven hundred Germans perished in the crossing; the normal mortality was about 10 per cent, although in the great year, 1847, it was closer to 20.

It was perhaps no consolation to these emigrants, but they were not the worst off. Among the Irish before 1850 there were some who had not the paltry price of a steerage passage, yet for whom there was no return from Liverpool. They had to find the means of a still cheaper crossing.

From Canada came awkward ships built expressly to bring eastward the tall timbers of American forests, lumbering vessels with great open holds not suited for the carriage of any west-bound cargo. From Nova Scotia and Newfoundland came fishing boats laden with the catch of the Grand Bank; these craft also could be entrusted with no cargo of value on their return. Formerly both types went back in ballast. Now they would bring the New World to Irishmen. The pittance these poor creatures could pay—ten to twenty shillings—was pure gain. As for the passengers, they would camp out in the empty stinking space below decks, spend an uneasy purgatory preparatory to the redemption by America.

From the harshness, the monotony, the misery of the journey, there was no effective relief. Government protection came late, was minimal, and lacked effective means of enforcement. After all, as the shipping agents argued, the emigrant had never known what it was to sleep in a bed. Give him pork and flour and you make the man sick. Let him lie on a good firm deck, eat salt herring, and he'll be hale and hearty.

Against the open brutalities, against the seamen who reckoned the women fair game, against the danger from within of petty theft and quarrels, the passengers formed spontaneous organizations of their own. The voluntary little associations were governed by codes of agreement, enforced by watchmen appointed from among themselves. But there was no power in these groups, on major matters, to resist the all-powerful captain and crew.

So they'd lie there, seafaring adventurers out to discover new continents, amidst the retching, noisome stench, the stomach-turning filth of hundreds of bodies confined to close quarters. Many nights, and many days that were indistinguishable from nights, they could see, by the sickly light of swinging lanterns, the creaking ugly timbers crowding in about them; they could hear the sounds of men in uneasy silence, of children in fitful rest; everywhere they could sense the menace of hostile winds and waves, of indifferent companions, of repressed passions.

There are times when a man can take no more. Incidents occur: ugly noises of childbirth; sopping disorder when the sea seeps in in a storm; unsuccessful rat-hunts; the splash of burials under a dark sky and without the consolation of a priest. *Ah, we thought we couldn't be worse off than we war; but now to our sorrow we know the differ; for supposin we war dyin of starvation, it would still not be dyin like rotten sheep thrown into a pit, and the minit the breath is out of our bodies, flung into the sea to be eaten up by them horrid sharks.* And a red rage takes hold of the sufferers, of their survivors. They pace about in the warm sticky passage. They clench fists. But against whom shall they raise them? Indeed they are helpless, and they fall into meaningless arguments among themselves. Furious blows are given by the wrestling mass of men in the narrow spaces; until, exhausted, they stand back, angry, ashamed, pick up the pitiful belongings kicked loose, broken, wet from the bilge water oozing up through the spaces of the floor boards. They laugh only at the greater misery of others.

Substantial improvements in the conditions of the crossing came only as indirect results of changes in the techniques of ocean travel. The introduction of steam in the transatlantic service in the 1840s was the first step. The Cunard Line and its imitators pre-empted the high-class passenger business and drove the sailing ships back upon the immigrant trade. Competition for that trade lowered the costs and improved the accommodations. By 1860 it was possible to buy reasonably priced prepaid tickets and to travel on a reliable schedule.

After 1870 the situation was even better. The new era in international relations emphasized navalism and drew the major European nations into a warship building race. Great merchant fleets seemed the necessary complements. England, France, Germany, and Italy hurried to build up their tonnage. Toward that end they were willing to grant heavy subsidies to the operators of the lines bearing their flags. Under those circumstances the price of steerage passage on a steamship fell to as little as twelve dollars, and included food. By the end of that decade, steam had displaced sail in the emigrant-carrying business.

Now the duration of the journey fell until it took ten days or less. Comfort and safety increased also. By 1900, the traveler could count on a crossing of little more than a week in vessels of ten to twenty thousand tons.

READING CRITICALLY FOR IDEAS, STRUCTURE, AND STYLE

1. Consider the measures that were taken by the U.S. and British governments to regulate the number of immigrants who boarded ships, the amount of food alloted, and the conditions of their passage. Why did these measures fail to protect the immigrants?

2. How does Handlin's use of statistics, and his description of the physical conditions in steerage during the forty-day journey from Liverpool to New York, make it possible for the reader to share the experience of the immigrants?

3. In paragraph 11, how effective is Handlin's change in writing style from an objective point of view to a subjective description that takes the reader into the world of the passengers in steerage? How does his use of descriptive imagery communicate this horrendous experience?

4. How does Handlin organize his description so as to lead the reader to descend with him below decks into the netherworld of steerage?

EXTENDING INSIGHTS THROUGH WRITING

1. Being an immigrant in the dehumanizing circumstances Handlin describes was made bearable only by the hope of a better life in the new world. In a short essay, discuss the meaning this journey had for the immigrants. If appropriate, draw on the experiences of your own family.

2. Many descendants of these immigrants now travel back to the Old World on cruise ships. Discuss the contrasting circumstances and symbolism of these very different kinds of voyages and their meanings in contemporary culture.

CONNECTING PERSPECTIVES ON THE HISTORICAL DIMENSION

1. How does Edward Said, in "Reflections on Exile," extend Handlin's description of the physical circumstances that confronted immigrants into an analysis of the psychological state of immigrants today?

2. In a few paragraphs, compare Handlin's account of this particular group of immigrants with Arnold J. Toynbee's mythic account of the movement of savages toward civilization. In what way are the courageous and risky voyages taken by these immigrants an example of "cliff-climbing" rather than "ledge-sitting" in Toynbee's analogy?

EDWARD SAID

Reflections on Exile

BACKGROUND

Edward Said (born in 1935) is a Palestinian who was educated in Palestine and Egypt when those countries were under British jurisdiction. Said is Parr professor of English and Comparative Literature at Columbia University. He is best known for his critical works, including *Orientalism* (1978), a lively analysis of how the West has created certain cultural stereotypes about the East; *The World, Text, and The Critic* (1983); *Culture and Imperialism* (1993); *Peace and Its Discontents* (1995); and *Out of Place: A Memoir* (1999). Said's influence has been enormous, and he is often credited as the founder of a new discipline that shares insights from literary theory, history, anthropology, and political science —the cultural study of colonialism. "Reflections on Exile," which first appeared in *Granta* (Autumn 1984), offers a penetrating analysis of the plight of the exiled and the role this condition has played in literature of the twentieth century.

APPROACHING SAID'S ESSAY

According to Said, exiles experience a sense of psychological dislocation because they do not feel connected to the new countries in which they reside. This feeling of isolation and detachment makes it difficult for exiles to adjust, and in this sense they live *between* countries rather than *in* any one place, as strangers in a strange land, caught between two cultures, at home in neither. They differ from refugees who feel a sense of communal bonding as they move into new countries *en masse* after being dispossessed by wars and natural disasters. Said links this state of exile with literary works by writers who attempt to compensate for a lost homeland, as James Joyce did (in *Ulysses*) after he left Ireland, and as Dante did (in *The Divine Comedy*) after he was exiled from Florence. The twentieth-century novel may even be said to be the chosen art form of the dispossessed intellectual. Said holds out the possibility that those who live as outsiders in a culture to which they have emigrated may achieve a level of detachment akin to that of a religious ascetic who has transcended worldly attachments. This piece might be considered an example of how the essay can develop an extended definition that brings into play a variety of rhetorical methods. Said uses memorable illustrations, comparisons and contrasts, and offers synonyms that clarify and define the basic nature of exile. He delves deeply into this concept by looking at its connotations, defining criteria, and offering variations in its meaning. His definition goes far beyond what people might initially associate with the term and broadens it to include the human condition in the twentieth century.

Reflections on Exile

Exile is strangely compelling to think about but terrible to experience. It is the unhealable rift forced between a human being and a native place, between the self and its true home: its essential sadness can never be surmounted. And while it is true that literature and history contain heroic, romantic, glorious, even triumphant episodes in an exile's life, these are no more than efforts meant to overcome the crippling sorrow of estrangement. The achievements of exile are permanently undermined by the loss of something left behind for ever.

Exiles look at non-exiles with resentment. *They* belong in their surroundings, you feel, whereas an exile is always out of place. What is it like to be born in a place, to stay and live there, to know that you are of it, more or less for ever?

Although it is true that anyone prevented from returning home is an exile, some distinctions can be made between exiles, refugees, expatriates and émigrés. Exile originated in the age-old practice of banishment. Once banished, the exile lives an anomalous and miserable life, with the stigma of being an outsider. Refugees, on the other hand, are a creation of the twentieth-century state. The word 'refugee' has become a political one, suggesting large herds of innocent and bewildered people requiring urgent international assistance, whereas 'exile' carries with it, I think, a touch of solitude and spirituality.

Expatriates voluntarily live in an alien country, usually for personal or social reasons. Hemingway and Fitzgerald were not forced to live in France. Expatriates may share in the solitude and estrangement of exile, but they do not suffer under its rigid proscriptions. Émigrés enjoy an ambiguous status. Technically, an émigré is anyone who emigrates to a new country. Choice in the matter is certainly a possibility. Colonial officials, missionaries, technical experts, mercenaries and military advisers on loan may in a sense live in exile, but they have not been banished. White settlers in Africa, parts of Asia and Australia may once have been exiles, but as pioneers and nation-builders the label 'exile' dropped away from them.

Much of the exile's life is taken up with compensating for disorient-   5
ing loss by creating a new world to rule. It is not surprising that so many exiles seem to be novelists, chess players, political activists, and intellectuals. Each of these occupations requires a minimal investment in objects and places a great premium on mobility and skill. The exile's new world, logically enough, is unnatural and its unreality resembles fiction. Georg Lukács, in *Theory of the Novel*, argued with compelling force that the novel, a literary form created out of the unreality of ambition and fantasy, is *the* form of 'transcendental homelessness.' Classical epics, Lukács wrote, emanate from settled cultures in which values are clear, identities stable, life unchanging. The European novel is grounded in precisely the opposite experience, that of a changing society in which an itinerant and disinherited middle-class hero or heroine seeks to construct a new world that somewhat resembles an old one left behind for ever. In the epic there is no *other* world, only the finality of *this* one. Odysseus returns to Ithaca after years of wandering; Achilles will die because he cannot escape his fate. The novel, however, exists because other worlds *may* exist, alternatives for bourgeois speculators, wanderers, exiles.

No matter how well they may do, exiles are always eccentrics who *feel* their difference (even as they frequently exploit it) as a kind of orphanhood. Anyone who is really homeless regards the habit of seeing estrangement in everything modern as an affectation, a display of modish attitudes. Clutching difference like a weapon to be used with stiffened will, the exile jealously insists on his or her right to refuse to belong.

This usually translates into an intransigence that is not easily ignored. Wilfulness, exaggeration, overstatement: these are characteristic styles of being an exile, methods for compelling the world to accept your vision— which you make more unacceptable because you are in fact unwilling to have it accepted. It is yours, after all. Composure and serenity are the last things associated with the work of exiles. Artists in exile are decidedly unpleasant, and their stubbornness insinuates itself into even their exalted works. Dante's vision in *The Divine Comedy* is tremendously powerful in its universality and detail, but even the beatific peace achieved in the *Paradiso* bears traces of the vindictiveness and severity of judgement embodied in the *Inferno*. Who but an exile like Dante, banished from Florence, would use eternity as a place for settling old scores?

James Joyce *chose* to be in exile: to give force to his artistic vocation. In an uncannily effective way—as Richard Ellmann has shown in his biography—Joyce picked a quarrel with Ireland and kept it alive so as to sustain the strictest opposition to what was familiar. Ellmann says that 'whenever his relations with his native land were in danger of improving, [Joyce] was to find a new incident to solidify his intransigence and to reaffirm the rightness of his voluntary absence.' Joyce's fiction concerns what in a letter he once described as the state of being 'alone and friendless.' And although it is rare to pick banishment as a way of life, Joyce perfectly understood its trials.

But Joyce's success as an exile stresses the question lodged at its very heart: is exile so extreme and private that any instrumental use of it is ultimately a trivialization? How is it that the literature of exile has taken its place as a *topos* of human experience alongside the literature of adventure, education or discovery? Is this the *same* exile that quite literally kills Yanko Goorall and has bred the expensive, often dehumanizing relationship between twentieth-century exile and nationalism? Or is it some more benign variety?

10　　Much of the contemporary interest in exile can be traced to the somewhat pallid notion that non-exiles can share in the benefits of exile as a redemptive motif. There is, admittedly, a certain plausibility and truth to this idea. Like medieval itinerant scholars or learned Greek slaves in the Roman Empire, exiles—the exceptional ones among them—do leaven their environments. And naturally 'we' concentrate on that enlightening aspect of 'their' presence among us, not on their misery or their demands. But looked at from the bleak political perspective of modern mass dislocations, individual exiles force us to recognize the tragic fate of homelessness in a necessarily heartless world.

A generation ago, Simone Weil posed the dilemma of exile as concisely as it has ever been expressed. 'To be rooted,' she said, 'is perhaps the most important and least recognized need of the human soul.' Yet Weil also saw that most remedies for uprootedness in this era of world wars, deportations and mass exterminations are almost as dangerous as what they purportedly remedy. Of these, the state—or, more accurately, statism—is one of the most insidious, since worship of the state tends to supplant all other human bonds.

Weil exposes us anew to that whole complex of pressures and constraints that lie at the centre of the exile's predicament, which, as I have suggested, is as close as we come in the modern era to tragedy. There is the sheer fact of isolation and displacement, which produces the kind of narcissistic masochism that resists all efforts at amelioration, acculturation and community. At this extreme the exile can make a fetish of exile, a practice that distances him or her from all connections and commitments. To live as if everything around you were temporary and perhaps trivial is to fall prey to petulant cynicism as well as to querulous lovelessness. More common is the pressure on the exile to join—parties, national movements, the state. The exile is offered a new set of affiliations and develops new loyalties. But there is also a loss—of critical perspective, of intellectual reserve, of moral courage.

It must also be recognized that the defensive nationalism of exiles often fosters self-awareness as much as it does the less attractive forms of self-assertion. Such reconstitutive projects as assembling a nation out of exile (and this is true in this century for Jews and Palestinians) involve constructing a national history, reviving an ancient language, founding national institutions like libraries and universities. And these, while they sometimes promote strident ethnocentrism, also give rise to investigations of self that inevitably go far beyond such simple and positive facts as 'ethnicity.' For example, there is the self-consciousness of an individual trying to understand why the histories of the Palestinians and the Jews have certain patterns to them, why in spite of oppression and the threat of extinction a particular ethos remains alive in exile.

Necessarily, then, I speak of exile not as a privilege, but as an *alternative* to the mass institutions that dominate modern life. Exile is not, after all, a matter of choice: you are born into it, or it happens to you. But, provided that the exile refuses to sit on the sidelines nursing a wound, there are things to be learned: he or she must cultivate a scrupulous (not indulgent or sulky) subjectivity.

Perhaps the most rigorous example of such subjectivity is to be found in the writing of Theodor Adorno, the German-Jewish philosopher and critic. Adorno's masterwork, *Minima Moralia*, is an autobiography written while in exile; it is subtitled *Reflexionen aus dem beschädigten Leben (Reflections from a Mutilated Life)*. Ruthlessly opposed to what he called the 'administered' world, Adorno saw all life as pressed into ready-made forms, prefabricated 'homes.' He argued that everything that one says or thinks, as well as every object one possesses, is ultimately a mere commodity. Language is jargon, objects are for sale. To refuse this state of affairs is the exile's intellectual mission.

Adorno's reflections are informed by the belief that the only home truly available now, though fragile and vulnerable, is in writing. Elsewhere, 'the house is past. The bombings of European cities, as well as the labour and concentration camps, merely precede as executors, with what the immanent development of technology had long decided was to be the fate of houses. These are now good only to be thrown away like old food cans.' In short, Adorno says with a grave irony, 'it is part of morality not to be at home in one's home.'

To follow Adorno is to stand away from 'home' in order to look at it with the exile's detachment. For there is considerable merit in the practice of noting the discrepancies between various concepts and ideas and what they actually produce. We take home and language for granted; they become nature, and their underlying assumptions recede into dogma and orthodoxy.

The exile knows that in a secular and contingent world, homes are always provisional. Borders and barriers, which enclose us within the safety of familiar territory, can also become prisons, and are often defended beyond reason or necessity. Exiles cross borders, break barriers of thought and experience.

Hugo of St Victor, a twelfth-century monk from Saxony, wrote these hauntingly beautiful lines:

> It is, therefore, a source of great virtue for the practised mind to learn, bit by bit, first to change about invisible and transitory things, so that afterwards it may be able to leave them behind altogether. The man who finds his homeland sweet is still a tender beginner; he to whom every soil is as his native one is already strong; but he is perfect to whom the entire world is as a foreign land. The tender soul has fixed his love on one spot in the world; the strong man has extended his love to all places; the perfect man has extinguished his.

Erich Auerbach, the great twentieth-century literary scholar who spent the war years as an exile in Turkey, has cited this passage as a model for any-

15

one wishing to transcend national or provincial limits. Only by embracing this attitude can a historian begin to grasp human experience and its written records in their diversity and particularity; otherwise he or she will remain committed more to the exclusions and reactions of prejudice than to the freedom that accompanies knowledge. But note that Hugo twice makes it clear that the 'strong' or 'perfect' man achieves independence and detachment by *working through* attachments, not by rejecting them. Exile is predicated on the existence of, love for, and bond with, one's native place; what is true of all exile is not that home and love of home are lost, but that loss is inherent in the very existence of both.

20   Regard experiences as if they were about to disappear. What is it that anchors them in reality? What would you save of them? What would you give up? Only someone who has achieved independence and detachment, someone whose homeland is 'sweet' but whose circumstances makes it impossible to recapture that sweetness, can answer those questions. (Such a person would also find it impossible to derive satisfaction from substitutes furnished by illusion or dogma.)

This may seem like a prescription for an unrelieved grimness of outlook and, with it, a permanently sullen disapproval of all enthusiasm or buoyancy of spirit. Not necessarily. While it perhaps seems peculiar to speak of the pleasures of exile, there are some positive things to be said for a few of its conditions. Seeing 'the entire world as a foreign land' makes possible originality of vision. Most people are principally aware of one culture, one setting, one home; exiles are aware of at least two, and this plurality of vision gives rise to an awareness of simultaneous dimensions, an awareness that—to borrow a phrase from music—is *contrapuntal*.

For an exile, habits of life, expression or activity in the new environment inevitably occur against the memory of these things in another environment. Thus both the new and the old environments are vivid, actual, occurring together contrapuntally. There is a unique pleasure in this sort of apprehension, especially if the exile is conscious of other contrapuntal juxtapositions that diminish orthodox judgement and elevate appreciative sympathy. There is also a particular sense of achievement in acting as if one were at home wherever one happens to be.

This remains risky, however: the habit of dissimulation is both wearying and nerve-racking. Exile is never the state of being satisfied, placid, or secure. Exile, in the words of Wallace Stevens, is 'a mind of winter' in which the pathos of summer and autumn as much as the potential of spring are nearby but unobtainable. Perhaps this is another way of saying that a life of exile moves according to a different calendar, and is less seasonal and settled than life at home. Exile is life led outside habitual order. It is nomadic, decentred, contrapuntal; but no sooner does one get accustomed to it than its unsettling force erupts anew.

READING CRITICALLY FOR IDEAS, STRUCTURE, AND STYLE

1. What distinctions does Said draw among exiles, immigrants, and refugees?
2. Why is being an exile an isolating psychological condition, whereas being a refugee is a communal experience that connects one with all other refugees in the same condition?
3. Why are so many exiles chess players, novelists, and intellectuals, according to Said? In what way is the exile's life "taken up with compensating for disorienting loss by creating a new world to rule?"

EXTENDING INSIGHTS THROUGH WRITING

1. Said mentions the great fictional works by Dante and James Joyce as examples of projections into imaginative form of the psychological characteristics of exile. In a few paragraphs, evaluate Said's analysis in relationship to a work by one of these authors or another writer who illustrates Said's thesis.
2. Does Said's analysis accurately describe the actual experiences you or any of the members of your family have had in terms of the psychological effects of being an exile, immigrant, or refugee? Explain your answer.

CONNECTING PERSPECTIVES ON THE HISTORICAL DIMENSION

1. In what way was Herodotus (see "Concerning Egypt"), as a Greek, able to be an objective observer of the customs of the Egyptians? Did Herodotus have the kind of dual perspective of the culture he was in (Egypt) and the culture he left behind (Greece) that Said says is characteristic of exiles?
2. The portrayal of Satan as the archetypal exile, as portrayed by Elaine Pagels in "The Social History of Satan," shares some interesting traits with the exile Said describes. What common characteristics do they share?

BOOK CONNECTIONS FOR CHAPTER 3

1. What features of Dava Sobel's account in "The Prize" (Chapter 5) use the principles outlined by R. G. Collingwood?

2. In what way do both Herodotus and Aristotle (see "Poetics" in Chapter 7) reveal the importance of analytical thought in ancient Greek civilization?

3. Compare the excavations of Howard Carter with those of Sir Leonard Woolley in "The Flood" in chapter 5 to gain insights into the methods of archeologists and the significance of what they find.

4. In what way do Arnold J. Toynbee and Sigmund Freud (see "Typical Dreams" Chapter 6) use myths as evidence to support their arguments?

5. In what way does Mark Twain satirize (see "The Lowest Animal" in Chapter 4) intolerance of the "other" in ways that correspond to Elaine Pagels' scholarly analysis?

6. According to Thomas Carlyle's criteria, could scientists, for example Charles Darwin (see "The Origin of Species" in Chapter 4) be considered heroes? Why or why not?

7. Does Walt Whitman put the events he describes into a meaningful context as Neil Postman (see "Information" in Chapter 5) recommends? Explain your answer.

8. Analyze Claude Eatherly's nightmares, as related by Maurizio Chierici, in terms of the theory presented by Sigmund Freud in "Typical Dreams" in Chapter 6.

9. How is the idea of liberty, as stated by Thomas Paine in "Rights of Man" in Chapter 2, re-expressed in John F. Kennedy's Inaugural Address over 200 years later?

10. Discuss the impact on one's life in America if one's ancestors were brought over as slaves, as discussed by James Baldwin (see "Letter to My Nephew" in Chapter 2), or came as immigrants, as described by Oscar Handlin.

11. In what way does being a victim of colonization, as described by Ngũgĩ wa Thiong'o (in "Decolonising the Mind" in Chapter 2), make one an exile, as discussed by Edward Said, in one's own country?

CHAPTER 4

THE NATURAL WORLD:
Instinct and Survival

INTRODUCTION

The natural world and the creatures within it are the focus of this chapter, beginning with investigations of migratory patterns, adaptive mechanisms, and the role of aggression in various animal species. We then move on to the relationship between human beings and other animal species and conclude by examining current genetic research that raises questions about what it means to be human.

The theme that informs the first group of selections is the role played by instinct and the adaptive capabilities displayed by different species in their quest to survive. Arthur D. Hasler and James A. Larsen reveal that individual salmon sacrifice themselves so that the species can survive, by being able to precisely navigate back to the exact stream in which they were hatched in order to spawn (after which they die). Charles Darwin identifies the basic mechanism operating in nature that ensures that species that possess advantageous mutations will thrive, whereas those less well-adapted will become extinct. His theories of "natural selection" and the "survival of the fittest" have had an incalculable effect on almost every field of study. The way we think about history, geology, psychology, physiology, linguistics, and even political science are profoundly indebted to Darwin's research. Konrad Lorenz extends Darwin's insights with his creative investigations of the role aggression plays and how innate inhibitions in certain species temper aggression and ensure the preservation of that species. The entomologist, Jean Henri Fabre, takes us into the world of the praying mantis and explores its predatory and cannibalistic habits (that includes the female devouring the male during procreation). These first four selections explore the most fundamental processes operating in the natural world and the way they ensure survival.

The next set of readings examine the place that human beings have tried to occupy in the order of nature and the often disastrous consequences of this competition to survive. Mark Twain satirizes (and misrepresents) Darwin's theory by parodying scientific experiments (which test assumptions and use control groups) and concludes that man is the "lowest animal." Hans Ruesch brings our attention to the experiments that use live animals in medical research and maintains that vivisection is a "pseudo-science."

The concluding three articles probe the essence of human identity and ask the crucial question of whether genetics or environment plays the most important role. The genetic basis of human identity is strongly suggested by the research on identical twins separated at birth reported by Constance Holden. But these results also raise the question as to how unique behavioral patterns (dipping buttered toast into coffee, remarrying women with the same names, wearing multiple rings and bracelets in unusual patterns, giving their children the same names) could be genetically pre-determined. The same question is raised by Matt Ridley in the realm of linguistics. He reports that the latest genetic research (connected with the Human Genome Project) has identified a particular gene on Chromosome 7 that actually makes it possible for us to acquire language—something previously believed to be solely a product of learning and culture. Gina Kolata continues this inquiry into the reassessment of what it means to be human in her discussion of the new technology of cloning. As these three selections illustrate, genetic research is the new frontier in which age-old questions of instinct and survival will be answered.

ARTHUR D. HASLER
AND JAMES A. LARSEN

The Homing Salmon

BACKGROUND

Arthur D. Hasler, born in 1908 in Ledi, Utah, earned a Ph. D. in zoology from the University of Wisconsin in 1937 and is professor emeritus of zoology at the University of Wisconsin, Madison. Hasler has served as the president of many scientific associations, including the American Society of Zoologists, Ecology Society of America, International Association of Ecologists, and the American Society of Limnology and Oceanography. Hasler's pioneering studies into the migration of fish and the study of fresh-water habitats (limnology) successfully illuminated the crucial role played by the sense of smell in orienting fishes in parent streams.

James A. Larsen, born in 1921 in Rhinelander, Wisconsin, earned a Ph.D. in ecology in 1968 and has distinguished himself both as a botanist, studying bioclimatology in the Arctic, and as a science writer. The classic essay "The Homing Salmon" (which first appeared in *Scientific American*, June 1955) joins the respective talents of these two researchers and describes an ingenious experiment designed to investigate the mysterious riddle of how the adult Chinook salmon finds its way back to the stream where it was born, nearly 900 miles away.

APPROACHING HASLER AND LARSEN'S ESSAY

Many species migrate annually. For example, Arctic terns travel 22,000 miles each year; and every year the Adelie penguins cross the Antarctic ice pack from a feeding area to the exact spot they nested the year before, often over distances of 1,200 miles. Hasler and Larsen's experiments were designed to solve the mystery of how salmon are able to navigate their way back over distances of sometimes nearly 900 miles to the very stream in which they were born. The migratory mechanism responsible for this had long baffled scientists. Moreover, an accurate understanding of this mechanism might make it possible to prevent wrong placement of dams, which could result in the extinction of certain species of salmon.

Their experiments were designed to test the assumption that each stage of salmon migration could be explained in terms of olfactory conditioning. That is, they hypothesized that salmon were able to perceive, and were conditioned to respond to, the particular smells of the streams in which they initially spawned. Hasler and Larsen's experiments were designed to test the crucial role played by olfactory conditioning in a number of ingenious ways that were designed to isolate and test one crucial variable—the role played by the salmon's sense of smell—as distinct from all other possible variables that might be responsible for the salmon's homing instincts. In their report, Hasler and Larsen clearly specify the question that their experiments are designed to answer. They describe exactly how each of the experiments is structured, provide pertinent technical information, and indicate why certain results are especially significant in proving the success of their theories. This model scientific experiment has become a classic study of the mechanisms underlying seasonal migration.

The Homing Salmon

A learned naturalist once remarked that among the many riddles of nature, not the least mysterious is the migration of fishes. The homing of salmon is a particularly dramatic example. The Chinook salmon of the U.S. Northwest is born in a small stream, migrates downriver to the Pacific Ocean as a young smolt and, after living in the sea for as long as five years, swims back unerringly to the stream of its birth to spawn. Its determination to return to its birthplace is legendary. No one who has seen a 100-pound Chinook salmon fling itself into the air again and again until it is exhausted in a vain effort to surmount a waterfall can fail to marvel at the strength of the instinct that draws the salmon upriver to the stream where it was born.

How do salmon remember their birthplace, and how do they find their way back, sometimes from 800 or 900 miles away? This enigma, which has fascinated naturalists for many years, is the subject of the research to be reported here. The question has an economic as well as a scientific interest, because new dams which stand in the salmon's way have cut heavily into salmon fishing along the Pacific Coast. Before long nearly every stream of any appreciable size in the West will be blocked by dams. It is true that the dams have fish lifts and ladders designed to help salmon to hurdle them. Unfortunately, and for reasons which are different for nearly every dam so far designed, salmon are lost in tremendous numbers.

There are six common species of salmon. One, called the Atlantic salmon, is of the same genus as the steelhead trout. These two fish go to sea and come back upstream to spawn year after year. The other five salmon species, all on the Pacific Coast, are the Chinook (also called the king salmon), the sockeye, the silver, the humpback and the chum. The Pacific salmon home only once: after spawning they die.

A young salmon first sees the light of day when it hatches and wriggles up through the pebbles of the stream where the egg was laid and fertilized. For a few weeks the fingerling feeds on insects and small aquatic animals. Then it answers its first migratory call and swims downstream to the sea. It must survive many hazards to mature: an estimated 15 percent of the young salmon are lost at every large dam, such as Bonneville, on the downstream strip; others die in polluted streams; many are swallowed up by bigger fish in the ocean. When, after several years in the sea, the salmon is ready to spawn, it responds to the second great migratory call. It finds the mouth of the river by which it entered the ocean and then swims steadily upstream, unerringly choosing the correct turn at each tributary fork, until it arrives at the stream, where it was hatched. Generation after generation, families of salmon return to the same rivulet so consistently that populations in streams not far apart follow distinctly separate lines of evolution.

The homing behavior of the salmon has been convincingly documented   5
by many studies since the turn of the century. One of the most elaborate was made by Andrew L. Pritchard, Wilbert A. Clemens and Russell E. Foerster in Canada. They marked 469,326 young sockeye salmon born in a tributary of the Fraser River, and they recovered nearly 11,000 of these in the same parent stream after the fishes' migration to the ocean and back. What is more, not one of the marked fish was ever found to have strayed to another stream. This remarkable demonstration of the salmon's precision in homing has presented an exciting challenge to investigators.

At the Wisconsin Lake Laboratory during the past decade we have been studying the sense of smell in fish, beginning with minnows and going on to salmon. Our findings suggest that the salmon identifies the stream of its birth by odor and literally smells its way home from the sea.

Fish have an extremely sensitive sense of smell. This has often been observed by students of fish behavior. Karl von Frisch showed that odors from the injured skin of a fish produce a fright reaction among its schoolmates. He once noticed that when a bird dropped an injured fish in the water, the school of fish from which it had been seized quickly dispersed and later avoided the area. It is well known that sharks and tuna are drawn to a vessel by the odor of bait in the water. Indeed, the time-honored custom of spitting on bait may be founded on something more than superstition; laboratory studies have proved that human saliva is quite stimulating to the taste buds of a bullhead. The sense of taste of course is closely allied to the sense of smell. The bullhead has taste buds all over the surface of its body; they are especially numerous on its whiskers. It will quickly grab a piece of meat that touches any part of its skin. But it becomes insensitive to taste and will not respond in this way if a nerve serving the skin buds is cut.

The smelling organs of fish have evolved in a great variety of forms. In the bony fishes the nose pits have two separate openings. The fish takes water into the front opening as it swims or breathes (sometimes assisting the intake with cilia), and then the water passes out through the second opening, which may be opened and closed rhythmically by the fish's breathing. Any odorous substances in the water stimulate the nasal receptors chemically, perhaps by an effect on enzyme reactions, and the resulting electrical impulses are relayed to the central nervous system by the olfactory nerve.

The human nose, and that of other land vertebrates, can smell a substance only if it is volatile and soluble in fat solvents. But in the final analysis smell is always aquatic, for a substance is not smelled until it passes into solution in the mucous film of the nasal passages. For fishes, of course, the odors are already in solution in their watery environment. Like any other animal, they can follow an odor to its source, as a hunting dog follows the scent of an animal. The quality or effect of a scent changes at the concentration changes; everyone knows that an odor may be pleasant at one concentration and unpleasant at another.

10   When we began our experiments, we first undertook to find out whether fish could distinguish the odors of different water plants. We used a special aquarium with jets which could inject odors into the water. For responding to one odor (by moving toward the jet), the fish were rewarded with food; for responding to another odor, they were punished with a mild electric shock. After the fish were trained to make choices between odors, they were tested on dilute rinses from 14 different aquatic plants. They proved able to distinguish the odors of all these plants from one another.

Plants must play an important role in the life of many freshwater fish. Their odors may guide fish to feeding grounds when visibility is poor, as in muddy water or at night, and they may hold young fish from straying from protective cover. Odors may also warn fish away from poisons. In fact, we discovered that fish could be put to use to assay industrial pollutants: our trained minnows were able to detect phenol, a common pollutant, at concentrations far below those detectable by man.

All this suggested a clear-cut working hypothesis for investigating the mystery of the homing of salmon. We can suppose that every little stream has its own characteristic odor, which stays the same year after year; that young salmon become conditioned to this odor before they go to sea; that they remember the odor as they grow to maturity, and that they are able to find it and follow it to its source when they come back upstream to spawn.

Plainly there are quite a few ifs in this theory. The first one we tested was the question: Does each stream have its own odor? We took water from two creeks in Wisconsin and investigated whether fish could learn to discriminate between them. Our subjects, first minnows and then salmon, were indeed able to detect a difference. If, however, we destroyed a fish's nose tissue, it was no longer able to distinguish between the two water samples.

Chemical analysis indicated that the only major difference between the two waters lay in the organic material. By testing the fish with various fractions of the water separated by distillation, we confirmed that the identifying material was some volatile organic substance.

The idea that fish are guided by odors in their migrations was further   15
supported by a field test. From each of two different branches of the
Issaquah River in the State of Washington we took a number of sexually ripe
silver salmon which had come home to spawn. We then plugged with cotton the noses of half the fish in each group and placed all the salmon in
the river below the fork to make the upstream run again. Most of the fish
with unplugged noses swam back to the stream they had selected the first
time. But the "odor-blinded" fish migrated back in random fashion, picking the wrong stream as often as the right one.

In 1949 eggs from salmon of the Horsefly River in British Columbia
were hatched and reared in a hatchery in a tributary called the Little
Horsefly. Then they were flown a considerable distance and released in the
main Horsefly River, from which they migrated to the sea. Three years later
13 of them had returned to their rearing place in the Little Horsefly, according to the report of the Canadian experimenters.

In our own laboratory experiments we tested the memory of fish for
odors and found that they retained the ability to differentiate between odors
for a long period after their training. Young fish remembered odors better
than the old. That animals "remember" conditioning to which they have
been exposed in their youth, and act accordingly, has been demonstrated
in other fields. For instance, there is a fly which normally lays its eggs on
the larvae of the flour moth, where the fly larvae then hatch and develop.
But if larvae of this fly are raised on another host, the beeswax moth, when
the flies mature they will seek out beeswax moth larvae on which to lay
their eggs, in preference to the traditional host.

With respect to the homing of salmon we have shown, then, that different streams have different odors, that salmon respond to these odors
and that they remember odors to which they have been conditioned. The
next question is: Is a salmon's homeward migration guided solely by its
sense of smell? If we could decoy homing salmon to a stream other than
their birthplace, by means of an odor to which they were conditioned artificially, we might have not only a solution to the riddle that has puzzled scientists but also a practical means of saving the salmon—guiding them to
breeding streams not obstructed by dams.

We set out to find a suitable substance to which salmon could be
conditioned. A student, W. J. Wisby, and I [Arthur Hasler] designed an
apparatus to test the reactions of salmon to various organic odors. It consists of a compartment from which radiate four runways, each with several steps which the fish must jump to climb the runway. Water cascades
down each of the arms. An odorous substance is introduced into one of the
arms, and its effect on the fish is judged by whether the odor appears to
attract fish into that arm, to repel them or to be indifferent to them.

We needed a substance which initially would not be either attractive   20
or repellent to salmon but to which they could be conditioned so that it
would attract them. After testing several score organic odors, we found that
dilute solutions of morpholine neither attracted nor repelled salmon but
were detectable by them in extremely low concentrations—as low as one
part per million. It appears that morpholine fits the requirements for the

substance needed: it is soluble in water; it is detectable in extremely low concentrations; it is chemically stable under stream conditions. It is neither an attractant nor a repellent to unconditioned salmon, and would have meaning only to those conditioned to it.

Federal collaborators of ours are now conducting field tests on the Pacific Coast to learn whether salmon fry and fingerlings which have been conditioned to morpholine can be decoyed to a stream other than that of their birth when they return from the sea to spawn. Unfortunately this type of experiment may not be decisive. If the salmon are not decoyed to the new stream, it may simply mean that they cannot be drawn by a single substance but will react only to a combination of subtle odors in their parent stream. Perhaps adding morpholine to the water is like adding the whistle of a freight train to the quiet strains of a violin, cello and flute. The salmon may still seek out the subtle harmonies of an odor combination to which they have been reacting by instinct for centuries. But there is still hope that they may respond to the call of the whistle.

READING CRITICALLY FOR IDEAS, STRUCTURE, AND STYLE

1. How was Hasler and Larsen's experiment designed to test their hypothesis as to how salmon were able to return to their exact birthplace over 900 miles away?

2. How did Hasler and Larsen's experiment demonstrate the scientific basis for a homing instinct that hitherto had been unexplained?

3. Describe the scientific model on which Hasler and Larsen based their research, the assumptions they wished to test, reports of past research, alternate theories, and control of key variables that would make it possible to duplicate their findings.

EXTENDING INSIGHTS THROUGH WRITING

1. Why would the results of Hasler and Larsen's research play a key role in decisions as to where to place dams in the Northwest?

2. As a research project, investigate explanations that have been tested to explain the homing instinct in other species (pets can be included). In a short paper evaluate one such instance.

CONNECTING PERSPECTIVES
ON THE NATURAL WORLD

1. In what way does Hasler and Larsen's experiment suggest that instinct plays a crucial role in the survival of the salmon through an adaptive mechanism of the kind Charles Darwin postulated in "The Origin of Species"?

2. Compare how sacrifice and cannibalism function as instincts peculiar to the homing salmon and to the praying mantis, as described by Jean Henri Fabre.

CHARLES ROBERT DARWIN

The Origin of Species

BACKGROUND

Charles Darwin (1809–1882), the eminent British naturalist and geologist, was born in Shrewsbury, England. Darwin initially studied medicine at Edinburgh University, but became so distressed at having to learn surgical skills by performing operations without anesthetics that he left medical school to study for the ministry at Cambridge. His growing interest in geology and natural history was encouraged by John Stevens Henslow, who acted as a mentor to the young Darwin. Henslow was responsible for Darwin's being invited to join the Admiralty survey ship *H. M. S. Beagle* as an unpaid naturalist. This voyage to different areas of South America and the Galapagos Islands, which would last some five years, provided Darwin with a wealth of observations, evidence, and a host of unanswered questions. Why, for example, did finches on different Galapagos Islands, identical in climate, foliage, and terrain, have different bill structures that were ideally suited to their respective diets (on some islands finches ate insects and on other islands they ate seeds). Darwin's answer was that in the competitive struggle for existence, those species possessing advantageous mutations (a bill well-suited to catch insects, for example) would thrive, whereas those less well-adapted would, over time, become extinct. His principal works include *On the Origin of Species by Means of Natural Selection* (1859); *The Variation of Animals and Plants Under Domestication* (1868); *The Descent of Man* (1971) (which proposed that both men and apes evolved separately—not, as is commonly thought, that man descended from the apes—from a common ancestor who today would be classified among the lower primates); and *The Expression of the Emotions in Man and Animals* (1872), a startling comparative study that began ethology, the science of animal behavior. In the following excerpt from *On the Origin of Species*, Darwin summarizes his theory of "natural selection" and replies to objections that the fossil record fails to show the full range of intermediary forms his theory postulates.

APPROACHING DARWIN'S ESSAY

Darwin's observations of finches and other species in the Galapagos Islands led him to realize that (a) slight variations always exist among individuals within a species and that (b) some of these variations (for example, beak structure in finches) allow individuals to survive and reproduce, thereby passing along these traits to the next generation. Over time, traits that proved particularly effective in allowing individuals to survive become widespread within that particular species. Thus, nature "selects" the varieties best adapted to survive and reproduce. This process, known as "natural selection," is, in essence, Darwin's theory of evolution.

Darwin had read the influential essay on population growth written in 1798 by the English clergyman and economist, Robert Thomas Malthus, who observed that human populations would double every twenty-five years unless limited by a shrinking food supply. Darwin concluded that all species are in a struggle to survive and that his theory of "natural selection" explained why only the most fit individuals, within a species, are likely to survive and pass on these traits. This process came to be known as the "survival of the fittest."

Darwin replies to objections that the fossil evidence fails to reflect the intermediary forms that must have existed if his theory of "natural selection" was correct. He answers his critics by pointing to the high probability of common ancestors that do not resemble amalgams of current forms and to the imperfect records of organisms in geological formations that have since crumbled. Darwin relies on the geological evidence assembled by Charles Lyell that the Earth was much older than the 6,000 years previously believed by the Creationists (who maintained that all species were created by God and had not changed biologically). If the world was indeed only 6,000 years old than the idea of the immutability of species was almost unavoidable. Once geological and fossil evidence proved that the world had existed for millions rather than thousands of years, the idea that species changed over such a vast period of time became more probable. Darwin also points out that the same principles that he describes were already used in procedures to develop certain domestic breeds.

In his argument, Darwin emphasizes the merits of his own position by pointing out the disadvantages of his opponents' views. He does this by putting his opponents in the untenable position of having to prove that nothing in nature has ever changed or can change. By contrast, Darwin asserts that his ideas of "natural selection" are based on easily observable phenomena, namely, the lack of any clear-cut distinction between a species and varieties of that species, and the continuing production through the centuries of new varieties of existing species.

Today, evolutionists believe that mutations in genes (whether called point mutation, genetic recombination, or random genetic drift) produce the variations that natural forces select for survival. And, indeed, geneticists have traced ancestral relationships among species from the presence of similar molecular structures and DNA patterns.

from *The Origin of Species*[1]

NATURAL SELECTION; OR THE SURVIVAL OF THE FITTEST

Summary of Chapter

If under changing conditions of life organic beings present individual differences in almost every part of their structure, and this cannot be disputed; if there be, owing to their geometrical rate of increase, a severe struggle for life at some age, season, or year, and this certainly cannot be disputed; then, considering the infinite complexity of the relations of all organic beings to each other and to their conditions of life, causing an infinite diversity in structure, constitution, and habits, to be advantageous to them, it would be a most extraordinary fact if no variations had ever occurred useful to each being's own welfare, in the same manner as so many variations have occurred useful to man. But if variations useful to any organic being ever do occur, assuredly individuals thus characterised will have the best chance of being preserved in the struggle for life; and from the strong principle of inheritance, these will tend to produce offspring similarly characterised. This principle of preservation, or the survival of the fittest, I have called Natural Selection. It leads to the improvement of each creature in relation to its organic and inorganic conditions of life; and consequently, in most cases, to what must be regarded as an advance in organisation. Nevertheless, low and simple forms will long endure if well fitted for their simple conditions of life.

Natural selection, on the principle of qualities being inherited at corresponding ages, can modify the egg, seed, or young, as easily as the adult. Amongst many animals, sexual selection[2] will have given its aid to ordinary selection, by assuring to the most vigorous and best adapted makes the greatest number of offspring. Sexual selection will also give characters useful to the males alone, in their struggles or rivalry with other males; and these characters will be transmitted to one sex or to both sexes, according to the form of inheritance which prevails.

Whether natural selection has really thus acted in adapting the various forms of life to their several conditions and stations, must be judged by the general tenor and balance of evidence given in the following chapters. But we have already seen how it entails extinction; and how largely extinction has acted in the world's history, geology plainly declares. Natural selection, also leads to divergence of character; for the more organic beings diverge in structure, habits, and constitution, by so much the more can a large

---

[1]This selection is excerpted from the sixth edition of Darwin's 1872 book, the last edition published during his lifetime.
[2]Sexual selection refers to the mating preferences within a species that ensure the most vigorous and best adapted offspring.

number be supported on the area,—of which we see proof by looking to the inhabitants of any small spot, and to the productions naturalised in foreign lands. Therefore, during the modification of the descendants of any one species, and during the incessant struggle of all species to increase in numbers, the more diversified the descendants become, the better will be their chance of success in the battle for life. Thus the small differences distinguishing varieties of the same species, steadily tend to increase, till they equal the greater differences between species of the same genus, or even of distinct genera. . . .

Natural selection, as has just been remarked, leads to divergence of character and to much extinction of the less improved and intermediate forms of life. On these principles, the nature of the affinities, and the generally well-defined distinctions between the innumerable organic beings in each class throughout the world, may be explained. It is a truly wonderful fact—the wonder of which we are apt to overlook from familiarity—that all animals and all plants throughout all time and space should be related to each other in groups, subordinate to groups, in the manner which we everywhere behold—namely, varieties of the same species most closely related, species of the same genus less closely and unequally related, forming sections and sub-genera, species of distinct genera much less closely related, and genera related in different degrees, forming sub-families, families, orders, sub-classes and classes. The several subordinate groups in any class cannot be ranked in a single file, but seem clustered round points, and these round other points, and so on in almost endless cycles. If species had been independently created, no explanation would have been possible of this kind of classification; but it is explained through inheritance and the complex action of natural selection, entailing extinction and divergence of character. . . .

The affinities of all the beings of the same class have sometimes been   5
represented by a great tree. I believe this simile largely speaks the truth. The green and budding twigs may represent existing species; and those produced during former years may represent the long succession of extinct species. At each period of growth all the growing twigs have tried to branch out on all sides, and to overtop and kill the surrounding twigs and branches, in the same manner as species and groups of species have at all times overmastered other species in the great battle for life. The limbs divided into great branches, and these into lesser and lesser branches, were themselves once, when the tree was young, budding twigs, and this connection of the former and present buds by ramifying branches may well represent the classification of all extinct and living species in groups subordinate to groups. Of the many twigs which flourished when the tree was a mere bush, only two or three, now grown into great branches, yet survive and bear the other branches; so with the species which lived during long-past geological periods, very few have left living and modified descendants. From the first growth of the tree, many a limb and branch has decayed and dropped off; and these fallen branches of various sizes may represent those whole orders, families, and genera which have now no living representatives, and which are known to us only in a fossil state. As we here and there see a thin straggling branch springing from a fork low down in a tree, and which

by some chance has been favoured and is still alive on its summit, so we occasionally see an animal like the Ornithorhynchus or Lepidosiren,[3] which in some small degree connects by its affinities two large branches of life, and which has apparently been saved from fatal competition by having inhabited a protected station. As buds give rise by growth to fresh buds, and these, if vigorous, branch out and overtop on all sides many a feebler branch, so by generation I believe it has been with the great Tree of Life, which fills with its dead and broken branches the crust of the earth, and covers the surface with its ever-branching and beautiful ramifications. . . .

ON THE IMPERFECTION OF THE GEOLOGICAL RECORD

In the sixth chapter I enumerated the chief objections which might be justly urged against the views maintained in this volume. Most of them have now been discussed. One, namely the distinctness of specific forms, and their not being blended together by innumerable transitional links, is a very obvious difficulty. I assigned reasons why such links do not commonly occur at the present day under the circumstances apparently most favourable for their presence, namely, on an extensive and continuous area with graduated physical conditions. I endeavoured to show, that the life of each species depends in a more important manner on the presence of other already defined organic forms, than on climate, and, therefore, that the really governing conditions of life do not graduate away quite insensibly like heat or moisture. I endeavoured, also, to show that intermediate varieties, from existing in lesser numbers than the forms which they connect, will generally be beaten out and exterminated during the course of further modification and improvement. The main cause, however, of innumerable intermediate links not now occurring everywhere throughout nature, depends on the very process of natural selection, through which new varieties continually take the places of and supplant their parentforms. But just in proportion as this process of extermination has acted on an enormous scale, so must the number of intermediate varieties, which have formerly existed, be truly enormous. Why then is not every geological formation and every stratum full of such intermediate links? Geology assuredly does not reveal any such finely-graduated organic chain; and this, perhaps, is the most obvious and serious objection which can be urged against the theory. The explanation lies, as I believe, in the extreme imperfection of the geological record.

In the first place, it should always be borne in mind what sort of intermediate forms must, on the theory, have formerly existed. I have found it difficult, when looking at any two species, to avoid picturing to myself forms *directly* intermediate between them. But this is a wholly false view: we should always look for forms intermediate between each species and a common but unknown progenitor; and the progenitor will generally have differed in some

[3]Ornithorhynchus anatinus refers to the duck-billed platypus, a semi-aquatic, egg-laying mammal of Tasmania and East Australia. It has a rubbery duck-bill-shaped muzzle; no teeth; no external ears; head, body, and tail are broad, flat, and covered with dark brown fur; its feet are webbed; and the adult male is about two feet long. Lepidosiren refers to a lung-bearing fish often resembling an eel that is found in rivers in South America, Africa, and Australia and ancestrally is related to four-footed land animals. They indicate a point of bifurcation in evolution since some species breathe through gills in water and other species will drown if held under water.

respects from all its modified descendants. To give a simple illustration: the fantail and pouter pigeons are both descended from the rock-pigeon; if we possessed all the intermediate varieties which have ever existed, we should have an extremely close series between both and the rock-pigeon; but we should have no varieties directly intermediate between the fantail and pouter; none, for instance, combining a tail somewhat expanded with a crop somewhat enlarged, the characteristic features of these two breeds. These two breeds, moreover, have become so much modified, that, if we had no historical or indirect evidence regarding their origin, it would not have been possible to have determined, from a mere comparison of their structure with that of the rock-pigeon, C. livia, whether they had descended from this species or from some allied form, such as C. oenas.

So, with natural species, if we look to forms very distinct, for instance to the horse and tapir, we have no reason to suppose that links directly intermediate between them ever existed, but between each and an unknown common parent. The common parent will have had in its whole organisation much general resemblance to the tapir and to the horse; but in some points of structure may have differed considerably from both, even perhaps more than they differ from each other. Hence, in all such cases, we should be unable to recognise the parent-form of any two or more species, even if we closely compared the structure of the parent with that of its modified descendants, unless at the same time we had a nearly perfect chain of the intermediate links.

It is just possible by the theory, that one of two living forms might have descended from the other; for instance, a horse from a tapir; and in this case *direct* intermediate links will have existed between them. But such a case would imply that one form had remained for a very long period unaltered, whilst its descendants had undergone a vast amount of change; and the principle of competition between organism and organism, between child and parent, will render this a very rare event; for in all cases the new and improved forms of life tend to supplant the old and unimproved forms.

By the theory of natural selection all living species have been connected with the parent-species of each genus, by differences not greater than we see between the natural and domestic varieties of the same species at the present day; and these parent-species, now generally extinct, have in their turn been similarly connected with more ancient forms; and so on backwards, always coverging to the common ancestor of each great class. So that the number of intermediate and transitional links, between all living and extinct species, must have been inconceivably great. But assuredly, if this theory be true, such have lived upon the earth.

10

On The Lapse of Time, as Inferred from the Rate of Deposition and Extent of Denudation

Independently of our not finding fossil remains of such infinitely numerous connecting links, it may be objected that time cannot have sufficed for so great an amount of organic change, all changes having been effected slowly. It is hardly possible for me to recall to the reader who is not a practical geologist, the facts leading the mind feebly to comprehend the lapse of time. He who can read Sir Charles Lyell's[4] grand work on the

---

[4]Sir Charles Lyell (1797–1875) English geologist whose research helped win acceptance of Darwin's theory of evolution.

Principles of Geology, which the future historian will recognise as having produced a revolution in natural science, and yet does not admit how vast have been the past periods of time, may at once close this volume. Not that it suffices to study the Principles of Geology, or to read special treatises by different observers on separate formations, and to mark how each author attempts to give an inadequate idea of duration of each formation, or even of each stratum. We can best gain some idea of past time by knowing the agencies at work, and learning how deeply the surface of the land has been denuded, and how much sediment has been deposited. As Lyell has well remarked, the extent and thickness of our sedimentary formations are the result and the measure of the denudation which the earth's crust has else-where undergone. Therefore a man should examine for himself the great piles of superimposed strata, and watch the rivulets bringing down mud, and the waves wearing away the sea-cliffs, in order to comprehend some-thing about the duration of past time, the monuments of which we see all around us. . . .

On The Poorness of Palaeontological Collections

Now let us turn to our richest geological museums, and what a pal-try display we behold! That our collections are imperfect is admitted by every one. The remark of that admirable paleontologist, Edward Forbes, should never be forgotten, namely, that very many fossil species are known and named from single and often broken specimens, or from a few speci-mens collected on some one spot. Only a small portion of the surface of the earth has been geologically explored, and no part with sufficient care, as the important discoveries made every year in Europe prove. No organism wholly soft can be preserved. Shells and bones decay and disappear when left on the bottom of the sea, where sediment is not accumulating.

. . . Those who believe that the geological record is in any degree per-fect, will undoubtedly at once reject the theory. For my part, following out Lyell's metaphor, I look at the geological record as a history of the world imperfectly kept, and written in a changing dialect; of this history we pos-sess the last volume alone, relating only to two or three countries. Of this volume, only here and there a short chapter has been preserved; and of each page, only here and there a few lines. Each word of the slowly-changing language, more or less different in the successive chapters, may represent the forms of life, which are entombed in our consecutive formations, and which falsely appear to have been abruptly introduced. On this view, the difficulties above discussed are greatly diminished, or even disappear. . . .

RECAPITULATION AND CONCLUSION

As this whole volume is one long argument, it may be convenient to the reader to have the leading facts and inferences briefly recapitulated.

That many and serious objections may be advanced against the the-ory of descent with modification through variation and natural selection, I do not deny. I have endeavored to give to them their full force. Nothing at

15

first can appear more difficult to believe than that the more complex organs and instincts have been perfected, not by means superior to, though analogous with, human reason, but by the accumulation of innumerable slight variations, each good for the individual possessor. Nevertheless, this difficulty, though appearing to our imagination insuperably great, cannot be considered real if we admit the following propositions, namely, that all parts of the organisation and instincts offer, at least, individual differences—that there is a struggle for existence leading to the preservation of profitable deviations of structure or instinct—and, lastly, that gradations in the state of perfection of each organ may have existed, each good of its kind. The truth of these propositions cannot, I think, be disputed.

Now let us turn to the other side of the argument. Under domestication we see much variability, caused, or at least excited, by changed conditions of life; but often in so obscure a manner, that we are tempted to consider the variations as spontaneous. Variability is governed by many complex laws,—by correlated growth, compensation, the increased use and disuse of parts, and the definite action of the surrounding conditions. There is much difficulty in ascertaining how largely our domestic productions have been modified; but we may safely infer that the amount has been large, and that modifications can be inherited for long periods. As long as the conditions of life remain the same, we have reason to believe that a modification, which has already been inherited for many generations, may continue to be inherited for an almost infinite number of generations. On the other hand, we have evidence that variability when it has once come into play, does not cease under domestication for a very long period; nor do we know that it ever ceases, for new varieties are still occasionally produced by our oldest domesticated productions.

Variability is not actually caused by man; he only unintentionally exposes organic beings to new conditions of life, and then nature acts on the organisation and causes it to vary. But man can and does select the variations given to him by nature, and thus accumulates them in any desired manner. He thus adapts animals and plants for his own benefit or pleasure. He may do this methodically, or he may do it unconsciously by preserving the individuals most useful or pleasing to him without any intention of altering the breed. It is certain that he can largely influence the character of a breed by selecting, in each successive generation, individual differences so slight as to be inappreciable except by an educated eye. This unconscious process of selection has been the great agency in the formation of the most distinct and useful domestic breeds. That many breeds produced by man have to a large extent the character of natural species, is shown by the inextricable doubts whether many of them are varieties or aboriginally distinct species.

There is no reason why the principles which have acted so efficiently under domestication should not have acted under nature. In the survival of favoured individuals and races, during the constantly-recurrent Struggle for Existence, we see a powerful and ever-acting form of Selection. The struggle for existence inevitably follows from the high geometrical ratio of increase which is common to all organic beings. This high rate of increase is proved by calculation,—by the rapid increase of many animals and plants during a succession of peculiar seasons, and when naturalised in new countries. More individuals are born than can possibly survive. A grain in the balance may determine which individuals shall live and which shall die,—which variety or species shall increase in number, and which shall decrease, or finally become extinct. As the individuals of the same species come in all respects into the closest competition with each other, the struggle will generally be most severe between them; it will be almost equally severe between the varieties of the same species, and next in severity between the species of the same genus. On the other hand the struggle will often be severe between beings remote in the scale of nature. The slightest advantage in certain individuals, at any age of during any season, over those with which they come into competition, or better adaptation in however slight a degree to the surrounding physical conditions, will, in the long run, turn the balance.

With animals having separated sexes, there will be in most cases a struggle between the males for the possession of the females. The most vigorous males, or those which have most successfully struggled with their conditions of life, will generally leave most progeny. But success will often depend on the males having special weapons, or means of defense, or charms; and a slight advantage will lead to victory. . . .

20   If then, animals and plants do vary, let it be ever so slightly or slowly, why should not variations or individual differences, which are in any way beneficial, be preserved and accumulated through natural selection, or the survival of the fittest? If man can by patience select variations useful to him, why, under changing and complex conditions of life, should not variations useful to nature's living products often arise, and be preserved or selected? What limit can be put to this power, acting during long ages and rigidly scrutinising the whole constitution, structure, and habits of each creature,— favouring the good and rejecting the bad? I can see no limit to this power, in slowly and beautifully adapting each form to the most complex relations of life. The theory of natural selection, even if we look no farther than this, seems to be in the highest degree probable. I have already recapitulated, as fairly as I could, the opposed difficulties and objections: now let us turn to the special facts and arguments in favour of the theory. . . .

It can hardly be supposed that a false theory would explain, in so satisfactory a manner as does the theory of natural selection, the several large classes of facts above specified. It has recently been objected that this is an unsafe method of arguing; but it is a method used in judging of the common events of life, and has often been used by the greatest natural philosophers. The undulatory theory of light has thus been arrived at; and the belief in the revolution of the earth on its own axis was until lately supported by hardly any direct evidence. It is no valid objection that science as yet throws no light on the far higher problem of the essence or origin of life. Who can explain what is the essence of the attraction of gravity? No one now objects to following out the results consequent on this unknown element of attraction; notwithstanding that Leibnitz[5] formerly accused Newton of introducing "occult qualities and miracles into philosophy."

[5]Wilhelm Leibnitz (1646–1716) German philosopher and mathematician who invented calculus concurrently with, but independently of, Newton. His optimistic belief that a divine plan made this the best of all possible worlds was satirized by Voltaire in *Candide*.

I see no good reason why the views given in this volume should shock the religious feelings of any one. It is satisfactory, as showing how transient such impressions are, to remember that the greatest discovery ever made by man, namely, the law of the attraction of gravity, was also attacked by Leibnitz, "as subversive of natural, and inferentially of revealed, religion." A celebrated author and divine has written to me that "he has gradually learnt to see that it is just as noble a conception of the Deity to believe that He created a few original forms capable of self-development into other and needful forms, as to believe that He required a fresh act of creation to supply the voids caused by the action of His laws." . . .

But the chief cause of our natural unwillingness to admit that one species has given birth to clear and distinct species, is that we are always slow in admitting great changes of which we do not see the steps. The difficulty is the same as that felt by so many geologists, when Lyell first insisted that long lines of inland cliffs had been formed, the great valleys excavated, by the agencies which we see still at work. The mind cannot possibly grasp the full meaning of the term of even a million years; it cannot add up and perceive the full effects of many slight variations, accumulated during an almost infinite number of generations.

Although I am fully convinced of the truth of the views given in this volume under the form of an abstract, I by no means expect to convince experenced naturalists whose minds are stocked with a multitude of facts all viewed, during a long course of years, from a point of view directly opposite to mine. It is so easy to hide our ignorance under such expressions as the "plan of creation," "unity of design," &c., and to think that we give an explanation when we only re-state a fact. Any one whose disposition leads him to attach more weight to unexplained difficulties than to the explanation of a certain number of facts will certainly reject the theory. A few naturalists, endowed with much flexibility of mind, and who have already begun to doubt the immutability of species, may be influenced by this volume; but I look with confidence to the future,—to young and rising naturalists, who will be able to view both sides of the question with impartiality. Whoever is led to believe that species are mutable will do good service by conscientiously expressing his conviction; for thus only can the load of prejudice by which this subject is overwheimed be removed. . . .

Authors of the highest eminence seem to be fully satisfied with the view that each species has been independently created. To my mind it accords better with what we know of the laws impressed on matter by the Creator, that the production and extinction of the past and present inhabitants of the world should have been due to secondary causes, like those determining the birth and death of the individual. When I view all beings not as special creations, but as the lineal descendants of some few beings which lived long before the first bed of the Cambrian system was deposited, they seem to me to become ennobled. Judging from the past, we may safely infer that no one living species will transmit its unaltered likeness to a distant futurity. And of the species now living very few will transmit progeny of any kind to a far distant futurity; for the manner in which all organic beings are grouped, shows that the greater number of species in each genus, and all the species in many genera, have left no descendants, but have become utterly extinct. We can so far take a prophetic glance into futurity as to foretell that it will be the common and widely-spread species, belonging to the larger and dominant groups within each class, which will ultimately prevail and procreate new and dominant species. As all the living forms of life are the lineal descendants of those which lived long before the Cambrian epoch, we may feel certain that the ordinary succession by generation has never once been broken, and that no cataclysm has desolated the whole world. Hence we may look with some confidence to a secure future of great length. And as natural selection works solely by and for the good of each being, all corporeal and mental endowments will tend to progress towards perfection.[6]

READING CRITICALLY FOR IDEAS, STRUCTURE, AND STYLE

1. In Darwin's view, how do natural forces operate to select the best variations within a species to enable it to survive?
2. Evaluate Darwin's explanation for the lack of adequate fossil records, which would show stages in adaptive evolution if his theory was correct.
3. How does Darwin reply to objections that his theories are incompatible with existing religious beliefs?

EXTENDING INSIGHTS THROUGH WRITING

1. How did Darwin's concept of "natural selection" pose a fundamental challenge to the anthropocentric view of nature, which was based on the assumption of a master plan for humanity?
2. Darwin's theories of "survival of the fittest" have been applied in innumerable areas (such as economics). Choose one of these areas and discuss whether his theory can realistically be applied.

CONNECTING PERSPECTIVES ON THE NATURAL WORLD

1. How is the ability to create clones, as reported by Gina Kolata, a positive or negative evolutionary development in terms of the adaptive survival mechanism described by Charles Darwin?
2. In what respects does Mark Twain misrepresent aspects of Darwin's theory?

---

[6]Progess towards perfection over time suggests Darwin, natural selection will produce forms better adapted to their particular environment rather than perfection as such.

KONRAD LORENZ

The Dove and the Wolf

BACKGROUND

Konrad Lorenz (1903–1989) was born in Vienna and was a joint recipient of the 1973 Nobel Prize for Physiology. He is considered an outstanding naturalist and zoologist and the father of the science of ethology, which he founded along with Niko Tinbergen in the late 1930s to study animal behavior under natural conditions. Lorenz's pioneering investigation of the instinctive behavior of animals in the wild has disclosed profound connections between animal instincts and behavior patterns, with wide-ranging implications for humans. The results of Lorenz's research have appeared in *King Solomon's Ring: New Light on Animal Ways* (1952); *Man Meets Dog* (1954); *Evolution and the Modification of Behavior* (1965); and his most widely known work, *On Aggression* (1966), a far-reaching investigation on the role of the instinct of aggression in a range of species. He has also written *Here Am I—Where Are You?: The Behavior of the Graylag Goose* (1988; trans. 1991). "The Dove and the Wolf," from his 1952 work, presents startling examples of aggressive instincts that discredit the traditional views regarding doves and wolves.

APPROACHING LORENZ'S ESSAY

Lorenz's insights into human behavioral patterns, based on the study of animals in their natural environment, are well-illustrated in this essay. Ethology, as a discipline, is based on the assumption that there are many overlapping patterns of behavior between animals and human beings. In this study, Lorenz investigates how innate inhibitions within certain species serve to temper the aggression and violence members of the species display towards each other, thereby ensuring preservation of that species.

Lorenz discovered that wolves, contrary to popular belief, do not fight each other to the death. Instead, the weaker of two combatants will offer his jugular vein in a submission gesture to the stronger—which paradoxically inhibits the victor from killing his defeated rival. Conversely, supposedly meek deer, hares, and doves will fight with members of their own species to the death, especially when avenues of escape have been cut off. Lorenz postulates that the lack of restraint in species that travel in packs, or act cooperatively, would have resulted in the self-destruction of that species. Thus, the innate inhibition against killing a defeated rival developed to ensure survival.

Lorenz's essay is filled with many illustrative examples that are not only scientifically accurate, but philosophically thought-provoking, and are presented in his typically literate and engaging style. From the parallels he draws between the social behavior of certain animals and human beings, we can see that Lorenz is particularly concerned about the ineffectiveness of legal, religious, and moral codes in restraining violence within the human species. For Lorenz, these codes are ineffective attempts to serve the same purpose for humans as innate inhibitions do for wolves and other species.

The Dove and the Wolf

It is early one Sunday morning at the beginning of March, when Easter is already in the air, and we are taking a walk in the Vienna forest whose wooded slopes of tall beeches can be equalled in beauty by few and surpassed by none. We approach a forest glade. The tall smooth trunks of the beeches soon give place to the Hornbeam which are clothed from top to bottom with pale green foliage. We now tread slowly and more carefully. Before we break through the last bushes and out of cover on to the free expanse of the meadow, we do what all wild animals and all good naturalists, wild boars, leopards, hunters and zoologists would do under similar circumstances: we reconnoitre, seeking, before we leave our cover, to gain from it the advantage which it can offer alike to hunter and hunted, namely, to see without being seen.

Here, too, this age-old strategy proves beneficial. We do actually see someone who is not yet aware of our presence, as the wind is blowing away from him in our direction: in the middle of the clearing sits a large fat hare. He is sitting with his back to us, making a big V with his ears, and is watching intently something on the opposite edge of the meadow. From this point, a second and equally large hare emerges and with slow dignified hops, makes his way towards the first one. There follows a measured encounter, not unlike the meeting of two strange dogs. This cautious mutual taking stock soon develops into sparring. The two hares chase each other round, head to tail, in minute circles. This giddy rotating continues for quite a long time. Then suddenly, their pent-up energies burst forth into a battle royal. It is just like the outbreak of war, and happens at the very moment when the long mutual threatening of the hostile parties has forced one to the conclusion that neither dares to make a definite move. Facing each other, the hares rear up on their hind legs and, straining to their full height, drum furiously at each other with their fore pads. Now they clash in flying leaps and, at last, to the accompaniment of squeals and grunts, they discharge a volley of lightning kicks, so rapidly that only a slow motion camera could help us to discern the mechanism of these hostilities. Now, for the time being, they have had enough, and they recommence their circling, this time much faster than before; then follows a fresh, more embittered bout. So engrossed are the two champions, that there is nothing to prevent myself and my little daughter from tiptoeing nearer, although that venture cannot be accomplished in silence. Any normal and sensible hare would have heard us long ago, but this is March and March Hares are mad! The whole box-ing match looks so comical that my little daughter, in spite of her iron upbringing in the matter of silence when watching animals, cannot restrain a chuckle. That is too much even for March Hares—two flashes in two dif-ferent directions and the meadow is empty, while over the battlefield floats a fistful of fluff, light as a thistledown.

It is not only funny, it is almost touching, this duel of the unarmed, this raging fury of the meek in heart. But are these creatures really so meek? Have they really got softer hearts than those of the fierce beasts of prey? If, in a zoo, you ever watched two lions, wolves or eagles in conflict, then, in all probability, you did not feel like laughing. And yet, these sov-ereigns come off no worse than the harmless hares. Most people have the habit of judging carnivorous and herbivorous animals by quite inapplica-ble moral criteria. Even in fairy-tales, animals are portrayed as being a community comparable to that of mankind, as though all species of ani-mals were beings of one and the same family, as human beings are. For this reason, the average person tends to regard the animal that kills animals in the same light as he would the man that kills his own kind. He does not judge the fox that kills a hare by the same standard as the hunter who shoots one for precisely the same reason, but with that severe censure that he would apply to the gamekeeper who made a practice of shooting farm-ers and frying them for supper! The "wicked" beast of prey is branded as a murderer, although the fox's hunting is quite as legitimate and a great deal more necessary to his existence than is that of the gamekeeper, yet nobody regards the latter's "bag" as his prey, and only one author, whose own stan-dards were indicted by the severest moral criticism, has dared to dub the fox-hunter "the unspeakable in pursuit of the uneatable."! In their dealing with members of their own species, the beasts and birds of prey are far more restrained than many of the "harmless" vegetarians.

Still more harmless than a battle of hares appears the fight between turtle- or ring-doves. The gentle pecking of the frail bill, the light flick of the fragile wing seems, to the uninitiated, more like a caress than an attack. Some time ago I decided to breed a cross between the African blond ring-dove and our own indigenous somewhat frailer turtle-dove, and, with this object, I put a tame, home-reared male turtle-dove and a female ring-dove together in a roomy cage. I did not take their original scrapping seriously. How could these paragons of love and virtue dream of harming one another? I left them in their cage and went to Vienna. When I returned, the next day, a horrible sight met my eyes. The turtle-dove lay on the floor of the cage;

the top of his head and neck, as also the whole length of his back, were not only plucked bare of feathers, but so frayed as to form a single wound dripping with blood. In the middle of this gory surface, like an eagle on his prey, stood the second harbinger of peace. Wearing that dreamy facial expression that so appeals to our sentimental observer, this charming lady pecked mercilessly with her silver bill in the wounds of her prostrated mate. When the latter gathered his last resources in a final effort to escape, she set on him again, struck him to the floor with a light clap of her wing and continued with her slow pitiless work of destruction. Without my interference she would undoubtedly have finished him off, in spite of the fact that she was already so tired that she could hardly keep her eyes open. Only in two other instances have I seen similar horrible lacerations inflicted on their own kind by vertebrates: once, as an observer of the embittered fights of cichlid fishes who sometimes actually skin each other, and again as a field surgeon, in the late war, where the highest of all vertebrates perpetrated mass mutilations on members of his own species. But to return to our "harmless" vegetarians. The battle of the hares which we witnessed in the forest clearing would have ended in quite as horrible a carnage as that of the doves, had it taken place in the confines of a cage where the vanquished could not flee the victor.

5   If this is the extent of the injuries meted out to their own kind by our gentle doves and hares, how much greater must be the havoc wrought amongst themselves by those beasts to whom nature has relegated the strongest weapons with which to kill their prey? One would certainly think so, were it not that a good naturalist should always check by observation even the most obvious-seeming inferences before he accepts them as truth. Let us examine that symbol of cruelty and voraciousness, the wolf. How do these creatures conduct themselves in their dealings with members of their own species? At Whipsnade, that zoological country paradise, there lives a pack of timber wolves. From the fence of a pine-wood of enviable dimensions we can watch their daily round in an environment not so very far removed from conditions of real freedom. To begin with, we wonder why the antics of the many woolly, fatpawed whelps have not led them to destruction long ago. The efforts of one ungainly little chap to break into a gallop have landed him in a very different situation from that which he intended. He stumbles and bumps heavily into a wicked-looking old sinner. Strangely enough, the latter does not seem to notice it, he does not even growl. But now we hear the rumble of battle sounds! They are low, but more ominous than those of a dog-fight. We are watching the whelps and have therefore only become aware of this adult fight now that it is already in full swing.

An enormous old timber wolf and a rather weaker, obviously younger one are the opposing champions and they are moving in circles round each other, exhibiting admirable "footwork." At the same time, the bared fangs flash in such a rapid exchange of snaps that the eye can scarcely follow them. So far, nothing has really happened. The jaws of one wolf close on the gleaming white teeth of the other who is on the alert and wards off the attack. Only the lips have received one or two minor injuries. The younger wolf is gradually being forced backwards. It dawns upon us that the older one is purposely manouvering him towards the fence. We wait with breathless anticipation what will happen when he "goes to the wall." Now he strikes the wire netting stumbles . . . and the old one is upon him. And now the incredible happens, just the opposite of what you would expect. The furious whirling of the grey bodies has come to a sudden standstill. Shoulder to shoulder they stand, pressed against each other in a stiff and strained attitude, both heads now facing in the same direction. Both wolves are growling angrily, the elder in a deep bass, the younger in higher tones, suggestive of the fear that underlies his threat. But notice carefully the position of the two opponents; the older wolf has his muzzle close, very close against the neck of the younger, and the latter holds away his head, offering unprotected to his enemy the bend of his neck, the most vulnerable part of his whole body! Less than an inch from the tensed neck-muscles, where the jugular vein lies immediately beneath the skin, gleam the fangs of his antagonist from beneath the wickedly retracted lips. Whereas, during the thick of the fight, both wolves were intent on keeping only their teeth, the one invulnerable part of the body, in opposition to each other, it now appears that the discomfited fighter proffers intentionally that part of his anatomy to which a bite must assuredly prove fatal. Appearances are notoriously deceptive, but in his case, surprisingly, they are not!

This same scene can be watched any time wherever street-mongrels are to be found. I cited wolves as my first example because they illustrate my point more impressively than the all-too familiar domestic dog. Two adult male dogs meet in the street. Stiff-legged, with tails erect and hair on end, they pace towards each other. The nearer they approach, the stiffer, higher and more ruffled they appear, their advance becomes slower and slower. Unlike fighting cocks they do not make their encounter head to head, front against front, but make as though to pass each other, only stopping when they stand at last flank to flank, head to tail, in close juxtaposition. Then a strict ceremonial demands that each should sniff the hind regions of the other. Should one of the dogs be overcome with fear at this juncture, down goes his tail between his legs and he jumps with a quick, flexible twist, wheeling at an angle of 180 degrees thus modestly retracting his former offer to be smelt, Should the two dogs remain in an attitude of self-display, carrying their tails as rigid as standards, then the sniffing process may be of a long protracted nature. All may be solved amicably and there is still the chance that first one tail and then the other may begin to wag with small but rapidly increasing beats and then this nerve-racking situation may develop into nothing worse than a cheerful canine romp. Failing this solution the situation becomes more and more tense, noses begin to wrinkle and to turn up with a vile, brutal expression, lips begin to curl, exposing the fangs on the side nearer the opponent. Then the animals scratch the earth angrily with their hind feet, deep growls rise from their chests, and, in the next moment, they fall upon each other with loud piercing yells.

But to return to our wolves, whom we left in a situation of acute tension. This was not a piece of inartistic narrative on my part, since the strained situation may continue for a great length of time which is minutes to the observer, but very probably seems hours to the losing wolf. Every second you expect violence and await with bated breath the moment when the winner's teeth will rip the jugular vein of the loser. But your fears are groundless, for it will not happen. In this particular situation, the victor will definitely not close on his less fortunate rival. You can see that he would like to, but he just cannot! A dog or wolf that offers its neck to its adversary in this way will never be bitten seriously. The other growls and grumbles, snaps with his teeth in the empty air and even carries out, without delivering so much as a bite, the movement of shaking something to death in the empty air. However, this strange inhibition from biting persists only so long as the defeated dog or wolf maintains his attitude of humility. Since the fight is stopped so suddenly by this action, the victor frequently finds himself straddling his vanquished foe in anything but a comfortable position. So to remain, with his muzzle applied to the neck of the "under-dog" soon becomes tedious for the champion, and, seeing that he cannot bite anyway, he soon withdraws. Upon this, the under-dog may hastily attempt to put distance between himself and his superior. But he is not usually successful in this, for, as soon as he abandons his rigid attitude of submission, the other again falls upon him like a thunderbolt and the victim must again freeze into his former posture. It seems as if the victor is only waiting for the moment when the other will relinquish his submissive attitude, thereby enabling him to give vent to his urgent desire to bite. But, luckily for the "under-dog," the top-dog at the close of the fight is overcome by the pressing need to leave his trade-mark on the battlefield, to designate it as his personal property—in other words, he must lift his leg against the nearest upright object. This right-of-possession ceremony is usually taken advantage of by the under-dog to make himself scarce.

By this commonplace observation, we are here, as so often, made conscious of a problem which is actual in our daily life and which confronts us on all sides in the most various forms. Social inhibitions of this kind are not rare, but so frequent that we take them for granted and do not stop to think about them. An old German proverb says that one crow will not peck out the eye of another and for once the proverb is right. A tame crow or raven will no more think of pecking at your eye than he will at that of one of his own kind. Often when Roah, my tame raven, was sitting on my arm, I purposely put my face so near to his bill that my open eye came close to its wickedly curved point. Then Roah did something positively touching. With a nervous, worried movement he withdrew his beak from my eye, just as a father who is shaving will hold back his razor blade from the inquisitive fingers of his tiny daughter. Only in one particular connection did Roah ever approach my eye with his bill during this facial grooming. Many of the higher, social birds and mammals, above all monkeys, will groom the skin of a fellow-member of their species in those parts of his body to which he himself cannot obtain access. In birds, it is particularly the head and the region of the eyes which are dependent on the attentions of a fellow. In my description of the jackdaw, I have already spoken of the gestures with which these birds invite one another to preen their head feathers. When, with

half-shut eyes, I held my head sideways towards Roah, just as corvine birds
do to each other, he understood this movement in spite of the fact that I
have no head feathers to ruffle, and at once began to groom me. While doing
so, he never pinched my skin, for the epidermis of birds is delicate and
would not stand such rough treatment. With wonderful precision, he submitted every attainable hair to a drycleaning process by drawing it separately through his bill. He worked with the same intensive concentration
that distinguishes the "lousing" monkey and the operating surgeon. This
is not meant as a joke: the social grooming of monkeys, and particularly of
anthropoid apes has not the object of catching vermin—these animals usually have none—and is not limited to the cleaning of the skin, but serves
also more remarkable operations, for instance the dexterous removal of
thorns and even the squeezing-out of small carbuncles.

The manipulations of the dangerous-looking corvine beak round the   10
open eye of a man naturally appear ominous and, of course, I was always
receiving warnings from on lookers at this procedure. "You never know—a
raven is a raven—" and similar words of wisdom. I used to respond with the
paradoxical observation that the warner was for me potentially more dangerous than the raven. It has often happened that people have been shot dead
by madmen who have masked their condition with the cunning and pretence
typical of such cases. There was always a possibility, though admittedly a
very small one, that our kind adviser might be afflicted with such a disease.
But a sudden and unpredictable loss of the eye-pecking inhibition in a healthy,
mature raven is more unlikely by far than an attack by a well-meaning friend.

Why has the dog the inhibition against biting his fellow's neck? Why
has the raven an inhibition against pecking the eye of his friend? Why has
the ring-dove no such "insurance" against murder? A really comprehensive answer to these questions is almost impossible. It would certainly
involve a *historical* explanation of the process by which these inhibitions
have been developed in the course of evolution. There is no doubt that they
have arisen side by side with the development of the dangerous weapons
of the beast of prey. However, it is perfectly obvious why these inhibitions
are necessary to all weapon-bearing animals. Should the raven peck, without compunction, at the eye of his nest-mate, his wife or his young, in the
same way as he pecks at any other moving and glittering object, there would,
by now, be no more ravens in the world. Should a dog or wolf unrestrainedly
and unaccountably bite the neck of his packmates and actually execute
the movement of shaking them to death, then his species also would certainly be exterminated within a short space of time.

The ring-dove does not require such an inhibition since it can only
inflict injury to a much lesser degree, while its ability to flee is so well developed that it suffices to protect the bird even against enemies equipped with
vastly better weapons. Only under the unnatural conditions of close confinement which deprive the losing dove of the possibility of flight does it
become apparent that the ring-dove has no inhibitions which prevent it
from injuring or even torturing its own kind. Many other "harmless" her-
bivores prove themselves just as unscrupulous when they are kept in narrow captivity. One of the most disgusting, ruthless and blood-thirsty

murderers is an animal which is generally considered as being second only to the dove in the proverbial gentleness of its nature, namely the roe-deer. The roe-buck is about the most malevolent beast I know and is possessed, into the bargain, of a weapon, its antlers, which it shows mighty little restraint in putting into use. The species can "afford" this lack of control since the fleeing capacity even of the weakest doe is enough to deliver it from the strongest buck. Only in very large paddocks can the roe-buck be kept with females of his own kind. In smaller enclosures, sooner or later he will drive his fellows, females and young ones included, into a corner and gore them to death. The only "insurance against murder" which the roe-deer possesses, is based on the fact that the onslaught of the attacking buck proceeds relatively slowly. He does not rush with lowered head at his adversary as, for example, a ram would do, but he approaches quite slowly, cautiously feeling with his antlers for those of his opponent. Only when the antlers are interlocked and the buck feels firm resistance does he thrust with deadly earnest. According to the statistics given by W. T. Hornaday, the former director of the New York Zoo, tame deer cause yearly more serious accidents than captive lions and tigers, chiefly because an uninitiated person does not recognize the slow approach of the buck as an earnest attack, even when the animal's antlers have come dangerously near. Suddenly there follows, thrust upon thrust, the amazingly strong stabbing movement of the sharp weapon, and you will be lucky if you have time enough to get a good grip on the aggressor's antlers. Now there follows a wrestling-match in which the sweat pours and the hands drip blood, and in which even a very strong man can hardly obtain mastery over the roe-buck unless he succeeds in getting to the side of the beast and bending his neck backwards. Of course, one is ashamed to call for help—until one has the point of an antler in one's body! So take my advice and if a charming, tame roe-buck comes playfully towards you, with a characteristic prancing step and flourishing his antlers gracefully, hit him, with your walking stick, a stone or the bare fist, as hard as you can, on the side of his nose, before he can apply his antlers to your person.

And now, honestly judged: who is really a "good" animal, my friend Roah to whose social inhibitions I could trust the light of my eyes, or the gentle ring-dove that in hours of hard work nearly succeeded in torturing its mate to death? Who is a "wicked" animal, the roe-buck who will slit the bellies even of females and young of his own kind if they are unable to escape him, or the wolf who cannot bite his hated enemy if the latter appeals to his mercy?

Now let us turn our mind to another question. Wherein consists the essence of all the gestures of submission by which a bird or animal of a social species can appeal to the inhibitions of its superior? We have just seen, in the wolf, that the defeated animal actually facilitates his own destruction by offering to the victor those very parts of his body which he was most anxious to shield as long as the battle was raging. All submissive attitudes with which we are so far familiar, in social animals, are based on the same principle: The supplicant always offers to his adversary the most vulnerable part of his body, or, to be more exact, that part *against which every killing attack is inevitably directed!* In most birds, this area is the base of the skull. If one jackdaw wants to show submission to another, he squats back on his hocks, turns away his head, at the same time drawing in his bill to make the nape of his neck bulge, and, leaning towards his superior, seems to invite him to peck at the fatal spot. Seagulls and herons present to their superior the top of their head, stretching their neck forward horizontally, low over the ground, also a position which makes the supplicant particularly defenceless.

With many gallinaceous birds, the fights of the males commonly end   15
by one of the combatants being thrown to the ground, held down and then scalped as in the manner described in the ring-dove. Only one species shows mercy in this case, namely the turkey: and this one only does so in response to a specific submissive gesture which serves to forestall the intent of the attack. If a turkey-cock has had more than his share of the wild and grotesque wrestling-match in which these birds indulge, he lays himself with outstretched neck upon the ground. Whereupon the victor behaves exactly as a wolf or dog in the same situation, that is to say, he evidently *wants* to peck and kick at the prostrated enemy, but simply cannot: he would if he could but he can't! So, still in threatening attitude, he walks around and around his prostrated rival, making tentative passes at him, but leaving him untouched.

This reaction—though certainly propitious for the turkey species— can cause a tragedy if a turkey comes to blows with a peacock, a thing which not infrequently happens in captivity, since these species are closely enough related to "appreciate" respectively their mutual manifestations of virility. In spite of greater strength and weight the turkey nearly always loses the match, for the peacock flies better and has a different fighting technique. While the red-brown American is muscling himself up for the wrestling-match, the blue East-Indian has already flown above him and struck at him with his sharply pointed spurs. The turkey justifiably considers this infringement of his fighting code as unfair and, although he is still in possession of his full strength, he throws in the sponge and lays himself down in the above depicted manner now. And a ghastly thing happens: the peacock does not "understand" this submissive gesture of the turkey, that is to say, it elicits no inhibition of his fighting drives. He pecks and kicks further at the helpless turkey, who, if nobody comes to his rescue, is doomed, for the more pecks and blows he receives, the more certainly are his escape reactions blocked by the psycho-physiological mechanism of the submissive attitude. It does not and cannot occur to him to jump up and run away.

The fact that many birds have developed special "signal organs" for eliciting this type of social inhibition, shows convincingly the blind instinctive nature and the great evolutionary age of these submissive gestures. The young of the water-rail, for example, have a bare red patch at the back of their head which, as they present it meaningly to an older and stronger fellow, takes on a deep red colour. Whether, in higher animals and man, social inhibitions of this kind are equally mechanical, need not for the moment enter into our consideration. Whatever may be the reasons that prevent the dominant individual from injuring the submissive one, whether he is prevented from doing so by a simple and purely mechanical reflex process or by a highly philosophical moral standard, is immaterial to the practical issue. The essential behaviour of the submissive as well as of the dominant partner remains the same: the humbled creature suddenly seems to lose his objections to being injured and removes all obstacles from the path of the killer, and it would seem that the very removal of these outer obstacles raises an insurmountable inner obstruction in the central nervous system of the aggressor.

And what is a human appeal for mercy after all? Is it so very different from what we have just described? The Homeric warrior who wishes to yield and plead mercy, discards helmet and shield, falls on his knees and inclines his head, a set of actions which should make it easier for the enemy to kill, but, in reality, hinders him from doing so. As Shakespeare makes Nestor say to Hector:

> "Thou hast hung thy advanced sword i' the air,
> Not letting it decline on the declined."

Even to-day, we have retained many symbols of such submissive attitudes in a number of our gestures of courtesy: bowing, removal of the hat, and presenting arms in military ceremonial. If we are to believe the ancient epics, an appeal to mercy does not seem to have raised an "inner obstruction" which was entirely insurmountable. Homer's heroes were certainly not as soft-hearted as the wolves of Whip-snade! In any case, the poet cites numerous instances where the supplicant was slaughtered with or without compunction The Norse heroic sagas bring us many examples of similar failures of the submissive gesture and it was not till the era of knight-errantry that it was no longer considered "sporting" to kill a man who begged for mercy. The Christian knight is the first who, for reasons of traditional and religious morals, is as chivalrous as is the wolf from the depth of his natural impulses and inhibitions. What a strange paradox!

20   Of course, the innate, instinctive, fixed inhibitions that prevent an animal from using his weapons indiscriminately against his own kind are only a functional analogy, at the most a slight foreshadowing, a genealogical predecessor of the social morals of man. The worker in comparative ethology does well to be very careful in applying moral criteria to animal behaviour. But here, I must myself own to harbouring sentimental feelings: I think it a truly magnificent thing that one wolf finds himself unable to bite the proffered neck of the other, but still more so that the other relies upon him for his amazing restraint. Mankind can learn a lesson from this, from the animal that Dante calls "la bestia senza pace."[1] I at least have extracted from it a new and deeper understanding of a wonderful and often

[1]The first Cante of Dante's *Inferno* represents a she-wolf, "the beast who cannot be placated."

misunderstood saying from the Gospel which hitherto had only awakened in me feelings of strong opposition: "And unto him that smiteth thee on the one cheek offer also the other" (St. Luke VI, 26). A wolf has enlightened me: not so that your enemy may strike you again do you turn the other cheek toward him, but to make him unable to do it.

When, in the course of its evolution, a species of animals develops a weapon which may destroy a fellow-member at one blow, then, in order to survive, it must develop, along with the weapon, a social inhibition to prevent a usage which could endanger the existence of the species. Among the predatory animals, there are only a few which lead so solitary a life that they can, in general, forego such restraint. They come together only at the mating season when the sexual impulse outweighs all others, including that of aggression. Such unsociable hermits are the polar bear and the jaguar and, owing to the absence of these social inhibitions, animals of these species, when kept together in Zoos, hold a sorry record for murdering their own kind. The system of special inherited impulses and inhibitions, together with the weapons with which a social species is provided by nature, form a complex which is carefully computed and self-regulating. All living beings have received their weapons through the same process of evolution that moulded their impulses and inhibitions; for the structural plan of the body and the system of behavior of a species are parts of the same whole.

> "If such a Nature's holy plan,
> Have I not reason to lament
> What man has made of man?"

Wordsworth is right: there is only one being in possession of weapons which do not grow on his body and of whose working plan, therefore, the instincts of his species know nothing and in the usage of which he has no correspondingly adequate inhibition. That being is man. With unarrested growth his weapons increase in monstrousness, multiplying horribly within a few decades. But innate impulses and inhibitions, like bodily structures, need time for their development, time on a scale in which geologists and astronomers are accustomed to calculate, and not historians. We did not receive our weapons from nature. We made them ourselves, of our own free will. Which is going to be easier for us in the future, the production of the weapons or the engendering of the feeling of responsibility that should go along with them, the inhibitions without which our race must perish by virtue of its own creations? We must build up these inhibitions purposefully for we cannot rely upon our instincts. Fourteen years ago, in November 1935, I concluded an article on "Morals and Weapons of Animals" which appeared in a Viennese journal, with the words, "The day will come when two warring factions will be faced with the possibility of each wiping the other out completely. The day may come when the whole of mankind is divided into two such opposing camps. Shall we then behave like doves or like wolves? The fate of mankind will be settled by the answer to this question." We may well be apprehensive.

READING CRITICALLY FOR IDEAS, STRUCTURE, AND STYLE

1. Much of Lorenz's essay is taken up with discrediting clichés about certain species such as rabbits, doves, and wolves. What does he discover that refutes conventional beliefs? How can each animal's behavior be understood as a form of adaptation for survival?

2. How does Lorenz use the last stages of combat between rival timber wolves as evidence of his theory?

3. What parallels or contrasts does Lorenz draw between animal instincts and human behavior? Do you agree with his conclusions? Why or why not?

EXTENDING INSIGHTS THROUGH WRITING

1. Closely observe the behavior of an animal and describe the patterns that suggest a particular kind of instinct that is uniquely adapted to ensure that species' survival. Write up your findings in a page or two; be as careful to document your observations as Lorenz is, and try to refute clichés about this species.

2. Apply Lorenz's methods of ethnographic observation to the human species at play in such symbolic ritual contests as prizefights or football games. Discuss the constraints involved that make these sports rather than a life or death contest.

CONNECTING PERSPECTIVES ON THE NATURAL WORLD

1. How do Lorenz's observations illustrate Darwin's theory of "survival of the fittest" and the different forms this takes in various species?

2. What do Lorenz and Arthur D. Hasler and James A. Larsen reveal about the role that instinct plays in ensuring the survival of the species?

JEAN HENRI FABRE

The Praying Mantis

BACKGROUND

Jean Henri Fabre (1823–1915), considered the father of entomology, received a doctorate in natural sciences in 1864 in Paris. Fabre published the first of his many distinctive works on the biology and behavior of insects in 1855. In the following year, Fabre was awarded the Prix Montyon for experimental physiology by the Institute of France, and Napoleon III awarded him the Legion of Honor. Fabre shared his passion for scientific discovery with Louis Pasteur and was visited by the leading scientists and intellectuals of his day, including John Stuart Mill. Charles Darwin praised the value of Fabre's research in his *On the Origin of Species* (1859) and described him as "that inimitable observer" because of his profound discoveries. Fabre disclosed the importance of instinct in the habits of many insects, including the dung beetle, and discovered how wasps paralyze their prey in response to specific stimulating zones. Fabre's major scientific work, the ten-volume *Souvenirs Entomologiques* (1878–1907), was accomplished between his retirement from academic life and the time of his death at age ninety-two. He was also a prolific poet and artist. In "The Praying Mantis," from *The Insect World* (1949), Fabre uses dramatic analogies to convey the cannibalistic mating habits of the praying mantis with his characteristic blend of meticulous observations and engaging style.

APPROACHING FABRE'S ESSAY

Fabre's blend of precise observations and exquisite literary style makes it easy for us to appreciate his discoveries of the importance of instinct among insects. To us, the mantis appears tiny and delicate, seeming in repose to assume a posture of prayer. But this insect is really fierce and appears huge and terrifying to other insects who may become its victims. Since Fabre is describing the fierce nature of the mantis, its methods of intimidation, the way it attacks and devours its prey, its cannibalism, and the eating of the male after fertilization of the female's eggs, it makes sense for Fabre to write of the mantis according to the scale of the insect world. Its fierceness would not make as deep an impression on the reader if he or she continued to view it as fragile and delicate. To make his points with maximum effect, Fabre carefully and graphically describes the mantis as it appears to other insects, a dangerous and formidable foe.

Throughout his essay, Fabre's accurate observations make the piece fascinating as well as informative. This is especially true of the mating habits of the mantis. Everything is described with such detail that the reader almost feels as if he were watching the process rather than reading about it.

Fabre uses analogies that are both dramatic and shocking to convey the predatory and cannabilistic habits of the praying mantis.

The Praying Mantis

Another creature of the south is at least as interesting as the Cicada, but much less famous, because it makes no noise. Had Heaven granted it a pair of cymbals, the one thing needed, its renown would eclipse the great musician's, for it is most unusual in both shape and habits. Folk hereabouts call it *lou Prègo-Diéu,* the animal that prays to God. Its official name is the Praying Mantis. . . .

The language of science and the peasant's artless vocabulary agree in this case and represent the queer creature as a pythoness[1] delivering her oracles or an ascetic rapt in pious ecstasy. The comparison dates a long way back. Even in the time of the Greeks the insect was called *Mántis,* the divine, the prophet. The tiller of the soil is not particular about analogies: where points of resemblance are not too clear, he will make up for their deficiencies. He saw on the sun-scorched herbage an insect of imposing appearance, drawn up majestically in a half-erect posture. He noticed its gossamer wings, broad and green, trailing like long veils of finest lawn; he saw its fore-legs, its arms so to speak, raised to the sky in a gesture of invocation. That was enough; popular imagination did the rest; and behold the bushes from ancient times stocked with Delphic priestesses, with nuns in orison.

Good people, with your childish simplicity, how great was your mistake! Those sanctimonious airs are a mask for Satanic habits; those arms folded in prayer are cut-throat weapons: they tell no beads, they slay whatever passes within range. Forming an exception which one would never have suspected in the herbivorous order of the Orthoptera, the Mantis feeds exclusively on living prey. She is the tigress of the peaceable entomological

[1]A reference to the priestess who served Apollo at Delphi and to the sacred serpent in the caves of Mount Parnassus from which the oracles were delivered.

tribes, the ogress in ambush who levies a tribute of fresh meat. Picture her with sufficient strength; and her carnivorous appetites, combined with her traps of horrible perfection, would make her the terror of the country-side. The *Prègo-Diéu* would become a devilish vampire.

Apart from her lethal implement, the Mantis has nothing to inspire dread. She is not without a certain beauty, in fact, with her slender figure, her elegant bust, her pale-green colouring and her long gauze wings. No ferocious mandibles, opening like shears; on the contrary, a dainty pointed muzzle that seems made for billing and cooing. Thanks to a flexible neck, quite independent of the thorax, the head is able to move freely, to turn to right or left, to bend, to lift itself. Alone among insects, the Mantis directs her gaze; she inspects and examines; she almost has a physiognomy.

Great indeed is the contrast between the body as a whole, with its very pacific aspect, and the murderous mechanism of the forelegs, which are correctly described as raptorial.[2] The haunch is uncommonly long and powerful. Its function is to throw forward the rat-trap, which does not await its victim but goes in search of it. The snare is decked out with some show of finery. The base of the haunch is adorned on the inner surface with a pretty, black mark, having a white spot in the middle; and a few rows of bead-like dots complete the ornamentation.

The thigh, longer still, a sort of flattened spindle, carries on the front half of its lower surface two rows of sharp spikes. In the inner row there are a dozen, alternately black and green, the green being shorter than the black. This alternation of unequal lengths increases the number of cogs and improves the effectiveness of the weapon. The outer row is simpler and has only four teeth. Lastly, three spurs, the longest of all, stand out behind the two rows. In short, the thigh is a saw with two parallel blades, separated by a groove in which the leg lies when folded back.

The leg, which moves very easily on its joint with the thigh, is likewise a double-edged saw. The teeth are smaller, more numerous and closer together than those on the thigh. It ends in a strong hook whose point vies with the finest needle for sharpness, a hook fluted underneath and having a double blade like a curved pruning-knife.

This hook, a most perfect instrument for piercing and tearing, has left me many a painful memory. How often, when Mantis-hunting, clawed by the insect which I had just caught and not having both hands at liberty, have I been obliged to ask somebody else to release me from my tenacious captive! To try to free yourself by force, without first disengaging the claws implanted in your flesh, would expose you to scratches similar to those produced by the thorns of a rose-tree. None of our insects is so troublesome to handle. The Mantis claws you with her pruning-hooks, pricks you with her spikes, seizes you in her vice and makes self-defence almost impossible if, wishing to keep your prize alive, you refrain from giving the pinch of the thumb that would put an end to the struggle by crushing the creature.

[2]Able to readily grasp victims.

When at rest, the trap is folded and pressed back against the chest and looks quite harmless. There you have the insect praying. But, should a victim pass, the attitude of prayer is dropped abruptly. Suddenly unfolded, the three long sections of the machine throw to a distance their terminal grapnel, which harpoons the prey and, in returning, draws it back between the two saws. The vice closes with a movement like that of the fore-arm and the upper arm; and all is over: Locusts, Grasshoppers and others even more powerful, once caught in the mechanism with its four rows of teeth, are irretrievably lost. Neither their desperate fluttering nor their kicking will make the terrible engine release its hold.

10   An uninterrupted study of the Mantis' habits is not practicable in the open fields; we must rear her at home. There is no difficulty about this: she does not mind being interned under glass, on condition that she be well fed. Offer her choice viands, served up fresh daily, and she will hardly feel her absence from the bushes.

As cages for my captives I have some ten large wire-gauze dishcovers, the same that are used to protect meat from the Flies. Each stands in a pan filled with sand. A dry tuft of thyme and a flat stone on which the laying may be done later constitute all the furniture. These huts are placed in a row on the large table in my insect laboratory, where the sun shines on them for the best part of the day. I install my captives in them, some singly, some in groups.

It is in the second fortnight of August that I begin to come upon the adult Mantis in the withered grass and on the brambles by the roadside. The females, already notably corpulent, are more frequent from day to day. Their slender companions, on the other hand, are rather scarce; and I some-times have a good deal of difficulty in making up my couples, for there is an appalling consumption of these dwarfs in the cages. Let us keep these atrocities for later and speak first of the females.

They are great eaters, whose maintenance, when it has to last for some months, is none too easy. The provisions, which are nibbled at dis-dainfully and nearly all wasted, have to be renewed almost every day. I trust that the Mantis is more economical on her native bushes. When game is not plentiful, no doubt she devours every atom of her catch; in my cages she is extravagant, often dropping and abandoning the rich morsel after a few mouthfuls, without deriving any further benefit from it. This appears to be her particular method of beguiling the tedium of captivity.

To cope with these extravagant ways I have to employ assistants. Two or three small local idlers, bribed by the promise of a slice of melon or bread-and-butter, go morning and evening to the grass-plots in the neighbourhood and fill their gamebags—cases made of reed-stumps—with live Locusts and Grasshoppers. I on my side, net in hand, make a daily circuit of my enclo-sure, in the hope of obtaining some choice morsel for my boarders.

15   These tit-bits are intended to show me to what lengths the Mantis' strength and daring can go. They include the big Grey Locust . . . , who is larger than the insect that will consume him; the White-faced Decticus, armed with a vigorous pair of mandibles whereof our fingers would do well to fight shy; the quaint Tryxalis, who wears a pyramid-shaped mitre on her

head; the Vine Ephippiger, who clashes cymbals and sports a sword at the bottom of her pot-belly. To this assortment of game that is not any too easy to tackle, let us add two monsters, two of the largest Spiders of the district: the Silky Epeira, whose flat, festooned abdomen is the size of a franc piece; and the Cross Spider, or Diadem Epeira, who is hideously hairy and obese.

I cannot doubt that the Mantis attacks such adversaries in the open, when I see her, under my covers, boldly giving battle to whatever comes in sight. Lying in wait among the bushes, she must profit by the fat prizes offered by chance even as, in the wire cage, she profits by the treasures due to my generosity. Those big hunts, full of danger, are no new thing: they form part of her normal existence. Nevertheless they appear to be rare, for want of opportunity, perhaps to the Mantis' deep regret.

Locusts of all kinds, Butterflies, Dragon-flies, large Flies, Bees and other moderatesized captures are what we usually find in the lethal limbs. Still the fact remains that, in my cages, the daring huntress recoils before nothing. Sooner or later, Grey Locust and Dectius, Epeira and Tryxalis are harpooned, held tight between the saws and crunched with gusto. The facts are worth describing.

At the sight of the Grey Locust who has heedlessly approached along the trelliswork of the cover, the Mantis gives a convulsive shiver and suddenly adopts a terrifying posture. An electric shock would not produce a more rapid effect. The transition is so abrupt, the attitude so threatening that the observer beholding it for the first time at once hesitates and draws back his fingers, apprehensive of some unknown danger. Old hand as I am, I cannot even now help being startled, should I happen to be thinking of something else.

You see before you, most unexpectedly, a sort of bogey-man or Jack-in-the-box. The wing-covers open and are turned back on either side, slantingly; the wings spread to their full extent and stand erect like parallel sails or like a huge heraldic crest towering over the back; the tip of the abdomen curls upwards like a crosier, rises and falls, relaxing with short jerks and a sort of sough, a "Whoof! Whoof!" like that of a Turkeycock spreading his tail. It reminds one of the puffing of a startled Adder.   [20]

Planted defiantly on its four hind-legs, the insect holds its long bust almost upright. The murderous legs, originally folded and pressed together upon the chest, open wide, forming a cross with the body and revealing the arm-pits decorated with rows of beads and a black spot with a white dot in the centre. These two faint imitations of the eyes in a Peacock's tail, together with the dainty ivory beads, are warlike ornaments kept hidden at ordinary times. They are taken from the jewelcase only at the moment when we have to make ourselves brave and terrible for battle.

Motionless in her strange posture, the Mantis watches the Locust, with her eyes fixed in his direction and her head turning as on a pivot whenever the other changes his place. The object of this attitudinizing is evident: the Mantis wants to strike terror into her dangerous quarry, to paralyze it with fright, for, unless demoralized by fear, it would prove too formidable.

Does she succeed in this? Under the shiny head of the Decticus, behind the long face of the Locust, who can tell what passes? No sign of excitement betrays itself to our eyes on those impassive masks. Nevertheless it is certain that the threatened one is aware of the danger. He sees standing before him a spectre, with uplifted claws, ready to fall upon him; he feels that he is face to face with death; and he fails to escape while there is yet time. He who excels in leaping and could so easily hop out of reach of those talons, he, the big-thighed jumper, remains stupidly where he is, or even draws nearer with a leisurely step.

They say that little birds, paralysed with terror before the open jaws of the Snake, spell-bound by the reptile's gaze, lose their power of flight and allow themselves to be snapped up. The Locust often behaves in much the same way. See him within reach of the enchantress. The two grapnels fall, the claws strike, the double saws close and clutch. In vain the poor wretch protests: he chews space with his mandibles and, kicking desperately, strikes nothing but the air. His fate is sealed. The Mantis furls her wings, her battle-standard; she resumes her normal posture; and the meal begins.

In attacking the Tryxalis and the Ephippiger, less dangerous game than the Grey Locust and the Decticus, the spectral attitude is less imposing and of shorter duration. Often the throw of the grapnels is sufficient. This is likewise so in the case of the Epeira, who is grasped round the body with not a thought of her poison-fangs. With the smaller Locusts, the usual fare in my cages as in the open fields, the mantis seldom employs her intimidation-methods and contents herself with seizing the reckless one that passes within her reach.

When the prey to be captured is able to offer serious resistance, the Mantis has at her service a pose that terrorizes and fascinates her quarry and gives her claws a means of hitting with certainty. Her rat-traps close on a demoralized victim incapable of defence. She frightens her victim into immobility by suddenly striking a spectral attitude.

The wings play a great part in this fantastic pose. They are very wide, green on the outer edge, colourless and transparent every elsewhere. They are crossed lengthwise by numerous veins, which spread in the shape of a fan. Other veins, transversal and finer, intersect the first at right angles and with them form a multitude of meshes. In the spectral attitude, the wings are displaced and stand upright in two parallel planes that almost touch each other, like the wings of a Butterfly at rest. Between them the curled tip of the abdomen moves with sudden starts. The sort of breath which I have compared with the puffing of an Adder in a posture of defence comes from this rubbing of the abdomen against the nerves of the wings. To imitate the strange sound, all that you need do is to pass your nail quickly over the upper surface of an unfurled wing.

Wings are essential to the male, a slender pigmy who has to wander from thicket to thicket at mating-time. He has a well-developed pair, more than sufficient for his flight, the greatest range of which hardly amounts to four or five of our paces. The little fellow is exceedingly sober in his appetites. On rare occasions, in my cages, I catch him eating a lean Locust, an insignificant, perfectly harmless creature. This means that he knows nothing of the spectral attitude which is of no use to an unambitious hunter of his kind.

On the other hand, the advantage of the wings to the female is not very obvious, for she is inordinately stout at the time when her eggs ripen. She climbs, she runs; but, weighed down by her corpulence, she never flies. Then what is the object of wings, of wings, too, which are seldom matched for breadth?

The question becomes more significant if we consider the Grey Mantis . . . . , who is closely akin to the Praying Mantis. The male is winged and is even pretty quick at flying. The female, who drags a great belly full of eggs, reduces her wings to stumps and, like the cheesemakers of Auvergne and Savory, wears a short-tailed jacket. For one who is not meant to leave the dry grass and the stones, this abbreviated costume is more suitable than superfluous gauze furbelows. The Grey Mantis is right to retain but a mere vestige of the cumbrous sails.

Is the other wrong to keep her wings, to exaggerate them, even though she never flies? Not at all. The Praying Mantis hunts big game. Sometimes a formidable prey appears in her hiding-place. A direct attack might be fatal. The thing to do is first to intimidate the new-comer, to conquer his resistance by terror. With this object she suddenly unfurls her wings into a ghost's winding-sheet. The huge sails incapable of flight are hunting-implements. This stratagem is not needed by the little Grey Mantis, who captures feeble prey, such as Gnats and newborn Locusts. The two huntresses, who have similar habits and, because of their stoutness, are neither of them able to fly, are dressed to suit the difficulties of the ambuscade. The first, an impetuous amazon, puffs her wings into a threatening standard; the second, a modest fowler, reduces them to a pair of scanty coat-tails.

In a fit of hunger, after a fast of some days' duration, the Praying Mantis will gobble up a Grey Locust whole, except for the wings, which are too dry; and yet the victim of her voracity is as big as herself, or even bigger. Two hours are enough for consuming this monstrous head of game. An orgy of the sort is rare. I have witnessed it once or twice and have always wondered how the gluttonous creature found room for so much food and how it reversed in its favour the axiom that the cask must be greater than its contents. I can but admire the lofty privileges of a stomach through which matter merely passes, being at once digested, dissolved and done away with.

The usual bill of fare in my cages consists of Locusts of greatly varied species and sizes. It is interesting to watch the Mantis nibbling her Acridian, firmly held in the grip of her two murderous fore-legs. Notwithstanding the fine, pointed muzzle, which seems scarcely made for this gorging, the whole dish disappears, with the exception of the wings, of which only the slightly fleshy base is consumed. The legs, the tough skin, everything goes down. Sometimes the Mantis seizes one of the big hinder thighs by the knuckle-end, lifts it to her mouth, tastes it and crunches it with a little air of satisfaction. The Locust's fat and juicy thigh may well be a choice morsel for her, even as a leg of mutton is for us.

The prey is first attacked in the neck. While one of the two lethal legs holds the victim transfixed through the middle of the body, the other presses the head and makes the neck open upwards. The Mantis' muzzle roots and nibbles at this weak point in the armour with some persistency. A large wound appears in the head. The Locust gradually ceases kicking and becomes a lifeless corpse; and, from this moment, freer in its movements, the carnivorous insect picks and chooses its morsel.

35   The Mantis naturally wants to devour the victuals in peace, without being troubled by the plunges of a victim who absolutely refuses to be devoured. A meal liable to interruptions lacks savour. Now the principal means of defence in this case are the hind-legs, those vigorous levers which can kick out so brutally and which moreover are armed with toothed saws that would rip open the Mantis' bulky paunch if by ill-luck they happen to graze it. What shall we do to reduce them to helplessness, together with the others, which are not dangerous but troublesome all the same, with their desperate gesticulations?

Strictly speaking, it would be practicable to cut them off one by one. But that is a long process and attended with a certain risk. The Mantis has hit upon something better. She has an intimate knowledge of the anatomy of the spine. By first attacking her prize at the back of the half-opened neck and munching the cervical ganglia, she destroys the muscular energy at its main seat; and inertia supervenes, not suddenly and completely, for the clumsily-constructed Locust has not the Bee's exquisite and frail vitality, but still sufficiently, after the first mouthfuls. Soon the kicking and the gesticulating die down, all movements ceases and the game, however big it be, is consumed in perfect quiet.

The little that we have seen of the Mantis' habits hardly tallies with what we might have expected from her popular name. To judge by the term *Prègo-Diéu*, we should look to see a placid insect, deep in pious contemplation; and we find ourselves in the presence of a cannibal, of a ferocious spectre munching the brain of a panic-stricken victim. Nor is even this the most tragic part. The Mantis has in store for us, in her relations with her own kith and kin, manners even more atrocious than those prevailing among the Spiders, who have an evil reputation in this respect.

To reduce the number of cages on my big table and give myself a little more space while still retaining a fair-sized menagerie, I install several females, sometimes as many as a dozen, under one cover. So far as accommodation is concerned, no fault can be found with the common lodging. There is room and to spare for the evolutions of my captives, who naturally do not want to move about much with their unwieldy bellies. Hanging to the trelliswork of the dome, motionless they digest their food or else await an unwary passer-by. Even so do they act when at liberty in the thickets.

Cohabitation has its dangers. I know that even Donkeys, those peace-loving animals, quarrel when hay is scarce in the manger. My boarders, who are less complaisant, might well, in a moment of dearth, become sour-tempered and fight among themselves. I guard against this by keeping the cages well supplied with Locusts, renewed twice a day. Should civil war break out, famine cannot be pleaded as the excuse.

At first, things go pretty well. The community lives in peace, each Mantis grabbing and eating whatever comes near her, without seeking strife with her neighbours. But this harmonious period does not last long. The bellies swell, the eggs are ripening in the ovaries, marriage and laying-time are at hand. Then a sort of jealous fury bursts out, though there is an entire absence of males who might be held responsible for feminine rivalry. The working of the ovaries seems to pervert the flock, inspiring its members with a mania for devouring one another. There are threats, personal encounters, cannibal feasts. Once more the spectral pose appears, the hissing of the wings, the fearsome gesture of the grapnels outstretched and uplifted in the air. No hostile demonstration in front of a Grey Locust or White-faced Decticus could be more menacing.

For no reason that I can gather, two neighbors suddenly assume their attitude of war. They turn their heads to right and left, provoking each other, exchanging insulting glances. The "Puff! Puff!" of the wings rubbed by the abdomen sounds the charge. When the duel is to be limited to the first scratch received, without more serious consequences, the lethal forearms, which are usually kept folded, open like the leaves of a book and fall back sideways, encircling the long bust. It is a superb pose, but less terrible than that adopted in a fight to the death.

Then one of the grapnels, with a sudden spring, shoots out to its full length and strikes the rival; it is no less abruptly withdrawn and resumes the defensive. The adversary hits back. The fencing is rather like that of two Cats boxing each other's ears. At the first blood drawn from her flabby paunch, or even before receiving the last wound, one of the duellists confesses herself beaten and retires. The other furls her battle-standard and goes off elsewhither to meditate the capture of a Locust, keeping apparently calm, but ever ready to repeat the quarrel.

Very often, events take a more tragic turn. At such times, the full posture of the duels to the death is assumed. The murderous fore-arms are unfolded and raised in the air. Woe to the vanquished! The other seizes her in her vice and then and there proceeds to eat her, beginning at the neck, of course. The loathsome feast takes place as calmly as though it were a matter of crunching up a Grasshopper. The diner enjoys her sister as she would a lawful dish; and those around do not protest, being quite willing to do as much on the first occasion.

Oh, what savagery! Why, even Wolves are said not to eat one another. The Mantis has no such scruples; she banquets off her fellows when there is plenty of her favorite game, the Locust, around her. She practises the equivalent of cannibalism, that hideous peculiarity of man.

These aberrations, these child-bed cravings can reach an even more revolting stage. Let us watch the pairing and, to avoid the disorder of a crowd, let us isolate the couples under different covers. Each pair shall have its own home, where none will come to disturb the wedding. And let us not forget the provisions, with which we will keep them well supplied, so that there may be no excuse of hunger.

It is near the end of August. The male, that slender swain, thinks the moment propitious. He makes eyes at his strapping companion; he turns his head in her direction; he bends his neck and throws out his chest. His little pointed face wears an almost impassioned expression. Motionless, in this posture, for a long time he contemplates the object of his desire. She does not stir, is as though indifferent. The lover, however, has caught a sign of acquiescence, a sign of which I do not know the secret. He goes nearer; suddenly he spreads his wings, which quiver with a convulsive tremor. This is his declaration. He rushes, small as he is, upon the back of his corpulent companion, clings on as best he can, steadies his hold. As a rule, the preliminaries last a long time. At last, coupling takes place and is also long drawn out, lasting for five or six hours.

Nothing worthy of attention happens between the two motionless partners. They end by separating, but only to unite again in a more intimate fashion. If the poor fellow is loved by his lady as the vivifier of her ovaries, he is also loved as a piece of highly-flavoured game. And, that same day, or at latest on the morrow, he is seized by his spouse, who first gnaws his neck, in accordance with precedent, and then eats him deliberately, by little mouthfuls, leaving only the wings. Here we have no longer a case of jealously in the harem, but simply a depraved appetite.

I was curious to know what sort of reception a second male might expect from a recently fertilized female. The result of my enquiry was shocking. The Mantis, in many cases, is never sated with conjugal raptures and banquets. After a rest that varies in length, whether the eggs be laid or not, a second male is accepted and then devoured like the first. A third succeeds him, performs his function in life, is eaten and disappears. A fourth undergoes a like fate. In the course of two weeks I thus see one and the same Mantis use up seven males. She takes them all to her bosom and makes them all pay for the nuptial ecstasy with their lives.

Orgies such as this are frequent, in varying degrees, though there are exceptions. On very hot days, highly charged with electricity, they are almost the general rule. At such times the Mantes are in a very irritable mood. In the cages containing a large colony, the females devour one another more than ever; in the cages containing separate pairs, the males, after coupling, are more than ever treated as an ordinary prey.

50   I should like to be able to say, in mitigation of these conjugal atrocities, that the Mantis does not behave like this in a state of liberty; that the male, after doing his duty, has time to get out of the way, to make off, to escape from his terrible mistress, for in my cages he is given a respite, lasting sometimes until next day. What really occurs in the thickets I do now know, chance, a poor resource, having never instructed me concerning the love-affairs of the Mantis when at large. I can only go by what happens in the cages, when the captives, enjoying plenty of sunshine and food and spacious quarters, do not seem to suffer from homesickness in any way. What they do here they must also do under normal conditions.

Well, what happens there utterly refutes the idea that the males are given time to escape. I find, by themselves, a horrible couple engaged as follows. The male, absorbed in the performance of his vital functions, holds the female in a tight embrace. But the wretch has no head; he has no neck; he has hardly a body. The other, with her muzzle turned over her shoulder continues very placidly to gnaw what remains of his gentle swain. And, all the time, that masculine stump, holding on firmly, goes on with the business!

Love is stronger than death, men say. Taken literally, the aphorism has never received a more brilliant confirmation. A headless creature, an insect amputated down to the middle of the chest, a very corpse persists in endeavouring to give life. It will not let go until the abdomen, the seat of the procreative organs, is attacked.

Eating the lover after consummation of marriage, making a meal of the exhausted dwarf, henceforth good for nothing, can be understood, to some extent, in the insect world, which has no great scruples in matters of sentiment; but gobbling him up during the act goes beyond the wildest dreams of the most horrible imagination. I have seen it done with my own eyes and have not yet recovered from my astonishment.

READING CRITICALLY FOR IDEAS, STRUCTURE, AND STYLE

1. Fabre's descriptive powers are so great that he almost makes us forget that the mantis is a slender fragile insect. What methods does he use to enhance suspense and dramatic conflict while being scrupulously accurate in his detailed observations?

2. How effectively does Fabre use analogies and references to tools and machinery to increase the readers' understanding of how the mantis functions?

3. Why is Fabre's description of the "courtship" and "wedding" of the mantis fascinating and at the same time shocking? In your opinion, does Fabre anthropomorphize his subject excessively? Why or why not?

EXTENDING INSIGHTS THROUGH WRITING

1. Observe any small insect for a long enough period of time to write a 300-word essay and describe it in the way Fabre might.

2. Do you feel Fabre's ability to make the world of insects interesting and entertaining makes him less credible as a scientific observer? Why or why not?

CONNECTING PERSPECTIVES
ON THE NATURAL WORLD

1. In what ways do Fabre and Konard Lorenz's observations in "The Dove and the Wolf" refute the clichéd symbolic meanings usually projected onto the insects and animals they discuss?

2. Discuss cruelty as part of nature, for example, the praying mantis as described by Fabre, in conjunction with Mark Twain's thesis about humans in "The Lowest Animal."

MARK TWAIN

The Lowest Animal

BACKGROUND

Mark Twain (1835–1910), the pseudonym of Samuel Langhorn Clemens, was brought up in Hannibal, Missouri. After serving as a printer's apprentice, Twain became a steamboat pilot on the Mississippi (1857–1861), adopting his pen name from the leadsman's call ("mark twain" means "by the mark two fathoms") sounding the river in shallow places. After an unsuccessful attempt to mine gold in Nevada, Twain edited the *Virginia City Enterprise*. In 1865, in the *New York Saturday Press,* Twain published "Jim Smiley and his Jumping Frog," which then became the title story of *The Celebrated Jumping Frog of Calaveras County and Other Sketches* (1867). His reputation as a humorist was enhanced by *Innocents Abroad* (1869), a comic account of his travels through France, Italy, Palestine, and by *Roughing It* (1872), a delightful spoof of his mining adventures. His acknowledged masterpieces are *The Adventures of Tom Sawyer* (1876) and its sequel, *The Adventures of Huckleberry Finn* (1885), works of great comic power and social insight. Twain's later works, including *The Man that Corrupted Hadleyburg* (1900), a fable about greed, and *The Mysterious Stranger* (1916), published six years after Twain's death, assail hypocrisy as endemic to the human condition. "The Lowest Animal" (1906) shows Twain at his most iconoclastic, formulating a scathing comparison between man and the so-called lower animals.

APPROACHING TWAIN'S ESSAY

Darwinian theory proposes that man evolved, or ascended, from the lower animals. All the results of Twain's "experiments," however, point to the opposite conclusion: After comparing the traits and dispositions of man with those of the "lower" animals, Twain concludes that man is by no means at the apex of all other species. In fact, to Twain, it appears that human beings must have descended from higher animals. Since this conclusion disputes Darwin's work, Twain's essay is a parody of Darwin's findings. Throughout the piece,

Twain provides clear stylistic signals to alert the reader that he is constructing an evaluative, rather than a merely informative, comparison as well as a
parody of an article in a scientific journal.

The point-by-point organization of the piece helps contribute to the
reader's sense of it as a scientific, scholarly article, in which everything is
organized by specific points and each point is discussed fully before going on
to the next one. This organization also makes for clarity and enables Twain to
state his conclusions, one by one, leading up to his final verdict on the "moral
sense."

Twain's final comment (a disparaging remark about the French) fits in
well with the humorous style of the piece as a whole and makes the point that
all humans have prejudices, even learned men (including Twain himself) who
write essays trying to tell their fellow humans what is wrong with mankind.

The Lowest Animal

I have been studying the traits and dispositions of the "lower animals"
(so-called), and contrasting them with the traits and dispositions of man.
I find the result humiliating to me. For it obliges me to renounce my allegiance to the Darwinian theory of the Ascent of Man from the Lower
Animals; since it now seems plain to me that that theory ought to be vacat-
ed in favor of a new and truer one, this new and truer one to be named the
Descent of Man from the Higher Animals.

In proceeding toward this unpleasant conclusion I have not guessed
or speculated or conjectured, but have used what is commonly called the
scientific method. That is to say, I have subjected every postulate that presented itself to the crucial test of actual experiment, and have adopted it
or rejected it according to the result. Thus I verified and established each
step of my course in its turn before advancing to the next. These experiments were made in the London Zoological Gardens, and covered many
months of painstaking and fatiguing work.

Before particularizing any of the experiments, I wish to state one or
two things which seem to more properly belong in this place than further
along. This in the interest of clearness. The massed experiments established to my satisfaction certain generalizations, to wit:

1. That the human race is of one distinct species. It exhibits slight
   variations—in color, stature, mental caliber, and so on—due to
   climate, environment, and so forth; but it is a species by itself,
   and not to be confounded with any other.

2. That the quadrupeds are a distinct family, also. This family
   exhibits variations—in color, size, food preferences and so on;
   but it is a family by itself.

3. That the other families—the birds, the fishes, the insects, the reptiles, etc.—are more or less distinct, also. They are in the procession. They are links in the chain which stretches down from the higher animals to man at the bottom.

Some of my experiments were quite curious. In the course of my reading I had come across a case where, many years ago, some hunters on our Great Plains organized a buffalo hunt for the entertainment of an English earl—that, and to provide some fresh meat for his larder. They had charming sport. They killed seventy-two of those great animals; and ate part of one of them and left the seventy-one to rot. In order to determine the difference between an anaconda and an earl—if any—I caused seven young calves to be turned into the anaconda's cage. The grateful reptile immediately crushed one of them and swallowed it, then lay back satisfied. It showed no further interest in the calves, and no disposition to harm them. I tried this experiment with other anacondas; always with the same result. The fact stood proven that the difference between an earl and an anaconda is that the earl is cruel and the anaconda isn't; and that the earl wantonly destroys what he has no use for, but the anaconda doesn't. This seemed to suggest that the anaconda was not descended from the earl. It also seemed to suggest that the earl was descended from the anaconda, and had lost a good deal in the transition.

I was aware that many men who have accumulated more millions of money than they can ever use have shown a rabid hunger for more, and have not scrupled to cheat the ignorant and the helpless out of their poor servings in order to partially appease that appetite. I furnished a hundred different kinds of wild and tame animals the opportunity to accumulate vast stores of food, but none of them would do it. The squirrels and bees and certain birds made accumulations, but stopped when they had gathered a winter's supply, and could not be persuaded to add to it either honestly or by chicane. In order to bolster up a tottering reputation the ant pretended to store up supplies, but I was not deceived. I know the ant. These experiments convinced me that there is this difference between man and the higher animals: he is avaricious and miserly, they are not.

In the course of my experiments I convinced myself that among the animals man is the only one that harbors insults and injuries, broods over them, waits till a chance offers, then takes revenge. The passion of revenge is unknown to the higher animals.

Roosters keep harems, but it is by consent of their concubines; therefore no wrong is done. Men keep harems, but it is by brute force, privileged by atrocious laws which the other sex is allowed no hand in making. In this matter man occupies a far lower place than the rooster.

Cats are loose in their morals, but not consciously so. Man, in his descent from the cat, has brought the cat's looseness with him but has left the unconsciousness behind—the saving grace which excuses the cat. The cat is innocent, man is not.

Indecency, vulgarity, obscenity—these are strictly confined to man; he invented them. Among the higher animals there is no trace of them. They hide nothing; they are not ashamed. Man, with his soiled mind, covers himself. He will not even enter a drawing room with his breast and back naked, so alive are he and his mates to indecent suggestion. Man is "The Animal that Laughs." But so does the monkey, as Mr. Darwin pointed out; and so does the Australian bird that is called the laughing jackass. No—Man is the Animal that Blushes. He is the only one that does it—or has occasion to.

10   At the head of this article we see how "three monks were burnt to death" a few days ago, and a prior "put to death with atrocious cruelty." Do we inquire into the details? No; or we should find out that the prior was subjected to unprintable multilations. Man—when he is a North American Indian—gouges out his prisoner's eyes; when he is King John, with a nephew to render untroublesome, he uses a red-hot iron; when he is a religious zealot dealing with heretics in the Middle Ages, he skins his captive alive and scatters salt on his back; in the first Richard's time he shuts up a multitude of Jew families in a tower and sets fire to it; in Columbus's time he captures a family of Spanish Jews and—but *that* is not printable; in our day in England a man is fined ten shillings for beating his mother nearly to death with a chair, and another man is fined forty shillings for having four pheasant eggs in his possession without being able to satisfactorily explain how he got them. Of all the animals, man is the only one that is cruel. He is the only one that inflicts pain for the pleasure of doing it. It is a trait that is not known to the higher animals. The cat plays with the frightened mouse; but she has this excuse, that she does not know that the mouse is suffering. The cat is moderate—unhumanly moderate: she only scares the mouse, she does not hurt it; she doesn't dig out its eyes, or tear off its skin, or drive splinters under its nails—man-fashion; when she is done playing with it she makes a sudden meal of it and puts it out of its trouble. Man is the Cruel Animal. He is alone in that distinction.

The higher animals engage in individual fights, but never in organized masses. Man is the only animal that deals in that atrocity of atrocities, War. He is the only one that gathers his brethren about him and goes forth in cold blood and with calm pulse to exterminate his kind. He is the only animal that for sordid wages will march out, as the Hessians[1] did in our Revolution, and as the boyish Prince Napoleon did in the Zulu war, and help to slaughter strangers of his own species who have done him no harm and with whom he has no quarrel.

Man is the only animal that robs his helpless fellow of his country—takes possession of it and drives him out of it or destroys him. Man has done this in all the ages. There is not an acre of ground on the globe that is in possession of its rightful owner, or that has not been taken away from owner after owner, cycle after cycle, by force and bloodshed.

Man is the only Slave. And he is the only animal who enslaves. He has always been a slave in one form or another, and has always held other

---

[1]Hessians: the German auxillary soldiers brought over by the British to fight the Americans during the Revolutionary War.

slaves in bondage under him in one way or another. In our day he is always some man's slave for wages, and does that man's work; and this slave has other slaves under him for minor wages, and they do *his* work. The higher animals are the only ones who exclusively do their own work and provide their own living.

Man is the only Patriot. He sets himself apart in his own country, under his own flag, and sneers at the other nations, and keeps multitudinous uniformed assassins on hand at heavy expense to grab slices of other people's countries, and keep *them* from grabbing slices of *his*. And in the intervals between campaigns he washes the blood off his hands and works for "the universal brotherhood of man"—with his mouth.

Man is the Religious Animal. He is the only Religious Animal. He is   15 the only animal that has the True Religion—several of them. He is the only animal that loves his neighbor as himself, and cuts his throat if his theology isn't straight. He has made a graveyard of the globe in trying his honest best to smooth his brother's path to happiness and heaven. He was at it in the time of the Caesars, he was at it in Mahomet's time, he was at it in the time of the Inquisition, he was at it in France a couple of centuries, he was at it in England in Mary's day, he has been at it ever since he first saw the light, he is at it today in Crete—as per the telegrams quoted above— he will be at it somewhere else tomorrow. The higher animals have no religion. And we are told that they are going to be left out, in the Hereafter. I wonder why? It seems questionable taste.

Man is the Reasoning Animal. Such is the claim. I think it is open to dispute. Indeed, my experiments have proven to me that he is the Unreasoning Animal. Note his history, as sketched above. It seems plain to me that whatever he is he is *not* a reasoning animal. His record is the fantastic record of a maniac. I consider that the strongest count against his intelligence is the fact that with that record back of him he blandly sets himself up as the head animal of the lot: whereas by his own standards he is the bottom one.

In truth, man is incurably foolish. Simple things which the other animals easily learn, he is incapable of learning. Among my experiments was this. In an hour I taught a cat and a dog to be friends. I put them in a cage. In another hour I taught them to be friends with a rabbit. In the course of two days I was able to add a fox, a goose, a squirrel and some doves. Finally a monkey. They lived together in peace; even affectionately.

Next, in another cage I confined an Irish Catholic from Tipperary, and as soon as he seemed tame I added a Scotch Presbyterian from Aberdeen. Next a Turk from Constantinople; a Greek Christian from Crete; an Armenian; a Methodist from the wilds of Arkansas; a Buddhist from China; a Brahman from Benares. Finally, a Salvation Army Colonel from Wapping. Then I stayed away two whole days. When I came back to note result, the cage of Higher Animals was all right, but in the other there was but a chaos of gory odds and ends of turbans and fezzes and plaids and bones and flesh—not a specimen left alive. These Reasoning Animals had disagreed on a theological detail and carried the matter to a Higher Court.

One is obliged to concede that in true loftiness of character, Man cannot claim to approach even the meanest of the Higher Animals. It is plain that he is constitutionally incapable of approaching that altitude; that he is constitutionally afflicted with a Defect which must make such approach forever impossible, for it is manifest that this defect is permanent in him, indestructible, ineradicable.

20   I find this Defect to be *the Moral Sense.* He is the only animal that has it. It is the secret of his degradation. It is the quality *which enables him to do wrong.* It has no other office. It is incapable of performing any other function. It could never have been intended to perform any other. Without it, man could do no wrong. He would rise at once to the level of the Higher Animals.

Since the Moral Sense has but the one office, the one capacity—to enable man to do wrong—it is plainly without value to him. It is as valueless to him as is disease. In fact, it manifestly is a disease. *Rabies* is bad, but it is not so bad as this disease. Rabies enables a man to do a thing which he could not do when in a healthy state: kill his neighbor with a poisonous bite. No one is the better man for having rabies. The Moral Sense enables a man to do wrong. It enables him to do wrong in a thousand ways. Rabies is an innocent disease, compared to the Moral Sense. No one, then, can be the better man for having the Moral Sense. What, now, do we find the Primal Curse to have been? Plainly what it was in the beginning: the infliction upon man of the Moral Sense; the ability to distinguish good from evil; and with it, necessarily, the ability to *do* evil; for there can be no evil act without the presence of consciousness of it in the doer of it.

And so I find that we have descended and degenerated, from some far ancestor—some microscopic atom wandering at its pleasure between the mighty horizons of a drop of water perchance—insect by insect, animal by animal, reptile by reptile, down the long highway of smirchless innocence, till we have reached the bottom stage of development—namable as the Human Being. Below us—nothing. Nothing but the Frenchman.

READING CRITICALLY FOR IDEAS, STRUCTURE, AND STYLE

1. How do Twain's experiments puncture the self-congratulatory illusions that the human species has about itself? In each case, why are animals superior to humans?

2. Twain adopts the mock scientific format of an experiment being performed with a control group of animals. How does the form of the essay parody not only the conclusions, but the scientific method itself?

3. Why does Twain believe that the "Moral Sense" would more appropriately be called a defect than an attribute? What do Twain's experiments reveal about the effects of this attribute?

EXTENDING INSIGHTS THROUGH WRITING

1. Doubtless there are altruistic sides to human behavior that would have undercut Twain's satire. What are they? Write a few paragraphs countering Twain's conclusions.

2. What contemporary satirist (cartoonist, essayist, stand-up comedian, rapper) displays the same scathing insights into human nature as Twain did? Describe this person and one of their most significant commentaries.

CONNECTING PERSPECTIVES
ON THE NATURAL WORLD

1. In what way does Twain parody, modify, and misrepresent Darwin's "the Origin of Species"? What clues suggest Twain read Darwin's work closely?

2. In what ways has Hans Ruesch's investigation of animal experimentation in "Slaughter of the Innocent" added another lamentable chapter to Twain's satire?

HANS RUESCH

Slaughter of the Innocent

BACKGROUND

Hans Ruesch (b. 1913) is a modern-day Renaissance man who is not only a scholar of the history of medicine, but has also written best-selling novels: *The Racer* (1953), *Savage Innocents* (1960), *Back to the Top of the World* (1973), and many short stories that have appeared in *The Saturday Evening Post, Esquire,* and *Redbook*. He is best known for his brilliant exposés of the animal experimentation industry, catalogued in such books as *Naked Empress: The Great Medical Fraud* (1982) and *Slaughter of the Innocent* (1983), from which the following chapter is reprinted. He currently lives in Milan and is the founder and director of Civis: The International Foundation Report Dedicated to the Abolition of Vivisection. Ruesch is currently defending himself against lawsuits instigated by the pharmaceutical companies whose practices he assails.

APPROACHING RUESCH'S ESSAY

Ruesch challenges the vivisectionist's position in a number of ways. The question at the heart of the vivisection controversy is whether the information obtained from experimentation on live animals can save human lives. Ruesch offers evidence that the results obtained from animal experiments cannot be generalized to apply to humans. Moreover, in many cases if the results were applied to humans, the consequences would be fatal. Ruesch condemns the attitude of laboratory experimenters who view animals as tools to be used and destroyed (often in unnecessary duplications of experiments) to test household cleansers, cosmetics, and preservatives. Ruesch reveals that vast amounts of money are at the heart of commercial testing and in research funded at universities throughout the world. Throughout his essay, Ruesch is careful to answer objections raised by his opponents.

Slaughter of the Innocent

SCIENCE OR MADNESS?

A dog is crucified in order to study the duration of the agony of Christ. A pregnant bitch is disemboweled to observe the maternal instinct in the throes of pain. Experimenters in an American university cause convulsions in dogs and cats, to study their brain waves during the seizures, which gradually become more frequent and severe until the animals are in a state of continual seizure that leads to their death in 3 to 5 hours; the experimenters then supply several charts of the brain waves in question, but no idea how they could be put to any practical use.

Another team of "scientists" submits to fatal scaldings 15,000 animals of various species, then administers to half of them a liver extract that is already known to be useful in case of shock: As expected, the treated animals agonize longer than the others.

Beagles, well-known for their mild and affectionate natures, are tortured until they start attacking each other. The "scientists" responsible for this announce that they were "conducting a study on juvenile delinquency."

Exceptions? Borderline cases? I wish they were.

Every day of the year, at the hands of white-robed individuals recognized as medical authorities, or bent on getting such recognition, or a degree, or at least a lucrative job, millions of animals—mainly mice, rats, guinea-pigs, hamsters, dogs, cats, rabbits, monkeys, pigs, turtles; but also horses, donkeys, goats, birds and fishes—are slowly blinded by acids, submitted to repeated shocks or intermittent submersion, poisoned, inoculated with deadly diseases, disemboweled, frozen to be revived and refrozen, starved or left to die of thirst, in many cases after various glands have been entirely or partially extirpated or the spinal cord has been cut.

The victims' reactions are then meticulously recorded, except during the long weekends, when the animals are left unattended to meditate about their sufferings; which may last weeks, months, years, before death puts an end to their ordeal—death being the only effective anesthesia most of the victims get to know.

But often they are not left in peace even then: Brought back to life—miracle of modern science—they are subjected to ever new series of tortures. Pain-crazed dogs have been seen devouring their own paws,

convulsions have thrown cats against the walls of their cages until the creatures collapsed, monkeys have clawed and gnawed at their own bodies or
killed their cage mates.

This and much more has been reported by the experimenters themselves in leading medical journals such as Britain's *Lancet* and its American,
French, German and Swiss counterparts, from which most of the evidence
here presented derives.

But don't stop reading just yet—because the purpose of this book is
to show you how you can, and why you should, put a stop to all that.

The Refinements

10   Each new experiment inspires legions of "researchers" to repeat it, in
the hope of confirming or debunking it; to procure the required tools or to
devise new, "better" ones. Apart from a long series of "restraining devices,"
derived from the "Czermak Table," the "Pavlov Stock" and other classic
apparatuses which decorate those pseudoscientific laboratories the world
over, there exist some particularly ingenious instruments, usually named
after their inventors.

One is the *Noble-Collip Drum,* a household word among physiologists
since 1942, when it was devised by two Toronto doctors, R. L. Noble and
J. B. Collip, who described it in *The Quarterly Journal of Experimental
Physiology* (Vol. 31, No. 3, 1942, p. 187) under the telltale title "A
Quantitative Method for the Production of Experimental Traumatic Shock
without Haemorrhage in Unanesthetized Animals": "The underlying principle of the method is to traumatize the animal by placing it in a revolving
drum in which are projections or bumps . . . The number of animals dying
showed a curve in proportion to the number of revolutions . . . When animals were run without having their paws taped they were found to give
irregular results, since some would at first jump over the bumps until
fatigued, and so protect themselves . . ."

There is the *Ziegler Chair,* an ingenious metal seat described in *Journal
of Laboratory and Clinical Medicine* (Sept. 1952), invented by Lt. James E.
Ziegler of the Medical Corps, U.S. Navy, Johnsville, Pa. One of the advantages claimed in the descriptive article for the apparatus is that "the head
and large areas of the monkey's body are exposed and thus accessible for
various manipulations." The uses of the chair include perforation of the
skull with stimulation of the exposed cortex, implantation of cranial windows, general restraint for dressings, and as a seat for the monkey in various positions on the large experimental centrifuge for periods that may
last uninterruptedly for years, until death.

There is the *Blalock Press,* so named after Dr. Alfred Blalock of the
famed Johns Hopkins Institute in Baltimore, Md. Constructed of heavy
steel, it resembles an ancient printing press. But the plates are provided
with steel ridges that mesh together when the top plate is forced against
the bottom plate. Pressure of up to 5,000 pounds is exerted by a heavy
automobile spring compressed by tightening four nuts. The purpose is to
crush the muscular tissue in a dog's legs without crushing the bone.

There is the *Collison Cannula*, designed to be implanted into the head of various animals to facilitate the repeated passage of hypodermic needles, electrodes, pressure gauges, etc., into the cranial cavity of the fully conscious animal—mostly cats and monkeys. The cannula is permanently fixed to the bone with acrylic cement anchored by four stainless-steel screws screwed into the skull. After undergoing this severe traumatic experience, the animal must be given at least a week to recover before the experiments proper can begin—as described in *Journal of Physiology*, October 1972. (In time, in an unsuccessful attempt to reject it, a purse of pus grows around the firmly anchored cannula and seeps into the victims' eyes and sinuses, eventually leading to blindness and death—sometimes one or two years later.)

There is the *Horsley-Clarke Stereotaxic Device*, so named after the two   15
doctors who designed it to immobilize small animals during the implantation of the aforementioned cannula, for the traditional brain "experiments" that have never led to any other practical result than procuring the Nobel Prize for Prof. Walter R. Hess of Zurich University in 1949, and fat subsidies for various colleagues all over the world.

It may as well be pointed out right now that Nobel prizes in biology, physiology and medicine—as well as the various grants for "medical research"—are conferred on the recommendations of committees of biologists, physiologists and doctors, who have either been similarly favored by the colleagues they recommend, or who hope to be repaid in kind.

What is Vivisection?

The term vivisection "is now used to apply to all types of experiments on living animals, whether or not cutting is done." So states the Encyclopedia Americana (International Edition, 1974). And the large Merriam-Webster (1963): ". . . broadly, any form of animal experimentation, especially if considered to cause distress to the subject." Thus the term also applies to experiments done with the administration of noxious substances, burns, electric or traumatic shocks, drawn-out deprivations of food and drink, psychological tortures leading to mental imbalance, and so forth. The term was employed in that sense by the physiologists of the last century who started this kind of "medical research," and so it will be used by me. By "vivisectionist" is usually meant every upholder of this method; by "vivisector" someone who performs such experiments or participates in them.

The "scientific" euphemism for vivisection is "basic research" or "research on models"—"model" being the euphemism for laboratory animal.

Though the majority of practicing physicians defend vivisection, most of them don't know what they are defending, having never set foot in a vivisection laboratory. Conversely, the great majority of vivisectors have never spent five minutes at a sick man's bedside, for the good reason that most of them decide to dedicate themselves to laboratory animals when they fail that most important medical examination, the one that would allow them to practice medicine. And many more take up "research" because that requires no formal studying. Any dunce can cut up live animals and report what he sees.

20   The number of animals dying of tortures through the practice of vivisection is estimated at around 400,000 a day world-wide at the time of this writing, and is growing at an annual rate of about 5 percent. Those experiments are performed in tens of thousands of clinical, industrial and university laboratories. All of them, without exception, deny access to channels of independent information. Occasionally, they take a journalist, guaranteed "tame," on a guided tour of a laboratory as carefully groomed as one of Potemkin's villages.

Today we no longer torture in the name of the Lord, but in the name of a new, despotic divinity—a so-called Medical Science which, although amply demonstrated to be false, successfully uses through its priests and ministers the tactics of terrorism: "If you don't give us plenty of money and a free hand with animals, you and your children will die of cancer"—well knowing that modern man does not fear God, but fears Cancer, and has never been told that most cancers, and maybe all, are fabricated through incompetence in the vivisection laboratories.

In the past, humanity was trained to tolerate cruelty to human beings on the grounds of a widespread superstition. Today humanity has been trained to tolerate cruelty to animals on the grounds of another superstition, equally widespread. There is a chilling analogy between the Holy Inquisitors who extracted confessions by torture from those suspected of witchcraft, and the priests of modern science who employ torture trying to force information and answers from animals. Meanwhile, the indifferent majority prefers to ignore what is going on around them, so long as they are left alone.

Vivisectors indignantly reject charges that their driving motive is avarice, ambition, or sadism disguised as scientific curiosity. On the contrary, they present themselves as altruists, entirely dedicated to the welfare of manking. But intelligent people of great humanity—from Leonardo da Vinci to Voltaire to Goethe to Schweitzer—have passionately declared that a species willing to be "saved" through such means would not be worth saving. And furthermore there exists by now a crushing documentation that vivisection is not only an inhuman and dehumanizing practice, but a continuing source of errors that have grievously damaged true science and the health of humanity at large.

If such a sordid approach to medical knowledge were as useful as advertised, the nation with the highest life expectancy should be the United States, where expenditures for vivisection are a multiple of those in any other country, where more "life-saving" operations are performed, and whose medical profession considers itself to be the world's finest, besides being the most expensive. In fact, "Among the nations that measure average life expectancy, America ranks a relatively low 17th—behind most of Western Europe, Japan, Greece, and even Bulgaria," reported *Time* magazine, July 21, 1975, after having reported on December 17, 1973, that "The US has twice as many surgeons in proportion to population as Great

Britain—and Americans undergo twice as many operations as Britons. Yet, on the average, they die younger."

All this in spite of Medicare and Medicaid and the formidable thera-   25
peutic arsenal at the disposal of American doctors and patients.

Man and Animals

Many of the medical men who have denounced the practice of vivisection as inhuman, fallacious and dangerous have been among the most distinguished in their profession. Rather than a minority, they ought to be called an élite. And in fact, opinions should not only be counted—they should also be weighed.

The first great medical man who indicated that vivisection is not just inhuman and unscientific, but that it is unscientific *because* it is inhuman was Sir Charles Bell (1774–1824), the Scottish physician, surgeon, anatomist and physiologist to whom medical science owes "Bell's law" on motor and sensory nerves. At the time the aberration of vivisection began to take root in its modern form, he declared that it could only be practiced by callous individuals, who couldn't be expected to penetrate the mysteries of life. Such individuals, he maintained, lack real intelligence—sensibility being a component, and certainly not the least, of human intelligence.

Those who hope to find remedies for human ills by inflicting deliberate sufferings on animals commit two fundamental errors in understanding. The first is the assumption that results obtained on animals are applicable to man. The second, which concerns the inevitable fallacy of experimental science in respect to the field of organic life, will be analyzed in the next chapter. Let us examine the first error now. Already the Pharaohs knew that to find out whether their food was poisoned they had to try it on the cook, not on the cat.

Since animals react differently from man, every new product or method tried out on animals must be tried out again on man, through careful clinical tests, before it can be considered safe. *This rule knows no exceptions.* Therefore, tests on animals are not only dangerous because they may lead to wrong conclusions, but they also retard clinical investigation, which is the only valid kind.

René Dubos; Pulitzer Prize-winner and professor of microbiology at the   30
Rockefeller Institute of New York, wrote in *Man, Medicine and Environment* (Praeger, New York, 1968, p. 107): "Experimentation on man is usually an indispensable step in the discovery of new therapeutic procedures or drugs ... The first surgeons who operated on the lungs, the heart, the brain were by necessity experimenting on man, since knowledge deriving from animal experimentation is never entirely applicable to the human species."

In spite of this universally recognized fact, not only the vivisectors, but also health authorities everywhere, having been trained in the vivisectionist mentality, which is a throwback to the last century, allow or prescribe animal tests, thus washing their hands of any responsibility if something goes wrong, as it usually does.

This explains the long list of products developed in laboratories, *and* presumed safe after extensive animal tests, which eventually prove deleterious for man:

Due to a "safe" painkiller named Paracetamol, 1,500 people had to be hospitalized in Great Britain in 1971. In the United States, Orabilex caused kidney damages with fatal outcome, MEL/29 caused cataracts, Metaqualone caused psychic disturbances leading to at least 366 deaths. Worldwide Thalidomide caused more than 10,000 deformed children. Chloramphenicol (Chloromycetin) caused leukemia, Stilbestrol cancer in young women. In the sixties a mysterious epidemic killed so many thousands of asthma sufferers in various countries that Dr. Paul D. Stolley of Johns Hopkins Hospital—who in July 1972 finally found the killer in Isoproterenol, packaged in England as an aerosol spray—spoke of the "worst therapeutic drug disaster on record." In the fall of 1975, Italy's health authorities seized the anti-allergic Trilergan, responsible for viral hepatitis. In early 1976 the laboratories Salvoxyl-Wander, belonging to Switzerland's gigantic Sandoz enterprise, withdrew their Flamanil, created to fight rheumatisms, but capable of causing loss of consciousness in its consumers— certainly one effective way to free them of all pains. A few months later, Great Britain's chemical giant, ICI (Imperial Chemical Industries), announced that it had started paying compensations to the victims (or their survivors) of its cardiotonic Eraldin, introduced on the market after 7 years of "very intensive" tests; but hundreds of consumers had then suffered serious damages to the eyesight or the digestive tract, and 18 had died.

The Great Drug Deception by Dr. Ralph Adam Fine (Stein and Day, New York, 1972) is just one of the many books published in the last decade on the subject of dangerous and often lethal drugs, but it achieved no practical results. Health authorities, as well as the public, stubbornly refused to take cognizance of the fact that all those drugs had been okayed and marketed after having been proved safe for animals. Actually it is unfair to single out just a few dangerous drugs, since there are thousands of them.

35   Of course the fallacy works both ways, precluding the acceptance of useful drugs. There is the great example of penicillin—if we want to consider this a useful drug. Its discoverers said they were fortunate. No guinea pigs were available for the toxicity tests, so they used mice instead. Penicillin kills guinea-pigs. But the same guinea pigs can safely eat strychnine, one of the deadliest poisons for humans—but not for monkeys.

Certain wild berries are deadly for human beings, but birds thrive on them. A dose of belladonna that would kill a man is harmless for rabbits and goats. Calomelan doesn't influence the secretion of bile in dogs, but can treble it in man. The use of digitalis—the main remedy for cardiac patients and the savior of countless lives the world over—was retarded for a long time because it was first tested on dogs, in which it dangerously raises blood pressure. And chloroform is so toxic to dogs that for many years this valuable anesthetic was not employed on patients. On the other hand a dose of opium that would kill a man is harmless to dogs and chickens.

Datura and henbane are poison for man, but food for the snail. The mushroom *amanita phalloides*, a small dose of which can wipe out a whole human family, is consumed without ill effects by the rabbit, one of the most common laboratory animals. A porcupine can *eat* in one lump without discomfort as much opium as a human addict *smokes* in two weeks, and wash it down with enough prussic acid to poison a regiment of soldiers.

The sheep can swallow enormous quantities of arsenic, once the murderers' favorite poison.

Potassium cyanide, deadly for us, is harmless for the owl, but one of our common field pumpkins can put a horse into a serious state of agitation. Morphine, which calms and anesthetizes man, causes maniacal excitement in cats and mice, but dogs can stand doses up to 20 times higher than man. On the other hand, our sweet almonds can kill foxes and chickens, and our common parsley is poison to parrots.

Robert Koch's Tuberkulin, once hailed as a vaccine against tuberculosis because it cured TB in guinea pigs, was found later on to *cause* TB in man. 40

There are enough such instances to fill a book—all proving that it would be difficult to find a more absurd and less scientific method of medical research.

Moreover, the anguish and sufferings of the animals, deprived of their natural habitat or habitual surroundings, terrorized by what they see in the laboratories and the brutalities they are subjected to, alter their mental balance and organic reactions to such an extent that *any* result is a priori valueless. The laboratory animal is a monster, made so by the experimenters. Physically and mentally it has very little in common with a normal animal, and much less with man.

As even Claude Bernard (1813–1878), founder of the modern vivisectionist method, wrote in his *Physiologie opératoire* (p. 152): "The experimental animal is never in a normal state. The normal state is merely a supposition, an assumption." (*Une pure conception de l'esprit.*)

Not only do all animals react differently—even kindred species like rat and mouse, or like the white rat and brown rat—not even two animals of the identical strain react identically; furthermore, they may be suffering from different diseases.

To counter this disadvantage, somebody launched the idea of breeding strains of bacteriologically sterile laboratory animals—mass-born by Caesarean section in sterile operating rooms, raised in sterile surroundings and fed with sterile foods—to provide what the researchers called a "uniform biological material," free of diseases. 45

One delusion spawned another. Consistent failures made certain of those misguided scientists realize—some haven't realized it yet—that organic "material" raised under such abnormal conditions differs more than ever from normal organisms. Animals so raised never develop the natural defense mechanism, the so-called immunological reaction, which is a salient characteristic of every living organism. So it would be difficult to devise a less reliable experimental material. Besides, animals are by nature immune to most human infections—diphtheria, typhus, scarlet fever, German measles, smallpox, cholera, yellow fever, leprosy, and bubonic plague, while other infections, such as TB and various septicemias, take up different forms in animals. So the claim that through animals we can learn to control human diseases could seem a sign of madness if we didn't know that it is just a pretext for carrying on "experiments" which, however dangerously misleading for medical science, are either intimately satisfying for those who execute them, or highly lucrative.

The Swiss nation illustrates well to what extent the profit motive promotes vivisection: With a population of less than 6 million, Switzerland uses up annually many times as many laboratory animals as does all of Soviet Russia with its 250 million inhabitants, but where there is no money in the making of medicines.

Experimental Research

Experimental research has brought about all human inventions and most discoveries—except in medicine.

When speaking of modern invention, the first name that comes to mind is Thomas Edison. His case is particularly interesting because Edison attended school for only three months, whereafter he had to start making a living. Thus Edison was not a well-educated man. But it was just this lack of formal education—the lack of notions blindly accepted by most educated people, including the scientists, inculcated into them at an early stage by rote—that enabled Edison to accomplish the extraordinary series of inventions that altered man's way of life.

50   For instance, in trying to perfect the first electric light bulb Edison wanted a wire that would remain incandescent for a reasonable length of time. No university professor, no metallurgical expert was able to help him. So Edison resorted to pure empiricism. He started trying out *every type of wire* he could think of—including the least likely ones, such as, say, a thread of charred cotton. Over a period of years, Edison spent $40,000 having his assistants trying out one material after another. Until he found a wire that remained incandescent for 40 consecutive hours. It was a charred cotton thread . . .

However, experimental science had started modifying the face of the earth two and a half centuries before Edison went about lighting up the nights. The beginning took place in 1637 with the publication of that *Discourse on Method* by Descartes which taught man a new way of thinking, and led to modern technology. But, who could foresee in this New World being born in the midst of widespread enthusiasm the danger of an exclusively mechanistic knowledge? Hardly Descartes, who was himself a negation of the arts and all human sentiments—his private life was a failure—and who believed in a mechanistic biology, establishing the basis for what may well be mankind's greatest error.

In his thirst for knowledge through experimentation, Descartes also practiced vivisection, making it a symbol of "progress" to succeeding mechanists. Descartes himself, of course, had learned nothing from this practice, as demonstrated by his statement that animals don't suffer, and that their cries mean nothing more than the creaking of a wheel. Then why not whip the cart instead of the horse? Descartes never troubled to explain that. But he gave as "proof" of his theory the fact that the harder one beats a dog, the louder it howls. Through him a new science was born, deprived of wisdom and humanity, thus containing the seed of defeat at birth.

Rid at last of the yoke of medieval obscurantism, man went all out for experimentation. The sensational conquests of technology led some doctors of limited mental power to believe that experimental science would bring about equally sensational results in their own field; that living organisms react like inanimate matter, enabling medical science to establish absolute, mathematical rules. And today's vivisectionists still cling to that belief, no matter how often it has proved tragically wrong.

The experiment Galileo made from Pisa's leaning tower, demonstrating that a light stone and a heavy stone fall at one and the same speed, established an absolute rule because it dealt with inanimate matter. But when we deal with living organisms, an infinity of different factors intervene, mostly unknown and not entirely identifiable, having to do with the mystery of life itself. It is difficult to disagree with Charles Bell that callous, dehumanized individuals are the least likely ever to penetrate these mysteries.

In his book *La sperimentazione sugli animali* (2nd ed., 1956,), Gennaro 55 Ciaburri, one of Italy's antivivisectionist doctors, provides among many others the following insight: "Normally, pressure on one or both eyeballs will slow down the pulse . . . This symptom has opened up a vast field for vivisection. Experimenters squashed the eyes of dogs to study this reflex, to the point of discovering that the heartbeat was slowing down—owing to the death of the animal . . ."

That such vivisectionist divertissements achieve nothing more than to provide a measure of human stupidity, has been declared repeatedly. The famed German doctor Erwin Liek—of whom the major German encyclopedia, *Der Grosse Brockhaus,* says, "he advocated a medical art of high ethical level, which takes into consideration the patient's psyche"—gives us the following information:

"Here is another example that animal experimentation sometimes can't answer even the simplest questions. I know personally two of Germany's most authoritative researchers, Friedberger of the Kaiser Wilhelm Institute for Nutritional Research and Prof. Scheunert of the Institute of Animal Physiology at Leipzig. Both wanted to investigate the simple question as to whether a diet of hardboiled eggs or of raw eggs is more beneficial. They employed the same animals: 28-day-old rats. Result: over an observation period of three months, Friedberger's animals prospered on a diet of raw eggs, while the control animals which got hardboiled eggs pined, lost their hair, developed eye troubles; several died after much suffering. At Scheunert's I witnessed the identical experiments, with exactly opposite results." (From *Gedanken eines Arztes,* Oswald Arnold, Berlin, 1949.)

Of course any disease deliberately provoked is unlike any disease that arises spontaneously.

Let's take the case of arthritis, a degenerative disease causing painful inflammation of the joints, and bringing about lesions or destruction of the cartilage. Overeating is one of its causes, regular exercise at an early stage of the malady is the only reliable cure we know to date. And yet the drug firms keep turning out "miracle" remedies based on animal tortures: mere palliatives that mask the symptoms, reducing the pain for a while but in the meantime ruining the liver or the kidneys or both, thus causing much more serious damage than the malady they pretend to cure—and eventually aggravating the malady.

60   While no solution to any medical problem has ever been found through animal experimentation, so on the other hand one can prove practically anything one sets out to prove using animals, as in the following case reported in the monthly *Canadian Hospital* (Dec. 1971): In the Montreal Heart Institute are thousands of cages full of rats used to determine the effects of specific diets on animals. One of the "researchers" in charge, Dr. Serge Renaud, "took one of the animals from its cage; its hair had fallen out; its arteries had hardened and it was ripe for a heart attack. This rat, with a normal life span of two years, was old at two months. 'We kill them with pure butter,' said Dr. Rensud."

So butter is poison! Science or idiocy?

Sometimes it is neither one nor the other, but a highly profitable business gimmick, as the cyclamate and the saccharin cases demonstrate. In the mid-sixties the new artificial sweeteners known as cyclamates had become a huge commercial success because they cost 5 times less than sugar and had 30 times the sweetening power, besides being non-fattening. So the American Sugar Manufacturers Association set about financing "research" on cyclamates, as did the sugar industries in some other countries. To "prove scientifically" what the sugar industry was determined to prove from the start—that cyclamates should be outlawed—hundreds of thousands of animals had to die painfully.

They were force-fed such massive, concentrated doses of the product that they were bound to become seriously sick, developing all sorts of diseases, including cancer. To consume the equivalent amount of artificial sweetener a human would have to drink more than 800 cans of diet soda every day of his life. In 1967 the British Sugar Bureau, a public relations organization set up by the sugar industry, was pressuring members of Parliament about the deadly dangers of cyclamates. The same was happening in the United States—the sugar lobby besieging the politicians. I am not saying that money changed hands, because I don't know. All I know is that in 1969 both the American and British Governments banned the sale of cyclamates. It wasn't banned in Switzerland, however, where there is no powerful sugar lobby, but a powerful chemical lobby instead. In Switzerland, cyclamates are still on sale, 8 years after they were taken off the shelves in America and Britain.

Then there was a repeat performance of the whole three-ring scientific circus in 1976 in regard to saccharin—and once more uncounted thousands of innocent animals were caught in the crossfire of embattled industrial glants.

65   Financed by a grant of $641,224 for 1971–72, researchers at the Center for Prevention and Treatment of Arteriosclerosis at Albany Medical College experimented with an initial group of 44 pigs. One by one these animals

were made to die of induced heart disease resulting from arteriosclerosis. Using an extreme form of diet known to be injurious to the vascular system, the process was further speeded up by X rays that damage the coronary arteries. Personnel were always on hand when an animal dropped dead; they hoped to pinpoint precisely what happens to the heart of a pig at this critical moment. Such, in essence, was a report in the *Times Union* of Buffalo, New York, Oct. 24, 1971.

Except for the money angle, the whole thing appears sophomoric. Yet similar programs utilizing various experimental animals were in progress at the same time at 12 other medical institutions all over the U.S. All of them proved adept at creating a wide range of diseases in animals, but were notable failures at coming up with a solution. Research of this nature has been practiced for decades, and millions of animals have died in the process, while the cures are still pies in the sky.

Today's pseudoscience proceeds similarly on all fronts. In the "fight against epilepsy," monkeys are submitted to a series of electroshocks that throw them into convulsions, until they become insane and manifest symptoms that may outwardly resemble epileptic fits in man—frothing at the mouth, convulsive movements, loss of consciousness, and such. Obviously the monkey's fits have nothing to do with human epilepsy, as they are artificially induced, whereas man's epilepsy arises inside from reasons deeply rooted in the individual's organism or psyche, and not from a series of electroshocks. And by trying out on these insane monkeys a variety of "new" drugs—always the same ones, in different combinations—vivisectionists promise to come up with "a remedy against epilepsy" some time soon, provided the grants keep coming. And such methods sail today under the flag of science—which is an insult to true science, as well as to human intelligence. Small wonder that epilepsy is another disease whose incidence is constantly increasing.

One of the latest shifts devised by medical research to make quick money is the invention of drugs that promise to prevent brain hemorrhages. How is it done? Easy. By now any attentive reader can do it. Take rats, dogs, rabbits, monkeys, and cats, and severely injure their brains. How? Our laboratory "Researchers" brilliantly solve that problem with hammer blows. Under the broken skulls, the animals' brains will form blood clots, whereafter various drugs are administered to the traumatized victim. As if blood clots due to hammer blows were the equivalent of circulation troubles which have gradually been building up in a human brain that is approaching the natural end of its vital arch, or has grown sclerotic through excessive intake of alcohol, food, tobacco, or from want of exercise, of fresh air, or mental activity. Everybody knows what to do to keep physically and mentally fit. But it is less fatiguing to swallow, before each rich meal, a couple of pills, and hope for the best.

Anybody suggesting that these pills are of no use would be in bad faith. They *are* useful: They help increase the profits of the world's most lucrative industry—and further ruin the organism, thus creating the necessity for still more "miracle" drugs.

The Solid Gold Source

70   The cancer bogy has become the vivisectionists' most powerful weapon. Dr. Howard M. Temin, a well-known scientist, said in a recent address at the University of Wisconsin that scientists are also interested in money, power, publicity and prestige, and that "some promise quick cures for human diseases, provided they are given more power and more money." He added that there is a tremendous advantage in the assertion that "If I am given 500 million dollars for the next five years, I can cure cancer," pointing out that if a rainmaker puts the time far enough in the future, no one can prove him wrong.

But so far as cancer is concerned, the rain may not come in our lifetime. It is obvious to anybody who has not been brainwashed in the western hemisphere's medical schools that an experimental cancer, one caused by grafting cancerous cells into an animal, or in other arbitrary ways, is entirely different from cancer that develops on its own and, furthermore, in a human being. A spontaneous cancer has an intimate relationship to the organism that developed it, and probably to the mind of that organism as well, whereas cancerous cells implanted into another organism have no "natural" relationship whatsoever to that organism, which merely acts as a soil for the culture of those cells.

However, the ably exploited fear of this dread disease has become an inexhaustible source of income for the researchers. In the course of our century, experimental cancer has become a source of solid gold without precedent.

It all started in France in 1773, when the Academy of Science in Lyon offered a prize for the best original essay on the subject: "What is Cancer?" The prize went to Bernard Peyrilhe, who described the first cancer experiment on record in which he inoculated a dog with "cancer fluid" from a breast cancer patient.

In the more than two centuries since then, during which not millions but billions of animals of every known species have been sacrificed to cancer research, the so-called scientists have not only failed to come up with any solution, but the problems have multiplied, the doubts proliferated. The results add up to the greatest confusion medical "science" has ever been able to create.

READING CRITICALLY FOR IDEAS, STRUCTURE, AND STYLE

1.   What moral objections does Ruesch raise to vivisection?
2.   According to Ruesch, why should the results obtained from vivisection not be used on humans?

3. What insight does Ruesch offer into the motives of the re-searchers and the companies who sponsor them?

EXTENDING INSIGHTS THROUGH WRITING

1. Implicit in Ruesch's essay is a critique of the *hubris* of the ex-perimental method as practiced by vivisectionists. Do some fur-ther research into one of the cases Ruesch mentions and either support or challenge his conclusions in a short essay.

2. Your college or university may have an active animal research program, sponsored by government grants and pharmaceutical companies. What guidelines and controls prevent the kind of abuses Ruesch describes from being practiced? You might in-terview a faculty member to get a response to Ruesch's article: Write a detailed report on your findings.

CONNECTING PERSPECTIVES ON THE NATURAL WORLD

1. Compare and contrast research that is dominated by financial incentive, as described by Ruesch, with research conducted to gain knowledge for its own sake as described by Matt Ridley in "Genome." How do the ends effect the means in both these arti-cles?

2. Draw on Arthur D. Hasler and James A. Larsen's "The Homing Salmon" and Ruesch's essay to write a short paper that defines the boundaries that researchers, who use live animals, should not exceed.

CONSTANCE HOLDEN

Identical Twins Reared Apart

BACKGROUND

Constance Holden (b.1941) is a writer for *Science* magazine, whose column, "News and Comment," discusses the implications of issues on the forefront of scientific research. Holden is particularly interested in questions regarding the relationship between mind and body. "Identical Twins Reared Apart," from *Science* (1980), reports on a comparative study conducted by Thomas J. Bouchard at the University of Minnesota, which points to the importance of heredity rather than environment in shaping human behavior. Holden develops a point-by-point comparison of the striking similarities in behavior between nine sets of identical twins who were separated at birth, raised in different environments, and then brought together. Bouchard is currently preparing his final report on his twin studies to be published in 2002.

APPROACHING HOLDEN'S ESSAY

Holden reports on a study that emphasizes the importance of heredity in shaping human behavior. She tells us that investigators were often astonished at similarities between long-separated twins, similarities that are ordinarily attributed to common environmental influences. The researchers who studied nine sets of identical twins (who were reared apart) discovered striking similarities in the livelihoods they chose, the school subjects they enjoyed, the names they selected for their children, their medical and psychiatric histories, sleep patterns, mannerisms and temperament, IQ scores, and idiosyncrasies. Although all nine sets of twins were reared in different socioeconomic circumstances, in various areas of the United States as well as in different countries, and under dissimilar emotional conditions, the researchers expected the differences to be more striking than the similarities. The implications of Bouchard's research for the social sciences are profound. Before reading

Holden's article, one might have thought that environment would be the crucial factor in shaping human behavior, but the results of the experiments described in this article suggest that heredity plays the more important role.

Identical Twins Reared Apart

Bridget and Dorothy are 39-year-old British housewives, identical twins raised apart who first met each other a little over a year ago. When they met, to take part in Thomas Bouchard's twin study at the University of Minnesota, the manicured hands of each bore seven rings. Each also wore two bracelets on one wrist and a watch and a bracelet on the other. Investigators in Bouchard's study, the most extensive investigation ever made of identical twins reared apart, are still bewitched by the seven rings. Was it coincidence, the result of similar influences, or is this small sign of affinity a true, even inevitable, manifestation of the mysterious and infinitely complex interaction of the genes the two women have in common?

Investigators have been bemused and occasionally astonished at similarities between long-separated twins, similarities that prevailing dogma about human behavior would ordinarily attribute to common environmental influences. How is it, for example, that two men with significantly different upbringings came to have the same authoritarian personality? Or another pair to have similar histories of endogenous depression? Or still another pair to have virtually identical patterns of headaches?

These are only bits and pieces from a vast amount of data, none of it yet analyzed, being collected by the University of Minnesota twin study that began last March. So provocative have been some of the cases that the study has already received much attention in the press, and it is bound to get a lot more. The investigation is extremely controversial, aimed, as it is, directly at the heart of the age-old debate about heredity versus environment. Identical twins reared apart have been objects of scrutiny in the past, notably in three studies conducted in England, Denmark, and the United States. An indication of the sensitivity of this subject is the fact that the last one in this country was completed more than 40 years ago,[1] although the rarity of cases has also made this type of research rather exotic. The Minnesota investigators, however, have been able to locate more twin pairs than they expected. So far they have processed nine pairs of identical or monozygotic twins (as well as several pairs of fraternal or dizygotic twins used as controls) and, owing to the publicity given the project, have managed to locate 11 additional pairs to take part in the study.

---

[1] A. H. Newman, F. N. Freeman, and K. J. Holzinger wrote up their study of 19 twin pairs in a 1937 book, *Twins: A Study of Heredity and Environment.*

The Minnesota study is unprecedented in its scope, using a team of psychologists, psychiatrists, and medical doctors to probe and analyze every conceivable aspect of the twins' life histories, medical histories and physiology, tastes, psychological inclinations, abilities, and intelligence. It began when Bouchard, a psychologist who specializes in investigating individual differences, heard of a pair of twins separated from birth, both coincidentally named Jim by their adoptive families, who were reunited at the age of 39. Bouchard did not have to look far to set up his study team, as Minnesota is a hotbed of twin research. There, ready to go to work, were Irving Gottesman, a behavioral geneticist who has spent his career studying twins and whose particular interest is the etiology of schizophrenia; psychologist David Lykken, who has been looking at the brain waves of twins for 10 years, psychologist Auke Tellegen, who recently completed a new personality questionnaire that is being used on the twins; and psychiatrist Leonard Heston, who has studied heritability of mental disorders with adopted children.

5   Bouchard has taken an eclectic approach in developing the battery of exercises through which the twins are run. Each pair goes through 6 days of intensive testing. In addition to detailed medical histories including diet, smoking, and exercise, the twins are given electrocardiograms, chest x-rays, heart stress tests, and pulmonary exams. They are injected with a variety of substances to determine allergies. They are wired to electroencephalographs to measure their brain wave responses to stimuli in the form of tones of varying intensity, and given other psychophysiological tests to measure such responses as reaction times. Several handedness tests are given to ascertain laterality.

The physiological probes are interspersed with several dozen pencil-and-paper tests, which over the week add up to about 15,000 questions; these cover family and childhood environment, fears and phobias, personal interests, vocational interests, values, reading and TV viewing habits, musical interests, aesthetic judgement tests, and color preferences. They are put through three comprehensive psychological inventories. Then there is a slew of ability tests: the Wechsler Adult Intelligence Scale (the main adult IQ test) and numerous others that reveal skills in information processing, vocabulary, spatial abilities, numerical processing, mechanical ability, memory, and so forth. Throughout the 6 days there is much overlap and repetition in the content of questions, the intent being to "measure the same underlying factor at different times," says Bouchard. Mindful of charges of investigator bias in the administration of IQ tests in past twin studies, Bouchard has contracted with outside professionals to come in just for the purpose of administering and scoring the Wechsler intelligence test.

And the upshot of all this probing? Although the data have not yet been interpreted, there have already been some real surprises. Bouchard told *Science:* "I frankly expected far more differences [between twins] than we have found so far. I'm a psychologist, not a geneticist. I want to find out how the environment works to shape psychological traits." But the most provocative morsels that have so far become available are those that seem to reveal genetic influences at work.

Take the "Jim twins," as they have come to be known. Jim Springer and Jim Lewis were adopted as infants into working-class Ohio families. Both liked math and did not like spelling in school. Both had law enforcement training and worked part-time as deputy sheriffs. Both vacationed in Florida, both drove Chevrolets. Much has been made of the fact that their lives are marked by a trail of similar names. Both had dogs named Toy. Both married and divorced women named Linda and had second marriages with women named Betty. They named their sons James Allan and James Alan, respectively. Both like mechanical drawing and carpentry. They have almost identical drinking and smoking patterns. Both chew their fingernails down to the nubs.

But what investigators thought "astounding" was their similar medical histories. In addition to having hemorrhoids and identical pulse and blood pressure and sleep patterns, both had inexplicably put on 10 pounds at the same time in their lives. What really gets the researchers is that both suffer from "mixed headache syndrome"—a combination tension headache and migraine. The onset occurred in both at the age of 18. They have these late-afternoon headaches with the same frequency and same degree of disability, and the two used the same terms to describe the pain.

The twins also have their differences. One wears his hair over his forehead, the other has it slicked back with sideburns. One expresses himself better orally, the other in writing. But although the emotional environments in which they were brought up were different, the profiles on their psychological inventories were much alike.

Another much-publicized pair are 47-year-old Oskar Stöhr and Jack Yufe. These two have the most dramatically different backgrounds of all the twins studied. Born in Trinidad of a Jewish father and a German mother, they were separated shortly after birth. The mother took Oskar back to Germany, where he was raised as a Catholic and a Nazi youth by his grandmother. Jack was raised in the Caribbean, as a Jew, by his father, and spent part of his youth on an Israeli kibbutz. The two men now lead markedly different lives. Oskar is an industrial supervisor in Germany, married, a devoted union man, a skier. Jack runs a retail clothing store in San Diego, is separated, and describes himself as a workaholic.

But similarities started cropping up as soon as Oskar arrived at the airport. Both were wearing wire-rimmed glasses and mustaches, both sported two-pocket shirts with epaulets. They share idiosyncrasies galore: they like spicy foods and sweet liqueurs, are absentminded, have a habit of falling asleep in front of the television, think it's funny to sneeze in a crowd of strangers, flush the toilet before using it, store rubber bands on their wrists, read magazines from back to front, dip buttered toast in their coffee. Oskar is domineering toward women and yells at his wife, which Jack did before he was separated. Oskar did not take all the tests because he speaks only German (some are scheduled to be administered to him in German), but the two had very similar profiles on the Minnesota Multi-phasic Personality

10

Inventory (the MMPI was already available in German). Although the two were raised in different cultures and speak different languages, investigator Bouchard professed himself struck by the similarities in their mannerisms, the questions they asked, their "temperament, tempo, the way they do things"—which are, granted, relatively intangible when it comes to measuring them. Bouchard also thinks the two supply "devastating" evidence against the feminist contention that children's personalities are shaped differently according to the sex of those who rear them, since Oskar was raised by women and Jack by men.

Other well-publicized twin pairs are Bridget and Dorothy, the British housewives with the seven rings, and Barbara and Daphne, another pair of British housewives. Both sets are now in their late 30's and were separated during World War II. Bridget and Dorothy are of considerable interest because they were raised in quite different socioeconomic settings—the class difference turns out mainly to be reflected in the fact that the one raised in modest circumstances has bad teeth. Otherwise, say the investigators, they share "striking similarities in all areas," including another case of coincidence in naming children. They named their sons Richard Andrew and Andrew Richard, respectively, and their daughters Catherine Louise and Karen Louise. (Bouchard is struck by this, as the likelihood of such a coincidence would seem to be lessened by the fact that names are a joint decision by husband and wife.) On ability and IQ tests the scores of the sisters were similar, although the one raised in the lower class setting had a slightly higher score.

The other British twins, Daphne and Barbara, are fondly remembered by the investigators as the "giggle sisters." Both were great gigglers, particularly together, when they were always setting each other off. Asked if there were any gigglers in their adoptive families, both replied in the negative. The sisters also shared identical coping mechanisms in the face of stress: they ignored it, managed to "read out" such stimuli. In keeping with this, both flatly avoided conflict and controversy—neither, for example, had any interest in politics. Such avoidance of conflict is "classically regarded as learned behavior," says Bouchard. Although the adoptive families of the two women were not terribly different, "we see more differences within families than between these two."

15   Only fragmentary information is available so far from the rest of the nine sets of twins, but it supplies abundant food for new lines of inquiry. Two 57-year-old women, for example, developed adult-onset diabetes at the same time in their lives. One of a pair of twins suffers from a rare neurological disease that has always been thought to be genetic in origin. Another area where identical twins differ is in their allergies.

Psychiatrically, according to Heston, who conducts personal interviews with all the twins, there has been remarkable agreement. "Twins brought up together have very high concordance in psychiatric histories," he says. (For example, if one identical twin has schizophrenia, the other one stands a 45 percent chance of developing it.) But what is surprising is that "what we see [with the twins in the study] is pretty much the same as in twins brought up together." By and large, he says, they share very similar phobias, and he has noted more than one case where both twins had histories of endogenous depression. In one case, twins who had been brought up in different emotional environments—one was raised in a strict disciplinarian household, the other had a warm, tolerant, loving mother—showed very similar neurotic and hypochondriacal traits. Says Heston, "things that I would never have thought of—mild depressions, phobias—as being in particular genetically mediated . . . now, at least, there are grounds for a very live hypothesis" on the role of genes not only in major mental illnesses, where chemistry clearly plays a part, but in lesser emotional disturbances.

Other odds and ends:

Two men brought up in radically different environments—one an uneducated manual laborer, the other highly educated and cosmopolitan—turned out to be great raconteurs. (They did, however, have very different IQ scores. The numbers are confidential but the difference was close to the largest difference on record for identical twins, 24 points.)

One of the greatest areas of discordance for twins was smoking. Of the nine pairs, there were four in which one twin smoked and the other did not. No one has an explanation for this. But, surprisingly, in at least one case a lifelong heavy smoker came out just as well on the pulmonary exam and heart stress test as did the nonsmoker.

In a couple of cases, one of a twin pair wore glasses and the other did not. But when their eyes were checked, it was found that both members of each pair required the same correction.

In the fascinating tidbit category: One pair of female twins was brought together briefly as children. Each wore her favorite dress for the occasion. The dresses were identical.

What is to be made of all this? As Tellegen warns, any conclusions at this point are "just gossip." The similarities are somehow more fascinating than the differences, and it could well be that the subjective impression they make on the investigators is heavier than is justified. Nonetheless, even the subjective impressions offer fertile grounds for speculation. Bouchard, for example, thinks that the team may discover that identical twins have a built-in penchant for a certain level of physical exertion. The latest pair to visit the laboratory, for example—23-year-old males—both eschew exercise (although both are thin as rails).

Lykken, who does the tests on the twins' central nervous systems, uses the case of the seven rings as an example for one of his tentative ideas. Fondness for rings is obviously not hereditary, but groups of unrelated genes on different chromosomes, producing pretty hands and other characteristics, may combine to result in beringedness. These traits, called idiographic—meaning particular to an individual rather than shared across a population—may not be as much a result of chance as has been thought. "There are probably other traits that are idiographic that may be almost inevitable given the [gene] combinations. . . . More of these unique characteristics than we previously thought may be determined by a particular combination of genes." Lykken adds, "people get so upset when you suggest that the wiring diagram can influence the mind." But to believe otherwise "requires a naïve dualism . . . an assumption that mental events occur independent of the physical substrate."

20   Such talk begins to sound pretty deterministic, but Lykken insists that when the mass of data has been ordered "there will be material that will make environmentalists very happy and material that will make hereditarians very happy." One thing that will not make the environmentalists happy is the fact that IQ seems to have a high degree of heritability, as indicated by the fact that of all the tests administered to identical twins separately reared, IQ shows the highest concordance. It is even higher than the introversion-extroversion personality trait, a venerable measure in psychological testing that shows higher concordance than other conventional categories such as sense of well-being, responsibility, dominance, and ego strength.

As several investigators mentioned to *Science*, the scores of identical twins on many psychological and ability tests are closer than would be expected for the same person taking the same test twice. Lykken also found this to be true of brain wave tracings, which is probably the most direct evidence that identical twins are almost identically wired. Several researchers also felt that there is something to the idea that identical twins reared apart may be even more similar in some respects than those reared together. The explanation is simple: competition between the two is inevitable; hence if the stronger or taller of the two excels at sports, the other twin, even if equal in inclination and ability, will avoid sports altogether in order not to be overshadowed. Or one twin will choose to be a retiring type in order not to compete with his extroverted sibling. In short, many twins, in the interest of establishing their individuality, tend to exaggerate their differences.

Although the tentativeness of the findings so far must be repeatedly emphasized, at least one of the Minnesota researchers believes it may be safe to hypothesize that only extreme differences in environment result in significant differences between identical twins. Lykken says, after observing so many similarities, that it is tempting to conclude that "native ability will show itself over a broad range" of backgrounds. So either a seriously impoverished or a greatly enriched environment is required "to significantly alter its expression."

Such an idea, if it gained broad acceptance, would have major impacts on social policies. But Bouchard wants to keep his study separate from politics, emphasizing instead that the research is "very much exploratory."

The data, once assembled and analyzed, should provide a gold mine of new hypotheses. If a great many pairs of twins are collected, says Bouchard, they may be able to present the findings quantitatively, otherwise, the findings will be in the form of case histories. Tellegen, however, whose main interest is the methodology, says "we want to invent methods for analyzing traits in an objective manner, so we can get statistically cogent conclusions from a single case." He points out that psychoanalytic theory was developed from intensive study of small numbers of people and that behavioral psychologist B. F. Skinner similarly was able to develop his theories by studying small numbers of animals. Take the twins with the identical headache syndromes: with just one pair of twins the door is opened to a new field of research.

The twin study may also make it clear that estimating the relative   25
contribution of heredity and environment to mental and psychological traits can never be boiled down to percentages. Some people, for example, may have authoritarian personalities no matter what their upbringing; the authoritarianism of others may be directly traceable to their environment. Similarly, with intelligence, some people may be smart or dumb regardless of outside influences, whereas the intelligence of others may be extremely malleable. Theoretically, variations from individual to individual in malleability and susceptibility may be so great that any attempt to make a generalization about the relative contribution of "innate" characteristics to a certain trait across a population would have no meaning.

Twin studies have been regarded with suspicion in some quarters because, according to Gottesman, the behavioral geneticist who worked with James Shields in England, they were "originally used to prove a genetic point of view." The most notorious of these were the studies of Cyril Burt on intelligence of twins reared separately, which were subsequently discredited. But, says Gottesman, "this study is a continuation of the efforts of Shields and Nielson [Niels Juel-Nielsen, a psychiatrist at the University of Odense in Denmark] to challenge received wisdom about the roles of genes and environment." Everyone, observes Gottesman, "seems to have made up their minds one way or the other." With such a dearth of data of the kind that can only be obtained by studying persons with identical genes raised in different environments, people have been free to be as dogmatic as they please.

Bouchard had a devil of a time getting funding for his study. Various probes at the National Institutes of Health were discouraged on the grounds that the study was too multidisciplinary for any institute to embrace it. He finally got some money from the National Science Foundation.

Although the ultimate conclusions of the study may well be susceptible to sensationalizing, Gordon Allen of the National Institute of Mental Health, head of the International Twin Society, does not believe it will find any "new and unique answers." The sample will not be large enough for that, and besides, too few of the twin pairs were reared in environments so radically different as to bring genetically based behavioral similarities into stark relief.

The most solid and unequivocal evidence will be that supplied by the physiological findings. Although the similarities are the most titillating to most observers, it is the discordances that will be the most informative. For any difference between a pair of identical twins is "absolute proof that that is not completely controlled by heredity."

At this point, no one can make any generalizations beyond that made   30
by James Shields, who died last year. Shields wrote that the evidence so far showed that "MZ [monozygotic] twins do not have to be brought up in

the same subtly similar family environment for them to be alike." He concluded, "I doubt if MZ's will ever be numerous and representative enough to provide the main evidence about environment, or about genetics, but . . . they can give unique real-life illustrations of some of the many possible pathways from genes to human behavior—and so will always be of human and scientific interest."

READING CRITICALLY FOR IDEAS, STRUCTURE, AND STYLE

1. What are some of the most striking examples where twins did not take on the learned behaviors of their adoptive families, but rather displayed traits that linked them with their siblings?

2. Which of the behaviors of the various sets of twins would you have thought was a result of choice or chance rather than being genetically determined? Explain your answer.

3. Why is the evidence found by Bouchard considered to be so significant? For example, what implications does it have for researchers in the social sciences and the way they study human behavior?

EXTENDING INSIGHTS THROUGH WRITING

1. Should twins be raised so as to emphasize their differences (for example, dress differently) or brought up to be exactly alike? Which approach would you use if you were the parent of twins? Explain your answer.

2. If you discovered that somewhere in the world you had a twin who you were separated from at birth and had the opportunity now to meet this person, would you do so? Why or why not?

CONNECTING PERSPECTIVES ON THE NATURAL WORLD

1. Why do clones raise ethical, moral, and practical questions in society (according to Gina Kolata in "A Clone Is Born") that identical twins do not?

2. How do the reports by Matt Ridley in "Genome" and Holden suggest that heredity is more important than environment?

MATT RIDLEY

Genome

BACKGROUND

Matt Ridley is a former science editor, Washington correspondent, and U.S. editor for the *Economist*. He is the author of *The Red Queen: Sex and the Evolution of Human Nature* (1994) and *The Origins of Virtue: Human Instincts and the Evolution of Cooperation* (1997). Ridley lives in England with his wife and two children. In the following chapter from *Genome: The Autobiography of a Species in 23 Chapters* (1999), Ridley explores the role of a particular gene in enabling us to acquire, use, and understand language.

APPROACHING RIDLEY'S ESSAY

Since Watson and Crick discovered the four-letter alphabet of DNA in 1953, scientists have attempted to decode the human genome—the complete set of genes housed in twenty-three pairs of chromosomes. The daunting nature of this task can be appreciated when we realize that this genome contains about a billion parcels of information expressed in this four-letter alphabet. In the foreword to his book, Ridley writes "If I wrote out the human genome, one letter per millimeter, my text would be as long as the River Danube. This is a gigantic document, an immense book, a recipe of extravagant length, and it all fits inside the microscopic nucleus of a tiny cell that fits easily upon the head of a pin."

With the decoding of a portion of the genome, biologists have begun to link specific genes with particular aspects of human behavior previously believed to be products of learning and culture. In this chapter, Ridley focuses on a gene on chromosome 7 that researchers believe guides our acquisition of language. The existence of this gene would prove the biological basis of a "language faculty" espoused by the pioneering linguist, Noam Chomsky. Chomsky theorizes that children possess (irrespective of the culture in which they are raised) a "deep structure" that allows them to acquire, use, and understand language—a set of inborn principles that speakers unconsciously draw on whenever they produce or understand sentences. Ridley builds the case for the existence of a language instinct in several ways and cites the research of Derek Bickerton and Myrna Gopnick, among others. Ridley also argues that Darwin's theory of "natural selection" can even apply to language, once a genetic basis has been established.

Genome

> The tabula of human nature was never rasa.
>
> W. D. Hamilton

Nobody doubts that genes can shape anatomy. The idea that they also shape behaviour takes a lot more swallowing. Yet I hope to persuade you that on chromosome 7 there lies a gene that plays an important part in equipping human beings with an instinct, and an instinct, moreover, that lies at the heart of all human culture.

Instinct is a word applied to animals: the salmon seeking the stream of its birth; the digger wasp repeating the behaviour of its long-dead parents; the swallow migrating south for the winter—these are instincts. Human beings do not have to rely on instinct; they learn instead; they are creative, cultural, conscious creatures. Everything they do is the product of free will, giant brains and brainwashing parents.

So goes the conventional wisdom that has dominated psychology and all other social sciences in the twentieth century. To think otherwise, to believe in innate human behaviour, is to fall into the trap of determinism, and to condemn individual people to a heartless fate written in their genes before they were born. No matter that the social sciences set about reinventing much more alarming forms of determinism to take the place of the genetic form: the parental determinism of Freud; the socio-economic determinism of Marx; the political determinism of Lenin; the peer-pressure cultural determinism of Franz Boas and Margaret Mead; the stimulus—response determinism of John Watson and B. F. Skinner; the linguistic determinism of Edward Sapir and Benjamin Whorf. In one of the great diversions of all time, for nearly a century social scientists managed to persuade thinkers of many kinds that biological causality was determinism while environmental causality preserved free will; and that animals had instincts, but human beings did not.

Between 1950 and 1990 the edifice of environmental determinism came tumbling down. Freudian theory fell the moment lithium first cured a manic depressive, where twenty years of psychoanalysis had failed. (In 1995 a woman sued her former therapist on the grounds that three weeks on Prozac had achieved more than three years of therapy.) Marxism fell when the Berlin wall was built, though it took until the wall came down before some people realised that subservience to an all-powerful state could not be made enjoyable however much propaganda accompanied it. Cultural determinism fell when Margaret Mead's conclusions (that adolescent behaviour was infinitely malleable by culture) were discovered by Derek Freeman to be based on a combination of wishful prejudice, poor data collection and adolescent prank-playing by her informants. Behaviourism fell with a famous 1950s experiment in Wisconsin in which orphan baby monkeys became emotionally attached to cloth models of their mothers even when fed only from wire models, thus refusing to obey the theory that we mammals can be conditioned to prefer the feel of anything that gives us food—a preference for soft mothers is probably innate.[1]

In linguistics, the first crack in the edifice was a book by Noam Chomsky, *Syntactic structures,* which argued that human language, the most blatantly cultural of all our behaviours, owes as much to instinct as it does to culture. Chomsky resurrected an old view of language, which had been described by Darwin as an 'instinctive tendency to acquire an art'. The early psychologist William James, brother of the novelist Henry, was a fervent protagonist of the view that human behaviour showed evidence of more separate instincts than animals, not fewer. But his ideas had been ignored for most of the twentieth century. Chomsky brought them back to life.

By studying the way human beings speak, Chomsky concluded that there were underlying similarities to all languages that bore witness to a universal human grammar. We all know how to use it, though we are rarely conscious of that ability. This must mean that part of the human brain comes equipped by its genes with a specialised ability to learn language. Plainly, the vocabulary could not be innate, or we would all speak one, unvarying language. But perhaps a child, as it acquired the vocabulary of its native society, slotted those words into a set of innate mental rules. Chomsky's evidence for this notion was linguistic: he found regularities in the way we spoke that were never taught by parents and could not be inferred from the examples of everyday speech without great difficulty. For example, in English, to make a sentence into a question we bring the main verb to the front of the statement. But how do we know which verb to bring? Consider the sentence, 'A unicorn that is eating a flower is in the garden.' You can turn that sentence into a question by moving the second 'is' to the front: 'Is a unicorn that is eating a flower in the garden?' But you make no sense if you move the first 'is': 'Is a unicorn that eating a flower is in the garden?' The difference is that the first 'is' is part of a noun phrase, buried in the mental image conjured by not just any unicorn, but any unicorn

[1]For the death of Freudianism: Wolf, T. (1997). Sorry but your soul just died. *The Independent on Sunday,* 2 February 1997. For the death of Meadism: Freeman, D. (1983). *Margaret Mead and Samoa: the making and unmaking of an anthropological myth.* Harvard University Press, Cambridge, MA; Freeman, D. (1997). *Frans Boas and 'The flower of heaven'.* Penguin, London. For the death of behaviourism: Harlow, H. F., Harlow, M. K. and Suomi, S. J. (1971). From thought to therapy: lessons from a primate laboratory. *American Scientist* 59: 538–49.

that is eating a flower. Yet four-year-olds can comfortably use this rule, never having been taught about noun phrases. They just seem to know the rule. And they know it without ever having used or heard the phrase 'a unicorn that is eating a flower' before. That is the beauty of language—almost every statement we make is a novel combination of words.

Chomsky's conjecture has been brilliantly vindicated in the succeeding decades by lines of evidence from many different disciplines. All converge upon the conclusion that to learn a human language requires, in the words of the psycho-linguist Steven Pinker, a human language instinct. Pinker (who has been called the first linguist capable of writing readable prose) persuasively gathered the strands of evidence for the innateness of language skills. There is first the universality of language. All human people speak languages of comparable grammatical complexity, even those isolated in the highlands of New Guinea since the Stone Age. All people are as consistent and careful in following implicit grammatical rules, even those without education and who speak what are patronisingly thought to be 'slang' dialects. The rules of inner-city black Ebonics are just as rational as the rules of the Queen's English. To prefer one to another is mere prejudice. For example, to use double negatives ('Don't nobody do this to me . . .') is considered proper in French, but slang in English. The rule is just as consistently followed in each.

Second, if these rules were learnt by imitation like the vocabulary, then why would four-year-olds who have been happily using the word 'went' for a year or so, suddenly start saying 'goed'? The truth is that although we must teach our children to read and write—skills for which there is no specialised instinct—they learn to speak by themselves at a much younger age with the least of help from us. No parent uses the word 'goed', yet most children do at some time. No parent explains that the word 'cup' refers to all cup-like objects, not this one particular cup, nor just its handle, nor the material from which it is made, nor the action of pointing to a cup, nor the abstract concept of cupness, nor the size or temperature of cups. A computer that was required to learn language would have to be laboriously equipped with a program that ignored all these foolish options—with an instinct, in other words. Children come pre-programmed, innately constrained to make only certain kinds of guess.

But the most startling evidence for a language instinct comes from a series of natural experiments in which children imposed grammatical rules upon languages that lacked them. In the most famous case, studied by Derek Bickerton, a group of foreign labourers brought together on Hawaii in the nineteenth century developed a pidgin language—a mixture of words and phrases whereby they could communicate with each other. Like most such pidgins, the language lacked consistent grammatical rules and remained both laboriously complex in the way it had to express things and relatively simple in what it could express. But all that changed when for the first time a generation of children learnt the language in their youth. The pidgin acquired rules of inflection, word order and grammar that made it a far more efficient and effective language—a creole. In short, as Bickerton concluded, pidgins become creoles only after they are learnt by a generation of children, who bring instinct to bear on their transformation.

Bickerton's hypothesis has received remarkable support from the study of sign language. In one case, in Nicaragua, special schools for the deaf, established for the first time in the 1980s, led to the invention, *de novo*, of a whole new language. The schools taught lip-reading with little success, but in the playground the children brought together the various hand signs they used at home and established a crude pidgin language. Within a few years, as younger children learnt this pidgin, it was transformed into a true sign language with all the complexity, economy, efficiency and grammar of a spoken language. Once again, it was children who made the language, a fact that seems to suggest that the language instinct is one that is switched off as the child reaches adulthood. This accounts for our difficulty in learning new languages, or even new accents, as adults. We no longer have the instinct. (It also explains why it is so much harder, even for a child, to learn French in a classroom than on holiday in France: the instinct works on speech that it hears, not rules that it memorises.) A sensitive period during which something can be learnt, and outside which it cannot, is a feature of many animals' instincts. For instance, a chaffinch will only learn the true song of its species if exposed to examples between certain ages. That the same is true of human beings was proved in a brutal way by the true story of Genie, a girl discovered in a Los Angeles apartment aged thirteen. She had been kept in a single sparsely furnished room all her life and deprived of almost all human contact. She had learnt two words, 'Stopit' and 'Nomore'. After her release from this hell she rapidly acquired a larger vocabulary, but she never learnt to handle grammar—she had passed the sensitive period when the instinct is expressed.

Yet even bad ideas take a lot of killing, and the notion that language is a form of culture that can shape the brain, rather than vice versa, has been an inordinate time a-dying. Even though the canonical case histories, like the lack of a concept of time in the Hopi language and hence in Hopi thought, have been exposed as simple frauds, the notion that language is a cause rather than consequence of the human brain's wiring survives in many social sciences. It would be absurd to argue that only Germans can understand the concept of taking pleasure at another's misfortune; and that the rest of us, not having a word for *Schadenfreude*, find the concept entirely foreign.[2]

Further evidence for the language instinct comes from many sources, not least from detailed studies of the ways in which children develop language in their second year of life. Irrespective of how much they are spoken to directly, or coached in the use of words, children develop language skills in a predictable order and pattern. And the tendency to develop language late has been demonstrated by twin studies to be highly heritable. Yet for many people the most persuasive evidence for the language instinct

[2]Pinker, S. (1994). *The Language Instinct: The New Science of Language and Mind.* Penguin, London.

comes from the hard sciences: neurology and genetics. It is hard to argue with stroke victims and real genes. The same part of the brain is consistently used for language processing (in most people, on the left side of the brain), even the deaf who 'speak' with their hands, though sign language also uses part of the right hemisphere.[3]

If a particular one of these parts of the brain is damaged, the effect is known as Broca's aphasia, an inability to use or understand all but the simplest grammar, even though the ability to understand sense remains unaffected. For instance, a Broca's aphasic can easily answer questions such as 'Do you use a hammer for cutting?' but has great difficulty with: 'The lion was killed by the tiger. Which one is dead?' The second question requires sensitivity to the grammar encoded in word order, which is known by just this one part of the brain. Damage to another area, Wernicke's area, has almost the opposite effect—people with such damage produce a rich but senseless stream of words. It appears as if Broca's area generates speech and Wernicke's area instructs Broca's area what speech to generate. This is not the whole story, for there are other areas active in language processing, notably the insula (which may be the region that malfunctions in dyslexia).[4]

There are two genetic conditions that affect linguistic ability. One is Williams syndrome, caused by a change in a gene on chromosome II, in which affected children are very low in general intelligence, but have a vivid, rich and loquacious addiction to using language. They chatter on, using long words, long sentences and elaborate syntax. If asked to refer to an animal, they are as likely to choose something bizarre like an aardvark as a cat or a dog. They have a heightened ability to learn language but at the expense of sense: they are severely mentally retarded. Their existence seems to undermine the notion, which most of us have at one time or another considered, that reason is a form of silent language.

15   The other genetic condition has the opposite effect: it lowers linguistic ability without apparently affecting intelligence, or at least not consistently. Known as specific language impairment (SLI), this condition is at the centre of a fierce scientific fight. It is a battle-ground between the new science of evolutionary psychology and the old social sciences, between genetic explanations of behaviour and environmental ones. And the gene is here on chromosome 7.

That the gene exists is not at issue. Careful analysis of twin studies unambiguously points to a strong heritability for specific language impairment. The condition is not associated with neurological damage during birth, is not associated with linguistically impoverished upbringings, and is not caused by general mental retardation. According to some tests—and depending on how it is defined—the heritability approaches one hundred

[3]Dale, P. S., Simonoff, E., Bishop, D. V. M., Eley, T. C., Oliver, B., Price, T. S., Purcell, S., Stevenson, J. and Plomin, R. (1998). Genetic influence on language delay in two-year-old children. *Nature Neuroscience* I: 324–8; Paulesu, E. and Mehler, J. (1998). Right on in sign language. *Nature* 392: 233–4.
[4]Carter, R. (1998). *Mapping the mind.* Weidenfeld and Nicolson, London.

per cent. That is, identical twins are roughly twice as likely to share the condition as fraternal twins.[5]

That the gene in question is on chromosome 7 is also not in much doubt. In 1997 a team of Oxford-based scientists pinned down a genetic marker on the long arm of chromosome 7, one form of which co-occurs with the condition of SLI. The evidence, though based only on one large English family, was strong and unambiguous.[6]

So why the battleground? The argument rages about what SLI is. To some it is merely a general problem with the brain that affects many aspects of language-producing ability, including principally the ability to articulate words in the mouth and to hear sounds correctly in the ear. The difficulty the subjects experience with language follow from these sensory problems, according to this theory. To others, this is highly misleading. The sensory and voice problems exist, to be sure, in many victims of the condition, but so does something altogether more intriguing: a genuine problem understanding and using grammar that is quite independent of any sensory deficits. The only thing both sides can agree upon is that it is thoroughly disgraceful, simplistic and sensationalist of the media to portray this gene, as they have done, as a 'grammar gene'.

The story centres on a large English family known as the Ks. There are three generations. A woman with the condition married an unaffected man and had four daughters and one son: all save one daughter were affected and they in turn had between them twenty-four children, ten of whom have the condition. This family has got to know the psychologists well; rival teams besiege them with a battery of tests. It is their blood that led the Oxford team to the gene on chromosome 7. The Oxford team, working with the Institute of Child Health in London, belongs to the 'broad' school of SLI, which argues that the grammar-deficient skills of the K family members stem from their problems with speech and hearing. Their principal opponent and the leading advocate of the 'grammar theory' is a Canadian linguist named Myrna Gopnik.

In 1990 Gopnik first suggested that the K family and others like them have a problem knowing the basic rules of English grammar. It is not that they cannot know the rules, but that they must learn them consciously and by heart, rather than instinctively internalise them. For example, if Gopnik shows somebody a cartoon of an imaginary creature and with it the words 'This is a Wug', then shows them a picture of two such creatures together with the words 'These are . . .', most people reply, quick as a flash, 'Wugs'. Those with SLI rarely do so, and if they do, it is after careful thought. The English plural rule, that you add an 's' to the end of most words, is one they seem not to know. This does not prevent those with SLI knowing the

20

[5]Bishop, D. V. M., North, T. and Donlan, C. (1995). Genetic basis of specific language impairment: evidence from a twin study. *Developmental Medicine and Child Neurology* 37: 56–71.

[6]Fisher, S. E., Vargha-Khadem, F., Watkins, K. E., Monaco, A. P. and Pembrey, M. E. (1998). Localisation of a gene implicated in a severe speech and language disorder. *Nature Genetics* 18: 168–70.

plural of most words, but they are stumped by novel words that they have not seen before, and they make the mistake of adding 's' to fictitious words that the rest of us would not, such as 'saess'. Gopnik hypothesises that they store English plurals in their minds as separate lexical entries, in the same way that we all store singulars. They do not store the grammatical rule.[7]

The problem is not, of course, confined to plurals. The past tense, the passive voice, various word-order rules, suffixes, word-combination rules and all the laws of English we each so unconsciously know, give SLI people difficulty, too. When Gopnik first published these findings, after studying the English family, she was immediately and fiercely attacked. It was far more reasonable, said one critic, to conclude that the source of the variable performance problems lay in the language-processing system, rather than the underlying grammar. Grammatical forms like plural and past tense were particularly vulnerable, in English, in individuals with speech defects. It was misleading of Gopnik, said another pair of critics, to neglect to report that the K family has a severe congenital speech disorder, which impairs their words, phonemes, vocabulary and semantic ability as well as their syntax. They had difficulty understanding many other forms of syntactical structure such as reversible passives, post-modified subjects, relative clauses and embedded forms.[8]

These criticisms had a whiff of territoriality about them. The family was not Gopnik's discovery: how dare she assert novel things about them? Moreover, there was some support for her idea in at least part of the criticism: that the disorder applied to all syntactical forms. And to argue that the grammatical difficulty must be caused by the mis-speaking problem, because mis-speaking goes with the grammatical difficulty, was circular.

Gopnik was not one to give up. She broadened the study to Greek and Japanese people as well, using them for various ingenious experiments designed to show the same phenomena. For example, in Greek, the word 'likos' means wolf. The word 'likanthropos' means wolfman. The word 'lik', the root of wolf, never appears on its own. Yet most Greek speakers automatically know that they must drop the '-os' to find the root if they wish to combine it with another word that begins with a vowel, like '-anthropos', or drop only the 's', to make 'liko-' if they wish to combine it with a word that begins with a consonant. It sounds a complicated rule, but even to English speakers it is immediately familiar: as Gopnik points out, we use it all the time in new English words like 'technophobia'.

Greek people with SLI cannot manage the rule. They can learn a word like 'likophobia' or 'likanthropos', but they are very bad at recognising that such words have complex structures, built up from different roots and suffixes. As a result, to compensate, they effectively need a larger vocabulary than other people. 'You have to think of them', says Gopnik, 'as people without a native language.' They learn their own tongue in the same laborious

[7]Gopnik, M. (1990). Feature-blind grammar and dysphasia. Nature 344: 715.
[8]Fletcher, P. (1990). Speech and language deficits. Nature 346: 226; Vargha-Khadem, F. and Passingham, R. E. (1990). Speech and language deficits. Nature 346: 226.

way that we, as adults, learn a foreign language, consciously imbibing the rules and words.[9]

Gopnik acknowledges that some SLI people have low IQ on non-verbal tests, but on the other hand some have above-average IQ. In one pair of fraternal twins, the SLI one had higher non-verbal IQ than the unaffected twin. Gopnik also acknowledges that most SLI people have problems speaking and hearing as well, but she contends that by no means all do and that the coincidence is irrelevant. For instance, people with SLI have no trouble learning the difference between 'ball' and 'bell', yet they frequently say 'fall' when they mean 'fell'—a grammatical, not a vocabulary difference. Likewise, they have no difficulty discerning the difference between rhyming words, like 'nose' and 'rose'. Gopnik was furious when one of her opponents described the K family members' speech as 'unintelligible' to outsiders. Having spent many hours with them, talking, eating pizza and attending family celebrations, she says they are perfectly comprehensible. To prove the irrelevance of speaking and hearing difficulties, she has devised written tests, too. For example, consider the following pair of sentences: 'He was very happy last week when he was first.' 'He was very happy last week when he is first.' Most people immediately recognise that the first is grammatical and the second is not. SLI people think they are both acceptable statements. It is hard to conceive how this could be due to a hearing or speaking difficulty.[10]

None the less, the speaking-and-hearing theorists have not given up. They have recently shown that SLI people have problems with 'sound masking', whereby they fail to notice a pure tone when it is masked by preceding or following noise, unless the tone is forty-five decibels more intense than is detectable to other people. In other words, SLI people have more trouble picking out the subtler sounds of speech from the stream of louder sounds, so they might, for example, miss the '-ed' on the end of a word.

But instead of supporting the view that this explains the entire range of SLI symptoms, including the difficulty with grammatical rules, this lends credence to a much more interesting, evolutionary explanation: that the speech and hearing parts of the brain are next door to the grammar parts and both are damaged by SLI. SLI results from damage to the brain caused in the third trimester of pregnancy by an unusual version of a gene on chromosome 7. Magnetic-resonance imaging confirms the existence of the brain lesion and the rough location. It occurs, not surprisingly, in one of the two areas devoted to speech and language processing, the areas known as Broca's and Wernicke's areas.

[9]Gopnik, M., Dalakis, J., Fukuda, S. E., Fukuda, S. and Kehayia, E. (1996). Genetic language impairment: unruly grammars. In Runciman, W. G., Maynard Smith, J. and Dunbar, R. I. M. (eds), *Evolution of social behaviour patterns in primates and man*, pp. 223–49. Oxford University Press, Oxford; Gopnik, M. (ed.) (1997). *The inheritance and innateness of grammars*. Oxford University Press, Oxford.

[10]Gopnik, M. and Goad, H. (1997). What underlies inflectional error patterns in genetic dysphasia? *Journal of Neurolinguistics* 10: 109–38; Gopnik, M. (1999). Familial language impairment: more English evidence. *Folia Phonetica et Logopaedia* 51: in press. Myrna Gopnik, e-mail correspondence with the author, 1998.

There are two areas in the brains of monkeys that correspond precisely to these areas. The Broca-homologue is used for controlling the muscles of the monkey's face, larynx, tongue and mouth. The Wernicke-homologue is used for recognising sound sequences and the calls of other monkeys. These are exactly the non-linguistic problems that many SLI people have: controlling facial muscles and hearing sounds distinctly. In other words, when ancestral human beings first evolved a language instinct, it grew in the region devoted to sound production and processing. That sound-production and processing module remained, with its connections to facial muscles and ears, but the language instinct module grew on top of it, with its innate capacity for imposing the rules of grammar on the vocabulary of sounds used by members of the species. Thus, although no other primate can learn grammatical language at all—and we are indebted to many diligent, sometimes gullible and certainly wishful trainers of chimpanzees and gorillas for thoroughly exhausting all possibilities to the contrary—language is intimately physically connected with sound production and processing. (Yet not too intimately: deaf people redirect the input and output of the language module to the eyes and hands respectively.) A genetic lesion in that part of the brain therefore affects grammatical ability, speech and hearing—all three modules.[11]

No better proof could be adduced for William James's nineteenth-century conjecture that human beings evolved their complex behaviour by adding instincts to those of their ancestors, not by replacing instincts with learning. James's theory was resurrected in the late 1980s by a group of scientists calling themselves evolutionary psychologists. Prominent among them were the anthropologist John Tooby, the psychologist Leda Cosmides and the psycho-linguist Steven Pinker. Their argument, in a nutshell, is this. The main goal of twentieth-century social science has been to trace the ways in which our behaviour is influenced by the social environment; instead, we could turn the problem on its head and trace the ways in which the social environment is the product of our innate social instincts. Thus the fact that all people smile at happiness and frown when worried, or that men from all cultures find youthful features sexually attractive in women, may be expressions of instinct, not culture. Or the universality of romantic love and religious belief might imply that these are influenced by instinct more than tradition. Culture, Tooby and Cosmides hypothesised, is the product of individual psychology more than vice versa. Moreover, it has been a gigantic mistake to oppose nature to nurture, because all learning depends on innate capacities to learn and innate constraints upon what is learnt. For instance, it is much easier to teach a monkey (and a man) to fear snakes than it is to teach it to fear flowers. But you still have to teach it. Fear of snakes is an instinct that has to be learnt.[12]

[11]Associated Press, 8 May 1997; Pinker, S. (1994). *The Language Instinct: The New Science of Language and Mind.* Penguin, London.
[12]Mineka, S. and Cook, M. (1993). Mechanisms involved in the observational conditioning of fear. *Journal of Experimental Psychology, General* 122: 23–38.

The 'evolutionary' in evolutionary psychology refers not so much to an interest in descent with modification, nor to the process of natural selection itself—interesting though these are, they are inaccessible to modern study in the case of the human mind, because they happen too slowly—but to the third feature of the Darwinian paradigm: the concept of adaptation. Complex biological organs can be reverse-engineered to discern what they are 'designed' to do, in just the same way that sophisticated machines can be so studied. Steven Pinker is fond of pulling from his pocket a complicated thing designed for pitting olives to explain the process of reverse engineering. Leda Cosmides prefers a Swiss-army knife to make a similar point. In each case, the machines are meaningless except when described in terms of their particular function: what is this blade for? It would be meaningless to describe the working of a camera without reference to the fact that it is designed for the making of images. In the same way, it is meaningless to describe the human (or animal) eye without mentioning that it is specifically designed for approximately the same purpose.

Pinker and Cosmides both contend that the same applies to the human brain. Its modules, like the different blades of a Swiss-army knife, are most probably designed for particular functions. The alternative, that the brain is equipped with random complexity, from which its different functions fall out as fortunate by-products of the physics of complexity—an idea still favoured by Chomsky—defies all evidence. There is simply nothing to support the conjecture that the more detailed you make a network of microprocessors, the more functions they will acquire. Indeed, the 'connectionist' approach to neural networks, largely misled by the image of the brain as a general-purpose network of neurons and synapses, has tested the idea thoroughly and found it wanting. Pre-programmed design is required for the solving of pre-ordained problems.

There is a particular historical irony here. The concept of design in nature was once one of the strongest arguments advanced against evolution. Indeed, it was the argument from design that kept evolutionary ideas at bay throughout the first half of the nineteenth century. Its most able exponent, William Paley, famously observed that if you found a stone on the ground, you could conclude little of interest about how it got there. But if you found a watch, you would be forced to conclude that somewhere there was a watchmaker. Thus the exquisite, functional design apparent in living creatures was manifest evidence for God. It was Darwin's genius to use the argument from design just as explicitly but in the service of the opposite conclusion: to show that Paley was wrong. A 'blind watchmaker' (in Richard Dawkin's phrase) called natural selection, acting step by step on the natural variation in the creature's body, over many millions of years and many millions of individuals, could just as easily account for complex adaptation. So successfully has Darwin's hypothesis been supported that complex adaptation is now considered the primary evidence that natural selection has been at work.[13]

---

[13]Dawkins, R. (1986). *The Blind Watchmaker*. Longman, Essex.

The language instinct that we all possess is plainly one such complex adaptation, beautifully designed for clear and sophisticated communication between individuals. It is easy to conceive how it was advantageous for our ancestors on the plains of Africa to share detailed and precise information with each other at a level of sophistication unavailable to other species. 'Go a short way up that valley and turn left by the tree in front of the pond and you will find the giraffe carcass we just killed. Avoid the brush on the right of the tree that is in fruit, because we saw a lion go in there.' Two sentences pregnant with survival value to the recipient; two tickets for success in the natural-selection lottery, yet wholly incomprehensible without a capacity for understanding grammar, and lots of it.

The evidence that grammar is innate is overwhelming and diverse. The evidence that a gene somewhere on chromosome 7 usually plays a part in building that instinct in the developing foetus's brain is good, though we have no idea how large a part that gene plays. Yet most social scientists remain fervently resistant to the idea of genes whose primary effect seems to be to achieve the development of grammar directly. As is clear in the case of the gene on chromosome 7, many social scientists prefer to argue, despite much evidence, that the gene's effects on language are mere side-effects of its direct effect on the ability of the brain to understand speech. After a century in which the dominating paradigm has been that instincts are confined to 'animals' and are absent from human beings, this reluctance is not surprising. This whole paradigm collapses once you consider the Jamesian idea that some instincts cannot develop without learnt, outside inputs.

35   This chapter has followed the arguments of evolutionary psychology, the reverse-engineering of human behaviour to try to understand what particular problems it was selected to solve. Evolutionary psychology is a new and remarkably successful discipline that has brought sweeping new insights to the study of human behaviour in many fields. Behaviour genetics, which was the subject of the chapter on chromosome 6, aims at roughly the same goal. But the approach to the subject is so different that behaviour genetics and evolutionary psychology are embarked on a collision course. The problem is' this: behaviour genetics seeks variation between individuals and seeks to link that variation to genes. Evolutionary psychology seeks common human behaviour—human universals, features found in every one of us—and seeks to understand how and why such behaviour must have become partly instinctive. It therefore assumes no individual differences exist, at least for important behaviours. This is because natural selection consumes variation: that is its job. If one version of a gene is much better than another, then the better version will soon be universal to the species and the worse version will soon be extinct. Therefore, evolutionary psychology concludes that if behaviour geneticists find a gene with common variation in it, then it may not be a very important gene, merely an auxiliary. Behaviour geneticists retort that every human gene yet investigated turns out to have variants, so there must be something wrong with the argument from evolutionary psychology.

In practice, it may gradually emerge that the disagreement between these two approaches is exaggerated. One studies the genetics of common, universal, species-specific features. The other studies the genetics of individual differences. Both are a sort of truth. All human beings have a language instinct, whereas all monkeys do not, but that instinct does not develop equally well in all people. Somebody with SLI is still far more capable of learning language than Washoe, Koko, Nim or any of the other trained chimpanzees and gorillas.

The conclusions of both behaviour genetics and evolutionary psychology remain distinctly unpalatable to many non-scientists, whose main objection is a superficially reasonable argument from incredulity. How can a gene, a stretch of DNA 'letters', cause a behaviour? What conceivable mechanism could link a recipe for a protein with an ability to learn the rule for making the past tense in English? I admit that this seems at first sight a mighty leap, requiring more faith than reason. But it need not be, because the genetics of behaviour is, at root, no different from the genetics of embryonic development. Suppose that each module of the brain grows its adult form by reference to a series of chemical gradients laid down in the developing embryo's head—a sort of chemical road map for neurons. Those chemical gradients could themselves be the product of genetic mechanisms. Hard though it is to imagine genes and proteins that can tell exactly where they are in the embryo, there is no doubting they exist. As I shall reveal when discussing chromosome 12, such genes are one of the most exciting products of modern genetic research. The idea of genes for behaviour is no more strange than the idea of genes for development. Both are mind-boggling, but nature has never found human incomprehension a reason for changing her methods.[14]

READING CRITICALLY FOR IDEAS, STRUCTURE, AND STYLE

1. How does Ridley construct his case that the acquisition of language is controlled by genes rather than culture? Why is Noam Chomsky so important in Ridley's argument?

2. How does the research of Derek Bickerton and Myrna Gopnick tend to confirm Ridley's thesis?

3. Ridley covers a lot of ground in trying to place this discovery in context of both social and biological sciences. Does Ridley have an observable bias in the way in which he makes his case? If so,

---

[14]Evolutionary psychology, the theme of this chapter, is explored in several books, including Jerome Barkow, Leda Cosmides and John Tooby's *The Adapted Mind* (Oxford University Press, 1992), Robert Wright's *The Moral Animal* (Pantheon, 1994), Steven Pinker's *How the Mind Works* (Penguin, 1998) and my own *The Red Queen* (Viking, 1993). The origin of human language is explored in Steven Pinker's *The Language Instinct* (Penguin, 1994) and Terence Deacon's *The Symbolic Species* (Penguin, 1997).

where do you see it? Take a close look at his word choices and the space he gives to opponents before you reply.

EXTENDING INSIGHTS THROUGH WRITING

1. Select one of the theorists or case studies Ridley cites and do some research to discover whether he fairly represents them or simplifies and distorts their conclusions. Present your findings in a short essay.

2. Ridley states that "all human beings have a language instinct, whereas all monkeys do not," an idea that is actively disputed by many researchers. Investigate the current research on this question and determine whether Ridley is correct.

CONNECTING PERSPECTIVES ON THE NATURAL WORLD

1. What important component of Ridley's argument applies Darwin's hypothesis as to the way "natural selection" functions to the evolution of the language instinct in humans? To what extent is modern research on this subject based on Darwin's assumptions?

2. Ridley's rhetoric is surprisingly aggressive (for example, "even bad ideas take a lot of killing," "the argument rages") given his subject. Evaluate whether this enhances his credibility or detracts from it when compared with Jean Henri Fabre's dramatic portrayal of "The Praying Mantis."

GINA KOLATA

A Clone Is Born

BACKGROUND

Gina Kolata (b. 1948) is a science journalist who has been writing for *The New York Times* since 1988. She studied molecular biology at the Massachusetts Institute of Technology and holds a master's degree in mathematics from the University of Maryland. Kolata is the author of *The Baby Doctors: Probing the Limits of Fetal Medicine* (1990) and *Clone: The Road to Dolly and the Path Ahead* (1998), from which "A Clone Is Born" is reprinted. Her latest work is *Flu: the Story of the Great Influenza Pandemic of 1918 and the Search for the Virus That Caused It* (1999).

APPROACHING KOLATA'S ESSAY

The ability to clone living beings has staggering consequences, which Kolata explores. Clones would require a rethinking of the relationship between a child and his or her parents. In this respect, clones are a radically different kind of child than one produced even by the most modern fertility treatments, including semen banks, donor eggs, frozen embryos, and artificial insemination. Secondly, cloning would challenge the view of many religions as to the existence of a unique soul inhabiting a particular body. It would also require a reformulation of the concept of an individual's mortality and pose many practical problems for society.

As a science journalist for *The New York Times*, Kolata maintains the objective attitude of a neutral observer. Her essay exemplifies the methods of effective cross-disciplinary research and fairly represents the perspectives of scientists, theologians, and ethicists. Since this article was written, Dolly (the cloned lamb) has given birth to three lambs who were not clones, other species such as goats and pigs have been cloned as well, and the cloning of humans is being actively debated and may actually have already taken place.

A Clone Is Born

Many people wonder if this is a miracle for which we can thank God, or an ominous new way to play God ourselves.
— *Nancy Duff, Princeton Theological Seminary*

On a soft summer night, July 5, 1996, at 5:00 P.M., the most famous lamb in history entered the world, head and forelegs first. She was born in a shed, just down the road from the Roslin Institute in Roslin, Scotland, where she was created. And yet her creator, Ian Wilmut, a quiet, balding fifty-two-year-old embryologist, does not remember where he was when he heard that the lamb, named Dolly, was born. He does not even recall getting a telephone call from John Bracken, a scientist who had monitored the pregnancy of the sheep that gave birth to Dolly, saying that Dolly was alive and healthy and weighed 6.6 kilograms, or 14.5 pounds.

It was a moment of remarkable insouciance. No one broke open champagne. No one took pictures. Only a few staff members from the institute and a local veterinarian who attended the birth were present. Yet Dolly, a fluffy creature with grayish-white fleece and a snow-white face, who looked for all the world like hundreds of other lambs that dot the rolling hills of Scotland, was soon to change the world.

When the time comes to write the history of our age, this quiet birth, the creation of this little lamb, will stand out. The events that change history are few and unpredictable. In the twentieth century, there was the discovery of quantum theory, the revolutionary finding by physicists that the normal rules of the visible world do not apply in the realm of the atom. There was Einstein's theory of general relativity, saying that space and time can be warped. There was the splitting of the atom, with its promise of good and evil. There was the often-overlooked theorem of mathematician Kurt Gödel, which said that there are truths that are unknowable, theorems that can be neither proved nor disproved. There was the development of computers that transformed Western society.

In biology and medicine, there was the discovery of penicillin in the 1940s, and there was James Watson and Francis Crick's announcement, in 1953, that they had found the structure of DNA, the genetic blueprint. There was the conquest of smallpox that wiped the ancient scourge from the face of the earth, and the discovery of a vaccine that could prevent the tragedy of polio. In the 1980s, there was the onslaught of AIDS, which taught us that plagues can afflict us still.

In politics, there were the world wars, the rise and fall of communism, and the Great Depression. There is the economic rise of Asia in the latter part of the century, and the ever-shifting balance of the world's powers.

But events that alter our very notion of what it means to be human are few and scattered over the centuries. The birth of Dolly is one of them. "Analogies to Copernicus, to Darwin, to Freud, are appropriate," said Alan Weisbard, a professor of law and medical ethics at the University of Wisconsin. The world is a different place now that she is born.

Dolly is a clone. She was created not out of the union of a sperm and an egg but out of the genetic material from an udder cell of a six-year-old sheep. Wilmut fused the udder cell with an egg from another sheep, after first removing all genetic material from the egg. The udder cell's genes took up residence in the egg and directed it to grow and develop. The result was Dolly, the identical twin of the original sheep that provided the udder cells, but an identical twin born six years later. In a moment of frivolity, as a wry joke, Wilmut named her Dolly after Dolly Parton, who also was known, he said, for her mammaries.

Until Dolly entered the world, cloning was the stuff of science fiction. It had been raised as a possibility decades ago, then dismissed, relegated to the realm of the kooky, the fringy, something that serious scientists thought was simply not going to happen anytime soon.

Yet when it happened, even though it involved but one sheep, it was truly fantastic, and at the same time horrifying in a way that is hard to define. In 1972, when Willard Gaylin, a psychiatrist and the founder of the Hastings Center, an ethics think tank, mistakenly thought that science was on the verge of cloning, he described its awesome power: "One could imagine taking a single sloughed cell from the skin of a person's hand, or even from the hand of a mummy (since cells are neither 'alive' nor 'dead,' but merely intact or not intact), and seeing it perpetuate itself into a sheet of skin tissue. But could one really visualize the cell forming a finger, let alone a hand, let alone an embryo, let alone another Amenhotep?"[1]

And what if more than one clone is made? Is it even within the realm of the imaginable to think that someday, perhaps decades from now, but someday, you could clone yourself and make tens, dozens, hundreds of genetically identical twins? Is it really science fiction to think that your cells could be improved beforehand, genetically engineered to add some genes and snip out others? These ideas, that so destroy the notion of the self, that touch on the idea of the soul, of human identity, seemed so implausible to most scientists that they had declared cloning off-limits for discussion.

Even ethicists, those professional worriers whose business it is to raise alarms about medicine and technology, were steered away from talk of cloning, though they tried to make it a serious topic. In fact, it was one of the first subjects mentioned when the bioethics field came into its own

---

[1]*Amenhotep:* King of Egypt of the XVIII dynasty, approximately 1570 B.C.

in the late 1960s and early 1970s. But scientists quashed the ethicists' ruminations, telling them to stop inventing such scary scenarios. The ethicists were informed that they were giving science a bad name to raise such specters as if they were real possibilities. The public would be frightened, research grants might dry up, scientists would be seen as Frankensteins, and legitimate studies that could benefit humankind could be threatened as part of an anti-science backlash.

Daniel Callahan, one of the founders of the bioethics movement and the founder, with Gaylin, of the Hastings Center, recalled that when he and others wanted to talk about cloning, scientists pooh-poohed them. They were told, he said, that "there was no real incentive for science to do this and it was just one of those scary things that ethicists and others were talking about that would do real harm to science."

Now, with the birth of Dolly, the ethicists were vindicated. Yes, it was a sheep that was cloned, not a human being. But there was nothing exceptional about sheep. Even Wilmut, who made it clear that he abhorred the very idea of cloning people, said that there was no longer any theoretical reason why humans could not clone themselves, using the same methods he had used to clone Dolly. "There is no reason in principle why you couldn't do it." But, he added, "all of us would find that offensive."

The utterly pragmatic approach of Wilmut and many other scientists, however, ignores the awesome nature of what was accomplished. Our era is said to be devoted to the self, with psychologists and philosophers battling over who can best probe the nature of our identities. But cloning pares the questions down to their essence, forcing us to think about what we mean by the self, whether we are our genes or, if not, what makes us *us*. "To thine own self be true" goes the popular line from Shakespeare—but what is the self?

15   We live in an age of the ethicist, a time when we argue about pragmatism and compromises in our quest to be morally right. But cloning forces us back to the most basic questions that have plagued humanity since the dawn of recorded time: What is good and what is evil? And how much potential for evil can we tolerate to obtain something that might be good? We live in a time when sin is becoming one of those quaint words that we might hear in church but that has little to do with our daily world. Cloning, however, with its possibilities for creating our own identical twins, brings us back to the ancient sins of vanity and pride: the sins of Narcissus, who so loved himself, and of Prometheus, who, in stealing fire, sought the powers of God. In a time when we hear rallying cries of reproductive freedom, of libertarianism and the rights of people to do what they want, so long as they hurt no one else, cloning, by raising the possibility that people could be made to order like commodities, places such ideas against the larger backdrop of human dignity.

So before we can ask why we are so fascinated by cloning, we have to examine our souls and ask, What exactly so bothers many of us about trying to replicate our genetic selves? Or, if we are not bothered, why aren't we?

We want children who resemble us. Even couples who use donor eggs because the woman's ovaries have failed or because her eggs are not easily fertilized, or who use donor sperm because the man's sperm is not viable, peruse catalogs of donors to find people who resemble themselves. We want to replicate ourselves. Several years ago, a poem by Linda Pastan, called "To a Daughter Leaving Home," was displayed on the walls of New York subways. It read:

> Knit two, purl two,
> I make of small boredoms
> a fabric
> to keep you warm.
> Is it my own image
> I love so
> in your face?
> I lean over your sleep,
> Narcissus over
> his clear pool,
> ready to fall in—
> to drown for you
> if necessary.

Yet if we so love ourselves, reflected in our children, why is it so terrifying to so many of us to think of seeing our exact genetic replicas born again, identical twins years younger than we? Is there a hidden fear that we would be forcing God to give us another soul, thereby bending God to our will, or, worse yet, that we would be creating soul-less beings that were merely genetic shells of humans? After all, in many religions, the soul is supposed to be present from the moment of conception, before a person is born and shaped by nurture as well as nature. If a clone is created, how could its soul be different from the soul of the person who is cloned? Is it possible, as molecular biologist Gunther Stendt once suggested, that "a human clone would nor consist of real persons but merely of Cartesian[2] automata in human shape"?

Or is it one thing for nature to form us through the vagaries of the genetic lottery, and another for us to take complete control, abandoning all thoughts of somehow, through the mixing of genes, having a child who is like us, but better? Normally, when a man and a woman have a child together, the child is an unpredictable mixture of the two. We recognize that, of course, in the hoary old joke in which a beautiful but dumb woman suggests to an ugly but brilliant man that the two have a child. Just think of how wonderful the baby would be, the woman says, with my looks and your brains. Aha, says the man. But what if the child inherited *my* looks and *your* brains?

Theologians speak of the special status of a child, born of an act of love between a man and a woman. Of course, we already routinely employ   20

[2]*Cartesian:* refers to French philosopher, mathematician, and scientist Rene Descartes (1596–1650).

infertility treatments, like donor eggs, semen banks, and frozen embryos, that have weakened these ties between the parents and the child. But, said Gilbert Meilaender, a Lutheran theologian, cloning would be "a new and decisive turn on this road." Cloning entails the *production*, rather than the creation, of a child. It is "far less a surrender to the mystery of the genetic lottery," he said, and "far more an understanding of the child as a product of human will."

Elliott Dorff, a rabbi at the University of Judaism in Los Angeles, said much the same thing. "Each person involved has to get out of himself or herself in order to make and have a child." But if a person can be reproduced through cloning, that self-surrender is lost, and there is danger of self-idolization.

Cloning also poses a danger to our notion of mortality, Dorff said. The biblical psalm says, "Teach us to number our days so that we can obtain a heart of wisdom," he recalled. "The sense that there is a deadline, that there is an end to all this, forces us to make good use of our lives."

In this age of entertainment, when philosophical and theological questions are pushed aside as too difficult or too deep, cloning brings us face-to-face with our notion of what it means to be human and makes us confront both the privileges and limitations of life itself. It also forces us to question the powers of science. Is there, in fact, knowledge that we do not want? Are there paths we would rather not pursue?

The time is long past when we can speak of the purity of science, divorced from its consequences. If any needed reminding that the innocence of scientists was lost long ago, they need only recall the comments of J. Robert Oppenheimer, the genius who was a father of the atomic bomb and who was transformed in the process from a supremely confident man, ready to follow his scientific curiosity, to a humbled and stricken soul, wondering what science had wrought.

25   Before the bomb was made, Oppenheimer said, "When you see something that is technically sweet you go ahead and do it." After the bomb was dropped on Hiroshima and Nagasaki, in a chilling speech at the Massachusetts Institute of Technology in 1947, he said: "In some sort of crude sense which no vulgarity, no humor, no overstatement can quite extinguish, the physicists have known sin; and this is a knowledge which they cannot lose."

As with the atom bomb, cloning is complex, multilayered in its threats and its promises. It offers the possibility of real scientific advances that can improve our lives and save them. In medicine, scientists dream of using cloning to reprogram cells so we can make our own body parts for transplantation. Suppose, for example, you needed a bone-marrow transplant. Some deadly forms of leukemia can be cured completely if doctors destroy your own marrow and replace it with healthy marrow from someone else. But the marrow must be a close genetic match to your own. If not, it will lash out at you and kill you. Bone marrow is the source of the white blood cells of the immune system. If you have someone else's marrow, you'll make their white blood cells. And if those cells think you are different from them, they will attack.

Today, if you need marrow, you have to hope that a sister, brother, parent, or child happens to have bone-marrow cells that are genetically compatible with your own. If you have no relative whose marrow matches yours, you can search in computer databases of people who have volunteered to donate their marrow, but your chances of finding someone who matches you are less than one in twenty thousand—or one in a million if you genetic type is especially rare.

But suppose, instead, that scientists could take one of your cells— any cell—and merge it with a human egg. The egg would start to divide, to develop, but it would not be permitted to divide more than a few times. Instead, technicians would bathe it in proteins that direct primitive cells, embryo cells, to become marrow cells. What started out to be a clone of you could grow into a batch of your marrow—the perfect match.

More difficult, but not inconceivable, would be to grow solid organs, like kidneys or livers, in the same way.

Another possibility is to create animals whose organs are perfect genetic matches for humans. If you needed a liver, a kidney, or even a heart, you might be able to get one from a pig clone that was designed so it had human proteins on the surface of its organs. The reason transplant surgeons steer away from using animal organs in humans, even though there is a dire shortage of human organs, is that animals are so genetically different from people. A pig kidney transplanted into a human is just so foreign that the person's immune system will attack it and destroy it. But cloning offers a different approach. Scientist could take pig cells, for example, and add human genes to them in the laboratory, creating pig cells that were coated with human proteins. Then they could make cloned pigs from those cells. Each pig would have organs that looked, to a human immune system, for all the world like a human organ. These organs could be used for transplantation.

Cloning could also be used to make animals that are living drug factories—exactly the experiment that Ian Wilmut's sponsor, a Scottish company called PPL Therapeutics, Ltd., wants to conduct. Scientists could insert genes into laboratory cells that would force the cells to make valuable drugs, like clotting factors for hemophiliacs. Then they could clone animals from those cells and create animals that made the drugs in their milk. The only step remaining would be to milk the clones and extract the drugs.

Another possibility would be to clone prize dairy cows. The average cow produces about fifteen thousand pounds of milk annually, but world champion milk producers make as much as forty thousand pounds of milk a year. The problem for breeders is that there are, apparently, so many genes involved in creating one of these phenomenal cows that no one has learned how to breed them the old-fashioned way. But if you had a cow that produced forty thousand pounds of milk a year, you could clone her and make a herd.

Zoologists might clone animals that are on the verge of extinction, keeping them alive and propagating when they might otherwise have vanished from the earth.

The possibilities are limitless, scientists say, and so, some argue, we should stop focusing on our hypothetical fears and think about the benefits that cloning could bring.

35   Others say that cloning is far from business as usual, far from a technical advance, and that we should be wary of heading down such a brambly path.

But was the cloning of Dolly really such a ground-shifting event? After all, the feat came as a climax to years of ever more frightening, yet dazzling, technological feats, particularly in the field of assisted reproduction. Each step, dreaded by some, cursed by others, welcomed by many more, soon grew to be part of the medical landscape, hardly worthy of comment. And so, with this history as background, some asked why, and how, anyone thought cloning could be controlled—or why anyone would want to. Besides, some asked, why was cloning any different in principle from some of the more spectacular infertility treatments that are accepted with hardly a raised eyebrow?

The infertility revolution began in 1978, when Louise Brown was born in England, the world's first test-tube baby. After more than a decade of futile efforts, scientists finally had learned to fertilize women's eggs outside their bodies, allowing the first stages of human life to begin in a petri dish in a laboratory. The feat raised alarms at the time. It was, said Moshe Tendler, a professor of medical ethics and chair of the biology department at Yeshiva University, "matchmaking at its most extreme, two reluctant gametes trying to be pushed together whether they liked it or not."

But in vitro fertilization flourished despite its rocky start, nourished by the plaintive cries of infertile couples so unjustly condemned to be barren, and justified by the miracle babies—children who were wanted so badly that their parents were willing to spend years in doctors' offices, take out loans for tens of thousands of dollars, and take their chances of finally, ultimately, failing and losing all hope of having a child who bore their genes. The doctors who ran the clinics soothed the public's fears. In vitro fertilization was not horrifying, they said. It was just a way to help infertile couples have babies.

The federal government quickly got out of the business of paying for any research that even peripherally contributed to the manipulation of human embryos, but in vitro fertilization clinics simply did research on their own, with money from the fees they charged women for infertility treatments, and so the field advanced, beyond the purview of university science, with its federal grants and accompanying strict rules and regulations.

40   "There are no hard-and-fast rules; there is no legislation," said Arthur Wisot, the executive director of the Center for Advanced Reproductive Care in Redondo Beach, California. "This whole area of medicine is totally unregulated. We don't answer to anyone but our peers."

Nearly every year, the fertility clinics would take another step. Recently, they began advertising something they called intercytoplasmic sperm injection, or I.C.S.I., in which they could get usable sperm even from men who seemed to make none, or whose sperm cells were misshapen or immotile and simply unable to fertilize an egg. The scientists would insert a needle into a man's testicle and remove immature sperm, which were little more than raw genes. They would inject these nascent sperm into an egg to create an embryo. Medical scientists later discovered that many of these men had such feeble sperm because the genes that controlled their sperm production were mutated. When the sperm, carrying the mutated gene, were used to make a baby boy, the boy would grow up with the same mutations and he, too, would need I.C.S.I. to have a baby. Some scientists worried that there might be other consequences of such a mutation.

But the infertility doctors and many infertile couples were unconcerned by the possibility that this technique might be less of an unqualified boon than it at first appeared. And the I.C.S.I. advertisements continued unabated.

Infertility doctors also learned to snip a cell from a microscopic embryo and analyze it for genetic defects, selecting only healthy embryos to implant in a woman's womb. They learned that there is no age barrier to pregnancy: Women who had passed the age of menopause could still carry a baby if they used eggs from a younger woman, fertilized in a laboratory. Even women in their early sixties have gotten pregnant, and while some doctors have said they do not want to participate in creating such pregnancies, others say that it is really up to the women whether they want to become mothers at such an advanced age.

Infertility clinics are even learning to do the ultimate prenatal testing: fishing fetal cells out of a pregnant woman's blood and analyzing them for genetic defects. It is, said Tendler, "the perfect child syndrome. We can now take 5 cc of a woman's blood when she is seven to nine weeks pregnant, do 191 genetic probes on that cell, and decide whether that baby is going to make it or not."

The latest development involves methods to sort sperm, separating   45
those sperm with Y chromosomes, which would create boys, from those with X chromosomes, which would create girls. Soon parents can have the ultimate control over the sex of their babies.

At the same time, molecular biologists learned to snip genes out of cells and to sew others in, engineering cells to order. Infertility clinics expect, before long, to be able to add genes to human embryos—or delete genes that could cause disease or disability—creating a perfect child before even implanting an embryo into a woman's womb.

At first, the feats of reproductive scientists were the objects of controversy and shock. But we have become accustomed to their achievements. And it is hard to argue against the cries that couples have a right to reproductive freedom. Many have suffered for years, yearning for a child of their own. If they want to create babies, and are paying with their own money, who has the right to tell them no?

These days, when infertility doctors introduce a new method to the public, or when their techniques disrupt what we have thought of as the natural order, there is, at first, a ripple of surprise, or sometimes dismay, but then that reaction fades and all we remember is that there seemed to be reports of one more incredible technological trick.

Even newspapers are becoming blasé. One Sunday in April, about six weeks after the cloning of Dolly was announced. I was attending a meeting of a federal commission that was assessing cloning. I crept out of the meeting to call a national news editor at *The New York Times* and inform him of the meeting's progress. He said there was something else he wanted to ask me about. There was a story out of Florida, he said, about a woman who just gave birth to her own grandchild. Was that news, he asked me?

50   I assured him that it was not news. Several years ago, another woman had done the same thing, and we'd reported it on page 1. The woman's daughter had been born with ovaries but not a uterus, so the mother carried the baby for the daughter. That story had come and gone, no longer even worth a raised eyebrow.

So when Dolly was born, in this age of ever-more-disarming scientific advances, some worried that her birth might be greeted with a brief shiver, then forgotten, like the woman who gave birth to her own grandchild. Leon Kass, a biochemist turned philosopher, at the University of Chicago, warned that to react as though cloning were just another infertility treatment would be to miss the point of Dolly. He worried that we may be too jaded by previous triumphs of technological wizardry to take cloning as seriously as we should. He quoted Raskolnikov, the protagonist of Fyodor Dostoyevsky's *Crime and Punishment:* "Man gets used to everything—the beast."

It is true, of course, that the revolution in infertility treatments set the stage for people to think about cloning a human. Were it not for the proficiency of doctors in manipulating human eggs and sperm, it would not be feasible to even think of transferring the chromosomes of an adult cell into a human egg. But there is an intellectual chasm between methods that result in a baby with half its genes from the mother and half from the father and cloning, which would result in a baby whose genes are identical to those of an adult who was cloned.

Human cloning, Kass said, would be "something radically new, both in itself and in its easily foreseeable consequences. The stakes here are very high indeed." Until now "we have benefited mightily from the attitude, let technology go where it will and we can fix any problems that might arise later." But, he said, "that paradigm is open to question." Now we are "threatened with really major changes in human life, even human nature." And even if an absolute prohibition on cloning cannot be made effective, "it would at least place the burden on the other side to show the necessity" of taking this awesome step.

What is at issue, Kass said, "is nothing less than whether human procreation is going to remain human, whether children are going to be made rather than begotten, and whether it is a good thing, humanly speaking, to say yes to the road which leads, at best, to the dehumanized rationality of *Brave New World.*" And so "What we have here is not business as usual, to be fretted about for a while and then given our seal of approval, not least because it appears to be unusual." Instead, he said, "the future of humanity may hang in the balance."

55   The cloning debate, Kass said, is so much more than just an argument about one more step in assisted reproduction. "This is really one of those critical moments where one gets a chance to think about terribly important things. Not just genetics and what is the meaning of mother and

father and kinship, but also the whole relationship between science and society and attitudes toward technology." Cloning, he said, "provides the occasion as well as the urgent necessity of deciding whether we shall be slaves of unregulated progress and ultimately its artifacts or whether we shall remain free human beings to guide our technique towards the enhancement of human dignity."

He quoted the theologian Paul Ramsey: "Raise the ethical questions with a serious and not a frivolous conscience. A man of frivolous conscience announces that there are ethical quandaries ahead that we must urgently consider before the future catches up with us. By this he often means that we need to devise a new ethics that will provide the rationalization for doing in the future what men are bound to do because of the new actions and interventions science will have made possible. In contrast, a man of serious conscience means to say in raising urgent ethical questions that there may be some things that men should never do. The good things that men do can be made complete only by the things they refuse to do."

Yet if there is one lesson of cloning it is that there is no uniformly accepted way to think about the ethical questions that it elicits, and no agreement, even among the most thoughtful and well-informed commentators, about what is right and what is wrong. Many—but by no means all—theologians tended to condemn the notion of human cloning. Many ethicists were similarly repelled, but others asked instead, who would be harmed, and why are we so sure that harm would ensue? While theologians cited religious traditions and biblical proscriptions, lawyers cited reproductive rights and said it would be very hard to argue that it was illegal to clone oneself. In the meantime, some ethicists said they'd heard from in vitro fertilization clinics, which—operating already outside the usual rules that bind scientists, and looking for paying customers—were extremely interested in investigating cloning.

The diversity of opinions extended even to interpretations of identical passages from the Bible. One priest and Catholic theologian argued from Genesis that cloning would be against God's will. An orthodox rabbi and theologian argued from the same passage that cloning should not be proscribed.

The priest, Albert Moraczewski, of the National Conference of Catholic Bishops, was invited to explain the Catholic point of view by a presidential commission that was asked to make recommendations on whether cloning should be permitted. He began by saying that the cloning of humans would be an affront to human dignity. Then he spoke of the familiar story of Adam and Eve, told in the Book of Genesis, in which God gave humans dominion "over the creatures that swim in the sea, that fly in the air, or that walk the earth." And he spoke of God's order. "The Lord God gave man this order: 'You are free to eat from any of the trees of the garden except the tree of knowledge of good and bad.' "

Moraczewski explained that according to the Catholic interpretation,   60
"Adam and Eve were given freedom in the garden but with one limitation, which if transgressed would lead to death. Accordingly, human beings have

been granted intelligence and free will so that human beings can search for, and recognize, the truth and freely pursue the good."

Cloning, he said, would exceed "the limits of the delegated dominion given to the human race. There is no evidence that humans were given the power to alter their nature or the manner in which they come into existence."

He added that couples who clone a child would be dehumanizing the act of procreating and treating their child as an object, attempting to "design and control the very identity of the child."

Moraczewski concluded by quoting John Paul II: "The biological nature of every person is untouchable."

The next day, Moshe Tendler, an Orthodox Jewish rabbi, spoke to the commission. He, too, started with Genesis, and with the same quotation. But his interpretation of it, from the Jewish tradition, was very different.

65   "This knowledge of good and evil has always confused theologians and certainly the layman," Tendler said. "If Adam and Eve did not know of good and evil, how could they have sinned? They knew good and evil. The tree of good and evil is the tree that allows you to think that you can reevaluate, you can set another yardstick for what is good and what is evil."

The Jewish tradition says that humans are obliged to help master our world, according to Tendler, as long as they do not transgress into areas where they would attempt to contravene God. It would not be in character with the Jewish tradition to have a technology that could have outcomes that are good—like preserving the family line of a Holocaust survivor who had no other living relatives—and decide, ahead of time, not to use it for fear of its evil consequences. "We are bound by good and evil as given to us by divine imperative. And we knew pretty well in most areas what is good and what is evil until cloning came along and now we are not so sure what is good and what is evil.

"So, cloning, it is not intrinsically good or evil," Tendler said. The question, really, is whether particular applications of cloning might be a transgression by humans into the domain of God.

"I will give you a simile or metaphor of a guest invited to your house," Tendler said. "You ask them to be comfortable, help themselves, there is cake in the cake box and fruits in the refrigerator, and coffee in the coffeemaker." When you wake up, he continued, you're pleased to see that your guest did as you suggested. "But if he should move your sofa to the other side of the wall because he thought that that is where it really belongs, you will not invite him again."

God, Tendler added, says, "Make yourselves comfortable in my world, but you are guests in my house, do not act as if you own the place. Don't you rearrange my furniture."

70   He spoke also of a metaphor from the Talmud. "The question was posed, 'Is there not a time when you say to the bee, neither your honey nor your sting?' And so, he asked, are we really prepared to ban cloning, to give up the honey, because we are so afraid of the sting?

On the other hand, some wonder whether we might not want to squash the bee. Nancy Duff, a theologian at the Princeton Theological Seminary, argued from Protestant tradition that, at the very least, all thoughts of human cloning should be put on hold. "Many people wonder if this is a miracle for which we can thank God, or an ominous new way to play God ourselves," she said. "At the very least, it represents the ongoing tension between faith and science."

But there is also a secular point of view, one that asks how persuasive, after all, are the hypothetical harms of cloning, and whether they are great enough to override the right that people have to reproductive freedom. John Robertson, a law professor at the University of Texas in Austin, who specializes in ethics and reproductive law, said he is unconvinced by those who argue that cloning is somehow too unnatural, too repugnant, too contrary to the laws of God, to proceed with. "In assessing harm, deviation from traditional methods of reproduction, including genetic selection of offspring characteristics, is not in itself a compelling reason for restriction when tangible harm to others is nor present." He argued that cloning is not significantly different from other methods our society now accepts as ethical, and which are now being actively studied in research laboratories throughout the world. He referred to methods for adding genes or correcting faulty ones, in an attempt to cure diseases like muscular dystrophy or cystic fibrosis, which, although not yet possible, is expected to occur before too long.

"Cloning enables a child with the genome of another embryo or person to be born," Robertson said. "The genome is taken as it is. Genetic alteration, on the other hand, will change the genome of a person who could have been born with their genome intact." So what is the greater intervention? Given a choice of a child who is a clone or no child at all—a choice that could befall infertile couples—how bad is it to allow them to have a clone? Robertson asked. "If a loving family will rear the child, it is difficult to see why cloning for genetic selection is per se unacceptable."

A compelling argument, said Daniel Brock, a philosopher and ethicist at Brown University, is the right to clone part of our right to reproductive freedom? he asked. He said that although he is not certain that cloning could be protected in this way because it is not, strictly speaking, reproduction, it might nonetheless fall into that broad category. And, he added, if the right to have yourself cloned is treated as a reproductive right, "that creates the presumption that it should be available to people who want to use it without government control."

Brock, for one, thinks that the public reaction to cloning is overblown. "The various harms are usually speculative," he said. "It is difficult to make the claim that these harms are serious enough and well-enough established to justify overriding the claim that cloning should be available." The public, he said, "has a tendency to want to leap ahead to possibilities that we're not even sure are possible."

Ruth Macklin, an ethicist at Albert Einstein College of Medicine, raised similar questions about whether fears of cloning are reasonable. "One incontestable ethical requirement is that no adult person should be cloned without his or her consent," Macklin said. "But if adult persons sought to have themselves cloned, would the resulting individual be harmed by being brought into existence in this way? One harm that some envisage is psychological or emotional distress to a person who is an exact replica of another. Some commentators have elevated this imagined harm to the level of a right: the right to control our own individual genetic identity. But it is not at all clear why the deliberate creation of an individual who is genetically identical to another living being (but separated in time) would violate anyone's rights."

After all, Macklin said, if the cloned person was not created from the cell of another, he or she would not have been born. Is it really better never to have existed than to exist as a clone? "Evidence, not mere surmise, is required to conclude that the psychological burdens of knowing that one was cloned would be of such magnitude that they would outweigh the benefits of life itself."

Macklin even took on those who argued that cloning violates human dignity. Those who hold that view, she said, "owe us a more precise account of just what constitutes a violation of human dignity if no individuals are harmed and no one's rights are violated. Dignity is a fuzzy concept and appeals to dignity are often used to substitute for empirical evidence that is lacking or sound arguments that cannot be mustered."

Kass argued, however, that such utterly pragmatic language obscures the moral significance of what is being contemplated. He quoted Bertrand Russell: "Pragmatism is like that warm bath that heats up so imperceptibly that you don't know when to scream."

80   The clashing viewpoints, said Ezekiel J. Emanuel, a doctor and ethicist at the Dana-Farber Cancer Institute in Boston, who was a member of the president's commission that was studying cloning, seem to indicate "a moral values gap." And so, he added, how people react to cloning "depends a lot on one's world outlook, as it were. How much you might weigh these other values depends a lot on how you understand yourself and your place in the world."

And that, in the end, is what cloning brings to the fore. Cloning is a metaphor and a mirror. It allows us to look at ourselves and our values and to decide what is important to us, and why.

It also reflects the place of science in our world. Do we see science as a threat or a promise? Are scientists sages or villains? Have scientists changed over the years from natural philosophers to technologists focused on the next trick that can be played on nature?

Freud once said that, sometimes, a cigar is just a cigar. But so far, we have not reached a point where a clone is just a clone. As the social and cultural history of cloning continues, the questions and the insights into who we are, who we are becoming, and who we want to be grow ever deeper. Dolly, it now seems, is more a beginning than an end.

READING CRITICALLY FOR IDEAS, STRUCTURE, AND STYLE

1. How has the new technology of cloning required ethicists, theologians, and social planners to answer age-old questions about the meaning and value of human life and new questions about a clone's civil rights and entitlements (for example, should your clone be able to share your social security benefits)?

2. Is Kolata's attitude toward cloning self-evident? Can you infer it from the way in which she describes the controversy?

3. What aspects of Kolata's discussion address the issue as to why people should not have the right to clone themselves? In your opinion, is the right to clone oneself part of the right to reproductive freedom? Explain your answer.

EXTENDING INSIGHTS THROUGH WRITING

1. If you had a choice of being cloned, would you? Why or why not?

2. Couples have had a child in order to serve as a bone-marrow doner for another of their children, who otherwise would die. Why, in principle, would this be different from creating a clone for the purpose of harvesting tissues and organs to be used by the donor? Explain your answer.

CONNECTING PERSPECTIVES ON THE NATURAL WORLD

1. How would "natural selection," as Darwin states it in "The Origin of Species," operate if the practice of cloning was widely adopted? What variations "useful to any organic being" could ever emerge?

2. Discuss how the ability to clone humans as organ banks, as described by Gina Kolata, raises many of the same ethical issues that Hans Ruesch explores in "Slaughter of the Innocent."

BOOK CONNECTIONS FOR CHAPTER 4

1. In what ways do the accounts by Hasler and Larsen and Sir Leonard Woolley (see "The Flood" in Chapter 5) illustrate how theories are formulated and tested in different disciplines?

2. In what ways did Thomas Robert Malthus's theory (see "The Principle of Population" in Chapter 2) about the relationship between population and food supply lead Darwin to understand how "natural selection" works?

3. In what respects might the ability to repress unpleasant feelings and thoughts, as described by Sigmund Freud (see "Typical Dreams" in Chapter 6), play a comparable role as a survival mechanism as does the inhibition against killing (in some species) described by Lorenz?

4. Discuss how both Fabre and Blaise Pascal (in "The Two Infinites" in Chapter 5) use the concept of scale in perception to explain their subjects.

5. In what way are many of the less desirable human traits Twain satirizes also the object of spiritual purification as described by Buddha (see "The Enlightenment of the Buddha: Buddhacarita" in Chapter 6)?

6. Compare the attitude towards animals subjected to experiments that Ruesch condemns with the assumptions of whalers that were challenged as reported by Nathaniel Philbrick in "The Attack" in Chapter 5.

7. In what respect does the research on twins reported by Holden challenge Jean Paul Sartre's assumption that people are free to shape their own destinies (see "Existentialism" in Chapter 6)?

8. Evaluate the forces that make it possible for us to acquire language, as discussed by Ridley, with those that shape the evolution of language as described by Paul Roberts in "Something About English" in Chapter 7.

9. Discuss some of the interesting theological issues raised by cloning (for example, where does the clone's soul come from?) as reported by Kolata in relation to St. Matthew's "Parables in *The New Testament*" (in Chapter 6) which presupposes a soul that can be "saved."

CHAPTER 5

THE PHYSICAL UNIVERSE:
Knowledge of Animate and Inanimate Worlds

INTRODUCTION

In this chapter we encounter different aspects of the physical universe in ways that shed light on the basic elements of the ocean, the Earth and its place in the universe, and world-altering applications of technology.

We begin with four very different perspectives on the impact of the ocean on various aspects of human life from biblical times to the present. We first discover that, according to the noted archeologist Sir Leonard Woolley, the biblical flood described in Genesis may not have been a universal deluge but rather a local flood within the valley of the Tigris and Euphrates's rivers. Then, Dava Sobel moves us to the eighteenth century, where the problem of measuring longitude accurately engaged the imagination of the best scientific minds of the era, but was solved by a self-educated clockmaker. Nathaniel Philbrick's account takes us to the early nineteenth century and tells the true story of the destruction of the *Essex* by a giant whale, an event that was retold by Herman Melville in his classic novel, *Moby Dick*. In the twentieth century, the famous Norwegian explorer, Thor Heyerdahl, undertook a series of voyages on his rafts, the *Kon-Tiki* and the *Ra I* and *Ra II*, that not only showed how ancient peoples could have migrated over vast distances, but revealed a hitherto unsuspected danger of ocean pollution. These first four selections tell a story of the timeless conflict between humanity and the sea and the changing conceptions of the ocean, as a mythic force, as a wily antagonist, as a realm to be exploited and finally, as an indispensable resource to be protected.

The next group of readings examine the changing conceptions of physicists and philosophers about the Earth and its place in the universe. The astrobiologists Peter D. Ward and Donald Brownlee correct the popular assumption that advanced forms of life are common throughout the universe by arguing that the rare set of circumstances that make complex life possible exist only on Earth. At the dawn of modern science, in the sixteenth century, philosopher and mathematician Blaise Pascal asks us to consider the place of human life admidst the infinity of universes visible in the night sky and the world of creatures visible only under the microscope. Pascal thereby sets the stage for the two directions modern physics has taken—the infinitely small world of subatomic particles and the macrocosmic sphere of galaxies—the subject of Sir Fred Hoyle's intriguing analysis of an ever-expanding universe. The common theme that threads its way through these three readings is the enduring question of how we can best know the universe and, more importantly, understand the place of human life between the vast extremes of the macrocosmic and microcosmic realms.

The last group of readings, by Charles H. Townes, Christopher Evans, Neil Postman, and Bill Gates, addresses the profound impact of technology and the information revolution on our lives. Knowledge of the physical universe in our culture is invariably pursued less for its own sake than for the ways it can be put into practice. Townes applied Einstein's theoretical insights to invent the laser, arguably one of the most important technological discoveries of our age, that has literally transformed almost every conceivable aspect of modern culture. Along with the laser, the computer also has had a monumental impact on every facet of our lives. Evans, who wrote in 1980, was something of a prophet in his praise of the microprocessor and defined our age as the "micromillennium"—which it certainly has become. The last two selections, by Neil Postman and Bill Gates, when taken together, offer a valuable dialogue on the real uses and meaning of such unlimited access to information made possible by the computer. Postman points out that the cult of information for its own sake is a relatively new phenomenon and recommends we recover the insights of important eighteenth-century thinkers and the spirit of the Enlightenment. Gates, by contrast, looks forward to a future where the computer will be an absolutely integral feature of work, leisure, education, and every other aspect of twenty-first century Western Culture.

SIR LEONARD WOOLLEY

The Flood

BACKGROUND

Sir Leonard Woolley (1880–1960) was born in London, England. He was educated at New College, Oxford, and was an assistant to Sir Arthur Evans at the Ashmolean Museum in 1905. After a period of field work in the Near East, Woolley was appointed director of the British Museum expedition to Carchemish in 1912. He was accompanied there by T. E. Lawrence (known as "Lawrence of Arabia"), with whom he co-authored *The Wilderness of Zin* (1915), an account of their discoveries. After directing a joint expedition of the British Museum and the Museum of the University of Pennsylvania, Woolley, in 1926, discovered and excavated the royal tombs at Ur, whose treasures invited comparisons with the discoveries by Schliemann (at Mycenae) and those of Howard Carter and Lord Carnarvon (of Tutankhamen's Tomb). Woolley's excavations at Ur reveal the existence and importance of Sumerian culture in Mesopotamia. His remarkably clear and readable accounts of his archeological discoveries were published in *Ur of the Chaldees* (1929), *The Sumerians* (1930), and *Excavations at Ur: A Record of Twelve Years Work* (1954). In "The Flood," from *Myth or Legend* (1968), Woolley describes the ingenious method he used to solve the problem of what actually occurred during the flood described in the Old Testament.

APPROACHING WOOLLEY'S ESSAY

Woolley first provides historical background into the story of the biblical flood, defines the archeological problem he was attempting to solve, and relates the procedures he uses to conduct his excavations. Woolley had compared the various texts of fables and legends to determine which elements contained in these stories agreed with each other. Woolley assumed that the truth lay in those portions of the stories that shared common elements, since these similarities remained constant through the various retellings of the flood story in the literatures of many cultures. He then describes his dig at Ur, which had been a flourishing city on the banks of the Euphrates in 3500 B.C. Previous archeological excavations in Mesopotamia had turned up tablets, which contained a Sumerian version of the flood story, which led Woolley to believe that the flood was actually an overflow of the Tigris and Euphrates rivers about 3200 B.C. that covered Sumerian villages over a large area.

Woolley's account shows a remarkable detective at work, whose findings offered an entirely new perspective on the ancient story from Genesis. His methods illustrate those used by scientists who express problems in the form of hypotheses and test them by empirical means. Moreover, the rhetorical structure of his essay follows a problem-solving format where the solution to the problem must take into account all the pertinent data his search has uncovered.

The Flood

There can be few stories more familiar to us than that of the Flood. The word "antediluvian" has passed into common speech, and Noah's Ark is still one of the favourite toys of the children's nursery.

The Book of Genesis tells us how the wickedness of man was such that God repented Him that He had made man upon the earth, and decided to destroy all flesh; but Noah, being the one righteous man, found grace in the eyes of the Lord. So Noah was bidden by God to build an ark, and in due time he and all his family went in, with all the beasts and the fowls of the air, going in two by two; and the doors of the ark were shut and the rain was upon the earth for forty days and forty nights, and the floods prevailed exceedingly and the earth was covered, and all flesh that moved upon the earth died, and Noah only remained alive and they that were with him in the ark. And then the floods abated. Noah sent out a raven and a dove, and at last the dove brought him back an olive leaf, proof that the dry land had appeared. And they all went forth out of the ark, and Noah built an altar and offered sacrifice, and the Lord smelt a sweet savour and promised that never again would He smite everything living, as He had done; and God set His bow in the clouds as a token of the covenant that there should not any more be a flood to destroy the earth.

For many centuries, indeed until only a few generations ago, the story of Noah was accepted as an historical fact; it was part of the Bible, it was the inspired Word of God, and therefore every word of it must be true. To deny the story was to deny the Christian faith.

Then two things happened. On the one hand scholars, examining the Hebrew text of Genesis, discovered that it was a composite narrative. There had been two versions of the Flood story which differed in certain small respects, and these two had been skillfully combined into one by the Jewish scribes four or five hundred years before the time of Christ, when they edited the sacred books of their people and gave to them the form which they have to-day. That discovery shook the faith of many old-fashioned believers, or was indignantly denied by them; they said that it was an attack on the Divine Word. Really, of course, it was nothing of the sort. Genesis is an historical book, and the writer of history does not weave the matter out of his imagination; he consults older authorities of every sort and quotes them as freely and as often as may be. The older the authorities are, and the more his account embodies theirs, the more reason we have to trust what he writes; if it be insisted that his writings are divinely inspired, the answer is that 'inspiration' consists not in dispensing with original sources but in making the right use of them. The alarm felt by the orthodox when confronted with the discoveries of scholarship was a false alarm.

The second shock came when from the ruins of the ancient cities of Mesopotamia archaeologists unearthed clay tablets on which was written another version of the Flood story—the Sumerian version. According to that, mankind had grown wicked and the gods in council decided to destroy the human race which they had made. But one of the gods happened to be a good friend of one mortal man, so he went down and warned him of what was to happen and counselled him to build an ark. And the man did so; and he took on board all his family, and his domestic animals, and shut the door, and the rain fell and the floods rose and covered all the earth. At last the storms abated and the ark ran aground, and the man sent out a dove and a swallow and a raven, and finally came forth from the ark and built an altar and did sacrifice, and the gods (who had had no food since the Flood started and were terribly hungry) "came round the altar like flies," and the rainbow is set in the clouds as a warrant that never again will the gods destroy all men by water.

It is clear that this is the same story as we have in Genesis. But the Sumerian account was actually written before the time of Moses (whom some people had, without reason, thought to be the author of Genesis), and not only that, but before the time of Abraham. Therefore the Flood story was not by origin a Hebrew story at all but had been taken over by the Hebrews from the idolatrous folk of Babylonia; it was a pagan legend, so why should we for a moment suppose that it was true? All sorts of attempts were made to show that the Bible story was independent, or was the older of the two, but all the attempts were in vain, and to some it seemed as if the battle for the Old Testament had been lost.

Once more, it was a false alarm. Nobody had ever supposed that the Flood had affected only the Hebrew people; other people had suffered by it, and a disaster of such magnitude was bound to be remembered in their traditions; in so far as the Sumerian legend was closer in time to the event, it might be said to strengthen rather than to weaken the case for the Biblical version. But it could well be asked, "Why should we believe a Sumerian legend which is, on the face of it, a fantastic piece of pagan mythology?" It is perfectly true that the Sumerian Flood story is a religious poem. It reflects the religious beliefs of a pagan people just as the biblical story reflects the religious beliefs of the Hebrews; and we cannot accept the Sumerian religion as true. Also, it is a poem, and everybody knows what poets are! Shakespeare certainly did:

> The poet's eye, in a fine frenzy rolling,
> Doth glance from heaven to earth, from earth to heaven,
> And, as imagination bodies forth
> The forms of things unknown, the poet's pen
> Turns them to shapes, and gives to airy nothing
> A local habitation and a name.

But the legend does not stand alone. Sober Sumerian historians wrote down a sort of skeleton of their country's history in the form of a list of its kings (like our "William I, 1066," and all that); starting at the very beginning there is a series of perhaps fabulous rulers, and, they say, "Then came the Flood. And after the Flood kingship again descended from heaven"; and they speak of a dynasty of kings who established themselves in the city of Kish, and next of a dynasty whose capital was Erech. Here, at least, we are upon historic ground, for archaeological excavation in modern times has recovered the material civilisation of those ancient days when Erech was indeed the chief city of Mesopotamia. The old historians were sure that not long before these days the course of their country's history had been interrupted by a great flood. If they were right, it does not, of course, mean that the Flood legend is correct in all its details, but it does at least give it a basis of fact.

In the year 1929, when we had been digging at Ur the famous "royal graves" with their extraordinary treasures, which can be dated to something like 2800 B.C., I determined to test still lower levels so as to get an idea of what might be found by digging yet deeper. We sank a small shaft below the stratum of soil in which the graves lay, and went down through the mixed rubbish that is characteristic of an old inhabited site—a mixture of decomposed mud-brick, ashes and broken pottery, very much like what we had been finding higher up. Then suddenly it all stopped: there were no more potsherds, no ashes, only clean, water-laid mud, and the workman in the shaft told me that he had reached virgin soil; there was nothing more to be found, and he had better go elsewhere.

I got down and looked at the evidence and agreed with him; but then I took my levels and found that "virgin soil" was not nearly as deep down as I expected. That upset a favourite theory of mine, and I hate having my theories upset except on the very best of evidence, so I told him to get back and go on digging. Most unwillingly he did so, turning up nothing but clean soil that contained no sign of human activity; he worked down through eight feet of it and then, suddenly, flint implements appeared and sherds of painted pottery which, we were fairly sure, was the earliest pottery made in southern Mesopotamia. I was convinced of what it meant, but I wanted to see whether others would arrive at the same conclusion. I brought up two of my staff and, after pointing out the facts, asked for their conclusions. They did not know what to say. My wife came along and looked and was asked the same question, and she turned away, remarking quite casually, "Well, of course it's the Flood."

So it was. But one could scarcely argue for the Deluge on the strength of a shaft a yard square; so the next season I marked out on the low ground where the graves had been a rectangle some seventy-five feet by sixty, and there dug a huge pit which went down, in the end, for sixty-four feet. The level at which we started had been the ground surface about 2600 B.C. Almost immediately we came on the ruins of houses slightly older than that; we cleared them away and found more houses below them. In the first twenty feet we dug through no fewer than eight sets of houses, each of which had been built over the ruins of the age before. Then the house ruins stopped and we were digging through a solid mass of potsherds wherein, at different levels, were the kilns in which the pots had been fired; the sherds represented those pots which went wrong in the firing and, having no commercial value, had been smashed by the potter and the bits left lying until they were so heaped up that the kilns were buried and new kilns had to be built. It was a vase factory which was running for so long a time that by the stratified sherds we could trace the course of history: near the bottom came the wares in use when Erech was the royal city, and at the very bottom was the painted ware of the land's earliest immigrants. And then came the clean, water-laid mud, eleven feet of it, mud which on analysis proved to be the silt brought down by the River Euphrates from its upper reaches hundreds of miles away; and under the silt, based on what really was virgin soil, the ruins of the houses that had been overwhelmed by the flood and buried deep beneath the mud carried by its waters.

This was the evidence we needed; a flood of magnitude unparalleled in any later phase of Mesopotamian history; and since, as the pottery proved, it had taken place some little while before the time of the Erech dynasty, this was the Flood of the Sumerian king-lists and that of the Sumerian legend and that of Genesis.

We have proved that the Flood really happened; but that does not mean that all the details of the Flood legend are true—we did not find Noah and we did not find his ark! But take a few details. The Sumerian version says (this is not mentioned in Genesis) that antediluvian man lived in huts made of reeds; under the Flood deposit we found the wreckage of reed huts. Noah built his ark of light wood and bitumen. Just on top of the Flood deposit we found a big lump of bitumen, bearing the imprint of the basket in which it had been carried, just as I have myself seen the crude bitumen from the pits of Hit on the middle Euphrates being put in baskets for export downstream. I reckoned that to throw up an eleven-foot pile of silt against the mound on which the primitive town of Ur stood the water would have to be at least twenty-five feet deep; the account in Genesis says that the depth of the flood water was fifteen cubits, which is roughly twenty-six feet. "Twenty-six feet?" you may say; "that's not much of a flood!" Lower Mesopotamia is so flat and low-lying that a flood having that depth at Ur would spread over an area 300 miles long and 100 miles wide.

Noah's Flood was not a universal deluge; it was a vast flood in the valley of the Rivers Tigris and Euphrates. It drowned the whole of the habitable land between the eastern and the western deserts; for the people who lived there that was all the world. It wiped out the villages and exterminated their inhabitants, and although some of the towns set upon mounds survived, it was but a scanty and dispirited remnant of the nation that watched the waters recede at last. No wonder that they saw in this disaster the gods' punishment of a sinful generation and described it as such in a great religious poem; and if, as may well have been the case, one household managed to escape by boat from the drowned lowlands, the head of that house would naturally be made the hero of the saga.

READING CRITICALLY FOR IDEAS, STRUCTURE, AND STYLE

1. What hypothesis did Woolley seek to prove? How would this hypothesis, if proven and accepted, change the prevailing beliefs about the biblical flood?

2. What procedures did Woolley use to conduct the archeological excavations? Why was the location of the pottery kilns, testing of silt, and the discovery of bitumen so important in providing pieces of the puzzle Woolley was trying to solve?

3. What did Woolley conclude, based on his excavations, about the story of the flood as related in the Bible and in ancient Sumarian texts?

EXTENDING INSIGHTS THROUGH WRITING

1. Read the biblical account of Noah and the flood in Genesis, Chapter 6–8 and discuss how Woolley's account offers a twentieth-century conjecture on this ancient legend. What new light did Woolley's research shed on the biblical account?

2. What would archeologists of the future conclude about our civilization if they unearthed and analyzed any of today's mass-produced artifacts, such as television sets, microwave ovens, or computers?

CONNECTING PERSPECTIVES ON THE PHYSICAL UNIVERSE

1. How do Woolley and Thor Heyerdahl (in "How to Kill an Ocean"), as scientists, challenge us to rethink our conceptions of the universal nature of the biblical flood and the boundless ocean?

2. How do Woolley and Fred Hoyle in "The Continuous Creation of the Universe" use the tools of science to address issues of religious belief, namely, the biblical flood and the Creation?

DAVA SOBEL

The Prize

BACKGROUND

Dava Sobel was born in 1947 in New York City and educated at the State University of New York at Binghamton. Sobel is an award-winning science reporter for *The New York Times* who has also written numerous articles for *Astronomy, Audubon, Discover,* and *Harvard* magazines, among others. The two books for which she is best known, *Longitude: The True Story of a Lone Genius Who Solved the Greatest Scientific Problem of His Time* (1995), and *Galileo's Daughter: A Historical Memoir of Science, Faith and Love* (1999), retrieve figures lost in obscurity and alert us to their significant contributions to the world of science. These books became best sellers and, in 1999, she received *The Los Angeles Times* Book Award for Science and Technology for *Galileo's Daughter.*

Longtitude in which the following chapter first appeared, has been translated into twenty-two languages and was adapted for television as a PBS special in 2001.

APPROACHING SOBEL'S ESSAY

In 1714, England's Parliament offered a prize of twenty thousand pounds (the equivalent of several million dollars today) to anyone who could solve the problem of measuring longitude correctly. A sea-worthy clock by which sailors could determine longitude had to withstand the vicissitudes of changes in climate and humidity to prevent them from sailing off-course, or even perishing at sea, because they were unable to calculate locations of land and thus, their destinations. In this chapter ("The Prize") Sobel describes how the scientific establishment, including Sir Isaac Newton and Edmund Halley (the astronomer who was the first to predict the return of a comet, now named for him), and scores of hopefuls unsuccessfully tackled the problem. The unlikely winner of the prize was John Harrison (the "lone genius" referred to in the subtitle of Sobel's book), a self-educated clockmaker who devoted more than forty-six years of his life to constructing clocks that were weather and motion-proof. Harrison not only figured out how to measure longitude, but, as an outsider, had to overcome the class prejudices of the establishment toward someone of his social position. Sobel's remarkable ability to involve her readers in such an esoteric subject and to explain technical matters so clearly is amply demonstrated in the following chapter from her book.

The Prize

Her cutty sark, o' Paisley harn,
That while a lassie she had worn,
In longitude tho' sorely scanty,
It was her best, and she was vauntie.
— *Robert Burns, "Tam o'Shanter"*

The merchants' and seamen's petition pressing for action on the matter of longitude arrived at Westminster Palace in May of 1714. In June a Parliamentary committee assembled to respond to its challenge.

Under orders to act quickly, the committee members sought expert advice from Sir Isaac Newton; by then a grand old man of seventy-two, and his friend Edmond Halley. Halley had gone to the island of St. Helena some years earlier to map the stars of the southern hemisphere—virtually virgin territory on the landscape of the night. Halley's published catalog of more than three hundred southern stars had won him election to the Royal Society. He had also traveled far and wide to measure magnetic variation, so he was well versed in longitude lore—and personally immersed in the quest.

Newton prepared written remarks for the committee members, which he read aloud to them, and also answered their questions, despite his "mental fatigue" that day. He summarized the existing means for determining longitude, saying that all of them were true in theory but "difficult to execute." This was of course a gross understatement. Here, for example, is Newton's description of the timekeeper approach:

"One [method] is by a Watch to keep time exactly. But, by reason of the motion of the Ship, the Variation of Heat and Cold, Wet and Dry, and the Difference of Gravity in different Latitudes, such a watch hath not yet been made." And not likely to be, either, he implied.

Perhaps Newton mentioned the watch first so as to set it up as a straw man, before proceeding to the somewhat more promising though still problematic field of astronomical solutions. He mentioned the eclipses of Jupiter's satellites, which worked on land, at any rate, though they left mariners in the lurch. Other astronomical methods, he said, counted on the predicted disappearances of known stars behind our own moon, or on the timed observations of lunar and solar eclipses. He also cited the grandiose "lunar distance" plan for divining longitude by measuring the distance between the moon and sun by day, between the moon and stars at night. (Even as Newton spoke, Flamsteed was giving himself a migraine at the Royal Observatory, trying to ascertain stellar positions as the basis for this much-vaunted method.)

The longitude committee incorporated Newton's testimony in its official report. The document did not favor one approach over another, or even British genius over foreign ingenuity. It simply urged Parliament to welcome potential solutions from any field of science or art, put forth by individuals or groups of any nationality, and to reward success handsomely.

The actual Longitude Act, issued in the reign of Queen Anne on July 8, 1714, did all these things. On the subject of prize money, it named first-, second-, and third-prize amounts, as follows:

£20,000 (the equivalent of millions of dollars today) for a method to determine longitude to an accuracy of half a degree of a great circle;

£15,000 for a method accurate to within two-thirds of a degree;

£10,000 for a method accurate to within one degree.

Since one degree of longitude spans sixty nautical miles (the equivalent of sixty-eight geographical miles) over the surface of the globe at the Equator, even a fraction of a degree translates into a large distance—and consequently a great margin of error when trying to determine the whereabouts of a ship vis-à-vis its destination. The fact that the government was willing to award such huge sums for "Practicable and Useful" methods that could miss the mark by many miles eloquently expresses the nation's desperation over navigation's sorry state.

The Longitude Act established a blue ribbon panel of judges that became known as the Board of Longitude. This board, which consisted of scientists, naval officers, and government officials, exercised sole discretion over the distribution of the prize money. The astronomer royal served as an ex-officio member, as did the president of the Royal Society, the first lord of the Admiralty, the speaker of the House of Commons, the first commissioner of the Navy, and the Savilian, Lucasian, and Plumian professors of mathematics at Oxford and Cambridge Universities. (Newton, a Cambridge man, had held the Lucasian professorship for thirty years; in 1714 he was president of the Royal Society.)

The board, according to the Longitude Act, could give incentive awards to help impoverished inventors bring promising ideas to fruition. This power over purse strings made the Board of Longitude perhaps the world's first official research-and-development agency. (Though none could have foreseen it at the outset, the Board of Longitude was to remain in existence for more than one hundred years. By the time it finally disbanded in 1828, it had disbursed funds in excess of £100,000.)

In order for the commissioners of longitude to judge the actual accuracy of any proposal, the technique had to be tested on one of Her Majesty's ships, as it sailed "over the ocean, from Great Britain to any such Port in the West Indies as those Commissioners Choose... without losing their Longitude beyond the limits before mentioned."

10

15   So-called solutions to the longitude problem had been a dime a dozen even before the act went into effect. After 1714, with their potential value exponentially raised, such schemes proliferated. In time, the board was literally besieged by any number of conniving and well-meaning persons who had heard word of the prize and wanted to win it. Some of these hopeful contenders were so galvanized by greed that they never stopped to consider the conditions of the contest. Thus the board received ideas for improving ships' rudders, for purifying drinking water at sea, and for perfecting special sails to be used in storms. Over the course of its long history, the board received all too many blueprints for perpetual motion machines and proposals that purported to square the circle or make sense of the value of pi.

In the wake of the Longitude Act, the concept of "discovering the longitude" became a synonym for attempting the impossible. Longitude came up so commonly as a topic of conversation—and the butt of jokes—that it rooted itself in the literature of the age. In *Gulliver's Travels*, for example, the good Doctor Lemuel Gulliver, when asked to imagine himself as an immortal Struldbrugg, anticipates the enjoyment of witnessing the return of various comets, the lessening of mighty rivers into shallow brooks, and "the discovery of the *longitude*, the *perpetual motion*, the *universal medicine*, and many other great inventions brought to the utmost perfection."

Part of the sport of tackling the longitude problem entailed ridiculing others in the competition. A pamphleteer who signed himself "R.B." said of Mr. Whiston, the fireball proponent, "[I]f he has any such Thing as Brains, they are really crackt."

Surely one of the most astute, succinct dismissals of fellow hopefuls came from the pen of Jeremy Thacker of Beverly, England. Having heard the half-baked bids to find longitude in the sound of cannon blasts, in compass needles heated by fire, in the moon's motion, in the sun's elevation, and what-else-have-you, Thacker developed a new clock ensconced in a vacuum chamber and declared it the best method of all: "In a word, I am satisfied that my Reader begins to think that the *Phonometers, Pyrometers, Selenometers, Heliometers,* and all the *Meters* are not worthy to be compared with my *Chronometer.*"

Thacker's witty neologism is apparently the first coinage of the word *chronometer.* What he said in 1714, perhaps in jest, later gained acceptance as the perfect moniker for the marine timekeeper. We still call such a device a chronometer today. Thacker's chronometer, however, was not quite as good as its name. To its credit, the clock boasted two important new advances. One was its glass house—the vacuum chamber that shielded the chronometer from troubling changes of atmospheric pressure and humidity. The other was a set of cleverly paired winding rods, configured so as to keep the machine going while being wound up. Until Thacker's introduction of this "maintaining power," spring-driven watches had simply stopped and lost track of time during winding. Thacker had also taken the precaution of suspending the whole machine in gimbals, like a ship's compass, to keep it from thumping about on a storm-tossed deck.

20   What Thacker's watch could *not* do was adjust to changes in temperature. Although the vacuum chamber provided some insulation against the effects of heat and cold, it fell short of perfection, and Thacker knew it.

Room temperature exerted a powerful influence on the going rate of any timekeeper. Metal pendulum rods expanded with heat, contracted when cooled, and beat out seconds at different tempos, depending on the temperature. Similarly, balance springs grew soft and weak when heated, stiffer and stronger when cooled. Thacker had considered this problem at great length when testing his chronometer. In fact, the proposal he submitted to the longitude board contained his careful records of the chronometer's rate at various temperature readings, along with a sliding scale showing the range of error that could be expected at different temperatures. A mariner using the chronometer would simply have to weigh the time shown on the clock's dial against the height of the mercury in the thermometer tube, and make the necessary calculations. This is where the plan falls apart: Someone would have to keep constant watch over the chronometer, noting all changes in ambient temperature and figuring them into the longitude reading. Then, too, even under ideal circumstances, Thacker owned that his chronometer occasionally erred by as many as six seconds a day.

Six seconds sound like nothing compared to the fifteen minutes routinely lost by earlier clocks. Why split hairs?

Because of the consequences—and the money—involved.

To prove worthy of the £20,000 prize, a clock had to find longitude within half a degree. This meant that it could not lose or gain more than three seconds in twenty-four hours. Arithmetic makes the point: Half a degree of longitude equals two minutes of time—the maximum allowable mistake over the course of a six-week voyage from England to the Caribbean. An error of only three seconds a day, compounded every day at sea for forty days, adds up to two minutes by journey's end.

Thacker's pamphlet, the best of the lot reviewed by members of the Board of Longitude during their first year, didn't raise anyone's hopes very high. So much remained to be done. And so little had actually been accomplished. 25

Newton grew impatient. It was clear to him now that any hope of settling the longitude matter lay in the stars. The lunar distance method that had been proposed several times over preceding centuries gained credence and adherents as the science of astronomy improved. Thanks to Newton's own efforts in formulating the Universal Law of Gravitation, the moon's motion was better understood and to some extent predictable. Yet the world was still waiting on Flamsteed to finish surveying the stars.

Flamsteed, meticulous to a fault, had spent forty years mapping the heavens—and had still not released his data. He kept it all under seal at Greenwich. Newton and Halley managed to get hold of most of Flamsteed's records from the Royal Observatory, and published their own pirated edition of his star catalog in 1712. Flamsteed retaliated by collecting three hundred of the four hundred printed copies, and burning them.

"I committed them to the fire about a fortnight ago," Flamsteed wrote to his former observing assistant Abraham Sharp. "If Sir I. N. would be sensible of it, I have done both him and Dr. Halley a very great kindness." In other words, the published positions, insufficiently verified as they were, could only discredit a respectable astronomer's reputation.

Despite the flap over the premature star catalog, Newton continued to believe that the regular motions of the clockwork universe would prevail in guiding ships at sea. A man-made clock would certainly prove a useful accessory to astronomical reckoning but could never stand in its stead. After seven years of service on the Board of Longitude, in 1721, Newton wrote these impressions in a letter to Josiah Burchett, the secretary of the Admiralty:

30

"A good watch may serve to keep a recconing at Sea for some days and to know the time of a celestial Observ[at]ion: and for this end a good Jewel watch may suffice till a better sort of Watch can be found out. But when the Longitude at sea is once lost, it cannot be found again by any watch."

Newton died in 1727, and therefore did not live to see the great longitude prize awarded at last, four decades later, to the self-educated maker of an over-sized pocket watch.

READING CRITICALLY FOR IDEAS, STRUCTURE, AND STYLE

1. As Sobel tells us, the prize established by the Longitude Board required the inventor to create a device that would be so accurate it could not lose or gain more than three seconds in twenty-four hours. Why was the creation of such a device of paramount importance for mariners down through the ages?

2. What details suggest that the concept of "discovering the longitude" pervaded almost every aspect of the culture of eighteenth-century England?

3. What kinds of class prejudices did John Harrison have to contend with especially in light of scientists of the caliber of Sir Isaac Newton having failed to solve the problem?

EXTENDING INSIGHTS THROUGH WRITING

1. In what respects was the longitude project as important in the era Sobel describes, as for example, going to the Moon was in the twentieth century? What practical and cultural meanings are invested in these accomplishments in terms of traversing and controlling the unknown (oceans or space)?

2. Watches that do unusual things besides tell the time often have iconic meanings. Look through online catalogues and describe the function and cultural significance of at least two watches that, for example, keep track of tides, are worn by pilots and scuba divers, receive e-mail, take photographs, monitor heart rates, and even contain miniature televisions.

CONNECTING PERSPECTIVES ON
THE PHYSICAL UNIVERSE

1. How do Sobel and Nathaniel Philbrick's accounts (see "The Attack") provide a composite portrait of the unimaginable challenges merchants and whaling fleets faced in the seventeen and eighteen-hundreds?

2. Compare and contrast the goal of precise measurement sought for by the Longitude Board, and achieved by the laser (as described by Charles H. Townes in "Harnessing Light") and discuss the transforming effects of these inventions in their eras.

NATHANIEL PHILBRICK

The Attack

BACKGROUND

Nathaniel Philbrick (b.1956) is the director of the Egan Institute of Maritime Studies and a research fellow at the Nantucket Historical Association. He graduated from Brown University in 1978. Philbrick, who is a leading authority on the history of Nantucket, has written *A Way Off Shore: Nantucket Island and Its People, 1602–1890* (1994) and *Abram's Eyes: The Native American Legacy of Nantucket Island* (1998). The following chapter is drawn from his bestselling account, *In the Heart of the Sea: the Tragedy of the Whale Ship Essex* (2000), of the real life events on which Herman Melville based his classic novel, *Moby Dick* (1851). Philbrick had been told this story by his father and did extensive research based on the narratives of surviving members of the crew of the *Essex*. A television special based on Philbrick's book was aired in 2001. In the 1800s, Nantucket, a fifteen-mile long island off southeast Massachusetts, was the center of the whaling industry and provided whale oil for use all over the world. Philbrick is still a resident of Nantucket where he is a champion sailboat racer.

APPROACHING PHILBRICK'S ESSAY

In this chapter, "The Attack," Philbrick describes an event that took place on November 20, 1820, thousands of miles off the coast of Chile, when a giant sperm whale rammed twice into a whale-hunting ship, called *The Essex*, and sank it. Such an event was unknown in the entire history of the Nantucket whaling industry. Philbrick theorizes that the attack was instigated by hammering aboard ship that the whale mistook for the clicking signals sperm whales use to communicate with each other. Three months after *The Essex* went down, of the twenty crew members who tried to survive on small life boats in the middle of the Pacific paddling their way back toward the coast of South America, more than 2,000 miles away, only eight survived. They clung to life by eating their dead comrades and drawing lots to determine who was next to be killed and eaten. The narrative of Philbrick's book is drawn from a number of written accounts by survivors including one by a 14-year-old ship's boy, Owen Chase. This horrifying and remarkable tale inspired a young seaman, Herman Melville, who had just begun his literary career. Melville not only drew on this incident for *Moby Dick* but interwove the themes of man against nature, leadership, class, and race into a work that has become a classic in American literature. Philbrick's compelling reenactment contains a wealth of information about the whaling practices of that era.

The Attack

Even today, in an age of instantaneous communication and high-speed transportation, the scale of the Pacific is difficult to grasp. Sailing due west from Panama, it is 11,000 miles to the Malay Peninsula—almost four times the distance Columbus sailed to the New World—and it is 9,600 miles from the Bering Strait to Antarctica. The Pacific is also deep. Hidden beneath its blue surface are some of the planet's most spectacular mountain ranges, with canyons that plunge more than six miles into the watery blackness. Geologically, the volcano-rimmed Pacific is the most active part of the world. Islands rise up; islands disappear. Herman Melville called this sixty-four-million-square-mile ocean the "tide-beating heart of the earth."

By November 16, 1820, the *Essex* had sailed more than a thousand miles west of the Galapagos, following the equator as if it were an invisible lifeline leading the ship ever farther into the largest ocean in the world. Nantucket whalemen were familiar with at least part of the Pacific. Over the last three decades the coast of South America had become their own backyard. They also knew the western edge of the Pacific quite well. By the early part of the century, English whalers, most of them captained by Nantucketers, were regularly rounding the Cape of Good Hope and taking whales in the vicinity of Australia and New Zealand. In 1815, Hezekiah Coffin, the father of Pollard's young cousin Owen, had died during a provisioning stop in the fever-plagued islands off Timor, between Java and New Guinea.

Lying between the island of Timor and the west coast of South America is the Central Pacific, what Owen Chase called "an almost untraversed ocean." The longitudes and latitudes of islands with names such as Ohevahoa, Marokinee, Owyhee, and Mowee might be listed in Captain Pollard's navigational guide, but beyond that they were—save for blood-chilling rumors of native butchery and cannibalism—a virtual blank.

All this was about to change. Unknown to Pollard, only a few weeks earlier, on September 29, the Nantucket whaleships *Equator* and *Balaena* stopped at the Hawaiian island of Oahu for the first time. In 1823, Richard Macy would be the first Nantucketer to provision his ship at the Society

Islands, now known as French Polynesia. But as far as Pollard and his men knew in November of 1820, they were at the edge of an unknown world filled with unimaginable dangers. And if they were to avoid the fate of the ship they'd encountered at Atacames, whose men had almost died of scurvy before they could reach the South American coast for provisions, there was no time for far-flung exploration. It had taken them more than a month to venture out this far, and it would take at least that to return. They had, at most, only a few months of whaling left before they must think about returning to South America and eventually to Nantucket.

5   So far, the whales they had sighted in this remote expanse of ocean had proved frustratingly elusive. "Nothing occurred worthy of note during this passage," Nickerson remembered, "with the exception of occasionally chasing a wild shoal of whales to no purpose." Tensions mounted among the *Essex's* officers. The situation prompted Owen Chase to make an adjustment aboard his whaleboat. When he and his boat-crew did finally approach a whale, on November 16, it was he, Chase reported, not his boatsteerer, Benjamin Lawrence, who held the harpoon.

This was a radical and, for Lawrence, humiliating turn of events. A mate took over the harpoon only after he had lost all confidence in his boatsteerer's ability to fasten to a whale. William Comstock told of two instances when mates became so disgusted with their boatsteerers' unsuccessful attempts to harpoon whales that they ordered them aft and took the iron themselves. One mate, Comstock wrote, screamed, "Who are you? What are you? Miserable trash, scum of Nantucket, a whimpering boy from the chimney corner. By Neptune I think you are afraid of a whale." When the boatsteerer finally burst into tears, the mate ripped the harpoon from his hands and ordered him to take the steering oar.

With Chase at the bow and Lawrence relegated to the steering oar, the first mate's boat approached a patch of water where, Chase predicted, a whale would surface. Chase was, in his own words, "standing in the fore part, with the harpoon in my hand, well braced, expecting every instant to catch sight of one of the shoal which we were in, that I might strike." Unfortunately, a whale surfaced directly under their boat, hurling Chase and his crew into the air. Just as had occurred after their first attempt at killing a whale, off the Falkland Islands, Chase and his men found themselves clinging to a wrecked whaleboat.

Given the shortage of spare boats aboard the *Essex,* caution on the part of the officers might have been expected, but caution, at least when it came to pursuing whales, was not part of the first mate's makeup. Taking to heart the old adage "A dead whale or a stove boat," Chase reveled in the risk and danger of whaling. "The profession is one of great ambition," he would boast in his narrative, "and full of honorable excitement: a tame man is never known amongst them."

Four days later, on November 20, more than 1,500 nautical miles west of the Galapagos and just 40 miles south of the equator, the lookout saw spouts. It was about eight in the morning of a bright clear day. Only a slight breeze was blowing. It was a perfect day for killing whales.

Once they had sailed to within a half mile of the shoal, the two ship-   10
keepers headed the *Essex* into the wind with the maintopsail aback, and
the three boats were lowered. The whales, unaware that they were being
pursued, sounded.

Chase directed his men to row to a specific spot, where they waited
"in anxious expectation," scanning the water for the dark shape of a sur-
facing sperm whale. Once again, Chase tells us, he was the one with the
harpoon, and sure enough, a small whale emerged just ahead of them and
spouted. The first mate readied to hurl the harpoon and, for the second
time in as many days of whaling, ran into trouble.

Chase had ordered Lawrence, the ex-harpooner, to steer the boat in
close to the whale. Lawrence did so, so close that as soon as the harpoon
sliced into it, the panicked animal whacked the already battered craft with
its tail, opening up a hole in the boat's side. As water poured in, Chase cut
the harpoon line with a hatchet and ordered the men to stuff their coats
and shirts into the jagged opening. While one man bailed, they rowed back
to the ship. Then they pulled the boat up onto the *Essex*'s deck.

By this time, both Pollard's and Joy's crews had fastened to whales.
Angered that he had once again been knocked out of the hunt, Chase began
working on his damaged boat with a fury, hoping to get the craft operable
while whales were still to be taken. Although he could have outfitted and
lowered the extra boat (the one they had bargained for in the Cape Verde
Islands, now lashed to the rack over the quarterdeck), Chase felt it would
be faster to repair the damaged boat temporarily by stretching some canvas across the hole. As he nailed the edges of the canvas to the boat, his
after oarsman, Thomas Nickerson—all of fifteen years old—took over the
helm of the *Essex* and steered the ship toward Pollard and Joy, whose
whales had dragged them several miles to leeward. It was then that
Nickerson saw something off the port bow.

It was a whale—a huge sperm whale, the largest they'd seen so far—
a male about eighty-five feet long, they estimated, and approximately eighty
tons. It was less than a hundred yards away, so close that they could see
that its giant blunt head was etched with scars, and that it was pointed
toward the ship. But this whale wasn't just large. It was acting strangely.
Instead of fleeing in panic, it was floating quietly on the surface of the water,
puffing occasionally through its blowhole, as if it were watching them. After
spouting two or three times, the whale dove, then surfaced less than thirty-
five yards from the ship.

Even with the whale just a stone's throw from the *Essex*, Chase did not   15
see it as a threat. "His appearance and attitude gave us at first no alarm," he
wrote. But suddenly the whale began to move. Its twenty-foot-wide tail pumped
up and down. Slowly at first, with a slight side-to-side waggle, it picked up
speed until the water crested around its massive barrel-shaped head. It was
aimed at the *Essex*'s port side. In an instant, the whale was only a few yards
away—"coming down for us," Chase remembered, "with great celerity."

In desperate hopes of avoiding a direct hit, Chase shouted to
Nickerson, "Put the helm hard up!" Several other crew members cried out

warnings. "Scarcely had the sound of the voices reached my ears," Nickerson remembered, "when it was followed by a tremendous crash." The whale rammed the ship just forward of the forechains.

The *Essex* shook as if she had struck a rock. Every man was knocked off his feet. Galapagos tortoises went skittering across the deck. "We looked at each other with perfect amazement," Chase recalled, "deprived almost of the power of speech."

As they pulled themselves up off the deck, Chase and his men had good reason to be amazed. Never before, in the entire history of the Nantucket whale fishery, had a whale been known to attack a ship. In 1807 the whaleship *Union* had accidentally plowed into a sperm whale at night and sunk, but something very different was happening here.

After the impact, the whale passed underneath the ship, bumping the bottom so hard that it knocked off the false keel—a formidable six-by-twelve-inch timber. The whale surfaced at the *Essex's* starboard quarter. The creature appeared, Chase remembered, "stunned with the violence of the blow" and floated beside the ship, its tail only a few feet from the stern.

20 Instinctively, Chase grabbed a lance. All it would take was one perfectly aimed throw and the first mate might slay the whale that had dared to attack a ship. This giant creature would yield more oil than two, maybe even three, normal-sized whales. If Pollard and Joy also proved successful that day, they would be boiling down at least 150 barrels of oil in the next week—more than 10 percent of the *Essex's* total capacity. They might be heading back to Nantucket in a matter of weeks instead of months.

Chase motioned to stab the bull—still lying hull-to-hull with the *Essex.* Then he hesitated. The whale's flukes, he noticed, were perilously close to the ship's rudder. If provoked, the whale might smash the delicate steering device with its tail. They were too far from land, Chase decided, to risk damaging the rudder.

For the first mate, it was a highly uncharacteristic display of caution. "But could [Chase] have foreseen all that so soon followed," Nickerson wrote, "he would probably have chosen the lesser evil and have saved the ship by killing the whale even at the expense of losing the rudder."

A sperm whale is uniquely equipped to survive a head-on collision with a ship. Stretching for a third of its length between the front of the whale's battering ram-shaped head and its vital organs is an oil-filled cavity perfectly adapted to cushioning the impact of a collision. In less than a minute, this eighty-ton bull was once again showing signs of life.

Shaking off its woozy lethargy, the whale veered off to leeward, swimming approximately six hundred yards away. There it began snapping its jaws and thrashing the water with its tail, "as if distracted," Chase wrote, "with rage and fury." The whale then swam to windward, crossing the *Essex's* bow at a high rate of speed. Several hundred yards ahead of the ship, the whale stopped and turned in the *Essex's* direction. Fearful that the ship might be taking on water, Chase had, by this point, ordered the men to rig the pumps. "[W]hile my attention was thus engaged," the first mate remembered, "I was aroused with the cry of a man at the hatchway,

'Here he is—he is making for us again.' " Chase turned and saw a vision of "fury and vengeance" that would haunt him in the long days ahead.

With its huge scarred head halfway out of the water and its tail beat-   25
ing the ocean into a white-water wake more than forty feet across, the whale approached the ship at twice its original speed—at least six knots. Chase, hoping "to cross the line of his approach before he could get up to us, and thus avoid what I knew, if he should strike us again, would prove our inevitable destruction," cried out to Nickerson, "Hard up!" But it was too late for a change of course. With a tremendous cracking and splintering of oak, the whale struck the ship just beneath the anchor secured at the cat-head on the port bow. This time the men were prepared for the hit. Still, the force of the collision caused the whalemen's heads to jounce on their muscled necks as the ship lurched to a halt on the slablike forehead of the whale. The creature's tail continued to work up and down, pushing the 238-ton ship backward until—as had happened after the knockdown in the Gulf Stream—water surged up over the transom.

One of the men who had been belowdecks ran up onto the deck shout-ing, "The ship is filling with water!" A quick glance down the hatchway revealed that the water was already above the lower deck, where the oil and provisions were stored.

No longer going backward, the *Essex* was now going down. The whale, having humbled its strange adversary, disengaged itself from the shattered timbers of the copper-sheathed hull and swam off to leeward, never to be seen again.

The ship was sinking bow-first. The forecastle, where the black sailors slept, was the first of the living quarters to flood, the men's sea chests and mattresses floating on the rising tide. Next the water surged aft into the blub-ber room, then into steerage, where Nickerson and the other Nantucketers slept. Soon even the mates' and captain's cabins were awash.

As the belowdecks creaked and gurgled, the black steward, William Bond, on his own initiative, returned several times to the rapidly filling aft cabins to retrieve Pollard's and Chase's trunks and—with great fore-sight—the navigational equipment. Meanwhile Chase and the rest of the crew cut the lashing off the spare whaleboat and carried it to the waist of the ship.

The *Essex* began to list dangerously to port. Bond made one last   30
plunge below. Chase and the others carried the whaleboat to the edge of the deck, now only a few inches above the ocean's surface. When the trunks and other equipment had been loaded aboard, everyone, including Bond, scrambled into the boat, the tottering masts and yards looming above them. They were no more than two boat lengths away when the *Essex*, with an appalling slosh and groan, capsized behind them.

Just at that moment, two miles to leeward, Obed Hendricks, Pollard's boatsteerer, casually glanced over his shoulder. He couldn't believe what he saw. From that distance it looked as if the *Essex* had been hit by a sudden squall, the sails flying in all directions as the ship fell onto her beam-ends.

"Look, look," he cried, "what ails the ship? She is upsetting!"

But when the men turned to look, there was nothing to see. "[A] general cry of horror and despair burst from the lips of every man," Chase wrote, "as their looks were directed for [the ship], in vain, over every part of the ocean." The *Essex* had vanished below the horizon.

The two boat-crews immediately released their whales and began rowing back toward the place the *Essex* should have been—all the time speculating frantically about what had happened to the ship. It never occurred to any of them that, in Nickerson's words, "a whale [had] done the work." Soon enough, they could see the ship's hull "floating upon her side and presenting the appearance of a rock."

35   As Pollard and Joy approached, the eight men crowded into Chase's boat continued to stare silently at the ship. "[E]very countenance was marked with the paleness of despair," Chase recalled. "Not a word was spoken for several minutes by any of us; all appeared to be bound in a spell of stupid consternation."

From the point at which the whale first attacked, to the escape from the capsizing ship, no more than ten minutes had elapsed. In only a portion of that time, spurred by panic, eight of the crew had launched an unrigged whaleboat from the rack above the quarterdeck, a process that would have normally taken at least ten minutes and required the effort of the entire ship's crew. Now, here they were, with only the clothes on their backs, huddled in the whaleboat. It was not yet ten in the morning.

It was then that Chase fully appreciated the service that William Bond had rendered them. He had salvaged two compasses, two copies of Nathaniel Bowditch's *New American Practical Navigator,* and two quadrants. Chase later called this equipment "the probable instruments of our salvation.... [W]ithout them," he added, "all would have been dark and hopeless."

For his part, Thomas Nickerson was swept by a sense of grief, not for himself, but for the ship. The giant black craft that he had come to know so intimately had been dealt a deathblow. "Here lay our beautiful ship, a floating and dismal wreck," Nickerson lamented, "which but a few minutes before appeared in all her glory, the pride and boast of her captain and officers, and almost idolized by her crew."

Soon the other two whaleboats came within hailing distance. But no one said a word. Pollard's boat was the first to reach them. The men stopped rowing about thirty feet away. Pollard stood at the steering oar, staring at the capsized hulk that had once been his formidable command, unable to speak. He dropped down onto the seat of his whaleboat, so overcome with astonishment, dread, and confusion that Chase "could scarcely recognize his countenance." Finally Pollard asked, "My God, Mr. Chase, what is the matter?"

40   Chase's reply: "We have been stove by a whale."

Even by the colossal standards of a sperm whale, an eighty-five-foot bull is huge. Today, male sperm whales, which are on average three to four times bulkier than females, never grow past sixty-five feet. Sperm whale expert Hal Whitehead has his doubts that the *Essex* whale could have been as large as Chase and Nickerson claimed it was. However, the logs of Nantucket whalemen are filled with references to bulls that, given the amount of oil they yielded, must have been on the order of the *Essex* whale.

It is an established fact that whalemen in both the nineteenth and twentieth centuries killed male sperm whales in disproportionate numbers: not only were they longer than the females but the males' oil-rich spermaceti organs accounted for a larger portion of that length. In 1820, before a century and a half of selective killing had rid the world of large bulls, it may have indeed been possible to encounter an eighty-five-foot sperm whale. Perhaps the most convincing evidence resides in the hallowed halls of the Nantucket Whaling Museum. There, leaning against the wall, is an eighteen-foot jaw taken from a bull that was estimated to have been at least eighty feet long.

The sperm whale has the largest brain of any animal that has ever lived on earth, dwarfing even that of the mighty blue whale. The large size of the sperm whale's brain may be related to its highly sophisticated ability to generate and process sound. Just beneath its blowhole, a sperm whale has what the whalemen referred to as a monkey's muzzle, a cartilaginous clapper system that scientists believe to be the source of the clicking sounds it uses to "see" the world through echolocation. Whales also use clicking signals to communicate over distances of up to five miles. Females tend to employ a Morse code-like series of clicks, known as a coda, and male sperm whales make slower, louder clicks called clangs. It has been speculated that males use clangs to announce themselves to eligible females and to warn off competing males.

Whalemen often heard sperm whales through the hulls of their ships. The sound—steady clicks at roughly half-second intervals—bore such a startling similarity to the tapping of a hammer that the whalemen dubbed the sperm whale "the carpenter fish." On the morning of November 20, 1820, sperm whales were not the only creatures filling the ocean with clicking sounds; there was also Owen Chase, busily nailing a piece of canvas to the bottom of an upturned whaleboat. With every blow of his hammer against the side of the damaged boat, Chase was unwittingly transmitting sounds down through the wooden skin of the whaleship out into the ocean. Whether or not the bull perceived these sounds as coming from another whale, Chase's hammering appears to have attracted the creature's attention.

Chase maintained that when the whale first struck the ship, it was going about three knots, the velocity of a whale at normal cruising speed. Whitehead, whose research vessel was once bumped into by a pregnant whale, speculates that the bull might have even initially run into the *Essex* by mistake.

Whatever prompted the encounter, the whale was clearly not prepared 45
for something as solid and heavy as a whaleship, which at 238 tons weighed approximately three times more than it did. The *Essex* might have been an old, work-worn whaleship, but she had been built to take her share of abuse. She was constructed almost entirely of white oak, one of the toughest and strongest of woods. Her ribs had been hewn from immense timbers, at least a foot square. Over that, laid fore and aft, were oak planks four inches thick. On top of the planks was a sheathing of yellow pine, more than half an inch thick. Extending down from the waterline (the point of

impact, according to Nickerson) was a layer of copper. The bull had slammed into a solid wooden wall.

What had begun as an experimental, perhaps unintentional jab with its head soon escalated into an all-out attack.

Like male elephants, bull sperm whales tend to be loners, moving from group to group of females and juveniles and challenging whatever males they meet along the way. The violence of these encounters is legendary. One whaleman described what happened when a bull sperm whale tried to move in on another bull's group:

> When the approaching bull attempted to join the herd, he was attacked by one of the established bulls, which rolled over on its back and attacked with its jaw... . Large pieces of blubber and flesh were taken out. Both bulls then withdrew and again charged at full tilt. They locked jaws and wrestled, each seemingly to try to break the other's jaw. Great pieces of flesh again were torn from the animals' heads. Next they either withdrew or broke their holds, and then charged each other again. The fight was even more strenuous this time, and little could be seen because of the boiling spray. The charge and withdrawal were repeated two or three times before the water quieted, and then for a few seconds the two could be seen lying head to head. The smaller bull then swam slowly away and did not attempt to rejoin the cows.... A whaleboat was dispatched, and the larger bull was captured. The jaw had been broken and was hanging by the flesh. Many teeth were broken and there were extensive head wounds.

Instead of fighting with its jaws and tail—the way whales commonly dispatched whaleboats—the *Essex* whale rammed the ship with its head, something that, Chase insisted, "has never been heard of amongst the oldest and most experienced whalers." But what most impressed the first mate was the remarkably astute way in which the bull employed its God-given battering ram. Both times the whale had approached the vessel from a direction "calculated to do us the most injury, by being made ahead, and thereby combining the speed of the two objects for the shock." Yet, even though it had come at the *Essex* from ahead, the whale had avoided striking the ship directly head-on, where the ship's heavily reinforced stem, the vertical timber at the leading edge of the bow, might have delivered a mortal gash.

Chase estimated that the whale was traveling at six knots when it struck the *Essex* the second time and that the ship was travelling at three knots. To bring the *Essex* to a complete standstill, the whale, whose mass was roughly a third of the ship's, would have to be moving at more than three times the speed of the ship, at least nine knots. One naval architect's calculations project that if the *Essex* had been a new ship, her oak planking would have withstood even this tremendous blow. Since the whale did punch a hole in the bow, the *Essex*'s twenty-one-year-old planking must have been significantly weakened by rot or marine growth.

Chase was convinced that the *Essex* and her crew had been the vic-   50
tims of "decided, calculating mischief" on the part of the whale. For a
Nantucketer, it was a shocking thought. If other sperm whales should start
ramming ships, it would be only a matter of time before the island's whaling
fleet was reduced to so much flotsam and jetsam.

Chase began to wonder what "unaccountable destiny or design" had
been at work. It almost seemed as if something—could it have been God?—
had possessed the beast for its own strange, unfathomable purpose.
Whatever or whoever might be behind it, Chase was convinced that "anything but chance" had sunk the *Essex.*

After listening to the first mate's account of the sinking, Pollard
attempted to take command of the dire situation. Their first priority, he
announced, was to get as much food and water out of the wreck as possible.
To do that, they needed to cut away the masts so that the still partially
floating hull could right. The men climbed onto the ship and began to hack
away at the spars and rigging with hatchets from the whaleboats. As noon
approached, Captain Pollard shoved off in his boat to take an observation
with his quadrant. They were at latitude 0 °40′ south, longitude 119° 0′
west, just about as far from land as it was possible to be anywhere on earth.

Forty-five minutes later, the masts had been reduced to twenty-foot
stumps and the *Essex* was floating partly upright again, at a forty-five-
degree angle. Although most of the provisions were unreachable in the lower
hold, there were two large casks of bread between decks in the waist of the
ship. And since the casks were on the *Essex*'s upper side, the men could
hope that they were still dry.

Through the holes they chopped into the deck they were able to extract
six hundred pounds of hardtack. Elsewhere they broke through the planks
to find casks of freshwater—more, in fact, than they could safely hold in
their whaleboats. They also scavenged tools and equipment, including two
pounds of boat nails, a musket, two pistols, and a small canister of pow-
der. Several Galapagos tortoises swam to the whaleboats from the wreck,
as did two skinny hogs. Then it began to blow.

In need of shelter from the mounting wind and waves, yet fearful the   55
Essex might at any moment break up and sink like a stone, Pollard ordered
that they tie up to the ship but leave at least a hundred yards of line between
it and themselves. Like a string of ducklings trailing their mother, they
spent the night in the lee of the ship.

The ship shuddered with each wave. Chase lay sleepless in his boat,
staring at the wreck and reliving the catastrophe over and over again in his
mind. Some of the men slept and others "wasted the night in unavailing mur-
murs," Chase wrote. Once, he admitted, he found himself breaking into tears.

Part of him was guilt-wracked, knowing that if he had only hurled the
lance, it might have all turned out differently. (When it came time to write
his own account of the attack, Chase would neglect to mention that he had
the chance to lance the whale—an omission Nickerson made sure to correct
in his narrative.) But the more Chase thought about it, the more he realized
that no one could have expected a whale to attack a ship, and not just once
but twice. Instead of acting as a whale was supposed to—as a creature "never

before suspected of premeditated violence, and proverbial for its inoffen-siveness"—this big bull had been possessed by what Chase finally took to be a very human concern for the other whales. "He came directly from the shoal which we had just before entered," the first mate wrote, "and in which we had struck three of his companions, as if fired with revenge for their sufferings."

As they bobbed in the lee of the wreck, the men of the *Essex* were of no mind to debate the whale's motives. Their overwhelming question was how twenty men in three boats could get out of a plight like this alive.

READING CRITICALLY FOR IDEAS, STRUCTURE, AND STYLE

1. The *Essex*'s disastrous encounter with an eighty-five foot long, eighty ton sperm whale is the central event in Philbrick's narra-tive. How does Philbrick frame his account to enable his readers to comprehend the formidable enigma of a whale attacking a ship, a hitherto unheard of event?

2. How does Philbrick use historical documents and other re-sources to give the reader insight into whaling practices of that era and the role of the *Essex*?

3. Why is it important that we come to know the crew as individu-als? How does this enhance the realism of Philbrick's account?

EXTENDING INSIGHTS THROUGH WRITING

1. Read the portions of Herman Melville's novel, *Moby Dick* (1851) that present a fictionalized version of this encounter and, in a short essay, discuss the tangible and symbolic dimensions with which Melville imbued this account. How does Melville use Owen Chase's observations about the whale's attack as a basis for the climactic scene in his novel?

2. How does the way in which whales are viewed today reveal a significant shift in the public's perception of their meaning from the 1820s (when this event took place)?

CONNECTING PERSPECTIVES ON THE PHYSICAL UNIVERSE

1. In what respects do both Philbrick and Thor Heyerdahl (see "How to Kill an Ocean") address the question of our dependence on the oceans and the human impact on biodiversity?

2. In what sense does the *Essex*'s encounter with the whale (in Philbrick's narrative) lead to the kind of philosophical perceptions about man's place in nature that lies at the heart of Blaise Pascal's reflections (as for example, "men have rashly rushed into the examination of nature, as though they bore some proportion to her")?

THOR HEYERDAHL

How to Kill an Ocean

BACKGROUND

Thor Heyerdahl, the daring Norwegian explorer and anthropologist, was born in 1914. In 1937 Heyerdahl went to the South Seas Island of Fatu-Hiva with his new bride to conduct botanical research and discovered plants and artifacts that led him to believe that people from South America had migrated to Polynesia thousands of years ago during the Stone Age. To test this hypothesis, Heyerdahl constructed a balsa raft and successfully navigated from Callao, Peru, to Tuamotu, a small island east of Tahiti in the South Pacific. In 1970, Heyerdahl sailed from Morocco in a papyrus boat, the *Ra II*, to the West Indies, a distance of 3,270 nautical miles in fifty-seven days. In a later voyage, in 1977–1978, he journeyed from Qurna, Iraq, to Djibouti, on the Gulf of Aden, in a boat, the *Tigris*, made entirely of reeds, a journey of 4,200 miles lasting five months. This voyage revealed the possibility of direct contact between the three oldest known civilizations: those of Mesopotamia, the Indus Valley, and Egypt.

Heyerdahl's fascinating adventures are recounted in *On the Hunt for Paradise* (1938), *The Kon-Tiki Expedition* (1948), *Aku-Aku* (1958), and *The Maldive Mystery* (1986), a true-life archaeological detective story. His most recent books include *Pyramids of Tucume* (1995), *Green Was the Earth On the Seventh Day* (1997), and *In the Footsteps of Adam* (2000). He died in 2002. "How to Kill an Ocean" originally appeared in *Saturday Review* (1975).

APPROACHING HEYERDAHL'S ESSAY

Heyerdahl's essay is designed to alert the public that the ocean is quite vulnerable to the effects of pollution. He redefines the conception of the ocean's unlimited "boundless" nature in ways that stress its fragility. Heyerdahl demonstrates that all of marine life is concentrated in only about 4 per cent of the ocean's total, that the average depth of all the oceans is only about 1,700 meters, slightly more than three times the height of the Empire State Building, and that many bodies of water (for example, the Baltic Sea), have been killed by pollutants such as waste contamination, chemicals, and pesticides that do not biograde over time. The United Nations has drawn on Heyerdahl's findings to issue warnings of the need for greater protection of the world's oceans.

How to Kill an Ocean

Since the ancient Greeks maintained that the earth was round and great navigators like Columbus and Magellan demonstrated that this assertion was true, no geographical discovery has been more important than what we all are beginning to understand today: that our planet has exceedingly restricted dimensions. There is a limit to all resources. Even the height of the atmosphere and the depth of soil and water represent layers so thin that they would disappear entirely if reduced to scale on the surface of a commonsized globe.

The correct concept of our very remarkable planet, rotating as a small and fertile oasis, two-thirds covered by life-giving water, and teeming with life in a solar system otherwise unfit for man, becomes clearer for us with the progress of moon travel and modern astronomy. Our concern about the limits to human expansion increases as science produces ever more exact data on the measurable resources that mankind has in stock for all the years to come.

Because of the population explosion, land of any nature has long been in such demand that nations have intruded upon each other's territory with armed forces in order to conquer more space for overcrowded communities. During the last few years, the United Nations has convened special meetings in Stockholm, Caracas, and Geneva in a dramatic attempt to create a "Law of the Sea" designed to divide vast sections of the global ocean space into national waters. The fact that no agreement has been reached illustrates that in our ever-shriveling world there is not even ocean space enough to satisfy everybody. And only one generation ago, the ocean was considered so vast that no one nation would bother to lay claim to more of it than the three-mile limit which represented the length of a gun shot from the shore.

It will probably take still another generation before mankind as a whole begins to realize fully that the ocean is but another big lake, landlocked on all sides. Indeed, it is essential to understand this concept for the survival of coming generations. For we of the 20th century still treat the ocean as the endless, bottomless pit it was considered to be in medieval times. Expressions like "the bottomless sea" and "the boundless ocean" are still in common use, and although we all know better, they reflect the mental image we still have of this, the largest body of water on earth. Perhaps one of the reasons why we subconsciously consider the ocean a sort of bottomless abyss is the fact that all the rain and all the rivers of the world keep pouring constantly into it and yet its water level always remains unchanged. Nothing affects the ocean, not even the Amazon, the Nile, or the Ganges. We know, of course, that this imperviousness is no indicator of size, because the sum total of all the rivers is nothing but the return to its own source of the water evaporated from the sea and carried ashore by drilling clouds.

5   What is it really then that distinguishes the ocean from the other more restricted bodies of water? Surely it is not its salt content. The Old and the New World have lakes with a higher salt percentage than the ocean has. The Aral Sea, the Dead Sea, and the Great Salt Lake in Utah are good examples. Nor is it the fact that the ocean lacks any outlet. Other great bodies of water have abundant input and yet no outlet. The Caspian Sea and Lake Chad in Central Africa are valid examples. Big rivers, among them the Volga, enter the Caspian Sea, but evaporation compensates for its lack of outlet, precisely as is the case with the ocean. Nor is it correct to claim that the ocean is open while inland seas and lakes are landlocked. The ocean is just as landlocked as any lake. It is flanked by land on all sides and in every direction. The fact that the earth is round makes the ocean curve around it just as does solid land, but a shoreline encloses the ocean on all sides and in every direction. The ocean is not even the lowest body of water on our planet. The surface of the Caspian Sea, for instance, is 85 feet below sea level, and the surface of the Dead Sea is more than 1,200 feet below sea level.

Only when we fully perceive that there is no fundamental difference between the various bodies of water on our planet, beyond the fact that the ocean is the largest of all lakes, can we begin to realize that the ocean has something else in common with all other bodies of water: it is vulnerable. In the long run the ocean can be affected by the continued discharge of all modern man's toxic waste. One generation ago no one would have thought that the giant lakes of America could be polluted. Today they are, like the largest lakes of Europe. A few years ago the public was amazed to learn that industrial and urban refuse had killed the fish in Lake Erie. The enormous lake was dead. It was polluted from shore to shore in spite of the fact that it has a constant outlet through Niagara Falls, which carries pollutants away into the ocean in a never-ending flow. The ocean receiving all this pollution has no outlet but represents a dead end, because only pure water evaporates to return into the clouds. The ocean is big; yet if 10 Lake Eries were taken and placed end to end, they would span the entire Atlantic from Africa to South America. And the St. Lawrence River is by no means the only conveyor of pollutants into the ocean. Today hardly a creek or a river in the world reaches the ocean without carrying a constant flow of nondegradable chemicals from industrial, urban, or agricultural areas. Directly by sewers or indirectly by way of streams and other waterways, almost every big city in the world, whether coastal or inland, makes use of the ocean as mankind's common sink. We treat the ocean as if we believed that it is not part of our own planet—as if the blue waters curved into space somewhere beyond the horizon where our pollutants would fall off the edge, as ships were believed to do before the days of Christopher Columbus. We build sewers so far into the sea that we pipe the harmful refuse away from public beaches. Beyond that is no man's concern. What we consider too dangerous to be stored under technical control ashore we dump forever out of sight at sea, whether toxic chemicals or nuclear waste. Our only excuse is the still-surviving image of the ocean as a bottomless pit.

It is time to ask: is the ocean vulnerable? And if so, can many survive on a planet with a dead ocean? Both questions can be answered, and they are worthy of our attention.

First, the degree of vulnerability of any body of water would of course depend on two factors: the volume of the water and the nature of the pollutants. We know the volume of the ocean, its surface measure, and its average depth. We know that it covers 71 percent of the surface of our planet, and we are impressed, with good reason, when all these measurements are given in almost astronomical figures. If we resort to a more visual image, however, the dimensions lose their magic. The average depth of all oceans is only 1,700 meters. The Empire State Building is 448 meters high. If stretched out horizontally instead of vertically, the average ocean depth would only slightly exceed the 1,500 meters than an Olympic runner can cover by foot in 3 minutes and 35 seconds. The average depth of the North Sea, however, is not 1,700 meters, but only 80 meters, and many of the buildings in downtown New York would emerge high above water level if they were built on the bottom of this sea. During the Stone Age most of the North Sea was dry land where roaming archers hunted deer and other game. In this shallow water, until only recently, all the industrial nations of Western Europe have conducted year-round routine dumping of hundreds of thousands of tons of their most toxic industrial refuse. All the world's sewers and most of its waste are dumped into waters as shallow as, or shallower than, the North Sea. An attempt was made at a recent ocean exhibition to illustrate graphically and in correct proportion the depths of the Atlantic, the Pacific, and the Indian oceans in relation to a cross section of the planet earth. The project had to be abandoned, for although the earth was painted with a diameter twice the height of a man, the depths of the world oceans painted in proportion became so insignificant that they could not be seen except as a very thin pencil line.

The ocean is in fact remarkably shallow for its size. Russia's Lake Baikal, for instance, less than 31 kilometers wide, is 1,500 meters deep, which compares well with the average depth of all oceans. It is the vast *extent* of ocean surface that has made man of all generations imagine a correspondingly unfathomable depth.

When viewed in full, from great heights, the ocean's surface is seen   10
to have definite, confining limits. But at sea level, the ocean seems to extend outward indefinitely, to the horizon and on into blue space. The astronauts have come back from space literally disturbed upon seeing a full view of our planet. They have seen at first hand how cramped together the nations are in a limited space and how the "endless" oceans are tightly enclosed within cramped quarters by surrounding land masses. But one need not be an astronaut to lose the sensation of a boundless ocean. It is enough to embark

on some floating logs tied together, as we did with the *Kon-Tiki* in the Pacific, or on some bundles of papyrus reeds, as we did with the *Ra* in the Atlantic. With no effort and no motor we were pushed by the winds and currents from one continent to another in a few weeks.

After we abandon the outworn image of infinite space in the ocean, we are still left with many wrong or useless notions about biological life and vulnerability. Marine life is concentrated in about 4 percent of the ocean's total body of water, whereas roughly 96 percent is just about as poor in life as is a desert ashore. We all know, and should bear in mind, that sunlight is needed to permit photosynthesis for the marine plankton on which all fishes and whales directly or indirectly base their subsistence. In the sunny tropics the upper layer of light used in photosynthesis extends down to a maximum depth of 80 to 100 meters. In the northern latitudes, even on a bright summer's day, this zone reaches no more than 15 to 20 meters below the surface. Because much of the most toxic pollutants are buoyant and stay on the surface (notably all the pesticides and other poisons based on chlorinated hydrocarbons), this concentration of both life and venom in the same restricted body of water is most unfortunate.

What is worse is the fact that life is not evenly distributed throughout this thin surface layer. Ninety percent of all marine species are concentrated above the continental shelves next to land. The water above these littoral shelves represents an area of only 8 percent of the total ocean surface, which itself represents only 4 percent of the total body of water, and means that much less than half a percent of the ocean space represents the home of 90 percent of all marine life. This concentration of marine life in shallow waters next to the coasts happens to coincide with the area of concentrated dumping and the outlet of all sewers and polluted river mouths, not to mention silt from chemically treated farm-land. The bulk of some 20,000 known species of fish, some 30,000 species of mollusks, and nearly all the main crustaceans lives in the most exposed waters around the littoral areas. As we know, the reason is that this is the most fertile breeding ground for marine plankton. The marine plant life, the phytoplankton, find here their mineral nutriments, which are brought down by rivers and silt and up from the ocean bottom through coastal upwellings that bring back to the surface the remains of decomposed organisms which have sunk to the bottom through the ages. When we speak of farmable land in any country, we do not include deserts or sterile rock in our calculations. Why then shall we decive ourselves by the total size of the ocean when we know that not even 1 percent of its water volume is fertile for the fisherman?

Much as been written for or against the activities of some nations that have dumped vast quantities of nuclear waste and obsolete war gases in the sea and excused their actions on the grounds that it was all sealed in special containers. In such shallow waters as the Irish Sea, the English Channel, and the North Sea there are already enough examples of similar "foolproof" containers moving about with bottom currents until they are totally displaced and even crack open with the result that millions of fish are killed or mutilated. In the Baltic Sea, which is shallower than many lakes and which—except for the thin surface layer—has already been killed by pollution, 7,000 tons of arsenic were dumped in cement containers some 40 years ago. These containers have now started to leak. Their combined contents are three times more than is needed to kill the entire population of the earth today.

Fortunately, in certain regions modern laws have impeded the danger of dumpings; yet a major threat to marine life remains—the less spectacular but more effective ocean pollution through continuous discharge from sewers and seepage. Except in the Arctic, there is today hardly a creek or a river in the world from which it is safe to drink at the outlet. The more technically advanced the country, the more devastating the threat to the ocean. A few examples picked at random will illustrate the pollution input from the civilized world:

French rivers carry 18 billion cubic meters of liquid pollution annually into the sea. The city of Paris alone discharges almost 1.2 million cubic meters of untreated effluent into the Seine every day.   15

The volume of liquid waste from the Federal Republic of Germany is estimated at over 9 billion cubic meters per year, or 25.4 million cubic meters per day, not counting cooling water, which daily amounts to 33.6 million cubic meters. Into the Rhine alone 50,000 tons of waste are discharged daily, including 30,000 tons of sodium chloride from industrial plants.

A report from the U.N. Economic and Social Council, issued prior to the Stockholm Conference on the Law of the Sea four years ago, states that the world had then dumped an estimated billion pounds of DDT into our environment and was adding an estimated 100 million more pounds per year. The total world production of pesticides was estimated at more than 1.3 billion pounds annually, and the United States alone exports more than 400 million pounds per year. Most of this ultimately finds its way into the ocean with winds, rain, or silt from land. A certain type of DDT sprayed on crops in East Africa a few years ago was found and identified a few months later in the Bay of Bengal, a good 4,000 miles away.

The misconception of a boundless ocean makes the man in the street more concerned about city smog than about the risk of killing the ocean. Yet the tallest chimney in the world does not suffice to send the noxious smoke away into space; it gradually sinks down, and nearly all descends, mixed with rain, snow, and silt, into the ocean. Industrial and urban areas are expanding with the population explosion all over the world, and in the United States alone, waste products in the form of smoke and noxious fumes amount to it total of 390,000 tons of pollutants every day, or 142 million tons every year.

With this immense concentration of toxic matter, life on the continental shelves would in all likelihood have been exterminated or at least severely decimated long since if the ocean had been immobile. The cause for the delayed action, which may benefit man for a few decades but will aggravate the situation for coming generations, is the well-known fact that the ocean rotates like boiling water in a kettle. It churns from east to west, from north to south, from the bottom to the surface, and down again, in perpetual motion. At a U.N. meeting one of the developing countries proposed that if ocean dumping were prohibited by global or regional law, they would offer friendly nations the opportunity of dumping in their own national waters—for a fee, of course!

20   It cannot be stressed too often, however, that it is nothing but a complete illusion when we speak of national waters. We can map and lay claim to the ocean bottom, but not to the mobile sea above it. The water itself is in constant transit. What is considered to be the national waters of Morocco one day turns up as the national waters of Mexico soon after. Meanwhile Mexican national water is soon on its way across the North Atlantic to Norway. Ocean pollution abides by no law.

My own transoceanic drifts with the *Kon-Tiki* raft and the reed vessels *Ra I* and *II* were eye-openers to me and my companions as to the rapidity with which so-called national waters displace themselves. The distance from Peru to the Tuamotu Islands in Polynesia is 4,000 miles when it is measured on a map. Yet the *Kon-Tiki* raft had only crossed about 1,000 miles of ocean surface when we arrived. The other 3,000 miles had been granted us by the rapid flow of the current during the 101 days our crossing lasted. But the same raft voyages taught us another and less pleasant lesson: it is possible to pollute the oceans, and it is already being done. In 1947, when the balsa raft *Kon-Tiki* crossed the Pacific, we towed a plankton net behind. Yet we did not collect specimens or even see any sign of human activity in the crystal-clear water until we spotted the wreck of an old sailing ship on the reef where we landed. In 1969 it was therefore a blow to us on board the papyrus raft-ship *Ra* to observe, shortly after our departure from Morocco, that we had sailed into an area filled with ugly clumps of hard asphalt-like material, brownish to pitch black in color, which were floating at close intervals on or just below the water's surface. Later on, we sailed into other areas so heavily polluted with similar clumps that we were reluctant to dip up water with our buckets when we needed a good scrub-down at the end of the day. In between these areas the ocean was clean except for occasional floating oil lumps and other widely scattered refuse such as plastic containers, empty bottles, and cans. Because the ropes holding the papyrus reeds of *Ra I* together burst, the battered wreck was abandoned in polluted waters short of the island of Barbados, and a second crossing was effectuated all the way from Safi in Morocco to Barbados in the West Indies in 1970. This time a systematic day-by-day survey of ocean pollution was carried out, and samples of oil lumps collected were sent to the United Nations together with a detailed report on the observations. This was published by Secretary-General U Thant as an annex to his report to the Stockholm Conference on the Law of the Sea. It is enough here to repeat that sporadic oil clots drifted by within reach of our dip net during 43 out of the 57 days our transatlantic crossing lasted. The laboratory analysis of the various samples of oil clots collected showed a wide range in the level of nickel and vanadium content, revealing that they originated from different geographical localities. This again proves that they represent not the homogeneous spill from a leaking oil drill or from a wrecked super-tanker, but the steadily accumulating waste from the daily routine washing of sludge from the combined world fleet of tankers.

The world was upset when the *Torrey Canyon's* unintentionally spilled 100,000 tons of oil into the English Channel some years ago; yet this is only a small fraction of the intentional discharge of crude oil sludge through less spectacular, routine tank cleaning. Every year more than *Torrey Canyon's* spill of a 100,000 tons of oil is intentionally pumped into the Mediterranean alone, and a survey of the sea south of Italy yielded 500 liters of solidified oil for every square kilometer of surface. Both the Americans and the Russians were alarmed by our observations of Atlantic pollution in 1970 and sent out specially equipped oceanographic research vessels to the area. American scientists from Harvard University working with the Bermuda Biological Station for Research found more solidified oil than seaweed per surface unit in the Sargasso Sea and had to give up their plankton catch because their nets were completely plugged up by oil sludge. They estimated, however, a floating stock of 86,000 metric tons of tar in the Northwest Atlantic alone. The Russians, in a report read by the representative of the Soviet Academy of Sciences at a recent pollution conference in Prague, found that pollution in the coastal areas of the Atlantic had already surpassed their tentative limit for what had been considered tolerable, and that a new scale of tolerability would have to be postulated.

The problem of oil pollution is in itself a complex one. Various types of crude oil are toxic in different degrees. But they all have one property in common: they attract other chemicals and absorb them like blotting paper, notably the various kinds of pesticides. DDT and other chlorinated hydrocarbons do not dissolve in water, nor do they sink: just as they are absorbed by plankton and other surface organisms, so are they drawn into oil slicks and oil clots, where in some cases they have been rediscovered in stronger concentrations than when originally mixed with dissolvents in the spraying bottles. Oil clots, used as floating support for barnacles, marine worms, and pelagic crabs, were often seen by us from the *Ra*, and these riders are attractive bait for filter-feeding fish and whales, which cannot avoid getting gills and baleens cluttered up by the tarlike oil. Even sharks with their rows of teeth plastered with black oil clots are now reported from the Caribbean Sea. Yet the oil spills and dumping of waste from ships represent a very modest contribution compared with the urban and industrial refuse released from land.

That the ocean, given time, will cope with it all, is a common expression of wishful thinking. The ocean has always been a self-purifying filter that has taken care of all global pollution for millions of years. Man is not the first polluter. Since the morning of time nature itself has been a giant workshop, experimenting, inventing, decomposing, and throwing away waste: the incalculable billions of tons of rotting forest products, decomposing flesh, mud, silt, and excrement. If this waste had not been recycled, the ocean would long since have become a compact soup after millions of years of death and decay, volcanic eruptions, and global erosion. Man is not the first large-scale producer, so why should he become the first disastrous polluter?

25   Man has imitated nature by manipulating atoms, taking them apart and grouping them together in different compositions. Nature turned fish into birds and beasts into man. It found a way to make fruits out of soil and sunshine. It invented radar for bats and whales, and shortwave transceivers for beetles and butterflies. Jet propulsion was installed on squids, and unsurpassed computers were made as brains, for mankind. Marine bacteria and plankton transformed the dead generations into new life. The life cycle of spaceship earth is the closest one can ever get to the greatest of all inventions, *perpetuum mobile*—the perpetual-motion machine. And the secret is that nothing was composed by nature that could not be recomposed, recycled, and brought back into service again in another form as another useful wheel in the smoothly running global machinery.

This is where man has sidetracked nature. We put atoms together into molecules of types nature had carefully avoided. We invent to our delight immediately useful materials like plastics, pesticides, detergents, and other chemical products hitherto unavailable on planet earth. We rejoice because we can get our laundry whiter than the snow we pollute and because we can exterminate every trace of insect life. We spray bugs and bees, worms and butterflies. We wash and flush the detergents down the drain out to the oysters and fish. Most of our new chemical products are not only toxic: they are in fact created to sterilize and kill. And they keep on displaying these same inherent abilities wherever they end up. Through sewers and seepage they all head for the ocean, where they remain to accumulate as undesired nuts and bolts in between the cog-wheels of a so far smoothly running machine. If it had not been for the present generation, man could have gone on polluting the ocean forever with the degradable waste he produced. But with ever-increasing speed and intensity we now produce and discharge into the sea hundreds of thousands of chemicals and other products. They do not evaporate nor do they recycle, but they grow in numbers and quantity and threaten all marine life.

We have long known that our modern pesticides have begun to enter the flesh of penguins in the Antarctic and the brains of polar bears and the blubber of whales in the Arctic, all subsisting on plankton and plankton-eating crustaceans and fish in areas far from cities and farmland. We all know that marine pollution has reached global extent in a few decades. We also know that very little or nothing is being done to stop it. Yet there are persons who tell us that there is no reason to worry, that the ocean is so big and surely science must have everything under control. City smog is being fought through intelligent legislation. Certain lakes and rivers have been improved by leading the sewers down to the sea. But where, may we ask, is the global problem of ocean pollution under control?

No breathing species could live on this planet until the surface layer of the ocean was filled with phytoplankton, as our planet in the beginning was only surrounded by sterile gases. These minute plant species manufactured so much oxygen that it rose above the surface to help form the atmosphere we have today. All life on earth depended upon this marine plankton for its evolution and continued subsistence. Today, more than ever before, mankind depends on the welfare of this marine plankton for his future survival as a species. With the population explosion we need to harvest even more protein from the sea. Without plankton there will be no fish. With our rapid expansion of urban and industrial areas and the continuous disappearance of jungle and forest, we shall be ever more dependent on the plankton for the very air we breathe. Neither man nor any other terrestrial beast could have bred had plankton not preceded them. Take away this indispensable life in the shallow surface areas of the sea, and life ashore will be unfit for coming generations. A dead ocean means a dead planet.

READING CRITICALLY FOR IDEAS, STRUCTURE, AND STYLE

1. How did Heyerdahl's voyages on the *Kon Tiki* (in the Pacific) and on the *Ra* (in the Atlantic) alert him to the potentially catastrophic changes in the ocean of which most people are unaware?

2. Why, according to Heyerdahl, is the common perception of the ocean as being limitless, incorrect? What means does he use to get his audience to understand how vulnerable the oceans are to pollution?

3. Heyerdahl's scenarios may strike some people as alarmist. Why are the combined effects of pollution far more destructive than people have anticipated?

EXTENDING INSIGHTS THROUGH WRITING

1. Heyerdahl's experiences on the *Kon Tiki* and the *Ra* make fascinating reading. Read one or both of these and discuss how either of these accounts provides a unique perspective on the effects of pollution on the oceans?

2. In a 300–500 word essay, discuss how the importance of convenience and disposable goods in our consumer culture has had an impact on ocean pollution.

CONNECTING PERSPECTIVES ON THE PHYSICAL UNIVERSE

1. In what respects do Heyerdahl and Peter D. Ward and Donald Brownlee alert us to the complex and precarious conditions necessary for life in the ocean and on Earth?

2. Discuss how Heyerdahl and Blaise Pascal, in "The Two Infinites," make their points by altering the scale of our perceptions?

PETER D. WARD AND DONALD BROWNLEE

Rare Earth

BACKGROUND

Peter D. Ward, a paleontologist (b. 1949) and Donald Brownlee, an astronomer (b. 1943) have examined the unique conditions and events that deposited life-forming chemicals on Earth, allowed elemental life to gain a foothold, and then protected the planet sufficiently to allow for the evolution and survival of higher forms of life. While it is widely believed that complex life is common, and even widespread throughout the billions of stars and galaxies of our universe, Ward and Brownlee argue, in *Rare Earth* (2000), that while microbial life may be more prevalent in the universe than previously believed, only Earth enjoys the precise balance of factors that make complex forms of life possible. Ward is professor of geological sciences at the University of Washington in Seattle and an authority on mass extinctions. His previous books include *On Methuselah's Trail: Living Fossils and the Great Extinctions* (1992), *The Call of Distant Mammoths: Why the Ice Age Mammals Disappeared* (1997), *Time Machines: Scientific Explorations in Deep Time* (1998), and *Rivers in Time: The Search for Clues to Earth's Mass Extinctions* (2000). Donald Brownlee is professor of astronomy at the University of Washington in Seattle and leads the NASA Stardust mission. He is a member of the National Academy of Sciences.

APPROACHING WARD AND BROWNLEE'S ESSAY

In this thought-provoking chapter from *Rare Earth*, Ward and Brownlee review key points in their argument. According to Ward and Brownlee, the improbable combination of factors that make the Earth unique, and let complex forms of life develop, includes its position in a safe part of the galaxy, orbiting a metal-rich star that has had liquid water for 4 billion years (just enough to cover some, but not all of the surface of the planet). They note that the presence of Jupiter keeps us safe from comets and asteroids by deflecting them away and that Earth's internal heat is just sufficient to allow plate tectonics (that is, linear mountain ranges) that regulate our temperature within a narrow range. Moreover, Earth has a large moon at the right distance that stabilizes tilt and ensures seasonal climate fluctations that are not too severe, and enough carbon to develop life, but not so much as to allow for runaway greenhouse conditions. This confluence of conditions is so rare that the authors conclude that we may, contrary to science-fiction fantasies, really be alone. Given this scenario, Ward and Brownlee draw attention to the destruction of tropical rain forests, the reduction in biodiversity, and the destablization of the environment that can result in species extinction, including our own.

Rare Earth

> Our planet is not in a special place in the solar system, our
> Sun is not in a special place in our galaxy and our galaxy is
> not in a special place in the Universe.
>
> —Marcello Gleiser, *The Dancing Universe*

Some things have to be experienced firsthand, for some wonders, no written description or photograph can substitute—the birth of one's child, for example, or the first music heard from an actual orchestra, love, sex, standing before a Monet canvas. One such revelation not so often experienced, is one's first glimpse of the starry night through a telescope.

VIEWING THE UNIVERSE

We have all seen photographs of endless star fields, galaxies, and nebulae. But no matter how great their beauty, the stars in photographs are lifeless, and no view of the night sky with the unaided eye, even in the clearest atmosphere, is like the first view through a small telescope. If looking at the Milky Way with the unaided eye is akin to snorkeling on a coral reef, then adding a telescope is like strapping on scuba tanks: We are no longer tied to the surface but can roam the depths of the star fields and see unimagined splendors amid stars whose numbers are beyond belief. Even with a low-power telescope a new vision emerges; the uncountable pinpricks of light now revealed are seemingly alive, in no way diminished by their passage through corrected lenses. In fact, the stars gain strength, color, and clarity. But the greatest and most lasting impression is the increase in their sheer numbers. The superb double-star cluster in Perscus changes from a dull, unresolvable glow to bountiful diamonds sprinkled on black velvet; the globular cluster in Hercules is transformed from a tiny smudge to scattered grains of light. With time and experience, even greater vistas open up. We discover the joys of other deep-space objects, galaxies and nebulae. And eventually, in the Northern hemisphere, we inevitably find ourselves slowly moving through the crowded star fields of Sagittarius on a dark summer night, the light from this luminous expanse of stars sweeping the senses like a wind, nebulae and galaxies an endless visual melody punctuated by staccatos of brighter suns. Those in the Southern hemisphere witness even more dramatic vistas: the two great Magellenic Clouds looming so close overhead. It becomes spectacle, overwhelming, and ultimately—diminishing. The myriad stars overcome us, so utterly do they trivialize (marginalize? minimize?) our small planet and we who stare out.

The Universe seems to be finite; there are not an infinite number of planets circling the vast number of stars in the ocean of space. But the numbers are immense beyond understanding. We are one of many planets. But as we have tried to show in this book, perhaps not so many as we might hope—and perhaps not so many that we will ever, however long the history of our species, find *any* extraterrestrial animals among the stars surrounding our sun. That is a fate not foreseen by Hollywood—that we may find nothing but bacteria, even on planets orbiting distant stars.

If the Rare Earth Hypothesis is correct—that is, if microbial life is common but animal life is rare—there will be societal implications, or at least some small personal implications. What will be the effect if news comes back from the next Mars mission that there is life on Mars after all—microbial to be sure, but life. Or what if, after astronauts voyage repeatedly to other planets in our solar system, or even to the dozen nearest stars, we find nothing more advanced than a bacterium? What if, at least in this quadrant of the galaxy, we are quite alone, not just as the only intelligent organisms but also as the only animals? How much of our striving to travel into space is the hope of discovering—and perhaps talking to—other *animalia*?

VIEWS OF EARTH THROUGH HUMAN HISTORY

5   Since the time of the Greeks, science has tried to make sense of the Universe and of our place in it. More than two millennia ago, a Greek named Thales of Miletus, credited by many as the founder of Western philosophy, was among the first to leave a record of his musings about the place of Earth in the cosmos. Thales thought that the cosmos was an organic, living thing, and in that he may not have been far wrong if bacteria or bacteria-like organisms are as common as we believe them to be in the Universe. Thales's student Anaximander was among the first to place Earth at the center of the cosmos, postulating that Earth was a floating cylinder with a series of large wheels with holes in them rotating around it. The Pythagoreans tried to break from this central-Earth motif, proposing that Earth moved in space and was not the center of the Universe. But Earth's centrality was restored by members of Plato's school and became exalted by the students of Aristotle. Eudoxus placed Earth at the center of 27 concentric spheres, each of which rotated around it. Soon two schools of thought competed: the

"sun-centered" model of Aristarchus and the Earth-centered model of Ptolemy. The latter held sway through the Middle Ages.

During the Middle Ages, Earth was not only regarded as the center of the Universe but was again believed to be flat. St. Thomas Aquinas made Earth a sphere again but codified its place as the center of the Universe. It was Nicholas Copernicus who finally shattered the notion of an Earth-centered. Universe and put the sun at the center of all orbits. But even with this great leap forward, the sun remained at the center of the Universe as well, according to Copernicus in his revolutionary book of 1514, *Commentariolus.*

Copernicus forever destroyed the myth that our Earth lay at the center of the Universe, with the sun and all other planets and stars revolving around us; his work eventually led to the concept of a "Plurality of Worlds"— the idea that our planet is but one among many. This has now been described as the "Principle of Mediocrity," also known as the Copernican Principle. Yet an even greater blow came with the invention of the telescope. There is still debate about who built the first optical telescope, although Dutch optician Johannes Lippershey obtained the first official license for construction of a telescope in 1608. The device was an immediate sensation, and by 1609 this revolutionary new instrument found its way into the hands of Galileo, who built his own soon after hearing of the concept. Before Galileo, telescopes had been used to assess the terrestrial world (and for various military applications), but Galileo pointed his into the heavens and forever changed our understanding of the cosmos.

Galileo quickly surmised that there are far more stars in the sky than anyone had guessed. He discovered that the Milky Way is made up of uncountable individual stars. He observed the Moon, discovered satellites revolving around Jupiter (and in so doing showed that our Earth could just as conceivably orbit the sun). Earth's central place in the Universe, the fervent belief of Aristotle, was now observationally shown to be wrong. Copernicus had dealt with theory; Galileo and his telescopes dealt with reality. Galileo's message, published in his booklet *Siderius nuncius,* or "Messenger from the Stars," was about the truth told by the stars: that Earth is but one of many cosmic objects. To illustrate his point, he noted the presence of faint patches of light just visible to the unaided eye—objects called nebulae. Even with his primitive and tiny telescopes, Galileo could see these curious objects far better than anyone before. He thought them to be great masses of stars, made indistinct by their very distance.

The decentralization of Earth continued in relentless fashion. In 1755 Immanuel Kant theorized that a rotating gas cloud would flatten into a disk as it contracted under its own gravity. Kant was familiar with the numerous nebulae of the night skies, the faint glowing patches of luminosity scattered through the heavens. All the early astronomers knew of the faint cloud in the constellation of Andromeda. He knew these objects to be one of many distant groups of stars he called "island Universes." But Kant didn't stop there: He theorized that the sun, Earth, and other planets might have formed in this swirling mass of gas. This concept was taken a step further by Pierre-Simon de Liplike, who speculated in detail about how planetary systems might form from nebular origins. He invoked a dynamical mechanism for the formation of stars and their planets. Earth and the solar system became one of many such systems all formed in the same way.

But how far away were these island Universes? Was there only a single galaxy in the Universe, of which our star was part, or were there many? This debate was not resolved until the early twentieth century, a time when gigantic new telescopes were being constructed and outer space was being probed as never before. The conflict came to a head on April 26, 1920, when Harlow Shapley from the Mount Wilson observatory in California and Heber Curtis from the Allegheny Observatory in Pittsburgh met before the members of the National Academy of Sciences, a clash that came to be known as the Great Debate. The debate ended inconclusively, because it was not yet possible to assess the distance of the nebulae. That soon changed, however, thanks to the efforts of astronomer Edwin Hubble. Using a newly constructed, 100-inch reflecting telescope, Hubble was able to make observations that proved conclusively that the island nebulae were not associated with our Milky Way but were far-distant objects. Even the closest, the Andromeda galaxy, was found to be at least 2 million light-years from Earth and similar in shape to our Milky Way galaxy. The debate was over. The Milky Way is one of a vast number of scattered and widely separated galaxies floating in space. We became even more trivialized—now our *galaxy* was but one of many.

Two millennia of astronomers and philosophers removed Earth from the center of the Universe and placed us orbiting a sun that is but one of hundreds of billions in a galaxy itself but one among billions in the Universe. And it was not only astronomers who changed the world view. Einstein showed that there is no preferred observer in the Universe, and quantum mechanics told us that chance is king. Charles Darwin and his powerful theory of evolution demoted humans from the crown of creation to a rather new species on an already animal-rich planet, the chance offspring of larger-scale evolutionary and ecological forces. Nothing special. And yet...

The great danger to our thesis (that Earth is rare because of its animal life, the factors and history necessary to arrive at this point as a teeming, animal- and plant-rich planet being highly improbable) is that it is a product of our lack of imagination. We assume in this book that animal life will be somehow Earth-like. We take the perhaps jingoistic stance that Earth-life is every-life, that lessons from Earth are not only guides but also *rules*. We assume that DNA is the only way, rather than only one way. Perhaps complex life—which we in this book have defined as animals (and higher plants as well)— is as widely distributed as bacterial life and as variable in its makeup. Perhaps Earth is not rare after all but is simply one variant in a nearly infinite assemblage of planets with life. Yet we do not believe this, for there is so much evidence and inference—as we have tried to show in the preceding pages—that such is not the case.

OUR RARE EARTH

Let us recap why we think Earth is rare. Our planet coalesced out of the debris from previous cosmic events at a position within a galaxy highly appropriate for the eventual evolution of animal life, around a star also highly appropriate—a star rich in metal, a star found in a safe region of a spiral galaxy, a star moving very slowly on its galactic pinwheel. Not in the center of the galaxy, not in a metal-poor galaxy, not in a globular cluster, not near an active gamma ray source, not in a multiple-star system, not even in a binary, or near a pulsar, or near stars too small, too large, or soon to go supernova. We became a planet where global temperatures have allowed liquid water to exist for more than 4 billion years—and for that, our planet had to have a nearly circular orbit at a distance from a star itself emitting a nearly constant energy output for a long period of time. Our planet received a volume of water sufficient to cover most—but not all—of the planetary surface. Asteroids and comets hit us but not excessively so, thanks to the presence of giant gas planets such as Jupiter beyond us. In the time since animals evolved over 600 million years ago, we have not been punched out, although the means of our destruction by catastrophic impact is certainly there. Earth received the right range of building materials—and had the correct amount of internal heat—to allow plate tectonics to work on the planet, shaping the continents required and keeping global temperatures within a narrow range for several billion years. Even as the Sun grew brighter and atmosphere composition changed, the Earth's remarkable thermostatic regulating process successfully kept the surface temperature within livable range. Alone among terrestrial planets we have a large moon, and this single fact, which sets us apart from Mercury, Venus, and Mars, may have been crucial to the rise and continued existence of animal life on Earth. The continued marginalization of Earth and its place in the Universe perhaps should be reassessed. We are not the center of the Universe, and we never will be. But we are not so ordinary as Western science has made us out to be for two millennia. Our global inferiority complex may be unwarranted. What if Earth is extremely rare because of its animals (or, to put it another way, because of its animal habitability)?

The possibility that animal life may be very rare in the Universe also heightens the tragedy of the current rate of extinction on our planet. Earlier, we suggested that the rise of an intelligent species on any planet might be a common source of mass extinction. That certainly seems to be the case on Earth. And if animals are as rare in the Universe as we suspect, it puts species extinction in a whole new light. Are we eliminating species not only from our planet but also from a quadrant of the galaxy as a whole?

To understand the rates of extinction on Earth today, one has only to examine the plight of tropical rainforests. Forests have been a part of this planet for more than 300 million years, and although the nature of species has changed over that long period, the nature of the forests has changed little. The forests are the great Noah's ark of species on this planet. Although the land surface of our globe is only one-third that of the oceans, it appears that 80% to 90% of the total animal and plant biodiversity of the planet inhabits the land, and most of that diversity is found in tropical forests. As we destroy these forests, we destroy species. It has been estimated that between 5 and 30 million species of *animals* live in the tropical rainforests and that only about 5% of these are known to science. The fossil record tells us quite clearly that the world has attained the highest level of biological diversity ever in its history. There are also disturbing and unmistakable signs that this plateau in the number of species on Earth has been crested and the biodiversity of Earth is diminishing.

There appear to be several forces driving a reduction of biodiversity—a *destruction* of biodiversity, to be less delicate. The most important seems to be the rapid increase in human population. Ten thousand years ago there may have been at most 2 to 3 million humans scattered around the globe. There were no cities, no great population centers. There were fewer people on the globe than are now found in virtually any large American city. Two thousand years ago the number had swelled to perhaps 130 to 200 million people. Our first billion was reached in the year 1800. If we take the time of origin of our species as about 100,000 years ago, it seems that it took our species 100,000 years to reach the billion-person population plateau. Then things sped up considerably. We reached 2 billion people in 1930, about 1000 times faster than it took to reach the first billion. But the rate of increase kept accelerating. By 1950, only 20 years later, we had reached 2.5 billion souls. In 1999, we hit 6 billion. There will be approximately 7 billion people by 2020 and perhaps 11 billion by 2050 to 2100.

Rainforest conversion, which changes forest to fields, and then (usually) to overgrazed, eroded, and infertile land within a generation, is perhaps the most direct executioner of biodiversity. It appears that 25% of the world's top soil has been lost since 1945. One-third of the world's forest area has disappeared in the same interval. The result is species extinction. A thousand years from now, when humanity reflects on the world that was, and looks out at the desert surrounding the rare and notably less diverse animals that remain, whom will it hold responsible?

President Theodore Roosevelt closed off the Yellowstone region to development in forming the first national park in the United States. Wouldn't it be ironic if some alien equivalent had done the same thing for our planet? Astrobiologists have suggested this—it is known as the Zoo Hypothesis. The joke would be on us: We are somebody's national park, our rare planet Earth stocked with animals for safekeeping. Perhaps that is why we have yet to hear any signals from space. A big fence surrounds our solar system: "Earth Intergalactic Park. Posted: No trespassing or tampering. The only planet with animals for the next 5000 light-years."

Twenty thousand years ago, Earth was locked in the glacial grip of the last ice age. Wooly mammoths and great mastodons, ground sloths, camels, and saber-toothed tigers roamed North America, people didn't. Humans were still thousands of years from crossing the land bridge from what would someday be called Siberia to the place we now know as Alaska. Humans were still 10,000 years from mastering agriculture. On some given yet forever anonymous day in that long ago time of 20,000 B.C., a distant neutron star in the constellation Aquila, part of the Summer Triangle so familiar to star watchers in the Northern hemisphere, underwent a violent cataclysm of some type and belched hard radiation into space, hurling an expanding sphere of poison at the speed of light in all directions. For 20,000 years it sped through space. It hit Earth over the Pacific Ocean on the evening of August 27, 1998, as it continued ever onward, its energy diminishing with each mile it traveled from its original source.

For 5 minutes on that late summer day, Earth was bombarded by gamma rays and X-rays, the lethal twins generated by thermonuclear bombs as well as by the interiors of stars. Even after traveling 20,000 light-years, the energy was sufficient to send radiation sensors on seven Earth satellites to maximum reading or off scale. Two of these satellites were shut down to save their instruments from burnout. The radiation penetrated to within 30 miles of Earth's surface and then was dissipated by the lower regions of our planet's atmosphere. This event was the first time that such high energy from outside the solar system was detected to have had a measurable effect on the atmosphere. But in all probability, it was not the first time Earth has been buffeted by energy from interstellar space. Perhaps a closer neutron star, or some other stellar demon not yet known to us, caused one or more of the mass extinctions in Earth's past. Perhaps we have only begun to see the demons surrounding us as we take our first tentative peeks through our planetary bedroom window into space.

Astronomers believe that the 1998 event was caused by the surface disruption of a kind of star that had only been theorized to exist: a magnetar. A type of neutron star, a magnetar is perhaps 20 miles in diameter but is more massive than our sun. It is estimated that a thimbleful of its material would weigh 100 million tons. It is matter compressed far beyond the point of human comprehension. The star has a surface of iron, but iron of a type never found in our solar system. The star spins, as all neutron stars spin, and the result is the formation of an intensely powerful magnetic field. For reasons we can only guess at, the surface of this star—20,000 years ago—underwent a massive disruption, sending energy into space as a consequence.

Energy dissipates with distance. Had the magnetar in question been only 10,000 light-years away, the energy reaching Earth would have been four times stronger—perhaps strong enough to damage the ozone layer. Did this particular event sterilize worlds within a light-year or less? Were there civilizations existing on worlds that were seared out of existence by gamma rays and a magnetic field pulse sufficient to tear the very molecules of living matter apart? Was another Earth sterilized? Perhaps life can flourish only in neighborhoods far from magnetars. Have magnetars—as well as so much else we have seen in the pages of this book—made animal life rare in the Universe? And what else is out there, lurking in the dark?

The discovery of a phenomenon such as the magnetar is an object lesson that suggests a great deal more than life's rarity: There is still so much more to learn about the heavens surrounding us. We humans are like 2-year-olds, just beginning to comprehend the immensity, wonder, and hazards of the wide world. So too with our understanding of astrobiology. It is clearly just beginning.

READING CRITICALLY FOR IDEAS, STRUCTURE, AND STYLE

1. How does the "rare earth" hypothesis rule out a universe populated by advanced extraterrestrial creatures?

2. Why do Ward and Brownlee take the reader through a successive view of the Earth since the time of the Greeks? How effective do you find this rhetorical strategy?

3. In the authors' view, how does the "rare earth" hypothesis make it even more imperative to protect Earth's biodiversity? What aspects of their essay are designed to underscore the uniqueness and fragility of life on Earth?

EXTENDING INSIGHTS THROUGH WRITING

1. After doing some research on the popular view that life exists elsewhere (such as Carl Sagan's argument that extraterrestrial civilizations probably number in the millions), create a dialogue between Carl Sagan (or another scientist with the same beliefs) with Ward and Brownlee. Be sure to fairly represent both sides of the argument and present your own opinion as well.

2. If Ward and Brownlee are correct and advanced life as we have come to expect it in the predictions of cosmologists is indeed simply wishful thinking, how would this change our perceptions of ourselves and our planet?

CONNECTING PERSPECTIVES ON THE PHYSICAL UNIVERSE

1. In what ways do Ward and Brownlee, and Sir Leonard Woolley (see "The Flood"), ask us to relinquish long-held beliefs, whether those of religion or of science?

2. How do Ward and Brownlee and Thor Heyerdahl (see "How To Kill an Ocean") use their discoveries to raise the public's awareness of the dangers facing the planet?

BLAISE PASCAL

The Two Infinites

BACKGROUND

Blaise Pascal (1623–1662), a French scientist and religious philosopher, was a precocious child who, before he was sixteen, composed a treatise on conic sections that won the praise of leading mathematicians. At nineteen he invented a calculating machine for his father to use in his tax computations. He founded the modern theory of probability, created what is known in mathematics as "Pascal's triangle," and was instrumental in developing differential calculus. In physics, his experiments in 1647 brought new knowledge of atmospheric pressure through barometric measurements and established what is known as "Pascal's law" on the equilibrium of fluids. Despite his many achievements in mathematics and physics, he is justly celebrated for his essays, notes, and memoranda in his personal journal called *Pensees* (thoughts) from which "The Two Infinites" is drawn.

APPROACHING PASCAL'S ESSAY

The insights in this essay (drawn from *Pensees*, published posthumously in 1670) stem from a mystical experience that Pascal underwent at the convent in Port Royale when he was thirty-one. Pascal, who was one of the great scientists of his era, frames an argument designed to question the limitations of knowledge gained solely through the senses. He leads us to understand that we live in "an infinity of universes" and evokes feelings of awe toward the cosmos. Once we have grasped the paradox of the human condition and have given up our conceit that science provides us with certainties, we can begin to understand, in a profound way, Pascal's statement that humanity "is in a dependent alliance with everything." He summarizes his case in the last four paragraphs by examining the division of human nature into the "spiritual and the corporeal" and returns to his theme that the tendency to value reason must be tempered by a need for religious faith.

The Two Infinites

Let man contemplate the whole of nature in her full and grand majesty, and turn his vision from the low objects which surround him. Let him gaze on that brilliant light, set like an eternal lamp to illumine the universe; let the earth appear to him a point in comparison with the vast circle described by the sun; and let him wonder at the fact that this vast circle is itself but a very fine point in comparison with that described by the stars in their revolution round the firmament. But if our view be arrested there, let our imagination pass beyond; it will sooner exhaust the power of conception than nature that of supplying material for conception. The whole visible world is only an imperceptible atom in the ample bosom of nature. No idea approaches it. We may enlarge our conceptions beyond all imaginable space; we only produce atoms in comparison with the reality of things. It is an infinite sphere, the centre of which is everywhere, the circumference nowhere. In short it is the greatest sensible mark of the almighty power of God, that imagination loses itself in that thought.

Returning to himself, let man consider what he is in comparison with all existence; let him regard himself as lost in this remote corner of nature; and from the little cell in which he finds himself lodged, I mean the universe, let him estimate at their true value the earth, kingdoms, cities, and himself. What is a man in the Infinite?

But to show him another prodigy equally astonishing, let him examine the most delicate things he knows. Let a mite be given him, with its minute body and parts incomparably more minute, limbs with their joints, veins in the limbs, blood in the veins, humours in the blood, drops in the humours,[1] vapours in the drops. Dividing these last things again, let him exhaust his powers of conception, and let the last object at which he can arrive be now that of our discourse. Perhaps he will think that here is the smallest point in nature. I will let him see therein a new abyss. I will paint for him not only the visible universe, but all that he can conceive of nature's immensity in the womb of this abridged atom. Let him see therein an infinity of universes, each of which has its firmament, its planets, its earth, in the same proportion as in the visible world; in each earth animals, and in the last mites, in which he will find again all that the first had, finding still in these others the same thing without end and without cessation. Let him

---

[1]Corresponding, in the older physiology, with glandular secretions.

lose himself in wonders as amazing in their littleness as the others in their vastness. For who will not be astounded at the fact that our body, which a little while ago was imperceptible in the universe, itself imperceptible in the bosom of the whole, is now a colossus, a world, or rather a whole, in respect of the nothingness which we cannot reach? He who regards himself in this light will be afraid of himself, and observing himself sustained in the body given him by nature between those two abysses of the Infinite and Nothing, will tremble at the sight of these marvels; and I think that, as his curiosity changes into admiration, he will be more disposed to contemplate them in silence than to examine them with presumption.

For in fact what is man in nature? A Nothing in comparison with the Infinite, an All in comparison with the Nothing, a mean between nothing and everything. Since he is infinitely removed from comprehending the extremes, the end of things and their beginning are hopelessly hidden from him in an impenetrable secret; he is equally incapable of seeing the Nothing from which he was made, and the Infinite in which he is swallowed up.

What will he do then, but perceive the appearance of the middle of things, in an eternal despair of knowing either their beginning or their end. All things proceed from the Nothing, and are borne towards the Infinite. Who will follow these marvellous processes? The Author of these wonders understands them. None other can do so.

Through failure to contemplate these Infinites, men have rashly rushed into the examination of nature, as though they bore some proportion to her. It is strange that they have wished to understand the beginnings of things, and thence to arrive at the knowledge of the whole, with a presumption as infinite as their object. For surely this design cannot be formed without presumption or without a capacity infinite like nature.

If we are well informed, we understand that, as nature has graven her image and that of her Author on all things, they almost all partake of her double infinity. Thus we see that all the sciences are infinite in the extent of their researches. For who doubts that geometry, for instance, has an infinite infinity of problems to solve? They are also infinite in the multitude and fineness of their premises; for it is clear that those which are put forward as ultimate are not self-supporting, but are based on others which, again having others for their support, do not permit of finality. But we represent some as ultimate for reason, in the same way as in regard to material objects we call that an indivisible point beyond which our senses can no longer perceive anything, although by its nature it is infinitely divisible.

Of these two Infinites of science, that of greatness is the most palpable, and hence a few persons have pretended to know all things. "I will speak of the whole," said Democritus.[2]

But the infinitely little is the least obvious. Philosophers have much oftener claimed to have reached it, and it is here they have all stumbled. This has given rise to such common titles as *First Principles, Principles of*

---

[2]One of the earliest Greek philosophers (born about 460 B.C.), founder of the atomic theory of nature.

Philosophy, and the like, as ostentatious in fact, though not in appearance, as that one which blinds us, *De omni scibili*.[3]

10   We naturally believe ourselves far more capable of reaching the centre of things than of embracing their circumference. The visible extent of the world visibly exceeds us; but as we exceed little things, we think ourselves more capable of knowing them. And yet we need no less capacity for attaining the Nothing than the All. Infinite capacity is required for both, and it seems to me that whoever shall have understood the ultimate principles of being might also attain to the knowledge of the Infinite. The one depends on the other, and one leads to the other. These extremes meet and reunite by force of distance, and find each other in God, and in God alone.

Let us then take our compass; we are something, and we are not everything. The nature of our existence hides from us the knowledge of first beginnings which are born of the Nothing; and the littleness of our being conceals from us the sight of the Infinite.

Our intellect holds the same position in the world of thought as our body occupies in the expanse of nature.

Limited as we are in every way, this state which holds the mean between two extremes is present in all our impotence. Our senses perceive no extreme. Too much sound deafens us; too much light dazzles us; too great distance or proximity hinders our view. Too great length and too great brevity of discourse tend to obscurity; too much truth is paralysing (I know some who cannot understand that to take four from nothing leaves nothing). First principles are too self-evident for us; too much pleasure disagrees with us. Too many concords are annoying in music; too many benefits irritate us....

...We feel neither extreme heat nor extreme cold. Excessive qualities are prejudicial to us and not perceptible by the senses; we do not feel but suffer them. Extreme youth and extreme age hinder the mind, as also too much and too little education. In short, extremes are for us as though they were not, and we are not within their notice. They escape us, or we them.

15   This is our true state; this is what makes us incapable of certain knowledge and of absolute ignorance. We sail within a vast sphere, ever drifting in uncertainty, driven from end to end. When we think to attach ourselves to any point and to fasten to it, it wavers and leaves us; and if we follow it, it eludes our grasp, slips past us, and vanishes for ever. Nothing stays for us. This is our natural condition, and yet most contrary to our inclination; we burn with desire to find solid ground and an ultimate sure foundation whereon to build a tower reaching to the Infinite. But our whole groundwork cracks, and the earth opens to abysses.

Let us therefore not look for certainty and stability. Our reason is always deceived by fickle shadows; nothing can fix the finite between the two Infinites, which both enclose and fly from it.

If this be well understood, I think that we shall remain at rest, each in the state wherein nature has placed him. As this sphere which has fallen to us as our lot is always distant from either extreme, what matters it that man should have a little more knowledge of the universe? If he has it, he

---

[3]Concerning all knowable things.

but gets a little higher. Is he not always infinitely removed from the end, and is not the duration of our life equally removed from eternity, even if it lasts ten years longer?

In comparison with these Infinites all finites are equal, and I see no reason for fixing our imagination on one more than on another. The only comparison which we make of ourselves to the finite is painful to us.

If man made himself the first object of study, he would see how incapable he is of going further. How can a part know the whole? But he may perhaps aspire to know at least the parts to which he bears some proportion. But the parts of the world are all so related and linked to one another, that I believe it impossible to know one without the other and without the whole.

Man, for instance, is related to all he knows. He needs a place wherein to abide, time through which to live, motion in order to live, elements to compose him, warmth and food to nourish him, air to breathe. He sees light; he feels bodies; in short, he is in a dependent alliance with everything. To know man, then, it is necessary to know how it happens that he needs air to live, and, to know the air, we must know how it is thus related to the life of man, etc. Flame cannot exist without air; therefore to understand the one, we must understand the other.   20

Since everything then is cause and effect, dependent and supporting, mediate and immediate, and all is held together by a natural though imperceptible chain, which binds together things most distant and most different, I hold it equally impossible to know the parts without knowing the whole, and to know the whole without knowing the parts in detail....

And what completes our incapability of knowing things, is the fact that they are simple, and that we are composed of two opposite natures, different in kind, soul and body. For it is impossible that our rational part should be other than spiritual; and if any one maintain that we are simply corporeal, this would far more exclude us from the knowledge of things, there being nothing so inconceivable as to say that matter knows itself. It is impossible to imagine how it should know itself.

So if we are simply material, we can know nothing at all; and if we are composed of mind and matter, we cannot know perfectly things which are simple, whether spiritual or corporeal. Hence it comes that almost all philosophers have confused ideas of things, and speak of material things in spiritual terms, and of spiritual things in material terms. For they say boldly that bodies have a tendency to fall, that they seek after their centre, that they fly from destruction, that they fear the void, that they have inclinations, sympathies, antipathies, all of which attributes pertain only to mind. And in speaking of minds, they consider them as in a place, and attribute to them movement from one place to another; and these are qualities which belong only to bodies.

Instead of receiving the ideas of these things in their purity, we colour them with our own qualities, and stamp with our composite being all the simple things which we contemplate.

Who would not think, seeing us compose all things of mind and body, but that this mixture would be quite intelligible to us? Yet it is the very thing we least understand. Man is to himself the most wonderful object in nature; for he cannot conceive what the body is, still less what the mind is,   25 and least of all how a body should be united to a mind. This is the consummation of his difficulties, and yet it is his very being.

READING CRITICALLY FOR IDEAS, STRUCTURE, AND STYLE

1. In what way is the paradox with which Pascal confronts us designed to help us understand that science in and of itself cannot answer the mysteries of the human condition? What features of Pascal's essay are designed to show the limits of reason and the distorting nature of the senses?

2. Why is it ironic that Pascal, who was a gifted mathematician and scientist, believes that religious faith rather than pure reason is the ultimate mode of inquiry?

3. In what way does Pascal express his insights with the precision of a mathematician and the imagination of a poet?

EXTENDING INSIGHTS THROUGH WRITING

1. Our culture is accustomed to believing in the certainties of scientific truth and knowledge, yet Pascal, who wrote 300 years ago, challenges the reliability of our sense perceptions. Do you agree or disagree with Pascal's doubts as to the validity of knowledge gained through the senses? Why or why not?

2. Looking out into the night sky or into a microscope makes us aware of our position as human beings between "two infinities." In a few paragraphs, let your imagination take you on a flight of fancy and reflect on how you exist between the two realms Pascal discusses.

CONNECTING PERSPECTIVES ON THE PHYSICAL UNIVERSE

1. In what ways do Pascal's reflections on the "abyss" of infinite space correspond to Fred Hoyle's analysis in "The Continuous Creation of the Universe"? Compare the ways in which both authors (then and now) represent the immensities of the physical universe in ways that appeal to our imagination?

2. Developments in micro-miniaturization of the kind described by Christopher Evans in "The Revolution Begins" suggest that we need a way to contemplate one of Pascal's two infinities. Extend Pascal's meditations to the realm of computers as they were in Evans's time and as they are now.

SIR FRED HOYLE

The Continuous Creation of the Universe

BACKGROUND

Sir Fred Hoyle (1915–2001), an astrophysicist, was born in Yorkshire, England, and earned an M. A. in 1939 from Cambridge University. He served as president of the Royal Astronomical Society from 1971 through 1973, the year in which he was knighted. Hoyle's theory of "continuous creation," which he espoused along with astronomers Thomas Gold and Hermann Bondi, was intended as an alternative to the "big bang" theory of creation. His book, *The Nature of the Universe* (1950; revised 1960), achieved wide popularity because of Hoyle's talent for clearly explaining the complex ideas in astronomy and physics. He also wrote a number of science-fiction novels, some in collaboration with his son, Geoffrey. Most recently, with G. Burbridge and J. V. Narlikar, Hoyle wrote *A Different Approach to Cosmology: From a Static Universe Through the Big-Bang Towards Reality* (2000). In "The Continuous Creation of the Universe" (1950), Hoyle creates analogies drawn from common experience to help his readers visualize the abstract concept of an expanding universe.

APPROACHING HOYLE'S ESSAY

Scientists and technical writers find analogies invaluable in aiding their audiences to grasp theories that require specialized mathematical knowledge. Hoyle uses a surprisingly mundane image to convey the size and placement of galaxies in respect to each other amidst an expanding universe whose immense distances exceed the grasp of our senses.

The "big bang" theory, which Hoyle challenges, proposes that in the beginning all the matter in the universe was concentrated into a single point at an extremely high temperature that exploded with tremendous force, creating an expanding superheated cloud of subatomic particles, from which

467

atoms formed, followed by stars, galaxies, planets, and life itself. The limitations of the "big bang" theory, according to Hoyle, is that it does not explain the problem of "missing mass," since galaxies interact with each other as though they had ten times the mass that is presently known. Thoughout his essay, Hoyle enables his audience to grasp these complex ideas by using everyday examples and easily understood analogies.

The Continuous Creation of the Universe

At the risk of seeming a little repetitive I should like to begin this chapter by recalling some of our previous results. One of the things I have been trying to do is to break up our survey of the Universe into distinct parts. We started with the Sun and our system of planets. To get an idea of the size of this system we took a model with the Sun represented by a ball about six inches in diameter. In spite of this enormous reduction of scale we found that our model would still cover the area of a small town. On the same scale the Earth has to be represented by a speck of dust, and the nearest stars are 2,000 miles away. So it is quite unwieldy to use this model to describe the positions of even the closest stars.

Some other means had to be found to get to grips with the distances of the stars in the Milky Way. Choosing light as our measure of distance, we saw that light takes several years to travel to us from near-by stars, and that many of the stars in the Milky Way are at a distance of as much as 1,000 light years. But the Milky Way is only a small bit of a great disk-shaped system of gas and stars that is turning in space like a great wheel. The diameter of the disk is about 60,000 light years. This distance is so colossal that there has only been time for the disk to turn round about twenty times since the oldest stars were born—about 4,000,000,000 years ago. And this is in spite of the tremendous speed of nearly 1,000,000 miles an hour at which the outer parts of the disk are moving. We also saw that the Sun and our planets lie together near the edge of our Galaxy, as this huge disk is called.

Now we shall go out into the depths of space far beyond the confines of our own Galaxy. Look out at the heavens on a clear night; if you want a really impressive sight do so from a steep mountainside or from a ship at sea. As I have said before, by looking at any part of the sky that is distant from the Milky Way you can see right out of the disk that forms our Galaxy. What lies out there? Not just scattered stars by themselves, but in every direction space is strewn with whole galaxies, each one like our own. Most of these other galaxies—or extra-galactic nebulae as astronomers often call them—are too faint to be seen with the naked eye, but vast numbers of them can be observed with a powerful telescope. When I say that these other galaxies are similar to our Galaxy, I do not mean that they are exactly alike. Some are much smaller than ours, others are not disk-shaped but nearly spherical in form. The basic similarity is that they are all enormous clouds of gas and stars, each one with anything from 100,000,000 to 10,000,000,000 or so members.

Although most of the other galaxies are somewhat different from ours, it is important to realize that some of them are indeed very like our Galaxy even so far as details are concerned. By good fortune one of the nearest of them, only about 700,000 light years away, seems to be practically a twin of our Galaxy. You can see it for yourself by looking in the constellation of Andromeda. With the naked eye it appears as a vague blur, but with a powerful telescope it shows up as one of the most impressive of all astronomical objects. On a good photograph of it you can easily pick out places where there are great clouds of dust. These clouds are just the sort of thing that in our own Galaxy produces the troublesome fog I mentioned in earlier talks. It is this fog that stops us seeing more than a small bit of our own Galaxy. If you want to get an idea of what our Galaxy would look like if it were seen from outside, the best way is to study this other one in Andromeda. If the truth be known I expect that in many places there living creatures are looking out across space at our Galaxy. They must be seeing much the same spectacle as we see when we look at their galaxy.

It would be possible to say a great deal about all these other galaxies: how they are spinning round like our own; how their brightest stars are supergiants, just like those of our Galaxy; and how in those where supergiants are common, wonderful spiral patterns are found. ...We can also find exploding stars in these other galaxies. In particular, supernovae[1] are so brilliant that they show up even though they are very far off. Now the existence of supernovae in other galaxies has implications for our cosmology. You will remember that in a previous chapter I described the way in which planetary systems like our own come into being; the basic requirement of the process was the supernova explosion. So we can conclude, since supernovae occur in the other galaxies, planetary systems must exist there just as in our own. Moreover, by observing the other galaxies we get a far better idea of the rate at which supernovae occur than we could ever get from our Galaxy alone. A general survey by the American observers Baade and Zwicky has shown that on the average there is a supernova explosion every four or five hundred years in each galaxy. So, remembering our previous argument, you will see that on the average each galaxy must contain more than 1,000,000 planetary systems.

How many of these gigantic galaxies are there? Well, they are strewn through space as far as we can see with the most powerful telescopes. Spaced apart at an average distance of rather more than 1,000,000 light years, they certainly continue out to the fantastic distance of 1,000,000,000 light years. Our telescopes fail to penetrate further than that, so we cannot be certain that the galaxies extend still deeper into space, but we feel pretty sure that they do. One of the questions we shall have to consider later is what lies beyond the range of our most powerful instruments. But even

---

[1]An extraordinarily bright star that radiates between ten million and one hundred million times as much energy as does our sun.

within the range of observation there are about 100,000,000 galaxies. With upward of 1,000,000 planetary systems per galaxy the combined total for the parts of the Universe that we can see comes out at more than a hundred million million. I find myself wondering whether somewhere among them there is a cricket team that could beat the Australians.

We now come to the important question of where this great swarm of galaxies has come from. Perhaps I should first remind you of what was said when we were discussing the origin of the stars. We saw that in the space between the stars of our Galaxy there is a tenuous gas, the interstellar gas. At one time our Galaxy was a whirling disk of gas with no stars in it. Out of the gas, clouds condensed, and then in each cloud further condensations were formed. This went on until finally stars were born. Stars were formed in the other galaxies in exactly the same way. But we can go further than this and extend the condensation idea to include the origin of the galaxies themselves. Just as the basic step in explaining the origin of the stars is the recognition that a tenuous gas pervades the space within a galaxy, so the basic step in explaining the origin of the galaxies is the recognition that a still more tenuous gas fills the whole of space. It is out of this general background material, as I shall call it, that the galaxies have condensed.

Here now is a question that is important for our cosmology. What is the present density of the background material? The average density is so low that a pint measure would contain only about one atom. But small as this is, the total amount of the background material exceeds about a thousandfold the combined quantity of material in all the galaxies put together. This may seem surprising but it is a consequence of the fact that the galaxies occupy only a very small fraction of the whole of space. You see here the characteristic signature of the New Cosmology. We have seen that inside our Galaxy the interstellar gas outweighs the material in all the stars put together. Now we see that the background material outweighs by a large margin all the galaxies put together. And just as it is the interstellar gas that controls the situation inside our Galaxy, so it is the background material that controls the Universe as a whole. This will become increasingly clear as we go on.

The degree to which the background material has to be compressed to form a galaxy is not at all comparable with the tremendous compression necessary to produce a star. This you can see by thinking of a model in which our Galaxy is represented by a fifty-cent piece. Then the blob of background material out of which our Galaxy condensed would be only about a foot in diameter. This incidentally is the right way to think about the Universe as a whole. If in your mind's eye you take the average galaxy to be about the size of a bee—a small bee, a honeybee, not a bumblebee—our Galaxy, which is a good deal larger than the average, would be roughly represented in shape and size by the fifty-cent piece, and the average spacing of the galaxies would be about three yards, and the range of telescopic vision about a mile. So sit back and imagine a swarm of bees spaced about three yards apart and stretching away from you in all directions for a distance of about a mile. Now for each honeybee substitute the vast bulk of a galaxy and you have an idea of the Universe that has been revealed by the large American telescopes.

Next I must introduce the idea that this colossal swarm is not static: it is expanding. There are some people who seem to think that it would be a good idea if it was static. I disagree with this idea, if only because a static universe would be very dull. To show you what I mean by this I should like to point out that the Universe is wound up in two ways—that is to say, energy can be got out of the background material in two ways. Whenever a new galaxy is formed, gravitation supplies energy. For instance, gravitation supplies the energy of the rotation that develops when a galaxy condenses out of the background material. And gravitation again supplies energy during every subsequent condensation of the interstellar gas inside a galaxy. It is because of this energy that a star becomes hot when it is born. The second source of energy lies in the atomic nature of the background material. It seems likely that this was originally pure hydrogen. This does not mean that the background material is now entirely pure hydrogen, because it gets slightly adulterated by some of the material expelled by the exploding supernovae. As a source of energy hydrogen does not come into operation until high temperatures develop—and this only arises when stars condense. It is this second source of energy that is more familiar and important to us on the Earth.

Now, why would a Universe that was static on a large scale, that was not expanding in fact, be uninteresting? Because of the following sequence of events. Even if the Universe were static on a large scale it would not be locally static: that is to say, the background material would condense into galaxies, and after a few thousand million years this process would be completed—no background would be left. Furthermore, the gas out of which the galaxies were initially composed would condense into stars. When this stage was reached hydrogen would be steadily converted into helium. After several hundreds of thousands of millions of years this process would be everywhere completed and all the stars would evolve toward the black dwarfs.[2] I mentioned in a previous chapter. So finally the whole Universe would become entirely dead. This would be the running down of the Universe that was described so graphically by Jeans.[3]

One of my main aims will be to explain why we get a different answer to this when we take account of the dynamic nature of the Universe. You might like to know something about the observational evidence that the Universe is indeed in a dynamic state of expansion. Perhaps you've noticed that a whistle from an approaching train has a higher pitch, and from a receding train a lower pitch, than a similar whistle from a stationary train. Light emitted by a moving source has the same property. The pitch of the light is lowered, or as we usually say reddened, if the source is moving away from us. Now we observe that the light from the galaxies is reddened, and the degree of reddening increases proportionately with the distance of a galaxy. The natural explanation of this is that the galaxies are rushing away

[2]Burned-out stars.
[3]Sir James Jeans (1877–1946), distinguished British astronomer and physicist.

from each other at enormous speeds, which for the most distant galaxies that we can see with the biggest telescopes become comparable with the speed of light itself.

My nonmathematical friends often tell me that they find it difficult to picture this expansion. Short of using a lot of mathematics I cannot do better than use the analogy of a balloon with a large number of dots marked on its surface. If the balloon is blown up the distances between the dots increase in the same way as the distances between the galaxies. Here I should give a warning that this analogy must not be taken too strictly. There are several important respects in which it is definitely misleading. For example, the dots on the surface of a balloon would themselves increase in size as the balloon was being blown up. This is not the case for the galaxies, for their internal gravitational fields are sufficiently strong to prevent any such expansion. A further weakness of our analogy is that the surface of an ordinary balloon is two dimensional—that is to say, the points of its surface can be described by two co-ordinates; for example, by latitude and longitude. In the case of the Universe we must think of the surface as possessing a third dimension. This is not as difficult as it may sound. We are all familiar with pictures in perspective—pictures in which artists have represented three-dimensional scenes on two-dimensional canvases. So it is not really a difficult conception to imagine the three dimensions of space as being confined to the surface of a balloon. But then what does the radius of the balloon represent, and what does it mean to say that the balloon is being blown up? The answer to this is that the radius of the balloon is a measure of time, and the passage of time has the effect of blowing up the balloon. This will give you a very rough, but useful, idea of the sort of theory investigated by the mathematician.

The balloon analogy brings out a very important point. It shows we must not imagine that we are situated at the center of the Universe, just because we see all the galaxies to be moving away from us. For, whichever dot you care to choose on the surface of the balloon, you will find that the other dots all move away from it. In other words, whichever galaxy you happen to be in, the other galaxies will appear to be receding from you.

15   Now let us consider the recession of the galaxies in a little more detail. The greater the distance of a galaxy the faster it is receding. Every time you double the distance you double the speed of recession. The speeds come out as vast beyond all precedent. Near-by galaxies are moving outward at several million miles an hour, whereas the most distant ones that can be seen with our biggest telescopes are receding at over 200,000,000 miles an hour. This leads us to the obvious question: If we could see galaxies lying at even greater distances; would their speeds be still vaster? Nobody seriously doubts that this would be so, which gives rise to a very curious situation that I will now describe.

Galaxies lying at only about twice the distance of the furthest ones that actually can be observed with the new telescope at Mount Palomar would be moving away from us at a speed that equalled light itself. Those at still greater distances would have speeds of recession exceeding that of light. Many people find this extremely puzzling because they have learned from

Einstein's special theory of relativity that no material body can have a speed greater than light. This is true enough in the special theory of relativity which refers to a particularly simple system of space and time. But it is not true in Einstein's general theory of relativity, and it is in terms of the general theory that the Universe has to be discussed. The point is rather difficult, but I can do something toward making it a little clearer. The further a galaxy is away from us the more its distance will increase during the time required by its light to reach us. Indeed, if it is far enough away the light never reaches us at all because its path stretches faster than the light can make progress. This is what is meant by saying that the speed of recession exceeds the velocity of light. Events occurring in a galaxy at such a distance can never be observed at all by anyone inside our Galaxy, no matter how patient the observer and no matter how powerful his telescope. All the galaxies that we actually see are ones that lie close enough for their light to reach us in spite of the expansion of space that's going on. But the struggle of the light against the expansion of space does show itself, as I said before, in the reddening of the light.

As you will easily guess, there must be intermediate cases where a galaxy is at such a distance that, so to speak, the light it emits neither gains ground nor loses it. In this case the path between us and the galaxy stretches at just such a rate as exactly compensates for the velocity of the light. The light gets lost on the way. It is a case, as the Red Queen remarked to Alice, of "taking all the running you can do to keep in the same place." We know fairly accurately how far away a galaxy has to be for this special case to occur. The answer is about 2,000,000,000 light years, which is only about twice as far as the distances that we expect the giant telescope at Mount Palomar to penetrate. This means that we are already observing about half as far into space as we can ever hope to do. If we built a telescope a million times as big as the one at Mount Palomar we could scarcely double our present range of vision. So what it amounts to is that owing to the expansion of the Universe we can never observe events that happen outside a certain quite definite finite region of space. We refer to this finite region as the observable Universe. The word "observable" here does not mean that we actually observe, but what we could observe if we were equipped with perfect telescopes.

READING CRITICALLY FOR IDEAS, STRUCTURE, AND STYLE

1. In order to communicate his theory, Hoyle relies on a number of ingenious analogies to explain the size and location of our galaxy and the ever-changing relationship between galaxies as they move away from each other. Choose one of these analogies

and explain how it enables you to understand an idea that otherwise would be hard to grasp.

2. What is the significance of the recession of the galaxies in terms of what can be directly observed even with the strongest telescopes?

3. According to Hoyle, why does the theory of an expanding universe provide a more adequate explanation for measurable physical phenomena, such as low-density background material and the shift in wave lengths emitted by increasingly distant galaxies?

EXTENDING INSIGHTS THROUGH WRITING

1. Hoyle compares the shifting red spectrum of light from receding galaxies to the whistle of a receding train that sounds lower as it moves farther away. In a paragraph or two, discuss the relevance of this to Hoyle's theory.

2. The universe has many mysterious phenomena, such as black holes, dark matter, missing mass, and quasars. Do some research into one of these and invent an analogy to explain it to someone who does not have a technical background.

CONNECTING PERSPECTIVES ON THE PHYSICAL UNIVERSE

1. Compare Hoyle's analogies to those of Christopher Evans (see "The Revolution Begins") in terms of the usefulness of analogies in communicating hard-to-understand scientific phenomena.

2. In what way do Hoyle's and Peter D. Ward and Donald Brownlee's accounts complement each other in terms of explaining the profusion of galaxies and planets, and the paradox of the very small possibility that animal life could exist elsewhere?

CHARLES H. TOWNES

Harnessing Light

BACKGROUND

Charles H. Townes (b.1915) received a Ph.D. in physics from the California Institute of Technology in 1939. He has been chairman of the physics department at Columbia University (1952–1955) and professor of physics and provost at Massachusetts Institute of Technology. Since 1967 Townes has been University Professor of Physics at the University of California at Berkeley. His investigation into molecular and nuclear structure, masers, lasers, and quantum electronics resulted in his being awarded the Nobel Prize in Physics in 1964. Townes's current research interests are in microwave spectoscopy and radio and infrared astronomy. In "Harnessing Light" (1984), Townes tells about the research that led to the discovery of the laser and defines the distinctive qualities possessed by this new technological phenomenon. His most recent work is *How the Laser Happened: Adventures of a Scientist* (1999).

APPROACHING TOWNES'S ESSAY

Charles H. Townes, whose research led to the development of the laser, provides a unique, behind-the-scenes account of an invention that changed the world. His account is engaging and, despite its specialized subject, is informative and easy-to-read. Townes uses an operational definition to give his readers insight into the distinctive nature of his invention. We learn what the laser is by what it does and are able to appreciate its many applications in medicine, industry, and communications.

Townes explains that all the energy in a beam of laser light is coherent, that is, all the energy released in a laser beam is composed of light waves of the same length, which reinforce the energy of the beam and add immeasurably to its concentrated force. By contrast, a normal beam of even very bright light is quickly diffused because it is composed of a multitude of light waves out of synchronization with each other. For example: "a laser emitting one watt of light has only a hundredth the power of a 100-watt light bulb. Yet, the beam of a one-watt laser directed at the moon was seen by television equipment on the lunar surface when all the lights of our greatest cities were undetectable—simply because the beam is so directional" (para.12). A normal beam of light might be pictured as a galley ship where rowers each put their oars into the water at different moments; by contrast, a laser might be seen as the same ship where all the oars of the rowers enter the water at the same time. There are as many rowers, but in the second case, the oars are synchronized; therefore their power is greatly amplified.

The extent to which the laser has changed our lives can be seen in many commonplace examples: The old-fashioned cash register has long since given way to optical scanning of bar codes, which manufacturers routinely place on almost all items. Surgeons use lasers to make finely controlled cuts, much as they had used scalpels in the past. Old fashioned copper wiring beneath streets and highways is being replaced by optical fiber phone lines, some 1/10 the size of a human hair, capable of carrying enormous numbers of messages in the form of coherent light beams. The known and potential applications of the laser qualify it as one of the most significant inventions, perhaps equal to the discovery of electricity.

Harnessing Light

The laser was born early one beautiful spring morning on a park bench in Washington, D.C. As I sat in Franklin Square, musing and admiring the azaleas, an idea came to me for a practical way to obtain a very pure form of electromagnetic waves from molecules. I had been doggedly searching for new ways to produce radio waves at very high frequencies, too high for the vacuum tubes of the day to generate. This short-wavelength radiation, I felt, would permit extremely accurate measurement and analysis, giving new insights into physics and chemistry.

As it turned out, I was much too conservative; the field has developed far beyond my imagination and along paths I could not have foreseen at the time. Surveyors use the laser to guarantee straight lines; surgeons to weld new corneas into place and burn away blood clots; industry to drill tiny, precise holes; communications engineers to send information in vast quantities through glass fiber pipes. It is even built into the supermarket checkout scanner that reads prices by bouncing a beam of laser light off a pattern imprinted on the item.

But in the spring of 1951, as I sat on my park bench, it was all yet to come. In the quest for short-wavelength radio waves, I built on the knowledge of the time. In general terms, it was this. Atoms and molecules can absorb radiation as light, as radio waves, or as heat. The radiation is absorbed in the form of a quantum, or tiny packet of energy, that pushes the atom from one energy level to a higher one by exactly the amount of absorbed energy. The atom excited in this way may spontaneously fall to a lower energy level. As it does, it gives up a quantum of radiant energy and releases a burst of electromagnetic radiation, usually in the form of light. This happens in the sun, where atoms are excited by heat agitation or radiation and then drop to a lower level of energy, releasing light. But I was focusing on another way of producing radiation, understood in theory since Einstein discussed it in 1917: the stimulated emission of radiation.

In this case, radiation such as light passing by stimulates an atom to give up its energy to the radiation, at exactly the same frequency and radiated in exactly the same direction, and then drop to a lower state. If this process happened naturally, light striking one side of a black piece of paper would emerge from the other side stronger than it went in—and that's what happens in a laser. But such extraordinary behavior requires an unusual condition: More atoms must be in an excited energy state than in a lower energy one.

That morning in the park, I realized that if man was to obtain wavelengths shorter than those that could be produced by vacuum tubes, he must use the ready-made small devices known as atoms and molecules. And I saw that by creating this effect in a chamber with certain critical dimensions, the stimulated radiation could be reinforced, becoming steady and intense.

Later discussions with my students at Columbia University over lunch produced a new vocabulary. We chose the name "maser," for microwave amplification by stimulated emission of radiation, for a device based on the fundamental principle. We also proposed, somewhat facetiously, the "iraser" (infrared amplification by stimulated emission of radiation), "laser" (light amplification), and "xaser" (X-ray amplification). Maser and laser stuck.

The first device to use the new amplifying mechanism was a maser built around ammonia gas, since the ammonia molecule was known to interact more strongly than any other with microwaves. A three-year thesis project of graduate student James Gordon, with assistance from Herbert Zeiger, a young postdoctoral physicist, succeeded and immediately demonstrated the extreme purity of the frequency of radiation produced by the natural vibrations of ammonia molecules. A pure frequency can be translated into accurate timekeeping. Suppose we know that the power from a wall outlet has a frequency of exactly 60 cycles per second. It then takes exactly 1/60th of a second to complete one cycle, one second to complete 60 cycles, one minute for 3,600 of them, and so on. To build an accurate clock, we have only to count the cycles. In the mid-1950s, when the first ammonia maser was completed, the best clocks had a precision of about one part in a billion, about the same accuracy of the Earth's rotation about its axis. Today, a hydrogen maser is the heart of an atomic clock accurate to one part in 100 trillion, an improvement by a factor of at least 10,000. Such a clock, if kept running, would be off by no more than one second in every few million years.

The new process also immediately provided an amplifier for radio waves much more sensitive than the best then available. Later refinements provided very practical amplifiers, and masers now are typically used to communicate in space over long distances and to pick up radio waves from distant galaxies. Astrophysicists recently have discovered *natural* masers in interstellar space that generate enormous microwave intensity from excited molecules.

Although my main interest in stimulated emission of radiation had been to obtain wavelengths shorter than microwaves, the new possibilities for superaccurate clocks and supersensitive amplifiers, and their scientific uses, occupied everyone's attention for some time. By 1957 I felt it was time to get back on the track of shorter wavelengths. I decided that it would actually be easier to make a big step than a small one and jump immediately to light waves—wavelengths in the visible or short infrared, almost 10,000 times higher in frequency than microwaves. But there was a sticky problem: What kind of resonating chamber would function at a single and precisely correct frequency but could be built using ordinary engineering techniques? My friend Arthur Schawlow, then at the Bell Telephone Laboratories, helped provide the answer: an elongated chamber with a mirror at each end.

10   In December of 1958 we published a paper that discussed this and other aspects of a practical laser and set off an intense wave of efforts to build one. In 1960 Theodore H. Maiman, a physicist with Hughes Aircraft Company, demonstrated the first operating laser, while Ali Javan, William R. Bennett Jr., and Donald R. Herriott at Bell Labs built a second, completely different type. Rather than using gas, Maiman's laser used a small cylinder of synthetic ruby, its ends polished into mirrored surfaces. The firing of a helical flashbulb surrounding the rod triggered the ruby to send out a brief, intense pulse of laser light. Soon there were many variations on the laser theme, using different atoms or molecules and different methods of providing them with energy, but all used a mirrored chamber.

The laser quickly gained great notoriety with the public as a "death ray"; it is a popular science fiction motif and one with undeniable dramatic appeal. Lasers certainly have the power to injure. Even a weak laser shone into the eye will be focused by the lens of the eye onto the retina and damage it. But laser beams are not very advantageous as military weapons. Guns are cheaper, easier to build and use, and, in most cases, much more effective. Science fiction's death ray is still mostly science fiction, and it is likely to remain so.

The laser is, however, extremely powerful. The reason is that stimulated amplification adds energy "coherently"—that is, in exactly the same direction as the initial beam. This coherence conveys surprising properties. A laser emitting one watt of light has only a hundredth the power of a 100-watt light bulb. Yet the beam of a one-watt laser directed at the moon was seen by television equipment on the lunar surface when all the lights of our greatest cities were undetectable—simply because the beam is so directional. A simple lens can focus the beam of light from an ordinary one-watt laser into a spot so small that it produces 100 million watts per square centimeter, enormously greater than the intensity from any other type of source.

But a one-watt laser is not even a particularly powerful one. Pulsed lasers can produce a *trillion* watts of power by delivering energy over a very short period but at enormous levels. This power may last only one ten-billionth of a second, but during that time a lens can concentrate it to a level of 100 million million million watts per square centimeter. The trillion watts that such a laser delivers is approximately equal to the average amount of electric power being used over the entire Earth at any one time. Focused by a lens, this concentration or power is 100 trillion times greater than the light at the surface of the sun. It will melt or tear apart any substance, including atoms themselves. Drilling through diamonds is easy for a laser beam and produces no wear. Lasers have been developed that can compact small pellets of material and then heat them in a sudden flash to reproduce conditions similar to those in the sun's interior, where nuclear fusion occurs.

The laser's directed intensity quickly made it an effective industrial tool. Lasers cut or weld delicate electronic circuits or heavy metal parts. They can melt or harden the surface of a piece of steel so quickly that under a very thin skin, the metal is still cool and undamaged. Industrial interest was especially high. By the end of the 1960s, most new lasers were being designed in industrial laboratories, though many are important tools in university laboratories.

How useful lasers and quantum electronics have been to scientists is 15 indicated by the fact that besides Nobel Prizes for work leading to the devices themselves, they have played an important role in other Nobel awards—for example, the one to Dennis Gabor of the University of London for the idea of holography (three-dimensional laser photography); the one to Schawlow of Stanford University for versatile new types of laser spectroscopy; to Nicolaas Bloembergen of Harvard University for discoveries in nonlinear optics made possible by high-intensity laser beams; and one to Arno Penzias and Robert W. Wilson of the Bell Telephone Laboratories for the discovery of microwave radiation from the Big Bang which initiated our universe. While the latter discovery might possible have been made by other techniques, it was facilitated by very sensitive maser amplification.

Because of the unswerving directionality of laser beams, probably more lasers have been sold for producing the straight lines needed in surveying than for any other single purpose. The laser is now a common surveying instrument that helps to lay out roads.

Laser beams also can measure distance conveniently. By bouncing the beam from a reflector, a surveyor can measure distances to high precision. Beams sent from Earth have been bounced off reflectors placed on the moon by astronauts. By generating a short light pulse and measuring the elapsed time before it returns, the distance to the moon can be measured within one inch. Such measurements have revealed effects of general relativity and thus refined our knowledge of the theory of gravitation.

In scientific equipment or simply in machine shops, the laser's pure frequency allows the beam to be reflected and the peaks and troughs of its wave matched with those of the first part of the beam, thus providing distance measurements to within a small fraction of one wavelength—40 millionths of an inch. In scientific experiments, changes of length as small as one hundredth of the diameter of an atom have been measured in this way. There are efforts to use such supersensitive measurements to detect the gravity waves due to motions of distant stars.

Because lasers can be so finely focused and their intensity adjusted to make controlled cuts, they are used as a surgeon's scalpel. Not only can they be very precisely directed, but a particular color can be chosen to destroy certain types of tissue while leaving others relatively intact, an especially valuable effect for some cancers. In cutting, the laser also seals off blood vessels so that there is relatively little bleeding. For the eye, laser light has the interesting ability to go harmlessly through the pupil and perform operations within.

20 Of all the ways our lives are likely to be affected by lasers, perhaps none will be so unobtrusive and yet more important than cheaper and more effective communications. Within many metropolitan areas, the number of radio or television stations must be limited because the number of available frequencies is limited. For the same reason, large numbers of conversations cannot simultaneously be carried on a single telephone wire. But light is a superhighway of frequencies; a single light beam can, in principle, carry all the radio and TV stations and all telephone calls in the world without interfering with one another. These light beams can be transmitted on glass fibers one-tenth the size of a human hair. In crowded cities where streets have been dug up for years and jammed beneath with all manner of pipes and wires, these tiny fibers can fit into the smallest spaces and provide enormous communication capacity. In long distance communication, they may replace most cables, and even satellites.

Even after the laser was invented and its importance recognized, it was by no means clear, even to those who worked on it, that it would see so many striking applications. And much undoubtedly lies ahead.

READING CRITICALLY FOR IDEAS, STRUCTURE, AND STYLE

1. Why is "the stimulated emission of radiation" a crucial concept in understanding how the laser became possible? What unique properties does the laser possess that makes it such an incredible invention?

2. How would you characterize the tone of Townes's essay? Does he present himself as a brilliant inventor or just another hardworking researcher who was lucky? How does his account give you insight into the *ethos* of scientists? Explain your answer.

3. How does the enormous range of applications of lasers directly depend on specific qualities of the laser beams?

EXTENDING INSIGHTS THROUGH WRITING

1. Although the present uses of the laser, including holography, fiber optics, microsurgery, and as surveying instruments, are quite familiar, Townes dismisses the possible use of the laser as a "death ray." Ironically, proposed strategic defense initiative systems (SDI) may make use of lasers in precisely this way. Do some research into the current state of these systems and the practical and political issues involved and discuss your findings.

2. What additional applications of the laser (that Townes does not mention) have permeated popular culture (for example, corrective eye surgery, scanning bar codes in supermarkets, and laser printers) since he wrote this in in 1984? How has the laser, in fact, transformed modern society since Townes invented it?

CONNECTING PERSPECTIVES ON
THE PHYSICAL UNIVERSE

1. If you had to choose, which would you say was a more significant invention that changed the world—lasers or computers (see Bill Gates "The Road Ahead")? Explain your answer in a short essay.

2. In what way do the numbers that Townes so casually includes as part of his account ("accurate to one part in 100 trillion") require the kind of imaginative analogies formulated by Christopher Evans (see "The Revolution Begins") to translate these ideas into a comprehensible framework? Explain your answer.

CHRISTOPHER EVANS

The Revolution Begins

BACKGROUND

Christopher Evans (1931–1979) was born in Aberdovey, Wales. Evans received his Ph.D. from the University at Reading, England, and served as the head of the Man-Computer Interaction Section, computer science division of the National Physical Laboratory, England, from 1963 until his untimely death in 1979. He was acknowledged as one of the world's leading experts on computers, and Evans's unique background in psychology and computer science are reflected in his wide range of published writings. He co-edited *Brain Physiology and Psychology* (1966), *Cybernetics* (1968), and *Attention in Neurophysiology* (1969). Evans wrote *Psychology: A Dictionary of the Mind, Brain, and Behavior* (1978), *The Mighty Micro: The Impact of the Computer Revolution* (1979), which became a six-part television series, and *The Micro Millennium* (1980) from which our selection is taken. In "The Revolution Begins," Evans uses an ingenious analogy to explain the incredible processing speed of the computer.

APPROACHING EVANS'S ESSAY

Evans realizes that the most difficult idea for readers to comprehend is the rapid switching speed of computers at over a billion times a second. Clock speed (measured today in MHz) for a microprocessor is one of the main factors that determines the power of the computer: the higher the number, the higher the speed. To most people, the word "billion" is just a word on paper; it is hard to comprehend what the number actually encompasses. To clarify this concept, Evans uses an analogy based on the amount of time it would take a billionaire to hand out one pound notes of his money to everyone he meets.

Evans also uses an ingenious way to explain the miniaturization process that makes it possible to increase the number of circuits that can be put on a microchip. His analogies and hypothetical scenarios help his readers to enter the world of minute dimensions and fantastic speeds.

The Revolution Begins

Miniaturization did not stop when it came to etching complete circuits on a chip. With the technique known as large-scale integration, first hundreds, then thousands, and even tens of thousands of individual units could be amassed on one slice of semi-conductor. And still the process of miniaturization continued, is continuing, and so far as one can see will continue into the foreseeable future. The units of which computers are made are getting smaller and smaller, shrinking beyond the range of ordinary microscopes into the infinities of the molecular world. So rapid is the rate of progress that advance seems to be following advance on almost a monthly basis. At the time of writing the very latest memories, effectively containing a hundred thousand switching units, are being squeezed onto a chip, and may well be on the market by the time this book is published. On the horizon, or to be more exact on the laboratory bench, and scheduled for operation within a year or so, are the first million-unit chips.

Now a million is a peculiar number which gets flung around more and more as inflation makes government budgets soar into the stratosphere. It is easy, therefore, to devalue the concept of a machine made up of a million individual components, and yet which would still nestle on a fingernail. To get a rough idea of what we're talking about, suppose one expanded these units up to the size of the tubes in the original ENIAC and laid them side by side on a flat surface so that they were two inches apart—what size would this turn out to be? The answer is that it would be as big as a football field.

But let us look at it another way. When the first big computers attracted the attention of the Press in the early '50s, they were given the not totally misleading name of "electronic brains." The human brain itself is made up of minute electronic binary switching units called neurones, and there are an awful lot of them—about ten thousand million in all. But even assuming that neurones and electronic switching units are functionally equivalent, it was ridiculous, scientists used to argue, to talk of computers as "brains" and even more ridiculous, scientists used to argue, to talk of computers as "brains" and even more ridiculous to imagine them doing brain-like things. Why, if you wanted to build a computer which contained the same number of functional elements as the brain, you would end up with something the size of New York City and drawing more power than the whole of the subway system!

This daunting example was generally used to silence the brain/computer parallelists in the all-tube days of the early '50s and it makes quaint reading when you come across it today. By the early '60s, with transistorization, the computer / brain had shrunk to the size of the Statue of Liberty, and a ten-kilowatt generator would have kept it ticking over nicely. By the early '70s, with integrated circuits, there had been a further compression: it was down to the size of a Greyhound bus, and you could ran it off a mains plug. By the mid '70s it was the size of a TV set, and at the time of writing is that of a typewriter. And such is the pace of development that, allowing a one-year lag between the time I write these words and the time you read them, the incredible shrinking brain will have continued to shrink—to what size? My guess is that it will be no bigger than a human brain, perhaps even smaller. And to power it, a portable radio battery will suffice.

5   These careering changes, which will shortly lead to computers paralleling the brain both in size and in the number of their individual components, do not allow one to draw other parallels. Assuming one makes such a brain model and it sits there, capable of calculating at computer-like speeds, it will still be unable to perform any of the functions of a human brain. To do so it would have to be programmed appropriately, and the programming problems would be colossal. But this does not imply that it could *never* be so programmed, a topic which we will be picking up later. It is also fair to say that the computer would have an enormous edge on switching speed. The human brain would be chugging along at a hundred cycles per second, while no computer could be satisfied with a switching speed of less than a million cycles! Here again we have to pause and contemplate just what we are talking about.

Most people reckon a second to be rather a short period. There is not much you can do with it—blink an eye, speak one short word or read about ten characters of text. The idea that an electromechanical relay can flick back and forth twenty times in a single second sets up an image of a blurring, clattering bit of metal, and when you get to tubes operating thousands of times a second you move into a scale of time with which you have no touch-points. But what about millions of times a second? Are we not in danger of losing contact with the concept altogether? But this is just the beginning, and if you have not thought much about these things you had better steel yourself for a shock when I tell you that computers already exist whose switching potential is in the nanosecond range—this is billions of times in each tick of the clock. Once again we need to at least try to get this in perspective and can perhaps manage it by spreading time out with a broader brush. Since we so frequently hear the word "billion" employed in terms of money (I am talking about the American billion—a thousand million), let us use a context which is both monetary and temporal.

Imagine a British billionaire who decides that he is going to hand out a pound note to everyone who comes up to him—just one pound each. A long line forms and the billionaire starts handing out his pounds. He moves quickly and manages to get rid of them at the rate of one every ten seconds, but being human he can only keep it up for eight hours a day, five days a week. How long will it take him to dispose of his billion? Suppose that he has just handed out his last note, how long ago would it have been since he handed over his first one? Ten years? Twenty? Most people, when asked this question, take a jump in the dark and come up with a figure between ten and fifty years in the past. Once in a while someone will give you a date in the nineteenth century. Does that seem plausible or might it be even earlier? Does it seem conceivable, for example, that the billionaire could have started as far back as the Battle of Waterloo? Well, in fact he would have had to start before that. The Great Fire of London? No, he would have been counting away while Old St Paul's blazed. The execution of Anne Boleyn? No, he would have been counting then too. Agincourt? No. Battle of Hastings? No, further still. To cut a long story short, you would have to go back to the year 640 or thereabouts before you would see the billionaire handing over his first pound note. But that is just a taste of the cake. A billion times per second is no longer considered to be anything like the upper limit of computer processing speeds. Some recent observations indicate that on the surfaces of some of the latest semi-conductor materials, tiny magnetic elements can be seen switching, admittedly in an uncontrolled way, at rates approaching a trillion a second.

Carry the analogy to a trillionaire who wants to get rid of his money and you dive back in time beyond Christ, beyond Rome, beyond Greece, Stonehenge, Egypt and the Pyramids, before architecture, literature and language, and back to the Pliocene Age when Europe was encrusted with ice and the mammoth and woolly rhinoceros were the kings. There is no other word for it—such switching speeds are fantastic. And yet they are real: computers can operate at such speeds, and Man will find a way of making use of them.

Which brings us to the question of just what possible use could be found for these extremely fast, extremely small computers and their even faster, even smaller progeny. Surely there must be an upper limit to the speed with which people would want to calculate? Is it really going to help a company whose total tax and wage structure is handled by its own computer in one hour, to have it dealt with by the next generation of machines in one second? Alternatively, supposing that, using current memory technologies, all personnel details could be recorded on a flat magnetic disc the size of a 45 rpm record, what possible advantage could there be in storing it all on something the size of a postage stamp? These may seem to be natural questions, as indeed they are, but they are not the most important ones and they miss one or two big points.

Firstly, while massive increases in processing speeds are helpful when it comes to number-crunching, they begin to have far more dramatic yield when the power of the computer is directed towards tasks of a non-numerical nature. The distinction between numerical and non-numerical needs to be made with care, but we are talking about tasks where the computer's intellectual potential, its capacity for problem-solving, for fact finding, for logical analysis rather than for purely routine calculation, come to the fore. The use of the word "intellectual" in connection with computers is also treading on dangerous ground, but once computers move from routine to analytical and integrative functions, the increases in processing speed will begin to pay off and they will be able to tackle more complex problems.

10

The second point concerns reductions in size. Why make computers so small that if you drop one on the floor you are in danger of walking off with it stuck to the heel of your shoe? There are three answers to this question and together they sum up one of the most important single factors about the pace of computer development over the next few years. Very small computers have enormous advantages: firstly, because they consume minute amounts of power; secondly, because they are very cheap, thirdly, because they are extremely portable and can therefore be put to use in all kinds of different places. Indeed, we are shortly moving into the phase where computers will become one of the cheapest pieces of technology on earth—cheaper than TV sets (they already are), cheaper than portable typewriters, cheaper even than transistor radios. They will also, for exactly the same reasons, become the most common pieces of technology in the world, and the most useful.

READING CRITICALLY FOR IDEAS, STRUCTURE, AND STYLE

1. Perhaps because he was writing at the very onset of the computer revolution in 1979, Evans was most amazed by the then phenomenal speeds of which computers were capable. How does his analogy, involving a billionaire, help the reader understand the concept of an unimaginably fast computing speed?

2. The other direction computers have taken, along with faster computing speeds, is towards miniaturization. How effective did you find his hypothetical scenario in explaining this phenomena?

3. Computers today have gone well beyond even what Evans could imagine. To what extent does he address the issue of ends versus means in assessing the direction the computer "revolution" has taken? Are there other issues he did not foresee that have become important (for example, privacy of data)?

EXTENDING INSIGHTS THROUGH WRITING

1. What functions would you like to see computers be able to perform in the future? Describe one or two of these in full detail.

2. How dependent are you on computers and being connected to the Internet? Try to live through a day without using a computer (or imagine what it would be like) and describe your experiences and conclusions about the extent to which computers are now an integral facet of modern life.

CONNECTING PERSPECTIVES ON
THE PHYSICAL UNIVERSE

1. Evans is obviously quite taken with the more "intellectual" analytical uses that computers would soon be capable of performing. How does Bill Gates (a real billionaire unlike Evans's imaginary one) in "The Road Ahead" extend this theme and project a range of applications Evans never even imagined?

2. In what way do analogies serve Evans, as they did Sir Fred Hoyle (see "The Continuous Creation of the Universe"), to put into concrete terms concepts of speed and distance that are beyond the grasp of the senses?

NEIL POSTMAN

Information

BACKGROUND

Neil Postman (b.1931) is University Professor, Paulette Goddard Chair of Media Ecology, and Chair of the Department of Culture and Communication at New York University and has investigated the effects of the media on our culture in books such as *Amusing Ourselves to Death* (1985) and *Conscientious Objections* (1992). Since the late 1960s he and Charles Weingartner have been active in calling for educational reform especially in their book *Teaching as a Subversive Activity* (1969). In *The End of Education* (1995), Postman looked back to the eighteenth century, and the Enlightenment, as providing the origins of many of today's most important ideas (concepts of political rights and religious and intellectual freedom). In his most recent book, *Building a Bridge to the 18th Century: How the Past Can Improve our Future* (1999), from which the following essay is drawn, Postman looks once again to the eighteenth century to recover the illuminating and enobling ideas he feels have been lost in modern culture.

APPROACHING POSTMAN'S ESSAY

Postman feels that the modern world moves so quickly that it has lost its sense of continuity with the past and needs to look back to the Enlightenment for the rich source of ideas that can still prove worthwhile. Central to these ideas is the concept of critical thinking, careful reading, and a healthy skepticism towards information devoid of context or purpose.

In "Information," Postman protests our addiction to information as an end in itself. Postman isn't uncritically nostalgic about the eighteenth century, but genuinely believes that modern culture has strayed from the efficient use of facts in the rush to indiscriminately obtain vast quantities of information (ironically, Bill Gates sees this as a defining positive feature of modern culture). Postman's research reveals that the famous encyclopedias, histories, and dictionaries of that era only presented information that was thought to be necessary and useful. Rather than simply being a curmudgeon, Postman is genuinely alarmed by what he perceives to be the insidious consequences of a culture drowning in a flood of indiscriminate data. By contrast, he discovers that the paramount concern of the eighteenth century, as expressed in the writings of Rousseau, Diderot, and Voltaire, was the meaning of human existence. These thinkers would have ridiculed our culture's obsession with information as an end in and of itself and were always alert to the applications of knowledge to improve our lives. Postman recommends we use the legacy of the eighteenth century to discover how far we have strayed from the ideals of rational, purposive thought.

Information

You can search the indexes of a hundred books on the Enlightenment (I have almost done it), and you will not find a listing for "information." This is quite remarkable, since the eighteenth century generated a tumult of new information, along with new media through which information is communicated. The newspaper had its origin in the beginning of the century, and by century's end, had taken on its modern form. Every country in Europe—indeed, most cities—had its own periodical, many following the pattern of England's *Spectator.* Unlike in England, censorship remained a problem on the Continent, but not sufficiently serious to prevent the proliferation of a variety of journals—for instance, *Diario, Zeitung, Almanache, Journal des Sciences et Beaux Arts, Tagebuch,* and scores of others, including the famous *Patriot,* a product of the city of Hamburg. Their purpose, in general, was to create a cosmopolitan citizenship, informed about the best ideas and most recent knowledge of the time. The same purpose was pursued, especially in France, through the creation of *salons*—gatherings of aristocratic and middle-class people who shared ideas and new information in social settings. As the century progressed, *salons* were established in many places, becoming of particular importance in Germany, Austria, and England. In England, the tradition of the exclusively male club took on the function of the *salon,* as in the case of the Scriblerus Club, founded in 1714 and frequented by Swift, Pope, and Boling-broke. The *salons* served especially well as media through which information about foreign lands could be shared. Beginning with Columbus's explorations, many European nations pursued policies of colonization so that, by the eighteenth century, explorers, merchants, and clerics from many European nations had stories to tell of exotic customs and strange people. All the major ports of Africa and India were frequented if not controlled by Europeans, who were also settling in North America and in newly discovered lands. They returned with original perspectives and startling information, and when Voltaire wrote his *History of the World,* he could include a chapter on China, about which much was beginning to be known. An era of new information was opened—about geography, social life, agriculture, history, and, of course, science and technology, the last of which required the establishment of academies for research and teaching: the Royal Society, the Académie des Sciences, the German Academia Naturae Curiosorum, the Berlin Academy. The eighteenth century also introduced engineering schools, commercial schools for training businessmen in accounting and foreign languages, and medical and surgical colleges. Indeed, beginning with John Locke's essay *Some Thoughts Concerning Education,* there followed a flood of books on the subject of children and learning.

All of this was accompanied by an unprecedented spread of literacy which had begun slowly in the seventeenth century and then accelerated in the eighteenth. Rousseau is the only major figure of the Enlightenment who was skeptical of the importance of literacy. In *Emile,* he requires the young to read only one book, *Robinson Crusoe,* and that only in order to learn how to survive in primitive conditions. Everyone else regarded the ability to read as the key to the cultivation of social, political, and moral consciousness. The English settlers in America provide a clear example of the obsession with literacy that characterized the age. Literacy rates are notoriously difficult to assess, but there is sufficient evidence that between 1640 and 1700 the literacy rate for men in Massachusetts and Connecticut was somewhere between eighty-nine and ninety-five percent, quite probably the highest concentration of literate males to be found anywhere in the world at that time. (The literacy rate for women in those colonies is estimated to have run as high as sixty-two percent in the years 1681–1697.)[1]

The Bible, of course, was the central reading matter in all households, since these people were Protestants who shared Luther's belief that printing was "God's highest and extremest act of Grace, whereby the business of the Gospel is driven forward." Of course, the business of the Gospel may be driven forward in books other than the Bible, as, for example, in the famous *Bay Psalm Book,* printed in 1640 and generally regarded as America's first best-seller.[2] But it is not to be assumed that these people confined their reading to religious matters. Probate records indicate that sixty percent of the estates in Middlesex County between the years 1654 and 1699 contained books, all but eight percent of them including more than the Bible. In fact, between 1682 and 1685, Boston's leading bookseller imported 3,421 books from *one* English dealer, most of these nonreligious books. The meaning of this fact may be appreciated when one adds that these books were intended for consumption by approximately 75,000 people then living in the northern colonies.[3] The modern equivalent would be ten million books.

The settlers came to America as readers who believed that reading was as important in the New World as it was in the Old. From 1650 onward almost all New England towns passed laws requiring the maintenance of a

---

[1]James D. Hart, *The Popular Book: A History of America's Literary Taste* (New York: Oxford University Press, 1950), p. 8.
[2]Ibid.
[3]Ibid., p. 15.

"reading and writing" school, the large communities being required to maintain a grammar school as well. In all such laws, reference is made to Satan, whose evil designs, it was supposed, could be thwarted at every turn by education. But there were other reasons why education was required, as suggested by the following ditty, popular in the late seventeenth century:

> From public schools shall general
> knowledge flow,
> For 'tis the people's
> sacred right to know.

These people, in other words, had more than the subjection of Satan on their minds. Beginning in the seventeenth century, a great epistemological shift had taken place in which knowledge of every kind was transferred to, and made manifest through, the printed page. "More than any other device," Lewis Mumford wrote of this shift, "the printed book released people from the domination of the immediate and the local;... print made a greater impression than actual events.... To exist was to exist in print: the rest of the world tended gradually to become more shadowy. Learning became book-learning."[4] In light of this, we may assume that the schooling of the young was understood by the colonists not only as a moral duty but as an intellectual imperative. (The England from which they came was an island of schools. By 1660, for example, there were 444 schools in England, one school approximately every twelve miles.)

It is clear that growth in literacy was closely connected to schooling, which in turn was connected to the enormous proliferation of information. We may wonder, then, why the late seventeenth century and eighteenth century are not commonly referred to as the age of information. The answer, I think, is that the concept of "information" was different from what it is today. Information was not thought of as a commodity to be bought and sold. It had no separate existence, as it does in our age; specifically, it was not thought to be worthwhile unless it was embedded in a context, unless it gave shape, texture, or authority to a political, social, or scientific concept, which itself was required to fit into some world-view. No one was ridiculed more in the eighteenth century, especially by Jonathan Swift, than the pedant, the person who collected information without purpose, without connection to social life.

A useful way to understand the Enlightenment conception of information is to peruse the famous *Encyclopédie*, the prospectus of which was launched in 1750 by Diderot. Among its predecessors was Pierre Bayle's *Dictionnaire historique et critique*, published in 1697, which had as its purpose promoting the importance—in fact, the virtue—of skepticism. Diderot's *Encyclopédie* had a similar purpose, which is to say that information was to be the vehicle through which skepticism, as a world-view, was to be advanced. (According to Diderot's daughter, the last words she heard him

---

[4]Lewis Mumford, *Technics and Civilization* (New York: Harcourt, Brace and World, 1934), p. 136.

speak, on the day before he died, were, "The first step toward philosophy is unbelief.")[5] This purpose was pursued in nearly every article that appeared in the *Encyclopédie,* including many of those that dealt with crafts, technology, and practical matters. Diderot wrote essays on cooking, on the art of whetting knives, on the reform of the alphabet, and on the different methods of catching fish worms. In most cases, these were what we would call today editorials. Diderot was, at heart, a revolutionary, and his conception of information was as a weapon of social and political change. The idea of information "for its own sake" was alien to him, as it was to all the Enlightenment philosophes. One can find something of the same utilitarian spirit in Voltaire's *History of the World* and even in Samuel Johnson's *Dictionary.* All lexicographers freely admit that, of necessity, they steal from one another, and Johnson is no exception. He mostly borrowed from Nathan Bailey's *An Universal Etymological English Dictionary,* generally regarded as the first English-language dictionary, published in 1721. But much more than Bailey, Johnson used his dictionary (published in 1755) as a vehicle to promote the stability of the English language. Most dictionaries today are *history* books, describing how words *have been* used. Johnson meant his dictionary to be a *law* book, asserting how words *ought* to be used. His purpose was to "purify" English. (He most likely was influenced by such enterprises as the French Academy, established for the preservation of the "purity" of French.) While Johnson did not deny that language changes, he left no doubt that he was against its doing so, and his dictionary represents, in a way, his protest. Johnson's dictionary was, in effect, a philosophy of language, and the information it contained had as its purpose the advancement of that philosophy.

What I am driving at is that it is hard to find a text of the Enlightenment that separates information from a specific purpose. All the newspapers of the age regarded information as a weapon. America's first paper, published in 1690, indicated that its purpose was to combat the spirit of lying which then prevailed in Boston (and, I am told, still does). One did not give information to make another "informed." One gave information to make another do something or feel something, and the doing and feeling were themselves part of a larger idea. Information was, in short, a rhetorical instrument, and this idea did not greatly change until the mid-nineteenth century.

The change in the meaning of information was largely generated by the invention of telegraphy and photography in the 1840s. Telegraphy, in particular, gave legitimacy to the idea of context-free information; that is, to the idea that the value of information need not be tied to any function it might serve in social and political life. It may exist by itself, as a means of satisfying curiosity and offering novelty. The telegraph made information into a commodity, a "thing," desirable in itself, separate from its possible uses or meaning. In the process, telegraphy made public discourse essentially incoherent. It brought into being a world of broken time and broken attention, to use Mumford's phrase. The principal strength of the telegraph

---

[5]Arthur M. Wilson, *Diderot* (New York: Oxford University Press, 1972), p. 140.

was its capacity to move information, not collect it, explain it, or analyze it. Photography joined with telegraphy in re-creating our conception of information, since photography is preeminently a world of fact, not of dispute about facts or of conclusions to be drawn from them. The way in which the photograph records experience is fundamentally different from the way of language. Language makes sense only when it is presented as a sequence of propositions. Meaning is distorted when a word or sentence is, as we say, taken out of context. But a photograph does not require one. In fact, the point of photography is to isolate images from context, so as to make them visible in a different way. In a world of photographic images, Susan Sontag writes, "all borders ... seem arbitrary. Anything can be separated, can be made discontinuous from anything else: All that is necessary is to frame the subject differently." She is remarking on the capacity of photographs to perform a peculiar kind of dismembering of reality, a wrenching of moments out of their contexts, and a juxtaposing of events and things that have no logical or historical connection with each other. Like telegraphy, photography re-creates the world as a series of idiosyncratic events. There is no beginning, middle, or end in a world of photographs, as there is none implied by telegraphy. The world is atomized. There is only a present, and it need not be part of any story that can be told.

Storyless information is an inheritance of the nineteenth century, not of the eighteenth. It emerged as a consequence of an extraordinarily successful effort to solve the problem of limitations in the speed with which information could be moved. In the early decades of the nineteenth century, messages could travel only as fast as a human being—about thirty-five miles per hour on a fast train. Moreover, the forms of information were largely confined to language, so that the forms of information were as limited as the speed of its movement. The problem addressed in the nineteenth century was how to get more information to more people, faster, and in more diverse forms. For 150 years, humanity has, worked with stunning ingenuity to solve this problem. The good news is that we have. The bad news is that, in solving it, we have created another problem, never before experienced: information glut, information as garbage, information divorced from purpose and even meaning. As a consequence, there prevails among us what Langdon Winner calls "mythinformation"—no lisp intended. It is an almost religious conviction that at the root of our difficulties—social, political, ecological, psychological—is the fact that we do not have enough information. This, in spite of everyone's having access to books, newspapers, magazines, radios, television, movies, photographs, videos, CDs, billboards, telephones, junk mail, and, recently, the Internet. If I have left out some source of information, you can supply it. The point is that having successfully solved the problem of moving information continuously, rapidly, and in diverse forms, we do not know, for the most part, what to do with it or about it—except to continue into the twenty-first century trying to solve a nineteenth-century problem that has already been solved. This is sheer foolishness, as any eighteenth-century savant would surely tell us. If there are people starving in the world—and there are—it is not caused by insufficient information. If crime is rampant in the streets, it is not caused by

10

insufficient information. If children are abused and wives are battered, that has nothing to do with insufficient information. If our schools are not working and democratic principles are losing their force, that too has nothing to do with insufficient information. If we are plagued by such problems, it is because something else is missing. That is to say, several things are missing. And one of them is some way to put information in its place, to give it a useful epistemological frame.

In the eighteenth century, the newspaper provided such a frame, and, given the present information flood, it may be the only medium capable of doing something like that for our use in the century ahead. Unlike more recent information media, the newspaper has a tradition as a public trust; it is given special protection by the Constitution (at least in America). It is more connected to community life than other media and, for all the imperial entrepreneurs who own them, newspapers still have editors and reporters whose interests are not wholly driven by the market. What follows, then, is an idea—hardly new—based on the retrieval of once useful definitions of and distinctions among information, knowledge, and wisdom. It is a proposal for redefining the place of information so that there might be at least one medium whose purpose is to help twenty-first-century citizens make sense of the world.

I should like to start the idea by referring to a cartoon that appeared some time ago in the *Los Angeles Times.* The cartoon is about an amazing new product that has just come on the market. The product is designed to be better than any computer or anything that one could use a computer for, including the Internet and web pages. The product is called a daily newspaper. And here are some of its selling points: It requires no batteries or wires; no maintenance contract is needed; it is lightweight, recyclable, and biodegradable; it is absolutely portable and will go with you on trains, buses, cars, airplanes, and even to bed; it is completely quiet, does not oink, buzz, or beep; no secret numbers, access codes, or modems are needed and it does not affect your telephone lines; one has unlimited use of it for about twenty dollars a month; it comes pre-edited for pornography, fraud, and typos; it requires no furniture space; and, last but not least, the product does not in any way contribute to the bank account of Bill Gates.

The cartoon makes a case for the importance of newspapers and for the reasons we may hope they will survive. But the cartoon largely concerns the *form* of newspapers and, except for the reference to the fact that the newspaper comes pre-edited for pornography, fraud, and typos, there is nothing suggested about the uniqueness of the *content* of newspapers. Perhaps this was omitted because the cartoonist assumed that the function of newspapers is to provide people with information; and when it comes to the distribution of information, computer technology can do it better than newspapers—that is, can do it faster, more voluminously, and more conveniently. In other words, if you want to promote the value of newspapers these days, perhaps it is best to avoid talking about information since the new technologies, including television, appear to be largely in charge of handling that.

Which brings us to the question: What is information and how much of it do people need? Obviously, information is not the same thing as knowledge, and it is certainly not anything close to what one might mean by wisdom. Information consists of statements about the facts of the world. There are, of course, an uncountable number of facts in the world. Facts are transformed into information only when we take note of them and speak of them, or, in the case of newspapers, write about them. By this definition, facts cannot be wrong. They are what they are. Statements about facts—that is, information—can be wrong, and often are. Thus, to say that we live in an unprecedented age of information is merely to say that we have available more statements about the world than we have ever had. This means, among other things, that we have available more *erroneous* statements than we have ever had. Has anyone been discussing the matter of how we can distinguish between what is true and what is false? Aside from schools, which are supposed to attend to the matter but largely ignore it, is there any institution or medium that is concerned with the problem of misinformation? Those who speak enthusiastically of the great volume of statements about the world available on the Internet do not usually address how we may distinguish the true from the false. By its nature, the Internet can have no interest in such a distinction. It is not a "truth" medium; it is an information medium. But in theory, at least, newspapers do have such an interest, and there are no editors anywhere who will claim that it is not their business to separate the true from the false. In fact, there is no problem older than this—how to know the difference between true and false statements. When Cain is asked where his brother is and he pretends not to know, God knows that he knows; indeed, he knew in advance that Cain would speak falsely. But for the rest of us the matter is not so simple. It is not my intention here to address the issue, although I will try in a later chapter. Here, I am addressing a problem no culture has faced before—the problem of what to do with too much information. One answer, of course, is to make oneself inaccessible to it. Some people do this, I among them. As I have mentioned, I do not have e-mail, to take only one example, because it would make me the target of carloads of messages, almost all of which have no fundamental bearing on my life. I have developed other means of withdrawal, as have many people, although it is not easy to do this. In America, especially, one is thought to be peculiar, if not worse, if one sidesteps the onrush of information. But I am not here concerned with individual strategies, some of which I have suggested in an earlier chapter. My focus here is on how at least one medium—the newspaper—can assist in helping everyone overcome information glut.

To say it simply, newspapers should, for a start, get out of the information business and into the knowledge business. What do I mean by "knowledge"? I define knowledge as organized information—information that is embedded in some context; information that has a purpose, that leads one to seek further information in order to understand something about the world. Without organized information, we may know something *of* the world, but very little *about* it. When one has knowledge, one knows how to make sense of information, knows how to relate information to one's life, and, especially, knows when information is irrelevant.

It is fairly obvious that some newspaper editors are aware of the distinction between information and knowledge, but not nearly enough of them. There are newspapers whose editors do not yet grasp that in a technological world, information is a problem, not a solution. They will tell us of things we already know about and will give little or no space to providing a sense of context or coherence. Let us suppose, for example, that a four-teen-year-old Palestinian boy hurls a Molotov cocktail at two eighteen-year-old Israeli soldiers in Jerusalem. The explosion knocks one of the soldiers down and damages his left eye. The other soldier, terrified, fires a shot at the Palestinian that kills him instantly. The injured soldier loses the sight of his eye. All of this we learn of on television or from radio the next day we are told about it again in the newspaper. Why? The newspaper will add nothing, unless it can tell something about the meaning of the event, including why this event is in the newspaper at all. There are at least forty wars presently going on someplace in the world, and we can assume that young people are being killed in all of them. Why do I need to know about *this* event? Why is what happens in Jerusalem more important than what happens in Ghana? Will this event in Jerusalem have an effect on other events? Is this something that has happened many times before? Is it likely to happen again? Is someone to blame for what happened there? In this context, what do we mean by "blame"?

A newspaper that does not answer these questions is useless. It is worse than useless. It contributes incoherence and confusion to minds that are already overloaded with information. After all, the next day someone will be killed in Bosnia, and the day after that, in Indonesia, and the day after that, someplace else. So what? If I were asked to say what is the worst thing about television news or radio news, I would say that it is just this: that there is no reason offered for why the information is there; no background; no connectedness to anything else; no point of view; no sense of what the audience is supposed to do with the information. It is as if the word "because" is entirely absent from the grammar of broadcast journalism. We are presented with a world of "and"s, not "because"s. This happened, *and* then this happened, *and* then something else happened. As things stand now, at least in America, television and radio are media for information junkies, not for people interested in "because"s. I might pause here to remark that it is one of the most crucial functions of social institutions—the church, the courts, the schools, political parties, families—to provide us with the "because"s; that is, help us to know why information is important or irrelevant, socially acceptable or blasphemous, conventional or weird, even true or false. Some of these institutions do not do this work with as much conviction as they once did, which makes it especially necessary that a knowledge medium be available. And there is no more fundamental requirement of a knowledge medium than that it make clear why we are being given information. If we do not know that, we know nothing worth knowing. But there is something else the newspapers must do for us in a technological age, and it has to do with the word "wisdom." I wish to suggest that it is time for newspapers to begin thinking of themselves as being not merely in the knowledge business but in the wisdom business as well.

You may be inclined to think I am going too far. But I wish to define "wisdom" in a way that will make it appear to you entirely practical. I mean by wisdom the capacity to know what body of knowledge is relevant to the solution of significant problems. Knowledge, as I have said, is only organized information. It is self-contained, confined to a single system of information about the world. One can have a great deal of knowledge about the world but entirely lack wisdom. That is frequently the case with scientists, politicians, entrepreneurs, academics, even theologians. Let us take, for example, a story about cloning. It is mere information to tell us that scientists in Scotland have cloned a sheep and that some scientists in the United States claim to have cloned a monkey. We will be provided with knowledge if we are told how cloning is done, and how soon we may expect humans to be cloned, and even something about the history of attempts at cloning. But it would be wisdom to advise us on what system of knowledge we need in order to evaluate the act of cloning. Science itself can give us no help in this matter. Science can only tell us how it works. What can tell us whether or not we should be happy or sad about this? What can tell us if there are policies that need to be developed to control such a process? What can tell us if this is progress or regress? To begin to think about such questions, we would have to be referred to the body of knowledge we call religion, or the body of knowledge we call politics, or the body of knowledge we call sociology. Knowledge cannot judge itself. Knowledge must be judged by other knowledge, and therein lies the essence of wisdom. There are, I have learned, children starving in Somalia. What system of knowledge do I need to know in order to have some idea about how to solve this problem? I have learned that our oceans are polluted and the rain forests are being depleted. What systems of knowledge can help us to know how these problems might be solved? Or the problems of racism and sexism? Or the problem of crime?

If you are thinking that this sort of thing is accomplished in newspapers on the editorial page, I say it is not. Editorials merely tell us *what* to think. I am talking about telling us what we need to know in order to think. That is the difference between mere opinion and wisdom. It is also the difference between dogmatism and education. Any fool can have an opinion; to know what one needs to know to *have* an opinion is wisdom; which is another way of saying that wisdom means knowing what questions to ask about knowledge. I do not mean, of course, technical questions, which are easy. I mean questions that come from a world other than the world from which the knowledge comes. And nowhere is this kind of wisdom needed more than in the story of technology itself. That story—the changeover from industrial machinery to electronic impulse—hasn't been well covered by most newspapers, in part because most editors do not have a clue about what questions need asking about technology. They seem unaware that significant technological change always involves a re-ordering of our moral presuppositions, of social life, of psychic habits, of political practices.

The closest editors ever come to conveying a sense of the nontechnological meaning of technological change is in their speculations about eco- 20 nomic consequences, which, I might say, they usually have wrong, mostly because they consult only with economists. But that is beside the point. Wisdom does not imply having the right answers. It implies only asking the right questions. Consider what most journalists might now do if given a chance to ask Bill Gates questions. What would they ask?— What is his latest project? How does his software work? How much money will he make? What mergers is he planning? I would probably ask him the same questions because, in fact, judging from his book, *The Road Ahead*, Gates may be the last person likely to have answers to the moral, psychological, and social questions that need to be asked about computer technology. Whom would we want to interview about *that*, and what would we ask? Consider who was interviewed by journalists during the U.S.-Iraqi war. On television and radio and in the press, generals, experts on weapons systems, and Pentagon officials dominated. No artists were interviewed—no historians, no novelists, no theologians, no schoolteachers, no doctors. Is war the business only of military experts? Is what they have to say about war the only perspective citizens need to have? I should think that weapons systems experts would be the last people to be interviewed on the matter of war. Perhaps the absence of any others may be accounted for by saying the first casualty of war is wisdom.

I can envision a future in which what I have been saying about wisdom will be commonplace in newspapers. I cannot envision exactly how this will be done, although I rather like imagining a time when, in addition to op-ed pages, we will have "wisdom pages," filled with relevant questions about the stories that have been covered, questions directed at those who offer different bodies of knowledge from those which the stories themselves confront. I can even imagine a time when the news will be organized, not according to the standard format of local, regional, national, and world news, but according to some other organizing principle—for example, the seven deadly sins of greed, lust, envy, and so on.

Do I ask too much of editors, too much of newspapers? Perhaps. But I say what I do because we live now in a world of too much information, confusing specialized knowledge, and too little wisdom. Journalists may think it is not their job to offer the wisdom. I say, Why not? Who can say where their responsibilities as journalists end?

This much we can say—and ought to: The problem to be solved in the twenty-first century is not how to *move* information, not the engineering of information. We solved that problem long ago. The problem is how to transform information into knowledge, and how to transform knowledge into wisdom. If we can solve that problem, all the rest will take care of itself.

READING CRITICALLY FOR IDEAS, STRUCTURE, AND STYLE

1. In what ways did "information" have an entirely different meaning in the eighteenth century than it does today?

2. What forces produced the modern way of looking at "information," and why, in Postman's view, is this an unfortunate development?

3. How does Postman's distinction between "information" and "wisdom" provide a useful way for him to illustrate what is missing in modern culture? In what ways can the writers (such as Rousseau, Diderot, Voltaire) he mentions from the eighteenth century provide guidance for the world today?

EXTENDING INSIGHTS THROUGH WRITING

1. Given the deluge of information available on the Internet, it might be interesting to try to do what Postman attempts, that is, to develop your own criteria by which to evaluate information on any subject of your choice. How do you gauge the objectivity and reliability of what you find on the Internet? How can you tell whether the sources are authoritative, timely, unbiased, or relevant? For example, what do domain names tell you about the source? In a few pages, discuss the criteria you use and analyze a sample Web site.

2. Along with interpreting what you find on the Net, being able to think and read critically would seem to be the requisite skill in today's culture because of all the information designed to influence what you think, believe, and buy. How do you understand the process of critical thinking and reading? Describe it in a few paragraphs and give an example of a text where you applied these skills.

CONNECTING PERSPECTIVES ON THE PHYSICAL UNIVERSE

1. Postman states that "[Bill] Gates may be the last person likely to have answers to the moral, psychological, and social questions that need to be asked about computer technology." Read Bill Gates's essay "The Road Ahead," which appears next in this chapter, and evaluate whether Postman's harsh criticism is warranted. If you wish, create a dialogue between Postman and Gates that expresses their viewpoints.

2. Would Blaise Pascal (see "The Two Infinites") be a writer whose way of thinking about things Postman would find applicable and instructive in the modern world? Why or why not?

BILL GATES

The Road Ahead

BACKGROUND

William (Bill) Henry Gates, III was born in 1955 in Seattle, Washington, and attended Harvard University from 1973 to 1975. He began to develop and market computer software while still in high school. In 1975 (with Paul Allen) he founded Microsoft Corporation, where he remains the Chief Executive Officer. Microsoft's phenomenal success (garnering half the revenues in PC software worldwide) has not only made Gates a multibillionaire, but has elevated him to the role of a visionary whose predictions about the information age are enormously influential. He is the author of *The Road Ahead* (1995), from which the following selection is drawn, and *Business @ the Speed of Thought: Using a Digital Nervous System* (with Collins Hemingway), 1999.

APPROACHING GATES'S ESSAY

Gates's tone in this essay (which is part business memoir and part high-tech manifesto), is upbeat and optimistic. He begins by tracing his own involvement in the early days of the computer industry and describes some of the intriguing new applications of this technology that are just over the horizon. Gates foresees the future not solely in terms of new gadgets (such as e-books), but in the fundamentally new way in which consumers can take advantage of new services to conduct business using the Internet. His model, which to some extent has already come to pass, envisages a future in which telecommuting will become common (lessening problems of urban congestion), and in which all imaginable sources of information will be instantly available according to individual needs and desires. Of course, the unspoken subtext of Gates's utopian vision is how Microsoft will produce, manage, and control this new future (a concern that prompted the U.S. government to bring an anti-trust action against the company and Bill Gates).

500

In Gates's view, the popular phrase "information superhighway" does not accurately characterize the future as he sees it. Instead, he proposes a scenario akin to a department store, stock exchange, or farmer's market where transactions take place directly between consumers and businesses, thereby eliminating the middle-men who were such a big part of the old industrial society.

The Road Ahead

I wrote my first software program when I was thirteen years old. It was for playing tic-tac-toe. The computer I was using was huge and cumbersome and slow and absolutely compelling. Letting a bunch of teenagers like me and my friend Paul Allen loose on a computer was the idea of the Mothers' Club at Lakeside, the private school I attended. The mothers decided that the proceeds from a rummage sale should be used to install a terminal and buy computer time for students, a pretty amazing choice at the time in Seattle—and one I'll always be grateful for.

I realized later part of the appeal was that here was an enormous, expensive, grown-up machine and we, the kids, could control it. We were too young to drive or to do any of the other fun-seeming adult activities, but we could give this big machine orders and it would always obey. It's feedback you don't get from many other things. That was the beginning of my fascination with software. And to this day it still thrills me to know that if I can get the program right it will always work perfectly, every time, just the way I told it to.

My parents paid my tuition at Lakeside and gave me money for books, but I had to take care of my own computer-time bills. This is what drove me to the commercial side of the software business. A bunch of us, including Paul, got entry-level software programming jobs. For high school students the pay was extraordinary—about $5,000 each summer, part in cash and the rest in computer time. One of the programs I wrote was the one that scheduled students in classes. I surreptitiously added a few instructions and found myself nearly the only guy in a class full of girls.

As a college sophomore, I stood in Harvard Square with Paul and pored over the description of a kit computer in Popular Electronics magazine. As we read excitedly about the first truly personal computer, Paul and I didn't know exactly how it would be used, but we were sure it would change us and the world of computing. We were right. The personal-computer revolution happened and it has affected millions of lives. It has led us to places we had barely imagined.

THE NEXT REVOLUTION

Now that computing is astoundingly inexpensive and computers inhabit every part of our lives, we stand at the brink of another revolution. This one   5 will involve unprecedentedly inexpensive communication; all the computers will join together to communicate with us and for us. Interconnected globally, they will form a network, which is being called the information highway. A direct precursor is the present Internet, which is a group of computers joined and exchanging information using current technology.

The revolution in communications is just beginning. It will take place over several decades, and will be driven by new "applications"—new tools, often meeting currently unforeseen needs. During the next few years, major decisions will have to be made by governments, companies, and individuals. These decisions will have an impact on the way the highway will roll out and how much benefit those deciding will realize. It is crucial that a broad set of people—not just technologists or those who happen to be in the computer industry—participate in the debate about how this technology should be shaped. If that can be done, the highway will serve the purposes users want. Then it will gain broad acceptance and become a reality.

In the United States, the connecting of all these computers has been compared to another massive project: the gridding of the country with interstate highways, which began during the Eisenhower era. This is why the new network was dubbed the "information superhighway." The highway metaphor isn't quite right, though. The phrase suggests landscape and geography, a distance between points, and embodies the implication that you have to travel to get from one place to another. In fact, one of the most remarkable aspects of this new communications technology is that it will eliminate distance. It won't matter if someone you're contacting is in the next room or on another continent, because this highly mediated network will be unconstrained by miles and kilometers.

A different metaphor that I think comes closer to describing a lot of the activities that will take place is that of the ultimate market. Markets from trading floors to malls are fundamental to human society, and I believe this new one will eventually be the world's central department store. It will be where we social animals will sell, trade, invest, haggle, pick stuff up, argue, meet new people, and hang out. Think of the hustle and bustle of the New York Stock Exchange or a farmers' market or of a bookstore full of people looking for fascinating stories and information. All manner of human activity takes place, from billion-dollar deals to flirtations.

The highway will enable capabilities that seem magical when they are described, but represent technology at work to make our lives easier and better. Because consumers already understand the value of movies and are used to paying to watch them, video-on-demand will be an important application on the information highway. It won't be the first, however. We already know that PCs will be connected long before television sets and that the quality of movies shown on early systems will not be very high. The systems will be able to offer other applications such as games, electronic mail, and home banking. When high-quality video can be transmitted, there won't be any intermediary VCR; you'll simply request what you want from a long list of available programs.

10   Television shows will continue to be broadcast as they are today for synchronous consumption—at the same time they are first broadcast. After

they air, these shows—as well as thousands of movies and virtually all other kinds of video—will be available whenever you want to view them. You'll be able to watch the new episode of "Seinfeld" at 9:00 p.m. on Thursday night, or at 9:13 p.m., or at 9:45 p.m., or at 11:00 a.m. on Saturday. If you don't care for his brand of humor, there will be thousands of other choices. Even if a show is being broadcast live, you'll be able to use your infrared remote control to start, stop, or go to any previous part of the program, at any time. If someone comes to you door, you'll be able to pause the program for as long as you like. You'll be in absolute control.

Your television set will not look like a computer and won't have a keyboard, but additional electronics inside or attached will make it architecturally like a PC. Television sets will connect to the highway via a set-top box similar to ones supplied today by most cable TV companies.

A WORLD OF 'E-BOOKS'

On the information highway, rich electronic documents will be able to do things no piece of paper can. The highway's powerful database technology will allow them to be indexed and retrieved using interactive exploration. It will be extremely cheap and easy to distribute them. In short, these new digital documents will replace many printed paper ones because they will be able to help us in new ways.

Ultimately, incremental improvements in computer and screen technology will give us a lightweight, universal electronic book or "e-book," which will approximate today's paperback book. Inside a case roughly the same size and weight as today's hardcover or paperback book, you'll have a display that can show high-resolution text, pictures, and video. You'll be able to flip pages with your finger or use voice commands.

The real point of electronic documents is not simply that we will read them on hardware devices. Going from paper book to e-book is just the final stage of a process already well under way. The exciting aspect of digital documentation is the redefinition of the document itself.

By the end of the decade a significant percentage of documents, even in offices, won't even be fully printable on paper. They will be like a movie or a song is today. You will still be able to print a two-dimensional view of its content, but it will be like reading a musical score instead of experiencing an audio recording. 15

Electronic documents will be interactive. Request a kind of information, and the document responds. Indicate that you've changed your mind, and the document responds again. Once you get used to this sort of system, you find that being able to look at information in different ways makes that information more valuable. The flexibility invites exploration, and the exploration is rewarded with discovery.

You'll be able to get your daily news in a similar way. You'll be able to specify how long you want your newscast to last because you'll be able to have each of the news stories selected individually. The newscast assembled for and delivered only to you might include world news from NBC, the

BBC, CNN, or the Los Angeles Times, with a weather report from a favorite local TV meteorologist—or from any private meteorologist who wanted to offer his or her own service. You will be able to request longer stories on the subjects that particularly interest you and just highlights on others. If, while you are watching the newscast, you want more than has been put together, you will easily be able to request more background or detail, either from another news broadcast or from file information.

Among all the types of paper documents, narrative fiction is one of the few that will not benefit from electronic organization. Almost every reference book has an index, but novels don't because there is no need to be able to look something up in a novel. Novels are linear. Likewise, we'll continue to watch most movies from start to finish. This isn't a technological judgment—it is an artistic one: Their linearity is intrinsic to the storytelling process.

The success of CD-ROM games has encouraged authors to begin to create interactive novels and movies in which they introduce the characters and the general outline of the plot, then the reader/player makes decisions that change the outcome of the story. No one suggests that every book or movie should allow the reader or viewer to influence its outcome. A good story that makes you just want to sit there for a few hours and enjoy it is wonderful entertainment. I don't want to choose an ending for "The Great Gatsby" or "La Dolce Vita."[1] F. Scott Fitzgerald and Federico Fellini[2] have done that for me.

20   Significant investments will be required to develop great on-line content that will delight and excite PC users and raise the number on-line from 10 percent up to 50 percent, or even the 90 percent I believe it will become. Part of the reason this sort of investment isn't happening today is that simple mechanisms for authors and publishers to charge their users or to be paid by advertisers are just being developed.

As the fidelity of visual and audio elements improves, reality in all its aspects will be more closely simulated. This "virtual reality," or VR, will allow us to "go" places and "do" things we never would be able to otherwise.

In order to work, VR needs two different sets of technology software that creates the scene and makes it respond to new information, and devices that allow the computer to transmit the information to our senses. The software will have to figure out how to describe the look, sound, and feel of the artificial world down to the smallest detail. That might sound overwhelmingly difficult but actually it's the easy part. We could write the software for VR today, but we need far more computer power to make it truly believable. At the pace technology is moving, though, that power will be available soon.

Inevitably, there has been more speculation (and wishful thinking) about virtual sex than about any other use for VR. Sexually explicit con-

---

[1] *La Dolce Vita* (1960).
[2] Federico Fellini (1920–1993), Italian film director whose works are known for their extravagant visual fantasy.

tent is as old as information itself. If historical patterns are a guide, a big early market for advanced virtual-reality documents will be virtual sex. But again, historically, as each of these markets grew, explicit material became a smaller and smaller factor.

THE IMPORTANCE OF EDUCATION

More than ever, an education that emphasizes general problem-solving skills will be important. In a changing world, education is the best preparation for being able to adapt. As the economy shifts, people and societies who are appropriately educated will tend to do best. The premium that society pays for skills is going to climb, so my advice is to get a good formal education and then keep on learning. Acquire new interests and skills throughout your life.

Some fear that technology will dehumanize formal education. But anyone who has seen kids working together around a computer, the way my friends and I first did in 1968, or watched exchanges between students in classrooms separated by oceans, knows that technology can humanize the educational environment. The same technological forces that will make learning so necessary will also make it practical and enjoyable. Just as information technology now allows Levi Strauss & Co. to offer jeans that are both mass-produced and custom fitted, information technology will bring mass customization to learning. Multimedia documents and easy-to-use authoring tools will enable teachers to "mass-customize" a curriculum for each student: computers will fine-tune the product—educational material, in this case—to allow students to follow somewhat divergent paths and learn at their own rates.

There is an often-expressed fear that technology will replace teachers. I can say emphatically and unequivocally, IT WON'T. The information highway won't replace or devalue any of the human educational talent needed for the challenges ahead: committed teachers, creative administrators, involved parents, and, of course, diligent students. However, technology will be pivotal in the future role of teachers.

Before the benefits of these advances can be realized, though, the way computers in the classroom are thought about will have to change. A lot of people are cynical about educational technology because it has been over-hyped and has failed to deliver on its promises. Many of the PCs in schools today are not powerful enough to be easy to use, and they don't have the storage capacity or network connections to permit them to respond to a child's curiosity with much information.

When teachers do excellent work and prepare wonderful materials now, only their few dozen students benefit each year. The network will enable teachers to share lessons and materials, so that the best educational practices can spread. The interactive network also will allow students to quiz themselves any time, in a risk-free environment. A self-administered quiz is a form of self-exploration. Testing will become a positive part of the learning process. A mistake won't call forth a reprimand; it will trigger the system

25

to help the student overcome his misunderstanding. The highway will also make home schooling easier. It will allow parents to select some classes from a range of quality possibilities and still maintain control over content.

THE IMPACT ON SOCIETY

Just because I'm optimistic doesn't mean I don't have concerns about what is going to happen to all of us. The broad benefits of advancing productivity are no solace for someone whose job is on the line. When a person has been trained for a job that is no longer needed, you can't just suggest he go out and learn something else. Adjustments aren't that simple or fast, but ultimately they are necessary.

30   The fully developed information highway will be affordable—almost by definition. An expensive system that connected a few big corporations and wealthy people simply would not be the information highway—it would be the information private road. The network will not attract enough great content to thrive if only the most affluent 10 percent of society choose to avail themselves of it. There are fixed costs to authoring material; so to make them affordable, a large audience is required. Advertising revenue won't support the highway if a majority of eligible people don't embrace it. If that is the case, the price for connecting will have to be cut or deployment delayed while the system is redesigned to be more attractive. The information highway is a mass phenomenon, or it is nothing.

The net effect will be a wealthier world, which should be stabilizing. Developed nations, and workers in those nations, are likely to maintain a sizable economic lead. However, the gap between the have and have-not nations will diminish. Starting out behind is sometimes an advantage. Those who adopt late skip steps, and avoid the mistakes of the trailblazers. Some countries will never have industrialization but will move directly into the Information Age.

The information highway is going to break down boundaries and may promote a world culture, or at least a sharing of cultural activities and values. The highway will also make it easy for patriots, even expatriates, deeply involved in their own ethnic communities to reach out to others with similar interests no matter where they may be located. This may strengthen cultural diversity and counter the tendency toward a single world culture.

A complete failure of the information highway is worth worrying about. Because the system will be thoroughly decentralized, any single outage is unlikely to have a widespread effect. If an individual server fails, it will be replaced and its data restored. But the system could be susceptible to assault. As the system becomes more important, we will have to design in more redundancy. One area of vulnerability is the system's reliance on cryptography—the mathematical locks that keep information safe. None of the protection systems that exist today, whether steering-wheel locks or steel vaults, are completely fail-safe. The best we can do is make it as difficult as possible for somebody to break in. Still, popular opinions to the contrary, computer security has a very good record.

Loss of privacy is another major concern about the highway. A great deal of information is already being gathered about each of us, by private companies as well as by government agencies, and we often have no idea how it is used or whether it is accurate. As more business is transacted using the highway and the amount of information stored there accrues, governments will consciously set policies regarding privacy and access to information. The potential problem is abuse, not the mere existence of information.

These privacy fears revolve around the possibility that someone else 　35 is keeping track of information about you. But the highway will also make it possible for an individual to keep track of his or her own whereabouts—to lead what we might call "a documented life." Your wallet PC will be able to keep audio, time, location, and eventually even video records of everything that happens to you. It will be able to record every word you say and every word said to you, as well as body temperature, blood pressure, barometric pressure, and a variety of other data about you and your surroundings. It will be able to track your interactions with the highway—all of the commands you issue, the messages you send, and the people you call or who call you. The resulting record will be the ultimate diary and autobiography, if you want one.

I find the prospect of documented lives a little chilling, but some people will warm to the idea. One reason for documenting a life will be defensive. If someone ever accused you of something, you could retort: "Hey, buddy, I have a documented life. These bits are stored away. I can play back anything I've ever said. So don't play games with me." Medical malpractice insurance might be cheaper, or only available, for doctors who record surgical procedures or even office visits. I can imagine proposals that every automobile, including yours and mine, be outfitted not only with a recorder but also with a transmitter that identifies the car and its location. If a car was reported stolen, its location would be known immediately. After a hit-and-run accident or a drive-by shooting, a judge could authorize a query: "What vehicles were in the following two-block area during this thirty-minute period?" The black box could record your speed and location, which would allow for the perfect enforcement of speeding laws. I would vote against that.

Even if the model of political decision making does not change explicitly, the highway will bestow power on groups who want to organize to promote causes or candidates. This could lead to an increased number of special-interest groups and political parties. Someone will doubtless propose total "direct democracy," having all issues put to a vote. Personally, I don't think direct voting would be a good way to run a government. There is a place in governance for representatives—middlemen—to add value. They are the ones who understand all the nuances of complicated issues. Politics involves compromise, which is nearly impossible without a relatively small number of representatives making decisions on behalf of the people who elected them.

We are watching something historic happen, and it will affect the world seismically, the same way the scientific method, the invention of printing, and the arrival of the Industrial Age did. Big changes used to take generations or centuries. This one won't happen overnight, but it will move much faster. The first manifestations of the information highway will be apparent in the United States by the millennium. Within a decade there will be widespread effects. If I had to guess which applications of the network will be embraced quickly and which will take a long time, I'd certainly get some wrong. Within twenty years virtually everything I've talked about will be broadly available in developed countries and in businesses and schools in developing countries.

READING CRITICALLY FOR IDEAS, STRUCTURE, AND STYLE

1. Gates assumes that the new information technology (which he ranks in importance to the development of the scientific method, the invention of the printing press, and the rise of the Industrial Age) will close the gap between the haves and have-nots and break down barriers between persons and countries. Do you agree with his assessment? Why or why not?

2. Why does Gates believe that the Internet should not be thought of as an "information superhighway" but rather as a kind of co-operative exchange? Does his view correspond with yours? Explain your answer.

3. To what extent does Gates address the question of who will control the flow of information over the Internet and in what ways does he assure his audience that the "documented life" he holds up as an ideal will not degenerate into a police state?

EXTENDING INSIGHTS THROUGH WRITING

1. Gates is very enthusiastic about potential applications of the information revolution (such as e-books, virtual reality programs [VR], and the documented life as a protection against false accusations). Where in his argument is Gates most persuasive, and where does he resort to unsubstantiated hyperbole? What kinds of ethical and moral problems has technology already created that Gates fails to address?

2. What role have computers come to play as part of your education, in and out of the classroom, and in what ways have they altered the traditional teaching paradigm?

CONNECTING PERSPECTIVES ON THE PHYSICAL UNIVERSE

1. In what respects was the ability to measure longitude, as described by Dava Sobel in "The Prize," as much a revolution in the past as computers are in our era, as discussed by Gates?

2. Postman's critique of information for its own sake—without a context in which to understand it or a reason for its dissemination—suggests Gates is erroneous in his belief that more information is always better. Do you agree with Gates or Neil Postman? Explain your answer.

BOOK CONNECTIONS FOR CHAPTER 5

1. In what ways do both Sir Leonard Woolley and Howard Carter (see "Finding the Tomb" in Chapter 3) shed light on the techniques archeologists use to uncover and assess the meaning of their findings?

2. The eighteenth century as Lord Chesterfield in "Letter to His Son" (in Chapter 1) represents it was overly class conscious. What insight does this give you into the difficulties John Harrison faced in getting a hearing for his theories, as described by Dava Sobel?

3. What insights do Nathaniel Philbrick and Oscar Handlin (see "Steerage" in Chapter 3) give you into the precarious nature of life aboard ships although in different contexts, in past centuries?

4. Although Thomas Robert Malthus in "The Principle of Population" (Chapter 2) frames his argument in terms of population versus resources, how does Thor Heyerdahl's essay provide an additional dimension to the problems Malthus discussed in 1803?

5. In what ways are Peter D. Ward and Donald Brownlee and Arnold J. Toynbee (see "Challenge and Response" in Chapter 3) concerned with the factors that determine success and failure in a cosmic context?

6. Discuss the similarities and differences in the outlooks of Blaise Pascal's meditations on the universe with those of Zen Buddists, as described by Alan Watts in "Beat Zen, Square Zen, and Zen" (Chapter 6).

7. Consider the scale of the universe in Fred Hoyle's account. If you already did not adhere to a religion, would this encourage you to accept the tenets, for example, of Hinduism (see "Readings from the Scriptures in Hinduism: *Rig-Veda*, the *Upanishads*, and the *Bhagavad-Gītā*" in Chapter 6)?

8. Although Charles H. Townes doesn't discuss the artistic uses of the laser, how has it influenced the visual arts (for example, holograms,

laser light shows) in ways that rely on the principle of *montage* as described by Sergei Eisenstein (see "The Cinematographic Principle and the Ideogram" in Chapter 7)?

9. Compare the ingenious analogies used by Christopher Evans and Jean Henri Fabre (see "The Praying Mantis" in Chapter 4) to humanize their very small, or very fast subjects.

10. One of Neil Postman's hypothetical wishes would be for some way to make cloning comprehensible in terms of moral and ethical choices. Does Gina Kolata in "A Clone Is Born" (in Chapter 4) provide the "wisdom" that Postman seeks? Why or why not?

11. Consider the computer as a tool much as Charles Darwin (see "the Origin of Species" in Chapter 4) viewed an elongated beak or some other evolutionary adaptation that conferred a survival advantage. Who wins and who loses in Gates's supposed cyberdemocracy of the future in terms of "survival of the fittest"?

CHAPTER 6

THE MIND AND THE SPIRIT:
Understanding the Unknown

INTRODUCTION

The selections in this chapter present the compelling philosophical ideas that have guided the human search for the meaning of existence. Although separated by 2,000 years, Plato and G. E. Moore look at the process by which we approach the spiritual order of knowledge. For Moore, writing in the early twentieth century, goodness is a self-evident quality that we can apprehend directly through the senses without sophisticated analyses. Plato, writing in the fifth century B.C., represents the idealist tradition of philosophy. He creates a memorable analogy to stress the difficulty of apprehending the ultimate good amidst the chaotic world of the senses.

Both Sigmund Freud and Marcel Proust investigate the mysterious relationship between the conscious and unconscious minds and the role played by dreams and memories. We owe our concept of the unconscious to Freud's discovery that many inexplicable behaviors were determined by hidden impulses repressed during childhood that reveal themselves only in dreams. Marcel Proust also found a corresponding parallel in the human psyche, a "bodily memory" that, once triggered, allows us to re-experience every facet of a past event as if it were occuring in the present (this insight served as a basis for his monumental novel, *The Remembrance of Things Past*).

The next six readings offer the defining moral and ethical beliefs of the world's major religions, including Hinduism, Judaism, Islam,

Christianity, Buddhism (and Zen Buddhism). Opposed to these are the skeptical viewpoints of Clarence Darrow and Jean-Paul Sartre.

The capacity to believe in the existence of a spiritual order is an act of faith that is the most fundamental aspect of all religions. The readings in this chapter illustrate a multiplicity of different responses to the universal or cosmic and reflect how people in many different cultures throughout the world, look at themselves in relationship to the absolute, the eternal, the supernatural, or the concept of an ultimate truth.

Hinduism, whose origins lie in prehistory, is the oldest of the world's major religions. It began in India and still provides the core of beliefs for Indian culture. Each act of daily life is woven into a complex scenario of lifetimes, or reincarnations, that chart a person's spiritual evolution under the laws of Karma.

Judaism, which dates its origin from the giving of the law at Mt. Sinai in thirteenth century B.C. in Palestine, also takes its name from a particular people, the Hebrews, who were captive in Egypt and Babylon and were exiled when the Roman emperor Titus occupied Jerusalem in 70 A.D. The teachings of Judaism are much more familiar than those of Hinduism, both because of the fundamental place the Hebrew Bible occupies in Western culture and because it also forms the foundation of Christianity. Judaism is defined by an uncompromising monotheism that reaches into every aspect of life—moral, social, and spiritual.

Islam (which is a form of the Arabic verb meaning "to submit"), the most recent of the world's great monotheistic religions, originated in Arabia in the seventh century A.D. Its founder, Muhammad, who is often referred to simply as the Prophet, preached the absolute sovereignty of a single God (Allah), the certainty of life to come, resurrection, hell, and the reward of the faithful, in paradise, and of his mission as the prophet of God. The revelations he received are recorded in the *Koran.*

Christianity (which claims the widest number of adherents of all religions) dates from 4 B.C., and also began in Palestine as an embodiment of the person and doctrine of its founder, Jesus Christ ("the annointed one"). The text we have chosen, the Parables in St. Matthew, draw their force from the role of Jesus as the Messiah (whom the Jews had long expected and whose coming was foretold) and from His power to forgive sins and promise salvation in a "Kingdom of Heaven."

Buddhism also originated in India and dates from the sixth century B.C. with the enlightenment of its founder, Siddhartha Guatama, known as the Buddha. He was born a Hindu and, although he accepted the doctrines of reincarnation and karma, Buddha placed less emphasis on theology as such and focused on the need to extinguish negative emotions, malice, and the force of desire to achieve a state of bliss, peace, and certainty known as Nirvana. We chose a text (the Enlightenment of the Buddha: Buddhacarita) that contains the key insight into the "Noble Eightfold Path" that forms the basis of Buddhist teaching.

Zen Buddhism emerged as an offshoot of Buddhism in the fifth century A.D. in China. It reached its golden age in the ninth century and was transmitted to Japan in the fourteenth century, where it greatly influenced every aspect of Japanese culture. Zen, as explained by one of its chief proponents, Alan Watts, emphasizes the practice of meditation and the achievement of sudden enlightenment (or *satori*) rather than an adherence to a particular scriptural doctrine.

The two readings with which we conclude, by Clarence Darrow and Jean-Paul Sartre, provide a sharp contrast to the expressions of faith recorded in the world's major religions. Darrow can find no reasonable basis to believe in the existence of a soul or in an afterlife; Sartre elevates this insight to serve as the basis for an entire philosophy, existentialism. Both writers express the vein of skepticism that has assumed such a large place in modern life (non-believers rank third after Christians and Muslims).

G. E. MOORE

The Indefinability of Good

BACKGROUND

G. E. (George Edward) Moore (1873–1958) the English philosopher, taught at Cambridge University for over forty years. From 1921 to 1947, he edited the prestigious British philosophical journal *Mind,* which inspired the school of analytical philosophy that has become the dominant philosophical tradition of the twentieth century. His critique of idealistic philosophy was presented in such essays as "The Nature of Judgment" (1899) and "The Refutation of Idealism" (1903). He developed his views in a later essay, "A Defense of Common Sense" (1925). Moore applied these methods of analysis to the realm of moral philosophy in *Principia Ethica* (1903), in which the following essay first appeared, and in *Ethics* (1912). In Moore's view, we possess a faculty of moral intuition that enables us to intuitively know if a person is good or if an action is correct. For Moore, "good" is a simple, self-evident, albeit, indefinable quality of certain things and includes personal friendships and aesthetic judgments. In its simplest form, Moore's thesis might be that just because we cannot define good does not mean that we cannot recognize it when we see it. Moore departed from the tradition of idealistic philosophy that goes back to Plato and is much closer to Aristotle's focus on evidence drawn from the senses. Although Moore is less well-known than his famous peers, Bertrand Russell and Ludwig Wittgenstein, he exercised an enormous influence on modern thought, especially in the branch of ethics called moral epistomology, which investigates how we come to know right from wrong and how moral beliefs are justified.

APPROACHING MOORE'S ESSAY

One way of approaching Moore's essay might be to place it in the context of the observation made by Lily Tomlin in the popular 1985 Broadway show "The Search for Signs of Intelligent Life in the Universe" (written by Jane Wagner and starring Lily Tomlin) that "reality is nothing but a collective hunch." This notion touches on the crucial role that commonsense should play in philosophy, according to Moore. In "A Defense of Common Sense," he argued that it is precisely because even the most sophisticated statements or propositions are expressed using concepts and, indeed language, that is shared by a community, that we are able to discuss and analyze what is "good." For Moore, definitions *per se* don't matter, since, as he says, goodness is a simple, indefinable non-natural quality that cannot be explained in terms of anything else. In Moore's view, as expressed in "The Indefinability of Good," good is a self-evident, fundamental quality that cannot be split into parts nor can it be reduced or subordinated to what we desire or need or what gives us pleasure. Moore makes his point by comparing the perception of good with the perception of a color, such as yellow. All attempts to define yellow in terms of light waves, or anything else, will fail to communicate the qualitative nature of our perception of yellow. Moore's commonsense approach to philosophy is evident in the direct, accessible style in which he writes.

The Indefinability of Good

"Good" Is a Simple Notion

. . . What, then, is good? How is good to be defined? Now, it may be thought that this is a verbal question. A definition does indeed often mean the expressing of one word's meaning in other words. But this is not the sort of definition I am asking for. Such a definition can never be of ultimate importance in any study except lexicography. If I wanted that kind of definition I should have to consider in the first place how people generally used the word "good," but my business is not with its proper usage, as established by custom. I should, indeed, be foolish, if I tried to use it for something which it did not usually denote: if, for instance, I were to announce that, whenever I used the word "good," I must be understood to be thinking of that object which is usually denoted by the word "table." I shall, therefore, use the word in the sense in which I think it is ordinarily used; but at the same time I am not anxious to discuss whether I am right in thinking that it is so used. My business is solely with that object or idea, which I hold, rightly or wrongly, that the word is generally used to stand for. What I want to discover is the nature of the object or idea, and about this I am extremely anxious to arrive at an agreement.

But, if we understand the question in this sense, my answer to it may seem a very disappointing one. If I am asked "What is good?" my answer is that good is good, and that is the end of the matter. Or if I am asked "How is good to be defined?" my answer is that it cannot be defined, and that is all I have to say about it. But disappointing as these answers may appear, they are of the very last importance. To readers who are familiar with philosophic terminology, I can express their importance by saying that they amount to this: That propositions about the good are all of them synthetic and never analytic; and that is plainly no trivial matter. And the same thing may be expressed more popularly, by saying that, if I am right, then nobody can foist upon us such an axiom as that "Pleasure is the only good" or that "The good is the desired" on the pretence that this is the very meaning of the word.

Let us, then, consider this position. My point is that "good" is a simple notion, just as "yellow" is a simple notion; that, just as you cannot, by any manner of means, explain to any one who does not already know it, what yellow is, so you cannot explain what good is. Definitions of the kind that I was asking for, definitions which describe the real nature of the object or notion denoted by a word, and which do not merely tell us what the word is used to mean, are only possible when the object or notion in question is something complex. You can give a definition of a horse, because a horse has many different properties and qualities, all of which you can enumerate. But when you have enumerated them all, when you have reduced a horse to his simplest terms, then you can no longer define those terms. They are simply something which you think of or perceive, and to any one who cannot think of or perceive them, you can never, by any definition, make their nature known. It may perhaps be objected to this that we are able to describe to others, objects which they have never seen or thought of. We can, for instance, make a man understand what a chimaera is, although he has never heard of one or seen one. You can tell him that it is an animal with a lioness's head and body, with a goat's head growing from the middle of its back, and with a snake in place of a tail. But here the object which you are describing is a complex object; it is entirely composed of parts, with which we are all perfectly familiar—a snake, a goat, a lioness; and we know, too, the manner in which those parts are to be put together, because we know what is meant by the middle of a lioness's back, and where her tail is wont to grow. And so it is with all objects, not previously known, which we are able to define; they are all complex; all composed of parts, which may themselves, in the first instance be capable of similar definition, but which must in the end be reducible to simplest parts, which can no longer be defined. But yellow and good, we say, are not complex; they are notions of that simple kind, out of which definitions are composed and with which the power of further defining ceases.

When we say, as Webster says, "The definition of horse is a 'hoofed quadruped of the genus Equus,'" we may, in fact, mean three different things. (1) We may mean merely: "When I say 'horse,' you are to understand that I am talking about a hoofed quadruped of the genus Equus." This might be called the arbitrary verbal definition: and I do not mean that good is indefinable in that sense. (2) We may mean, as Webster ought to mean: "When most English people say 'horse,' they mean a hoofed quadruped of the genus Equus." This may be called the verbal definition proper, and I do not say that good is indefinable in this sense either; for it is certainly possible to discover how people use a word: otherwise, we could never have known that "good" may be translated by "gut" in German and by "bon" in French. But (3) we may, when we define horse, mean something much more important. We may mean that a certain object, which we all of us know, is composed in a certain manner; that it has four legs, a head, a heart, a liver, etc., etc., all of them arranged in definite relations to one another. It is in this sense that I deny good to be definable. I say that it is not composed of any parts, which we can substitute for it in our minds when we are thinking of it. We might think just as clearly and correctly about a horse, if we thought of all its parts and their arrangement instead of thinking of the whole: we could, I say, think how a horse differed from a donkey just as well, just as truly, in this way, as now we do, only not so easily; but there is nothing whatsoever which we could so substitute for good; and that is what I mean, when I say that good is indefinable.

But I am afraid I have still not removed the chief difficulty which may   5
prevent acceptance of the proposition that good is indefinable. I do not mean to say that *the* good, that which is good, is thus indefinable; if I did think so, I should not be writing on Ethics, for my main object is to help towards discovering that definition. It is just because I think there will be less risk of error in our search for a definition of "the good," that I am now insisting that *good* is indefinable. I must try to explain the difference between these two. I suppose it may be granted that "good" is an adjective. Well "the good," "that which is good," must therefore be the substantive to which the adjective "good" will apply: it must be the whole of that to which the adjective will apply, and the adjective must *always* truly apply to it. But if it is that to which the adjective will apply, it must be something different from that adjective itself; and the whole of that something different, whatever it is, will be our definition of *the* good. Now it may be that this something will have other adjectives, besides "good," that will apply to it. It may be full of pleasure, for example; it may be intelligent: and if these two adjectives are really part of its definition, then it will certainly be true, that pleasure and intelligence are good. And many people appear to think that, if we say "Pleasure and intelligence are good," or if we say "Only pleasure and intelligence are good," we are defining "good." Well, I cannot deny that propositions of this nature may sometimes be called definitions; I do not know well enough how the word is generally used to decide upon this point. I only wish it to be understood that that is not what I mean when I say there is no possible definition of good, and that I shall not mean this if I use the word again. I do most fully believe that some true proposition of the form "Intelligence is good and intelligence alone is good" can be found; if none could be found, our definition of *the* good would be impossible. As it is, I believe *the* good to be definable; and yet I still say that good itself is indefinable.

"Good," then, if we mean by it that quality which we assert to belong to a thing, when we say that the thing is good, is incapable of any definition, in the most important sense of that word. The most important sense of "definition" is that in which a definition states what are the parts which invariably compose a certain whole; and in this sense "good" has no definition because it is simple and has no parts. It is one of those innumerable objects of thought which are themselves incapable of definition, because they are the ultimate terms by reference to which whatever *is* capable of definition must be defined. That there must be an indefinite number of such terms is obvious, on reflection; since we cannot define anything except by analysis, which, when carried as far as it will go, refers us to something, which is simply different from anything else, and which by that ultimate difference explains the peculiarity of the whole which we are defining: for every whole contains some parts which are common to other wholes also. There is, therefore, no intrinsic difficulty in the contention that "good" denotes a simple and indefinable quality. There are many other instances of such qualities.

Consider yellow, for example. We may try to define it, by describing its physical equivalent; we may state what kind of light-vibrations must stimulate the normal eye, in order that we may perceive it. But a moment's reflection is sufficient to show that those light-vibrations are not themselves what we mean by yellow. *They* are not what we perceive. Indeed we should never have been able to discover their existence, unless we had first been struck by the patent difference of quality between the different colours. The most we can be entitled to say of those vibrations is that they are what corresponds in space to the yellow which we actually perceive.

Yet a mistake of this simple kind has commonly been made about "good." It may be true that all things which are good are *also* something else, just as it is true that all things which are yellow produce a certain kind of vibration in the light. And it is a fact, that Ethics aims at discovering what are those other properties belonging to all things which are good. But far too many philosophers have thought that when they named those other properties they were actually defining good; that these properties, in fact, were simply not "other," but absolutely and entirely the same with goodness.

READING CRITICALLY FOR IDEAS, STRUCTURE, AND STYLE

1. In Moore's view, what kinds of problems arise when people try to define what is good in terms of something else (for example, pleasure and intelligence)?

2. In Moore's view, why should common sense play a dominant role in our attempts to perceive what is good?

3. How does Moore's analogy use attempts to define the color yellow to illustrate his thesis about the indefinability of good?

EXTENDING INSIGHTS THROUGH WRITING

1. Since goodness is a moral property quite unlike other natural properties, such as roundness or hardness, what faculty do we

rely on to tell us what is good or bad, right or wrong? In a few paragraphs, discuss this question and try to avoid circular definitions.

2. Moore believed that good was a simple, indefinable non-natural quality of many things we can recognize and appreciate, such as friendship and works of art. Name some instances when you can recognize the presence of goodness or any other concept, such as consciousness.

CONNECTING PERSPECTIVES ON THE MIND AND THE SPIRIT

1. How do Moore and Plato (see "The Allegory of the Cave") use analogies to express exactly opposite views on what goodness is and whether we can know it? How do these analogies reflect their respective philosophical schools of realism and idealism?

2. Buddhism, as depicted in "The Enlightenment of the Buddha: Buddhacarita," implies a variety of moral obligations. In what ways are these designed to instill a perception of goodness that can be defined?

PLATO

The Allegory of the Cave

BACKGROUND

Plato (428–347 B.C.), whose theories stress reason as a way of perceiving the truth, can be considered the founder of Western philosophy. He was born in Athens into an aristocratic family of statesmen at a time when Athens, the most influential city-state of its era, was embroiled in political turmoil. The Peloponnesian War (431–404 B.C.) with Sparta had ended disastrously, and the unsettled political climate made it increasingly difficult for Plato to have a career in politics. As a boy, Plato had been friends with Socrates and became his pupil. When Socrates was brought to trial in 399 B.C., charged with corrupting the youth of Athens and with impiety, and was condemned and executed (an event described in Plato's *Apology*), Plato abandoned whatever political ambitions he harboured. Until philosophers, said Plato, became kings or kings became philosophers, an honest man had no place in politics. He then traveled several times to Italy and to Sicily in the attempt to foster his concept of the ideal state.

He returned to Athens in 387 B.C. to establish his school, known as the Academy (that became a model for universities of the future), where he taught for the next forty years. Among the many young men who were his pupils was Aristotle, who joined the school when he was eighteen. Most of Plato's works are cast in the form of dialogues between Socrates and his students. The earliest of these, the *Ion, Euthyphro, Protagoras,* and *Gorgias,* illustrate the so-called Socratic Method, in which questions are asked until contradictions in the answers given disclose the truth. Later in his life, Plato also wrote the *Crito, Apology, Phaedo, Symposium,* and *Timaeus,* among other dialogues, as well as his influential treatises, *The Republic* and *The Laws.* Plato's formative influence on Western thought can be traced to his belief that the soul and the body had distinct and separate existences, and that beyond the world of the senses existed an eternal, changeless order of Ideal Forms. Only by grasping these Forms was real knowledge possible. In "The Allegory of the Cave" from *The Republic,* Plato creates an extended analogy to dramatize the importance

520

of recognizing that the "unreal" world of the senses, and physical phenomena, are merely shadows cast by the immortal light of the "real" world of Ideal Forms.

APPROACHING PLATO'S ESSAY

An extended analogy, or allegory, provides a way to shed light on hidden, difficult or complex ideas by relating them to everyday human experience. One of the most famous analogies ever conceived, Plato's "Allegory of the Cave," uses a series of comparisons to express Plato's view that lifelong conditioning deludes man into mistakening illusions for reality. Plato formulated this analogy to illustrate his theory about the relationship between the realm of Ideas and the world of the senses. Plato believed that ultimate reality is apprehended solely by reason and equated this journey toward the truth with the experience of a prisoner who emerges from a dark cave into the light.

Plato's theme is a complex one; he attempts to define things that are intangible, which constitutes the search for truth. To ensure that his ideas will be understood, he uses an analogy in which each point of his theme is compared to tangible, everyday things that would be familiar to his audience. He likens truth to the sun and those seeking it to prisoners emerging from a cave; the cave's darkness, in the allegory, equals naiveté and ignorance. Each element in the analogy, the fire, the prisoners, the shadows, the dazzling light, offers Plato a means for teaching the existence of truth as a greater reality beyond the illusory shadows of what we mistake as the "real world."

The Allegory of the Cave

Socrates: And now, I said, let me show in a figure[1] how far our nature is enlightened or unenlightened:— Behold! human beings living in an underground den, which has a mouth open towards the light and reaching all along the den: here they have been from their childhood, and have their legs and necks chained so that they cannot move, and can only see before them, being prevented by the chains from turning round their heads. Above and behind them a fire is blazing at a distance, and between the fire and the prisoners there is a raised way; and you will see, if you look, a low wall built along the way, like the screen which marionette players have in front of them, over which they show the puppets.

The den, the prisoners; the light at a distance.

[1]*Figure:* a picture or image.

Glaucon: I see.

And do you see, I said, men passing along the wall carrying all sorts of vessels, and statues and figures of animals made of wood and stone and various materials, which appear over the wall? Some of them are talking, others silent.

You have shown me a strange image, and they are strange prisoners.

5   Like ourselves, I replied; and they see only their own shadows, or the shadows of one another, which the fire throws on the opposite wall of cave?

The low wall, and the moving figures of which the shadows are seen on the opposite wall of the den.

True, he said; how could they see anything but the shadows if they were never allowed to move their heads?

And of the objects which are being carried in like manner they would only see the shadows?

Yes, he said.

And if they were able to converse with one another, would they not suppose that they were naming what was actually before them?

10   Very true.

And suppose further that the prison had an echo which came from the other side, would they not be sure to fancy when one of the passers-by spoke that the voice which they heard came from the passing shadow?

The prisoners would mistake the shadows for realities.

No question, he replied.

To them, I said, the truth would be literally nothing but the shadows of the images.

That is certain.

15   And now look again, and see what will naturally follow if the prisoners are released and disabused of their error. At first, when any of them is liberated and compelled suddenly to stand up and turn his neck round and walk and look towards the light, he will suffer sharp pains; the glare will distress him, and he will be unable to see the realities of which in his former state he had seen the shadows; and then conceive some one saying to him, that what he saw before was an illusion, but that now, when he is approaching nearer to being and his eye is turned towards more real existence, he has a clearer vision,—what will be his reply? And you may further imagine that his instructor is pointing to the objects as they pass and requiring him to name them,—will he not be perplexed? Will he not fancy that the shadows which he formerly saw are truer than the objects which are now shown to him?

And when released, they would still persist in maintaining the superior truth of the shadows.

Far truer.

And if he is compelled to look straight at the light, will he not have a pain in his eyes which will make him turn away to take refuge in the objects of vision which he can see, and which he will conceive to be in reality clearer than the things which are now being shown to him?

True, he said.

And suppose once more, that he is reluctantly dragged up a steep and rugged ascent, and held fast until he is forced into the presence of the sun himself, is he not likely to be pained and irritated. When he approaches the light his eyes will be dazzled, and he will not be able to see anything at all of what are now called realities.

When dragged upwards, they would be dazzled by excess of light.

Not all in a moment, he said.

20

He will require to grow accustomed to the sight of the upper world. And first he will see the shadows best, next the reflections of men and other objects in the water, and then the objects themselves; then he will gaze upon the light of the moon and the stars and the spangled heaven; and he will see the sky and the stars by night better than the sun or the light of the sun by day?

Certainly.

Last of all he will be able to see the sun, and not mere reflections of him in the water, but he will see him in his own proper place, and not in another; and he will contemplate him as he is.

At length they will see the sun and understand his nature.

Certainly.

He will then proceed to argue that this is he who gives the season and the years, and is the guardian of all that is in the visible world, and in a certain way the cause of all things which he and his fellows have been accustomed to behold?

25

Clearly, he said, he would first see the sun and then reason about him.

And when he remembered his old habitation, and the wisdom of the den and his fellow-prisoners, do you not suppose that he would felicitate himself on the change, and pity them?

They would then pity their old companions of the den.

Certainly, he would.

And if they were in the habit of conferring honours among themselves on those who were quickest to observe the passing shadows and to remark which of them went before, and which followed after, and which were together; and who were therefore best able to draw conclusions as to the future, do you think that he would care for such honours and glories, or envy the possessors of them? Would he not say with Homer, "Better to be the poor servant of a poor master," and to endure anything, rather than think as they do and live after their manner?

30   Yes, he said, I think that he would rather suffer anything than entertain those false notions and live in this miserable manner.

Imagine once more, I said, such an one coming suddenly out of the sun to be replaced in his old situation; would he not be certain to have his eyes full of darkness?

To be sure, he said.

And if there were a contest, and he had to compete in measuring the shadows with the prisoners who had never moved out of the den, while his sight was still weak, and before his eyes had become steady (and the time which would be needed to acquire this new habit of sight might be very considerable), would he not be ridiculous? Men would say of him that up he went and down he came without his eyes; and that it was better not even to think of ascending; and if any one tried to loose another and lead him up to the light, let them only catch the offender, and they would put him to death.

But when they returned to the den they would see much worse than those who had never left it.

No question, he said.

35   This entire allegory, I said, you may not append, dear Glaucon, to the previous argument; the prison-house is the world of sight, the light of the fire is the sun, and you will not misapprehend me if you interpret the journey upwards to be the ascent of the soul into the intellectual world according to my poor belief, which, at your desire, I have expressed—whether rightly or wrongly God knows. But, whether true or false, my opinion is that in the world of knowledge the idea of good appears last of all, and is seen only with an effort; and when seen, is also inferred to be the universal author of all things beautiful and right, parent of light and of the lord of light in this visible world, and the immediate source of reason and truth in the intellectual; and that this is the power upon which he who would act rationally either in public or private life must have his eye fixed.

The prison is the world of sight, the light of the fire is the sun.

I agree, he said, as far as I am able to understand you.

READING CRITICALLY FOR IDEAS, STRUCTURE, AND STYLE

1. Plato used this allegory as a teaching tool. If you were one of his philosophy students, what would the allegorical equivalent, or meaning, of the cave, the prisoners, the fire, the sun, and the shadows reveal about the human condition?

2. How is the allegory designed to convey a process of education that moves from ignorance to enlightenment?

3. When the prisoner returns to the cave and is initially unable to see in the dark as are the others, how do those in the cave respond to his claim of greater light outside? Why are they unwilling to let other prisoners follow him into the light?

EXTENDING INSIGHTS THROUGH WRITING

1. Plato's allegory is particularly poignant in view of the way the Athenians reacted to the truth-seeking efforts of Plato's teacher, Socrates. Read Plato's *Apology* and in a short paper discuss the picture you get of Socrates, especially his role as an individual whose life embodied what Plato discusses as an abstract ideal.

2. Plato's allegory is particularly well-suited to describe deprogramming experiences, whether those of a state, or a cult. Apply his method to any form of propaganda or advertising in which one must sift through the lies, deceptions, and misrepresentations in order to discover the truth.

CONNECTING PERSPECTIVES ON THE MIND AND THE SPIRIT

1. Compare Plato's allegory, as a teaching tool designed to convey subtle meanings as to the nature of absolute good, to the parables of St. Matthew in the *New Testament*, which are designed to convey something as profound as the Kingdom of Heaven. In what way is the form of the parable, or extended allegory, uniquely suited to this task?

2. In what way is Plato's concept of Ideal Forms similar to or different from the Torah's concept of God as a personal being who communicates with individuals and intervenes in human history?

SIGMUND FREUD

Typical Dreams

BACKGROUND

Sigmund Freud (1856–1939), the founder of psychoanalysis, whose theories revolutionized our understanding of human nature, was born in Moravia
(what is now the Czech Republic). He received his M.D. from the University of
Vienna in 1891 and joined the resident staff of Vienna General Hospital where
he began his studies in clinical neurology. Freud then studied with J. M.
Charcot, a French neurologist who alerted Freud to the possibility that hysteria might be caused by underlying sexual problems. Freud adapted methods of hypnosis used by Joseph Breuer in treating a patient known as "Anna
O" (described in Freud and Breuer's collaborative work *Studies in Hysteria*,
1895) and developed the technique of "free association," whereby patients, in
the process of talking freely about their symptoms, would reveal the true
source of their neuroses.

Freud discovered the essential concept of psychoanalytical thought—
that the repression of ideas unacceptable to the conscious mind could manifest as slips of the tongue, memory lapses, hysteria, and dream images. The
role played by the unconscious is the basis for Freud's most important works,
The Interpretation of Dreams (1901), *The Psychopathology of Everyday Life*
(1904), and *Three Essays on the Theory of Sexuality* (1905).

Freud's key concepts of the oral, anal, and phallic stages of development
and personality types, his three-part division of personality into the id, ego,
and superego, and terms such as the "Oedipus complex," "defense mechanisms," "castration anxiety," and "libido" developed from his research have
become part of the vocabulary of the twentieth century. In "Typical Dreams,"
from *The Interpretation of Dreams* (1913), Freud argues that adult dreams of
the death of a loved one are disguised forms of wish-fulfillments stemming
from repressed sexual drives and jealousies from childhood. Freud supports
his argument with evidence drawn from his analysis of the classic tragedies,
Oedipus Rex and *Hamlet*.

APPROACHING FREUD'S ESSAY

Freud's theories of the human mind are based on a number of assumptions validated by the empirical evidence he gathered in his many years of practice. He believed that many of our thoughts and actions (which we believe to be the result of free choice) are in reality determined by unconscious impulses that act as hidden causes of our behavior. This theory allowed him to explain otherwise puzzling human phenomena such as hysterical paralyses, neurotic behavior, obsessive thoughts, dreams, and even slips of the tongue (still referred to as "Freudian slips"). To promote acceptance of his theories, Freud draws on extensive research, carefully documented by the numerous examples of dreams of the patients that he has analyzed. He also draws on examples from works of literature, such as *The Odyssey, Hamlet,* and *Oedipus Rex,* to reveal the persisting themes he explores. He also emphasizes that otherwise disturbing dreams (such as the death of a sibling) reflect unconscious wishes from childhood.

Freud's argument moves from specific facts to the elaboration of a general hypothesis. This process, called inductive reasoning, depends on observing similarities among a number of specific cases and then making inferences about other similar cases that have not been observed. In this way, Freud builds his case for the existence of "sibling rivalry," "repression," and other psychological phenomena.

Typical Dreams

THE EMBARRASSMENT-DREAM OF NAKEDNESS

In a dream in which one is naked or scantily clad in the presence of strangers, it sometimes happens that one is not in the least ashamed of one's condition. But the dream of nakedness demands our attention only when shame and embarrassment are felt in it, when one wishes to escape or to hide, and when one feels the strange inhibition of being unable to stir from the spot, and of being utterly powerless to alter the painful situation. It is only in this connection that the dream is typical; otherwise the nucleus of its content may be involved in all sorts of other connections, or may be replaced by individual amplifications. The essential point is that one has a painful feeling of shame, and is anxious to hide one's nakedness, usually by means of locomotion, but is absolutely unable to do so. I believe that the great majority of my readers will at some time have found themselves in this situation in a dream.

The nature and manner of the exposure is usually rather vague. The dreamer will say, perhaps, "I was in my chemise," but this is rarely a clear image; in most cases the lack of clothing is so indeterminate that it is described in narrating the dream by an alternative: "I was in my chemise or my petticoat." As a rule the deficiency in clothing is not serious enough to justify the feeling of shame attached to it. For a man who has served in the army, nakedness is often replaced by a manner of dressing that is contrary to regulations. "I was in the street without my sabre, and I saw some officers approaching," or "I had no collar," or "I was wearing checked civilian trousers," etc.

The persons before whom one is ashamed are almost always strangers, whose faces remain indeterminate. It never happens, in the typical dream, that one is reproved or even noticed on account of the lack of clothing which causes one such embarrassment. On the contrary, the people in the dream appear to be quite indifferent; or, as I was able to note in one particularly vivid dream, they have stiff and solemn expressions. This gives us food for thought.

The dreamer's embarrassment and the spectator's indifference constitute a contradiction such as often occurs in dreams. It would be more in keeping with the dreamer's feelings if the strangers were to look at him in astonishment, or were to laugh at him, or be outraged. I think, however, that this obnoxious feature has been displaced by wish-fulfilment, while the embarrassment is for some reason retained, so that the two components are not in agreement. We have an interesting proof that the dream which is partially distorted by wish-fulfilment has not been properly understood; for it has been made the basis of a fairy-tale familiar to us all in Andersen's version of *The Emperor's New Clothes,* and it has more recently received poetical treatment by Fulda in *The Talisman.* In Andersen's fairy-tale we are told of two imposters who weave a costly garment for the Emperor, which shall, however, be visible only to the good and true. The Emperor goes forth clad in this invisible garment, and since the imaginary fabric serves as a sort of touchstone, the people are frightened into behaving as though they did not notice the Emperor's nakedness.

5   But this is really the situation in our dream. . . . The imposter is the dream, the Emperor is the dreamer himself, and the moralizing tendency betrays a hazy knowledge of the fact that there is a question, in the latent dream-content, of forbidden wishes, victims of repression. The connection in which such dreams appear during my analyses of neurotics proves beyond a doubt that a memory of the dreamer's earliest childhood lies at the foundation of the dream. Only in our childhood was there a time when we were seen by our relatives, as well as by strange nurses, servants and visitors, in a state of insufficient clothing, and at that time we were not ashamed of our nakedness. In the case of many rather older children it may be observed that being undressed has an exciting effect upon them, instead of making them feel ashamed. They laugh, leap about, slap or thump their own bodies; the mother, or whoever is present, scolds them, saying: "Fie, that is shameful—you mustn't do that!" Children often show a desire to display themselves; it is hardly possible to pass through a village in country districts

without meeting a two- or three-year-old child who lifts up his or her blouse or frock before the traveller, possibly in his honour. One of my patients has retained in his conscious memory a scene from his eighth year, in which, after undressing for bed, he wanted to dance into his little sister's room in his shirt, but was prevented by the servant. In the history of the childhood of neurotics exposure before children of the opposite sex plays a prominent part; in paranoia the delusion of being observed while dressing and undressing may be directly traced to these experiences; and among those who have remained perverse there is a class in whom the childish impulse is accentuated into a symptom: the class of *exhibitionists*.

This age of childhood, in which the sense of shame is unknown, seems a paradise when we look back upon it later, and paradise itself is nothing but the mass-phantasy of the childhood of the individual. This is why in paradise men are naked and unashamed, until the moment arrives when shame and fear awaken; expulsion follows, and sexual life and cultural development begin. Into this paradise dreams can take us back every night; we have already ventured the conjecture that the impressions of our earliest childhood (from the prehistoric period[1] until about the end of the third year) crave reproduction for their own sake, perhaps without further reference to their content, so that their repetition is a wish-fulfilment. Dreams of nakedness, then, are *exhibition-dreams*.

The nucleus of an exhibition-dream is furnished by one's own person, which is seen not as that of a child, but as it exists in the present, and by the idea of scanty clothing which emerges indistinctly, owing to the superimposition of so many later situations of being partially clothed, or out of consideration for the censorship,[2] to these elements are added the persons in whose presence one is ashamed. I know of no example in which the actual spectators of these infantile exhibitions reappear in a dream; for a dream is hardly ever a simple recollection. Strangely enough, those persons who are the objects of our sexual interest in childhood are omitted from all reproductions, in dreams, in hysteria or in obsessional neurosis; paranoia alone restores the spectators, and is fanatically convinced of their presence, although they remain unseen. The substitute for these persons offered by the dream, the "number of strangers" who take no notice of the spectacle offered them, is precisely the *counter-wish* to that single intimately-known person for whom the exposure was intended. "A number of strangers," moreover, often occur in dreams in all sorts of other connections; as a *counter-wish* they always signify "a secret." It will be seen that even that restitution of the old state of affairs that occurs in paranoia complies with this counter-tendency. One is no longer alone; one is quite positively being watched; but the spectators are "a number of strange, curiously indeterminate people."

Furthermore, repression finds a place in the exhibition-dream. For the disagreeable sensation of the dream is, of course, the reaction. . . to the

---

[1]That is, the period before the child develops a capacity for conscious memory.
[2]The function of the mind that prevents threatening unconscious materials or thoughts from entering the conscious mind, or only admits them in disguised forms to prevent conscious recognition of forbidden, repressed wishes.

fact that the exhibitionistic scene which has been condemned by the censorship has nevertheless succeeded in presenting itself. The only way to avoid this sensation would be to refrain from reviving the scene.

In a later chapter we shall deal once again with the feeling of inhibition. In our dreams it represents to perfection *a conflict of the will, a denial.* According to our unconscious purpose, the exhibition is to proceed; according to the demands of the censorship, it is to come to an end.

The relation of our typical dreams to fairy-tales and other fiction and poetry is neither sporadic nor accidental. Sometimes the penetrating insight of the poet has analytically recognized the process of transformation of which the poet is otherwise the instrument, and has followed it up in the reverse direction; that is to say, has traced a poem to a dream. A friend has called my attention to the following passage in G. Keller's *Der Grüne Heinrich:* "I do not wish, dear Lee, that you should ever come to realize from experience the exquisite and piquant truth in the situation of Odysseus when he appears, naked and covered with mud, before Nausicaä and her playmates![3] Would you like to know what it means? Let us for a moment consider the incident closely. If you are ever parted from your home, and from all that is dear to you, and wander about in a strange country; if you have seen much and experienced much; if you have cares and sorrows, and are, perhaps, utterly wretched and forlorn, you will some night inevitably dream that you are approaching your home; you will see it shining and glittering in the loveliest colours; lovely and gracious figures will come to meet you; and then you will suddenly discover that you are ragged, naked, and covered with dust. An indescribable feeling of shame and fear overcomes you; you try to cover yourself, to hide, and you wake up bathed in sweat. As long as humanity exists, this will be the dream of the care-laden, tempest-tossed man, and thus Homer has drawn this situation from the profoundest depths of the eternal nature of humanity."

What are the profoundest depths of the eternal nature of humanity, which the poet commonly hopes to awaken in his listeners, but these stirrings of the psychic life which are rooted in that age of childhood, which subsequently becomes prehistoric? Childish wishes, now suppressed and forbidden, break into the dream behind the unobjectionable and permissibly conscious wishes of the homeless man, and it is for this reason that the dream which is objectified in the legend of Nausicaä regularly develops into an anxiety-dream.

---

[3]Odysseus, as Homer depicts him in Book VI of *The Odyssey,* has been shipwrecked by a storm brought about by Poseidon and has barely managed to reach the shore of the land of the Phaecians. Naked and bruised, he falls asleep, only to be discovered by the Princess Nausicaä and her handmaidens. Although embarrassed by his nakedness, Odysseus wins Nausicaä's confidence with a speech praising her beauty and is washed, fed, and clothed before being presented to her father, King Alcinous.

DREAMS OF THE DEATH OF BELOVED PERSONS

Another series of dreams which may be called typical are those whose content is that a beloved relative, a parent, brother, sister, child, or the like, has died. We must at once distinguish two classes of such dreams: those in which the dreamer remains unmoved, and those in which he feels profoundly grieved by the death of the beloved person, even expressing this grief by shedding tears in his sleep.

We may ignore the dreams of the first group; they have no claim to be reckoned as typical. If they are analysed, it is found that they signify something that is not contained in them, that they are intended to mask another wish of some kind. . . .

It is otherwise with those dreams in which the death of a beloved relative is imagined, and in which a painful affect is felt. These signify, as their content tells us, the wish that the person in question might die; and since I may here expect that the feelings of all my readers and of all who have had such dreams will lead them to reject my explanation, I must endeavour to rest my proof on the broadest possible basis.

We have already cited a dream from which we could see that the   15
wishes represented as fulfilled in dreams are not always current wishes. They may also be bygone, discarded, buried and repressed wishes, which we must nevertheless credit with a sort of continued existence, merely on account of their reappearance in a dream. They are not dead, like persons who have died, in the sense that we know death, but are rather like the shades in the Odyssey which awaken to a certain degree of life so soon as they have drunk blood. . . .[4]

If anyone dreams that his father or mother, his brother or sister, has died, and his dream expresses grief, I should never adduce this as proof that he wishes any of them dead *now*. The theory of dreams does not go as far as to require this; it is satisfied with concluding that the dreamer has wished them dead at some time or other during his childhood. I fear, however, that this limitation will not go far to appease my critics; probably they will just as energetically deny the possibility that they ever had such thoughts, as they protest that they do not harbour them now. I must, therefore, reconstruct a portion of the submerged infantile psychology on the basis of the evidence of the present.

Let us first of all consider the relation of children to their brothers and sisters. I do not know why we presuppose that it must be a loving one, since examples of enmity among adult brothers and sisters are frequent in everyone's experience, and since we are so often able to verify the fact that this estrangement originated during childhood, or has always existed. Moreover, many adults who to-day are devoted to their brothers and sisters, and support them in adversity, lived with them in almost continuous

---

[4]Freud's reference is to Homer's epic, *The Odyssey*, Book XI, where Odysseus makes it possible for the spirits of the dead, thronging about him, to communicate, by feeding them with the blood of a sheep he has just killed.

enmity during their childhood. The elder child ill-treated the younger, slandered him, and robbed him of his toys; the younger was consumed with helpless fury against the elder, envied and feared him, or his earliest impulse toward liberty and his first revolt against injustice were directed against his oppressor. The parents say that the children do not agree, and cannot find the reason for it. It is not difficult to see that the character even of a well-behaved child is not the character we should wish to find in an adult. A child is absolutely egotistical; he feels his wants acutely, and strives remorselessly to satisfy them, especially against his competitors, other children, and first of all against his brothers and sisters. And yet we do not on that account call a child "wicked"—we call him "naughty"; he is not responsible for his misdeeds, either in our own judgment or in the eyes of the law. And this is as it should be; for we may expect that within the very period of life which we reckon as childhood, altruistic impulses and morality will awake in the little egoist. . . .

Many persons, then, who now love their brothers and sisters, and who would feel bereaved by their death, harbour in their unconscious hostile wishes, survivals from an earlier period, wishes which are able to realize themselves in dreams. It is, however, quite especially interesting to observe the behaviour of little children up to their third and fourth year towards their younger brothers or sisters. So far the child has been the only one; now he is informed that the stork has brought a new baby. The child inspects the new arrival, and expresses his opinion with decision: "The stork had better take it back again!"

I seriously declare it as my opinion that a child is able to estimate the disadvantages which he has to expect on account of a new-comer. A connection of mine, who now gets on very well with a sister, who is four years her junior, responded to the news of this sister's arrival with the reservation: "But I shan't give her my red cap, anyhow." If the child should come to realize only at a later stage that its happiness may be prejudiced by a younger brother or sister, its enmity will be aroused at this period. I know of a case where a girl, not three years of age, tried to strangle an infant in its cradle, because she suspected that its continued presence boded her no good. Children at this time of life are capable of a jealousy that is perfectly evident and extremely intense. . . .

20   Feelings of hostility towards brothers and sisters must occur far more frequently in children than is observed by their obtuse elders.

In the case of my own children, who followed one another rapidly, I missed the opportunity of making such observations, I am now retrieving it, thanks to my little nephew, whose undisputed domination was disturbed after fifteen months by the arrival of a feminine rival. I hear, it is true, that the young man behaves very chivalrously toward his little sister, that he kisses her hand and strokes her; but in spite of this I have convinced myself that even before the completion of his second year he is using his new command of language to criticize this person, who, to him, after all, seems superfluous. Whenever the conversation turns upon her he chimes in, and cries angrily: "Too (l)ittle, too (l)ittle!" During the last few months, since the child has outgrown this disparagement, owing to her splendid development, he has found another reason for his insistence that she does not deserve so much attention. He reminds us, on every suitable pretext: "She hasn't any teeth.". . . .

I have never failed to come across this dream of the death of brothers or sisters, denoting an intense hostility, e.g. I have met it in all my female patients. I have met with only one exception, which could easily be interpreted into a confirmation of the rule. Once, in the course of a sitting, when I was explaining this state of affairs to a female patient, since it seemed to have some bearing on the symptoms under consideration that day, she answered, to my astonishment, that she had never had such dreams. But another dream occurred to her, which presumably had nothing to do with the case—a dream which she had first dreamed at the age of *four*, when she was the youngest child, and had since then dreamed repeatedly. "*A number of children, all her brothers and sisters with her boy and girl cousins, were romping about in a meadow. Suddenly they all grew wings, flew up, and were gone.*" She had no idea of the significance of this dream; but we can hardly fail to recognize it as a dream of the death of all the brothers and sisters, in its original form, and but little influenced by the censorship. I will venture to add the following analysis of it: on the death of one out of this large number of children—in this case the children of two brothers were brought up together as brothers and sisters—would not our dreamer, at that time not yet four years of age, have asked some wise, grown-up person: "What becomes of children when they are dead?" The answer would probably have been: "They grow wings and become angels." After this explanation, all the brothers and sisters and cousins in the dream now have wings, like angels and—this is the important point—they fly away. Our little angel-maker is left alone: just think, the only one out of such a crowd! That the children romp about a meadow, from which they fly away, points almost certainly to butterflies—it is as though the child had been influenced by the same association of ideas which led the ancients to imagine Psyche, the soul, with the wings of a butterfly.

Perhaps some readers will now object that the inimical impulses of children toward their brothers and sisters may perhaps be admitted, but how does the childish character arrive at such heights of wickedness as to desire the death of a rival or a stronger playmate, as though all misdeeds could be atoned for only by death? Those who speak in this fashion forget that the child's idea of "being dead" has little but the word in common with our own. This child knows nothing of the horrors of decay, of shivering in the cold grave, of the terror of the infinite Nothing, the thought of which the adult, as all the myths of the hereafter testify, finds so intolerable. The fear of death is alien to the child; and so he plays with the horrid word, and threatens another child: "If you do that again, you will die, just like Francis died;" at which the poor mother shudders, unable perhaps to forget that the greater proportion of mortals do not survive beyond the years of childhood. Even at the age of eight, a child returning from a visit to a natural history museum may say to her mother: "Mamma, I do love you so; if you ever die, I am going to have you stuffed and set you up here in the room, so that I can always, always see you!" So different from our own is the childish conception of being dead.

Being dead means, for the child, who has been spared the sight of the suffering that precedes death, much the same as "being gone," and ceasing to annoy the survivors. The child does not distinguish the means by which this absence is brought about, whether by distance, or estrangement, or death. If, during the child's prehistoric years, a nurse has been dismissed, and if his mother dies a little while later, the two experiences, as we discover by analysis, form links of a chain in his memory. The fact that the child does not very intensely miss those who are absent has been realized, to her sorrow, by many a mother, when she has returned home from an absence of several weeks, and has been told, upon inquiry: "The children have not asked for their mother once." But if she really departs to "that undiscovered country from whose bourne no traveller returns," the children seem at first to have forgotten her, and only *subsequently* do they begin to remember their dead mother.

25   While, therefore, the child has its motives for desiring the absence of another child, it is lacking in all those restraints which would prevent it from clothing this wish in the form of a death-wish; and the psychic reaction to dreams of a death-wish proves that, in spite of all the differences of content, the wish in the case of the child is after all identical with the corresponding wish in an adult.

If, then, the death-wish of a child in respect of his brothers and sisters is explained by his childish egoism, which makes him regard his brothers and sisters as rivals, how are we to account for the same wish in respect of his parents, who bestow their love on him, and satisfy his needs, and whose preservation he ought to desire for these very egoistical reasons?

Towards a solution of this difficulty we may be guided by our knowledge that the very great majority of dreams of the death of a parent refer to the parent of the same sex as the dreamer, so that a man generally dreams of the death of his father, and a woman of the death of her mother. I do not claim that this happens constantly; but that it happens in a great majority of cases is so evident that it requires explanation by some factor of general significance. Broadly speaking, it is as though a sexual preference made itself felt at an early age, as though the boy regarded his father, and the girl her mother, as a rival in love—by whose removal he or she could but profit.

Before rejecting this idea as monstrous, let the reader again consider the actual relations between parents and children. We must distinguish between the traditional standard of conduct, the filial piety expected in this relation, and what daily observation shows us to be the fact. More than one occasion for enmity lies hidden amidst the relations of parents and children; conditions are present in the greatest abundance under which wishes which cannot pass the censorship are bound to arise. Let us first consider the relation between father and son. In my opinion the sanctity with which we have endorsed the injunctions of the Decalogue[5] dulls our perception of the reality. Perhaps we hardly dare permit ourselves to perceive that the greater part of humanity neglects to obey the fifth commandment. In the

---

[5]The Decalogue are the Ten Commandments, given to Moses on Mt. Sinai (Exodus 20:1–17). The Fifth Commandment states: "Honor thy father and thy mother."

lowest as well as in the highest strata of human society, filial piety towards parents is wont to recede before other interests. The obscure legends which have been handed down to us from the primeval ages of human society in mythology and folklore give a deplorable idea of the despotic power of the father, and the ruthlessness with which it was exercised. Kronos devours his children,[6] as the wild boar devours the litter of the sow; Zeus emasculates his father and takes his place as ruler. The more tyrannically the father ruled in the ancient family, the more surely must the son, as his appointed successor, have assumed the position of an enemy, and the greater must have been his impatience to attain to supremacy through the death of his father. Even in our own middle-class families the father commonly fosters the growth of the germ of hatred which is naturally inherent in the paternal relation, by refusing to allow the son to be a free agent or by denying him the means of becoming so. A physician often has occasion to remark that a son's grief at the loss of his father cannot quench his gratification that he has at last obtained his freedom. Fathers, as a rule, cling desperately to as much of the sadly antiquated *potestas patris familias*[7] as still survives in our modern society, and the poet who, like Ibsen, puts the immemorial strife between the father and son in the foreground of his drama is sure of his effect. The causes of conflict between mother and daughter arise when the daughter grows up and finds herself watched by her mother when she longs for real sexual freedom, while the mother is reminded by the budding beauty of her daughter that for her the time has come to renounce sexual claims.

All these circumstances are obvious to everyone, but they do not help us to explain dreams of the death of their parents in persons for whom filial piety has long since come to be unquestionable. We are, however, prepared by the foregoing discussion to look for the origin of a death-wish in the earliest years of childhood.

In the case of psychoneurotics, analysis confirms this conjecture beyond all doubt. For analysis tells us that the sexual wishes of the child— in so far as they deserve this designation in their nascent state—awaken at a very early age, and that the earliest affection of the girl-child is lavished on the father, while the earliest infantile desires of the boy are directed upon the mother. For the boy the father, and for the girl the mother, becomes an obnoxious rival, and we have already shown, in the case of brothers and sisters, how readily in children this feeling leads to the death-wish. As a general rule, sexual selection soon makes its appearance in the parents; it is a natural tendency for the father to spoil his little daughters, and for the mother to take the part of the sons, while both, so long as the glamour of

30

---

[6]Because Kronos, the father of Zeus, feared that his sons would displace him and seize power, he devoured each of them as they were born. Zeus's mother, Rhea, protected Zeus by hiding him in a cave and substituted a stone for Kronos to swallow instead of the infant.

[7]"The authority of the father." Freud is probably referring to Ibsen's play, *Ghosts*, a pioneering psychological drama that used themes of heredity and venereal disease to explore the conflict of fathers and sons and the past with the present.

sex does not prejudice their judgment, are strict in training the children. The child is perfectly conscious of this partiality, and offers resistance to the parent who opposes it. To find love in an adult is for the child not merely the satisfaction of a special need; it means also that the child's will is indulged in all other respects. Thus the child is obeying its own sexual instinct, and at the same time reinforcing the stimulus proceeding from the parents, when its choice between the parents corresponds with their own.

The signs of these infantile tendencies are for the most part over-looked; and yet some of them may be observed even after the early years of childhood. An eight-year-old girl of my acquaintance, whenever her mother is called away from the table, takes advantage of her absence to proclaim herself her successor. "Now I shall be Mamma; Karl, do you want some more vegetables? Have some more, do," etc. A particularly clever and live-ly little girl, not yet four years of age, in whom this trait of child psycholo-gy is unusually transparent, says frankly: "Now mummy can go away; then daddy must marry me, and I will be his wife." Nor does this wish by any means exclude the possibility that the child may most tenderly love its mother. If the little boy is allowed to sleep at his mother's side whenever his father goes on a journey, and if after his father's return he has to go back to the nursery, to a person whom he likes far less, the wish may read-ily arise that his father might always be absent, so that he might keep his place beside his dear, beautiful mamma; and the father's death is obviously a means for the attainment of this wish; for the child's experience has taught him that "dead" folks, like grandpapa, for example, are always absent; they never come back. . . .

According to my already extensive experience, parents play a leading part in the infantile psychology of all persons who subsequently become psy-choneurotics. Falling in love with one parent and hating the other forms part of the permanent stock of the psychic impulses which arise in early childhood, and are of such importance as the material of the subsequent neurosis. But I do not believe that psychoneurotics are to be sharply dis-tinguished in this respect from other persons who remain normal—that is, I do not believe that they are capable of creating something absolutely new and peculiar to themselves. It is far more probable—and this is confirmed by incidental observations of normal children—that in their amorous or hostile attitude toward their parents, psychoneurotics do no more than reveal to us, by magnification, something that occurs less markedly and intensively in the minds of the majority of children. Antiquity has furnished us with legendary matter which corroborates this belief, and the profound and universal validity of the old legends is explicable only by an equally uni-versal validity of the above-mentioned hypothesis of infantile psychology.

I am referring to the legend of King Oedipus and the *Oedipus Rex* of Sophocles. Oedipus, the son of Laius, king of Thebes, and Jocasta, is exposed as a suckling, because an oracle had informed the father that his son, who was still unborn, would be his murderer. He is rescued, and grows up as a king's son at a foreign court, until, being uncertain of his origin, he too, consults the oracle, and is warned to avoid his native place, for he is destined to become the murderer of his father and the husband of his mother. On the road leading away from his supposed home he meets King Laius, and in a sudden quarrel strikes him dead. He comes to Thebes, where he solves the riddle of the Sphinx, who is barring the way to the city, whereupon he is elected king by the grateful Thebans, and is rewarded with the hand of Jocasta. He reigns for many years in peace and honour, and begets two sons and two daughters upon his unknown mother, until at last a plague breaks out—which causes the Thebans to consult the oracle anew. Here Sophocles' tragedy begins. The messengers bring the reply that the plague will stop as soon as the murderer of Laius is driven from the country. But where is he?

> "Where shall be found,
> Faint, and hard to be known, the trace of the ancient guilt?"

The action of the play consists simply in the disclosure, approached step by step and artistically delayed (and comparable to the work of a psychoanalysis) that Oedipus himself is the murderer of Laius, and that he is the son of the murdered man and Jocasta. Shocked by the abominable crime which he has unwittingly committed, Oedipus blinds himself, and departs from his native city. The prophecy of the oracle has been fulfilled. . . .

If the *Oedipus Rex* is capable of moving a modern reader or playgoer no less powerfully than it moved the contemporary Greeks, the only possible explanation is that the effect of the Greek tragedy does not depend upon the conflict between fate and human will, but upon the peculiar nature of the material by which this conflict is revealed. There must be a voice within us which is prepared to acknowledge the compelling power of fate in the *Oedipus*. . . . And there actually is a motive in the story of King Oedipus which explains the verdict of this inner voice. His fate moves us only because it might have been our own, because the oracle laid upon us before our birth the very curse which rested upon him. It may be that we were all destined to direct our first sexual impulses toward our mothers, and our first impulses of hatred and violence toward our fathers; our dreams convince us that we were. King Oedipus, who slew his father Laius and wedded his mother Jocasta, is nothing more or less than a wish-fulfilment—the fulfilment of the wish of our childhood. But we, more fortunate than he, in so far as we have not become psychoneurotics, have since our childhood succeeded in withdrawing our sexual impulses from our mothers, and in forgetting our jealousy of our fathers. We recoil from the person for whom this primitive wish of our childhood has been fulfilled with all the force of the repression which these wishes have undergone in our minds since childhood. As the poet brings the guilt of Oedipus to light by his investigation, he forces us to become aware of our own inner selves, in which the same impulses are still extant, even though they are suppressed. The antithesis with which the chorus departs:—

35

> ". . . Behold, this is Oedipus,
> Who unravelled the great riddle, and was first in power,
> Whose fortune all the townsmen praised and envied;
> See in what dread adversity he sank!"

—this admonition touches us and our own pride, us who since the years of our childhood have grown so wise and so powerful in our own estimation. Like Oedipus, we live in ignorance of the desires that offend morality, the desires that nature has forced upon us and after their unveiling we may well prefer to avert our gaze from the scenes of our childhood.

In the very text of Sophocles' tragedy there is an unmistakable reference to the fact that the Oedipus legend had its source in dream-material of immemorial antiquity, the content of which was the painful disturbance of the child's relation to its parents caused by the first impulses of sexuality. Jocasta comforts Oedipus—who is not yet enlightened, but is troubled by the recollection of the oracle—by an allusion to a dream which is often dreamed, though it cannot, in her opinion, mean anything:—

> "For many a man hath seen himself in dreams
> His mother's mate, but he who gives no heed
> To suchlike matters bears the easier life.". . .

Another of the great poetic tragedies, Shakespeare's *Hamlet*, is rooted in the same soil as *Oedipus Rex*. But the whole difference in the psychic life of the two widely separated periods of civilization, and the progress, during the course of time, of repression in the emotional life of humanity, is manifested in the differing treatment of the same material. In *Oedipus Rex* the basic wish-phantasy of the child is brought to light and realized as it is in dreams; in *Hamlet* it remains repressed, and we learn of its existence—as we discover the relevant facts in a neurosis—only through the inhibitory effects which proceed from it. In the more modern drama, the curious fact that it is possible to remain in complete uncertainty as to the character of the hero has proved to be quite consistent with the overpowering effect of the tragedy. The play is based upon Hamlet's hesitation in accomplishing the task of revenge assigned to him; the text does not give the cause or the motive of this hesitation, nor have the manifold attempts at interpretation succeeded in doing so. According to the still prevailing conception, a conception for which Goethe was first responsible, Hamlet represents the type of man whose active energy is paralysed by excessive intellectual activity: "Sicklied o'er with the pale cast of thought." According to another conception, the poet has endeavoured to portray a morbid, irresolute character, on the verge of neurasthenia. The plot of the drama, however, shows us that Hamlet is by no means intended to appear as a character wholly incapable of action. On two separate occasions we see him assert himself: once in a sudden outburst of rage, when he stabs the eavesdropper behind the arras, and on the other occasion when he deliberately, and even craftily, with the complete unscrupulousness of a prince of the Renaissance, sends the two courtiers to the death which was intended for himself. What is it, then, that inhibits him in accomplishing the task which his father's ghost has laid upon him? Here the explanation offers itself that it is the peculiar nature of this task. Hamlet is able to do anything but take vengeance upon the man who did away with his father and has taken his father's place with his mother—the man who shows him in realization the repressed desires of his own childhood. The loathing which should have driven him to revenge is thus replaced by self-reproach, by conscientious scruples, which tell him that he himself is no better than the murderer whom he is required to punish. I have here translated into consciousness what had to remain unconscious in the mind of the hero; if anyone wishes to call Hamlet an hysterical subject I cannot but admit that this is the deduction to be drawn from my interpretation. The sexual aversion which Hamlet expresses in conversation with Ophelia is perfectly consistent with this deduction—the same sexual aversion which during the next few years was increasingly to take possession of the poet's soul, until it found its supreme utterance in *Timon of Athens.* It can, of course, be only the poet's own psychology with which we are confronted in *Hamlet*; and in a work on Shakespeare by Georg Brandes (1896) I find the statement that the drama was composed immediately after the death of Shakespeare's father (1601)—that is to say, when he was still mourning his loss, and during a revival, as we may fairly assume, of his own childish feelings in respect of his father. It is known, too, that Shakespeare's son, who died in childhood, bore the name of Hamnet (identical with Hamlet). . . . I have here attempted to interpret only the deepest stratum of impulses in the mind of the creative poet.

READING CRITICALLY FOR IDEAS, STRUCTURE, AND STYLE

1. How do the children's dreams about the death or disappearance of brothers and sisters prove the existence of what Freud termed "sibling rivalry"?

2. How does the mechanism of "repression" operate in dreams where one appears naked before an indifferent public?

3. How does Freud interpret the Greek legend of Oedipus as a more intense form of the psychological conflict that most children work through successfully?

4. How does Freud's theory of "Oedipal conflict" help explain the longstanding question as to why Hamlet delays taking revenge on Claudius (in Shakespeare's play)?

EXTENDING INSIGHTS THROUGH WRITING

1. Freud discusses how "censorship" works in the dreams of one of his patients who dreamt her siblings and cousins "flew away." If you have any siblings, can you recall any dreams of yours that might express, although not in the same form, the phenomenon of "sibling rivalry?" Try to analyze one of your dreams as Freud might.

2. The dream of appearing naked is so common that you can probably recall having this dream yourself. Describe the circumstances of the dream and what it might have referred to in your everyday life.

CONNECTING PERSPECTIVES
ON THE MIND AND THE SPIRIT

1. Compare the similarities between Freud's analysis of the need to understand the origin of neuroses and to achieve self-consciousness with Plato's description of the sense of liberation the prisoners experienced when they left the cave. In what sense do both thinkers believe that individual well-being, mental and spiritual, are possible only if false perceptions are corrected? Discuss how the cave might be seen as the unconscious (a withdrawal from reality) and the prisoners as suffering from repression (in the grip of defense mechanisms).

2. Discuss the ways in which both Freud and Jean-Paul Sartre (see "Existentialism") set the tone for modern thinking in terms of the responsibilites we must take for our own actions, lives, and thoughts.

MARCEL PROUST

The Bodily Memory

BACKGROUND

Marcel Proust (1871–1922), the French novelist, is undisputably one of the great literary figures of the twentieth century. He was born in Auteuil, France, graduated from the Sorbonne, and briefly served in the French Army (where he was ranked 73rd in a company of 74). As a young man, he was active in the Paris social scene and became friends with Anatole France and other literary celebrities. His health deteriorated so greatly (from asthma and bronchitis) that from 1905 until his death in 1922 he lived as an invalid, spending most of his days propped up in bed, with the windows closed and shuttered, in the now famous cork-lined room. On the few occasions when he went out, always after sundown, he was muffled in a heavy overcoat, even in summer, and carried an umbrella. Although Proust attempted to go beyond friendship with a number of women, he realized he was incapable of heterosexual romantic love and the theme of homosexuality begins to enter his life and work.

The paradox of Proust is that, although so enfeebled, he undertook and created the most astounding and monumental novel, *Remembrance of Things Past,* in seven volumes (3,300 pages in the English translation). The first volume appeared in 1913, and the succeeding six parts (three were published after his death) contain a wealth of brilliant social and psychological observations expressed in rich metaphors and meticulous and intricate prose. In this work, he formulated the fundamental idea that memory is the link between external and internal reality. The picture of society he presents is of a world of fleeting loyalties, snobbery, and treachery, in which only the artist is uniquely capable of genuine devotion—to his craft. The selection reprinted here are the last pages of the "Overture" from volume one, "Swann's Way," and contains the most famous passage in Proust (the madeleine cake dipped in tea) that explores the connection between the conscious and unconscious mind.

APPROACHING PROUST'S ESSAY

The experience of "*deja vu*" described in this excerpt is familiar to all of us, but rarely does anyone attempt to trace it back to its source, as does Proust. Proust's protagonist, Marcel, discovers that we have two kinds of memory, "intellectual memory," through which we remember the fact that something happened, and "bodily memory," that can be triggered by something as trivial as the taste of a certain kind of cake dipped in lime-flower tea, through which we relive a past experience. By contrast with "intellectual memory" (which is thin, two-dimensional, and abstract), "bodily memory" is a three-dimensional, concrete, sensory experience in which we literally relive the moment. When Proust first presented "Swann's Way" to publishers, they complained that it was too convoluted and precious and rejected it. Proust finally had to publish the manuscript at his own expense. Today, we can appreciate the way his style communicates the sensory experience he describes: the narrator tastes a pastry dipped in tea and is overwhelmed by memories of his childhood.

The Bodily Memory

I feel that there is much to be said for the Celtic belief that the souls of those whom we have lost are held captive in some inferior being, in an animal, in a plant, in some inanimate object, and so effectively lost to us until the day (which to many never comes) when we happen to pass by the tree or to obtain possession of the object which forms their prison. Then they start and tremble, they call us by our name, and as soon as we have recognised their voice the spell is broken. We have delivered them: they have overcome death and return to share our life.

And so it is with our own past. It is a labour in vain to attempt to recapture it: all the efforts of our intellect must prove futile. The past is hidden somewhere outside the realm, beyond the reach of intellect, in some material object (in the sensation which that material object will give us) which we do not suspect. And as for that object, it depends on chance whether we come upon it or not before we ourselves must die.

Many years had elapsed during which nothing of Combray,[1] save what was comprised in the theatre and the drama of my going to bed there, had any existence for me, when one day in winter, as I came home, my mother, seeing that I was cold, offered me some tea, a thing I did not ordinarily take. I declined at first, and then, for no particular reason, changed my mind. She sent out for one of those short, plump little cakes called 'petites madeleines,' which look as though they had been moulded in the fluted

---

[1]The village where the hero of *Remembrance of Things Past* spent much of his childhood.

scallop of a pilgrim's shell. And soon, mechanically, weary after a dull day with the prospect of a depressing morrow, I raised to my lips a spoonful of the tea in which I had soaked a morsel of the cake. No sooner had the warm liquid, and the crumbs with it, touched my palate than a shudder ran through my whole body, and I stopped, intent upon the extraordinary changes that were taking place. An exquisite pleasure had invaded my senses, but individual, detached, with no suggestion of its origin. And at once the vicissitudes of life had become indifferent to me, its disasters innocuous, its brevity illusory—this new sensation having had on me the effect which love has of filling me with a precious essence; or rather this essence was not in me, it was myself. I had ceased now to feel mediocre, accidental, mortal. Whence could it have come to me, this all-powerful joy? I was conscious that it was connected with the taste of tea and cake, but that it infinitely transcended those savours, could not, indeed, be of the same nature as theirs. Whence did it come? What did it signify? How could I seize upon and define it?

I drink a second mouthful, in which I find nothing more than in the first, a third, which gives me rather less than the second. It is time to stop; the potion is losing its magic. It is plain that the object of my quest, the truth, lies not in the cup but in myself. The tea has called up in me, but does not itself understand, and can only repeat indefinitely with a gradual loss of strength, the same testimony; which I, too, cannot interpret, though I hope at least to be able to call upon the tea for it again and to find it there presently, intact and at my disposal, for my final enlightenment. I put down my cup and examine my own mind. It is for it to discover the truth. But how? What an abyss of uncertainty whenever the mind feels that some part of it has strayed beyond its own borders; when it, the seeker, is at once the dark region through which it must go seeking, where all its equipment will avail it nothing. Seek? More than that: create. It is face to face with something which does not so far exist, to which it alone can give reality and substance, which it alone can bring into the light of day.

And I begin again to ask myself what it could have been, this unre-   5
membered state which brought with it no logical proof of its existence, but only the sense that it was a happy, that it was a real state in whose presence other states of consciousness melted and vanished. I decide to attempt to make it reappear. I retrace my thoughts to the moment at which I drank the first spoonful of tea. I find again the same state, illumined by no fresh light. I compel my mind to make one further effort, to allow and recapture once again the fleeting sensation. And that nothing may interrupt it in its course I shut out every obstacle, every extraneous idea, I stop my ears and inhibit all attention to the sounds which come from the next room. And then, feeling that my mind is growing fatigued without having any success to report, I compel it for a change to enjoy that distraction which I have just denied it, to think of other things, to rest and refresh itself before the supreme attempt. And then for the second time I clear an empty space in front of it. I place in position before my mind's eye the still recent taste of that first mouthful, and I feel something start within me, something that leaves its resting-place and attempts to rise, something that has been

embedded like an anchor at a great depth; I do not know yet what it is, but I can feel it mounting slowly; I can measure the resistance, I can hear the echo of great spaces traversed.

Undoubtedly what is thus palpitating in the depths of my being must be the image, the visual memory which, being linked to that taste, has tried to follow it into my conscious mind. But its struggles are too far off, too much confused; scarcely can I perceive the colourless reflection in which are blended the uncapturable whirling medley of radiant hues, and I cannot distinguish its form, cannot invite it, as the one possible interpreter, to translate to me the evidence of its contemporary, its inseparable paramour, the taste of cake soaked in tea; cannot ask it to inform me what special circumstance is in question, of what period in my past life.

Will it ultimately reach the clear surface of my consciousness, this memory, this old, dead moment which the magnetism of an identical moment has travelled so far to importune, to disturb, to raise up out of the very depths of my being? I cannot tell. Now that I feel nothing, it has stopped, has perhaps gone down again into its darkness, from which who can say whether it will ever rise? Ten times over I must essay the task, must lean down over the abyss. And each time the natural laziness which deters us from every difficult enterprise, every work of importance, has urged me to leave the thing alone, to drink my tea and to think merely of the worries of to-day and of my hopes for to-morrow, which let themselves be pondered over without effort or distress of mind.

And suddenly the memory returns. The taste was that of the little crumb of madeleine which on Sunday mornings at Combray (because on those mornings I did not go out before church-time), when I went to say good day to her in her bedroom, my aunt Léonie used to give me, dipping it first in her own cup of real or of lime-flower tea. The sight of the little madeleine had recalled nothing to my mind before I tasted it; perhaps because I had so often seen such things in the interval, without tasting them, on the trays in pastry-cooks' windows, that their image had disociated itself from those Combray days to take its place among others more recent; perhaps because of those memories, so long abandoned and put out of mind, nothing now survived, everything was scattered; the forms of things, including that of the little scallop-shell of pastry, so richly sensual under its severe, religious folds, were either obliterated or had been so long dormant as to have lost the power of expansion which would have allowed them to resume their place in my consciousness. But when from a long-distant past nothing subsists, after the people are dead, after the things are broken and scattered, still, alone, more fragile, but with more vitality, more unsubstantial, more persistent, more faithful, the smell and taste of things remain poised a long time, like souls, ready to remind us, waiting and hoping for their moment, amid the ruins of all the rest; and bear unfaltering, in the tiny and almost impalpable drop of their essence, the vast structure of recollection.

And once I had recognized the taste of the crumb of madeleine soaked in her decoction of lime-flowers which my aunt used to give me (although I did not yet know and must long postpone the discovery of why this memory made me so happy) immediately the old grey house upon the street, where her room was, rose up like the scenery of a theatre to attach itself to the little pavilion, opening on to the garden, which had been built out behind it for my parents (the isolated panel which until that moment had been all that I could see); and with the house the town, from morning to night and in all weathers, the Square where I was sent before luncheon, the streets along which I used to run errands, the country roads we took when it was fine. And just as the Japanese amuse themselves by filling a porcelain bowl with water and steeping in it little crumbs of paper which until then are without character or form, but, the moment they become wet, stretch themselves and bend, take on colour and distinctive shape, become flowers or houses or people, permanent and recognisable, so in that moment all the flowers in our garden and in M. Swann's park, and the water-lilies on the Vivonne and the good folk of the village and their little dwellings and the parish church and the whole of Combray and of its surroundings, taking their proper shapes and growing solid, sprang into being, town and gardens alike, from my cup of tea.

READING CRITICALLY FOR IDEAS, STRUCTURE, AND STYLE

1. What is the relationship between the "Celtic" belief Proust mentions in the first paragraph and the episode of the madeleine cake and the lime-flower tea?

2. How does Marcel's experience show him the difference between "intellectual memory" and "bodily memory" and illustrate the mysterious connection between the conscious and the unconscious mind?

3. Stylistically, how does Proust capture the sensation of the difficulty in retrieving deeply submerged memories and the value in doing so?

EXTENDING INSIGHTS THROUGH WRITING

1. Proust's sentences are so complex that it might be worth the effort to paraphrase a paragraph or even a single sentence (for example, what is he saying in the last part of the fourth paragraph beginning "What an abyss of uncertainty . . .")?

2. In the second paragraph Proust says that one's personal past is "beyond the reach of intellect" and is hidden "in some material object." Describe, in full detail, a particular sensory trigger that is your "madeleine" cupcake dipped in "lime-flower tea" that re-

evokes an experience in its three-dimensional, concrete form as though you were reliving it. What were the circumstances in which you first realized its power?

CONNECTING PERSPECTIVES ON THE MIND AND THE SPIRIT

1. The preceding piece by Sigmund Freud ("Typical Dreams") explores how the workings of the unconscious mind are sometimes available to us. Compare Freud's theories to Marcel's experience in "The Bodily Memory."

2. Discuss Marcel's experience in Proust's work in terms of Plato's extended analogy (see "The Allegory of the Cave"). What would be the cave from which the prisoner is released, in Proust's account?

Readings from the Scriptures in Hinduism: Rig-Veda, Upanishads, and the Bhagavad-Gītā

BACKGROUND

Hinduism, which is more accurately thought of as a way of life than a religion, is the term applied to the beliefs and practices of its 900 million followers. The word "Hindu" derives from a Greek mispronunciation of Sindhu, a river that was the center of the civilization of Northwest India 5000 years ago. Hinduism is based on Dharma, a social and moral code that governs every aspect of life. Since Hinduism has no founder, anyone who practices Dharma can call himself or herself a Hindu. The two principal concepts that underlie Hindu religious thought are a belief in reincarnation and caste. The social position into which one is born is a consequence of karma (the laws governing reincarnation). The caste system is akin to a hereditary class structure composed of the Brahman (priests and scholars), the Kshatriya (warriors and rulers), the Vaisya, or Bania (farmers and merchants), and the Sudra (peasants and laborers); below these were the Untouchables—a category now outlawed.

As members of the highest caste, Brahmans are presumed to have the closest relationship to the Divine and are therefore appointed as priests. Hindus believe that the individual human soul (or *atman*) originates, and ultimately merges with, the world spirit (or *Brahman*). The central idea is that one is directly responsible for one's Fate, through a succession of incarnations (estimated at 8,400,000) that extend from the distant past into the future. Hindus believe that only desirelessness, detachment, and moderation, can liberate us from the "Wheel of Karma."

The history of Hinduism is complex (including, as it does, pantheism, polytheism, and monotheism), but inextricably linked to sacred texts, the oldest of which are the Vedas, a collection of hymns that date from about 1000 B.C. The first of these, the *Rig-Veda*, describes an indwelling spirit named Brahm (which literally means "breath") that permeates everything. The caste of priests and scholars responsible for teaching rituals and correct forms of observance are known as Brahmans who, in 800 B.C., set down laws governing correct behavior in all social and religious matters. For example, the glorification of the cow as a living symbol of Mother Earth dates from this period: The Vedas prohibit killing a Brahman's cow and even today they are free to wander the streets of towns and cities, protected from all harm even when they obstruct traffic.

In the next stage of Hinduism, nature spirits (such as the God of the Rain, the Dawn, the Sun, and the Sky) described in the *Rig-Veda*, have evolved into two major deities: Vishnu, the preserver, and Shiva, the destroyer. Vishnu had been associated with the Sun and represents permanence, while Shiva came from a mountain god and represents the tumultuous and destructive forces of existence. Vishnu is usually depicted as blue-colored, with four or more hands, two of which hold the wheel and the conch-shell, clothed in yellow. Shiva is shown holding a trident, naked except for a tiger skin, with matted hair that holds the sacred River Ganges, a blue throat, two to four arms, and wearing a garland of skulls. These images may appear bizarre to Westerners, but we must remember that image worship is a key feature of Hindu rituals. Sculptors and artists often merged two or more deities (hence, more than two arms) in these extravagant and symbolically meaningful postures.

The esoteric philosophy of the Brahmans is fully expounded in the *Upanishads* (which means "to sit down near," and refers to the method of teaching students who would sit near the feet of their teacher). There are also many epics and stories that dramatize the relationship between men and gods, and the human manifestations of the Divine. Two of the most widely read are the *Ramayana* and the *Mahabharata* that relate episodes in the lives of two incarnations of Lord Vishnu, as Rama and as Krishna. "Maha" in Sanskrit means great, and "Bharata" is the name of a family or clan, but in a more extended sense, means Hindu or even mankind. Thus, the *Mahabharata* (composed between the fifth and second centuries) can be understood as the "great history of humankind." At 100,000 stanzas (fifteen times longer than the Bible) it tells the story of an epic battle between two great families, the Kauravas and the Pandavas.

The *Bhagavad-Gītā* or "Song of God" section of this epic, is considered by many to be the epitome of Hindu philosophy and tells the story of Prince Arjuna, a great warrior related to both families, who is torn by the prospect of killing his own kinsmen. The "*Gītā*," as it is known, defines the essential principles by which one should live one's life. It takes the form of a dialogue between Lord Krishna (as the eighth incarnation of Vishnu) and Arjuna, for whom Krishna acts as a charioteer in the battle.

The selections below reflect the evolution of Hinduism from its earliest stages through an account of the Creation from the *Rig-Veda*,[1] the account of Brahman as an imperishable spirit from the *Upanishads*,[2] and a crucial dialogue between Arjuna and Krishna from *The Bhagavad-Gītā*[3]

[1]Trans. R.T.H. Griffith. *The Hymns of the Rig-Veda* (1889; rpt. Delhi: Motilal Banarsidass, 1973).

[2]Trans. R.E. Hume. *The Thirteen Principal Upanishads* 2nd rev.ed. (Oxford: Oxford University Press, 1931).

[3]*A New Translation*, trans. K.W. Bolle (Berkeley: University of California Press, 1979).

APPROACHING READINGS FROM THE SCRIPTURES
IN HINDUISM: RIG-VEDA, UPANISHADS,
AND THE BHAGAVAD-GĪTĀ

The four Vedas are the oldest Indian scriptures and were originally a body of orally preserved literature divided into hymns, texts describing correct procedures for sacrifices, and philosophical musings about the purpose and meaning of life. The word *Veda* comes from the Sanskrit verb meaning "to know" and thus, the Vedas mean "body of knowledge." In the Creation narrative following (from the *Rig-Veda*), the world originates as a negation of non-being; this account closely resembles the Creation described in Genesis of the Hebrew Bible.

The Upanishads expound the esoteric spiritual philosophy of the Brahmans. In the following excerpt from the Svetasvatara Upanishad, we find a description of Brahman as the "one" who is the "source of all," a transcendent God who sustains and supports the world around us in all its diverse guises. Yet, as the passage implies, true knowledge (of the kind the Vedas provide) enables us to go beyond the world of the senses and leave "the body behind." The concept of an impersonal World-Spirit (Brahman) may have proven too abstract, because the next stage in the evolution of Hinduism witnesses the new element of *bhakti*, or passionate devotion to a personal God who is also an aspect of one's self. The most dramatic illustration of the concept of *bhakti* can be seen in the *Bhagavad-Gītā* where Lord Krishna is a God who takes human form. The *Bhagavad-Gītā* consists of 650 Sanskrit verses, divided into 18 chapters, and takes place on the eve of a fratricidal civil war between the Kauravas and Pandavas. Arjuna is overcome with anguish at the prospect of slaying his kinsmen and friends. Krishna teaches him that there is no such thing as death since the soul is immortal and that spiritual detachment is possible even in the midst of the most violent encounters. Arjuna learns that union with God is possible through selfless action, discipline (or Yoga), knowledge, and devotion.

In the following dialogue (from the eleventh chapter of the *Bhagavad-Gītā*), Krishna reveals his true form to Arjuna who is stupified by the glorious and terrifying experience and discovers that God is "the absolute foundation of all things." This dialogue, which is narrated by Samjaya (who has been given clairvoyant powers to describe everything taking place on the distant battlefield), is crucial because it reveals Krishna as an incarnation of the Divine World Spirit in human form (much as the *New Testament* reveals Jesus as an incarnation of Divinity). The *Bhagavad-Gītā* is the most accessible and popular of all Hindu religious literature and has profoundly influenced such figures as Mohandas K. Gandhi (1869–1948), who led the nonviolent civil disobedience movement that resulted in India's independence (in 1947) from the British, as well as Henry David Thoreau (1817-1862), and Ralph Waldo

Emerson (1803–1882), who incorporated Hindu beliefs into the American Transcendentalist movement.

Rig-Veda

In the beginning there was neither naught nor aught;
Then there was neither sky nor atmosphere above.
What then enshrouded all this teeming Universe?
In the receptacle of what was it contained?
Was it enveloped in the gulf profound of water?
Then was there neither death nor immortality,
Then was there neither day, nor night, nor light, nor dark-
     ness,
Only the existent One breathed calmly, self-contained.
Naught else than him there was—naught else above, beyond.
Then first came darkness hid in darkness, gloom in gloom.
Next all was water, all a chaos indiscrete,
In which the One lay void, shrouded in nothingness.
Then turning inwards, He by self-developed force
Of inner fervour and intense abstraction, grew.
And now in Him Desire, the primal germ of mind
Arose, which learned men, profoundly searching, say
Is the first subtle bond, connecting Entity
With Nullity. This ray that kindled dormant life,
Where was it then? before? or was it found above?
Were there parturient powers and latent qualities,
And fecund principle beneath, and active forces
That energized aloft? Who knows? Who can declare?
How and from what has sprung this Universe? The gods
Themselves are subsequent to its development.
Who then can penetrate the secret of its rise?
Whether t'was framed or not, made or not made, He only
Who in the highest heaven sits, the omniscient Lord,
Assuredly knows all, or haply knows He not.

The One God and the Phenomenal World: Śvetāśvatara Upanishad

In the imperishable, infinite,
  supreme Brahman are two
  things;
 For therein are knowledge and ignorance placed hidden.
Now ignorance is a thing perishable,
  but knowledge is a thing immortal.
And He who rules the ignorance and
  the knowledge is another,
 [Even] the One who rules over
  every single source,
All forms and all sources;
Who bears in his thoughts, and be-
  holds when born,
 That red [*kapila*] seer who was en-
  gendered in the beginning.
That Gods spreads out each single
  net [of illusion] manifoldly,
 And draws it together here in the
  world.
Thus again, having created his
  Yatis,[1] the Lord [*īśa*],
 The Great Soul [*mahātman*],
  exercises universal overlordship.
As the illumining sun shines upon
  All regions, above, below,
  and across,
 So that One God, glorious, adorable,
Rules over whatever creatures are
  born from a womb.
The source of all, who develops his
  own nature,

Who brings to maturity whatever
  can be ripened,
And who distributes all qualities
  [*guna*]—Over this whole world
  rules the One.
That which is hidden in the secret
  of the Vedas, even the Mystic
  Doctrines [*upanishad*]—
 Brahmā knows That as the source
  of the sacred word [*brahman*].
The gods and seers of old who knew
  That,
 They, [coming to be] of Its nature,
  verily, have become immortal.
Whoever has qualities [*guna*, dis-
  tinctions] is the doer of deeds
  that bring recompense;
 And of such action surely he experiences the consequence.
Undergoing all forms, characterized
  by the three Qualities,[2] treading
  the three paths,[3]
 The individual self roams about according to its deeds [*karman*].
He is the measure of a thumb, of
  sun-like appearance,
 When coupled with conception
  [*samkalpa*] and egoism
  [*ahamkāra*].
But with only the qualities of intellect and of self,
 The lower [self] appears of the size
  of the point of an awl.
This living self is to be known as a
  part Of the hundredth part

---

[1]Yatis, according to the Rgveda, are lower deities who assisted in the creation of the
  world.
[2]The three qualities are pureness, passion, and darkness.
[3]The three paths are religiousness, irreligiousness, and knowledge.

of the point of a hair Subdivided
a hundredfold;
And yet it partakes of infinity.
Not female, nor yet male is it;
Nor yet is this neuter.
Whatever body he takes to himself,
With that he becomes connected.
By the delusions [moha] of imagina-
tion, touch, and sight,
And by eating, drinking, and im-
pregnation there is a birth and
development of the self [ātman].
According unto his deeds [karman]
the embodied one
successively assumes forms in
various conditions.
Coarse and fine, many in number,
The embodied one chooses forms
according to his own qualities.
[Each] subsequent cause of his
union with them is seen to be

Because of the quality of his acts
and of himself.
Him who is without beginning and
without end, in the midst of
confusion,
The Creator of all, of manifold form,
The One embracer of the universe—
By knowing God [deva] one is released from all fetters.
Him who is to be apprehended in
existence, who is called
'incorporeal',
The maker of existence [bhâva] and
non-existence, the kindly one
[śiva].
God [deva], the maker of the creation and its parts—
They who know Him, have left the
body behind.

'The Absolute Foundation of All Things': Bhagavad-Gītā

Arjuna:
You have favoured me by disclosing
the highest secret, concerning the
self.
Your words have cleared away the
darkness of my mind,
For you have taught me at length
the origin and end of creatures,
And also about your glory, which is
endless.
O highest Lord, I wish I could see
you,
your form as Lord,
Just as you yourself say you are,
Supreme Divine Being.
O Lord, if you think it is possible
that I might see you—
Then, Lord of Mystic power, show
to me your changeless self.

The Lord:
Open your eyes and see my hundreds, my thousands of forms,
In all their variety, heavenly splendour,
in all their colours and semblances.
Look upon the Gods of Heaven, the
Radiant Gods,
the terrifying Gods, the Kind Celestial Twins.
See Arjuna, countless marvels never
seen before.
Here in my body, in one place, now
the whole world—
All that moves and does not
move—
and whatever else you want to see.
Of course, with the ordinary eye you
cannot see me.

I give you divine vision.
Behold my absolute power!

Samjaya:
With these words, Visnu, the great
 Lord of mystic power,
  Gave Arjuna the vision of his high-
  est, absolute form—
His form with many mouths and
 eyes,
  appearing in many miraculous
  ways,
   With many divine ornaments and
   divine, unsheathed weapons.
He wore garlands and robes and
 ointments of divine fragrance.
He was a wholly wonderful god,
 infinite, facing in every direction.
If the light of a thousand suns
 should effulge all at once,
  It would resemble the radiance of
  that god of overpowering reality.
Then and there, Arjuna saw the entire world unified,
  Yet divided manifold, embodied in
  the God of gods.
Bewildered and enraptured,
 Arjuna, the Pursuer of Wealth,
 bowed his head to the god,
 joined his palms, and said:

Arjuna:
Master! Within you I see the gods,
 and all classes of beings,
  the Creator on his lotus seat,
  and all seers and divine serpents.
Far and near, I see you without
 limit,
  Reaching, containing everything,
  and with innumerable mouths
  and eyes.
I see no end to you, no middle,
 And no beginning—
  O universal Lord and form of all!
You, Wearer of Crown, Mace and
 Discus,
  You are a deluge of brilliant light
  all around.

I see you,
 Who can hardly be seen,
 With the splendour of radiant fires
 and suns,
 Immeasurable.
You are the one imperishable Para-
 mount necessary core of knowl-
 edge,
  The world's ultimate foundation;
  You never cease to guard the eter-
  nal tradition.
You are the everlasting Divine Being.
There is no telling what is begin-
 ning, middle or end in you.
Your power is infinite.
Your arms reach infinitely far.
Sun and moon are your eyes.
This is how I see you.
Your mouth is a flaming sacrificial
 fire.
You burn up the world with your ra-
 diance.
For you alone fill the quarters of
 heaven And the space between
 heaven and earth.
The world above, man's world,
 And the world in between Are
 frightened at the awesome sight
 of you, O mighty being!
There I see throngs of gods entering
 you.
Some are afraid,
 They join their palms and call
 upon your name.
Throngs of great seers and perfect
 sages hail you with magnificent
 hymns,
The Terrifying Gods,
The Gods of Heaven, the Radiant
 Gods,
Also the Celestial Spirits,
The All-Gods, the Celestial Twins,
The Storm-Gods and the Ancestors;
Multitudes of heavenly musicians,
Good sprites, demons and perfect
 sages All look upon you in wonder.
When the worlds see your form
 Of many mouths and eyes,

Of many arms, legs and feet,
  Many torsos, many terrible tusks,
  They tremble, as do I.
For seeing you ablaze with all the
    colours of the rainbow,
  Touching the sky,
  With gaping mouths and wide,
    flaming eyes,
  My heart in me is shaken.
O God, I have lost all certainty, all
    peace.
Your mouths and their terrible tusks
  evoke The world in conflagration.
Looking at them I can no longer ori-
  ent myself.
There is no refuge.
O Lord of gods, dwelling place of the
    world,
  Give me your grace.
And there the sons of Dhṛtarāṣṭra
    enter you,
  All of them,
  Together with a host of kings,
  Bhīsma, Drona,
  And also the charioteer's son,
  Karna—
  And our own commanders,
  Even they are with them!
They rush into your awful mouths
  With those terrible rusks.
Some can be seen stuck between
  your teeth,
  Their heads crushed.
As the many river torrents rush to-
  ward one sea,
  Those worldly heroes enter your
  flaming mouths.
As moths hasten frantically into the
  fire To meet their end,
  So men enter your jaws.
Devouring all with the flames of
    your mouths Lapping and licking
  all around,
  You fill the world with effulgence,
  And your awesome splendour is
    scorching, O God!
I bow before you, supreme God. Be
  gracious.

You, who are so awesome to see,
  Tell me, who are you?
I want to know you, the very first
  Lord,
  For I do not understand what it is
  you are doing.

The Lord:
I am Time who destroys man's
  world.
I am the time that is now ripe To
  gather in the people here;
  That is what I am doing.
Even without you, all these warriors
    Drawn up for battle in opposing
  ranks Will cease to exist.
Therefore rise up! Win glory!
When you conquer your enemies,
  Your kingship will be fulfilled.
Enjoy it.
Be just an instrument,
  You, who can draw the bow with
    the left as well as the right hand!
I myself have slain your enemies
  long ago.
Do not waver.
Conquer the enemies whom I have
    already slain—
  Drona and Bhīṣma and
  Jayadratha,
  And Karna also, and the other he-
  roes at arms.
Fight! You are about to defeat your
  rivals in war.

Samjaya:
After these words of Kṛṣṇa,
  The wearer of the crown was over-
  whelmed.
Joining his palms he honoured
  Kṛṣṇa.
He bowed down, then spoke again,
  Stammering, overcome by fear:

Arjuna:
It is right, Kṛṣṇa, that the world Rev-
  els in your glory,

That demons are frightened And flee
in all directions,
And all the host of perfect sages
honour your.
Why should they not bow to you, O
mighty one!
For you are most worthy of honour;
You impelled even the creator.
O infinite Lord of the gods and
abode of the world,
You are the imperishable beginning,
You are what exists and what does
not exist,
And you are beyond both.
You are the very first god,
The primal Divine Being,
The absolute foundation of all
things,
Knower and known,
And the highest estate.
You of infinite form stretched out
the world.
You who are Wind, Death, Fire,
The God of Streams, the Moon,
The Lord of living beings, of cre-
ation,
You should receive honour
A thousandfold—Time and again,
Honour, honour to you!
Let honour be given to you
Before you and behind
And on all sides.
You who are all,
Your might is boundless,
Your strength unmeasured.
You are all, for you fulfill all.
Whatever I blurted out, carelessly or
out of affection—
Kṛṣṇa! Son of Yadhu! My Friend!—
Thinking of you as my companion,
And unaware of this, of your great-
ness,
And whatever I did improperly to
you, jokingly,
In playing, resting, sitting, or eating,
Either by myself or in public—
O imperishable Lord, I ask your
pardon for it.

You are immeasurable.
You are the father of the world With
all its moving and unmoving
things.
You are its spiritual guide,
Most venerable and worthy of wor-
ship.
There is none like you.
How could there be anyone higher
In the world above, in man's
world,
And in the realm between the two,
O paramount Lord!
Therefore, I bow,
I prostrate myself,
I beg your grace,
For your are the Lord to be wor-
shipped.
Please, God, be patient with me As a
father with his son, a friend with
his friend A lover with his
beloved.
I have seen what no one saw before,
And I rejoice.
But my heart is stricken with fear.
Show me that one usual form of
yours, O God,
Be gracious, Lord of gods,
Refuge of the world.
I would like to see you just like that
With your crown and club and
the discus in your hand.
O you with thousand arms and of
all forms,
Appear again in that four-armed
shape of yours.

The Lord:
I am pleased with you, Arjuna,
And by my own will I have shown
you my supreme form.
This is the form of my majesty,
It is my universal form, primordial
and endless.
No one but you has ever seen it.
No one but you, foremost of the
Kurus,

In the world of men can see me in
this form,
Whether by knowledge of Sacred
Texts,
Or by sacrifices, study, or acts of
generosity,
Or rituals, or grim austerities.
Having no fear, no anxieties,
When you see this shape of mine,
However terrifying it is.
See, here is my usual form again.
Your fear is dispelled, your heart at
ease.

Samjaya:
Thus Kṛṣṇa spoke to Arjuna And
showed his own form again.
The mighty being took on his agreeable form,
And he comforted that frightened
man.

Arjuna:
Now that I see this pleasant, human
shape of yours, Kṛṣṇa,

I regain my senses and become normal again.

The Lord:
Even the gods long to see this form
of mine That is very difficult to
see and that you have seen.
The way you have seen me I cannot
be seen By knowing sacred texts,
by austerity, generosity, or sacrifice,
But I can be known and seen in
this way, as I really am;
I am accessible through devotion
directed to me alone.
Who does his rites for me and is intent on me,
Who loves me without other desires,
And has no ill will toward any creatures at all,
He comes to me.

READING CRITICALLY FOR IDEAS, STRUCTURE, AND STYLE

1. Taken as a series, what values emerge from these texts that are
   essential to Hinduism?

2. The concept of a divine spirit incarnated in human form provides one of the most dramatic moments of the *Bhagavad-Gîtā*.
   How does this dialogue serve as a vehicle for the expression of
   important spiritual truths? What does Arjuna learn?

3. The language in these texts is both dramatic and poetic. What
   metaphors, similes, and images do the writers create in order to
   communicate the experiences that otherwise would be beyond
   comprehension?

EXTENDING INSIGHTS THROUGH WRITING

1. The concepts of reincarnation and karma are outside traditional Western religions and may be difficult to grasp. In a few paragraphs, explain how you understand these concepts and describe how they would apply to you or people you know.

2. For a research project, obtain the three-part video that Peter Brook made of *The Mahabharata* (1989) and, after watching it, write a short essay in which you analyze three or four of the characters in relationship to the concepts you have read about in the scriptures. This prize-winning video can be obtained from the Parabola Video Library, 656 Broadway, New York, New York 10012.

CONNECTING PERSPECTIVES
ON THE MIND AND THE SPIRIT

1. Hinduism at first glance would seem to present a very different view of human existence than does Jean-Paul Sartre. But, in what ways do both philosophies (Hinduism and Existentialism) emphasize the concept of personal responsibility for one's fate?

2. Hindus and Muslims have been at odds with each other for many centuries. Is there anything intrinsic in the tenets of Hinduism as reflected in these readings and/or in the *Koran* that would explain this longstanding antagonism?

Three Texts from the Torah: Genesis, Burning Bush, and the Ten Commandments

BACKGROUND

The religious beliefs, practices, and way of life of both the Israelites in the Bible and of contemporary Jews (who number 14 million) is based on the teachings of the Torah (the law) or Hebrew Bible. The five books, or Pentateuch, that comprise the Torah consist of Genesis, Exodus, Leviticus, Numbers, and Deuteronomy. Genesis tells of the creation of the world by God and of the deeds of the "Patriarchs"—Abraham, Isaac, Jacob, and Joseph. Exodus includes the story of the Israelites in Egypt, their escape under Moses, and the giving of the Ten Commandments at Mount Sinai. Interestingly, the exodus of Moses is date zero in the Jewish calendar, which begins at this time. Leviticus further explains the detailed laws given at Mount Sinai, as does Numbers, which then relates the story of the departure of the Israelites from Sinai towards the borders of the promised land. Deuteronomy contains the final words of Moses to the Israelites, giving them laws to be observed in the promised land, and includes the description of his death. Collectively, the scrolls that comprise the Torah are an indispensable guide as to how to live a correct life as a Jew and serve as a liturgy (that is, as a publicly read text) that provides the core of religious ritual in the synagogue, or temple.

Judaism is a monotheistic religion (as are Christianity and Islam) and throughout its history, the Torah was considered the binding word of God that covered all aspects of human conduct. God (or Yahweh) is the Prime Cause of everything that exists in the universe. For Jews, God is without rivals, incarnations, and needs no representation. Thus, Jews would consider the worship of any other deity as a form of blasphemy. Ancient Israelites made no distinction between civil codes of law and religious codes. The thirty-nine books (that include the five books of the Torah) are commonly referred to as the Old Testament. But this designation reflects the Christian view that sees the New Testament, or testimony of Jesus, as the fulfillment of the old covenant.

God, in the Torah, is very much a personal being who requires obedience and submission to His will. Various dramatic stories (such as God instructing Abraham to sacrifice his only son, Isaac, in Genesis Chapter 22) demonstrate this obligation, which transcends every other consideration. Conversely, other episodes illustrate the consequences of humanity's perverse use of God-given free will to choose evil over good.

Rituals and observances play a crucial role in Judaism. There are seven major holidays in the Jewish calender, whose zero date corresponds to 3761

B.C. and include such holy days and festivals as Hanukkah (the Festival of Lights, in December), Passover (recalling the exodus of the Jews from Egypt, in March/April) and Rosh Hashanah (the Jewish New Year, in September), which begins ten days of penitence that ends with Yom Kippur (a day of fasting and praying for forgiveness for the past year's sins).

The texts that follow are drawn from the Torah and encompass the Creation narrative (from Genesis, *King James Version,* New York: American Bible Society) and the encounter of Moses with God at the Burning Bush and the Decalogue, or Ten Commandments, given by God to Moses (from Exodus, Chapter 3 and Chapter 20, *The Holy Bible,* rev.standard edition, ed. H.G. May, New York and London: Collins, 1971).

APPROACHING THE TORAH

In the biblical account of the creation of the world, as related in Genesis, we can understand that events that took place instantaneously are expressed in the narrative form to make the account more comprehensible. In this narrative, God creates the sky, the Earth, light, the succession of days and nights, the firmament, plant life, the Moon and the Sun, animals and, finally, man. Beginning with the fourth verse of the second chapter, the emphasis shifts to a very personal kind of deity who nurtures, tends, and supervises His creations, including man. Subtle differences between the account related in the first chapter and the beginning of the second (to the middle of the fourth verse) and the retelling of the same story from the fourth verse onward may be due to the fact that portions of the Bible were transmitted orally for unknown periods of time before these stories were preserved in writing. Inconsistencies that have troubled scholars may be due to the nature of the text as an amalgam of overlapping accounts told from slightly different perspectives.

The account continues with one of the most famous examples of a human confrontation with the Divine. Moses is tending the sheep of Jethro and is startled and terrified by the Burning Bush. From this time onward, Moses is given the task of bringing the Israelites out of bondage in Egypt and vested with the power to accomplish this by God as the successor to the "Patriarchs."

The Ten Commandments given by God to Moses and Israel (recorded in Exodus, Chapter 20) are divided into two broad categories: While the first five define the expected relationship between man and God, the last five define relationships between human beings. Sages and scholars in ancient and medieval periods have found the Torah to contain 613 commandments and see the Ten Commandments as broad categories under which the others can be included. These moral codes are designed to reinforce the ties between man and God.

The First Book of Moses, called Genesis

THE CREATION

¹ In the beginning God created the heaven and the earth. ² And the earth was without form, and void; and darkness *was* upon the face of the deep. And the Spirit of God moved upon the face of the waters.

³ And God said, Let there be light:[a] and there was light. ⁴ And God saw the light, that *it was* good: and God divided the light from the darkness. ⁵ And God called the light Day, and the darkness he called Night. And the evening and the morning were the first day.

⁶ And God said, Let there be a firmament in the midst of the waters, and let it divide the waters from the waters. ⁷ And God made the firmament, and divided the waters which *were* under the firmament from the waters which *were* above the firmament: and it was so. ⁸ And God called the firmament Heaven.[b] And the evening and the morning were the second day.

⁹ And God said, Let the waters under the heaven be gathered together unto one place, and let the dry *land* appear: and it was so. ¹⁰ And God called the dry *land* Earth; and the gathering together of the waters called he Seas: and God saw that *it was* good. ¹¹ And God said, Let the earth bring forth grass, the herb yielding seed, *and* the fruit tree yielding fruit after his kind, whose seed *is* in itself, upon the earth: and it was so. ¹² And the earth brought forth grass, *and* herb yielding seed after his kind, and the tree yielding fruit, whose seed *was* in itself, after his kind: and God saw that *it was* good. ¹³ And the evening and the morning were the third day.

¹⁴ And God said, Let there be lights in the firmament of the heaven to divide the day from the night; and let them be for signs, and for seasons, and for days, and years: ¹⁵ and let them be for lights in the firmament of the heaven to give light upon the earth: and it was so. ¹⁶ And God made two great lights; the greater light to rule the day, and the lesser light to rule the night: *he made* the stars also. ¹⁷ And God set them in the firmament of the heaven to give light upon the earth, ¹⁸ and to rule over the day and over the night, and to divide the light from the darkness: and God saw that *it was* good. ¹⁹ And the evening and the morning were the fourth day.

²⁰ And God said, Let the waters bring forth abundantly the moving creature that hath life, and fowl *that* may fly above the earth in the open firmament of heaven. ²¹ And God created great whales, and every living creature that moveth, which the waters brought forth abundantly, after their kind, and every winged fowl after his kind: and God saw that *it was* good. ²² And God blessed them, saying, Be fruitful, and multiply, and fill the waters in the seas,

[a]1:3 2 Cor. 4:6.
[b]1:6-8 2 Pet. 3:5. [Eds Note: Letters refer to parallel passages].

and let fowl multiply in the earth. [23] And the evening and the morning were the fifth day.

[24] And God said, Let the earth bring forth the living creature after his kind, cattle, and creeping thing, and beast of the earth after his kind: and it was so. [25] And God made the beast of the earth after his kind, and cattle after their kind, and every thing that creepeth upon the earth after his kind: and God saw that *it was* good.

[26] And God said, Let us make man in our image,[c] after our likeness: and let them have dominion over the fish of the sea, and over the fowl of the air, and over the cattle, and over all the earth, and over every creeping thing that creepeth upon the earth. [27] So God created man in his *own* image, in the image of God created he him; male and female created he them.[d] [28] And God blessed them,[e] and God said unto them, Be fruitful, and multiply, and replenish* the earth, and subdue it: and have dominion over the fish of the sea, and over the fowl of the air, and over every living thing that moveth upon the earth. [29] And God said, Behold, I have given you every herb bearing seed, which *is* upon the face of all the earth, and every tree, in the which *is* the fruit of a tree yielding seed; to you it shall be for meat. [30] And to every beast of the earth, and to every fowl of the air, and to every thing that creepeth upon the earth, where-in *there is* life, *I have given* every green herb for meat: and it was so. [31] And God saw every thing that he had made, and, behold, *it was* very good. And the evening and the morning were the sixth day.

GENESIS 1–3

[2] Thus the heavens and the earth were finished, and all the host of them. [2] And on the seventh day God ended his work which he had made; and he rested on the seventh day from all his work which he had made.[a] [3] And God blessed the seventh day, and sanctified it:[b] because that in it he had rested from all his work which God created and made.

Man in the Garden of Eden

[4] These *are* the generations of the heavens and of the earth when they were created, in the day that the LORD God made the earth and the heavens, [5] and every plant of the field before it was in the earth, and every herb of the field before it grew: for the LORD God had not caused it to rain upon the earth, and *there was* not a man to till the ground. [6] But there went up a mist from the earth, and watered the whole face of the ground. [7] And the LORD God formed man *of* the dust of the ground, and breathed into his nostrils the breath

[c]1:26 1 Cor. 11:7.
[d]1:27 Mt. 19:4; Mk. 10:6.
[e]1:27–28 Gen. 5:1-2.
[a]2:2 Heb 4:4, 10.
[b]2.2–3 Ex. 20:11.

of life; and man became a living soul.[c] [8] And the LORD God planted a garden eastward in Eden; and there he put the man whom he had formed. [9] And out of the ground made the LORD God to grow every tree that is pleasant to the sight, and good for food; the tree of life[d] also in the midst of the garden, and the tree of knowledge of good and evil.

THE BURNING BUSH: EXODUS 3

Now Moses was keeping the flock of his father-in-law, Jethro, the priest of Mid'ian; and he led his flock to the west side of the wilderness, and came to Horeb, the mountain of God. And the angel of the Lord appeared to him in a flame of fire out of the midst of a bush; and he looked, and lo, the bush was burning, yet it was not consumed. And Moses said, 'I will turn aside and see this great sight, why the bush is not burnt.' When the Lord saw that he turned aside to see, God called to him out of the bush, 'Moses, Moses!' And he said, 'Here am I.' Then he said, 'Do not come near; put off your shoes from your feet, for the place on which you are standing is holy ground.' And he said, 'I am the God of your father, the God of Abraham, the God of Isaac, and the God of Jacob.' And Moses hid his face, for he was afraid to look at God.

Then the Lord said, 'I have seen the affliction of my people who are in Egypt, and have heard their cry because of their taskmasters; I know their sufferings, and I have come down to deliver them out of the hand of the Egyptians, and to bring them up out of that land to a good and broad land, a land flowing with milk and honey, to the place of the Canaanites, the Hittites, the Amorites, and Per'izzites, the Hivites, and the Jeb'usites. And now, behold, the cry of the people of Israel has come to me, and I have seen the oppression with which the Egyptians oppress them. Come, I will send you to Pharaoh that you may bring forth my people, the sons of Israel, out of Egypt.' But Moses said to God, 'Who am I that I should go to Pharaoh, and bring the sons of Israel out of Egypt?' He said, 'But I will be with you; and this shall be the sign for you, that I have sent you: when you have brought forth the people out of Egypt, you shall serve God upon this mountain.'

Then Moses said to God, 'If I come to the people of Israel and say to them, "The God of your fathers has sent me to you," and they ask me, "What is his name?" what shall I say to them?' God said to Moses, 'I AM WHO I AM.' And he said, 'Say this to the people of Israel, "I AM has sent me to you."' God also said to Moses, 'Say this to the people of Israel, "The Lord, the God of your fathers, the God of Abraham, the God of Isaac, and the God of Jacob, has sent me to you": this is my name for ever, and thus I am to be remembered throughout all generations. Go and gather the elders of Israel together, and say to them, "The Lord, the God of your fathers, the God of Abraham of Isaac, and of Jacob, has appeared to me, saying, "I have observed you and what has been

[c]2:7 1 Cor. 15:45.
[d]2:9 Rev. 2:7; 22:2, 14.

done to you in Egypt; and I promise that I will bring you up out of the affliction of Egypt, to the land of the Canaanites, the Hittites, the Amorites, the
Per'izzites, the Hivites, and the Jeb'usites, a land flowing with milk and honey."
And they will hearken to your voice; and you and the elders of Israel shall go
to the king of Egypt and say to him, "The Lord, the God of the Hebrews, has
met with us; and now, we pray you, let us go a three days' journey into the
wilderness, that we may sacrifice to the Lord our God." I know that the king
of Egypt will not let you go unless compelled by a mighty hand. So I will stretch
out my hand and smite Egypt with all the wonders which I will do in it; after
that he will let you go. And I will give this people favour in the sight of the
Egyptians; and when you go, you shall not go empty, but each woman shall
ask of her neighbour, and of her who sojourns in her house, jewellery of silver and gold, and clothing, and you shall put them on your sons and on your
daughters; thus you shall despoil the Egyptians.'

THE TEN COMMANDMENTS: EXODUS 20

And God spoke all these words, saying,
I am the Lord your God, who brought you out of the land of Egypt, out
of the house of bondage.
You shall have no other gods before me.
You shall not make for yourself a graven image, or any likeness of anything that is in heaven above, or that is in the earth beneath, or that is in the
water under the earth; you shall not bow down to them or serve them; for I
the Lord your God am a jealous God, visiting the iniquity of the fathers upon
the children to the third and the fourth generation of those who hate me, but
showing steadfast love to thousands of those who love me and keep my
commandments.
You shall not take the name of the Lord your God in vain; for the Lord
will not hold him guiltless who takes his name in vain.
Remember the sabbath day, to keep it holy. Six days you shall labour,
and do all your work; but the seventh day is a sabbath to the Lord your God;
in it you shall not do any work, you, or your son, or your daughter, your manservant, or your maidservant, or your cattle, or the sojourner who is within your
gates; for in six days the Lord made heaven and earth, the sea, and all that is
in them, and rested the seventh day; therefore the Lord blessed the sabbath
day and hallowed it.
Honour your father and your mother, that your days may be long in the
land which the Lord your God gives you.
You shall not kill.
You shall not commit adultery.
You shall not steal.
You shall not bear false witness against your neighbour.
You shall not covet your neighbour's house; you shall not covet your
neighbour's wife, or his manservant, or his maidservant, or his ox, or his ass,
or anything that is your neighbour's.

READING CRITICALLY FOR IDEAS, STRUCTURE, AND STYLE

1. In what way does the account of the Creation (in Genesis, Chapter 1) propose that man must exercise dominion over the created order of the world just as God exercises dominion over the universe?

2. With what obligation is Moses charged in the episode of the Burning Bush? How would you characterize the way Yahweh is made manifest in this episode?

3. What different kinds of expectations are contained in the Ten Commandments, and how do they define the relationship between the Israelites and Yahweh?

EXTENDING INSIGHTS THROUGH WRITING

1. Do some research into the aspects of the Torah that are designed to counter the prevailing trend towards polytheism among the people surrounding the Jews. What episodes in the Bible are intended to keep the Jews as the only ancient people who were monotheistic?

2. The Psalms are a collection of 150 poetic pieces, many of which are attributed to King David and King Solomon, and have had enormous cultural and literary influence. Read several of these, such as 8, 19, 23, 27, 95, 121, and discuss the themes and the imagery employed.

CONNECTING PERSPECTIVES ON THE MIND AND THE SPIRIT

1. The two ideas that unite Hindu religious thought are reincarnation and the principle of caste. Compare and contrast these concepts with the ethical injunctions and doctrines of Judaism.

2. In a short essay, discuss the differences between proselytizing religions (for example, Christianity and Islam) and non-proselytizing religions, such as Judaism, Hinduism, and Shintoism (the major religion of Japan) in terms of the acceptance or nonacceptance of outsiders.

THE PROPHET MUHAMMAD

From the Koran

BACKGROUND

Islam is a monotheistic religion whose members worship the one God of Jews and Christians (God is called Allah in Arabic) and follow the teachings of the *Koran* (or *Qur'an*), which is believed to be the revelation of God to Muhammad. For many Westerners, Islam (which ranks second, after Roman Catholicism, among the major religions of the world with 1.3 billion followers) remains a rather mysterious system of belief. Islam (which means "submission to the will of God") is the religion founded by Muhammad about 600 years after the inception of Christianity. Muhammad (570–632 A.D.) was born into the Kuraish tribe, which ruled Mecca, an important caravan city in western Saudi Arabia, and began receiving visions and revelations when he was about forty, which he believed were given to him by the Archangel Gabriel. These revelations and teachings (which form the basis of Islam and are recorded in the *Koran*) had a profoundly transforming effect on his life. Initially, he made few converts and attracted many enemies. In 622, he escaped a potential assassination by journeying from Mecca to Medina. It is from this event of the flight (*Hejira*) that Islam begins it calendar. Muhammad spent the rest of his life at the city he named Medina and built a theocratic state from which he governed a rapidly expanding empire. Muslims believe that Muhammad is the last and the greatest of God's prophets, who also include Adam, Noah, Abraham, Moses, and Jesus.

Muslims are required to pray five times a day (facing Mecca), to fast in the daytime during the holy month of Ramadan (the 9th month of the Muslim year), to abstain from pork and alcohol, and to give alms to the poor. They are also expected to make a pilgrimage to Mecca (Muhammad's birthplace in western Saudi Arabia) at least once in their lives. Thus, Islam is not only a system of beliefs and rituals, but a way of life.

565

APPROACHING THE *KORAN*

The *Koran* consists of 114 *surahs*, or chapters, of varying lengths that were taken down as they were spoken by Muhammad and are written in a form of Arabic that is close to that of rhymed prose or poetry. It differs from any other scripture in the world (such as the Hebrew Bible or the *New Testament*) in that it is the work of one man and contains every kind of advice about every conceivable subject (doctrines, morals, civil laws, manners), as well as astonishing descriptions of Heaven and Hell. The following excerpt is drawn from the surah or chapter of the *Koran* called "the Believer" and describes the characteristics of those who follow Allah and contrasts their fate with the fate awaiting unbelievers.

From the Koran

The Believer

In the Name of God, the Compassionate, the Merciful

Hā' mīm. This Book is revealed by God, the Mighty One, the All-knowing, who forgives sin and accepts repentance.

His punishment is stern, and His bounty infinite. There is no god but Him. All shall return to Him.

None but the unbelievers dispute the revelations of God. Do not be deceived by their prosperous dealings in the land. Long before them the people of Noah denied Our revelations, and so did the factions after them. Every nation strove to slay their apostle, seeking with false arguments to refute the truth; but I smote them, and how stern was My punishment! Thus shall the word of your Lord be fulfilled concerning the unbelievers: they are the heirs of the Fire.

Those who bear the Throne and those who stand around it give glory to their Lord and believe in Him. They implore forgiveness for the faithful, saying: "Lord, you embrace all things with Your mercy and Your knowledge. Forgive those that repent and follow Your path. Shield them from the scourge of Hell. Admit them, Lord, to the gardens of Eden which You have promised them, together with all the righteous among their fathers, their spouses, and their descendants. You are the Almighty, the Wise One. Deliver them from all evil. He whom You will deliver from evil on that day will surely earn Your mercy. That is the supreme triumph."

5   But to the unbelievers a voice will cry: "God's abhorrence of you is greater than your hatred of yourselves. You were called to the Faith, but you denied it."

They shall say: "Lord, twice have You made us die, and twice have You given us life. We now confess our sins. Is there no way out?"

They shall be answered: "This is because when God was invoked alone, you disbelieved; but when you were bidden to serve other gods besides Him you believed in them. Today judgement rests with God, the Most High, the Supreme One."

It is He who reveals His signs to you, and sends down sustenance from the sky for you. Yet none takes heed except the repentant. Pray, then, to God and worship none but Him, however much the unbelievers may dislike it.

Exalted and throned on high. He lets the Spirit descend at His behest on those of His servants whom He chooses, that He may warn them of the day when they shall meet Him; the day when they shall rise up from their graves with nothing hidden from God. And who shall reign supreme on that day? God, the One, the Almighty.

On that day every soul shall be paid back according to what it did. On   10
that day none shall be wronged. Swift is God's reckoning.

Forewarn them of the approaching day, when men's hearts will leap up to their throats and choke them; when the wrongdoers will have neither friend nor intercessor to be heard. He knows the furtive look and the secret thought. God will judge with fairness, but the idols to which they pray besides Him can judge nothing. God alone hears all and observes all.

Have they never journeyed through the land and seen what was the end of those who have gone before them, nations far greater in prowess and in splendour? God scourged them for their sins, and from God they had none to protect them. That was because their apostles had come to them with clear revelations and they denied them. So God smote them. Mighty is God, and stern His retribution.

We sent forth Moses with Our signs and with clear authority to Pharaoh, Haman, and Korah. But they said: "A sorcerer, a teller of lies."

And when he brought them the Truth from Ourself, they said: "Put to death the sons of those who share his faith, and spare only their daughters." Futile were the schemes of the unbelievers.

Pharaoh said: "Let me slay Moses, and then let him invoke his god! I fear   15
that he will change your religion and spread disorder in the land."

Moses said: "I take refuge in my Lord and in your Lord from every tyrant who denies the Day of Reckoning."

But one of Pharaoh's kinsmen, who in secret was a true believer, said: "Would you slay a man merely because he says: 'My Lord is God?' He has brought you evident signs from your Lord. If he is lying, may his lie be on his head; but if he is speaking the truth, a part at least of what he threatens will smite you. God does not guide the lying transgressor. Today you are the masters, my people, illustrious throughout the earth. But who will save us from the might of God when it bears down upon us?"

Pharaoh said: "I have told you what I think. I will surely guide you to the right path."

He who was a true believer said: "I warn you, my people, against the fate which overtook the factions: the people of Noah, 'Ād, and Thamūd, and those that came after them. God does not seek to wrong His servants.

"I warn you, my people, against the day when men will cry out to one   20
another, when you will turn and flee, with none to defend you against God.

He whom God confounds shall have none to guide him. Long before this, Joseph came to you with veritable signs, but you never ceased to doubt them; and when he died you said: 'After him God will never send another apostle.' Thus God confounds the doubting transgressor. Those who dispute God's revelations, with no authority vouchsafed to them, are held in deep abhorrence by God and by the faithful. Thus God seals up the heart of every scornful tyrant."

Pharaoh said to Haman: "Build me a tower that I may reach the highways—the very highways—of the heavens, and look upon the god of Moses. I am convinced that he is lying."

Thus was Pharaoh seduced by his foul deeds, and he was turned away from the right path. Pharaoh's cunning led to nothing but perdition.

He who was a true believer said: "Follow me, my people, that I may guide you to the right path. My people, the life of this world is a fleeting comfort, but the life to come is an everlasting mansion. Those that do evil shall be rewarded with like evil; but those that have faith and do good works, both men and women, shall enter the gardens of Paradise and therein receive blessings without number.

"My people, how is it that I call you to salvation, while you call me to the Fire? You bid me deny God and serve other gods I know nothing of; while I exhort you to serve the Almighty, the Benignant One. Indeed, the gods to whom you call me can be invoked neither in this world nor in the hereafter. To God we shall return. The transgressors are the heirs of the Fire.

25   "Bear in mind what I have told you. To God I commend myself. God is cognizant of all His servants."

God delivered him from the evils which they planned, and a grievous scourge encompassed Pharaoh's people. They shall be brought before the Fire morning and evening, and on the day the Hour strikes, a voice will cry: "Mete out to the people of Pharaoh the sternest punishment!"

And when they argue in the Fire, the humble will say to those who deemed themselves mighty: "We have been your followers: will you now ward off from us some of these flames?" But those who deemed themselves mighty will reply: "Here are all of us now. God has judged His servants."

And those in the Fire will say to the keepers of Hell: "Implore your Lord to relieve our torment for one day!"

"But did your apostles not come to you with undoubted signs?" they will ask.

30   "Yes," they will answer. And their keepers will say: "Then offer your prayers." But vain shall be the prayers of the unbelievers.

We shall help Our apostles and the true believers both in this world and on the day when the witnesses rise to testify. On that day no excuse will avail the guilty. The Curse shall be their lot, and the scourge of the hereafter.

We gave Moses Our guidance and the Israelites the Book[1] to inherit: a guide and an admonition to men of understanding. Therefore have patience; God's promise is surely true. Implore forgiveness for your sins, and celebrate the praise of your Lord evening and morning.

---

[1]The Book: The Bible.

As for those who dispute the revelations of God, with no authority vouch-safed to them, they nurture in their hearts ambitions they shall never attain. Therefore seek refuge in God; it is He that hears all and observes all.

Surely, the creation of the heavens and the earth is greater than the creation of man; yet most men have no knowledge.

The blind and the seeing are not equal, nor are the wicked the equal of those that have faith and do good works. Yet do you seldom give thought.   35

The Hour of Doom is sure to come: of this there is no doubt; and yet most men do not believe.

Your Lord has said: "Call on me and I will answer you. Those that disdain My service shall enter Hell with all humility."

It was God who made for you the night to rest in and the day to give you light. God is bountiful to men, yet most men do not give thanks.

Such is God your Lord, the Creator of all things. There is no god but Him. How then can you turn away from Him? Yet even thus the men who deny God's revelations turn away from Him.

It is God who has made the earth a dwelling-place for you, and the sky   40
a ceiling. He has moulded your bodies into a comely shape and provided you with good things.

Such is God, your Lord. Blessed be God, Lord of the Universe.

He is the Living One; there is no god but Him. Pray to Him, then, and worship none besides Him. Praise be to God, Lord of the Universe!

Say: "I am forbidden to serve your idols, now that clear proofs have been given me from my Lord. I am commanded to surrender myself to the Lord of the Universe."

It was He who created you from dust, then from a little germ, and then from a clot of blood. He brings you infants into the world; you reach manhood, then decline into old age (though some of you die young), so that you may complete your appointed term and grow in wisdom.

It is He who ordains life and death. If He decrees a thing, He need only   45
say: "Be," and it is.

Do you not see how those who dispute the revelations of God turn away from the right path? Those who have denied the Book and the message We sent through Our apostles shall realize the truth hereafter: when, with chains and shackles round their necks, they shall be dragged through scalding water and burnt in the fire of Hell.

They will be asked: "Where are the gods whom you have served besides God?"

"They have forsaken us," they will reply. "Indeed, they were nothing, those gods to whom we prayed." Thus God confounds the unbelievers.

And they will be told: "That is because on earth you took delight in falsehoods, and led a wanton life. Enter the gates of Hell and stay therein for ever. Evil is the home of the arrogant."

Therefore have patience: God's promise is surely true. Whether We let   50
you[2] glimpse in some measure the scourge We threaten them with, or call you back to Us before We smite them, to Us they shall return.

---

[2]Muhammad. [Translator's note]

We sent forth other apostles before your time; of some We have already told you, of others We have not yet told you. None of those apostles could bring a sign except by God's leave. And when God's will was done, justice prevailed and there and then the disbelievers lost.

It is God who has provided you with beasts, that you may ride on some and eat the flesh of others. You put them to many uses; they take you where you wish to go, carrying you by land as ships carry you by sea.

He reveals to you His signs. Which of God's signs do you deny?

Have they never journeyed through the land and seen what was the end of those who have gone before them? More numerous were they in the land, and far greater in prowess and in splendour; yet all their labours proved of no avail to them.

55   When their apostles brought them veritable signs they proudly boasted of their own knowledge; but soon the scourge at which they scoffed encompassed them. And when they beheld Our might they said: "We now believe in God alone. We deny the idols which We served besides Him."

But their new faith was of no use to them, when they beheld Our might: such being the way of God with His creatures; and there and then the unbelievers lost.

READING CRITICALLY FOR IDEAS, STRUCTURE, AND STYLE

1. What are the characteristics of the believer, and what does God promise to the believer?
2. What behaviors merit punishment?
3. What features of this *surah* are designed to counter the worship of idols?

EXTENDING INSIGHTS THROUGH WRITING

1. The kind of faith promoted in this surah is designed to supplant the belief in idols with belief in a monotheistic God. How might the concept of idol worship be broadened to include our worship of cultural icons?
2. Discuss the way the fate of unbelievers is similar to or different from that which awaits unbelievers in other religions, as represented in this chapter.

DIFFERENT PERSPECTIVES ON GREAT IDEAS

1. Compare how Allah reveals himself to Muhammad in this *surah* with the way Lord Krishna reveals himself to Arjuna in the *Bhagavad-Gītā*. What different sets of concerns underlie each portrayal?

2. In what respects is the *Koran's* portrait of the true believer similar to those who follow the word of Jesus in St. Matthew's "Parables in the *New Testament*."

ST. MATTHEW

Parables in the New Testament

BACKGROUND

The New Testament, or the distinctively Christian portion of the Bible, consists of twenty-seven books dating from the earliest Christian period, transmitted in a popular form of Greek spoken in the biblical regions from the fourth century B.C. The word *testament* refers to the testimony of Jesus as the Christ or fulfillment prophesied in the Hebrew Bible, which Christians refer to as the Old Testament. In the Gospels, that is, in the four biographies of Jesus in the New Testament, which are attributed to Matthew, Mark, Luke, and John, parables are short, illustrative narratives and figurative statements. The teaching that Christ gives in the New Testament takes different forms. The symbolic language of the parables is designed to lead from the literal world to the hidden spiritual dimension. The literal and figurative meaning of the parables is meant to make us aware of this higher dimension. In the thirteenth chapter of Matthew, Christ begins to speak in parables to the multitude.[1] His disciples ask why he suddenly has begun to use parables, and he responds that it is because he is speaking about the Kingdom of Heaven—that is, about a spiritual reality that would be otherwise impossible to grasp. The "Parable of the Sower and the Seed" is the starting point of Christ's teaching about the Kingdom of Heaven. Not surprisingly, this master parable is about the way people differ in their ability to understand this teaching. Differences in receptivity are presented in the parable by analogy as differences in the kinds of ground or earth into which the seed is sown: the wayside, stony places, ground where the seed does not take root, seed planted among thorns, and varying quantities of harvest grown from the seed. From this analysis about people's different capacities for receiving the teach-

---

[1]The Gospel according to St. Matthew is one of the first four books of the New Testament, a collection of documents from the early Christian community, written in the first two centuries after Jesus. This Gospel, which is believed to have been written between 80 and 95 A.D., stresses the ways in which Jesus fulfills the prophecies of the Old *Testament.* This Gospel also contains the Sermon on the Mount.

ings, there follow parables about "The Grain of Mustard Seed," "The Woman and the Leaven," "The Wheat and the Tares," "The Net," "The Pearl of Great Price," and "The Net Cast into the Sea."

Each in its own way deals with the Kingdom of Heaven and the teaching concerning it. The twentieth chapter of Matthew, in "The Parable of the Laborers in the Vineyard," presents a seemingly paradoxical idea that challenges conventional concepts of what is just and what is unjust. Laborers who have spent a whole day in the scorching heat of the fields are angry that those who have simply labored one hour are paid the same. The parable teaches that the Kingdom of Heaven cannot be thought of in terms of conventional rewards. The seeming injustice of the parable—that those who work longer do not gain a greater reward—hints that the Kingdom of Heaven has to do with eternity. The context in which the parable is given suggests that it is meant as an answer to the disciples who have abandoned all they had to follow Jesus and now want a reward in the conventional sense. The parables reprinted are drawn from the 1611 *King James* Version.

APPROACHING *THE NEW TESTAMENT*

Christianity (which ranks first among the major religions of the world and has 2 billion followers), the religion based on the life and teachings of Jesus Christ, is about 500 years younger than Buddhism and incorporates the name of the founder just as Buddhism does. The name Christ comes from *Christos,* the Greek word for the Hebrew Messiah, or "annointed one," and reminds us that Christianity arose out of Judaism. The first Christians were Jews by birth, who observed the rituals of Judaism and attended the synagogue. The life of Jesus is so familiar to Westerners as to need no recounting. But the key points of Christianity stress Jesus's role as the Messiah sent by God, who by dying and rising from the dead, made up for the sin of Adam, and by doing so, redeemed all of mankind. Belief in Jesus as the Messiah is a precondition to enter the Kingdom of Heaven, a spiritual state that the parables (reprinted here) attempt to define.

Parables in the New Testament

CHAPTER 13

1. The same day went Jesus out of the house, and sat by the sea side.

2. And great multitudes were gathered together unto him, so that he went into a ship, and sat; and the whole multitude stood on the shore.

3. And he spake many things unto them in parables, saying, Behold, a sower went forth to sow:

4. And when he sowed, some seeds fell by the way side, and the fowls came and devoured them up.

5. Some fell upon stony places, where they had not much earth: and forthwith they sprung up, because they had no deepness of earth.

6. And when the sun was up, they were scorched; and because they had no root, they withered away.

7. And some fell among thorns; and the thorns sprung up, and choked them;

8. But other fell into good ground, and brought forth fruit, some an hundredfold, some sixtyfold, some thirtyfold.

9. Who hath ears to hear, let him hear.

10. And the disciples came, and said unto him, Why speakest thou unto them in parables?

11. He answered and said unto them: Because it is given unto you to know the mysteries of the kingdom of heaven, but to them it is not given.

12. For whosoever hath, to him shall be given, and he shall have more abundance, but whosoever hath not, from him shall be taken away even that he hath.

13. Therefore speak I to them in parables: because they seeing see not; and hearing they hear not, neither do they understand.

14. And in them is fulfilled the prophecy of Esaias[2] which saith: By hearing ye shall hear, and shall not understand; and seeing ye shall see, and shall not perceive.

15. For this people's heart is waxed gross, and their ears are dull of hearing, and their eyes they have closed; lest at any time they should see with their eyes, and hear with their ears, and should understand with their heart, and should be converted, and I should heal them.

16. But blessed are your eyes, for they see, and your ears, for they hear.

17. For verily I say unto you, That many prophets and righteous men have desired to see those things which ye see, and have not seen them; and to hear those things which ye hear, and have not heard them.

18. Hear ye therefore the parable of the sower.

---

[2]*Esaias:* Isaiah 5:9-10.

19. When any one heareth the word of the kingdom, and understandeth it not, then cometh the wicked one, and catcheth away that which was sown in his heart. This is he which received seed by the way side.

20. But he that received the seed into stony places, the same is he that heareth the word, and anon with joy receiveth it;

21. Yet hath he not root in himself, but dureth for a while: for when tribulation or persecution ariseth because of the word, by and by he is offended.[3]

22. He also that received seed among the thorns is he that heareth the word; and the care of this world, and the deceitfulness of riches, choke the word, and he becometh unfruitful.

23. But he that received seed into the good ground is he that heareth the word, and understandeth it; which also beareth fruit, and bringeth forth, some an hundredfold, some sixty, some thirty.

24. Another parable put he forth unto them, saying, The kingdom of heaven is likened unto a man which sowed good seed in his field.

25. But while men slept, his enemy came and sowed tares among the wheat, and went his way.[4]

26. But when the blade was sprung up, and brought forth fruit, then appeared the tares also.

27. So the servants of the householder came and said unto him, Sir, didst not thou sow good seed in thy field? from whence then hath it tares?

28. He said unto them, An enemy hath done this. The servants said unto him, Wilt thou then that we go and gather them up?

29. But he said, Nay; lest while ye gather up the tares, ye root up also the wheat with them.

30. Let both grow together until the harvest; and in the time of harvest I will say to the reapers, Gather ye together first the tares, and bind them in bundles to burn them: but gather the wheat into my barn.

31. Another parable put he forth unto them, saying, The kingdom of heaven is like to a grain of mustard seed, which a man took, and sowed in his field:

[3]*Offended:* falls away.
[4]*Tares:* a noxious weed, probably the darnel.

32. Which indeed is the least of all seeds: but when it is grown, it is the greatest among herbs, and becometh a tree, so that the birds of the air come and lodge in the branches thereof.

33. Another parable spake he unto them: The kingdom of heaven is like unto leaven, which a woman took, and hid in three measures of meal, till the whole was leavened.

34. All these things spake Jesus unto the multitude in parables; and without a parable spake he not unto them,

35. That it might be fulfilled which was spoken by the prophet, saying, I will open my mouth in parables; I will utter things which have been kept secret from the foundation of the world.

36. Then Jesus sent the multitude away, and went into the house: and his disciples came unto him, saying, Declare unto us the parable of the tares of the field.

37. He answered and said unto them; He that soweth the good seed is the Son of man;

38. The field is the world; the good seed are the children of the kingdom; but the tares are the children of the wicked one.

39. The enemy that sowed them is the devil; the harvest is the end of the world; and the reapers are the angels.

40. As therefore the tares are gathered and burned in the fire; so shall it be in the end of this world.

41. The Son of man shall send forth his angels, and they shall gather out of his kingdom all things that offend, and them which do iniquity;

42. And shall cast them into a furnace of fire: there shall be wailing and gnashing of teeth.

43. Then shall the righteous shine forth as the sun in the kingdom of their Father. Who hath ears to hear, let him hear.

44. Again, the kingdom of heaven is like unto treasure hid in a field; the which when a man hath found, he hideth, and for joy thereof goeth and selleth all that he hath, and buyeth that field.

45. Again, the kingdom of heaven is like unto a merchant man, seeking goodly pearls:

46. Who, when he had found one pearl of great price, went and sold all that he had, and bought it.

47. Again, the kingdom of heaven is like unto a net, that was cast into the sea, and gathered of every kind:

48. Which, when it was full, they drew to shore, and sat down, and gathered the good into vessels, but cast the bad away.

49. So shall it be at the end of the world: the angels shall come forth, and sever the wicked from among the just,

50. And shall cast them into the furnace of fire: there shall be wailing and gnashing of teeth.

51. Jesus saith unto them, Have ye understood all these things? They say unto him, Yea, Lord.

52. Then said he unto them, Therefore every scribe which is instructed unto the kingdom of heaven is like unto a man that is an householder, which bringeth forth out of his treasure things new and old.

53. And it came to pass, that when Jesus had finished these parables, he departed thence.

54. And when he was come into his own country, he taught them in their synagogue, insomuch that they were astonished, and said, Whence hath this man this wisdom, and these mighty works?

55. Is not this the carpenter's son? is not his mother called Mary? and his brethren, James, and Joses, and Simon, and Judas?

56. And his sisters, are they not all with us? Whence then hath this man all these things?

57. And they were offended in him. But Jesus said unto them, A prophet is not without honour, save in his own country, and in his own house.

58. And he did not many mighty works there because of their unbelief.

CHAPTER 20

1. For the kingdom of heaven is like unto a man that is an householder, which went out early in the morning to hire labourers into his vineyard.

2. And when he had agreed with the labourers for a penny a day, he sent them into his vineyard.

3. And he went out about the third hour, and saw others standing idle in the marketplace,

4. And said unto them; Go ye also into the vineyard, and whatsoever is right I will give you. And they went their way.

5. Again he went out about the sixth and ninth hour, and did likewise.

6. And about the eleventh hour he went out, and found others standing idle, and saith unto them, Why stand ye here all the day idle?

7. They say unto him, Because no man hath hired us. He saith unto them, Go ye also into the vineyard; and whatsoever is right, that shall ye receive.

8. So when even was come, the lord of the vineyard saith unto his steward, Call the labourers, and give them their hire, beginning from the last unto the first.

9. And when they came that were hired about the eleventh hour, they received every man a penny.

10. But when the first came, they supposed that they should have received more; and they likewise received every man a penny.

11. And when they had received it, they murmured against the goodman of the house,

12. Saying, These last have wrought but one hour, and thou hast made them equal unto us, which have borne the burden and heat of the day.

13. But he answered one of them, and said, Friend, I do thee no wrong: didst not thou agree with me for a penny?

14. Take that thine is, and go thy way: I will give unto this last, even as unto thee.

15. Is it not lawful for me to do what I will with mine own? Is thine eye evil, because I am good?

16. So the last shall be first, and the first last: for many be called, but few chosen.

READING CRITICALLY FOR IDEAS, STRUCTURE, AND STYLE

1. In what sense is the parable of "The Sower and the Seed" the master parable that provides an indispensable starting point in any attempt to understand the other parables? For example, what do the differences among the four conditions in which seed is sown imply about different people's capacity to respond to Christ's teachings?

2. How is the parable of "The Laborers in the Vineyard" framed as a paradox? How does it introduce a concept of a threshold necessary to attain the "Kingdom of Heaven"?

3. The language into which the parables are cast may seem elliptical or obscure, especially since this was Jesus's chosen vehicle for promulgating his teaching. Discuss why you think he used

parables rather than continuing to teach as he had done in "The Sermon on the Mount."

EXTENDING INSIGHTS THROUGH WRITING

1. In a short essay discuss how any of these parables (or another in the *New Testament*) uses literal frames of reference to communicate spiritual meanings. For example, why is it significant that the mustard seed looks the smallest, but when grown is the greatest among herbs?

2. Create your own parable to express your understanding of what the Kingdom of Heaven means or how it might be attained.

CONNECTING PERSPECTIVES
ON THE MIND AND THE SPIRIT

1. To what extent does Christ's teaching differ from those of the Buddha? In what respects are they similar? How is the Kingdom of Heaven similar to and different from the Buddhist concept of Nirvana?

2. In the *Bhagavad-Gītā* in Hinduism, Krishna is a human incarnation of the Divine. Compare and contrast the messages of Jesus with those of Krishna and the correct moral perceptions and procedures one must follow to become one with God or enter the Kingdom of Heaven.

The Enlightenment of the Buddha: Buddhacarita

BACKGROUND

The Buddha is the title given to the founder of Buddhism, Siddhartha (which means "desire accomplished") Gautama (563–483 B.C.), who was born into a family of wealth and power in southern Nepal. Although reared in great luxury, Siddhartha renounced his life of privilege at the age of twenty-nine to become a wandering ascetic and to seek an answer to the problems of death and human suffering. After six years of intense spiritual discipline, he achieved enlightenment while meditating under a pipal or Bohdi tree (a fig tree, somewhat resembling the banyan) at Bodh Gaya (a town in central India). He spent the remainder of his life teaching and established a community of monks to carry on his work.

According to Buddhism, life as we know it is completely bound up with the consequences of our thoughts and actions in an endless cycle of birth, death, and rebirth known as *samsara.* The laws of cause and effect that keep us in this form of bondage is known as karma. In Buddha's view, the key to extricating oneself from this cycle of desire, suffering, and rebirth is to accept what came to be called the "Four Noble Truths": (1) existence is suffering; (2) the cause of suffering is desire; (3) there is a cessation of suffering called Nirvana (or total transcendence); and (4) there is a path that leads to the end of suffering, the "Noble Eightfold Path" of right views, right resolve, right speech, right action, right livelihood, right effort, right mindfulness, and right concentration.

Implicit in this program are the core values of Buddhism: the need to divest oneself of ill-will, sensuality, and personal cravings; the desire to wish others well; a refusal to injure other creatures (human and otherwise), hence vegetarianism is required; and the need to maintain constant intellectual awareness, hence the importance of meditation using techniques and principles employed by Buddha himself to reach enlightenment.

Buddha is said to have died at eighty (around 480 B.C.). The concepts of Buddhism were initially quite strong in India where, in the third century B.C., the emperor Asoka made it the official religion; it was, however, later absorbed into Hinduism. Over the next 200 years it became the major religion in China and was adopted in Japan, Sri Lanka, Burma, Thailand, and Tibet. At one time, Buddhism could claim more adherents than any other religion, but today its followers number approximately 360 million, which places it after Christianity, Islam, and Hinduism in number of believers.

The following selection, "The Enlightenment of the Buddha: Buddhacarita" (ed. by E. Conze, *Buddhist Texts Through the Ages*, London: Faber & Faber, 1954) is drawn from a second century A.D. text written by Asvaghosa, which provides an account of the Buddha's coming to awareness of the nature and purpose of human existence through a nightlong meditation marked by the ancient methods used to keep time ("the watches of the night"). Just prior to the events described here, Buddha had decided to give up severe self-mortification, during which he is said to have eaten only one grain of rice a day and came near to the point of death, without receiving enlightenment. At this point, he is tempted by Mara, the evil one, to give up his quest, but Gautama remained unmoved, sat down under a Bohdi tree (the tree of wisdom), and entered into a state of deep meditation.

During the third watch of the night, which corresponds to the early morning hours, Buddha gains insight into the principles that will become the foundation of his teaching: the Four Noble Truths and the Eightfold Noble Path. This moment when the meaning of existence is revealed to him along with the causes of human sorrow and the way in which release might be obtained is one of the most significant events in the Buddhist canon.

APPROACHING BUDDHISM

We recall that as a young man Siddhartha Gautama could have easily remained ensconced in a privileged life as a prince. Instead, he began a lifelong search for a way to extricate himself from the unceasing cycle of birth, death, and rebirth (reincarnation, or the wheel of *karma*).

Through the meditation recounted here he discovered that we suffer because we cling to desires that lead us to frustration and suffering. This led him quite naturally to the revelatory insight that suffering ceases through selflessness. But to achieve this, we must reach the realization that despite what our ego tells us (with all its needs and wants and desires and expectations), we, as a self, do not literally exist. We mistake the bundle of cravings and traces of effects set in motion from past lifetimes as a substantial permanent self when in reality it is simply an illusion. The state of Nirvana (that literally means "blowing out") is a perfect description of the extinction of selfish desires and the illusion that happiness can be gained through greed or sensual pleasures. *Nirvana* refers to a condition of absolute peace and certainty that is attainable in this life, about which very little can be said because words are not adequate to describe it.

In the following passage, Buddha moves through a progression of increasingly concentrated mental states, in which he truly perceives the nature of human existence. In the third Watch, he gains insight into the principles that can release us from our delusions (that we exist as a self and that the world exists) and from the negative emotions of greed and hatred, that are the root cause of all suffering.

We notice that Buddhism doesn't involve a belief in God, as such, nor does it place an emphasis on original sin. Nor is there any discussion of the origin (creation) or the end (apocalypse) of the world—features that are prominent in the Hebrew Bible and the *New Testament*. In Buddhism, the only way out of our predicament is through the renunciation of the self and by following the Noble Eightfold Path.

The Enlightenment of the Buddha: Buddhacarita

Now that he had defeated Mâra's[1] violence by his firmness and calm, the Bodhisattva,[2] possessed of great skill in Transic meditation,[3] put himself into trance, intent of discerning both the ultimate reality of things and the final goal of existence. After he had gained complete mastery over all the degrees and kinds of trance:

1. In the first watch of the night he recollected the successive series of his former births. 'There was I so and so; that was my name; deceased from there I came here'—in this way he remembered thousands of births, as though living them over again. When he had recalled his own births and deaths in all these various lives of his, the Sage, full of pity, turned his compassionate mind towards other living beings, and he thought to himself: 'Again and again they must leave the people they regard as their own, and must go on elsewhere, and that without ever stopping. Surely this world is unprotected and helpless, and like a wheel it turns round and round.' As he continued steadily to recollect the past thus, he came to the definite conviction that this world of samsâra[4] is as unsubstantial as the pith of a plantain tree.

2. Second to none in valour, he then, in the second watch of the night, acquired the supreme heavenly eye, for he himself was the best of all those who have sight. Thereupon with the perfectly pure heavenly eye he looked upon the entire world, which appeared to him as though reflected in a spotless mirror. He saw that the decease and rebirth of beings depend on whether they have done superior or inferior deeds. And his compassionateness grew still further. It became clear to him that no security can be found in this flood of samsâric existence, and that the

---

[1]*Mâra* Literally "death dealer": the Buddhist equivalent of Satan.
[2]*Bodhisattva* Literally a being destined for enlightenment: a person who has attained enlightenment but postpones Nirvana in order to help others attain it.
[3]*Transic meditation* A spiritual discipline that leads the practitioner through increasingly concentrated mental states that progess toward complete psychic equilibrium and composure.
[4]*samsara* The endless cycle of birth, death, and rebirth.

threat of death is ever-present. Beset on all sides, creatures can find no resting place. In this way he surveyed the five places of rebirth with his heavenly eye. And he found nothing substantial in the world of becoming, just as no core of heartwood is found in a plantain tree when its layers are peeled off one by one.

3. Then, as the third watch of that night drew on, the supreme master of trance turned his meditation to the real and essential nature of this world: 'Alas, living beings wear themselves out in vain! Over and over again they are born, they age, die, pass on to a new life, and are reborn! What is more, greed and dark delusion obscure their sight, and they are blind from birth. Greatly apprehensive, they yet do not know how to get out of this great mass of ill.' He then surveyed the twelve links of conditioned co-production,[5] and saw that, beginning with ignorance, they lead to old age and death, and, beginning with the cessation of ignorance, they lead to the cessation of birth, old age, death and all kinds of ill.

When the great seer had comprehended that where there is no ignorance whatever, there also the karma[6]-formations are stopped—then he had achieved a correct knowledge of all there is to be known, and he stood out in the world as a Buddha. He passed through the eight stages of Transic Insight, and quickly reached their highest point. From the summit of the world downwards he could detect no self anywhere. Like the fire, when its fuel is burnt up, he became tranquil. He had reached perfection, and he thought to himself: 'This is the authentic Way on which in the past so many great seers, who also knew all higher and all lower things, have travelled on to ultimate and real truth. And now I have obtained it!'

4. At that moment, in the fourth watch of the night, when dawn broke and all the ghosts that move and those that move not went to rest, the great seer took up the position which knows no more alteration, and the leader of all reached the state of all-knowledge. When, through his Buddhahood, he had cognized this fact, the earth swayed like a woman drunken with wine, the sky shone bright with the Siddhas[7] who appeared in crowds in all the directions, and the mighty drums of thunder resounded through the air. Pleasant breezes blew softly, rain fell from a cloudless sky, flowers and fruits dropped from the trees out of

[5]*conditioned co-production* Buddha is referring to a concept elaborated in his First Sermon delivered to five monks who became his disciples. This refers to the ways in which we are enmeshed in illusory cravings and desires. Doctrines were taught through disciples and not through books.
[6]*karma* A natural and personal law of moral cause and effect in which actions in past incarnations determine the conditions of one's present life.
[7]*Siddhas* Enlightened sages

season—in an effort, as it were, to show reverence for him. Mandarava flowers and lotus blossoms, and also water lilies made of gold and beryl, fell from the sky on to the ground near the Shakya sage, so that it looked like a place in the world of the gods. At that moment no one anywhere was angry, ill, or sad; no one did evil, none was proud; the world became quite quiet, as though it had reached full perfection. Joy spread through the ranks of those gods who longed for salvation; joy also spread among those who lived in the regions below. Everywhere the virtuous were strengthened, the influence of Dharma[8] increased, and the world rose from the dirt of the passions and the darkness of ignorance. Filled with joy and wonder at the Sage's work, the seers of the solar race who had been protectors of men, who had been royal seers, who had been great seers, stood in their mansions in the heavens and showed him their reverence. The great seers among the hosts of invisible beings could be heard widely proclaiming his fame. All living things rejoiced and sensed that things went well. Mâra alone felt deep displeasure, as though subjected to a sudden fall.

For seven days he dwelt there—his body gave him no trouble, his eyes never closed, and he looked into his own mind. He thought: 'Here I have found freedom', and he knew that the longings of his heart had at last come to fulfilment. Now that he had understood the principle of causation and had become certain of the lack of self in all that is, he roused himself again from his deep trance, and in his great compassion he surveyed the world with his Buddha-eye, intent on giving it peace. When, however, he saw on the one side of the world lost in low views and confused efforts, thickly covered with the dirt of the passions, and saw on the other side the exceeding subtlety of the Dharma of emancipation, he felt inclined to take no action. But when he weighed up the significance of the pledge to enlighten all beings he had taken in the past, he became again more favourable to the idea of proclaiming the path to Peace. Reflecting in his mind on this question, he also considered that, while some people have a great deal of passion, others have but little. As soon as Indra and Brahmâ, the two chiefs of those who dwell in the heavens, had grasped the Sugata's[9] intention to proclaim the path to Peace, they shone brightly and came up to him, the weal of the world their concern. He remained there on his seat, free from all evil and successful in his aim. The most excellent Dharma which he had seen was his most excellent companion. His two visitors gently and reverently spoke to him these words, which were meant for the weal of the world: 'Please do not con-

[8]*Dharma* Righteousness or good ethical practices as taught by the Buddha.
[9]*Sugata* Literally "one who has gone well," another title given the Buddha.

demn all those that live as unworthy of such treasure! Oh, please engender pity in your heart for beings in this world! So varied is their endowment, and while some have much passion, others have only very little. Now that you, O Sage, have yourself crossed the ocean of the world of becoming, please rescue also the other living beings who have sunk so deep into suffering! As a generous lord shares his wealth, so may also you bestow your own virtues on others! Most of those who know what for them is good in this world and the next, act only for their own advantage. In the world of men and in heaven it is hard to find anyone who is impelled by concern for the weal of the world.' Having made this request to the great seer, the two gods returned to their celestial abode by the way they had come. And the sage pondered over their words. In consequence he was confirmed in his decision to set the world free.

READING CRITICALLY FOR IDEAS, STRUCTURE, AND STYLE

1. How do the insights Buddha gained during the first and second watches of the night lead him to discover a way to escape the cycle of birth, death, and rebirth? What is the central principle that would allow one to escape from the unceasing round of incarnations?

2. What features of this account stress how anguished Buddha is over the human predicament, while at the same time he is remarkably compassionate, yet detached? How does this humanize what otherwise might be considered an unreachable state?

3. What physical signs in the world reflect Buddha's enlightenment? Why does he decide to share the knowledge of the path that has allowed him to attain Nirvana?

EXTENDING INSIGHTS THROUGH WRITING

1. Everybody at one time or another has tried to meditate. Describe your experiences. If you have not attempted this, do so and describe the results.

2. In a few paragraphs, translate the tenets of Buddhism for a modern audience. Be sure to include a definition of selflessness with some examples that demonstrate its nature.

CONNECTING PERSPECTIVES
ON THE SPIRIT AND THE MIND

1. Buddha's encounter with Mâra (the devil), who tries to persuade him to leave the world since mankind will never understand his doctrine, offers an interesting contrast with the temptations offered to Christ by Satan in the *New Testament* (as in Luke 1:1–12). How do these temptations differ and what do they tell you respectively about Buddhism and Christianity?

2. The series of results that pass on from one incarnation to the next are not to be mistaken for the soul, which is believed to not exist, in Buddhism; nor are there gods or rituals that can save one—only renunication of the self and the Noble Eightfold Path can accomplish this. In these respects, how does Hinduism differ from Buddhism, although Buddhists and Hindus both believe in reincarnation and karma?

ALAN WATTS

Beat Zen, Square Zen, and Zen

BACKGROUND

Alan Wilson Watts (1915–1973), the philosopher, writer, and probably the single-most influential figure in popularizing Eastern religious philosophy in the United States, was born in Chislehurst, England, and came to America in 1938. He was an ordained Anglican minister but left the church to devote himself to the study of Eastern religions including Mahayana Buddhism (Zen), Taoism, religious symbolism, and psychology. He was only twenty-one when his first book, *The Spirit of Zen*, was published and he embarked on his lifelong mission of interpreting Asian philosophy for Westerners. He founded the American Academy of Asian Studies in San Francisco in 1951 and became the resident guru (not a role he coveted) for such counterculture figures as Jack Kerouac, Gary Snyder, and Allen Ginsberg. He gave radio broadcasts and conducted classes at the Academy and held seminars in the Buddhist church in Berkeley. His many works include *The Way of Zen* (1957), *Psychotherapy East and West* (1961), and *The Art of Contemplation* (1972). The following essay was first published in *Chicago Review* (Summer 1958) and is critical of the then popular "beat-Zen," which according to Watts, exploited disenchantment with society in a way that was contrary to the basic tenets of Zen Buddhism.

APPROACHING WATTS'S ESSAY

In one sense, Watts's essay might be understood as an effort to explain how the Asian religions of Zen Buddhism and Taoism differ from the Western religions of Christianity and Judaism, with their emphasis on societal rules of conduct that produce and exploit mental states of guilt and anxiety. Zen and Taoism do not proscribe rules of moral conduct and instead lead the mind to a state of liberation ("enlightenment") from enslavement to social conventions—with minimal guidelines about how one should live. In Watts's view,

587

much of the pain of human existence is based on identifying with the unnecessary polarities of good and bad, male and female, right and wrong, success and failure, self and non-self, and other seeming oppositions with which people berate and torture themselves.

As the title of this essay implies, Watts further distinguishes the form of Zen practiced by the Bohemians of the beat-generation from more authentic forms of Zen. He understands why the idea of having no fixed moral codes or standards to conflict with the kinds of free-spirited, spontaneous lifestyles they have chosen would appeal to writers such as Jack Kerouac. But, Watts also feels that Zen, for this group, has simply become an excuse or "pretext for license," in both lifestyles and the taking of drugs.

At the other extreme, "square Zen" is defined by an "esoteric discipline and degrees of initiation," comparable to degrees in the martial arts. This form of Zen is conducted as a formal school with tests and certificates of achievement. But, for Watts, the kind of of Zen that appeals to him is the "no fuss Zen" that permits one to stand outside the deceptive value system of modern society, based as it is on competition, acquisitition, and self-judgment.

Beat Zen, Square Zen, and Zen

IT IS as difficult for Anglo-Saxons as for the Japanese to absorb anything quite so Chinese as Zen. For though the word "Zen" is Japanese and though Japan is now its home, Zen Buddhism is the creation of T'ang dynasty[1] China. I do not say this as a prelude to harping upon the incommunicable subtleties of alien cultures. The point is simply that people who feel a profound need to justify themselves have difficulty in understanding the viewpoints of those who do not, and the Chinese who created Zen were the same kind of people as Lao-tzu,[2] who, centuries before, had said, "Those who justify themselves do not convince." For the urge to make or prove oneself right has always jiggled the Chinese sense of the ludicrous, since as both Confucians and Taoists—however different these philosophies in other ways—they have invariably appreciated the man who can "come off it." To Confucius it seemed much better to be human-hearted than righteous, and to the great Taoists, Lao-tzu and Chuang-tzu,[3] it was obvious that one could

---

[1] The T'ang dynasty lasted from about A.D. 618 to 906. It was distinguished by wide territorial expansion, great wealth, the invention of printing, and the flourishing of art and poetry.

[2] Lao-tzu (ca. 604-531 B.C.) was the legendary founder of Taoism.

[3] Chuang-tzu, or Chuang-chou, was a Taoist philosopher flourishing in China ca. 290 B.C. See Lin Yutang. *The Wisdom of Lao-tse* (New York: Modern Library, 1948).

not be right without also being wrong, because the two were as inseparable as back and front. As Chuang-tzu said, "Those who would have good
government without its correlative misrule, and right without its correlative wrong, do not understand the principle of the universe."

To Western ears such words may sound cynical, and the Confucian
admiration of "reasonableness" and compromise may appear to be a weak-
kneed lack of commitment to principle. Actually they reflect a marvelous
understanding and respect for what we call the balance of nature, human
and otherwise—a universal vision of life is the Tao or way of nature in which
the good and the evil, the creative and the destructive, the wise and the
foolish are the inseparable polarities of existence. "Tao," said the *Chung-
Yung*,[4] "is that from which one cannot depart. That from which one can
depart is not the Tao." Therefore wisdom did not consist in trying to wrest
the good from the evil but in learning to "ride" them as a cork adapts itself
to the crests and troughs of the waves. At the roots of Chinese life there is
a trust in the good-and-evil of one's own nature which is peculiarly foreign
to those brought up with the chronic uneasy conscience of the Hebrew-
Christian cultures. Yet it was always obvious to the Chinese that a man who
mistrusts himself cannot even trust his mistrust, and must therefore be
hopelessly confused.

For rather different reasons, Japanese people tend to be as uneasy
in themselves as Westerners, having a sense of social shame quite as acute
as our more metaphysical sense of sin. This was especially true of the class
most attracted to Zen, the *samurai*.[5] Ruth Benedict, in that very uneven
work *Chrysanthemum and Sword*, was, I think, perfectly correct in saying
that the attraction of Zen to the *samurai* class was its power to get rid of
an extremely awkward self-consciousness induced in the education of the
young. Part-and-parcel of this self-consciousness is the Japanese compulsion to compete with oneself—a compulsion which turns every craft
and skill into a marathon of self-discipline. Although the attraction of Zen
lay in the possibility of liberation from self-consciousness, the Japanese
version of Zen fought fire with fire, overcoming the "self observing the self"
by bringing it to an intensity in which it exploded. How remote from the
regimen of the Japanese Zen monastery are the words of the great T'ang
master Lin-chi:

> In Buddhism there is no place for using effort. Just be ordinary
> and nothing special. Eat your food, move your bowels, pass water,
> and when you're tired go and lie down. The ignorant will laugh at
> me, but the wise will understand.

. . . The Buddha or awakened man of Chinese Zen is "ordinary and
nothing special"; he is humorously human like the Zen tramps portrayed

---

[4]The *Chung-yung* or *The Book of the Unwobbling Pivot* is one of the principal Confucian
classics, dating from the fourth century B.C.
[5]Warrior class of feudal Japan.

by Mu-chi and Liang-k'ai.[6] We like this because here, for the first time, is a conception of the holy man and sage who is not impossibly remote, not superhuman but fully human, and, above all, not a solemn and sexless ascetic. Furthermore, in Zen the *satori* experience of awakening to our "original inseparability" with the universe seems, however elusive, always just round the corner. One has even met people to whom it has happened, and they are no longer mysterious occultists in the Himalayas nor skinny *yogis* in cloistered *ashrams*.[7] They are just like us, and yet much more at home in the world, floating much more easily upon the ocean of transience and insecurity.

Above all, I believe that Zen appeals to many in the post-Christian West because it does not preach, moralize, and scold in the style of Hebrew-Christian prophetism. Buddhism does not deny that there is a relatively limited sphere in which human life may be improved by art and science, reason and good-will. However, it regards this sphere of activity as important but nonetheless subordinate to the comparatively limitless sphere in which things are as they are, always have been, and always will be—a sphere entirely beyond the categories of good and evil, success and failure, and individual health and sickness. On the one hand, this is the sphere of the great universe. Looking out into it at night, we make no comparisons between right and wrong stars, nor between well and badly arranged constellations. Stars are by nature big and little, bright and dim. Yet the whole thing is a splendor and a marvel which sometimes makes our flesh creep with awe. On the other hand, this is also the sphere of human, every-day life which we might call existential.

5

For there is a standpoint from which human affairs are as much beyond right and wrong as the stars, and from which our deeds, experiences, and feelings can no more be judged than the ups and downs of a range of mountains. Though beyond moral and social valuation, this level of human life may also be seen to be just as marvelous and uncanny as the great universe itself. This feeling may become particularly acute when the individual ego tries to fathom its own nature, to plumb the inner sources of its own actions and consciousness. For here it discovers a part of itself—the inmost and greatest part—which is strange to itself and beyond its understanding and control. Odd as it may sound, the ego finds that its own center and nature is beyond itself. The more deeply I go into myself, the more I am not myself, and yet this is the very heart of me. Here I find my own inner workings functioning of themselves, spontaneously, like the rotation of the heavenly bodies and the drifting of the clouds. Strange and foreign as this aspect of myself at first seems to be, I soon realize that it *is* me, and much more me than my superficial ego. This is not fatalism or determinism, because there is no longer anyone being pushed around or determined; there is nothing that this deep "I" is not doing. The configuration of

---

[6]Outstanding Chinese painters in the Zen tradition of black-ink brushwork. They flourished in the thirteenth century.
[7]Ascetic practitioners of yoga, living in hermitages.

my nervous-system, like the configuration of the stars, happens of itself, and this "itself" is the real "myself."

From this standpoint—and here language reveals its limitations with a vengeance—I find that I cannot help doing and experiencing, quite freely, what is always "right," in the sense that the stars are always in their "right" places. As Hsiang-yen[8] put it,

> There's no use for artificial discipline, For, move as I will, I manifest the ancient Tao.

At this level, human life is beyond anxiety, for it can never make a mistake. If we live, we live; if we die, we die; if we suffer, we suffer; if we are terrified, we are terrified. There is no problem about it. A Zen "master" was once asked, "It is terribly hot, and how shall we escape the heat?" "Why not," he answered, "go to the place where it is neither hot or cold?" "Where is that place?" "In summer we sweat; in winter we shiver." In Zen one does not feel guilty about dying, or being afraid, or disliking the heat. At the same time, Zen does not insist upon this point of view as something which one *ought* to adopt; it does not preach it as an ideal. For if you don't understand it, your very not understanding is also IT. There would be no bright stars without dim stars, and, without the surrounding darkness, no stars at all.

The Hebrew-Christian universe is one in which moral urgency, the anxiety to be right, embraces and penetrates everything. God, the Absolute itself, is good as against bad, and thus to be immoral or in the wrong is to feel oneself an outcast not merely from human society but also from existence itself, from the root and ground of life. To be in the wrong therefore arouses a metaphysical anxiety and sense of guilt—a state of eternal damnation—utterly disproportionate to the crime. This metaphysical guilt is so insupportable that it must eventually issue in the rejection of God and of his laws—which is just what has happened in the whole movement of modern secularism, materialism, and naturalism. Absolute morality is profoundly destructive of morality, for the sanctions which it invokes against evil are far, far too heavy. One does not cure the headache by cutting off the head. The appeal of Zen, as of other forms of Eastern philosophy, is that it unveils behind the urgent realm of good and evil a vast region of oneself about which there need be no guilt or recrimination, where at last the self is indistinguishable from God.

But the Westerner who is attracted by Zen and who would understand it deeply must have one indispensable qualification: he must understand his own culture so thoroughly that he is no longer swayed by its premises unconsciously. He must really have come to terms with the Lord God Jehovah and with his Hebrew-Christian conscience so that he can take it or leave it without fear or rebellion. He must be free of the itch to justify

---

[8]A Chinese Zen master of the ninth to tenth centuries A.D., disciple of the great master Lin-chi, who originated the Rinzai school of Zen, the form of Zen most widely known in the West.

himself. Lacking this, his Zen will be either "beat" or "square," either a revolt from the culture and social order or a new form of stuffiness and respectability. For Zen is above all the liberation of the mind from conventional thought, and this is something utterly different from rebellion against convention, on the one hand, or adapting foreign conventions, on the other. . . .

10

The "beat" mentality as I am thinking of it is something much more extensive and vague than the hipster life of New York and San Francisco. It is a younger generation's nonparticipation in "the American Way of Life," a revolt which does not seek to change the existing order but simply turns away from it to find the significance of life in subjective experience rather than objective achievement. . . .

Beat Zen is a complex phenomenon. It ranges from a use of Zen for justifying sheer caprice in art, literature, and life to a very forceful social criticism and "digging of the universe" such as one may find in the poetry of Ginsberg, Whalen and Snyder, and, rather unevenly, in Kerouac, who is always a shade too self-conscious, too subjective, and too strident to have the flavor of Zen.

When Kerouac gives his philosophical final statement, "I don't know. I don't care. And it doesn't make any difference"—that cat is out of the bag, for there is a hostility in these words which clangs with self-defense. But just because Zen truly surpasses convention and its values, it has no need to say "To hell with it," nor to underline with violence the fact that anything goes.

It is indeed the basic intuition of Zen that there is an ultimate standpoint from which "anything goes." In the celebrated words of the master Yun-men, "Every day is a good day." Or as is said in the *Hsin-hsin Ming:*

> If you want to get the plain truth,
> Be not concerned with right and wrong.
> The conflict between right and wrong
> Is the sickness of the mind.[9]

But this standpoint does not exclude and is not hostile towards the distinction between right and wrong at other levels and in more limited frames of reference. The world is seen to be beyond right and wrong when it is not framed: that is to say, when we are not looking at a particular situation by itself—out of relation to the rest of the universe. Within this room there is a clear difference between up and down; out in interstellar space there is not. Within the conventional limits of a human community there are clear distinctions between good and evil. But these disappear when human affairs are seen as part and parcel of the whole realm of nature. Every framework sets up a restricted field of relationships, and restriction is law or rule.

[9]*Hsin-hsin Ming,* the *Treatise on Faith in Mind,* by the Chinese Zen master Sengts' an (d. A.D. 606). Translated by D. T. Suzuki, in *Manual of Zen Buddhism.* (There is an American paperback.)

Now a skilled photographer can point his camera at almost any scene   15
or object and create a marvelous composition by the way in which he frames
and lights it. An unskilled photographer attempting the same thing creates
only messes, for he does not know how to place the frame, the border of
the picture, where it will be in relation to the contents. How eloquently this
demonstrates that as soon as we introduce a frame anything does *not* go.
But every work of art involves a frame. A frame of some kind is precisely
what distinguishes a painting, a poem, a musical composition, a play, a
dance, or a piece of sculpture from the rest of the world. Some artists may
argue that they do not want their works to be distinguishable from the total
universe, but if this be so they should not frame them in galleries and concert halls. Above all they should not sign them nor sell them. This is as
immoral as selling the moon or signing one's name to a mountain. (Such
an artist may perhaps be forgiven if he knows what he is doing, and prides
himself inwardly, not on being a poet or painter, but a competent crook.)
Only destructive little boys and vulgar excursionists go around initialling
the trees.

Today there are Western artists avowedly using Zen to justify the indiscriminate framing of simply anything—blank canvases, totally silent music,
torn up bits of paper dropped on a board and stuck where they fall, or
dense masses of mangled wire. The work of the composer John Cage[10] is
rather typical of this tendency. In the name of Zen, he has forsaken his
earlier and promising work with the "prepared piano," to confront audiences with eight Ampex tape-recorders simultaneously bellowing forth random noises. There is, indeed, a considerable therapeutic value in allowing
oneself to be deeply aware of any sight or sound that may arise. For one thing,
it brings to mind the marvel of seeing and hearing as such. For another, the
profound willingness to listen to or gaze upon anything at all frees the mind
from fixed preconceptions of beauty, creating, as it were, a free space in
which altogether new forms and relationships may emerge. But this is therapy; it is not yet art. It is on the level of the random ramblings of a patient
on the analyst's couch: very important indeed as therapy, though it is by
no means the aim of psychoanalysis to substitute such ramblings for conversation and literature. Cage's work would be redeemed if he framed and
presented it as a kind of group session in audio-therapy, but as a concert
it is simply absurd. One may hope, however, that *after* Cage has, by such
listening, set his own mind free from the composer's almost inevitable plagiarism of the forms of the past, he will present us with the new musical
patterns and relationships which he has not yet uttered.

Just as the skilled photographer often amazes us with his lighting
and framing of the most unlikely subjects, so there are painters and writers in the West, as well as in modern Japan, who have mastered the authen-
tically Zen art of controlling accidents. Historically this first arose in the
Far-East in the appreciation of the rough texture of brush-strokes in calligraphy and painting, and in the accidental running of the glaze on bowls

[10]John Cage (1912–1992) American avant-garde composer famous for his controversial
theories and experimental compositions and performances.

made for the tea-ceremony. One of the classical instances of this kind of thing came about through the shattering of a fine ceramic tea-caddy, belonging to one of the old Japanese tea-masters. The fragments were cemented together with gold, and its owner was amazed at the way in which the random network of thin gold lines enhanced its beauty. It must be remembered, however, that this was an *objet trouvé*[11]—an accidental effect *selected* by a man of exquisite taste, and treasured as one might treasure and exhibit a marvelous rock or a piece of driftwood. For in the Zen-inspired art of *bonseki* or rock-gardening, the stones are selected with infinite care, and though the hand of man may never have changed them it is far from true that any old stone will do. Furthermore, in calligraphy, painting, and ceramics, the accidental effects of running glaze or of flying hair-lines of the brush were only accepted and presented by the artist when he felt them to be fortuitous and unexpected marvels within the context of the work as a whole.

What governed his judgment? What gives *certain* accidental effects in painting the same beauty as the accidental outlines of clouds? According to Zen feeling there is no precise rule, no rule, that is to say, which can be formulated in words and taught systematically. On the other hand, there is in all these things a principle of order which in Chinese philosophy is termed *li,* and which Joseph Needham has translated "organic pattern."[12] *Li* originally meant the markings in jade, the grain in wood, and the fiber in muscle. It designates a type of order which is too multi-dimensional, too subtly interrelated, and too squirmingly vital to be represented in words or mechanical images. The artist has to know it as he knows how to grow his hair. He can do it again and again, but can never explain how. In Taoist philosophy this power is called *te,* or "magical virtue." It is the element of the miraculous which we feel both at the stars in heaven and at our own ability to be conscious.

It is the possession of *te,* then, which makes all the difference between mere scrawls and the "white writing" of Mark Tobey[13] which admittedly derived its inspiration from Chinese calligraphy. It was by no means a purely haphazard drooling of paint or uncontrolled wandering of the brush, for the character and taste of such an artist is visible in the grace (a possible equivalent of *te*) with which his strokes are formed even when he is not trying to represent anything except strokes . . . .

20   The real genius of Chinese and Japanese Zen artists in their use of controlled accidents goes beyond the discovery of fortuitous beauty. It lies in being able to express, at the level of artistry, the realization of that ultimate standpoint from which "anything goes" and at which "all things are of one suchness." The mere selection of any random shape to stick in a frame simply confuses the metaphysical and the artistic domains; it does not express the one in terms of the other. Set in a frame, any old mess is

---

[11]An object discovered to have artistic merit even though not deliberately designed for that effect; literally, a "found" object.

[12]See Joseph Needham, *Science and Civilization in China,* Vol. 2 (Cambridge University Press, 1956).

[13]Distinguished modern American painter. Calligraphy is handwriting developed as an art in itself.

at once cut off from the totality of its natural context, and for this very reason its manifestation of the Tao is concealed. The formless murmur of night noises in a great city has an enchantment which immediately disappears when formally presented as music in a concert hall. A frame outlines a universe, a microcosm, and if the contents of the frame are to rank as art they must have the same quality of relationship to the whole and to each other as events in the great universe, the macrocosm of nature. In nature the accidental is always recognized in relation to what is ordered and controlled. The dark *yin* is never without the bright *yang*.[14] Thus the painting of Sesshu,[15] the calligraphy of Ryokwan,[16] and the ceramic bowls of the Hagi or Karatsu schools[17] reveal the wonder of accidents in nature through accidents in a context of highly disciplined art.

The realization of the unswerving "rightness" of whatever happens is no more manifested by utter lawlessness in social conduct than by sheer caprice in art. As Zen has been used as a pretext for the latter in our times, its use as a pretext for the former is ancient history. Many a rogue has justified himself with the Buddhist formula, "Birth-and-death (*samsara*) is Nirvana; worldly passions are Enlightenment." This danger is implicit in Zen because it is implicit in freedom. Power and freedom can never be safe. They are dangerous in the same way that fire and electricity are dangerous. But it is quite pitiful to see Zen used as a pretext for license when the Zen in question is no more than an idea in the head, a simple rationalization. To some extent "Zen" is so used in the underworld which often attaches itself to artistic and intellectual communities. After all, the Bohemian way of life is primarily the natural consequence of artists and writers being so absorbed in their work that they have no interest in keeping up with the Joneses. It is also a symptom of creative changes in manners and morals which at first seem as reprehensible to conservatives as new forms in art. But every such community attracts a number of weak imitators and hangers-on, especially in the great cities, and it is mostly in this class that one now finds the stereotype of the "beatnik" with his phony Zen. . . . .

One of the most problematic characteristics of beat Zen, shared to some extent both by the creative artists and their imitators, is the fascination for marijuana and peyote, and the notion that the states of consciousness produced by these substances have some affinity with *satori*. That many of these people "take drugs" naturally lays them wide open to the most extreme forms of righteous indignation, despite the fact that marijuana and peyote (or its derivative, mescaline) are far less harmful and habit-forming than whiskey or tobacco. But while it is true that these drugs induce states of great aesthetic insight and, perhaps, therapeutic value, the *satori*-experience is so startlingly different from anything of this kind that no one who had shared both could possibly confuse them. Both states

---

[14]Two basic forces in the universe according to Chinese philosophy: Yin is passive, negative, Yang is active, positive. Their interaction underlies all phenomena.

[15]Fifteenth-century Japanese master of black-ink (*sumi*) painting who was also a Zen priest.

[16]Japanese Zen priest and calligrapher (1758–1831).

[17]Schools of Japanese pottery celebrated for their "rough" naturalistic style.

of consciousness require an apparently paradoxical type of language to describe them, for which reason one might easily confuse the drug-induced states with written accounts of *satori*. But *satori* is always marked by a kind of intense clarity and simplicity from which complex imagery, jazzed-up sense perceptions, and the strange "turned-on" feeling invariably produced by these drugs are absent. It is not by chance that *satori* is called *fu-sho* or "unproduced," which means among other things, that there is no gimmick whether psychological or chemical for bringing it about. *Satori* always remains inaccessible to the mind preoccupied with its own states or with the search for ecstasy.

Now the underlying protestant lawlessness of beat Zen disturbs the square Zennists very seriously. For square Zen is the Zen of established tradition in Japan with its clearly defined hierarchy, its rigid discipline, and its specific tests of *satori*. More particularly, it is the kind of Zen adopted by Westerners studying in Japan, who will before long be bringing it back home. But there is an obvious difference between square Zen and the common-or-garden squareness of the Rotary Club or the Presbyterian Church. It is infinitely more imaginative, sensitive and interesting. But it is still square because it is a quest for the *right* spiritual experience, for a *satori* which will receive the stamp (*inka*) of approval and established authority. There will even be certificates to hang on the wall.

If square Zen falls into any serious excess it is in the direction of spiritual snobbism and artistic preciousness, though I have never known an orthodox Zen teacher who could be accused of either. These gentlemen seem to take their exalted office rather lightly, respecting its dignity without standing on it. The faults of square Zen are the faults of any spiritual in-group with an esoteric discipline and degrees of initiation. Students in the lower ranks can get unpleasantly uppity about inside knowledge which they are not at liberty to divulge—"and you wouldn't understand even if I could tell you"—and are apt to dwell rather sickeningly on the immense difficulties and iron disciplines of their task. There are times, however, when this is understandable, especially when someone who is just goofing-off claims that he is following the Zen ideal of "naturalness."

25   The student of square Zen is also inclined at times to be niggling in his recognition of parallels to Zen in other spiritual traditions. Because the essentials of Zen can never be accurately and fully formulated, being an experience and not a set of ideas, it is always possible to be critical of anything anyone says about it, neither putting up nor shutting up. Any statement about Zen, or about spiritual experience of any kind, will always leave some aspect, some subtlety, unexpressed. No one's mouth is big enough to utter the whole thing. . . .

There was never a spiritual movement without its excesses and distortions. The experience of awakening which truly constitutes Zen is too timeless and universal to be injured. The extremes of beat Zen need alarm no one since, as Blake said, "the fool who persists in his folly will become wise." As for square Zen, "authoritative" spiritual experiences have always had a way of wearing thin, and thus of generating the demand for something genuine and unique which needs no stamp.

I have known followers of both extremes to come up with perfectly clear *satori* experiences, for since there is no real "way" to *satori* the way you are following makes very little difference. . . .

The old Chinese Zen masters were steeped in Taoism. They saw nature in its total interrelatedness, and saw that every creature and every experience is in accord with the Tao of nature just as it is. This enabled them to accept themselves as they were, moment by moment, without the least need to justify anything. They didn't do it to defend themselves or to find an excuse for getting away with murder. They didn't brag about it and set themselves apart as rather special. On the contrary, their Zen was *wu-shih*, which means approximately "nothing special" or "no fuss." But Zen is "fuss" when it is mixed up with Bohemian affectations, and "fuss" when it is imagined that the only proper way to find it is to run off to a monastery in Japan or to do special exercises in the lotus posture for five hours a day. And I will admit that the very hullabaloo about Zen, even in such an essay as this, is also fuss—but a little less so.

Having said that, I would like to say something for all Zen fussers, beat or square. Fuss is all right, too. If you are hung on Zen, there's no need to try to pretend that you are not. If you really want to spend some years in a Japanese monastery, there is no earthly reason why you shouldn't. Or if you want to spend your time hopping freight cars and digging Charlie Parker, it's a free country.

> In the landscape of Spring there is neither better
>   nor worse;
> The flowering branches grow naturally, some long,
>   some short.

READING CRITICALLY FOR IDEAS, STRUCTURE, AND STYLE

1. In what way is Zen designed to liberate one from the mind-set that Watts refers to as "the chronic uneasy conscience of the Hebrew-Christian cultures"?

2. What criticism does Watts make of the "beat" interpretation of Zen? How does he use the analogy of the "frame" in photography, painting, and music to point out the difference between true Zen and "beat" Zen?

3. How does he define "square" Zen, and what does he mean by the "no fuss" approach to Zen he mentions at the end of this piece?

EXTENDING INSIGHTS THROUGH WRITING

1. A key concept in Watts's essay is the idea of the "awakened man" who has experienced *satori*. How would you define this state, and do you agree it would be a desirable condition to achieve? Why or why not?

2. It is ironic that Watts, who was thought of as the resident guru of the "beat" generation, was quite critical of the way they misapplied Zen. Do some research on the "beat" generation, for example, you might wish to read the works of Jack Kerouac, Gary Snyder, or Allen Ginsberg and discuss the appeal Zen had for them.

CONNECTING PERSPECTIVES
ON THE SPIRIT AND THE MIND

1. Discuss the expectations for believers in the *Koran* with those of Zen as Watts explains them. Would Watts's characterization of the Hebrew-Christian universe also extend to Islam? Why or why not?

2. In what respects is Zen close to the core beliefs of Hinduism as expressed in the *Bhagavad-Gîtā?* How does it differ?

CLARENCE DARROW

The Myth of Immortality

BACKGROUND

Clarence Darrow (1857–1938), one of the most colorful and controversial attorneys of his time, was born in Farmdale, Ohio, into an abolitionist family. He began his career as a country lawyer, but later moved to Chicago where he defended the socialist Eugene V. Debs in connection with the 1894 strike of railway workers against the Pullman Company. Darrow gained reknown as an opponent of capital punishment, and of his more than 100 clients, none was ever sentenced to death. His defense in 1924 of the sadistic murderers Nathan Leopold, Jr. and Richard Loeb, (who had killed a thirteen-year-old on a whim), won them life imprisonment on the grounds of insanity, and is cited by opponents of capital punishment to this day. In 1925, he defended biology teacher John T. Scopes over whether Charles Darwin's theory of evolution should be taught in United States public schools (known as the infamous "monkey trial") in Dayton, Tennessee. The attorney representing Christian fundamentalism was the Democratic populist William Jennings Bryan. This trial was the basis for the award-winning motion picture, *Inherit the Wind* (1960). Darrow's best-known books are *An Eye for An Eye* (1905), a novel that explored the social roots of crime; *Crime: Its Cause and Treatment* (1922), in which he argued for the rehabilitation of criminals; and *The Story of My Life* (1932). The following selection, which originally appeared under the title "The Myth of the Soul," and was published in *The Forum* (October 1928), spells out Darrow's defense of agnosticism.

APPROACHING DARROW'S ESSAY

In this essay, Darrow takes the same pragmatic, humane approach he did as a criminal attorney defending unpopular clients, since he is clearly arguing against a widely held belief. Darrow's reputation as an independent thinker willing to champion unpopular positions was amply demonstrated in

the Debs, Leopold and Loeb, and Scopes trials. Darrow reveals an equally
independent point-of-view in his argument against a belief in immortality.
Although he is certainly sympathetic to the emotional basis of the desire to
believe in this idea, he can find no evidence to support it. His acute capacity
for reasoning is evident in the skill with which he questions assumptions on
which a belief in immortality is based, and dissects each of the arguments a
believer might propose. Darrow concludes that there is no reasonable basis
for believing in the existence of a soul, and therefore, no reason to believe in
its survival after death, or in the reality of places called heaven or hell. He further assails the Christian belief in resurrection and concludes that compassion for the living is the appropriate approach to take rather than deferring
our hopes to an afterlife. In this, he is thoroughly consistent with the here-
and-now approach he took in understanding the basis of crime as due to injus-
tices in society that we ought to address rather than dwelling on the evil of
the individuals who commit crimes.

The Myth of Immortality

There is, perhaps, no more striking example of the credulity of man
than the widespread belief in immortality. This idea includes not only the
belief that death is not the end of what we call life, but that personal identity involving memory persists beyond the grave. So determined is the ordinary individual to hold fast to this belief that, as a rule, he refuses to read
or to think upon the subject lest it cast doubt upon his cherished dream.
Of those who may chance to look at this contribution, many will do so with
the determination not to be convinced, and will refuse even to consider the
manifold reasons that might weaken their faith. I know that this is true,
for I know the reluctance with which I long approached the subject and my
firm determination not to give up my hope. Thus the myth will stand in the
way of a sensible adjustment to facts.

Even many of those who claim to believe in immortality still tell themselves and others that neither side of the question is susceptible of proof.
Just what can these hopeful ones believe that the word "proof" involves?
The evidence against the persistence of personal consciousness is as strong
as the evidence of gravitation, and much more obvious. It is as convincing
and unassailable as the proof of the destruction of wood or coal by fire. If
it is not certain that death ends personal identity and memory, then almost
nothing that man accepts as true is susceptible of proof. . . .

It is customary to speak of a "belief in immortality." First, then, let us
see what is meant by the word "belief." If I take a train in Chicago at noon,
bound for New York, I believe I will reach that city the next morning. I believe
it because I have been to New York. I have read about the city, I have known
many other people who have been there, and their stories are not inconsistent with any known facts in my own experience. I have even examined

the timetables, and I know just how I will go and how long the trip will take. In other words, when I board the train for New York, I believe I will reach that city because I have *reason* to believe it.

But if I am told that next week I shall start on a trip to Goofville; that I shall not take my body with me; that I shall stay for all eternity: can I find a single fact connected with my journey—the way I shall go, the part of me that is to go, the time of the journey, the country I shall reach, its location in space, the way I shall live there—or anything that would lead to a rational belief that I shall really make the trip? Have I ever known anyone who has made the journey and returned? If I am really to believe, I must try to get some information about all these important facts.

But people hesitate to ask questions about life after death. They do not ask, for they know that only silence comes out of the eternal darkness of endless space. If people really believed in a beautiful, happy, glorious land waiting to receive them when they died; if they believed that their friends would be waiting to meet them; if they believed that all pain and suffering would be left behind: why should they live through weeks, months, and even years of pain and torture while a cancer eats its way to the vital parts of the body? Why should one fight off death? Because he does *not* believe in any real sense: he only hopes. Everyone knows that there is no real evidence of any such state of bliss; so we are told not to search for proof. We are to accept through faith alone. But every thinking person knows that faith can only come through belief. Belief implies a condition of mind that accepts a certain idea. This condition can be brought about only by evidence. True, the evidence may be simply the unsupported statement of your grandmother; it may be wholly insufficient for reasoning men; but, good or bad, it must be enough for the believer or he could not believe.

Upon what evidence, then, are we asked to believe in immortality? There is no evidence. One is told to rely on faith, and no doubt this serves the purpose so long as one can believe blindly whatever he is told. But if there is no evidence upon which to build a positive belief in immortality, let us examine the other side of the question. Perhaps evidence can be found to support a positive conviction that immortality is a delusion.

THE SOUL

The belief in immortality expresses itself in two different forms. On the one hand, there is a belief in the immortality of the "soul." This is sometimes interpreted to mean simply that the identity, the consciousness, the memory of the individual persists after death. On the other hand, many religious creeds have formulated a belief in "the resurrection of the body"— which is something else again. It will be necessary to examine both forms of this belief in turn.

The idea of continued life after death is very old. It doubtless had its roots back in the childhood of the race. In view of the limited knowledge of primitive man, it was not unreasonable. His dead friends and relatives visited him in dreams and visions and were present in his feeling and imagination until they were forgotten. Therefore the lifeless body did not raise

5

the question of dissolution, but rather of duality. It was thought that man was a dual being possessing a body and a soul as separate entities, and that when a man died, his soul was released from his body to continue its life apart. Consequently, food and drink were placed upon the graves of the dead to be used in the long journey into the unknown. In modified forms, this belief in the duality of man persists to the present day.

But primitive man had no conception of life as having a beginning and an end. In this he was like the rest of the animals. Today, everyone of ordinary intelligence knows how life begins, and to examine the beginnings of life leads to inevitable conclusions about the way life ends. If a man has a soul, it must creep in somewhere during the period of gestation and growth.

10   All the higher forms of animal life grow from a single cell. Before the individual life can begin its development, it must be fertilized by union with another cell; then the cell divides and multiplies until it takes the form and pattern of its kind. At a certain regular time the being emerges into the world. During its term of life millions of cells in its body are born, die, and are replaced until, through age, disease, or some catastrophe, the cells fall apart and the individual life is ended.

It is obvious that but for the fertilization of the cell under right conditions, the being would not have lived. It is idle to say that the initial cell has a soul. In one sense it has life; but even that is precarious and depends for its continued life upon union with another cell of the proper kind. The human mother is the bearer of probably ten thousand of one kind of cell, and the human father of countless billions of the other kind. Only a very small fraction of these result in human life. If the unfertilized cells of the female and the unused cells of the male are human beings possessed of souls, then the population of the world is infinitely greater than has ever been dreamed. Of course no such idea as belief in the immortality of the germ cells could satisfy the yearnings of the individual for a survival of life after death.

If that which is called a "soul" is a separate entity apart from the body, when, then, and where and how was this soul placed in the human structure? The individual began with the union of two cells, neither of which had a soul. How could these two soulless cells produce a soul? I must leave this search to the metaphysicians. When they have found the answer, I hope they will tell me, for I should really like to know.

We know that a baby may live and fully develop in its mother's womb and then, through some shock at birth, may be born without life. In the past, these babies were promptly buried. But now we know that in many cases, where the bodily structure is complete, the machine may be set to work by artificial respiration or electricity. Then it will run like any other human body through its allotted term of years. We also know that in many cases of drowning, or when some mishap virtually destroys life without hopelessly impairing the body, artificial means may set it in motion once more, so that it will complete its term of existence until the final catastrophe comes. Are we to believe that somewhere around the stillborn child and somewhere in the vicinity of the drowned man there hovers a detached soul waiting to be summoned back into the body by a pulmotor? This, too, must be left to the metaphysicians.

The beginnings of life yield no evidence of the beginnings of a soul. It is idle to say that the something in the human being which we call "life" is the soul itself, for the soul is generally taken to distinguish human beings from other forms of life. There is life in all animals and plants, and at least potential life in inorganic matter. This potential life is simply unreleased force and matter—the great storehouse from which all forms of life emerge and are constantly replenished. It is impossible to draw the line between inorganic matter and the simpler forms of plant life, and equally impossible to draw the line between plant life and animal life, or between other forms of animal life and what we human beings are pleased to call the highest form. If the thing which we call "life" is itself the soul, then cows have souls; and, in the very nature of things, we must allow souls to all forms of life and to inorganic matter as well.

Life itself is something very real, as distinguished from the soul. Every   15
man knows that his life had a beginning. Can one imagine an organism that has a beginning and no end? If *I did not exist in the infinite past, why should I, or could I, exist in the infinite future?* "But," say some, "your consciousness, your memory may exist even after you are dead. This is what we mean by the soul." Let us examine this point a little.

I have no remembrance of the months that I lay in my mother's womb. I cannot recall the day of my birth nor the time when I first opened my eyes to the light of the sun. I cannot remember when I was an infant, or when I began to creep on the floor, or when I was taught to walk, or anything before I was five or six years old. Still, all of these events were important, wonderful, and strange in a new life. What I call my "consciousness," for lack of a better word and a better understanding, developed with my growth and the crowding experiences I met at every turn. I have a hazy recollection of the burial of a boy soldier who was shot toward the end of the Civil War. He was buried near the schoolhouse when I was seven years old. But I have no remembrance of the assassination of Abraham Lincoln, although I must then have been eight years old. I must have known about it at the time, for my family and my community idolized Lincoln, and all America was in mourning at his death. Why do I remember the dead boy soldier who was buried a year before? Perhaps because I knew him well. Perhaps because his family was close to my childish life. Possibly because it came to me as my first knowledge of death. At all events, it made so deep an impression that I recall it now.

"Ah, yes," say the believers in the soul, "what you say confirms our own belief. You certainly existed when these early experiences took place. You were conscious of them at the time, even though you are not aware of it now. In the same way, may not your consciousness persist after you die, even though you are not aware of the fact?"

On the contrary, my fading memory of the events that filled the early years of my life lead me to the opposite conclusion. So far as these incidents are concerned, the mind and consciousness of the boy are already dead. Even now, am I fully alive? I am seventy-one years old. I often fail to recollect the names of some of those I knew full well. Many events do not make the lasting impression that they once did. I know that it will be only a few years, even if my body still survives decay, when few important matters will even register in my mind. I know how it is with the old. I know that physical life can persist beyond the time when the mind can fully function. I know that if I live to an extreme old age, my mind will fail. I shall eat and drink and go to my bed in an automatic way. Memory—which is all that binds me to the past—will already be dead. All that will remain will be a vegetative existence; I shall sit and doze in the chimney corner, and my body will function in a measure even though the ego will already be practically dead. I am sure that if I die of what is called "old age," my consciousness will gradually slip away with my failing emotions; I shall no more be aware of the near approach of final dissolution than is the dying tree.

In primitive times, before men knew anything about the human body or the universe of which it is a part, it was not unreasonable to believe in spirits, ghosts, and the duality of man. For one thing, celestial geography was much simpler then. Just above the earth was a firmament in which the stars were set, and above the firmament was heaven. The place was easy of access, and in dreams the angels were seen going up and coming down on a ladder. But now we have a slightly more adequate conception of space and the infinite universe of which we are so small a part. Our great telescopes reveal countless worlds and planetary systems which make our own sink into utter insignificance in comparison. We have every reason to think that beyond our sight there is endless space filled with still more planets, so infinite in size and number that no brain has the smallest conception of their extent. Is there any reason to think that in this universe, with its myriads of worlds, there is no other life so important as our own? Is it possible that the inhabitants of the earth have been singled out for special favor and endowed with souls and immortal life? Is it at all reasonable to suppose that any special account is taken of the human atoms that forever come and go upon this planet?

20   If man has a soul that persists after death, that goes to a heaven of the blessed or to a hell of the damned, where are these places? It is not so easily imagined as it once was. How does the soul make its journey? What does immortal man find when he gets there, and how will he live after he reaches the end of endless space? We know that the atmosphere will be absent; that there will be no light, no heat—only the infinite reaches of darkness and frigidity. In view of modern knowledge, can anyone *really* *believe* in the persistence of individual life and memory?

THE RESURRECTION OF THE BODY

There are those who base their hope of a future life upon the resurrection of the body. This is a purely religious doctrine. It is safe to say that few intelligent men who are willing to look obvious facts in the face hold any such belief. Yet we are seriously told that Elijah was carried bodily to heaven in a chariot of fire, and that Jesus arose from the dead and ascended into heaven. The New Testament abounds in passages that support this doctrine.

St. Paul states the tenet over and over again. In the fifteenth chapter of First Corinthians he says: "If Christ be preached that he arose from the dead, how say some among you that there is no resurrection of the dead? . . . And if Christ be not risen, then is our preaching vain. . . . For if the dead rise not, then is not Christ raised." The Apostles' Creed says: "I believe in the resurrection of the body." This has been carried into substantially all the orthodox creeds; and while it is more or less minimized by neglect and omission, it is still a cardinal doctrine of the orthodox churches.

Two thousand years ago, in Palestine, little was known of man, of the earth, or of the universe. It was then currently believed that the earth was only four thousand years old, that life had begun anew after the deluge about two thousand years before, and that the entire earth was soon to be destroyed. Today it is fairly well established that man has been upon the earth for a million years. During that long stretch of time the world has changed many times; it is changing every moment. At least three or four ice ages have swept across continents, driving death before them, carrying human beings into the sea or burying them deep in the earth. Animals have fed on man and on each other. Every dead body, no matter whether consumed by fire or buried in the earth, has been resolved into its elements, so that the matter and energy that once formed human beings has fed animals and plants and other men. As the great naturalist, Fabre[1] has said: "At the banquet of life each is in turn a guest and a dish." Thus the body of every man now living is in part made from the bodies of those who have been dead for ages.

Yet we are still asked to believe in the resurrection of the body. By what alchemy, then, are the individual bodies that have successfully fed the generations of men to be separated and restored to their former identities? And if I am to be resurrected, what particular *I* shall be called from the grave, from the animals and plants and the bodies of other men who shall inherit this body I now call my own? My body has been made over and over, piece by piece, as the days went by, and will continue to be so made until the end. It has changed so slowly that each new cell is fitted into the living part, and will go on changing until the final crisis comes. Is it the child in the mother's womb or the tottering frame of the old man that shall be brought back? The mere thought of such a resurrection beggars reason, ignores facts, and enthrones blind faith, wild dreams, hopeless hopes, and cowardly fears as sovereign of the human mind.

THE INDESTRUCTABILITY OF MATTER AND FORCE

Some of those who profess to believe in the immortality of man— whether it be of his soul or of his body—have drawn what comfort they could from the modern scientific doctrine of the indestructibility of matter and force. This doctrine, they say, only confirms in scientific language what they have always believed. This, however, is pure sophistry. It is probably

---

[1]The reference is to Jean H. C. Fabre (1823–1915), a French biologist, renowned for his observations and experiments on insects, spiders, and scorpions.

true that no matter or force has even been or ever can be destroyed. But it is likewise true that there is no connection whatever between the notion that personal consciousness and memory persist after death and the scientific theory that matter and force are indestructible. For the scientific theory carries with it a corollary, that the forms of matter and energy are constantly changing through an endless cycle of new combinations. Of what possible use would it be, then, to have a consciousness that was immortal, but which, from the moment of death, was dispersed into new combinations so that no two parts of the original identity could ever be reunited again?

25   These natural processes of change, which in the human being take the forms of growth, disease, senility, death, and decay, are essentially the same as the processes by which a lump of coal is disintegrated in burning. One may watch the lump of coal burning in the grate until nothing but ashes remains. Part of the coal goes up the chimney in the form of smoke; part of it radiates through the house as heat; the residue lies in the ashes on the hearth. So it is with human life. In all forms of life nature is engaged in combining, breaking down, and recombining her store of energy and matter into new forms. The thing we call "life" is nothing other than a state of equilibrium which endures for a short span of years between the two opposing tendencies of nature—the one that builds up, and the one that tears down. In old age, the tearing-down process has already gained the ascendency, and when death intervenes, the equilibrium is finally upset by the complete stoppage of the building-up process, so that nothing remains but complete disintegration. The energy thus released may be converted into grass or trees or animal life; or it may lie dormant until caught up again in the crucible of nature's laboratory. But whatever happens, the man—the *You* and the *I*—like the lump of coal that has been burned, is gone, irrevocably dispersed. All the King's horses and all the King's men cannot restore it to its former unity.

The idea that man is a being set apart, distinct from all the rest of nature, is born of man's emotions, of his loves and hates, of his hopes and fears, and of the primitive conceptions of undeveloped minds. The *You* or the *I* which is known to our friends does not consist of an immaterial something called a "soul" which cannot be conceived. We know perfectly well what we mean when we talk about this *You* and this *Me*: and it is equally plain that the whole fabric that makes up our separate personalities is destroyed, dispersed, disintegrated beyond repair by what we call "death."

THE DESIRE FOR ANOTHER LIFE

Those who refuse to give up the idea of immortality declare that nature never creates a desire without providing the means for its satisfaction. They likewise insist that all people, from the rudest to the most civilized, yearn for another life. As a matter of fact, nature creates many desires which she does not satisfy; most of the wishes of men meet no fruition. But nature does not create any emotion demanding a future life. The only yearning that the individual has is to keep on living—which is a very different thing. This urge is found in every animal, in every plant. It is simply the momentum of a living structure: or, as Schopenhauer[2] put it, "the will to live." What we long for is a continuation of our present state of existence, not an uncertain reincarnation in a mysterious world of which we know nothing.

THE BELIEVER'S LAST RESORT

All men recognize the hopelessness of finding any evidence that the individual will persist beyond the grave. As a last resort, we are told that it is better that the doctrine be believed even if it is not true. We are assured that without this faith, life is only desolation and despair. However that may be, it remains that many of the conclusions of logic are not pleasant to contemplate; still, so long as men think and feel, at least some of them will use their faculties as best they can. For if we are to believe things that are not true, who is to write our creed? Is it safe to leave it to any man or organization to pick out the errors that we must accept? The whole history of the world has answered this question in a way that cannot be mistaken.

And after all, is the belief in immortality necessary or even desirable for man? Millions of men and women have no such faith; they go on with their daily tasks and feel joy and sorrow without the lure of immortal life. The things that really affect the happiness of the individual are the matters of daily living. They are the companionship of friends, the games and contemplations. They are misunderstandings and cruel judgments, false friends and debts, poverty and disease. They are our joys in our living companions and our sorrows over those who die. Whatever our faith, we mainly live in the present—in the here and now. Those who hold the view that man is mortal are never troubled by metaphysical problems. At the end of the day's labor we are glad to lose our consciousness in sleep; and intellectually, at least, we look forward to the long rest from the stresses and storms that are always incidental to existence.

When we fully understand the brevity of life, its fleeting joys and unavoidable pains; when we accept the fact that all men and women are approaching an inevitable doom: the consciousness of it should make us more kindly and considerate of each other. This feeling should make men and women use their best efforts to help their fellow travellers on the road, to make the path brighter and easier as we journey on. It should bring a closer kinship, a better understanding, and a deeper sympathy for the wayfarers who must live a common life and die a common death.

30

[2]Schopenhauer (1788–1860): German philosopher who believed in the primacy of the will.

READING CRITICALLY FOR IDEAS, STRUCTURE, AND STYLE

1. What baseless assumptions, in Darrow's view, are responsible for the widespread belief in immortality? According to Darrow, what are the real questions people should ask? Do you agree with him? Why or why not?

2. Is Darrow fair in representing the opinions, perspectives, and beliefs of those who hold the opposite view? Explain your answer.

3. How does the language and evidence, drawn from everyday experience, Darrow uses reflect his pragmatic, no-nonsense skepticism? If you were a member of the jury listening to his presentation on immortality, would you be persuaded by his argument? Why or why not?

EXTENDING INSIGHTS THROUGH WRITING

1. Since Darrow was seventy-one when he wrote this, he might be expected to have become more religious as he reached the end of his life. In your experience, are Darrow's viewpoints uncommon? Do you know anyone like him? If so, describe this person.

2. In a short essay, write a rebuttal to Darrow or support his argument with additional points.

CONNECTING PERSPECTIVES ON THE SPIRIT AND THE MIND

1. Darrow and Jean-Paul Sartre, in "Existentialism," may seem to be making the same kind of argument, but each emphasizes different aspects of a world without transcendent possibilities. Compare these two positions and discuss whether Sartre's philosophy is merely a highbrow version of Darrow's.

2. Do the tenets of Hinduism, as embodied in the *Bhagavad-Gītā,* that stress the immortality of the soul through repeated incarnations encourage the same kind of engagment in the here and now, and compassion toward others as does Darrow (who doesn't believe in the existence of the soul, or in immortality)? Explain your answer.

JEAN-PAUL SARTRE

Existentialism

BACKGROUND

Jean-Paul Sartre (1905–1980), the French philosopher, author, and leading exponent of existentialism, was born in Paris. His father died in Indo-China while Sartre was still a child, and he grew up in the home of his maternal grandfather, a German-language teacher in whose book-lined study Sartre taught himself to read (by the age of eight he had read *Madame Bovary*.) He attended the prestigious École Normale Supérieure and taught for many years in the French secondary schools. While studying for his examinations in 1929, he met Simone de Beauvoir, and they began a lifelong relationship outside the bounds of the "bourgeois" institution of marriage. In the years that followed, Sartre briefly served in the army, studied in Berlin (where he was influenced by the philosophies of Martin Heidegger and Søren Kierkeggard), and developed his ideas on the basic tenets of existentialism. In his view, the individual is a responsible, but lonely, being, set loose in a universe without meaning, but with the terrifying freedom to choose. His early works include the philosophical novel *Nausea* (1938) and a collection of short stories, *The Wall* (1939). In the same year, he was called up for active duty, sent to the Maginot line, and in June 1940, was taken prisoner by the Germans. Sartre was released nine months later and became a member of the French Resistance, writing for *Combat*, the underground newspaper edited by Albert Camus. Sartre wrote his most important work, *Being and Nothingness* (1943), while he was a prisoner of war. After Paris was liberated from the Germans in 1945, Sartre delivered a lecture later published as a book, *Existentialism and Humanism* (1946), from which the following excerpt is drawn.

In his play *No Exit* (1944), he dramatized the consequences of those who failed to assume responsibility for their own lives: Hell is an ordinary living room where people who fail to act in life must endure each other's conversations throughout eternity, a situation he expressed in the famous idea that "Hell is other people." In 1946, he, Simone de Beauvoir, and Maurice

Merleau Ponty, founded and edited *Les Temps Modernes,* a monthly review. He continued to express his philosophy in many novels, including *The Age of Reason* (1945), *The Reprieve* (1945), and *Troubled Sleep* (1949), and proposed a synthesis of Marxism and Existentialism in *The Criticique of Dialectical Reason* (1960). Sartre was awarded the Nobel Prize for literature in 1964, which he refused to accept.

APPROACHING SARTRE'S ESSAY

Many key concepts in Sartre's philosophy are expressed here in a stylish and accessible manner. His now classic statement that man's "existence precedes his essence" (para. 1) means that human beings simply exist and have not been created as part of any particular plan, either divine or evolutionary—we simply happen to exist and therefore must consciously decide at each moment of our lives what to make of ourselves. In this sense each of us, in every action we take and decision we make, must create who we are—that is our "essence." Since this situation, or predicament as Sartre thinks of it, is fraught with constant awareness of our freedom, it produces such anguish that we typically avoid thinking about it (or relapse into more comfortable beliefs). Every aspect of Sartre's philosophy is designed to lead us to accept responsibility, not only for our actions, but for our feelings, inclinations, temperament, and in fact, every aspect of our being.

Existentialism

Atheistic existentialism, which I represent, . . . states that if God does not exist, there is at least one being in whom existence precedes essence, a being who exists before he can be defined by any concept, and that this being is man, or, as Heidegger says, human reality. What is meant here by saying that existence precedes essence? It means that, first of all, man exists, turns up, appears on the scene, and, only afterwards, defines himself. If man, as the existentialist conceives him, is indefinable, it is because at first he is nothing. Only afterward will he be something, and he himself will have made what he will be. Thus, there is no human nature, since there is no God to conceive it. Not only is man what he conceives himself to be, but he is also only what he wills himself to be after this thrust toward existence.

Man is nothing else but what he makes of himself. Such is the first principle of existentialism. It is also what is called subjectivity. But what do we mean by this, if not that man has a greater dignity than a stone or table? For we mean that man first exists, that is, that man first of all is the being who hurls himself toward a future and who is conscious of imagining himself as being in the future. Man is at the start a plan which is aware of itself, rather than a patch of moss, a piece of garbage, or a cauliflower; nothing exists prior to this plan; there is nothing in heaven; man will be what he will have planned to be. Not what he will want to be. Because by the word "will" we generally mean a conscious decision, which is subsequent to what we have already made of ourselves. I may want to belong to a political party, write a book, get married; but all that is only a manifestation of an earlier, more spontaneous choice that is called "will." But if existence really does precede essence, man is responsible for what he is. Thus, existentialism's first move is to make every man aware of what he is and to make the full responsibility of his existence rest on him. And when we say that a man is responsible for himself, we do not only mean that he is responsible for his own individuality, but that he is responsible for all men.

The word "subjectivism" has two meanings. Subjectivism means, on the one hand, that an individual chooses and makes himself; and, on the other, that it is impossible for man to transcend human subjectivity. The second of these is the essential meaning of existentialism. When we say that man chooses his own self, we mean that every one of us does likewise; but we also mean by that that in making this choice he also chooses all men. In fact, in creating the man that we want to be, there is not a single one of our acts which does not at the same time create an image of man as we think he ought to be. To choose to be this or that is to affirm at the same time the value of what we choose, because we can never choose evil. We always choose the good, and nothing can be good for us without being good for all.

If, on the other hand, existence precedes essence, and if we grant that we exist and fashion our image at one and the same time, the image is valid for everybody and for our whole age. Thus, our responsibility is much greater than we might have supposed, because it involves all mankind. If I am a workingman and choose to join a Christian trade union rather than be a Communist, and if by being a member, I want to show that the best thing for a man is resignation, that the kingdom of man is not of this world, I am not only involving my own case—I want to be resigned for everyone. As a result, my action has involved all humanity. To take a more individual matter, if I want to marry, to have children, even if this marriage depends solely on my own circumstances or passion or wish, I am involving all humanity in monogamy and not merely myself. Therefore, I am responsible for myself and for everyone else. I am creating a certain image of man of my own choosing. In choosing myself, I choose man.

The existentialist thinks it very distressing that God does not exist, because all possibility of finding values in a heaven of ideas disappears along with Him; there can no longer be an a priori Good, since there is no infinite and perfect consciousness to think it. Nowhere is it written that the good exists, that we must be honest, that we must not lie; because the fact is we are on a plane where there are only men. Dostoievsky said, "If God didn't exist, everything would be possible." That is the very starting point of existentialism. Indeed, everything is permissible if God does not exist, and as a result man is forlorn, because neither within him or without does he find anything to cling to. He can't start making excuses for himself.

If existence really does precede essence, there is no explaining things away by reference to a fixed and given nature. In other words, there is no determinism, man is free, man is freedom. On the other hand, if God does not exist, we find no values or commands to turn to which legitimize our conduct. So, in the bright realm of values, we have no excuse behind us, nor justification before us. We are alone, with no excuses.

That is the idea I shall try to convey when I say that man is condemned to be free. Condemned, because he did not create himself, yet, in other respects is free; because, once thrown into the world, he is responsible for everything he does.

To give you an example which will enable you to understand forlornness better, I shall cite the case of one of my students who came to see me under the following circumstances: his father was on bad terms with his mother, and, moreover, was inclined to be a collaborationist, his older brother had been killed in the German offensive of 1940, and the young man, with somewhat immature but generous feelings, wanted to avenge him. His mother lived alone with him, very much upset by the half-treason of her husband and the death of her older son; the boy was her only consolation.

The boy was faced with the choice of leaving for England joining the Free French forces—that is, leaving his mother behind—or remaining with his mother and helping her to carry on. He was fully aware that the woman lived only for him and that his going off—and perhaps his death—would plunge her into despair. He was also aware that every act that he did for his mother's sake was a sure thing, in the sense that it was helping her to carry on, whereas every effort he made toward going off and fighting was an uncertain move which might run aground and prove completely useless; for example, on his way to England he might, while passing through Spain, be detained indefinitely in a Spanish camp; he might reach England or Algiers and be stuck in an office at a desk job. As a result, he was faced with two very different kinds of action: one, concrete, immediate, but concerning only one individual; the other concerned an incomparably vaster group, a national collectivity, but for that very reason was dubious, and might be interrupted en route. And, at the same time, he was wavering between two kinds of ethics. On the one hand, an ethics of sympathy, of personal devotion; on the other, a broader ethics, but one whose efficacy was more dubious. He had to choose between the two.

Who could help him choose? Christian doctrine? No. Christian doctrine says, "Be charitable, love your neighbor, take the more rugged path, etc., etc." But which is the more rugged path? Whom should he love as a brother? The fighting man or his mother? Which does the greater good, the vague act of fighting in a group, or the concrete one of helping a particular human being to go on living? Who can decide a priori? Nobody. No book of ethics can tell him. The Kantian ethics says, "Never treat any person as a means, but as an end." Very well, if I stay with my mother, I'll treat her as an end and not as a means; but by virtue of this very fact, I'm running the risk of treating the people around me who are fighting, as means; and conversely, if I go to join those who are fighting, I'll be treating them as an end, and, by doing that, I run the risk of treating my mother as a means.

If values are vague, and if they are always too broad for the concrete and specific case that we are considering, the only thing left for us is to trust our instincts. That's what this young man tried to do; and when I saw him, he said, "In the end, feeling is what counts. I ought to choose whichever pushes me in one direction. If I feel that I love my mother enough to sacrifice everything else for her—my desire for vengeance, for action, for adventure—then I'll stay with her. If, on the contrary, I feel that my love for my mother isn't enough, I'll leave."

But how is the value of a feeling determined? What gives his feeling for his mother value? Precisely the fact that he remained with her. I may say that I like so-and-so well enough to sacrifice a certain amount of money for him, but I may say so only if I've done it. I may say "I love my mother well enough to remain with her" if I have remained with her. The only way to determine the value of this affection is, precisely, to perform an act which confirms and defines it. But, since I require this affection to justify my act, I find myself caught in a vicious circle.

Given that men are free and that tomorrow they will freely decide what man will be, I cannot be sure that, after my death, fellow-fighters will carry on my work to bring it to its maximum perfection. Tomorrow, after my death, some men may decide to set up Fascism, and the others may be cowardly and muddled enough to let them do it. Fascism will then be the human reality, so much the worse for us.

Actually, things will be as man will have decided they are to be. Does that mean that I should abandon myself to quietism? No. First, I should involve myself; then, act on the old saw, "Nothing ventured, nothing gained." Nor does it mean that I shouldn't belong to a party, but rather that I shall have no illusions and shall do what I can. For example, suppose I ask myself, "Will socialization, as such, ever come about?" I know nothing about it. All I know is that I'm going to do everything in my power to bring it about. Beyond that, I can't count on anything. Quietism is the attitude of people who say, "Let others do what I can't do." The doctrine I am presenting is the very opposite of quietism, since it declares, "There is no reality except in action." Moreover, it goes further, since it adds, "Man is nothing else than his plan; he exists only to the extent that he fulfills himself; he is therefore nothing else than the ensemble of his acts, nothing else than his life."

Now, for the existentialist there is really no love other than one which manifests itself in a person's being in love. There is no genius other than one which is expressed in works of art; the genius of Proust is the sum of Proust's works; the genius of Racine is his series of tragedies. Outside of that, there is nothing. Why say that Racine could have written another tragedy, when he didn't write it? A man is involved in life, leaves his impress on it, and outside of that there is nothing. To be sure, this may seem a harsh thought to someone whose life hasn't been a success. But, on the other hand, it prompts people to understand that reality alone is what counts, that dreams, expectations, and hopes warrant no more than to define a man as a disappointed dream, as miscarried hopes, as vain expectations. In other words, to define him negatively and not positively. However, when we say, "You are nothing else than your life," that does not imply that the artist will be judged solely on the basis of his works of art; a thousand other things will contribute toward summing him up. What we mean is that a man is nothing else than a series of undertakings, that he is the sum, the organization, the ensemble of the relationships which make up these undertakings.

When all is said and done, what we are accused of, at bottom, is not our pessimism, but an optimistic toughness. If people throw up to us our works of fiction in which we write about people who are soft, weak, cowardly, and sometimes even downright bad, it's not because these people are soft, weak, cowardly, or bad; because if we were to say, as Zola did, that they are that way because of heredity, the workings of environment, society, because of biological or psychological determinism, people would be reassured. They would say, "Well, that's what we're like, no one can do anything about it." But when the existentialist writes about a coward, he says that this coward is responsible for his cowardice. He's not like that because he has a cowardly heart or lung or brain; he's not like that on account of his physiological make-up; but he's like that because he has made himself a coward by his acts. There's no such thing as a cowardly constitution; there are nervous constitutions; there is poor blood, as the common people say, or strong constitutions. But the man whose blood is poor is not a coward on that account, for what makes cowardice is the act of renouncing or yielding. A constitution is not an act; the coward is defined on the basis of the acts he performs. People feel, in a vague sort of way, that this coward we're talking about is guilty of being a coward, and the thought frightens them. What people would like is that a coward or a hero be born that way.

Existentialism is nothing else than an attempt to draw all the consequences of a coherent atheistic position. It isn't trying to plunge man into despair at all. But if one calls every attitude of unbelief despair, like the Christians, then the word is not being used in its original sense. Existentialism isn't so atheistic that it wears itself out showing that God doesn't exist. Rather, it declares that even if God did exist, that would change nothing. There you've got our point of view. Not that we believe that God exists, but we think that the problem of His existence is not the issue. In this sense existentialism is optimistic, a doctrine of action, and it is plain dishonesty for Christians to make no distinction between their own despair and ours and then to call us despairing.

READING CRITICALLY FOR IDEAS, STRUCTURE, AND STYLE

1. Sartre assumes, as an atheistic existentialist, that there is no divine creator or, indeed, any predetermined plan for human existence. What kind of burden does this impose upon us, and, correspondingly, what freedoms does it give us? In what way might the same questions be asked of those who believe in God?

2. In what way does Sartre's style (which might be characterized as intellectual and self-aware) aptly express his views?

3. Sartre cites the example of one of his students who is faced with a dilemma. How does Sartre use this case to illustrate his philosophy?

EXTENDING INSIGHTS THROUGH WRITING

1. Have you ever faced a choice comparable to that confronting the young man in Sartre's example or any instance of temptation or indecision? What aspects of the situation dramatized the uselessness of preexisting value systems? Discuss how, in making the decision, you created yourself.

2. In your opinion, who is this essay designed to persuade? Where in it does Sartre take into account the views of his opponents?

CONNECTING PERSPECTIVES ON GREAT IDEAS

1. How does Sartre's belief in our freedom to choose contradict Sigmund Freud's theory that much of our behavior is determined by unconscious motivations?

2. In what respects do both Sartre and Alan Watts (see "Beat Zen, Square Zen, and Zen") put a premium on the individual's need to choose, without reference to traditional moral codes or conventional value systems?

BOOK CONNECTIONS FOR CHAPTER 6

1. Compare the insights offered by G. E. Moore with Elaine Pagels's (see "The Social History of Satan" in Chapter 3) analysis to discover how we represent, and thus define, the concepts of good and evil.

2. In what ways might Plato's allegory be applied to Neil Postman's discussion in "Information" (in Chapter 5) of our need to renew contact with eighteenth-century thought?

3. Konrad Lorenz (see "The Dove and the Wolf" in Chapter 4) says that the more we know about the nature of human aggression, the greater chance we have to redirect it. In what respects are Lorenz's views about the power of instincts and our need to un-

derstand them comparable to Sigmund Freud's theory of the unconscious?

4. Does nineteenth-century music, as discussed by Edward Rothstein in "Why We Live in the Musical Past," serve the same function for modern culture that Marcel Proust's madeleine cupcake dipped in lime-flower tea did for him? Explain your answer.

5. In what way is tragedy, as described by Aristotle, designed to liberate one from worldly illusions in much the same way as the concepts and tenets of Hinduism (see "Readings from the Scriptures in Hinduism: *Rig-Veda*, the *Upanishads*, and the *Bhagavad-Gītā*").

6. Compare the different perspectives on the Creation, as embodied in the Torah and hypothesized by Peter D. Ward and Donald Brownlee in "Rare Earth" (Chapter 5).

7. Compare P. D. Ouspensky's description of the architecture and designs in the Taj Mahal (in Chapter 7) with the prohibition against worshipping idols, as revealed to the Prophet Muhammad in the *Koran*? How does this help explain why there are no human forms or statues in the Taj Mahal?

8. Discuss the use of analogies to explain difficult concepts in physics, as Fred Hoyle does in "The Continuous Creation of the Universe" (in Chapter 5) with the use of extended analogies as reported by St. Matthew in "Parables in the New Testament."

9. Compare and contrast the advice on how to live one's life according to Lord Chesterfield in "Letter to My Son" (in Chapter 1) with the precepts of the Noble Eightfold Path contained in the "The Enlightenment of the Buddha: Buddhacarita."

10. Discuss the ways in which Alan Watts and Sergei Eisenstein (in "The Cinematographic Principle and the Ideogram" in Chapter 7) explore the influence of Japanese culture and philosophy on the arts.

11. Discuss the skepticism and humanism of Clarence Darrow and of George Bernard Shaw as expressed in "She Would Have Enjoyed It" (in Chapter 1).

12. Compare Anne Frank's view in "from The Diary of Anne Frank" (in Chapter 1) with those of Jean-Paul Sartre on the points of taking individual responsibility and religious faith in the context of World War II.

CHAPTER 7

THE ARTS OF CIVILIZATION:
The Human Element

INTRODUCTION

The selections in the final chapter look at the profound meaning that the arts—painting, sculpture, architecture, music, dance literature—and the commercial forms of advertising, have played in defining the cultural component of civilization.

We begin with the oldest and most durable critical theory of art as *mimesis* or "imitation" as described by Aristotle. The art of the ancient Greek theater, particularly tragedies, according to Aristotle, served a religious function quite different from the way theater functions today—as a diversion and form of entertainment. Giorgio Vasari in the fifteenth-century and David Sylvester's interview in the twentieth-century with the celebrated English sculptor, Henry Moore, contrast the power of the ideals of Renaissance art with modern abstract art. Vasari describes the life and work of Leonardo da Vinci and the famous portrait of the *Mona Lisa* in terms of the Renaissance commitment to Aristotle's dictum that art should imitate life. In the twentieth century we learn that Moore, a great modern sculptor, can find much to admire in the Renaissance practices of Michelangelo, and sees him as a beacon of artistic integrity. The next two selections, by John Ruskin and P. D. Ouspensky, create an interesting contrast between two great architectural wonders of Christianity and Islam and analyze the function each serves. Ruskin takes us on a tour through St. Mark's Cathedral and reveals how its ornate decorations and mosaics served as a kind of visual Bible for those who could not read or write. Then Ouspensky describes his experience of spiritual enlightenment when he visited the majestic Taj Mahal. These two accounts instruct us in the language of architecture in two very different traditions and in the service of different faiths and cultures.

No chapter on the arts of civilization would be complete without an account of the evolution and impact of language. Paul Roberts traces the development of English over 1,400 years and identifies the most significant forces that have shaped it into the capacious, malleable, and infinitely expressive form that has made it a universal language. Then, Gustav Flaubert tells us of his struggles to use his native language (French) to render a true account of human experience in his great novel, *Madame Bovary*. Since the nineteenth century, Flaubert has represented the symbol of commitment to the artist's vocation (and the need to find the perfect word or phrase) and *Madame Bovary* has set the standard for the realistic novel.

Next, the music critic Edward Rothstein explores the cultural impact of Romantic nineteenth-century composers on twentieth-century audiences. Our nostalgia for the musical past he believes arises from the same impulse that make the novels of Jane Austen, Charles Dickens, and George Eliot still popular today. Sergei Eisenstein, whose pioneering work was responsible for the development of film as an art form, arguably *the* art form of the twentieth-century, shows how the principle of cinematic *montage* he originated (and perfected in such movies as *The Battleship Potemkin* [1925]) was similar to Chinese and Japanese ideograms and styles of drawing. Then Agnes De Mille, in "Pavlova" describes the inspiring influence of the famous Russian ballerina on her life and art. Last, John Berger investigates the way the symbols of affluence depicted in oil paintings from the past serve as a visual language used by advertisers to enhance the image of their products and offer consumers the chance to live the "good life." In this sense, advertising can be considered a parody of the traditional arts—or, the defining "art" of modern civilization.

ARISTOTLE

Poetics

BACKGROUND

Aristotle (384–323 B.C.) was born at Stagira in Macedon and was sent by his family in 367 B.C. to be educated in Athens, where he studied under Plato for twenty years. Although a Platonist initially, Aristotle later became convinced of the need for empirical observation, rejected the Platonic doctrine of Ideal Forms, and developed his own views on philosophical, political, and scientific issues. He tutored the future Alexander the Great in 342 B.C., after which he returned to Athens to establish his school, the Lyceum. Aristotle's existing works covering logic, ethics, metaphysics, physics, zoology, politics, rhetoric, and poetics, were transcribed from notes he used for his lectures. His writings were crucial in shaping the thought of many cultures and were regarded as the basis of all knowledge for over 1,400 years. In the "Poetics" Aristotle elaborates what has proven to be one of the most influential pieces of criticism ever written. Aristotle framed the discussion, which is actually a set of notes written for his lectures on the subject, as an examination of key elements in works of literature (including the epic works, the *Iliad* and the *Odyssey* by Homer and the tragic cycle *Oedipus Rex* by Sophocles) he had studied. In the following excerpt, he addresses the key question as to what function the arts serve, how they go about achieving this purpose, and offers a definition of tragedy that has endured.

APPROACHING ARISTOTLE'S ESSAY

Although his first sentence refers to "poetry" in general, in making his observations Aristotle talks mainly about drama and its distinctive divisions into tragedy and comedy. The impulse underlying the arts is "mimesis," or imitation, although the types of characters imitated in comedy and tragedy are

619

quite different. Tragedy focuses on noble actions and fated consequences while comedy represents noncatastrophic mix-ups. Aristotle identifies and defines six important elements in tragedy (plot, character, thought, diction, spectacle, and music) and discusses the role played by "reversal" and "recognition" that elicit pity and fear from the audience. Theater played a vital role in the Greek society of Aristotle's day. Twenty thousand to 40,000 people (the population of an average city in ancient Greece) would attend plays in specially constructed theaters. Aristotle, in formulating his theory of "catharsis," was making explicit one of the underlying values of Athenian society in which theater had a quasi-religious function. Each spring Athenians undertook a public and private ritual purification. This period concluded with the performance of plays whose attendance was seen as a civic obligation.

Thus, Aristotle most likely drew on the important ritual function of theater in formulating his theory of "catharsis."

Poetics

Poetry in general[1] seems to have sprung from two causes, each of them lying deep in our nature. First, the instinct of imitation is implanted in man from childhood, one difference between him and other animals being that he is the most imitative of living creatures, and through imitation learns his earliest lessons; and no less universal is the pleasure felt in things imitated. We have evidence of this in the facts of experience. Objects which in themselves we view with pain, we delight to contemplate when reproduced with minute fidelity: such as the forms of the most ignoble animals and of dead bodies. The cause of this again is, that to learn gives the liveliest pleasure, not only to philosophers but to men in general; whose capacity, however, of learning is more limited. Thus the reason why men enjoy seeing a likeness is, that in contemplating it they find themselves learning or inferring, and saying perhaps, "Ah, that is he." For if you happen not to have seen the original, the pleasure will be due not to the imitation as such, but to the execution, the colouring, or some such other cause.

Imitation, then, is one instinct of our nature. Next, there is the instinct for "harmony" and rhythm, metres being manifestly sections of rhythm. Persons, therefore, starting with this natural gift developed by

---

[1]"Poetry" has wider reference here than it has to us. Aristotle is going to talk chiefly about drama, and one must remember that classical Greek dramas, both tragedy and comedy, were in the form of poetry.

degrees their special aptitudes, till their rude improvisations gave birth to Poetry.

Poetry now diverged in two directions, according to the individual character of the writers. The graver spirits imitated noble actions, and the actions of good men. The more trivial sort imitated the actions of meaner persons, at first composing satires, as the former did hymns to the gods and the praises of famous men. . . .

But when Tragedy and Comedy came to light, the two classes of poets still followed their natural bent: the lampooners became writers of Comedy, and the Epic poets were succeeded by Tragedians, since the drama was a larger and higher form of art. . . .

Tragedy—as also Comedy—was at first mere improvisation. The one originated with the authors of the Dithyramb, the other with those of the phallic songs,[2] which are still in use in many of our cities. Tragedy advanced by slow degrees; each new element that showed itself was in turn developed. Having passed through many changes, it found its natural form, and there it stopped. . . .

Comedy is, as we have said, an imitation of characters of a lower type—not, however, in the full sense of the word bad, the Ludicrous being merely a subdivision of the ugly. It consists in some defect or ugliness which is not painful or destructive. To take an obvious example, the comic mask is ugly and distorted, but does not imply pain.

Epic poetry agrees with Tragedy in so far as it is an imitation in verse of characters of a higher type. They differ, in that Epic poetry admits but one kind of metre, and is narrative in form. They differ, again, in their length: for Tragedy endeavours, as far as possible, to confine itself to a single revolution of the sun, or but slightly to exceed this limit; whereas the Epic action has no limits of time. . . .

Of their constituent parts some are common to both, some peculiar to Tragedy: whoever, therefore, knows what is good or bad Tragedy, knows also about Epic poetry. All the elements of an Epic poem are found in Tragedy, but the elements of a Tragedy are not all found in the Epic poem. . . .

Let us now discuss Tragedy, resuming its formal definition, as resulting from what has been already said.

Tragedy then, is an imitation of an action that is serious, complete, and of a certain magnitude; in language embellished with each kind of artistic ornament, the several kinds being found in separate parts of the play; in the form of action, not of narrative; through pity and fear effecting the proper purgation[3] of these emotions. By "language embellished," I mean language into which rhythm, "harmony," and song enter. By "the

---

[2]Both dithyramb and phallic songs originated in the religious ritual of Dionysus. The former was a choric hymn; the latter were boisterous choruses and dialogues performed by players in phallic costumes and animal masks.

[3]In Aristotle's view of tragedy, "pity" draws the audience to empathize with the plight of the characters while "terror" repels them through the idea that such events can occur. The combined tension has a cathartic effect on the audience and readjusts their moral perspective.

several kinds in separate parts," I mean, that some parts are rendered through the medium of verse alone, others again with the aid of song.

Now as tragic imitation implies persons acting, it necessarily follows, in the first place, that Spectacular equipment[4] will be a part of Tragedy. Next, Song and Diction, for these are the medium of imitation. By "Diction" I mean the mere metrical arrangement of the words: as for "Song," it is a term whose sense every one understands.

Again, Tragedy is the imitation of an action; and an action implies personal agents, who necessarily possess certain distinctive qualities both of character and thought; for it is by these that we qualify actions themselves, and these—thought and character—are the two natural causes from which actions spring, and on actions again all success or failure depends. Hence, the Plot is the imitation of the action:—for by plot I here mean the arrangement of the incidents. By Character I mean that in virtue of which we ascribe certain qualities to the agents. Thought is required wherever a statement is proved, or, it may be, a general truth enunciated. Every Tragedy, therefore, must have six parts, which parts determine its quality—namely, Plot, Character, Diction, Thought, Spectacle, Song. Two of the parts constitute the medium of imitation, one the manner, and three the objects of imitation. And these complete the list. These elements have been employed, we may say, by the poets to a man; in fact, every play contains Spectacular elements as well as Character, Plot, Diction, Song, and Thought. . . .

But most important of all is the structure of the incidents. For Tragedy is an imitation, not of men, but of an action and of life, and life consists in action, and its end is a mode of action, not a quality. Now character determines men's qualities, but it is by their actions that they are happy or the reverse. Dramatic action, therefore, is not with a view to the representation of character: character comes in as subsidiary to the actions. Hence the incidents and the plot are the end of a tragedy; and the end is the chief thing of all. Again, without action there cannot be a tragedy; there may be without character. . . .

Again, if you string together a set of speeches expressive of character, and well finished in point of diction and thought, you will not produce the essential tragic effect nearly so well as with a play which, however deficient in these respects, yet has a plot and artistically constructed incidents. Besides which, the most powerful elements of emotional interest in Tragedy—Peripeteia or Reversal of the Situation, and Recognition scenes—are parts of the plot. A further proof is, that novices in the art attain to finish of diction and precision of portraiture before they can construct the plot. It is the same with almost all the early poets.

15   The Plot, then, is the first principle, and, as it were, the soul of a tragedy: Character holds the second place. . . .

[4]By this Aristotle means spectacle (what we call setting, costumes, and props) and music (which had an important function in drama, through the chorus).

Thus Tragedy is the imitation of an action, and of the agents, mainly with a view to the action.

Third in order is Thought—that is, the faculty of saying what is possible and pertinent in given circumstances. In the case of oratory, this is the function of the political art and of the art of rhetoric: and so indeed the older poets make their characters speak the language of civic life; the poets of our time, the language of the rhetoricians.

Character is that which reveals moral purpose, showing what kind of things a man chooses or avoids. Speeches, therefore, which do not make this manifest, or in which the speaker does not choose or avoid anything whatever, are not expressive of character. Thought, on the other hand, is found where something is proved to be or not to be, or a general maxim is enunciated.

Fourth among the elements enumerated comes Diction; by which I mean, as has been already said, the expression of the meaning in words; and its essence is the same both in verse and prose.

Of the remaining elements Song holds the chief place among the embellishments.   20

The Spectacle has, indeed, an emotional attraction of its own, but, of all the parts, it is the least artistic, and connected least with the art of poetry. For the power of Tragedy, we may be sure, is felt even apart from representation and actors. Besides, the production of spectacular effects depends more on the art of the stage machinist than on that of the poet.

These principles being established, let us now discuss the proper structure of the Plot, since this is the first and most important part of Tragedy.

Now, according to our definition, Tragedy is an imitation of an action that is complete, and whole, and of a certain magnitude; for there may be a whole that is wanting in magnitude. A whole is that which has a beginning, a middle, and an end. A beginning is that which does not itself follow anything by causal necessity, but after which something naturally is or comes to be. An end, on the contrary, is that which itself naturally follows some other thing, either by necessity, or as a rule, but has nothing following it. A middle is that which follows something as some other thing follows it. A well constructed plot, therefore, must neither begin nor end at haphazard, but conform to these principles.

Again, a beautiful object, whether it be a living organism or any whole composed of parts, must not only have an orderly arrangement of parts, but must also be of a certain magnitude; for beauty depends on magnitude and order. Hence an exceedingly small picture cannot be beautiful; for the view of it is confused, the object being seen in an almost imperceptible moment of time. Nor, again, can one of vast size be beautiful; for as the eye cannot take it all in at once, the unity and sense of the whole is lost for the spectator; as for instance if there were a picture a thousand miles long. As, therefore, in the case of animate bodies and pictures a certain magnitude is necessary, and a magnitude which may be easily embraced in one view; so in the plot, a certain length is necessary, and a length which can be easily embraced by the memory.

The limit of length in relation to dramatic competition and sensuous presentment, is no part of artistic theory. For had it been the rule for a hundred tragedies to compete together, the performance would have been regulated by the water-clock—as indeed we are told was formerly done. But the limit as fixed by the nature of the drama itself is this:—the greater the length, the more beautiful will the piece be by reason of its size, provided that the whole be perspicuous. And to define the matter roughly, we may say that the proper magnitude is comprised within such limits, that the sequence of events, according to the law of probability or necessity, will admit of a change from bad fortune to good, or from good fortune to bad.

25   Unity of plot does not, as some persons think, consist in the unity of the hero. For infinitely various are the incidents in one man's life, which cannot be reduced to unity; and so, too, there are many actions of one man out of which we cannot make one action. Hence the error, as it appears, of all poets who have composed a *Heracleid,* a *Theseid,*[5] or other poems of the kind. They imagine that as Heracles was one man, the story of Heracles must also be a unity. But Homer, as in all else he is of surpassing merit, here too—whether from art or natural genius—seems to have happily discerned the truth. In composing the *Odyssey* he did not include all the adventures of Odysseus—such as his wound on Parnassus, or his feigned madness at the mustering of the host—incidents between which there was no necessary or probable connexion: but he made the *Odyssey,* and likewise the *Iliad,* to centre round an action that in our sense of the word is one.[6] As therefore, in the other imitative arts, the imitation is one when the object imitated is one, so the plot, being an imitation of an action, must imitate one action and that a whole, the structural union of the parts being such that, if any one of them is displaced or removed, the whole will be disjointed and disturbed. For a thing whose presence or absence makes no visible difference, is not an organic part of the whole.

It is, moreover, evident from what has been said, that it is not the function of the poet to relate what has happened, but what may happen— what is possible according to the law of probability or necessity. The poet and the historian differ not by writing in verse or in prose. The work of Herodotus might be put into verse, and it would still be a species of history, with metre no less than without it. The true difference is that one relates what has happened, the other what may happen. Poetry, therefore, is a more philosophical and a higher thing than history: for poetry tends to express the universal, history the particular. . . .

---

[5]Poems about the adventures of Hercules and Theseus.
[6]In Aristotle's sense of "an action that is one," the action of the *Odyssey* may be said to center on the efforts of Odysseus to get back home to Ithaca and resume his kingship there; while the action of the *Iliad* is centered on the problem of getting Achilles into the fight after his quarrel with Agamemnon.

It clearly follows that the poet or "maker"[7] should be the maker of plots rather than of verses; since he is a poet because he imitates, and what he imitates are actions. And even if he chances to take an historical subject, he is none the less a poet; for there is no reason why some events that have actually happened should not conform to the law of the probable and possible, and in virtue of that quality in them he is their poet or maker.

Of all plots and actions the episodic are the worst. I call a plot "episodic" in which the episodes or acts succeed one another without probable or necessary sequence. Bad poets compose such pieces by their own fault, good poets, to please the players; for, as they write show pieces for competition, they stretch the plot beyond its capacity, and are often forced to break the natural continuity.

But again, Tragedy is an imitation not only of a complete action, but of events terrible and pitiful. Such an effect is best produced when the events come on us by surprise; and the effect is heightened when, at the same time, they follow as cause and effect. The tragic wonder will then be greater than if they happened of themselves or by accident; for even coincidences are most striking when they have an air of design. We may instance the statue of Mitys at Argos, which fell upon his murderer while he was a spectator at a festival, and killed him. Such events seem not to be due to mere chance. Plots, therefore, constructed on these principles are necessarily the best.

Plots are either Simple or Complex, for the actions in real life, of which the plots are an imitation, obviously show a similar distinction. An action which is one and continuous in the sense above defined, I call Simple, when the change of fortune takes place without Reversal of the Situation and without Recognition.

A Complex action is one in which the change is accompanied by such Reversal, or by Recognition, or by both. These last should arise from the internal structure of the plot, so that what follows should be the necessary or probable result of the preceding action. . . .

Reversal of the Situation is a change by which the action veers round to its opposite, subject always to our rule of probability or necessity. Thus in the *Oedipus,* the messenger comes to cheer Oedipus and free him from his alarms about his mother, but by revealing who he is, he produces the opposite effect. . . .

Recognition, as the name indicates, is a change from ignorance to knowledge, producing love or hate between the persons destined by the poet for good or bad fortune. The best form of recognition is coincident with a Reversal of the Situation as in the *Oedipus.* There are indeed other forms. Even inanimate things of the most trivial kind may sometimes be objects of recognition. Again, we may recognise or discover whether a person has done a thing or not. But the recognition which is

30

---

[7]The words "poet" and "poetry" come from the Greek verb *poiein,* "to make" (in the sense of "create").

most intimately connected with the plot and action is, as we have said, the recognition of persons. This recognition, combined with Reversal, will produce either pity or fear; and actions producing these effects are those which, by our definition, Tragedy represents. Moreover, it is upon such situations that the issues of good or bad fortune will depend. Recognition, then, being between persons, it may happen that one person only is recognised by the other—when the latter is already known—or it may be necessary that the recognition should be on both sides. Thus Iphigenia is revealed to Orestes by the sending of the letter; but another act of recognition is required to make Orestes known to Iphigenia.

Two parts, then, of the Plot—Reversal of the Situation and Recognition—turn upon surprises. A third part is the Tragic Incident. The Tragic Incident is a destructive or painful action, such as death on the stage, bodily agony, wounds, and the like. . . .

As the sequel to what has already been said, we must proceed to consider what the poet should aim at, and what he should avoid, in constructing his plots; and by what means the specific effect of Tragedy will be produced.

A perfect Tragedy should, as we have seen, be arranged not on the simple but on the complex plan. It should, moreover, imitate actions which excite pity and fear, this being the distinctive mark of tragic imitation. It follows plainly, in the first place, that the change of fortune presented must not be the spectacle of a virtuous man brought from prosperity to adversity: for this moves neither pity nor fear; it merely shocks us. Nor, again, that of a bad man passing from adversity to prosperity: for nothing can be more alien to the spirit of Tragedy; it possesses no single tragic quality; it neither satisfies the moral sense, nor calls forth pity or fear. Nor, again, should the downfall of the utter villain be exhibited. A plot of this kind would, doubtless, satisfy the moral sense, but it would inspire neither pity nor fear; for pity is aroused by unmerited misfortune, fear by the misfortune of a man like ourselves. Such an event, therefore, will be neither pitiful nor terrible. There remains, then, the character between these two extremes—that of a man who is not eminently good and just, yet whose misfortune is brought about not by vice or depravity, but by some error or frailty. He must be one who is highly renowned and prosperous—a personage like Oedipus, Thyestes, or other illustrious men of such families.

A well constructed plot should, therefore, be single in its issue, rather than double as some maintain. The change of fortune should be not from bad to good, but, reversely, from good to bad. It should come about as the result not of vice, but of some great error or frailty, in a character either such as we have described, or better rather than worse. The practice of the stage bears out our view. At first the poets recounted any legend that came in their way. Now, the best Tragedies are founded on the story of a few houses—on the fortunes of Alcmaeon, Oedipus, Orestes, Meleager, Thyestes, Telephus, and those others who have done or suffered something terrible. A Tragedy, then, to be perfect according to the rules of

35

art should be of this construction. Hence they are in error who censure Euripides just because he follows this principle in his plays, many of which end unhappily. It is, as we have said, the right ending. The best proof is that on the stage and in dramatic competition, such plays, if well worked out, are the most tragic in effect; and Euripides, faulty though he may be in the general management of his subject, yet is felt to be the most tragic of the poets.

In the second rank comes the kind of Tragedy which some place first. Like the *Odyssey* it has a double thread of plot, and also an opposite catastrophe for the good and for the bad. It is accounted the best because of the weakness of the spectators; for the poet is guided in what he writes by the wishes of his audience. The pleasure, however, thence derived is not the true tragic pleasure. It is proper rather to Comedy, where those who, in the piece, are the deadliest enemies—like Orestes and Aegisthus— quit the stage as friends at the close, and no one slays or is slain.

Fear and pity may be aroused by spectacular means; but they may also result from the inner structure of the piece, which is the better way, and indicates a superior poet. For the plot ought to be so constructed that, even without the aid of the eye, he who hears the tale told will thrill with horror and melt to pity at what takes place. This is the impression we should receive from hearing the story of the *Oedipus.* But to produce this effect by the mere spectacle is a less artistic method, and dependent on extraneous aids. Those who employ spectacular means to create a sense not of the terrible but only of the monstrous, are strangers to the purpose of Tragedy; for we must not demand of Tragedy any and every kind of pleasure, but only that which is proper to it. And since the pleasure which the poet should afford is that which comes from pity and fear through imitation, it is evident that this quality must be impressed upon the incidents.

Let us then determine what are the circumstances which strike us 40 as terrible or pitiful.

Actions capable of this effect must happen between persons who are either friends or enemies or indifferent to one another. If an enemy kills an enemy, there is nothing to excite pity either in the act or the intention— except so far as the suffering in itself is pitiful. So again with indifferent persons. But when the tragic incident occurs between those who are near or dear to one another—if, for example, a brother kills, or intends to kill, a brother, a son his father, a mother her son, a son his mother, or any other deed of the kind is done—these are the situations to be looked for by the poet. . . .

In respect of Character there are four things to be aimed at. First, and most important, it must be good. Now any speech or action that manifests moral purpose of any kind will be expressive of character: the character will be good if the purpose is good. This rule is relative to each class. Even a woman may be good, and also a slave; though the woman may be said to be an inferior being, and the slave quite worthless. The second thing to aim at is propriety. There is a type of manly valour; but valour in a woman, or unscrupulous cleverness, is inappropriate. Thirdly, character must be true to life: for this is a distinct thing from goodness and propriety, as here described. The fourth point is consistency: for though the subject of the imitation, who suggested the type, be inconsistent, still he must be consistently inconsistent. . . .

As in the structure of the plot, so too in the portraiture of character, the poet should always aim either at the necessary or the probable. Thus a person of a given character should speak or act in a given way, by the rule either of necessity or of probability; just as this event should follow that by necessary or probable sequence. It is therefore evident that the unravelling of the plot, no less than the complication, must arise out of the plot itself, it must not be brought about by the *Deus ex Machina*[8]—as in the *Medea*. . . . The *Deus ex Machina* should be employed only for events external to the drama—for antecedent or subsequent events, which lie beyond the range of human knowledge, and which require to be reported or foretold; for to the gods we ascribe the power of seeing all things. Within the action there must be nothing irrational. If the irrational cannot be excluded, it should be outside the scope of the tragedy. Such is the irrational element in the *Oedipus* of Sophocles. . . .

READING CRITICALLY FOR IDEAS, STRUCTURE, AND STYLE

1. How does Aristotle's definition of tragedy elaborate a theory as to why people should be emotionally moved by witnessing the unexpected fate of someone who is neither "perfectly virtuous" or "thoroughly evil"?

2. What principle explains Aristotle's ranking of the six elements that comprise tragedy? Would you use a different ranking? Explain your answer.

3. Why would "reversal" and "recognition" be the key elements in tragedy? Why would these elements be capable of eliciting pity and fear?

EXTENDING INSIGHTS THROUGH WRITING

1. Write a short essay and apply Aristotle's discussion to any literary work (for example, *Hamlet*) or historical event (for example, the destruction of the World Trade Center in New York) and define what makes it tragic.

---

[8]Literally, the god from the machine—the "machine" being any stage contraption, such as pulleys, by which supernatural beings are brought on the scene. The term has come to be used for artificial or makeshift means of resolving a plot.

2. Rewrite part or all of Aristotle's argument and substitute your own examples and illustrations for a contemporary audience.

CONNECTING PERSPECTIVES ON THE ARTS OF CIVILIZATION

1. Compare Aristotle's theory that art should imitate life with Leonardo da Vinci's working methods (as, for example, in *The Last Supper*) as described by Giorgio Vasari.

2. Compare Aristotle's discussion of the function theater should serve with Gustav Flaubert's analysis of what he tried to achieve in writing *Madame Bovary* (see "Letters to Louise Colete").

GIORGIO VASARI

The Life of Leonardo da Vinci

BACKGROUND

Italian painter, architect, and art historian, Giorgio Vasari (1511–1574) was born in Arezzo, and at thirteen moved to Florence where he studied under Michelangelo, Andrea Del Sarto, and Bacchio Bandinelli, and gained the patronage of the powerful Medici family. The commissions he undertook for them included redesigning the interior of the Palazzo degli Uffizi, now a famous museum in Florence. Although Vasari's paintings can be found in the Duomo (cathedral) in Florence, he is most famous for his work, *Lives of the Greatest Painters, Sculptors, and Architects,* first published in 1550 (revised in 1568) and translated into English, in ten volumes, in 1912–1914. His renown as an art historian is based on his invaluable insight into the lives of the major Italian Renaissance artists, including Leonardo da Vinci (1452–1519). In the following essay, Vasari draws on firsthand sources of information to create a compelling portrait of the famous artist.

APPROACHING VASARI'S ESSAY

Vasari offers an invaluable portrait of the great painter and inventive genius that is filled with a wealth of facts and is shaped to express Vasari's finely honed critical sense of the importance of Leonardo da Vinci's works. Vasari was a child of eight when Leonardo da Vinci died, and thus was still able to draw on contemporary sources for his biography of Leonardo da Vinci. The fact that Vasari had studied under Michelangelo gives greater credence to his stories of the rivalry between Leonardo da Vinci and Michelangelo ("there was no love lost between him and Michelanglo Buonarroti, so that the latter, left Florence owing to their rivalry"). From Vasari's account, we learn of Leonardo's capriciousness in beginning projects and not finishing them and are given memorable examples of da Vinci's gift for mechanics and engineering. Vasari interprets Leonardo's paintings as illustrating the Renaissance doctrine that art should imitate life and discusses this idea in relationship to the famous portrait of Mona Lisa. Vasari's insights about Renaissance painters are unequalled and his writing style is so natural, fluid, and easy-to-read that we feel instantly connected to his subject.

The Life of Leonardo da Vinci

The heavens often rain down the richest gifts on human beings, naturally, but sometimes with lavish abundance bestow upon a single individual beauty, grace and ability, so that, whatever he does, every action is so divine that he distances all other men, and clearly displays how his genius is the gift of God and not an acquirement of human art. Men saw this in* Lionardo da Vinci, whose personal beauty could not be exaggerated, whose every movement was grace itself and whose abilities were so extraordinary that he could readily solve every difficulty. He possessed great personal strength, combined with dexterity, and a spirit and courage invariably royal and magnanimous, and the fame of his name so spread abroad that, not only was he valued in his own day, but his renown has greatly increased since his death.

This marvellous and divine Lionardo was the son of Piero da Vinci. He would have made great profit in learning had he not been so capricious and fickle, for he began to learn many things and then gave them up. Thus in arithmetic, during the few months that he studied it, he made such progress that he frequently confounded his master by continually raising doubts and difficulties. He devoted some time to music, and soon learned to play the lyre, and, being filled with a lofty and delicate spirit, he could sing and improvise divinely with it. Yet though he studied so many different things, he never neglected design and working in relief, those being the things which appealed to his fancy more than any other. When Ser Piero perceived this, and knowing the boy's soaring spirit, he one day took some of his drawings to Andrea del Verrocchio, who was his close friend, and asked his opinion whether Lionardo would do anything by studying design. Andrea was so amazed at these early efforts that he advised Ser Piero to have the boy taught. So it was decided that Lionardo should go to Andrea's workshop.* The boy was greatly delighted, and not only practised his profession, but all those in which design has a part. Possessed of a divine and marvellous intellect, and being an excellent geometrician, he not only worked in sculpture, doing some heads of women smiling, which were casts, and children's heads also, executed like a master, but also prepared many architectural plans and elevations, and he was the first, though so young, to propose to canalise the Arno from Pisa

*About 1468.
*Italian spelling

to Florence. He made designs for mills, fulling machines, and other engines to go by water, and as painting was to be his profession he studied drawing from life. He would make clay models of figures, draping them with soft rags dipped in plaster, and would then draw them patiently on thin sheets of cambric or linen, in black and white, with the point of the brush. He did these admirably, as may be seen by specimens in my book of designs. He also drew upon paper so carefully and well that no one has ever equalled him. I have a head in grisaille[1] which is divine. The grace of God so possessed his mind, his memory and intellect formed such a mighty union, and he could so clearly express his ideas in discourse, that he was able to confound the boldest opponents. Every day he made models and designs for the removal of mountains with ease and to pierce them to pass from one place to another, and by means of levers, cranes and winches to raise and draw heavy weights; he devised a method for cleansing ports, and to raise water from great depths, schemes which his brain never ceased to evolve. Many designs for these notions are scattered about, and I have seen numbers of them. He spent much time in making a regular design of a series of knots so that the cord may be traced from one end to the other, the whole filling a round space. There is a fine engraving of this most difficult design, and in the middle are the words: *Leonardus Vinci Academia.* Among these models and designs there was one which he several times showed to many able citizens who then ruled Florence, of a method of raising the church of S. Giovanni and putting steps under it without it falling down. He argued with so much eloquence that it was not until after his departure that they recognised the impossibility of such a feat.

His charming conversation won all hearts, and although he possessed nothing and worked little, he kept servants and horses of which he was very fond, and indeed he loved all animals, and trained them with great kindness and patience. Often, when passing places where birds were sold, he would let them out of their cages and pay the vendor the price asked. Nature had favoured him so greatly that in whatever his brain or mind took up he displayed unrivalled divinity, vigour, vivacity, excellence, beauty and grace. His knowledge of art, indeed, prevented him from finishing many things which he had begun, for he felt that his hand would be unable to realise the perfect creations of his imagination, as his mind formed such difficult, subtle and marvellous conceptions that his hands, skilful as they were, could never have expressed them. His interests were so numerous that his inquiries into natural phenomena led him to study the properties of herbs and to observe the movements of the heavens, the moon's orbit and the progress of the sun.

Lionardo was placed, as I have said, with Andrea del Verrocchio in his childhood by Ser Piero, and his master happened to be painting a picture of St. John baptising Christ.[*] For this Lionardo did an angel holding some clothes, and, although quite young, he made it far better than the

[1]Gray monochrome painting.
[*]About 1470.

figures of Andrea. The latter would never afterwards touch colours, chagrined that a child should know more than he. Lionardo was next employed to draw a cartoon of the Fall[2] for a portière in tapestry, to be made in Flanders of gold and silk, to send to the King of Portugal. Here he did a meadow in grisaille, with the lights in white lead, containing much vegetation and some animals, unsurpassed for finish and naturalness. There is a fig-tree, the leaves and branches beautifully fore-shortened and executed with such care that the mind is amazed at the amount of patience displayed. There is also a palm-tree, the rotundity of the dates being executed with great and marvellous art, due to the patience and ingenuity of Lionardo. This work was not carried farther, and the cartoon is now in Florence in the fortunate house of Ottaviano de' Medici the Magnificent, to whom it was given not long ago by Lionardo's uncle.

It is said that when Ser Piero was at his country-seat he was requested by a peasant of his estate to get a round piece of wood painted for him at Florence, which he had cut from a fig-tree on his farm. Piero readily consented, as the man was very skilful in catching birds and fishing, and was very useful to him in such matters. Accordingly Piero brought the wood to Florence and asked Lionardo to paint something upon it, without telling him its history. Lionardo, on taking it up to examine it one day, found it warped, badly prepared and rude, but with the help of fire he made it straight, and giving it to a turner, had it rendered soft and smooth instead of being rough and rude. Then, after preparing the surface in his own way, he began to cast about what he should paint on it, and resolved to do the Medusa head[3] to terrify all beholders. To a room, to which he alone had access, Lionardo took lizards, newts, maggots, snakes, butterflies, locusts, bats, and other animals of the kind, out of which he composed a horrible and terrible monster, of poisonous breath, issuing from a dark and broken rock, belching poison from its open throat, fire from its eyes, and smoke from its nostrils, of truly terrible and horrible aspect. He was so engrossed with the work that he did not notice the terrible stench of the dead animals, being absorbed in his love for art. His father and the peasant no longer asked for the work, and when it was finished Lionardo told his father to send for it when he pleased, as he had done his part. Accordingly Ser Piero went to his rooms one morning to fetch it. When he knocked at the door Lionardo opened it and told him to wait a little, and, returning to his room, put the round panel in the light on his easel, and having arranged the window to make the light dim, he called his father in. Ser Piero, taken unaware, started back, not thinking of the round piece of wood, or that the face which he saw was painted, and was beating a retreat when Lionardo detained him and said, "This work has served its purpose; take it away, then, as it has produced the effect intended." Ser Piero indeed thought it more than miraculous, and he warmly praised Lionardo's idea. He then quietly went and bought another round wheel with a

5

---

[2]A "cartoon" is a sketch or preliminary drawing. The "Fall" refers to the Biblical story of the temptation of Adam and Eve—the "Fall of Man."
[3]The Medusa was one of the snake-haired Gorgons, whose look turned men to stone.

heart transfixed by a dart painted upon it, and gave it to the peasant, who was grateful to Piero all his life. Piero took Lionardo's work secretly to Florence and sold it to some merchants for 100 ducats, and in a short time it came into the hands of the Duke of Milan, who bought it of them for 300 ducats.

Lionardo next did a very excellent Madonna, which afterwards belonged to Pope Clement VII. Among other things it contained a bowl of water with some marvellous flowers, the dew upon them seeming actually to be there, so that they looked more real than reality itself. For his good friend Antonio Segni he drew a Neptune on paper, with so much design and care that he seemed alive. The sea is troubled and his car is drawn by sea-horses, with the sprites, monsters, and south winds and other fine marine creatures. . . .

Lionardo was so delighted when he saw curious heads, whether bearded or hairy, that he would follow about anyone who had thus attracted his attention for a whole day, acquiring such a clear idea of him that when he went home he would draw the head as well as if the man had been present. In this way many heads of men and women came to be drawn, and I have several such pen-and-ink drawings in my book, so often referred to. Among them is the head of Amerigo Vespucci, a fine old man, drawn in carbon, and that of Scaramuccia, the gipsy captain.

On the death of Giovan. Galeazzo, Duke of Milan, and the accession of Ludovico Sforza in the same year, 1493, Lionardo was invited to Milan with great ceremony by the duke to play the lyre, in which that prince greatly delighted. Lionardo took his own instrument, made by himself in silver, and shaped like a horse's head, a curious and novel idea to render the harmonies more loud and sonorous, so that he surpassed all the musicians who had assembled there. Besides this he was the best reciter of improvised rhymes of his time. The duke, captivated by Lionardo's conversation and genius, conceived an extraordinary affection for him. He begged him to paint an altar-picture of the Nativity, which was sent by the duke to the emperor. Lionardo then did a Last Supper for the Dominicans at S. Maria delle Grazie in Milan, endowing the heads of the Apostles with such majesty and beauty that he left that of Christ unfinished, feeling that he could not give it that celestial divinity which it demanded. This work left in such a condition has always been held in the greatest veneration by the Milanese and by other foreigners, as Lionardo has seized the moment when the Apostles are anxious to discover who would betray their Master. All their faces are expressive of love, fear, wrath or grief at not being able to grasp the meaning of Christ, in contrast to the obstinacy, hatred and treason of Judas, while the whole work, down to the smallest details, displays incredible diligence, even the texture of the tablecloth being clearly visible so that actual cambric would not look more real. It is said that the prior incessantly importuned Lionardo to finish the work, thinking it strange that the artist should pass half a day at a time lost in thought. He would have desired him never to lay down the brush, as if he were digging a garden. Seeing that his importunity produced no effect, he had recourse to the duke, who felt compelled to send for Lionardo to inquire about the work, showing tactfully that he was driven to act by the importunity of the prior. Lionardo, aware of the acuteness and discretion of the duke, talked with him fully about the picture, a thing which he had never done with the prior. He spoke freely of his art, and explained how men of genius really are doing most when they work least, as they are thinking out ideas and perfecting the conceptions, which they subsequently carry out with their hands. He added that there were still two heads to be done, that of Christ, which he would not look for on the earth, and felt unable to conceive the beauty of the celestial grace that must have been incarnate in the divinity. The other head was that of Judas, which also caused him thought, as he did not think he could express the face of a man who could resolve to betray his Master, the Creator of the world, after having received so many benefits. But he was willing in this case to seek no farther, and for lack of a better he would do the head of the importunate and tactless prior. The duke was wonderfully amused, and laughingly declared that he was quite right. Then the poor prior, covered with confusion, went back to his garden and left Lionardo in peace, while the artist indeed finished his Judas, making him a veritable likeness of treason and cruelty. The head of Christ was left unfinished, as I have said. The nobility of this painting, in its composition and the care with which it was finished, induced the King of France to wish to take it home with him. Accordingly he employed architects to frame it in wood and iron, so that it might be transported in safety, without any regard for the cost, so great was his desire. But the king was thwarted by its being done on the wall, and it remained with the Milanese.

He afterwards devoted even greater care to the study of the anatomy of men, aiding and being aided by M. Marcantonio della Torre, a profound philosopher, who then professed at Padua and wrote upon the subject.[4] I have heard it said that he was one of the first who began to illustrate the science of medicine, by the learning of Galen, and to throw true light upon anatomy, up to that time involved in the thick darkness of ignorance. In this he was marvellously served by the genius, work and hands of Lionardo, who made a book about it with red crayon drawings* outlined with the pen, in which he foreshortened and portrayed with the utmost diligence. He did the skeleton, adding all the nerves and muscles, the first attached to the bone, the others keeping it firm and the third moving, and in the various parts he wrote notes in curious characters, using his left hand, and writing from right to left, so that it cannot be read without practice, and only at a mirror.

When Lionardo was at Milan the King of France came there and   10
desired him to do something curious; accordingly he made a lion whose chest opened after he had walked a few steps, discovering himself to be full of lilies. At Milan Lionardo took Salai of that city as his pupil. This was a graceful and beautiful youth with fine curly hair, in which Li-

---

[4]The word "professed" is used here in the sense of "taught" (compare the word "professor"). Galen, mentioned below, was a Greek physician of the second century A.D.
*Between 1495 and 1498.

onardo greatly delighted. He taught him many things in art, and some works which are attributed in Milan to Salai were retouched by Lionardo. He returned to Florence, where he found that the Servite friars had allotted to Filippino[5] the picture of the high altar of the Nunziata. At this Lionardo declared that he should like to have done a similar thing. Filippino heard this, and being very courteous, he withdrew. The friars, wishing Lionardo to paint it, brought him to their house, paying all his expenses and those of his household. He kept them like this for a long time, but never began anything. At length he drew a cartoon of the Virgin and St. Anne with a Christ, which not only filled every artist with wonder, but, when it was finished and set up in the room, men and women, young and old, flocked to see it for two days, as if it had been a festival, and they marvelled exceedingly. The face of the Virgin displays all the simplicity and beauty which can shed grace on the Mother of God, showing the modesty and humility of a Virgin contentedly happy, in seeing the beauty of her Son, whom she tenderly holds in her lap. As she regards it the little St. John at her feet is caressing a lamb, while St. Anne smiles in her great joy at seeing her earthly progeny become divine, a conception worthy of the great intellect and genius of Lionardo. . . .

For Francesco del Giocondo Lionardo undertook the portrait of Mona Lisa, his wife, and left it incomplete after working at it for four years. This work is now in the possession of Francis, King of France, at Fontainebleau. This head is an extraordinary example of how art can imitate Nature, because here we have all the details painted with great subtlety. The eyes possess that moist lustre which is constantly seen in life, and about them are those livid reds and hair which cannot be rendered without the utmost delicacy. The lids could not be more natural, for the way in which the hairs issue from the skin, here thick and there scanty, and following the pores of the skin. The nose possesses the fine delicate reddish apertures seen in life. The opening of the mouth, with its red ends, and the scarlet cheeks seem not colour but living flesh. To look closely at her throat you might imagine that the pulse was beating. Indeed, we may say that this was painted in a manner to cause the boldest artists to despair. Mona Lisa was very beautiful, and while Lionardo was drawing her portrait he engaged people to play and sing, and jesters to keep her merry, and remove that melancholy which painting usually gives to portraits. This figure of Lionardo's has such a pleasant smile that it seemed rather divine than human, and was considered marvellous, an exact copy of Nature.

The fame of this divine artist grew to such a pitch by the excellence of his works that all who delighted in the arts and the whole city wished him to leave some memorial, and they endeavoured to think of some noteworthy decorative work through which the state might be adorned and honoured by the genius, grace and judgment characteristic of his work. The great hall of the council was being rebuilt . . . ., and being finished with great speed, it was ordained by public decree that Lionardo should be employed to paint

[5]Filippino Lippi, fifteenth-century painter.

some fine work. . . . He designed a group of horsemen fighting for a standard, a masterly work on account of his treatment of the fight, displaying the wrath, anger and vindictiveness of men and horses; two of the latter, with their front legs involved, are waging war with their teeth no less fiercely than their riders are fighting for the standard. One soldier, putting his horse to the gallop, has turned round and, grasping the staff of the standard, is endeavouring by main force to wrench it from the hands of four others, while two are defending it, trying to cut the staff with their swords; an old soldier in a red cap has a hand on the staff, as he cries out, and holds a scimetar in the other and threatens to cut off both hands of the two, who are grinding their teeth and making every effort to defend their banner. On the ground, between the legs of the horses, are two foreshortened figures who are fighting together, while a soldier lying prone has another over him who is raising his arm as high as he can to run his dagger with his utmost strength into his adversary's throat; the latter, whose legs and arms are helpless, does what he can to escape death. The manifold designs Lionardo made for the costumes of his soldiers defy description, not to speak of the scimetars and other ornaments, and his incredible mastery of form and line in dealing with horses, which he made better than any other master, with their powerful muscles and graceful beauty. It is said that for designing the cartoon he made an ingenious scaffolding which rose higher when pressed together and broadened out when lowered. Thinking that he could paint on the wall in oils, he made a composition so thick for laying on the wall that when he continued his painting it began to run and spoil what had been begun, so that in a short time he was forced to abandon it.

He went to Rome with Duke Giuliano de' Medici on the election of Leo X,[6] who studied philosophy and especially alchemy. On the way he made a paste with wax and constructed hollow animals which flew in the air when blown up, but fell when the wind ceased. On a curious lizard found by the vine-dresser of Belvedere he fastened scales taken from other lizards, dipped in quicksilver, which trembled as it moved, and after giving it eyes, a horn and a beard, he tamed it and kept it in a box. All the friends to whom he showed it ran away terrified. He would often dry and purge the guts of a wether[7] and make them so small that they might be held in the palm of the hand. In another room he kept a pair of smith's bellows, and with these he would blow out one of the guts until it filled the room, which was a large one, forcing anyone there to take refuge in a corner. The fact that it had occupied such a little space at first only added to the wonder. He perpetrated many such follies, studied mirrors and made curious experiments to find oil for painting and varnish to preserve the work done. It is said that, on being commissioned by the Pope to do a work, he straightway began to distil oil and herbs to make the varnish, which induced Pope Leo to say: "This man will never do anything, for he begins to think of the end before the beginning!"

---

[6]Giovanni de' Medici, elected Pope in 1513.
[7]A castrated male sheep.

There was no love lost between him and Michelangelo Buonarroti, so that the latter left Florence owing to their rivalry, Duke Giuliano excusing him by saying that he was summoned by the Pope to do the façade of S. Lorenzo. When Lionardo heard this, he left for France, where the king had heard of his works and wanted him to do the cartoon of St. Anne in colours. But Lionardo, as was his wont, gave him nothing but words for a long time. At length, having become old, he lay sick for many months, and seeing himself near death, he desired to occupy himself with the truths of the Catholic Faith and the holy Christian religion. Then, having confessed and shown his penitence with much lamentation, he devoutly took the Sacrament out of his bed, supported by his friends and servants, as he could not stand. The king arriving, for he would often pay him friendly visits, he sat up in bed from respect, and related the circumstances of his sickness, showing how greatly he had offended God and man in not having worked in his art as he ought. He was then seized with a paroxysm, the harbinger of death, so that the king rose and took his head to assist him and show him favour as well as to alleviate the pain. Lionardo's divine spirit, then recognising that he could not enjoy a greater honour, expired in the king's arms, at the age of seventy-five. The loss of Lionardo caused exceptional grief to those who had known him, because there never was a man who did so much honour to painting. By the splendour of his magnificent mien he comforted every sad soul, and his eloquence could turn men to either side of a question. His personal strength was prodigious, and with his right hand he could bend the clapper of a knocker or a horseshoe as if they had been of lead. His liberality warmed the hearts of all his friends, both rich and poor, if they possessed talent and ability. His presence adorned and honoured the most wretched and bare apartment. Thus Florence received a great gift in the birth of Lionardo, and its loss in his death was immeasurable.

READING CRITICALLY FOR IDEAS, STRUCTURE, AND STYLE

1. What aspects of Leonardo da Vinci's life and career illustrate why Vasari venerated him? What insight does he provide into da Vinci's working methods and wide-ranging inventive genius?

2. In what way is Vasari's style surprisingly accessible and quite contemporary although he wrote this so long ago.

3. How important was it for Vasari that da Vinci's paintings were done so as to imitate life as the painter had observed it? What can you infer about the importance of "mimesis" for the arts during the Renaissance?

EXTENDING INSIGHTS THROUGH WRITING

1. Reproductions of the *Mona Lisa* are readily available. Study one of these carefully and discuss how Vasari's description adds to your understanding of this painting.

2. Further insights on Leonardo da Vinci can be gained if you consult his Notebooks, or web sites devoted to him. How do the ideas contained in these Notebooks amplify the inventive side of his personality that Vasari discusses?

CONNECTING PERSPECTIVES
ON THE ARTS OF CIVILIZATION

1. Compare the significance of oil painting as a way of seeing the world, as Leonardo da Vinci practiced it, with John Berger's analysis (in "Ways of Seeing") of how contemporary society uses this traditional form in a new way.

2. Many of the architectural wonders in Venice that John Ruskin describes are contemporaneous with Leonardo da Vinci's life. What conclusions can you draw about the function of public religious art in Italian culture in the mid-1500s?

DAVID SYLVESTER

The Genius of Michelangelo:
An Interview with Henry Moore

BACKGROUND

On the 400th anniversary of Michelangelo's death in 1964, David Sylvester, the British critic and art historian, interviewed the renowned English sculptor, Henry Moore (1898–1986). The resulting dialogue which first appeared in *The New York Times Magazine*, March 8, 1964 illuminates both Moore's own work as well as Michelangelo's. Henry Moore first studied at the Royal College of Art. His early sculpture was inspired by a pre-Colombian style that was jagged and unfinished. Beginning in 1928, he evolved a style characterized by smooth organic shapes, empty hollows, and circular forms that often depicted a mother and child and reclining figures. His monumental sculptures are found in the leading museums of the world. He was also commissioned to do public sculptures, including one for the University of Chicago.

Michelangelo Buonarroti (1475–1564), the painter, architect, sculptor, and poet's impact on the Italian Renaissance and the world's culture is incalculable. Initially he was sponsored by Lorenzo de' Medici (of the Medici family who helped make Florence a center of European culture from the early 1400s through 1737). But in his life of nearly ninety years, Michelangelo accepted many commissions. He sculpted the *David* and several versions of the *Pietà*, painted the ceiling and rear wall of the *Sistene Chapel* in the Vatican (1508–1512), and was one of the chief architects of St. Peter's Basilica, designing its famous dome. The *Moses*, discussed by Moore in his interview, was part of the tomb of Pope Julius II; the "Night" and "Day" are reclining figures on the sarcophagi of Giuliano and Sorenzo dé Medici.

APPROACHING SYLVESTER'S INTERVIEW

Since this selection is an interview rather than an essay, we might expect to find different qualities than in a piece of writing that was planned, edited, and revised. But several themes unite Moore's conversation with Sylvester. One is the authenticity of Michelangelo's artistic vision and how true to it he remained throughout his life. Much of Moore's discussion concerns the Rondanini *Pieta* (which is not the more famous one in which the Virgin holds the dead Christ across her knees). We learn that Michelangelo, who was then near eighty, was dissatisfied with this work, although it was finished, and took a hammer one night and knocked the whole top part off because it did not meet his standards. The portrait of Michelangelo that emerges from this interview is of a sculptor whose works express, on a grand scale, his own tragic sense of human destiny. Ironically, according to Moore, Michelangelo came to value "the expression of the spirit of the person . . . more than a finished or a beautiful or a perfect work of art." Sylvester's own responses are crucial to the way the interview develops and imparts a feeling of naturalness and spontaneity. The interview shows how a great sculptor of the twentieth century, whose own works in the abstract style express a distinctive modern perspective on art, contrast profoundly with the ideals of Renaissance art, embodied in Michelangelo's work.

The Genius of Michelangelo: An Interview with Henry Moore

SYLVESTER: Your generation of *avant-garde* artists tended to react against Renaissance art. I know that you yourself as a student were especially interested in things like pre-Columbian and African art. Where did you see Michelangelo in relation to this?

MOORE: I still knew that as an individual he was an absolute superman. Even before I became a student, I'd taken a peculiar obsessive interest in him, though I didn't know what his work was like until I won a traveling scholarship and went to Italy. And then I saw he had such ability that beside him any sculptor must feel as a miler would knowing someone had once run a three-minute mile.

Take the "Moses." The way he builds up a mass of detail yet keeps the same vision and dignity throughout it—it really is staggering that anyone should do that out of such an intractable material as marble. There's an ability to realize his conception completely in the material and to find no restrictions or difficulties in doing it. You look at any of the parts and it's absolutely perfect: there's no hesitation—it's by someone who can do just what he wants to do. But later his technical achievement became less important to him, when he knew that the technical thing was something he could do without worrying.

I do dislike in some of his sculptures, like the figures of "Night" and "Day," the kind of leathery thickness of the skin. You feel that the bodies are covered with a skin that is half an inch thick rather than a skin such as you see in the Ilissus of the Parthenon. The skin there is exactly skin thick, whereas in some of Michelangelo's middle-period sculptures there's a thick leatheriness that looks to me a little bit repellent. Nevertheless in a work like the "Night," there's a grandeur of gesture and scale that for me is what great sculpture is. The reason I can't look at Bernini, or even Donatello,[1] beside him is his tremendous monumentality, his over-life-size vision. What sculpture should have for me is this monumentality rather than details that are sensitive.

SYLVESTER: Do you ever find yourself put off by that high polish on his marble?

MOORE: Sometimes. But in the "Night" or the "Moses" you'd lose something without that high polish. In some of his works he used contrast between a highly finished part and a part that is not so finished, and this is something one likes.

I would say that all young sculptors would be better if they were made to finish their early works to the very utmost. It's like a singer learning to sing higher than he can readily go, so that he can then sing within his own range. In the same way, if you can finish a sculpture, later you can afford to leave some parts unfinished. And for me Michelangelo's greatest work is one that was in his studio partly finished, partly unfinished, when he died—the Rondanini "Pietà." I don't know of any other single work of art by anyone that is more poignant, more moving. It isn't the most powerful of Michelangelo's works—it's a mixture, in fact, of two styles.

It must have been started at least 10 years before his death and at some stage was probably nearly finished throughout, in the style that the legs are in still. Then Michelangelo must have decided that he was dissatisfied with it or wanted to change it. And the changing became so drastic that I think he knocked the head off the sculpture. Because, if you look at that arm, which hangs there detached from the body of Christ, you see that it ends less than halfway up the biceps, yet this brings it nearly level to the shoulder of the existing figure. So the figure must originally have been a good deal taller. And if we also see the proportion of the length of the body of Christ compared with the length of the legs, there's no doubt that the whole top of the original sculpture has been cut away.

Now this to me is a great question. Why should I and other sculptors I know, my contemporaries—I think that Giacometti feels this, I know Marino Marini feels it—find this work one of the most moving and greatest works we know of when it's a work which has such disunity in it? There's a fragment—the arm—of the sculpture in a previous stage still left there; here are the legs

[1]Bernini was an Italian sculptor of the seventeenth century, Donatello of the fifteenth.

finished as they were perhaps 10 years previously, but the top recarved so that the hand of the Madonna on the chest of Christ is only a paper-thin ribbon.

But that's so moving, so touching; the position of the heads, the whole tenderness of the top part of the sculpture, is in my opinion more what it is by being in contrast with the rather finished, tough, leathery, typical Michelangelo legs. The top part is Gothic and the lower part is sort of Renaissance. So it's a work of art that for me means more because it doesn't fit in with all the theories of critics and estheticians who say that one of the great things about a work of art must be its unity of style.

SYLVESTER: It has been called by some historians a wreck—which seems obtuse.

MOORE: It does to me, because it's like finding the altered work of all old men a wreck. I think the explanation is perhaps that by this time Michelangelo knew he was near death and his values were more spiritual than they had been. I think also he came to know that, in a work of art, the expression of the spirit of the person—the expression of the artist's outlook on life—is what matters more than a finished or a beautiful or a perfect work of art.

I'm sure that had he taken away the nearly detached arm we should find it less moving because that part is near the new part. And undoubtedly, in my opinion, had he recarved the legs to have the same quality as the top, the whole work would have lost its point. This contrast, this disunity of style, brings together two of the Ages of Man, as it were.

SYLVESTER: It's not great in spite of its disunity but because of it?

MOORE: For me it's great because the very things that a lot of art writers would find wrong in it are what give it its greatness. There's something of the same principle in his unfinished "Slaves"—so-called unfinished: I don't think they're unfinished, because though Michelangelo might have gone on a bit more, I can't conceive that he would ever have wanted to finish them in the high way he finished other works.

Here again it's that same contrast—a contrast between two opposites, like the rough and the smooth, the old and the new, the spiritual and the anatomic. Here in this "Pietà" is the thin expressionist work set against the realistic style of the arm. Why should that hand, which scarcely exists, be so expressive? Why should Michelangelo, out of nothing, achieve that feeling of somebody touching another body with such tenderness? I just don't know. But it comes, I think, from the spirit. And it seems to me to have something of the same quality as the late "Crucifixion" drawings.

SYLVESTER: They are certainly the other works by Michelangelo to which the Rondanini "Pietà" relates. For one thing, they have the same stark up-and-down movement.

MOORE: Yes, I think that toward the end of his life he was someone who knew that a lot of the swagger didn't count. His values had changed to more deeply fundamental human values.

SYLVESTER: By the way, the arm that remains from the earlier state echoes the vertical movement of the group.

MOORE: Yes, that's maybe why he left it and didn't want to lose it. He wasn't dissatisfied. But I think there was no such conscious kind of design. I think that the parts he disliked he would alter and the parts he didn't dislike he'd leave.

And this is how artists work. It isn't that they work out—at least I don't—a theory, like saying, "This is upright and I'm going to leave it because it fits in with my new thing." It's because you *see* it fits in that you leave it—you're satisfied with it. It's that you work from satisfaction and dissatisfaction. You alter the things that don't seem right and you leave the things that are more right to go on with sometime later.

SYLVESTER: But why does this kind of simplicity in Michelangelo produce such a different effect from the kind you get in archaic forms of sculpture?

MOORE: Well, I think that if you do the opposite of something which you have a full experience of doing, the seeds of the previous thing will still be there. That is, nothing is ever lost, nothing is ever missing. The "Crucifixion" drawings are very simplified, without the twisting and turning of the earlier Michelangelo, yet they have a slight movement, a slight hang and turn that give a sense of agonized weight. All his past experience is in them.

This is the kind of quality you get in the work of old men who are really great. They can simplify; they can leave out. Even someone like Matisse can just sit in his bed, ill and sick, nearly dying, and with a pair of scissors and so on he can cut out things—and why they're so good is because of the past history of Matisse. There's this little difference that he makes which some young man trying to imitate him would never make.

25   SYLVESTER: But what is it that makes you like the unfinished "Slaves" better than the finished ones?

MOORE: I prefer them because they have more power in them, to me, much more power than the finished ones. That one in the Louvre is much too weary and sleepy and lackadaisical.

SYLVESTER: Well, it's meant to be dying.

MOORE: I know, but I mean you can have a thing that's dying and yet it has the vitality of the sculptor in it.

SYLVESTER: Maybe the more finished works are often less sympathetic just because they express Michelangelo's fantasy more clearly and we find certain things in his fantasy repellent. For instance, that leathery skin in the figure of "Night." With the unfinished "Slaves," you don't refer them back in a literal way to life in the same way as you do the "Night."

30   MOORE: No. And when one compares her breasts to a real woman's breasts, one finds them unpleasant. And I think in some of Michelangelo there can be a kind of melancholic, lazy slowness: I admire that, but I don't like it, and that's perhaps why, when he hasn't arrived at that, like it the unfinished "Slaves"—where that can't come in because he hasn't had the time to put it in—they appeal to one more.

But one still admires "Night." I mean, this is still an unbelievable pose. The whole attitude of the figure, the grandeur, the magnificence of the conception is still a wonderful thing. In all his work—early, middle, late—there's no sculptor of more ability. He could do anything he wanted.

READING CRITICALLY FOR IDEAS, STRUCTURE, AND STYLE

1. What qualities does Moore most admire in Michelangelo's sculpting? What influence did Michelangelo have on Moore's conception of art?

2. What significance does Moore attach to the presence of "finished" and "unfinished" parts in Michelangelo's later work?

3. How does the incident Sylvester reports about the Rondinini *Pietà* illustrate the increasing importance of "more spiritual" values for Michelangelo, as he grew old?

EXTENDING INSIGHTS THROUGH WRITING

1. After obtaining a reproduction of the Rondinini *Pietà* on a web site devoted to Michelangelo, reread Moore's description and, in a paragraph or two, discuss the relevance of his observations.

2. Obtain reproductions on web sites devoted to both Moore's and Michelangelo's works and discuss the differences between the modern idea of abstract art and the Renaissance ideal of "mimesis."

CONNECTING PERSPECTIVES ON THE ARTS OF CIVILIZATION

1. After reading Giorgio Vasari's account of Leonardo da Vinci and Sylvester's interview, and looking at reproductions of each artist's work, discuss any important similarities and contrasts between these two great Italian Renaissance artists.

2. Aristotle emphasized the importance of unity in a work of art (see "Poetics"), yet Henry Moore praises Michelangelo for precisely the opposite quality. What does Moore's assessment suggest about how artistic values have changed?

JOHN RUSKIN

The Stones of St. Mark's

BACKGROUND

John Ruskin (1819–1900), the English critic and social theorist, was born in London into a prosperous family; his father was a founder of Pedro Domecq sherries, while his mother was a devout Evangelical Protestant who hoped her son would become an Anglican bishop. He was educated at Oxford and while there wrote a pamphlet defending landscape painter, J. M. W. Turner, from which evolved his first work, *Modern Painters* (five vols., 1843–1860). In it, he espoused the theory that art is a "universal language" that can express moral truths. Ruskin applied this view to architecture in *The Seven Lamps of Architecture* (1849) and *The Stones of Venice* (1851–1853) from which the following selection is taken. He broadened his focus from art criticism to social and political issues and in *Unto This Last* (1860), *Sesame and Lilies* (1865), *The Crown of Wild Olive* (1866), and especially in *Fors Clavigera* (1871–1884) was the first to propose social reforms, including old-age pensions, nationalization of education, and organization of labor. As a reformer, Ruskin helped found the Working Men's College in London in 1854 where he lectured and gave lessons in drawing. In 1870, Ruskin was appointed Slade Professor at Oxford and became the first professor of art in England.

APPROACHING RUSKIN'S ESSAY

Ruskin begins this essay on St. Mark's by briefly surveying an English cathedral, before moving on to St. Mark's Cathedral in Venice. The contrast between a staid English cathedral town and the splendor, scale, and drama of St. Mark's Square in Venice prepares us to appreciate its many unique architectural features and their meaning. He defends St. Mark's against the charge that it is gaudy, incrusted (and insincere) by pointing out that its mosaics serve as a "great Book of Common Prayer." Ruskin is known as one of the great English stylists, and although his sentence structure is rather convoluted for modern tastes, it is perfectly suited to describe the fantastic jumble of forms, colors, and textures that is St. Mark's.

The Stones of St. Mark's

And now I wish that the reader, before I bring him into St. Mark's Place,[1] would imagine himself for a little time in a quiet English cathedral town, and walk with me to the west front of its cathedral. Let us go together up the more retired street, at the end of which we can see the pinnacles of one of the towers, and then through the low grey gateway, with its battlemented top and small latticed window in the centre, into the inner private-looking road or close, where nothing goes in but the carts of the tradesmen who supply the bishop and the chapter,[2] and where there are little shaven grass-plots, fenced in by neat rails, before old-fashioned groups of somewhat diminutive and excessively trim houses, with little oriel and bay windows, jutting out here and there, and deep wooden cornices and eaves painted cream colour and white, and small porches to their doors in the shape of cockle-shells, or little, crooked, thick, indescribable wooden gables warped a little on one side; and so forward till we come to larger houses, also old-fashioned, but of red brick, and with garden behind them, and fruit walls, which show here and there, among the nectarines, the vestiges of an old cloister arch or shaft, and looking in front on the cathedral square itself, laid out in rigid divisions of smooth grass and gravel walk, yet not uncheerful, especially on the sunny side, where the canons'[3] children are walking with their nurserymaids. And so, taking care not to tread on the grass, we will go along the straight walk to the west front, and there stand for a time, looking up at its deep-pointed porches and the dark places between their pillars where there were statues once, and where the fragments, here and there, of a stately figure are still left, which has in it the likeness of a king, perhaps indeed a king on earth, perhaps a saintly king long ago in heaven; and so higher and higher up to the great mouldering wall of rugged sculpture and confused arcades, shattered, and grey, and grisly with heads of dragons and mocking fiends, worn by the rain and swirling winds into yet unseemlier shape, and coloured on their stony scales by the deep russet-orange lichen, melancholy gold; and so, higher still, to the bleak towers, so far above that the eye loses itself among the bosses[4] of their traceries, though they are rude and strong, and only sees like a drift of eddying

---

[1]The great square in Venice before the cathedral.
[2]The clergy associated with the cathedral.
[3]Chapter members (see preceding note).
[4]Protruberant ornamental carvings marking centers of architectural design.

black points, now closing, now scattering, and now settling suddenly into invisible places among the bosses and flowers, the crowd of restless birds that fill the whole square with that strange clangour of theirs, so harsh and yet so soothing, like the cries of birds on a solitary coast between the cliffs and sea.

Think for a little while of that scene, and the meaning of all its small formalisms, mixed with its serene sublimity. Estimate its secluded, continuous, drowsy felicities, and its evidence of the sense and steady performance of such kind of duties as can be regulated by the cathedral clock; and weigh the influence of those dark towers on all who have passed through the lonely square at their feet for centuries, and on all who have seen them rising far away over the wooded plain, or catching on their square masses the last rays of the sunset, when the city at their feet was indicated only by the mist at the bend of the river. And then let us quickly recollect that we are in Venice, and land at the extremity of the Calle Lunga San Moisè, which may be considered as there answering to the secluded street that led us to our English cathedral gateway.

We find ourselves in a paved alley, some seven feet wide where it is widest, full of people, and resonant with cries of itinerant salesmen,—a shriek in their beginning, and dying away into a kind of brazen ringing, all the worse for its confinement between the high houses of the passage along which we have to make our way. Overhead an inextricable confusion of rugged shutters, and iron balconies and chimney flues pushed out on brackets to save room, and arched windows with projecting sills of Istrian stone, and gleams of green leaves here and there where a fig-tree branch escapes over a lower wall from some inner cortile,[5] leading the eye up to the narrow stream of blue sky high over all. On each side, a row of shops, as densely set as may be, occupying, in fact, intervals between the square stone shafts, about eight feet high, which carry the first floors: intervals of which one is narrow and serves as a door; the other is, in the more respectable shops, wainscotted to the height of the counter and glazed above, but in those of the poorer tradesmen left open to the ground, and the wares laid on benches and tables in the open air, the light in all cases entering at the front only, and fading away in a few feet from the threshold into a gloom which the eye from without cannot penetrate, but which is generally broken by a ray or two from a feeble lamp at the back of the shop, suspended before a print of the Virgin.

A yard or two farther, we pass the hostelry of the Black Eagle, and glancing as we pass through the square door of marble, deply moulded, in the outer wall, we see the shadows of its pergola of vines resting on an ancient well, with a pointed shield carved on its side; and so presently emerge on the bridge and Campo San Moisè, whence to the entrance into St. Mark's Place, called the Bocca di Piazza (mouth of the square), the Venetian character is nearly destroyed, first by the frightful façade of San Moisè and then by the modernising of the shops as they near the piazza, and the mingling with the lower Venetian populace of lounging groups of

---

[5]Small patio or courtyard.

English and Austrians. We will push fast through them into the shadow of the pillars at the end of the "Bocca di Piazza," and then we forget them all; for between those pillars there opens a great light, and, in the midst of it, as we advance slowly, the vast tower of St. Mark seems to lift itself visibly forth from the level field of chequered stones; and, on each side, the countless arches prolong themselves into ranged symmetry, as if the rugged and irregular houses that pressed together above us in the dark alley had been struck back into sudden obedience and lovely order, and all their rude casements and broken walls had been transformed into arches charged with goodly sculpture, and fluted shafts of delicate stone.

And well may they fall back, for beyond those troops of ordered arches   5
there rises a vision out of the earth, and all the great square seems to have opened from it in a kind of awe, that we may see it far away;—a multitude of pillars and white domes, clustered into a long low pyramid of coloured light; a treasure-heap, it seems, partly of gold, and partly of opal and mother-of-pearl, hollowed beneath into five great vaulted porches, ceiled with fair mosaic, and beset with sculpture of alabaster, clear as amber and delicate as ivory,—sculpture fantastic and involved, of palm leaves and lilies, and grapes and pomegranates, and birds clinging and fluttering among the branches, all twined together into an endless network of buds and plumes; and in the midst of it, the solemn forms of angels, sceptred, and robed to the feet, and leaning to each other across the gates, their figures indistinct among the gleaming of the golden ground through the leaves beside them, interrupted and dim, like the morning light as it faded back among the branches of Eden, when first its gates were angel-guarded long ago. And round the walls of the porches there are set pillars of variegated stones, jasper and porphyry, and deep-green serpentine spotted with flakes of snow, and marbles, that half refuse and half yield to the sunshine, Cleopatra-like, "their bluest veins to kiss"—the shadow, as it steals back from them, revealing line after line of azure undulation, as a receding tide leaves the waved sand; their capitals rich with interwoven tracery, rooted knots of herbage, and drifting leaves of acanthus and vine, and mystical signs, all beginning and ending in the Cross; and above them, in the broad archivolts,[6] a continuous chain of language and of life—angels, and the signs of heaven, and the labours of men, each in its appointed season upon the earth; and above these, another range of glittering pinnacles, mixed with white arches edged with scarlet flowers,—a confusion of delight, amidst which the breasts of the Greek horses are seen blazing in their breadth of golden strength, and the St. Mark's lion, lifted on a blue field covered with stars, until at last, as if in ecstasy, the crests of the arches break into a marble foam, and toss themselves far into the blue sky in flashes and wreaths of sculptured spray, as if the breakers on the Lido shore had been frost-bound before they fell, and the sea-nymphs had inlaid them with coral and amethyst.

Between that grim cathedral of England and this, what an interval! There is a type of it in the very birds that haunt them; for, instead of the

---

[6]Parts of the masonry making up an arch.

restless crowd, hoarse-voiced and sable-winged, drifting on the bleak upper air, the St. Mark's porches are full of doves, that nestle among the marble foliage, and mingle the soft iridescence of their living plumes, changing at every motion, with the tints, hardly less lovely, that have stood unchanged for seven hundred years.

And what effect has this splendour on those who pass beneath it? You may walk from sunrise to sunset, to and fro, before the gateway of St. Mark's, and you will not see an eye lifted to it, nor a countenance brightened by it. Priest and layman, soldier and civilian, rich and poor, pass by it alike regardlessly. Up to the very recesses of the porches, the meanest tradesmen of the city push their counters; nay, the foundations of its pillars are themselves the seats—not "of them that sell doves" for sacrifice, but of the vendors of toys and caricatures. Round the whole square in front of the church there is almost a continuous line of cafés, where the idle Venetians of the middle classes lounge, and read empty journals; in its centre the Austrian bands play during the time of vespers, their martial music jarring with the organ notes,—the march drowning the miserere,[7] and the sullen crowd thickening round them,—a crowd, which, if it had its will, would stiletto every soldier that pipes to it. And in the recesses of the porches, all day long, knots of men of the lowest classes, unemployed and listless, lie basking in the sun like lizards; and unregarded children,— every heavy glance of their young eyes full of desperation and stony depravity, and their throats hoarse with cursing,—gamble, and fight, and snarl, and sleep, hour after hour, clashing their bruised centesimi[8] upon the marble ledges of the church porch. And the images of Christ and His angels look down upon it continually.

Let us enter the church. It is lost in still deeper twilight, to which the eye must be accustomed for some moments before the form of the building can be traced; and then there opens before us a vast cave, hewn out into the form of a Cross, and divided into shadowy aisles by many pillars. Round the domes of its roof the light enters only through narrow apertures like large stars; and here and there a ray or two from some far-away casement wanders into the darkness, and casts a narrow phosphoric stream upon the waves of marble that heave and fall in a thousand colours along the floor. What else there is of light is from torches, or silver lamps, burning ceaselessly in the recesses of the chapels; the roof sheeted with gold, and the polished walls covered with alabaster, give back at every curve and angle some feeble gleaming to the flames; and the glories round the heads of the sculptured saints flash out upon us as we pass them, and sink again into the gloom. Under foot and over head, a continual succession of crowded imagery, one picture passing into another, as in a dream; forms beautiful and terrible mixed together; dragons and serpents, and ravening beasts of prey, and graceful birds that in the midst of them drink from running fountains and feed from vases of crystal; the passions and the pleasures of human life symbolised together, and the

[7]The 50th psalm in the Vulgate, named for its first word.
[8]Very small coins, like pennies.

mystery of its redemption; for the mazes of interwoven lines and changeful pictures lead always at last to the Cross, lifted and carved in every place and upon every stone; sometimes with the serpent of eternity wrapt round it, sometimes with doves beneath its arms, and sweet herbage growing forth from its feet; but conspicuous most of all on the great rood that crosses the church before the altar, raised in bright blazonry against the shadow of the apse.[9]

Now the first broad characteristic of the building, and the root nearly of every other important peculiarity in it, is its confessed *incrustation.* It is the purest example in Italy of the great school of architecture in which the ruling principle is the incrustation of brick with more precious materials; and it is necessary, before we proceed to criticise any one of its arrangements, that the reader should carefully consider the principles which are likely to have influenced, or might legitimately influence the architects of such a school, as distinguished from those whose designs are to be executed in massive materials. This incrusted school appears *insincere* at first to a Northern builder, because, accustomed to build with solid blocks of freestone, he is in the habit of supposing the external superficies of a piece of masonry to be some criterion of its thickness. But, as soon as he gets acquainted with the incrusted style, he will find that the Southern builders had no intention to deceive him. He will see that every slab of facial marble is fastened to the next by a confessed *rivet,* and that the joints of the armour are so visibly and openly accommodated to the contours of the substance within that he has no more right to complain of treachery than a savage would have, who, for the first time in his life seeing a man in armour, had supposed him to be made of solid steel. Acquaint him with the customs of chivalry, and with the uses of the coat of mail, and he ceases to accuse of dishonesty either the panoply or the knight.

These laws and customs of the St. Mark's architectural chivalry it must be our business to develop.   10

First, consider the natural circumstances which give rise to such a style. Suppose a nation of builders, placed far from any quarries of available stone, and having precarious access to the mainland where they exist; compelled therefore either to build entirely with brick, or to import whatever stone they use from great distances, in ships of small tonnage, and, for the most part, dependent for speed on the oar rather than the sail. The labour and cost of carriage are just as great, whether they import common or precious stone, and therefore the natural tendency would always be to make each shipload as valuable as possible. But in proportion to the preciousness of the stone, is the limitation of its possible supply; limitation not determined merely by cost, but by the physical conditions of the material, for of many marbles pieces above a certain size are not to be had for money. There would also be a tendency in such circumstances to import as much

[9]"Rood" is an ancient Anglo-Saxon word for the cross or crucifix, which was often placed on a large ornamental screen (the rood screen). The apse is the termination of the nave, traditionally the east end, beyond the altar, semicircular or polygonal in plan and with a vaulted or domed roof.

stone as possible ready sculptured, in order to save weight; and therefore, if the traffic of their merchants led them to places where there were ruins of ancient edifices, to ship the available fragments of them home. Out of this supply of marble, partly composed of pieces of so precious a quality that only a few tons of them could be on any terms obtained, and partly of shafts, capitals, and other portions of foreign buildings, the island architect has to fashion, as best he may, the anatomy of his edifice. It is at his choice either to lodge his few blocks of precious marble here and there among his masses of brick, and to cut out of the sculptured fragments such new forms as may be necessary for the observance of fixed proportions in the new building; or else to cut the coloured stones into thin pieces, of extent suffi-cient to face the whole surface of the walls, and to adopt a method of con-struction irregular enough to admit the insertion of fragmentary sculptures; rather with a view of displaying their intrinsic beauty, than of setting them to any regular service in the support of the building.

An architect who cared only to display his own skill, and had no re-spect for the works of others, would assuredly have chosen the former al-ternative, and would have sawn the old marbles into fragments in order to prevent all interference with his own designs. But an architect who cared for the preservation of noble work, whether his own or others', and more regarded the beauty of his building than his own fame, would have done what those old builders of St. Mark's did for us, and saved every relic with which he was entrusted.

But these were not the only motives which influenced the Venetians in the adoption of their method of architecture. It might, under all the cir-cumstances above stated, have been a question with other builders, whether to import one shipload of costly jaspers, or twenty of chalk flints; and whether to build a small church faced with porphyry and paved with agate, or to raise a vast cathedral in freestone. But with the Venetians it could not be a question for an instant; they were exiles from ancient and beautiful cities, and had been accustomed to build with their ruins, not less in affection than in admiration; they had thus not only grown familiar with the practice of inserting older fragments in modern buildings, but they owed to that practice a great part of the splendour of their city, and whatever charm of association might aid its change from a Refuge into a Home. The practice which began in the affections of a fugitive nation, was prolonged in the pride of a conquering one; and besides the memorials of departed happiness, were elevated the trophies of returning victory. The ship of war brought home more marble in triumph than the merchant ves-sel in speculation; and the front of St. Mark's became rather a shrine at which to dedicate the splendour of miscellaneous spoil, than the orga-nized expression of any fixed architectural law or religious emotion.

It is on its value as a piece of perfect and unchangeable colouring, that the claims of this edifice to our respect are finally rested; and a deaf man might as well pretend to pronounce judgment on the merits of a full orches-tra, as an architect trained in the composition of form only, to discern the beauty of St. Mark's. It possesses the charm of colour in common with the greater part of the architecture, as well as of the manufactures, of the East;

but the Venetians deserve especial note as the only European people who appear to have sympathized to the full with the great instinct of the Eastern races. They indeed were compelled to bring artists from Constantinople to design the mosaics of the vaults of St. Mark's, and to group the colours of its porches; but they rapidly took up and developed, under more masculine conditions, the system of which the Greeks had shown them the example: while the burghers and barons of the North were building their dark streets and grisly castles of oak and sandstone, the merchants of Venice were covering their palaces with porphyry and gold; and at last, when her mighty painters had created for her a colour more priceless than gold or porphyry, even this, the richest of her treasures, she lavished upon walls whose foundations were beaten by the sea; and the strong tide, as it runs beneath the Rialto, is reddened to this day by the reflection of the frescoes of Giorgione.[10]

If, therefore, the reader does not care for colour, I must protest against his endeavour to form any judgment whatever of this church of St. Mark's. But, if he both cares for and loves it let him remember that the school of incrusted architecture is *the only one in which perfect and permanent chromatic decoration is possible;* and let him look upon every piece of jasper and alabaster given to the architect as a cake of very hard colour, of which a certain portion is to be ground down or cut off, to paint the walls with. Once understand this thoroughly, and accept the condition that the body and availing strength of the edifice are to be in brick, and that this under muscular power of brickwork is to be clothed with the defence and the brightness of the marble, as the body of an animal is protected and adorned by its scales or its skin, and all the consequent fitnesses and laws of the structure will be easily discernible.

There are those who suppose the mosaics of St. Mark's, and others of the period, to be utterly barbarous as representations of religious history. Let it be granted that they are so; we are not for that reason to suppose they were ineffective in religious teaching. The whole church may be seen as a great Book of Common Prayer; the mosaics were its illuminations, and the common people of the time were taught their Scripture history by means of them, more impressively perhaps, though far less fully, than ours are now by Scripture reading. They had no other Bible, and—Protestants do not often enough consider this—*could* have no other. We find it somewhat difficult to furnish our poor with printed Bibles; consider what the difficulty must have been when they could be given only in manuscript. The walls of the church necessarily became the poor man's Bible, and a picture was more easily read upon the walls than a chapter. Under this view, and considering them merely as the Bible pictures of a great nation in its youth, I have to deprecate the idea of their execution being in any sense barbarous. I have conceded too much to modern prejudice, in permitting them to be rated as mere childish efforts at coloured portraiture: they have characters in them of a very noble kind; nor are they by any means devoid of the remains of the science of the later Roman empire. The character of the features is almost always fine, the expression stern and quiet, and very

15

---

[10]Venetian painter of the fifteenth century.

solemn, the attitudes and draperies always majestic in the single figures, and in those of the groups which are not in violent action; while the bright colouring and disregard of chiaroscuro[11] cannot be regarded as imperfections, since they are the only means by which the figures could be rendered clearly intelligible in the distance and darkness of the vaulting. So far am I from considering them barbarous, that I believe of all works of religious art whatsoever, these, and such as these, have been the most effective.

Missal-painting[12] could not, from its minuteness, produce the same sublime impressions, and frequently merged itself in mere ornamentation of the page. Modern book illustration has been so little skilful as hardly to be worth naming. Sculpture, though in some positions it becomes of great importance, has always a tendency to lose itself in architectural effect; and was probably seldom deciphered, in all its parts, by the common people, still less the traditions annealed in the purple burning of the painted window. Finally, tempera pictures and frescoes were often of limited size or of feeble colour. But the great mosaics of the twelfth and thirteenth centuries covered the walls and roofs of the churches with inevitable lustre; they could not be ignored or escaped from; their size rendered them majestic, their distance mysterious, their colour attractive. They did not pass into confused or inferior decorations; neither were they adorned with any evidences of skill or science, such as might withdraw the attention from their subjects. They were before the eyes of the devotee at every interval of his worship; vast shadowings forth of scenes to whose realization he looked forward, or of spirits whose presence he invoked. And the man must be little capable of receiving a religious impression of any kind, who, to this day, does not acknowledge some feeling of awe, as he looks up to the pale countenances and ghastly forms which haunt the dark roofs of the Baptisteries of Parma and Florence, or remains altogether untouched by the majesty of the colossal images of apostles, and of Him who sent apostles, that look down from the darkening gold of the domes of Venice and Pisa.

READING CRITICALLY FOR IDEAS, STRUCTURE, AND STYLE

1. How does the contrast between the plain English cathedral and St. Mark's set the stage for Ruskin's thesis about the public educative function St. Mark's played in the life of the common people in Venice?

---

[11]From the Italian words for "clear" and "dark," referring to the perspective or sense of dimension in depth achieved by the light and dark areas in drawing.
[12]Medieval decoration of books of the Mass.

2. What function did the ornate cathedrals and stained glass windows play, because of the stories they told, in the lives of the people? How does Ruskin attempt to communicate their impact and significance? Has this impact changed since most of the population are now literate?

3. What argument does Ruskin formulate against those who dismiss the incrusted style of St. Mark's as "insincere"? What other criterion aside from "composition of form" does he suggest should be applied?

EXTENDING INSIGHTS THROUGH WRITING

1. Analyze the syntax of one of Ruskin's sentences, for example, the third sentence in the first paragraph, or the first sentence in the fifth paragraph, and discuss how he recreates the experience for his readers through the pace and changing focus of his description.

2. Visit a cathedral or church near you and try to emulate Ruskin's style in conveying the psychological effects of what you see at every moment in your description. Pay particular attention to the effects of light and shadow as Ruskin does.

CONNECTING PERSPECTIVES
ON THE ARTS OF CIVILIZATION

1. Compare the descriptions by Ruskin of St. Mark's and P. D. Ouspensky's of the Taj Mahal in terms of the different architectural styles they embody, their effects on visitors, and the function each serves within their respective cultures.

2. Compare the way in which cathedrals are designed to create memorable impressions and communicate ideas and feelings to the masses, as described by Ruskin, with the popular art form of our era—the cinema—whose principle of *montage* was first stated by Sergei Eisenstein in "The Cinematographic Principle and the Ideogram." How does *montage* depend on time while mosaics, described by Ruskin, produce their effects in space? How does each express the era in which they were perfected?

P. D. OUSPENSKY

The Taj Mahal

BACKGROUND

Peter Demianovich Ouspensky (1878–1947) was born in Moscow. His first book *The Fourth Dimension* (1909) established him as one of the foremost writers on abstract mathematical theory. His subsequent works *Tertium Organum* (1912), *A New Model of the Universe* (1914), and *In Search of the Miraculous*, which appeared posthumously in 1949, have been acclaimed as among the most important philosophical works of the twentieth century. The current essay, on the Taj Mahal, drawn from the 1914 volume, is a provocative reassessment of one of the world's great architectural wonders.

APPROACHING OUSPENSKY'S ESSAY

Ouspensky opens his essay by creating an expectation of discovery of the secrets of the Taj Mahal. Because Ouspensky first sees the Taj Mahal by moonlight, his descriptions are filled with a sense of mystery. In the moonlight, the structure appears larger than it actually is because the lighting makes it difficult to tell where the building ends and the gardens begin. Ouspensky's sensation that he has moved into another realm becomes even more significant later as he concludes that the mystery and beauty of the Taj Mahal lie in the mystery of death and the beauty of the soul. He sees the little light inside the Taj Mahal as symbolic of life, which can easily be extinguished. The permanence and beauty of the Taj Mahal lead him to the comforting philosophy that, in eternity, as in the visual perception of the Taj Mahal, everything is united and dimensions are merged. He comes to the belief that the Taj Mahal is so radiantly beautiful because it is a place where life merges with eternity: The soul is in contact with the living world and life flows into the soul.

Ouspensky attempts to communicate the profound nature of his experience using language that becomes increasingly mystical and testifies to his

inability to express his feelings in words. As Ouspensky describes how the Taj
Mahal appears at different times of the day and from different angles, we can
imagine what it would be like to encounter the ethereal architecture, strange
echoes, intricate floral designs, and the unceasing flow of visitors in their robes
and turbans.

The Taj Mahal:
The Soul Of The Empress Mumtaz-i-Mahal

It was my last summer in India. The rains were already beginning when
I left Bombay for Agra and Delhi. For several weeks before that I had been collecting and reading everything I could find about Agra, about the palace of
the Great Moguls and about the Taj Mahal, the famous mausoleum of the
Empress who died at the beginning of the 17th century.

But everything that I had read, either then or before, left me with a kind
of indefinite feeling as though all who had attempted to describe Agra and the
Taj Mahal had missed what was most important.

Neither the romantic history of the Taj Mahal, nor the architectural
beauty, the luxuriance and opulence of the decoration and ornaments, could
explain for me the impression of fairy-tale unreality, of something beautiful,
but infinitely remote from life, the impression which was felt behind all the
descriptions, but which nobody has been able to put into words or explain.

And it seemed to me that here there was a mystery. The Taj Mahal had
a secret which was felt by everybody but to which nobody could give a name.

Photographs told me nothing at all. A large and massive building, and four   5
tapering minarets, one at each corner. In all this I saw no particular beauty, but
rather something incomplete. And the four minarets, standing separate, like four
candles at the corners of a table, looked strange and almost unpleasant.

In what then lies the strength of the impression made by the Taj Mahal?
Whence comes the irresistible effect which it produces on all who see it?
Neither the marble lace-work of the trellises, nor the delicate carving which
covers its walls, neither the mosaic flowers, nor the fate of the beautiful
Empress, none of these by itself could produce such an impression. It must
lie in something else. But in what? I tried not to think of it, in order not to create a preconceived idea. But something fascinated me and agitated me. I could
not be sure, but it seemed to me that the enigma of the Taj Mahal was connected with the mystery of death, that is, with the mystery regarding which,
according to the expression of one of the Upanishads,[1] "even the gods have
doubted formerly."

---

[1]*Upanishads*: speculative and mystical scriptures of Hinduism composed circa 900 B.C.,
regarded as the foundation of Hindu religion and philosophy.

The creation of the Taj Mahal dates back to the time of the conquest of India by the Mahomedans. The grandson of Akbar,[2] Shah Jehan, was one of the conquerors who changed the very face of India. Soldier and statesman, Shah Jehan was at the same time a fine judge of art and philosophy; and his court at Agra attracted all the most eminent scholars and artists of Persia, which was at that time the center of culture for the whole of Western Asia.

Shah Jehan passed most of his life, however, on campaign and in fighting. And on all his campaigns he was invariably accompanied by his favorite wife, the beautiful Arjumand Banu, or, as she was also called, Mumtaz-i-Mahal—"The Treasure of the Palace." Arjumand Banu was Shah Jehan's constant adviser in all matters of subtle and intricate Oriental diplomacy, and she also shared his interest in the philosophy to which the invincible Emperor devoted all his leisure.

During one of these campaigns the Empress, who as usual was accompanying Shah Jehan, died, and before her death she asked him to build for her a tomb—"the most beautiful in the world."

10　　And Shah Jehan decided to build for the interment of the dead Empress an immense mausoleum of white marble on the bank of the river Jumna in his capital Agra, and later to throw a silver bridge across the Jumna and on the other bank to build a mausoleum of black marble for himself.

Only half these plans was destined to be realised, for twenty years later, when the building of the Empress' mausoleum was being completed, a rebellion was raised against Shah Jehan by his son Aurungzeb, who later destroyed Benares.[3] Aurungzeb accused his father of having spent on the building of the mausoleum the whole revenue of the state for the last twenty years. And having taken Shah Jehan captive Aurungzeb shut him up in a subterranean mosque in one of the inner courts of the fortress-palace of Agra.

Shah Jehan lived seven years in this subterranean mosque and when he felt the approach of death, he asked to be moved to the fortress wall into the so-called "Jasmine Pavilion," a tower of lace-like marble, which had contained the favourite room of the Empress Arjumand Banu. And on the balcony of the "Jasmine Pavilion" overlooking the Jumna, whence the Taj Mahal can be seen in the distance, Shah Jehan breathed his last.

Such, briefly, is the history of the Taj Mahal. Since those days the mausoleum of the Empress has survived many vicissitudes of fortune. During the constant wars that took place in India in the 17th and 18th centuries, Agra changed hands many times and was frequently pillaged. Conquerors carried off from the Taj Mahal the great silver doors and the precious lamps and candlesticks; and they stripped the walls of the ornaments of precious stones. The building itself, however, and the greater part of the interior decoration has been preserved.

In the thirties of the last century the British Governor-General proposed to sell the Taj Mahal for demolition. The Taj Mahal has now been restored and is carefully guarded.

---

[2]Akbar (1542–1605): the third Mogul emperor of India, known for his religious tolerance and enlightenment, whose grandson built the Taj Mahal.

[3]*Benares*: now called Varanasi, the holiest Hindu city, is in north central India on the Ganges River and is one of the oldest continuously inhabited cities in the world.

I arrived at Agra in the evening and decided to go at once to see the Taj 15
Mahal by moonlight. It was not full moon, but there was sufficient light.

Leaving the hotel, I drove for a long time through the European part of
Agra, along broad streets all running between gardens. At last we left the town
and, driving through a long avenue, on the left of which the river could be
seen, we came out upon a broad square paved with flagstones and surrounded
by red stone walls. In the walls, right and left, there were gates with high towers.
The gate on the right, my guide explained, led into the old town, which had
been the private property of the Empress Arjumand Banu, and remains in
almost the same state as it was during her lifetime. The gate in the left-hand
tower led to the Taj Mahal.

It was already growing dark, but in the light of the broad crescent of the
moon every line of the buildings stood out distinctly against the pale sky. I
walked in the direction of the high, dark-red gate-tower with its arrow-shaped
arch and horizontal row of small white characteristically Indian cupolas surmounted by sharp-pointed spires. A few broad steps led from the square to
the entrance under the arch. It was quite dark there. My footsteps along the
mosaic paving echoed resoundingly in the side niches from which stairways
led up to a landing on the top of the tower, and to the museum which is inside
the tower.

Through the arch the garden is seen, a large expanse of verdure and in
the distance some white outlines resembling a white cloud that had descended
and taken symmetrical forms. These were the walls, cupolas and minarets of
the Taj Mahal.

I passed through the arch and out on to the broad stone platform, and
stopped to look about me. Straight in front of me and right across the garden
led a long broad avenue of dark cypresses, divided down the middle by a strip
of water with a row of jutting arms of fountains. At the further end the avenue
of cypresses was closed by the white cloud of the Taj Mahal. At the sides of
the Taj, a little below it, the cupolas of two large mosques could be seen under
the trees.

I walked slowly along the main avenue in the direction of the white build- 20
ing, by the strip of water with its fountains. The first thing that struck me, and
that I had not foreseen, was the immense size of the Taj. It is in fact a very
large structure, but it appears even larger than it is, owing chiefly to the ingenious design of the builders, who surrounded it with a garden and so arranged
the gates and avenues that the building from this side is not seen all at once,
but is disclosed little by little as you approach it. I realised that everything
about it had been exactly planned and calculated, and that everything was
designed to supplement and reinforce the chief impression. It became clear to
me why it was that in photographs the Taj Mahal had appeared unfinished
and almost plain. It cannot be separated from the garden and from the
mosques on either side, which appear as its continuation. I saw now why the
minarets at the corners of the marble platform on which the main building
stands had given me the impression of a defect. For in photographs I had seen
the picture of the Taj as ending on both sides with these minarets. Actually,
it does not end there, but imperceptibly passes into the garden and the adjacent buildings. And again, the minarets are not actually seen in all their height

as they are in photographs. From the avenue along which I walked only their tops were visible behind the trees.

The white building of the mausoleum itself was still far away, and as I walked towards it, it rose before me higher and higher. Though in the uncertain and changing light of the crescent moon I could distinguish none of the details, a strange sense of expectation forced me to continue looking intently, as if something was about to be revealed to me.

In the shadow of the cypresses it was nearly dark; the garden was filled with the scent of flowers, above all with that of jasmine, and peacocks were miauing. And this sound harmonised strangely with the surroundings, and somehow still further intensified the feeling of expectation which was coming over me.

Already I could see, brightly outlined in front of me, the central portion of the Taj Mahal rising from the high marble platform. A little light glimmered through the doors.

I reached the middle of the path leading from the arched entrance to the mausoleum. Here, in the centre of the avenue, is a square tank with lotuses in it and with marble seats on one side.

25   In the faint light of the half moon the Taj Mahal appeared luminous. Wonderfully soft, but at the same time quite distinct, white cupolas and white minarets came into view against the pale sky, and seemed to radiate a light of their own.

I sat on one of the marble seats and looked at the Taj Mahal, trying to seize and impress on my memory all the details of the building itself as I saw it and of everything else around me.

I could not have said what went on in my mind during this time, nor could I have been sure whether I thought about anything at all, but gradually, growing stronger and stronger; a strange feeling stole over me, which no words can describe.

Reality, that everyday actual reality in which we live, seemed somehow to be lifted, to fade and float away; but it did not disappear, it only underwent some strange sort of transformation, losing all actuality; every object in it, taken by itself, lost its ordinary meaning and became something quite different. In place of the familiar, habitual reality another reality opened out, a reality which usually we neither know, nor see, nor feel, but which is the one true and genuine reality.

I feel and know that words cannot convey what I wish to say. Only those will understand me who have themselves experienced something of this kind, who know the "taste" of such feelings.

30   Before me glimmered the small light in the doors of the Taj Mahal. The white cupolas and white minarets seemed to stir in the changing light of the white half moon. From the garden came the scent of jasmine and the miauing of the peacocks.

I had the sensation of being in two worlds at once. In the first place, the ordinary world of things and people had entirely changed, and it was ridiculous even to think of it; so imaginary, artificial and unreal did it appear now. Everything that belonged to this world had become remote, foreign and unintelligible to me—and I myself most of all, this very I that had arrived two hours before with all sorts of luggage and had hurried off to see the Taj Mahal by moonlight. All this—and the whole of the life of which it formed a part—seemed a puppet-show, which moreover was most clumsily put together and crudely painted, thus not resembling any reality whatsoever. Quite as grotesquely senseless and tragically ineffective appeared all my previous thoughts about the Taj Mahal and its riddle.

The riddle was here before me, but now it was no longer a riddle. It had been made a riddle only by that absurd, non-existent reality from which I had looked at it. And now I experienced the wonderful joy of liberation, as if I had come out into the light from some deep underground passages.

Yes, this was the mystery of death! But a revealed and visible mystery. And there was nothing dreadful or terrifyng about it. On the contrary, it was infinite radiance and joy.

Writing this now, I find it strange to recall that there was scarcely any transitional state. From my usual sensation of myself and everything else I passed into this new state immediately, while I was in this garden, in the avenue of cypresses, with the white outline of the Taj Mahal in front of me.

I remember that an unusually rapid stream of thoughts passed through my mind, as if they were detached from me and choosing or finding their own way. 35

At one time my thought seemed to be concentrated upon the artists who had built the Taj Mahal. I knew that they had been Sufis,[4] whose mystical philosophy, inseparable from poetry, has become the esotericism of Mahomedanism and in brilliant and earthly forms of passion and joy expressed the ideas of eternity, unreality and renunciation. And here the image of the Empress Arjumand Banu and her memorial, "the most beautiful in the world," became by their invisible sides connected with the idea of death, yet death not as annihilation, but as a new life.

I got up and walked forward with my eyes on the light glimmering in the doors, above which rose the immense shape of the Taj Mahal.

And suddenly, quite independently of me, something began to be formulated in my mind.

The light, I knew, burned above the tomb where the body of the Empress lay. Above it and around it are the marble arches, cupolas and minarets of the Taj Mahal, which carry it upwards, merging it into one whole with the sky and the moonlight.

I felt that precisely here was the beginning of the solution of the riddle. 40

The light—glimmering above the tomb where lies the dust of her body—this light that is so small and insignificant in comparison with the marble shape of the Taj Mahal, this is life, the life which we know in ourselves and others, in contrast with that other life which we do not know, which is hidden from us by the mystery of death.

The light which can so easily be extinguished, that is the little, transitory, earthly life. The Taj Mahal—that is the future or *eternal* life.

I began to understand the idea of the artists who had built the mausoleum of the Empress, who had surrounded it with this garden, with these

[4]*Sufis*: Muslim philosophical and literary movement that emerged in Persia (present-day Iran) in the early eleventh century.

gates, towers, pavilions, fountains, mosques—who had made it so immense, so white, so unbelievably beautiful, merging into the sky with its cupolas and minarets.

Before me and all around me was the soul of the Empress Mumtaz-i-Mahal.

The soul, so infinitely great, radiant and beautiful in comparison with the little body that had lived on earth and was now enclosed in the tomb.

In that moment I understood that the soul is not enclosed in the body, but that the body lives and moves in the soul. And then I remembered and understood a mystical expression which had arrested my attention in old books:

The soul and the future life are one and the same.

It even seemed strange to me that I had not been able to understand this before. Of course they were the same. Life, as a process, and that which lives, can be differentiated in our understanding only so long as there is the idea of disappearance, of death. Here, as in eternity, everything was united, dimensions merged, and our little earthly world disappeared in the infinite world.

I cannot reconstruct all the thoughts and feelings of those moments, and I feel that I am expressing a negligible part of them.

I now approached the marble platform on which stands the Taj Mahal with its four minarets at the corners. Broad marble stairs at the sides of the cypress avenue lead up to the platform from the garden.

I went up and came to the doors where the light was burning. I was met by Mahomedan gate-keepers, with slow, quiet movements, dressed in white robes and white turbans.

One of them lit a lantern, and I followed him into the interior of the mausoleum.

In the middle, surrounded by a carved marble trellis, were two white tombs; in the centre the tomb of the Empress, and beside it that of Shah Jehan. The tombs were covered with red flowers, and above them a light burned in a pierced brass lantern.

In the semi-darkness the indistinct outlines of the white walls vanished into the high dome, where the moonlight, penetrating from without, seemed to form a mist of changing colour.

I stood there a long time without moving, and the calm, grave Mahomedans in their white turbans left me undisturbed, and themselves stood in silence near the trellis which surrounded the tombs.

This trellis is itself a miracle of art. The word "trellis" conveys nothing, because it is really not a trellis, but a lace of white marble of wonderful workmanship. It is difficult to believe that the flowers and decorative ornamentation of this white filigree lace are neither moulded nor cast, but carved directly in thin marble panels.

Observing that I was examining the trellis, one of the gate-keepers quietly approached me and began to explain the plan of the interior of the Taj Mahal.

The tombstones before me were not real tombs. The real tombs in which the bodies lay were underneath in the crypt.

The middle part of the mausoleum, where we now stood, was under the great central dome; and it was separated from the outer walls by a wide corridor running between the four corner recesses, each beneath one of the four smaller cupolas.

"It is never light here," said the man, lifting up his hand. "Light only comes through the trellises of the side galleries. 60

"Listen, master."

He stepped back a few paces and, raising his head, cried slowly in a loud voice:

"Allah!"

His voice filled the whole of the enormous space of the dome above our heads, and as it began slowly, slowly, to die away, suddenly a clear and powerful echo resounded in the side cupolas from all four sides simultaneously:

"Allah!"

The arches of the galleries immediately responded, but not all at once; 65 one after another voices rose from every side as though calling to one another.

"Allah! Allah!"

And then, like the chorus of a thousand voices or like an organ, the great dome itself resounded, drowning everything in its solemn, deep bass:

"Allah!"

Then again, but more quietly, the side-galleries and cupolas answered, 70 and the great dome, less loudly, resounded once more, and the faint, almost whispering tones of the inner arches re-echoed its voice.

The echo fell into silence. But even in the silence it seemed as if a far, far-away note went on sounding.

I stood and listened to it, and with an intensified sense of joy I felt that this marvellous echo also was a calculated part of the plan of the artists who had given to the Taj Mahal a voice, bidding it repeat for ever the name of God.

Slowly I followed the guide, who, raising his lantern, showed me the ornaments covering the walls: violet, rose, blue, yellow and bright red flowers mingled with the green, some life-size and others larger than life-size, stone flowers that looked alive and that were beyond the reach of time; and after that, the whole of the walls covered with white marble flowers, carved doors and carved windows—all of white marble.

The longer I looked and listened, the more clearly, and with a greater and greater sense of gladness, I felt the idea of the artists who had striven to express the infinite richness, variety and beauty of the *soul* or of *eternal life* as compared with the small and insignificant earthly life.

We ascended to the roof of the Taj Mahal, where the cupolas stand at the 75 corners, and from there I looked down on the broad, dark Jumna. Right and left stood large mosques of red stone with white cupolas. Then I crossed to the side of the roof which overlooks the garden. Below, all was still, only the trees rustled in the breeze, and from time to time there came from afar the low and melodious miauing of the peacocks.

All this was so like a dream, so like the "India" one may see in dreams, that I should not have been in the least surprised had I suddenly found myself flying over the garden to the gate-tower, which was now growing black, at the end of the cypress avenue.

Then we descended and walked round the white building of the Taj Mahal on the marble platform, at the corners of which stand the four minarets, and by the light of the moon we examined the decorations and ornaments of the outer walls.

Afterwards we went below into the white marble crypt, where, as above, a lamp was burning and where red flowers lay on the white tombs of the Emperor and Empress.

The following morning I drove to the fortress, where the palace of Shah Jehan and the Empress Arjumand Banu is still preserved.

80   The fortress of Agra is a whole town in itself. Enormous towers built of brick stand above the gates. The walls are many feet thick, and enclose a labyrinth of courtyards, barracks, warehouses and buildings of all kinds. A considerable part of the fortress indeed is devoted to modern uses and is of no particular interest. At last I came upon the Pearl Mosque, which I had known from Verestchagin's picture. Here begins the kingdom of white marble and blue sky. There are only two colours, white and blue. The Pearl Mosque is very much larger than I had imagined. Great heavy gates encased in copper, and behind them, under a glittering sky, a dazzling white marble yard with a fountain, and further on a hall for sermons, with wonderful carved arches with gold ornaments and with marble latticed windows into the inner parts of the palace, through which the wives of the Emperor and the ladies of the court could see into the mosque.

Then the palace itself. This is not one building, but a whole series of marble buildings and courts contained within the brick buildings and courts of the fortress itself.

The throne of Akbar, a black marble slab in the fortress wall on a level with the higher battlements, and in front of it the "Court of Justice." Then Shah Jehan's "Hall of Audience," with more carved arches similar to those in the Pearl Mosque, and finally the residential quarters of the palace and the Jasmine Pavilion.

These palace apartments are situated on the fortress wall which looks out over the Jumna. They consist of a series of rooms, not very large according to modern standards, but the walls of which are covered with rare and beautiful carving. Everything is so wonderfully preserved that it might have been only yesterday that here, with their women, lived those emperor-conquerors, philosophers, poets, sages, fanatics, madmen, who destroyed one India and created another. Most of the residential part of the palace is under the floor of the marble courts and passages which extend from the Hall of Audience to the fortress wall. The rooms are joined by corridors and passages and by small courts enclosed in marble trellises.

Beyond the fortress wall there is a deep inner court where tourneys of warriors were held, and where wild beasts fought with one another or with men. Above is the small court surrounded by lattices, from which the ladies of the palace viewed the combats of elephants against tigers and gazed at the contests of the warriors. Here, too, with their wares, came merchants from far countries, Arabians, Greeks, Venetians and Frenchmen. A "chessboard" court paved with rows of black and white slabs in chess-board pattern, where dancers and dancing-girls in special costumes acted as chess-men. Further on, the apartments of the Emperor's wives; in the walls carved cupboards for jewelry still exist, as well as small round apertures, leading to secret cupboards, into which only very small hands could penetrate. A bathroom lined with rock crystal which causes its walls to sparkle with changing colours when a light is lit. Small, almost toy rooms, like bonbonnières. Tiny balconies. Rooms under the floor of the inner court, into which the light passes only through thin marble panels, and where it is never hot—and then at last, the miracle of miracles, the Jasmine Pavilion, which used to contain the favourite apartment of the Empress Mumtaz-i-Mahal.

It is a circular tower, surrounded by a balcony hanging over the fortress wall above the Jumna. Eight doors lead within from the balcony. There is literally not one inch of the walls of the Jasmine Pavilion or of the balustrades and pillars of the balcony, that is not covered with the most delicate, beautiful carving. Ornament within ornament, and again in every ornament still another ornament, almost like jewellers' work. The whole of the Jasmine Pavilion is like this, and so is the small hall with a fountain and rows of carved columns.

In all this there is nothing grandiose or mystical, but the whole produces an impression of unusual intimacy. I felt the life of the people who had lived there. In some strange way I seemed to be in touch with it, as if the people were still living, and I caught glimpses of the most intimate and secret aspects of their lives. In this palace time is not felt at all. The past connected with these marble rooms is felt as the present, so real and living does it stand out, and so strange is it even to think while here that it is no more.

As we were leaving the palace the guide told me of the subterranean maze beneath the whole fortress where, it is said, innumerable treasures lie concealed. And I remembered that I had read about it before. But the entrances to these underground passages had been closed and covered over many years ago, after a party of curious travellers had lost their way and perished in them. It is said that there are many snakes there, among them some gigantic cobras larger than any to be found elsewhere, which were perhaps alive in the days of Shah Jehan. And they say that sometimes on moonlight nights they crawl out to the river.

From the palace I drove again to the Taj Mahal, and on the way I bought photographs taken from old miniatures, portraits of Shah Jehan and the Empress Arjumand Banu. Once seen, their faces remain in the memory. The Empress' head is slightly inclined, and she holds a rose in her delicate hand. The portrait is very much stylised, but in the shape of the mouth and in the large eyes one feels a deep inner life, strength and thought; and in the whole face the irresistible charm of mystery and fairy-tale. Shah Jehan is in profile. He has a very strange look, ecstatic yet at the same time balanced. In this portrait he sees something which no one but himself could see or perhaps would dare to see. Also he appears to be looking at himself, observing his every thought and feeling. It is the look of a clairvoyant, a dreamer, as well as that of a man of extraordinary strength and courage.

The impression of the Taj Mahal not only is not weakened by the light of day, rather it is strengthened. The white marble amidst the green stands out so astonishingly against the deep blue sky; and in a single glance you seize more particulars and details than at night. Inside the building you are still more struck by the luxuriance of the decoration, the fairy-tale flowers, red, yellow and blue, and the garlands of green; the garlands of marble leaves and marble flowers and lace-work trellises. And all this is the soul of the Empress Mumtaz-i-Mahal.

90   I spent the whole of the next day until evening in the garden that surrounds the Taj Mahal. Above all things I liked to sit on the wide balcony on the top of the gate-tower. Beneath me lay the garden intersected by the cypress avenue and the line of fountains reaching as far as the marble platform on which the Taj Mahal stands. Under the cypresses slowly moved groups of Mahomedan visitors in robes and turbans of soft colours that can only be imagined: turquoise, lemon-yellow, pale green, yellow-rose. For a long time I watched through my glasses a pale orange turban side by side with an emerald shawl. Every now and again they vanished behind the trees, again they appeared on the marble stairs leading to the mausoleum. Then they disappeared in the entrances to the Taj Mahal, and again could be seen amongst the cupolas on the roof. And all the time along the avenue of cypresses moved the procession of coloured robes and turbans, blue, yellow, green, rose turbans, shawls and caftans—not a single European was in sight.

The Taj Mahal is the place of pilgrimage and the place for promenades from the town. Lovers meet here; you see children with their large dark eyes, calm and quiet, like all Indian children; ancient and decrepit men, women with babies, beggars, fakirs,[5] musicians. . . .

All faces, all types of Mahomedan India pass before you.

And I had a strange feeling all the time that this, too, was part of the plan of the builders of the Taj Mahal, part of their mystical idea of the contact of the *soul* with the whole world and with all the life that from all sides unceasingly flows into the soul.

READING CRITICALLY FOR IDEAS, STRUCTURE, AND STYLE

1. How does the nature of the enigma that confronts Ouspensky in paragraph 5 serve as the focus of his investigation?

2. How would you characterize Ouspensky's tone, and what sense do you get of him as a person? Does he make an ideal observer of the Taj Mahal? Why or why not?

---

[5]*fakirs:* religious ascetics in India who perform spiritual and physical feats of endurance and subsist through begging.

3. What conclusion does Ouspensky reach after visiting the Taj Mahal at different times, in different light, and deeply considering its effect on him?

EXTENDING INSIGHTS THROUGH WRITING

1. The Taj Mahal plays an important part in Ouspensky's work as an example of an "objective" work of art, that is, a work that produces the same emotional reaction on all who see it. In a few paragraphs discuss the way an "objective" work of art differs from the more familiar "subjective" art we are used to. Have you ever encountered a work of art that you would classify as "objective"? Describe it and your experiences. For further information on his theory, you might consult Ouspensky's *A New Model of the Universe* (1950).

2. Many Web sites are devoted to the Taj Mahal. Visit one and compare Ouspensky's observations, and what he learned from delving into its history, with your impressions. Do you think you would have had the same reaction? Why or why not?

CONNECTING PERSPECTIVES
ON THE ARTS OF CIVILIZATION

1. From what you learned from David Sylvester's interview with Henry Moore about Michelangelo's sculptures, do you think one of those could effect people in the same way as does the Taj Mahal? Why or why not?

2. In what respects might one of the great symphonies of the past, as discussed by Edward Rothstein, produce an impression comparable to that produced on Ouspensky when he saw the Taj Mahal?

PAUL ROBERTS

Something About English

BACKGROUND

Paul Roberts (1917–1967) was a linguist, teacher, and writer. After teaching at San Jose State and Cornell University, he became director of language at the Center of American Studies in Rome. His published works include *Understanding Grammar* (1954), *Patterns of English* (1956), *Cornflakes and Beaujolais* (1958), and in the same year, *Understanding English*, from which the following essay is drawn.

APPROACHING ROBERTS'S ESSAY

From its beginnings, as an obscure Anglo-Saxon dialect to its current status as a world language spoken by 400 million people, English has been shaped by historical events at every stage in its evolution. This is the amazing story, covering 1,400 years, that Roberts relates in a concise and very readable form. In Roberts's view, four main kinds of events shaped the history of the English language. Through trade, Latin words were added to the basic Anglo-Saxon vocabulary and English became the language of business. Religion, too, was a decisive force, especially, the conversion of England to Christianity in 597 A.D. Multiple invasions were the decisive catalyst: Anglo-Saxon tribes brought a Germanic form of language, later, Vikings added words from Old Norse, and still later, the Norman invasion led by William the Conquerer in 1066 brought a large influx of French words and contributed to the breakdown of Germanic grammatical inflections. The printing press was the fourth factor that resulted in English being standardized and led to improved communication so that English did not ultimately break up into mutually unintelligible languages. Throughout, Roberts organizes his narrative so as to carefully make the connections between historical events and the development of English.

Something About English

HISTORICAL BACKGROUNDS

No understanding of the English language can be very satisfactory without a notion of the history of the language. But we shall have to make do with just a notion. The history of English is long and complicated, and we can only hit the high spots.

The history of our language begins a little after A.D. 600. Everything before that is pre-history, which means that we can guess at it but can't prove much. For a thousand years or so before the birth of Christ our linguistic ancestors were savages wandering through the forests of northern Europe. Their language was a part of the Germanic branch of the Indo-European family.

At the time of the Roman Empire—say, from the beginning of the Christian Era to around A.D. 400—the speakers of what was to become English were scattered along the northern coast of Europe. They spoke a dialect of Low German. More exactly, they spoke several different dialects, since they were several different tribes. The names given to the tribes who got to England are *Angles, Saxons,* and *Jutes.* For convenience, we can refer to them all as Anglo-Saxons.

Their first contact with civilization was a rather thin acquaintance with the Roman Empire on whose borders they lived. Probably some of the Anglo-Saxons wandered into the Empire occasionally, and certainly Roman merchants and traders traveled among the tribes. At any rate, this period saw the first of our many borrowings from Latin. Such words as *kettle, wine, cheese, butter, cheap, plum, gem, bishop, church* were borrowed at this time. They show something of the relationship of the Anglo-Saxons with the Romans. The Anglo-Saxons were learning, getting their first taste of civilization.

They still had a long way to go, however, and their first step was to help smash the civilization they were learning from. In the fourth century the Roman power weakened badly. While the Goths were pounding away at the Romans in the Mediterranean countries, their relatives, the Anglo-Saxons, began to attack Britain.

The Romans had been the ruling power in Britain since A.D. 43. They had subjugated the Celts whom they found living there and had succeeded

5

in setting up a Roman administration. The Roman influence did not extend to the outlying parts of the British Isles. In Scotland, Wales, and Ireland the Celts remained free and wild, and they made periodic forays against the Romans in England. Among other defense measures, the Romans built the famous Roman Wall to ward off the tribes in the north.

Even in England the Roman power was thin. Latin did not become the language of the country as it did in Gaul and Spain. The mass of people continued to speak Celtic, with Latin and the Roman civilization it contained in use as a top dressing.

In the fourth century, troubles multiplied for the Romans in Britain. Not only did the untamed tribes of Scotland and Wales grow more and more restive, but the Anglo-Saxons began to make pirate raids on the eastern coast. Furthermore, there was growing difficulty everywhere in the Empire, and the legions in Britain were siphoned off to fight elsewhere. Finally, in A.D. 410, the last Roman ruler in England, bent on becoming emperor, left the islands and took the last of the legions with him. The Celts were left in possession of Britain but almost defenseless against the impending Anglo-Saxon attack.

Not much is surely known about the arrival of the Anglo-Saxons in England. According to the best early source, the eighth-century historian Bede, the Jutes came in 449 in response to a plea from the Celtic king, Vortigern, who wanted their help against the Picts attacking from the north. The Jutes subdued the Picts but then quarreled and fought with Vortigern, and, with reinforcements from the Continent, settled permanently in Kent. Somewhat later the Angles established themselves in eastern England and the Saxons in the south and west. Bede's account is plausible enough, and these were probably the main lines of the invasion.

We do know, however, that the Angles, Saxons, and Jutes were a long time securing themselves in England. Fighting went on for as long as a hundred years before the Celts in England were all killed, driven into Wales, or reduced to slavery. This is the period of King Arthur, who was not entirely mythological. He was a Romanized Celt, a general, though probably not a king. He had some success against the Anglo-Saxons, but it was only temporary. By 550 or so the Anglo-Saxons were firmly established. English was in England.

OLD ENGLISH

10   All this is pre-history, so far as the language is concerned. We have no record of the English language until after 600, when the Anglo-Saxons were converted to Christianity and learned the Latin alphabet. The conversion began, to be precise, in the year 597 and was accomplished within thirty or forty years. The conversion was a great advance for the Anglo-Saxons, not only because of the spiritual benefits but because it reëstablished contact with what remained of Roman civilization. This civilization didn't amount to much in the year 600, but it was certainly superior to anything in England up to that time.

It is customary to divide the history of the English language into three periods: Old English, Middle English, and Modern English. Old English runs from the earliest records—i.e., seventh century—to about 1100; Middle English from 1100 to 1450 or 1500; Modern English from 1500 to the present day. Sometimes Modern English is further divided into Early Modern, 1500–1700, and Late Modern, 1700 to the present.

When England came into history, it was divided into several more or less autonomous kingdoms, some of which at times exercised a certain amount of control over the others. In the century after the conversion the most advanced kingdom was Northumbria, the area between the Humber River and the Scottish border. By A.D. 700 the Northumbrians had developed a respectable civilization, the finest in Europe. It is sometimes called the Northumbrian Renaissance, and it was the first of the several renaissances through which Europe struggled upward out of the ruins of the Roman Empire. It was in this period that the best of the Old English literature was written, including the epic poem *Beowulf.*

In the eighth century, Northumbrian power declined, and the center of influence moved southward to Mercia, the kingdom of the Midlands. A century later the center shifted again, and Wessex, the country of the West Saxons, became the leading power. The most famous king of the West Saxons was Alfred the Great, who reigned in the second half of the ninth century, dying in 901. He was famous not only as a military man and administrator but also as a champion of learning. He founded and supported schools and translated or caused to be translated many books from Latin into English. At this time also much of the Northumbrian literature of two centuries earlier was copied in West Saxon. Indeed, the great bulk of Old English writing which has come down to us is in the West Saxon dialect of 900 or later.

In the military sphere, Alfred's great accomplishment was his successful opposition to the viking invasions. In the ninth and tenth centuries, the Norsemen emerged in their ships from their homelands in Denmark and the Scandinavian peninsula. They traveled far and attacked and plundered at will and almost with impunity. They ravaged Italy and Greece, settled in France, Russia, and Ireland, colonized Iceland and Greenland, and discovered America several centuries before Columbus. Nor did they overlook England.

After many years of hit-and-run raids, the Norsemen landed an   15
army on the east coast of England in the year 866. There was nothing much to oppose them except the Wessex power led by Alfred. The long struggle ended in 877 with a treaty by which a line was drawn roughly from the northwest of England to the southeast. On the eastern side of the line Norse rule was to prevail. This was called the Danelaw. The western side was to be governed by Wessex.

The linguistic result of all this was a considerable injection of Norse into the English language. Norse was at this time not so different from English as Norwegian or Danish is now. Probably speakers of English could understand, more or less, the language of the newcomers who had

moved into eastern England. At any rate, there was considerable inter-
change and word borrowing. Examples of Norse words in the English language are *sky, give, law, egg, outlaw, leg, ugly, scant, sly, crawl, scowl,
take, thrust*. There are hundreds more. We have even borrowed some pronouns from Norse—*they, their*, and *them*. These words were borrowed first
by the eastern and northern dialects and then in the course of hundreds
of years made their way into English generally.

It is supposed also—indeed, it must be true—that the Norsemen influenced the sound structure and the grammar of English. But this is
hard to demonstrate in detail.

A SPECIMEN OF OLD ENGLISH

We may now have an example of Old English. The favorite illustration
is the Lord's Prayer, since it needs no translation. This has come to us in
several different versions. Here is one:

Fæder ure þu ðe eart on heofonum si þin nama gehalgod. Tobecume
þin rice. Gewurðe þin willa on eorðan swa swa on heofonum. Urne
gedæghwamlican hlaf syle us to dæg. And forgyf us ure gyltas swa
swa we forgyfaþ urum gyltendum. And ne gelæd þu us on cost-
nunge ac alys us of yfele. Soðlice.

Some of the differences between this and Modern English are merely
differences in orthography. For instance, the sign æ is what Old English
writers used for a vowel sound like that in modern *hat* or *and*. The th
sounds or modern *thin* or *then* are represented in Old English by þ or ð.
But of course there are many differences in sound too. *Ure* is the ancestor
of modern *our*, but the first vowel was like that in *too* or *ooze*. *Hlaf* is modern *loaf*; we have dropped the h sound and changed the vowel, which in
hlaf was pronounced something like the vowel in *father*. Old English had
some sounds which we do not have. The sound represented by y does not
occur in Modern English. If you pronounce the vowel in *bit* with your lips
rounded, you may approach it.

20   In grammar, Old English was much more highly inflected than Modern English is. That is, there were more case endings for nouns, more person and number endings for verbs, a more complicated pronoun system,
various endings for adjectives, and so on. Old English nouns had four
cases—nominative, genitive, dative, accusative. Adjectives had five—all
these and an instrumental case besides. Present-day English has only two
cases for nouns—common case and possessive case. Adjectives now have
no case system at all. On the other hand, we now use a more rigid word
order and more structure words (prepositions, auxiliaries, and the like) to
express relationships than Old English did.

Some of this grammar we can see in the Lord's Prayer. *Heofonum*, for
instance, is a dative plural; the nominative singular was *heofon*. *Urne* is
an accusative singular; the nominative is *ure*. In *urum gyltendum* both
words are dative plural. *Forgyfaþ* is the third person plural form of the

verb. Word order is different: "urne gedæghwamlican hlaf syle us" in place of "Give us our daily bread." And so on.

In vocabulary Old English is quite different from Modern English. Most of the Old English words are what we may call native English: that is, words which have not been borrowed from other languages but which have been a part of English ever since English was a part of Indo-European. Old English did certainly contain borrowed words. We have seen that many borrowings were coming in from Norse. Rather large numbers had been borrowed from Latin, too. Some of these were taken while the Anglo-Saxons were still on the Continent (*cheese, butter, bishop, kettle,* etc.); a larger number came into English after the Conversion (*angel, candle, priest, martyr, radish, oyster, purple, school, spend,* etc.). But the great majority of Old English words were native English.

Now, on the contrary, the majority of words in English are borrowed, taken mostly from Latin and French. Of the words in *The American College Dictionary* only about 14 percent are native. Most of these, to be sure, are common, high-frequency words—*the, of, I, and, because, man, mother, road,* etc.; of the thousand most common words in English, some 62 percent are native English. Even so, the modern vocabulary is very much Latinized and Frenchified. The Old English vocabulary was not.

MIDDLE ENGLISH

Sometime between the years 1000 and 1200 various important changes took place in the structure of English, and Old English became Middle English. The political event which facilitated these changes was the Norman Conquest. The Normans, as the name shows, came originally from Scandinavia. In the early tenth century they established themselves in northern France, adopted the French language, and developed a vigorous kingdom and a very passable civilization. In the year 1066, led by Duke William, they crossed the Channel and made themselves masters of England. For the next several hundred years, England was ruled by kings whose first language was French.

One might wonder why, after the Norman Conquest, French did not become the national language, replacing English entirely. The reason is that the Conquest was not a national migration, as the earlier Anglo-Saxon invasion had been. Great numbers of Normans came to England, but they came as rulers and landlords. French became the language of the court, the language of the nobility, the language of polite society, the language of literature. But it did not replace English as the language of the people. There must always have been hundreds of towns and villages in which French was never heard except when visitors of high station passed through.

But English, though it survived as the national language, was profoundly changed after the Norman Conquest. Some of the changes—in sound structure and grammar—would no doubt have taken place whether there had been a Conquest or not. Even before 1066 the case system of English nouns and adjectives was becoming simplified; people came to rely more on word order and prepositions than on inflectional endings to communicate their meanings. The process was speeded up by sound changes which caused many of the endings to sound alike. But no doubt the Conquest facilitated the change. German, which didn't experience a Norman Conquest, is today rather highly inflected compared to its cousin English.

But it is in vocabulary that the effects of the Conquest are most obvious. French ceased, after a hundred years or so, to be the native language of very many people in England, but it continued—and continues still—to be a zealously cultivated second language, the mirror of elegance and civilization. When one spoke English, one introduced not only French ideas and French things but also their French names. This was not only easy but socially useful. To pepper one's conversation with French expressions was to show that one was well-bred, elegant, *au courant*. The last sentence shows that the process is not yet dead. By using *au courant* instead of, say, *abreast of things*, the writer indicates that he is no dull clod who knows only English but an elegant person aware of how things are done in *le haut monde*.

Thus French words came into English, all sorts of them. There were words to do with government: *parliament, majesty, treaty, alliance, tax, government;* church words: *parson, sermon, baptism, incense, crucifix, religion;* words for foods: *veal, beef, mutton, bacon, jelly, peach, lemon, cream, biscuit;* colors: *blue, scarlet, vermilion;* household words: *curtain, chair, lamp, towel, blanket, parlor;* play words: *dance, chess, music, leisure, conversation;* literary words: *story, romance, poet, literary;* learned words: *study, logic, grammar, noun, surgeon, anatomy, stomach;* just ordinary words of all sorts: *nice, second, very, age, bucket, gentle, final, fault, flower, cry, count, sure, move, surprise, plain.*

All these and thousands more poured into the English vocabulary between 1100 and 1500, until at the end of that time many people must have had more French words than English at their command. This is not to say that English became French. English remained English in sound structure and in grammar, though these also felt the ripples of French influence. The very heart of the vocabulary, too, remained English. Most of the high-frequency words—the pronouns, the prepositions, the conjunctions, the auxiliaries, as well as a great many ordinary nouns and verbs and adjectives—were not replaced by borrowings.

30   Middle English, then, was still a Germanic language, but it differed from Old English in many ways. The sound system and the grammar changed a good deal. Speakers made less use of case systems and other inflectional devices and relied more on word order and structure words to express their meanings. This is often said to be a simplification, but it isn't really. Languages don't become simpler; they merely exchange or kind of complexity for another. Modern English is not a simple language, as any foreign speaker who tries to learn it will hasten to tell you.

For us Middle English is simpler than Old English just because it is closer to Modern English. It takes three or four months at least to learn to read Old English prose and more than that for poetry. But a week of good study should put one in touch with the Middle English poet Chaucer. Indeed, you may be able to make some sense of Chaucer straight off, though you would need instruction in pronunciation to make it sound like poetry. Here is a famous passage from the *General Prologue to the Canterbury Tales*, fourteenth century:

> Ther was also a nonne, a Prioresse,
> That of hir smyling was ful symple and coy,
> Hir gretteste oath was but by Seinte Loy,
> And she was cleped Madame Eglentyne.
> Ful wel she song the service dyvyne,
> Entuned in hir nose ful semely.
> And Frenshe she spak ful faire and fetisly,
> After the scole of Stratford-atte-Bowe,
> For Frenshe of Parys was to hir unknowe.

EARLY MODERN ENGLISH

Sometime between 1400 and 1600 English underwent a couple of sound changes which made the language of Shakespeare quite different from that of Chaucer. Incidentally, these changes contributed much to the chaos in which English spelling now finds itself.

One change was the elimination of a vowel sound in certain unstressed positions at the end of words. For instance, the words *name, stone, wine, dance* were pronounced as two syllables by Chaucer but as just one by Shakespeare. The e in these words became, as we say, "silent." But it wasn't silent for Chaucer; it represented a vowel sound. So also the words *laughed, seemed, stored* would have been pronounced by Chaucer as two-syllable words. The change was an important one because it affected thousands of words and gave a different aspect to the whole language.

The other change is what is called the Great Vowel Shift. This was a systematic shifting of half a dozen vowels and diphthongs in stressed syllables. For instance, the word *name* had in Middle English a vowel something like that in the modern word *father; wine* had the vowel of modern *mean; he* was pronounced something like modern *hey; mouse* sounded like *moose; moon* had the vowel of *moan.* Again the shift was thoroughgoing and affected all the words in which these vowel sounds occurred. Since we still keep the Middle English system of spelling these words, the differences between Modern English and Middle English are often more real than apparent.

The vowel shift has meant also that we have come to use an entirely   35
different set of symbols for representing vowel sounds than is used by writers of such languages as French, Italian, or Spanish, in which no such vowel shift occurred. If you come across a strange word—say, *bine*—in an English book, you will pronounce it according to the English system, with the vowel of *wine* or *dine.* But if you read *bine* in a French, Italian, or Spanish book, you will pronounce it with the vowel of *mean* or *seen.*

These two changes, then, produced the basic differences between Middle English and Modern English. But there were several other developments that had an effect upon the language. One was the invention of printing, an invention introduced into England by William Caxton in the year 1475. Where before books had been rare and costly, they suddenly became cheap and common. More and more people learned to read and write. This was the first of many advances in communication which have worked to unify languages and to arrest the development of dialect differences, though of course printing affects writing principally rather than speech. Among other things it hastened the standardization of spelling.

The period of Early Modern English—that is, the sixteenth and seventeenth centuries—was also the period of the English Renaissance, when people developed, on the one hand, a keen interest in the past and, on the other, a more daring and imaginative view of the future. New ideas multiplied, and new ideas meant new language. Englishmen had grown accustomed to borrowing words from French as a result of the Norman Conquest; now they borrowed from Latin and Greek. As we have seen, English had been raiding Latin from Old English times and before, but now the floodgates really opened, and thousands of words from the classical languages poured in. *Pedestrian, bonus, anatomy, contradict, climax, dictionary, benefit, multiply, exist, paragraph, initiate, scene, inspire* are random examples. Probably the average educated American today has more words from French in his vocabulary than from native English sources, and more from Latin than from French.

The greatest writer of the Early Modern English period is of course Shakespeare, and the best-known book is the King James Version of the Bible, published in 1611. The Bible (if not Shakespeare) has made many features of Early Modern English perfectly familiar to many people down to present times, even though we do not use these features in present-day speech and writing. For instance, the old pronouns *thou* and *thee* have dropped out of use now, together with their verb forms, but they are still familiar to us in prayer and in Biblical quotation: "Whither thou goest, I will go." Such forms as *hath* and *doth* have been replaced by *has* and *does;* "Goes he hence tonight?" would now be "Is he going away tonight?"; Shakespeare's "Fie on't, sirrah" would be "Nuts to that, Mac." Still, all these expressions linger with us because of the power of the works in which they occur.

It is not always realized, however, that considerable sound changes have taken place between Early Modern English and the English of the present day. Shakespearian actors putting on a play speak the words, properly enough, in their modern pronunciation. But it is very doubtful that this pronunciation would be understood at all by Shakespeare. In Shakespeare's time, the word *reason* was pronounced like modern *raisin;* *face* had the sound of modern *glass;* the l in *would, should, palm* was pronounced. In these points and a great many others the English language has moved a long way from what it was in 1600.

RECENT DEVELOPMENTS

The history of English since 1700 is filled with many movements and 40
counter-movements, of which we can notice only a couple. One of these is
the vigorous attempt made in the eighteenth century, and the rather half-
hearted attempts made since, to regulate and control the English language.
Many people of the eighteenth century, not understanding very well the
forces which govern language, proposed to polish and prune and restrict
English, which they felt was proliferating too wildly. There was much talk
of an academy which would rule on what people could and could not say
and write. The academy never came into being, but the eighteenth century
did succeed in establishing certain attitudes which, though they haven't had
much effect on the development of the language itself, have certainly
changed the native speaker's feeling about the language.

In part a product of the wish to fix and establish the language was
the development of the dictionary. The first English dictionary was published in 1603; it was a list of 2500 words briefly defined. Many others
were published with gradual improvements until Samuel Johnson published his *English Dictionary* in 1755. This, steadily revised, dominated
the field in England for nearly a hundred years. Meanwhile in America,
Noah Webster published his dictionary in 1828, and before long dictionary
publishing was a big business in this country. The last century has seen
the publication of one great dictionary: the twelve-volume *Oxford English
Dictionary*, compiled in the course of seventy-five years through the labors
of many scholars. We have also, of course, numerous commercial dictionaries which are as good as the public wants them to be if not, indeed,
rather better.

Another product of the eighteenth century was the invention of
"English grammar." As English came to replace Latin as the language of
scholarship it was felt that one should also be able to control and dissect
it, parse and analyze it, as one could Latin. What happened in practice
was that the grammatical description that applied to Latin was removed
and superimposed on English. This was silly, because English is an entirely different kind of language, with its own forms and signals and
ways of producing meaning. Nevertheless, English grammars on the
Latin model were worked out and taught in the schools. In many schools
they are still being taught. This activity is not often popular with school
children, but it is sometimes an interesting and instructive exercise in
logic. The principal harm in it is that it has tended to keep people from
being interested in English and has obscured the real features of English
structure.

But probably the most important force on the development of English in the modern period has been the tremendous expansion of English-
speaking peoples. In 1500 English was a minor language, spoken by a few
people on a small island. Now it is perhaps the greatest language of the
world, spoken natively by over a quarter of a billion people and as a second language by many millions more. When we speak of English now, we

must specify whether we mean American English, British English, Australian English, Indian English, or what, since the differences are considerable. The American cannot go to England or the Englishman to America confident that he will always understand and be understood. The Alabaman in Iowa or the Iowan in Alabama shows himself a foreigner every time he speaks. It is only because communication has become fast and easy that English in this period of its expansion has not broken into a dozen mutually unintelligible languages.

READING CRITICALLY FOR IDEAS, STRUCTURE, AND STYLE

1. How does Roberts organize his essay to reveal a connection among trade and commerce, religion, invasions and territorial conquests, the invention of the printing press, and the development of the English language? Which examples seem to you to be especially persuasive in demonstrating this connection?

2. What is the significance of the linguistic phenomenon known as the "great vowel shift," and how did it change the way thousands of words were pronounced and represented through symbols?

3. Does Roberts appear to give preferential weight to English as a medium of communication more than other languages? Do you see him as a reporter or an advocate?

EXTENDING INSIGHTS THROUGH WRITING

1. As a research project, trace the evolution or history of any term (you might consult *The Oxford English Dictionary*) and give illustrations of this term as it originally was used and as it is used today. For example, "peddling your wares" meant your goods or your merchandise in the 1400s, whereas we know the term today as "software" which refers to programs for computers.

2. Roberts mentions that many everyday words are of French origin and were brought into English by the Norman invaders. In a 300–500 word essay, discuss why some of these words are thought to carry an aura of sophistication and refinement (especially, in literature, cuisine, and fashion), which their English counterparts do not.

**CONNECTING PERSPECTIVES
ON THE ARTS OF CIVILIZATION**

1. According to Edward Rothstein (see "Why We Live in the Musical Past") people prefer music from the nineteenth century, but they do not choose to speak as people did then. How does this reflect the different ways music and the English language have evolved?

2. Is what is going on in advertising today, according to John Berger, the same process that the English language has displayed, that is, the assimilation of sources, that Roberts discusses? Explain your answer.

GUSTAV FLAUBERT

Letters to Louise Colete

BACKGROUND

Gustav Flaubert (1821–1880), whose work has been perhaps the single most important influence on the technique of the modern novel, was born in Rouen, France, where he was educated at the College Royal. He studied law but abandoned the idea of becoming an attorney and became committed to literature. Each of his works is undoubtedly a masterpiece, but he is best known for his novel *Madame Bovary* (1857), which realistically and objectively depicts with enormous finesse and stylistic precision the yearnings of a sensitive young woman. Flaubert's other works include *Salammbo* (1862), *A Sentimental Education* (1869), *The Temptation of Saint Anthony* (1874), and *Bouvard et Pecuchet* (1881), as well as volumes of short stories and travel sketches. Flaubert's lifelong stormy relationship with the poetess Louise Colete is reflected in his candid correspondence with her in which he discusses his literary philosophy and the painstaking effort he expended in creating the characters and incidents for *Madame Bovary*. The following series of letters were written to her between July 6, 1852 and July 15, 1853.

APPROACHING FLAUBERT'S ESSAY

The origins of *Madame Bovary* lie in the reactions of Flaubert's friends, Maxim Du Camp and Louis Bouilhet, in 1849, to a draft of *The Temptation of Saint Anthony*, who found it to be imprecise, flowery, excessively vague, and too detached from modern times. Instead, they urged him to consider writing a novel that would be realistic and more accessible to his audience. Du Camp maintained that he told Flaubert the true story of a local tragedy in which a wife committed suicide after having an affair and her husband, a doctor, killed himself. Other sources have been cited, but the germ of this story—which became Emma Bovary's attempts to find romance and the resulting tragedy —fixed itself in Flaubert's imagination. When it was published, the novel became something of a scandal since the French government had already tried to censor the magazine (for blasphemy and offending public morals) in which several installments had appeared. Flaubert was brought to trial in February 1857 on the grounds of his novel's alleged immorality, but narrowly escaped conviction. Its success became something of a touchy subject to Flaubert who felt his later works were overshadowed by the success of *Madame Bovary*, which was widely acclaimed by critics who instantly recognized it as a masterpiece. Flaubert's practice of scrupulously trying to find the exact word and revising to achieve objectivity is expressed in his statement to Colete—"Art is not interested in the personality of the artist."

Letters to Louise Colet

Tuesday, [Croisset, July 6, 1852]

Musset[1] has never separated poetry from the sensations of which it is the consummate expression. Music, according to him, was made for serenades, painting for portraits, and poetry for consoling the heart. But if you put the sun inside your trousers, all you do is burn your trousers and wet the sun. That is what happened to him. Nerves, magnetism: for him poetry is those things. Actually, it is something less turbulent. If sensitive nerves were the only requirement of a poet, I should be superior to Shakespeare and to Homer, whom I picture as a not very nervous individual. Such confusion is blasphemy. I know whereof I speak: I used to be able to hear what people were saying in low voices behind closed doors thirty paces away; all my viscera could be seen quivering under my skin; and sometimes I experienced in the space of a single second a million thoughts, images, associations of all kinds which exploded in my mind like a grand display of fireworks. But all this, closely related though it is to the emotions, is mere parlor talk.

Poetry is by no means an infirmity of the mind; whereas these nervous susceptibilities are. Extreme sensitivity is a weakness. Let me explain:

If my mind had been stronger, I shouldn't have fallen ill as a result of studying law and being bored. I'd have turned those circumstances to good account instead of being worsted by them. My unhappiness, instead of confining itself to my

---

[1]Alfred de Musset, French writer contemporary with Flaubert.

brain, affected the rest of my body and threw me into convulsions. It was a "deviation." One often sees children whom music hurts physically: they have great talent, retain melodies after but one hearing, become over-excited when they play the piano; their hearts pound, they grow thin and pale and fall ill, and their poor nerves writhe in pain at the sound of notes—like dogs. These are never the future Mozarts. Their vocation has been misplaced: the idea has passed into the flesh, and there it remains sterile and causes the flesh to perish; neither genius nor health results.

It is the same with art. Passion does not make poetry, and the more personal you are, the weaker. I have always sinned in that direction myself, because I have always put myself into what I was doing. Instead of Saint Anthony,[2] for example, *I* am in my book; and I, rather than the reader, underwent the temptation. *The less you feel a thing, the fitter you are to express it as it is* (as it *always* is, in itself, in its essence, freed of all ephemeral contingencies). But you must have the capacity to *make yourself feel it.* This capacity is what we call genius: the ability to *see,* to have your model constantly posing in front of you.

That is why I detest so-called poetic language. When there are no words, a glance is enough. Soulful effusions, lyricism, descriptions—I want all these embodied in Style. To put them elsewhere is to prostitute art and feeling itself.

> *Thursday, 4 A.M., [Croisset, July 22, 1852]*
> I am in the process of copying and correcting the entire first part of *Bovary.* My eyes are smarting. I should like to be able to read these 158 pages at a single glance and grasp them with all their details in a single thought. A week from Sunday I shall read the whole thing to Bouilhet, and a day or two later you will see me. What a bitch of a thing prose is! It is never finished; there is always something to be done over. Still, I think it is possible to give it the consistency of verse. A good prose sentence should be like a good line of poetry—*unchangeable,* just as rhythmic, just as sonorous. Such, at least, is my ambition (I am sure of one thing: no one has ever conceived a more perfect type of prose than I; but as to the execution, how weak, how weak, oh God!). Nor does it seem to me impossible to give psychological analysis[3] the swiftness, clarity, and impetus of a strictly dramatic narrative. That has never been attempted, and it would be beautiful. Have I succeeded a little in this? I

---

[2]The reference is to Flaubert's *Temptations of Saint Anthony*, a magnificent fantasy about the trials of the famous anchorite.
[3]Flaubert refers here to his *Madame Bovary.*

have no idea. At this moment I have no definite opinion about my work.

> *Monday, 1 A.M., [Croisset, July 27, 1852]*

Yes, it is a strange thing, the relation between one's writing and one's personality. Is there anyone more in love with antiquity than I, anyone more haunted by it, anyone who has made a greater effort to understand it? And yet in my books I am as far from antiquity as possible. From my appearance one would think me a writer of epic, drama, brutally factual narrative; whereas actually I feel at home only in analysis—in anatomy, if I may call it such. By natural disposition I love what is vague and misty; and it is only patience and study that have rid me of all the white fat that clogged my muscles. The books I most long to write are precisely those for which I am least endowed. *Bovary,* in this sense, is an unprecedented tour de force (a fact of which I alone shall ever be aware): its subject, characters, effects, etc.— all are alien to me. It should make it possible for me to take a great step forward later. Writing this book I am like a man playing the piano with leaden balls attached to his fingers. But once I have mastered my technique, and find a piece that's to my taste and that I can play at sight, the result will perhaps be good. In my case, I think I am doing the right thing. What one does is not for one's self, but for others. Art is not interested in the personality of the artist. So much the worse for him if he doesn't like red or green or yellow: all colors are beautiful, and his task is to use them. . . .

> *Sunday, 11 P.M., [Croisset, September 19, 1852]*

What trouble my *Bovary* is giving me! Still, I am beginning to see my way a little. Never in my life have I written anything more difficult than what I am doing now—trivial dialogue. . . . I have to portray, simultaneously and in the same conversation, five or six characters who speak, several others who are spoken about, the scene, and the whole town, giving physical descriptions of people and objects; and in the midst of all that I have to show a man and a woman who are beginning (through a similarity in tastes) to fall in love with each other.[4] If only I had space! But the whole thing has to be swift without being dry, and well worked out without taking up too much room; and many details which would be more striking here I have to keep in reserve for use elsewhere. I am going to put the whole thing down quickly, and then proceed by a series of increasingly drastic revisions; by going over and

---

[4]The reference is to the scene of the Agricultural Fair in *Madame Bovary.*

over it I can perhaps pull it together. The language itself is a great stumbling-block. My characters are completely commonplace, but they have to speak in a literary style, and politeness of language takes away so much picturesqueness from any speech!

Night of Friday-Saturday, 2 A.M., [Croisset, October 1-2, 1852]
The other day I learned that a young man I knew at school had been interned at Saint-Yon (the Rouen insane asylum). A year ago I read a book of stupid poems by him; but I was moved by the sincerity, enthusiasm, and faith expressed in the preface. I was told that like me he lived in the country, secluded and working as hard as he could. The bourgeois had the greatest contempt for him. He complained of being constantly slandered and insulted; he suffered the common ordeal of unrecognized geniuses. Eventually he lost his mind, and now he is raving and screaming and treated with cold baths. Who can assure me that I am not on the same path? What is the line of demarcation between inspiration and madness, between stupidity and ecstasy? To be an artist is it not necessary to *see everything* differently from other men? Art is no mere game of the intellect; it is a special atmosphere that we breathe. But if in search of more and more potent air we descend ever deeper into art's subterranean recesses, who knows that we may not end by breathing deadly miasmas? It would make a nice book—the story of a man whose mind is sound (quite possibly my young friend is sane) locked up as insane and treated by stupid doctors.

Sunday, 4 o'clock, Easter Day [Croisset, March 27, 1853]
As for me, the more I realize the difficulties of writing, the more daring I become; this is what keeps me from pedantry, into which I should otherwise doubtless fall. I have plans for writing that will keep me busy till the end of my life, and though I sometimes have moments of bitterness that make me almost scream with rage (so acutely do I feel my own impotence and weakness) I have others when I can scarcely contain myself for joy. Something deep and extra-voluptuous gushes out of me, like an ejaculation of the soul. I feel transported, drunk with my own thought, as though a hot gust of perfume were being wafted to me through some inner conduit. I shall never go very far; I know my limitations. But the goal I have set for myself will be achieved by others: thanks to me someone more talented, more instinctive, will be set on the right path. It is perhaps absurd to want to give prose the rhythm of verse (keeping it distinctly prose, however) and to write of ordinary life as one writes history or epic (but without falsifying the subject). I often wonder about this. But on the other hand

it is perhaps a great experiment, and very original too. I know where I fail. (Ah, if only I were fifteen!) No matter: I shall always be given some credit for my stubbornness. And then, who can tell? Some day I may find a good motif, an air completely suited to my voice, neither too high nor too low. In any case I shall have lived nobly and often delightfully.

There is a saying by La Bruyère that serves me as a guide: "A good author likes to think that he writes sensibly."[5] That is what I ask—to write sensibly; and it is asking a good deal. Still, one thing is depressing, and that is to see how easily the great men achieve their effects by means extraneous to Art. What is more badly put together than much of Rabelais, Cervantes, Molière, and Hugo? But such quick punches! Such power in a single word! We have to pile up a lot of little pebbles to build our pyramids; theirs, a hundred times greater, are made with a single block. But to seek to imitate the method of these geniuses would be fatal. They are great for the very reason that they have no method.

> *Friday night, 1 A.M., [Croisset, July 15, 1853]*
What artists we should be if we had never read, seen, or loved anything that was not beautiful; if from the outset some guardian angel of the purity of our pens had kept us from all contamination; if we had never known fools or read newspapers! The Greeks were like that. . . . But classic form is insufficient for our needs, and our voices are not made to sing such simple tunes. Let us be as dedicated to art as they were, if we can, but differently. The human mind has broadened since Homer. Sancho Panza's belly has burst the seams of Venus' girdle. Rather than persisting in copying old modes we should exert ourselves to invent new ones. I think Leconte de Lisle[6] is unaware of all this. He has no instinct for modern life; he lacks heart. By this I do not mean personal or even humanitarian feelings, no—but *heart*, almost in the medical sense of the word. His ink is pale; his muse suffers from lack of fresh air. Thoroughbred horses and thoroughbred styles have plenty of blood in their veins, and it can be seen pulsing everywhere beneath the skin and the words. Life! Life! . . .That is the only thing that counts! That is why I love lyricism so much. It seems to me the most natural form of poetry—poetry in all its nakedness and freedom. All the power of a work of art lies in this mystery, and it is this primordial quality, this *motus animi continuus* (vibration, continual movement of the mind—Cicero's definition of eloquence), which gives conciseness, distinctness, form, energy, rhythm, diversity. It doesn't require

[5]Seventeenth-century French author and moralist.
[6]French poet, contemporary with Flaubert.

much brains to be a critic: you can judge the excellence of a book by the strength of its punches and the time it takes you to recover from them. And then the excesses of the great masters! They pursue an idea to its furthermost limits. In Molière's *Monsieur de Pourceaugnac* there is a question of giving a man an enema, and a whole troop of actors carrying syringes pour down the aisles of the theatre. Michelangelo's figures have cables rather than muscles; in Rubens' bacchanalian scenes men piss on the ground; and think of everything in Shakespeare, etc., etc., and the most recent representative of the family, old Hugo. What a beautiful thing *Notre-Dame* is! I lately reread three chapters in it, including the sack of the church by the vagabonds. That's the sort of thing that's strong! I think that the greatest characteristic of genius is, above all, *energy*. Hence, what I detest most of all in the arts, what sets me on edge, is the *ingenious*, the clever. This is not at all the same as bad taste, which is a good quality gone wrong. In order to have what is called bad taste, you must have a sense for poetry; whereas cleverness, on the contrary, is incompatible with genuine poetry. Who was cleverer than Voltaire, and who less a poet? In our darling France, the public will accept poetry only if it is disguised. If it is given to them raw they protest. They have to be treated like the horses of Abbas-Pasha, who are fed a tonic of meat balls covered with flour. That's what Art is: knowing how to make the covering! But have no fear: if you offer this kind of flour to lions, they will recognize the smell twenty paces away and spring at it.

READING CRITICALLY FOR IDEAS, STRUCTURE, AND STYLE

1. Flaubert's philosophy of style is so unusual because it departs from conventional views that the artist expresses his or her own personality through the work. What rationale does Flaubert offer for his very opposite view of style?

2. What kind of a relationship did Flaubert have with Louise Colete as far as you can gather from these letters? Was she his confidante, critic, sounding board, best friend, lover?

3. What is Flaubert's attitude toward his novel *Madame Bovary*, and how does it incorporate the qualities he strives to achieve?

EXTENDING INSIGHTS THROUGH WRITING

1. Attempt the kind of stylistic evaluation Flaubert recommends on another selection in this book. Can you find a few sentences that would meet the standards he sets forth in his second letter ("a good prose sentence should be just like a good line of poetry —*unchangable*, just as rhythmic, just as sonorous").

2. Revision is essential in Flaubert's method of writing. How important is it in your own writing? Revise a passage you have recently written so that it possesses the qualities Flaubert praises.

CONNECTING PERSPECTIVES
ON THE ARTS OF CIVILIZATION

1. Compare P. D. Ouspensky's description of the Taj Mahal with Flaubert's discussion of style. In what respect is the best art, whether in writing or architecture, the least personal?

2. In what sense is Flaubert's theory that art should exist separately from the artist the opposite of the relationship of nineteenth-century composers to their music as described by Edward Rothstein?

EDWARD ROTHSTEIN

Why We Live in the Musical Past

BACKGROUND

Edward Rothstein, born in 1952, was the chief music critic for *The New York Times*. Rothstein graduated from Yale University in 1973 and pursued grad-uate studies in mathematics, literature, and philosophy at Brandeis, Columbia, and the University of Chicago. His essays on literature, science, culture, and all aspects of musical history and performance have appeared in the *New York Review of Books*, the *New Republic*, *Vanity Fair*, *Commentary*, the *American Scholar*, *Musical Quarterly*, and the *Washington Post*. His essay, "The Body of Bach," was chosen to appear in *The Best American Essays 1986*. He has also received many awards including the Ingram Merrill Foundation Award in 1990 and a Guggenheim Fellowship in 1991. Rothstein's discussions of how the quality of musical reproduction varies with different kinds of audio technology have also appeared in *The Absolute Sound*. His latest work is *Emblems of Mind: The Inner Life of Music and Mathematics* (1995). "Why We Live in the Musical Past," which originally appeared in *The New York Times* (1982), analyzes the programmatic, narrative, and mythic qualities that define nineteenth-century music. In this article, Rothstein offers a provocative theory as to why twentieth-century concert-goers have an overwhelming preference for nineteenth-century music.

APPROACHING ROTHSTEIN'S ESSAY

Prior to the nineteenth-century, music was written for church services, court performances, wealthy patrons, and folk celebrations. With the rise of the middle-class public, music composed during this century was the first to be specifically written to satisfy the musical tastes of the bourgeoise. The New York Philharmonic, the Metropolitan Opera, the symphony orchestra, the concert hall, and the grand opera all originated, in the form in which we know them today, during the nineteenth century. Thus, in some sense, we all still live in a nineteenth-century musical culture (for example, the most heavily represented composers in the New York Philharmonic concert season [1982] are those from the nineteenth century, such as Beethoven and Brahms).

Nineteenth-century music (characterized by a narrative style or "story" line, elaborate orchestration, and a strong melodic line) appeals to modern audiences for the same reasons it was popular with audiences of the last two centuries. Musical narratives (and the novels written during this time) spoke directly to the emerging middle-class.

Rothstein also explains the desire of twentieth-century audiences to hear nineteenth-century music in the context of Freud's observations, in *Beyond the Pleasure Principle,* where Freud analyzes the desire of children to have stories told to them repeatedly and without alteration. In much the same way, concert goers find reassurance and comfort in hearing works by nineteenth-century composers repeatedly played as the main part of all concert programs. Throughout his essay, Rothstein draws on a wide range of sources including statistics, historical analysis, and theories of anthropologists and psychologists to support his thesis.

Why We Live in the Musical Past

We are living in a most peculiar musical age. Musical life is booming, audiences are growing, seasons are expanding, conservatories are turning out virtuosos. In New York, well over a *hundred* concerts are given every week. There is an extraordinary bustle and whirl in the music world and its accompanying business. But in the midst of all that activity, there is a certain stillness, an immovable center. For our musical life is based upon repetition.

In recent weeks, for example, the New York Philharmonic and the Metropolitan Opera have announced their programs for the coming season. At the Philharmonic, there are, of course, some unusual offerings. A concert performance of Janacek's "From the House of the Dead" is planned as are programs devoted to Shostakovich and to the Polish modern, Witold Lutoslawski—all reflecting growing interest in Slavic and Eastern European composers. There is also a "retrospective" of six compositions by Schoenberg planned, concentrating on his earliest music.

But the repertory of the Philharmonic is actually dominated by familiarly repeated works of the 19th-century musical tradition—including Mozart on one end and a few moderns like Rachmaninoff on the other. Out of the more than 90 compositions the Philharmonic is performing in 125 concerts with more than 35 different programs, only *six* works will be new to New York; *three* of those will be world premieres. The most heavily represented composers are Mozart, with seven works, including four popular piano concertos, and Beethoven with six works, including three familiar symphonies. Brahms is among the next most often scheduled composers, represented by the First Piano Concerto, First Symphony, Violin Concerto and Tragic Overture. Schumann is also heavily represented.

Many of the scheduled works—including Schubert's "Unfinished" Symphony, Mussorgsky's "Pictures at an Exhibition," Tchaikovsky's Fifth Symphony—are the musical equivalents of "best-sellers." Each season they are repeatedly played, if not by the Philharmonic then by another local or visiting orchestra. Apart from such other 19th-century masters as Berlioz, Bruckner, Liszt, Wagner, Strauss and Dvorak, there are a few familiar "modern" works—Barber's "Adagio for Strings," Debussy's "La Mer"—a few selections by other repeated moderns like Elgar, Walton, Sibelius and Bernstein, and a handful of novelties by Carter, Druckman and others.

5   At the Metropolitan Opera, programming is similar. There are new productions of Strauss's "Arabella," Verdi's "Macbeth" and Mozart's "Idomeneo." The acclaimed production of Mussorgsky's "Boris Godunov" will return as will Debussy's "Pelléas et Mélisande" and the "Parade" trilogy, with its ballet and two 20th-century operas. But 12 out of the 21 operatic productions being offered next season—over *half* the repertory—were premiered in the 55 years between 1830 and 1885, five of those are by Verdi. Only *three* works premiered after 1905, one is the familiar "Der Rosenkavalier."

The seasons of both the Met and the Philharmonic, then, are intensely focussed on the 19th-century repertory. That policy is a resounding success: halls are filled to over 90 percent of capacity; at least 12,000 seats are filled at the four weekly Philharmonic concerts; more than 25,000 tickets are sold to the seven weekly Met performances. This programming speaks for the tastes of the musical mainstream.

Elsewhere, the same repertory is also repeated by popular demand. The Mostly Mozart Festival will soon return as well, with its repetitive festivities. The massive replays and Romantic music, occasionally interrupted by a new or recent work, have become an accepted part of the musical scene.

But as we know, in previous centuries new works were the rule and not the exception. Bach had a new cantata ready every Sunday, Mozart composed new concertos for his important appearances. 19th-century concert halls and opera houses thrived on premieres. Something changed in this century. The repertory congealed. Our institutions have become repetitive museums.

There is, of course, repetition in the other arts as well. But only in music is the new so sweepingly rejected and the old so worshipfully celebrated. New plays are at the heart of every theater season, new paintings appear on living room walls with insouciant ease, fiction is read hot off the presses. To get an idea of the peculiarity of our musical life, imagine most movie theaters as re-run houses; imagine if most publishers specialized in Dickens and Thackeray.

Still more peculiar is the restricted historical range of our musical   10
life. The 19th-century supplies nearly all of our repertory. For most audiences, the Baroque era is worth only an occasional visit, the Renaissance
is a novelty, the Middle Ages an eccentricity.

Of course, the 19th-century repertory is a great achievement of
Western European culture; it is extraordinarily profound and exciting,
worthy of living with, not just listening to. Given its immense riches many
listeners hardly will risk an evening on a third-rate new composition. The
repetitive musical culture has, in fact, been attributed to a failure of contemporary composition. Other explanations blame the lack of adventur-
ous listeners, the stodgy institutions, the commercialization of classical
music or the stagnation of the recording industry.

Each of these explanations has some validity. But they reduce an
exceedingly complex cultural phenomenon to matters of taste and commerce. They do not explain why repetition has become so extensive in its
own right, and why those repetitions should be so exclusively centered
upon the 19th-century tradition.

We do not, for example, turn to this repertory simply because the
"new" is unappreciated; in fact, for most audiences, the "new" is unnecessary. The 19th century satisfies our musical needs; it has a special meaning.
This is not just because 19th-century music is "great" or has beautiful
melodies—the melodies of the Renaissance are just as beautiful, largely
unperformed early music just as "great." The point is that the 19th-centu-
ry has actually come to *define* our ideas of what music should be. The
Philharmonic and the Metropolitan Opera were founded in the 19th-cen-
tury; the symphony orchestra, the concert hall and grand opera have their
origins in the same period. We live in a 19th-century musical culture.

Why then, is this music so tirelessly repeated? There are the obvious
reasons—because it is pleasurable, rewarding, beautiful. But our repetitions are also similar to the demands made in childhood, demands to hear
a story told again and again; such demands are echoed in many of the
repetitions of culture and religion.

As children we did not ask for retellings in order to learn more; we   15
simply wanted to hear tales told again. Children ask to hear the stories
they know the best, stories they know so well, they could easily tell them
themselves.

Sigmund Freud referred to the "child's peculiar pleasure in constant
repetition." In *Beyond the Pleasure Principle*, he writes: "If a child has been
told a nice story, he will insist on hearing it over and over again rather
than a new one; and he will remorselessly stipulate that the repetition
shall be an identical one and will correct any alterations of which the narrator may be guilty."

Of course, contemporary musical audiences are not merely children
listening to papa composers tell stories. But the requests are similar; certain works are selected as "favorites"—Beethoven's Fifth Symphony,
Chopin's Waltzes, Verdi's "La Traviata." These are known best, demanded
most and varied least. Recordings also offer musical tales in precise, unaltered repetitions.

Freud linked compulsions to repeat to the nature of instinct—the effort "to restore an earlier state of things." Repetition of a story, in this view, involves an attempt to comprehend or restore a dramatic or psychological situation contained within the tale.

Both Bruno Bettelheim and Erich Fromm have continued this argument, demonstrating that stories contain conflicts and situations which the child is attempting to master or understand. In "Hansel and Gretel," for example, a struggle with parental figures is enacted in the children's exile from home and their overcoming of the witch. Particular moments are always psychologically significant to a child—when the prince rescues the sleeping beauty, when the wolf in grandma's clothing bares his teeth. "Tell it to me again," says the child, "the part where. . . ." Psychologists remind us: the child is never just listening to a story; he is dreaming of his own life.

20   The story involves not just fantasy, but the real world of parents, authority, conflict; that is why children prefer that stories be told by a parent instead of read in a book or recited by a friend. It may be that our repeated listening to music involves a similar state-of-mind. "Play it again," say our concert audiences, "the Beethoven 'Emperor'." We reflect on psychological or social situations embodied in the music, which take on additional power when told in their social setting, the concert hall.

What is special about our chosen repertory? First of all, 19th-century music really is written in the form of a story, with elaborate narrative programs. While programs in Baroque repertory centered on *images,* such as the warbling of a bird, Romantic and late Classical programs allude to narrative *journeys,* invoking Faust, Shakespeare, literary adventures.

These programs are supported by a narrative musical style. In a Baroque fugue, basic thematic material is an unchanged part of a complex musical architecture; but the dominant musical forms of our repertory treat a theme as if it were a character in a novel, subject to events which affect is character, until it is restored, transformed, all tensions resolved. Early sonatas by Haydn, for example, with their surprising wit and dramatic character can be compared to picaresque novels or opera buffa; later sonatas, by Lizst or Brahms, with their passionate mediations, can be compared to the Romantic confessional literature.

That is why we treat these works as stories and listen with rapt attention. If we also respond so strongly, it is because of their meanings. Music after early Classicism was not written for a patron, a court performance, church service or folk celebration; it was the first music written for "the public"—the new middle class—to be heard in concert halls. These musical narratives are similar to the novel which came to maturity in the same period. The novels of Austen, Dickens, or George Eliot were precisely observed tales about the social order and the willful individual, about the middle-class public and its ambitious, desirous and reflective citizens. Musical narratives by middle-class composers have the same spirit.

The symphonic repertory is suffused with psychological detail and epic tension, with encounters between public order (massive blocks of sound, regular harmonics, sturdy resolutions) and more unstable private passions (surprising dissonances, melancholy melodies, rhythmic disruption). These conflicts are the themes of grand opera as well. In "Don-Carlo," an individual's desires threaten the social and familial order; in "Macbeth," ambition does the same. The heroic Siegried is the savior and destroyer of the order of the gods. In grand opera, stable social hierarchies are threatened by the hero's yearning, or (as in "Carmen") by a woman outside the social order who inspires troubling desires and ambitions.

These were then, forms of bourgeois theater that spoke directly to   25
the new public. The 19th-century concerto, with its heroic soloist pitted against a grand orchestral order, can be almost Dickensian in its melodramatic confrontations and coincidences. The charismatic conductor binding the orchestra into a single society, and the flamboyant virtuoso, victoriously braving instrumental dangers, embody the dreams of the middle-class.

Music has always been written for a specific audience. The music of the 19th-century was directed at the bourgeoisie. Even today, a century later, we treasure these tales; our audience is still the middle-class. As children do with resonant stories, we demand the repetition of this music, attempting to savor and master its situations and resolutions.

But this music is more than just social adventure. The anthropologist Claude Lévi-Strauss has suggested that this repertory has a *mythological* function in society.

In "Myth and Meaning," Mr. Lévi Strauss asserts that after the 16th-century, myth receded in importance; the novel and music took its place. "The music that took over the traditional function of mythology," he argues, "reached its full development with Mozart, Beethoven, and Wagner in the 18th and 19th centuries."

One function of myth, in Mr. Lévi-Strauss's view, is to show how a culture's customs of marriage, government or economy are related to more universal natural forces. Prometheus brings fire from the gods; Moses brings down laws from Mt. Sinai; medicine, in many myths, is taught to man by animals. In his musical analogy the anthropologist suggests that our repertory serves this mythological function: it dramatizes how bourgeois society is connected to the primal forces which lie outside it.

In opera, this was, in fact a major theme, not just in Wagner's overtly   30
mythic "Ring." Again and again, opera shows the social order both animated and threatened by primal passions. The bourgeois family, for example, is one arena for mythic tensions. Carmen—a gypsy on the outskirts of the social order—seduces the soldier away from familial responsibilities; in "Il Trovatore," another gypsy steals a child from an aristocratic father; in "La Traviata," the "fallen woman" is a threat to Germont, the bourgeois father; in "Robert le Diable" the father is the devil himself.

Similar concerns with irrational forces lying behind a rational order can be heard throughout the symphonic music of the 19th-century. The figure of the devil in 19th-century music is just one example of the music's mythic concerns—in Berlioz's "Symphonie Fantastique," in Liszt's "Faust" and "Mephisto." Even the "virtuoso"—a favorite 19th-century persona—was a figure with frightening powers from outside the musical and social order; Paganini was considered demonic.

So when we listen to this repertory with as much avidity and passion as we do, it is not merely because it is "great." The foundations of contemporary society lie in the 19th-century; we share its mythology. Even today, musical myths speak with authority about our rational bourgeois society, its fragility and its strengths.

The mythological nature of the repertory also provides insight into our musical repetitions. Mircea Eliade, a historian of religion, has explained that in ancient cultures, myths are connected with ritualist repetitions. Even in contemporary religion, for example, the ritual of Mass regularly enacts the myth of the Eucharist, Sabbath rituals regularly recall the myth of God's rest after the Creation. Through these repetitions, societies act "to regenerate themselves periodically."

This is precisely what happens in our secular musical world. If 19th-century music has the function of myth in our society, the concert hall is a cross between a theater and a temple. The concert has the airs of a repeated ritual, communally celebrated in our modern religion of high art. The musical myths, telling of our social origins and our connections with primal forces, are told and retold.

35   The "great" 19th-century composer himself becomes a mythic figure in these rituals. The heroes of myth, Mr. Eliade points out, are not just individuals who lived at a particular time and place; they are representative of primal forces. Moses and Jesus and Mohammed, in the mythologies of three religions, speak for the divine realm. So too with Mozart, Beethoven, Wagner; no matter how program notes describe their lives or surroundings, we treat the music as if it derived from a transcendental source. In Peter Shaffer's Broadway play "Amadeus," this split between music and the historical individual is taken as self-evident: Mozart is crude and awful; his music is magical, a revelation.

Musically, then, we have turned these "great" composers into a pantheon of gods who lived at the beginning of our musical age. They stand outside of history, delivering regenerative messages from the musical beyond. And we honor their messages with unstinting devotion at every concert. When we repeat these myths we invoke our gods and celebrate our mythological past, regenerating ourselves with the concert ritual.

Of course, nuances and qualifications have to be added to these speculations about myth and story in the 19th-century; Mozart, for example, needs slightly different treatment. Clearly, the art works of a century cannot be treated only with sweeping abstractions. But in repeating this repertory with such regularity, we have already acknowledged its shared meanings. The expansion of middle-class audiences in recent decades has solidified the repertory's secure position.

Meanwhile the 19th-century forms of grand opera and symphony orchestra remain alien to the mainstream of contemporary expression. Music has moved on to other things, alienated and private statements, complex illuminations, attempts to recreate ritual in the repetitions of Minimalism. The middle-class is no longer its subject or its audience.

So our repetitions of 19th-century repertory have a darker, more disturbing side. On a vast scale, we mythologize the 19th-century. We anxiously savor music at its most heroic moment, before it went awry with the beginnings of modernism. We attempt, perhaps, to "restore an earlier state of things." We define what music should be by repeating the works of a single European century. Like myths, these works give our origins; like fairy tales, they offer us promises. But there is something in the present that they miss; they do not show us the future.

READING CRITICALLY FOR IDEAS, STRUCTURE, AND STYLE

1. What qualities define nineteenth-century music? In Rothstein's view, how does it differ from the kind of music written previously?

2. What evidence does Rothstein offer to document its popularity in the twentieth century?

3. What kinds of theories does Rothstein propose to explain why music written in the nineteenth century appeals so greatly to modern audiences? How does he use evidence drawn from psychology, anthropology, and comparative mythology to support his thesis?

EXTENDING INSIGHTS THROUGH WRITING

1. After listening to some musical works by nineteenth-century composers, evaluate Rothstein's thesis and draw your own conclusions. Some of these musical forms and works that you might choose were developed by Wagner (music as drama), Liszt (symphonic tone poems), Brahms (art songs or *lieder* and symphonies), Schubert (songs and symphonies), Strauss (waltzes and symphonic poems), Tchaikovsky (symphonies and ballets), and Berlioz (program music in symphonic form).

2. Now that we are in the twenty-first century, what twentieth-century composers have begun to be viewed in the same way as the nineteenth-century ones discussed by Rothstein (for example, Gershwin's *Rhapsody in Blue* is now considered a staple in concerts). What stories do these modern works express that appeal to audiences today?

CONNECTING PERSPECTIVES
ON THE ARTS OF CIVILIZATION

1. Although he didn't think of himself as an artist in the grand tradition of the nineteenth century, Gustav Flaubert has come to be viewed this way (see "Letters to Louise Colete"). After reading Rothstein's essay, discuss whether we do the same thing for works of literature written in the nineteenth century that we did for its music. In your opinion, are these "classics" really better or just simply older and more familiar?

2. How does nineteenth-century music rely on a conflict between orchestra and soloist in much the same way as *montage,* according to Sergei Eisenstein (see "The Cinematographic Principle and the Ideogram"), relies on visual conflicts to tell its story in films?

SERGEI EISENSTEIN

The Cinematographic Principle and the Ideogram

BACKGROUND

Sergei Eisenstein (1898–1948), the Russian film director and motion picture theorist, was born in Riga, Latvia. Before the Russian Revolution in 1917, he attended the Institute of Civil Engineering in Petrograd. After the fall of the Czar, he was an engineer in the Red Army and joined the Moscow Proletkult Theater, first as a set designer and later as a director. He was influenced by the theories of Vsevolod Meyerhold, whose concept of "biomechanics" led Eisenstein to formulate his theory of a "montage of attractions." This refers to the practice of quick-cutting or juxtaposition of images to create an emotional response in the viewer. Prior to this, movies were simply filmed versions of stage plays: The camera remained fixed and only the actors moved. He perfected this technique of *montage* in his pioneering films, *Strike* (1924), *The Battleship Potemkin* (1925), and *Alexander Nevsky* (1938). Eisenstein was a supporter of the Communist revolution in its early stages and filmmaking for him was a form of political statement; he even theorized that *montage* was the cinematic equivalent of Marxist dialectic (thesis, antithesis, synthesis). Ironically, he was increasingly subject to harrassment by the authorities and became a victim of Stalin's purges along with millions of ordinary citizens. In the following essay from *Film Form* (1949), edited and translated by Jay Leyda, Eisenstein elaborates his theory of *montage* and explains its connection to the Japanese methods of teaching drawing.

APPROACHING EISENSTEIN'S ESSAY

Eisenstein's revolutionary concept of *montage*—or the technique of film editing in which several contrasting shots or sequences are juxtaposed to present an idea or to create an emotional response—fundamentally changed the way motion pictures were made. For Eisenstein, *montage* was a way to reach the common man in much the same way as the mosaics and stained glass windows in St. Mark's Cathedral in Venice (as discussed by John Ruskin earlier in this chapter) could teach biblical stories to the illiterate. A good example of *montage* is the famous scene in *The Battleship Potemkin* where a baby carriage rolls down the Odessa steps out of control with a cross-cut shot of apprehensive onlookers standing helplessly by while the battleship races to save the citizens. This scene has been alluded to in countless movies, including a scene in *The Untouchables* (1987) directed by Brian De Palma that starred Kevin Costner. In 1998, the Russian government issued coins commemorating the 100th anniversary of Eisenstein's birth with his image on one side and the "Battleship Potemkin" on the other. This essay was originally published as an afterword to a pamphlet *Japanese Cinema* in Moscow, in 1929, and relates Eisenstein's own theories of cinematic montgage to the stylistic pictures or ideograms characteristic of Japanese drawing and writing. He equates these to hieroglyphs (not unlike the ones Howard Carter found in the tomb of Tutankhamen described in "Finding the Tomb" in Chapter 3) as examples of images that function as *montage* before cinema existed. Since conflicting or contrasting images are the essence of *montage,* Eisenstein explains some of the many different kinds of cinematic conflict that the film director has at his or her disposal. The form in which these observations appear is not an essay as such but is similar to the notes that Eisenstein jotted down for his own use.

The Cinematographic Principle and the Ideogram

IT IS a weird and wonderful feat to have written a pamphlet on something that in reality does not exist. There is, for example, no such thing as a cinema without cinematography. And yet the author of the pamphlet preceding this essay[*] has contrived to write a book about the *cinema* of a country that has no *cinematography*. About the cinema of a country that has, in its culture, an infinite number of cinematographic traits, strewn everywhere with the sole exception of—its cinema.

This essay is on the cinematographic traits of Japanese culture that lie outside the Japanese cinema. . . .

Cinema is: so many corporations, such and such turnovers of capital, so and so many stars, such and such drams.

Cinematography is, first and foremost, montage.[1]

---

[*]Eisenstein's essay was originally published as an "afterword" to N. Kaufman's pamphlet, *Japanese Cinema* (Moscow, 1929).
[1]This term is explained fully in the essay.

The Japanese cinema is excellently equipped with corporations, ac-   5
tors, and stories. But the Japanese cinema is completely unaware of montage. Nevertheless the principle of montage can be identified as the basic
element of Japanese representational culture.

Writing—for their writing is primarily representational.

The hieroglyph.

The naturalistic image of an object, as portrayed by the skilful Chinese
hand of Ts'ang Chieh 2650 years before our era, becomes slightly formalized
and, with its 539 fellows, forms the first "contingent" of hieroglyphs.
Scratched out with a stylus on a slip of bamboo, the portrait of an object
maintained a resemblance to its original in every respect.

But then, by the end of the third century, the brush is invented. In
the first century after the "joyous event" (A.D.)—paper. And, lastly, in the
year 220— India ink.

A complete upheaval. A revolution in draughtsmanship. And, after   10
having undergone in the course of history no fewer than fourteen different
styles of handwriting, the hieroglyph crystallized in its present form. The
means of production (brush and India ink) determined the form.

The fourteen reforms had their way. As a result:

In the fierily cavorting hieroglyph *ma* (a horse) it is already impossible to recognize the features of the dear little horse sagging pathetically in
its hindquarters, in the writing style of Ts'ang Chieh, so well-known from
ancient Chinese bronzes.

But let it rest in the Lord, this dear little horse, together with the
other *607* remaining *hsiang cheng* symbols—the earliest extant category
of hieroglyphs.

The real interest begins with the second category of hieroglyphs—the
huei-i, i.e., "copulative."

The point is that the copulation (perhaps we had better say, the com-   15
bination) of two hieroglyphs of the simplest series is to be regarded not as
their sum, but as their product, i.e., as a value of another dimension, another degree; each, separately, corresponds to an *object,* to a fact, but
their combination corresponds to a *concept.* From separate hieroglyphs

has been fused—the ideogram. By the combination of two "depictables" is achieved the representation of something that is graphically undepictable.

For example: the picture for water and the picture of an eye signifies "to weep"; the picture of an ear near the drawing of a door = "to listen";

a dog + a mouth = "to bark";

a mouth + a child = "to scream";

a mouth + a bird = "to sing";

a knife + a heart = "sorrow," and so on.

But this is—montage!

Yes. It is exactly what we do in the cinema, combining shots that are *depictive*, single in meaning, neutral in content—into *intellectual* contexts and series.

This is a means and method inevitable in any cinematographic exposition. And, in a condensed and purified form, the starting point for the "intellectual cinema."

For a cinema seeking a maximum laconism[2] for the visual representation of abstract concepts.

And we hail the method of the long-lamented Ts'ang Chieh as a first step along these paths.

We have mentioned laconism. Laconism furnishes us a transition to another point. Japan possesses the most laconic form of poetry: the *haikai* (appearing at the beginning of the thirteenth century and known today as "haiku" or "hokku") and the even earlier *tanka* (mythologically assumed to have been created along with heaven and earth).

Both are little more than hieroglyphs transposed into phrases. . . .

As the ideogram provides a means for the laconic imprinting of an abstract concept, the same method, when transposed into literary exposition, gives rise to an identical laconism of pointed imagery. . . .

But let us turn to examples.

The *haiku* is a concentrated impressionist sketch:

> A lonely crow
> On leafless bough,
> One autumn eve.
>
> BASHŌ[3]

> What a resplendent moon!
> It casts the shadow of pine boughs
> Upon the mats.
>
> KIKAKU

> An evening breeze blows.
> The water ripples
> Against the blue heron's legs.
>
> BUSON

[2]Originally referring to the speech of the ancient Laconians (Spartans), the word means a short, concise, condensed form of utterance; it is more familiar in its adjectival form, "laconic."

[3]Bashō, Kikaku, etc., are the names of the poets who composed these *haiku*.

It is early dawn.
The castle is surrounded
By the cries of wild ducks.

KYOROKU

The earlier *tanka* is slightly longer (by two lines):

O mountain pheasant
long are the feathers trail'st thou
on the wooded hill-side—as
long the nights seem to me
on lonely couch sleep seeking.

HITOMARO[?]

From our point of view, these are montage phrases. Shot lists.[4] The simple combination of two or three details of a material kind yields a perfectly finished representation of another kind—psychological. . . .

We should observe that the emotion is directed towards the reader, for, as Yone Noguchi has said, "it is the readers who make the *haiku's* imperfection a perfection of art."

Exactly the same method (in its depictive aspect) operates also in the most perfect examples of Japanese pictorial art.

Sharaku—creator of the finest prints of the eighteenth century, and especially of an immortal gallery of actors' portraits. The Japanese Daumier.[5] Despite this, almost unknown to us. The characteristic traits of his work have been analyzed only in our century. One of these critics, Julius Kurth, in discussing the question of the influence on Sharaku of sculpture, draws a parallel between his wood-cut portrait of the actor Nakayama Tomisaburō and an antique mask of the semi-religious Nō theater, the mask of a Rozo.

30

[4]The word "shot" is used in the photographic sense.
[5]Nineteenth-century French caricaturist.

The faces of both the print and the mask wear an *identical expres-sion.* . . . Features and masses are similarly arranged although the mask represents an old priest, and the print a young woman. This relationship is striking, yet these two works are otherwise totally dissimilar; this in itself is a demonstration of Sharaku's originality. While the carved mask was constructed according to fairly accurate anatomical proportions, the proportions of the portrait print are simply impossible. The space between the eyes comprises a width that makes mock of all good sense. The nose is almost twice as long in relation to the eyes as any normal nose would dare to be, and the chin stands in no sort of relation to the mouth; the brows, the mouth, and every feature—is hopelessly misrelated. *This observation may be made in all the large heads by Sharaku.* That the artist was unaware that all these proportions are false is, of course, out of the question. It was with a full awareness that he repudiated normalcy, and, while the drawing of the separate features depends on severely concentrated naturalism, their proportions have been subordinated to purely intellectual considerations. *He set up the essence of the psychic expression as the norm for the proportions of the single features.*

Is not this process that of the ideogram, combining the independent "mouth" and the dissociated symbol of "child" to form the significance of "scream"?

Is this not exactly what we of the cinema do temporally, just as Sharaku in simultaneity, when we cause a monstrous disproportion of the parts of a normally flowing event, and suddenly dismember the event into "close-up of clutching hands," "medium shots of the struggle," and "extreme close-up of bulging eyes," in making a montage disintegration of the event in various planes? In making an eye twice as large as a man's full figure?! By combining these monstrous incongruities we newly collect the disintegrated event into one whole, but in *our* aspect. According to the treatment of our relation to the event.

The disproportionate depiction of an event is organically natural to us from the beginning. Professor Luriya, of the Psychological Institute in Moscow, has shown me a drawing by a child of "lighting a stove." Everything is represented in passably accurate relationship and with great care. Firewood. Stove. Chimney. But what are those zigzags in that huge central rectangle? They turn out to be—matches. Taking into account the crucial importance of these matches for the depicted process, the child provides a proper scale for them. . . .**

***It is possible to trace this particular tendency from its ancient, almost pre-historical source (". . .in all ideational art, objects are given size according to their importance, the king being twice as large as his subjects, or a tree half the size of a man when it merely informs us that the scene is out-of-doors. Something of this principle of size according to significance persisted in the Chinese tradition. The favorite disciple of Confucius looked like a little boy beside him and the most important figure in any group was usually the largest.") through the highest development of Chinese art, parent of Japanese graphic arts: ". . . natural scale always had to bow to pictorial scale . . . size according to distance never followed the laws of geometric perspective but the needs of the design. Foreground features might be diminished to avoid obstruction and overemphasis, and far distant objects, which were too minute to count pictorially, might be enlarged to act as a counterpoint to the middle distance or foreground." [Author's note.]

Both in painting and sculpture there is a periodic and invariable re-   35
turn to periods of the establishment of absolutism. Displacing the expres-
siveness of archaic disproportion for regulated "stone tables" of officially
decreed harmony.

Absolute realism is by no means the correct form of perception. It is
simply the function of a certain form of social structure. Following a state
monarchy, a state uniformity of thought is implanted. Ideological uniformity of a sort that can be developed pictorially in the ranks of colors and
designs of the Guards regiments. . . .

A shot. A single piece of celluloid. A tiny rectangular frame in which
there is, organized in some way, a piece of an event. . . .

The shot is a montage *cell.*

Just as cells in their division form a phenomenon of another order,
the organism or embryo, so, on the other side of the dialectical leap from
the shot, there is montage.

By what, then, is montage characterized and, consequently, its cell—   40
the shot?

By collision. By the conflict of two pieces in opposition to each other.
By conflict. By collision. . . .

As the basis of every art is conflict (an "imagist" transformation of
the dialectical principle). The shot appears as the *cell* of montage. Therefore it also must be considered from the viewpoint of *conflict.*

Conflict within the shot is potential montage, in the development of
its intensity shattering the quadrilateral cage of the shot and exploding its
conflict into montage impulses *between* the montage pieces. . . .

If montage is to be compared with something, then a phalanx of
montage pieces, of shots, should be compared to the series of explosions
of an internal combustion engine, driving forward its automobile or trac-
tor: for similarly, the dynamics of montage serve as impulses driving forward the total film.

Conflict within the frame. . . .
Conflict of graphic directions.
(Lines—either static or dynamic)

Conflict of scales.
Conflict of volumes.
Conflict of masses.
(Volumes filled with various intensities of light)
Conflict of depths.
Close shots and long shots.
Pieces of darkness and pieces of lightness.
And, lastly, there are such unexpected conflicts as:
*Conflicts between an object and its dimension—and conflicts between an
event and its duration.*

These may sound strange, but both are familiar to us. The first is ac-   45
complished by an optically distorted lens, and the second by stop-motion
or slow-motion. . . .

Whereas we know a good deal about montage, in the theory of the shot we are still floundering about amidst the most academic attitudes, some vague tentatives, and the sort of harsh radicalism that sets one's teeth on edge.

To regard the frame as a particular, as it were, molecular case of montage makes possible the direct application of montage practice to the theory of the shot.

And similarly with the theory of lighting. To sense this as a collision between a stream of light and an obstacle, like the impact of a stream from a fire-hose striking a concrete object, or of the wind buffeting a human figure, must result in a usage of light entirely different in comprehension from that employed in playing with various combinations of "gauzes" and "spots."

Thus far we have one such significant principle of conflict: *the principle of optical counterpoint.*

50   And let us not now forget that soon we shall face another and less simple problem in counterpoint: *the conflict in the sound film of acoustics and optics.*

Let us return to one of the most fascinating of optical conflicts: the conflict between the frame of the shot and the object. . . .

And once again we are in Japan! For the cinematographic method is used in teaching drawing in Japanese schools.

What is our method of teaching drawing? Take any piece of white paper with four corners to it. Then cram onto it, usually even without using the edges (mostly greasy from the long drudgery!), some bored caryatid, some conceited Corinthian capital, or a plaster Dante.

The Japanese approach this from a quite different direction: Here's the branch of a cherry-tree. And the pupil cuts out from this whole, with a square, and a circle, and a rectangle—compositional units:

55   He frames a shot!

These two ways of teaching drawing can characterize the two basic tendencies struggling within the cinema of today. One—the expiring method of artificial spatial organization of an event in front of the lens. . . .

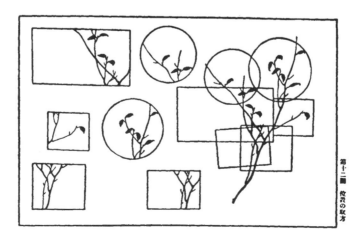

The other—a "picking-out" by the camera: organization by means of the camera. Hewing out a piece of actuality with the ax of the lens. . . .

Let us turn back to the question of methods of montage in the Japanese theater, particularly in acting.

The first and most striking example, of course, is the purely cinematographic method of "acting without transitions." Along with mimic transitions carried to a limit of refinement, the Japanese actor uses an exactly contrary method as well. At a certain moment of his performance he halts; the black-shrouded *kurogo* obligingly conceals him from the spectators. And lo! —he is resurrected in a new make-up. And in a new wig. Now characterizing another stage (degree) of his emotional state.

Thus, for example, in the Kabuki play *Narukami*, the actor Sadanji   60
must change from drunkenness to madness. This transition is solved by a mechanical cut. And a change in the arsenal of grease-paint colors on his face, emphasizing those streaks whose duty it is to fulfill the expression of a higher intensity than those used in his previous make-up.

This method is organic to the film. The forced introduction into the film, by European acting traditions, of pieces of "emotional transitions" is yet another influence forcing the cinema to mark time. Whereas the method of "cut" acting makes possible the construction of entirely new methods. Replacing one changing face with a whole scale of facial types of varying moods affords a far more acutely expressive result than does the changing surface, too receptive and devoid of organic resistance, of any single professional actor's face.

In our new film [*Old and New*] I have eliminated the intervals between the sharply contrasting polar stages of a face's expression. . . . Here the psychological process of mingled faith and doubt is broken up into its two extreme states of joy (confidence) and gloom (disillusionment). Furthermore, this is sharply emphasized by light—illumination in no wise conforming to actual light conditions. This brings a distinct strengthening of the tension.

Another remarkable characteristic of the Kabuki theater is the principle of "disintegrated" acting. Shocho, who played the leading female rôles in the Kabuki theater that visited Moscow, in depicting the dying daughter in *Yashaō (The Mask-Maker)*, performed his rôle in pieces of acting completely detached from each other: Acting with only the right arm. Acting with one leg. Acting with the neck and head only. (The whole process of the death agony was disintegrated into solo performances of each member playing its own rôle: the rôle of the leg, the rôle of the arms, the rôle of the head.) A breaking-up into shots. With a gradual shortening of these separate, successive pieces of acting as the tragic end approached. . . .

So, it has been possible to establish (cursorily) the permeation of the most varied branches of Japanese culture by a pure cinematographic element—its basic nerve, montage. . . .

Instead of learning how to extract the principles and technique of   65
their remarkable acting from the traditional feudal forms of their materials, the most progressive leaders of the Japanese theater throw their energies

into an adaptation of the spongy shapelessness of our own "inner" naturalism. The results are tearful and saddening. In its cinema Japan similarly pursues imitations of the most revolting examples of American and European entries in the international commercial film race.

To understand and apply her cultural peculiarities to the cinema, this is the task of Japan! Colleagues of Japan, are you really going to leave this for us to do?

READING CRITICALLY FOR IDEAS, STRUCTURE, AND STYLE

1. How does *montage* enable the film director to link shots together to form symbolic associations in order to express the filmmaker's message?

2. What connections does Eisenstein draw between *montage* and different aspects of Asian art forms and culture? What analogy does Eisenstein draw between his concept of cinematography and Japanese art forms such as *haiki* and *kabuki* theater?

3. What aspects of Eisenstein's article make it clear that he intends his new technique to have a political application quite different from the way movies are made in decadent Western cultures?

EXTENDING INSIGHTS THROUGH WRITING

1. The case might be made that most Internet web sites are at the stage movies were before Eisenstein thought of a creative way to cross-cut images to tell a story? Are you aware of web sites that are on the cutting edge and go beyond the documents-on-paper paradigm? Describe one of these and explain how *montage* functions in this web site.

2. Rent one of Eisenstein's movies and slow the shots down so that you can describe the collisions, contrasts, and conflicts in adjacent cuts and how they are edited so as to create an emotional response. Alternatively, you might rent Alfred Hitchcock's 1965 film *Psycho* and study the classic shower scene for a masterful example of *montage* (in which the knife never actually strikes the character played by actress Janet Leigh).

CONNECTING PERSPECTIVES
ON THE ARTS OF CIVILIZATION

1. How does *montage* make it possible to communicate a story that someone who cannot read or write can understand in the same way as the mosaics function in St. Mark's Cathedral, as discussed by John Ruskin in "The Stones of St. Mark's"?

2. Both Eisenstein and John Berger (in "Ways of Seeing") criticize Western culture and its commercial art forms from a Marxist perspective. Compare Berger's analysis of how modern ads "quote" the language of oil paintings and the paintings themselves to sell products with Eisenstein's conception of *montage*. Is "quoting" actually another form of *montage?* why or why not?

AGNES DE MILLE

Pavlova

BACKGROUND

Agnes De Mille (1908–1993), a principal figure in American dance, was born in New York city. She created distinctive American ballets, such as *Rodeo* (1942) and Tally-Ho (1944), and brought her talents as an innovative chore-ographer to *Oklahoma!* (1943 and 1980), *Carousel* (1945), *Brigadoon* (1947), *Paint Your Wagon* (1951), *Gentlemen Prefer Blondes* (1949), and other musicals. De Mille's entertaining autobiographies, *Dance to the Piper* (1952) and *Reprieve: A Memoir* (1981) describe many exciting moments in her life. "Pavlova," from *Dance to the Piper,* contains De Mille's recollection of what she felt when she saw Anna Pavlova, the famed Russian ballerina, for the first time.

APPROACHING DE MILLE'S ESSAY

Pavlova's performance left a deep, spiritual impression on the young Agnes De Mille that inspired her to reach the highest goals in her own career. For De Mille, the performance as an "unworldly experience" made her lose forever her "irresponsibility" and created an intense yearning to achieve the kind of beauty and passion in dance as Pavlova had done. Pavlova's performance became "the vision and the impulse and the goal," and served as a catalyst for De Mille's desire to achieve excellence in the field of dance. The reader gains the impression that De Mille saw Pavlova as an almost superhuman figure, bird-like, having an energy of her own that enabled her to almost seem to fly. As Pavlova dances, the reader envisions her as a bird flying and "flashing" through the air. Pavlova's dance is as breathtaking and as beautiful as a bird in flight, an impression De Mille reinforces with images which make the reader see Pavlova as almost belonging to another species.

Pavlova

Anna Pavlova! My life stops as I write that name. Across the daily preoccupation of lessons, lunch boxes, tooth brushings and quarrelings with Margaret flashed this bright, unworldly experience and burned in a single afternoon a path over which I could never retrace my steps. I had witnessed the power of beauty, and in some chamber of my heart I lost forever my irresponsibility. I was as clearly marked as though she had looked me in the face and called my name. For generations my father's family had loved and served the theater. All my life I had seen actors and actresses and had heard theater jargon at the dinner table and business talk of box-office grosses. I had thrilled at Father's projects and watched fascinated his picturesque occupations. I took a proprietary pride in the profitable and hasty growth of "The Industry." But nothing in his world or my uncle's prepared me for theater as I saw it that Saturday afternoon.

Since that day I have gained some knowledge in my trade and I recognize that her technique was limited; that her arabesques were not as pure or classically correct as Markova's, that her jumps and batterie were paltry, her turns not to be compared in strength and number with the strenuous durability of Baronova or Toumanova. I know that her scenery was designed by second-rate artists, her music was on a level with restaurant orchestrations, her company definitely inferior to all the standards we insist on today, and her choreography mostly hack. And yet I say that she was in her person the quintessence of theatrical excitement.

As her little bird body revealed itself on the scene, either immobile in trembling mystery or tense in the incredible arc which was her lift, her instep stretched ahead in an arch never before seen, the tiny bones of her hands in ceaseless vibration, her face radiant, diamonds glittering under her dark hair, her little waist encased in silk, the great tutu balancing, quickening and flashing over her beating, flashing, quivering legs, every man and woman sat forward, every pulse quickened. She never appeared to rest static, some part of her trembled, vibrated, beat like a heart. Before our dazzled eyes, she flashed with the sudden sweetness of a hummingbird in action too quick for understanding by our gross utilitarian standards, in action sensed rather than seen. The movie cameras of her day could not record her allegro. Her feet and hands photographed as a blur.

Bright little bird bones, delicate bird sinews! She was all fire and steel wire. There was not an ounce of spare flesh on her skeleton, and the life force used and used her body until she died of the fever of moving, gasping for breath, much too young.

She was small, about five feet. She wore a size one and a half slipper, but her feet and hands were large in proportion to her height. Her hand could cover her whole face. Her trunk was small and stripped of all anatomy but the ciphers of adolescence, her arms and legs relatively long, the neck extraordinarily long and mobile. All her gestures were liquid and possessed of an inner rhythm that flowed to inevitable completion with the finality of architecture or music. Her arms seemed to lift not from the elbow or the arm socket, but from the base of the spine. Her legs seemed to function from the waist. When she bent her head

5

her whole spine moved and the motion was completed the length of the arm through the elongation of her slender hand and the quivering reaching fingers. I believe there has never been a foot like hers, slender, delicate and of such an astonishing aggressiveness when arched as to suggest the ultimate in human vitality. Without in any way being sensual, being, in fact, almost sexless, she suggested all exhilaration, gaiety and delight. She jumped, and we broke bonds with reality. We flew. We hung over the earth, spread in the air as we do in dreams, our hands turning in the air as in water—the strong forthright taut plunging leg balanced on the poised are of the foot, the other leg stretched to the horizon like the wing of a bird. We lay balancing, quivering, turning, and all things were possible, even to us, the ordinary people.

I have seen two dancers as great or greater since, Alicia Markova and Margot Fonteyn, and many other women who have kicked higher, balanced longer or turned faster. These are poor substitutes for passion. In spite of her flimsy dances, the bald and blatant virtuosity, there was an intoxicated rapture, a focus of energy, Dionysian in its physical intensity, that I have never seen equaled by a performer in any theater of the world. Also she was the *first* of the truly great in our experience.

I sat with the blood beating in my throat. As I walked into the bright glare of the afternoon, my head ached and I could scarcely swallow. I didn't wish to cry. I certainly couldn't speak. I sat in a daze in the car oblivious to the grownups' ceaseless prattle. At home I climbed the stairs slowly to my bedroom and, shutting myself in, placed both hands on the brass rail at the foot of my bed, then rising laboriously to the tips of my white buttoned shoes I stumped the width of the bed and back again. My toes throbbed with pain, my knees shook, my legs quivered with weakness. I repeated the exercise. The blessed, relieving tears stuck at last on my lashes. Only by hurting my feet could I ease the pain in my throat.

Standing on Ninth Avenue under the El, I saw the headlines on the front page of *The New York Times.* It did not seem possible. She was in essence the denial of death. My own life was rooted to her in a deep spiritual sense and had been during the whole of my growing up. It mattered not that I had only spoken to her once and that my work lay in a different direction. She was the vision and the impulse and the goal.

READING CRITICALLY FOR IDEAS, STRUCTURE, AND STYLE

1. What features of Pavlova's appearance and dance does De Mille find so enthralling? How did seeing Pavlova's performance change De Mille's life?

2. What qualities distinguish Pavlova from the other famous dancers that De Mille had seen perform? What details does De Mille

include to focus the reader's attention on Pavlova's diminuative size and her ability to express emotion through gesture?

3. What words and phrases make the reader aware that De Mille has been inspired by Pavlova's performance?

EXTENDING INSIGHTS THROUGH WRITING

1. Describe a performance you have seen that you would call inspiring. It might be a country, rock, or classical performance or something you have seen on television or on film. Describe the performer and the event and pay particular attention to the gestures, physical appearance, voice quality, musical instruments and any special effects as well as the mood the performer created. Organize your description, your main impression, and use specific details of sight and sound that will allow your readers to share your experience as De Mille did in "Pavlova."

2. If you could appear on the cover of any magazine for an achievement or quality for which you are celebrated, what would it be—*Sports Illustrated, Time Magazine's* person of the year, *Rolling Stone, Business Week, Gourmet*?

CONNECTING PERSPECTIVES
ON THE ARTS OF CIVILIZATION

1. In what respect does Henry Moore find Michelanglo a source of inspiration (as described in David Sylvester's interview) comparable to Pavlova's influence on Agnes De Mille in terms of defining the spirit of sculpture and the dance, respectively?

2. In what sense did seeing Pavlova dance produce the same kinds of feelings on De Mille that seeing the Taj Mahal did for P. D. Ouspensky?

JOHN BERGER

Ways of Seeing

BACKGROUND

John Berger was born in 1926 in London and studied at the Central and Chelsea Schools of Art. Although he is known primarily as an art critic and novelist, Berger is also a poet, essayist, translator, playwright, screenwriter, painter (his work has been exhibited in galleries in London), and teacher of drawing. His novel *G* (1992) about migrant workers in Europe won the Booker Prize. He was an art critic for the *New Statesman* and the *Sunday Times*. A prolific author, he has written nine novels and fourteen works of nonfiction, including *Ways of Seeing* (1972), which was composed in association with a television series created for the BBC. This is essentially an argument against the dehumanizing process of consumerism that Berger, as a Marxist, sees as a defining feature of contemporary Western culture. The following reading is drawn from this book. Berger currently lives in a peasant farming community in the French Jura.

APPROACHING BERGER'S ESSAY

Berger demonstrates how many of the distinctive qualities of a particular advertising campaign are, in reality, borrowed from traditional art and sculpture from the past. He analyzes, from a Marxist perspective, the values that underlie ads and argues that advertising's fundamental ideology is the way it commodifies values by suggesting that middle-class consumers can share, through the purchase of an item, the lifestyles of the rich. How ads do this is by instilling envy and the feeling that life has value only insofar as we are able to purchase things. Berger points out that without "publicity" (his word for advertising) capitalism could not survive and that advertising undermines democracy by diverting people's attention away from the possibility of changing society toward how to change their place within that society. It forces them "to define their own interests as narrowly as possible," so that they focus on obtaining material possessions rather than on what is happening in the world: "the act of acquiring has taken the place of all other actions," in Berger's view.

Structurally, the essay is arranged quite logically. Readers are first asked to acknowledge the ubiquity of advertising images all around them. This is followed by Berger's thesis about the way publicity works, its true message. The rest of the essay is an extended comparison between the visual "language" of oil painting and that of advertising. This comparison serves to highlight the ways that advertising arouses envy in the spectator in order to get its message across ("you are what you have"). Finally, the consequences of this envy are laid out in the final paragraphs that form the conclusion. Berger shows how advertising is successful by playing on daydreams that stem from and serve to perpetuate powerlessness.

Ways of Seeing

In the cities in which we live, all of us see hundreds of publicity images every day of our lives. No other kind of image confronts us so frequently.

In no other form of society in history has there been such a concentration of images, such a density of visual messages.

One may remember or forget these messages but briefly one takes them in, and for a moment they stimulate the imagination by way of either memory or expectation. The publicity image belongs to the moment. We see it as we turn a page, as we turn a corner, as a vehicle passes us. Or we see it on a television screen whilst waiting for the commercial break to end. Publicity images also belong to the moment in the sense that they must be continually renewed and made up-to-date. Yet they never speak of the present. Often they refer to the past and always they speak of the future.

We are now so accustomed to being addressed by these images that we scarcely notice their total impact. A person may notice a particular image or place of information because it corresponds to some particular interest he has. But we accept the total system of publicity images as we accept an element of climate. For example, the fact that these images belong to the moment but speak of the future produces a strange effect which has become so familiar that we scarcely notice it. Usually it is *we* who pass the image—walking, travelling, turning a page; on the tv screen it is somewhat different but even then we are theoretically the active agent—we can look away, turn down the sound, make some coffee. Yet despite this, one has the impression that publicity images are continually passing us, like express trains on their way to some distant terminus. We are static; they are dynamic—until the newspaper is thrown away, the television programme continues or the poster is posted over.

Publicity is usually explained and justified as a competitive medium which ultimately benefits the public (the consumer) and the most efficient manufacturers—and thus the national economy. It is closely related to certain ideas about freedom: freedom of choice for the purchaser: freedom

5

of enterprise for the manufacturer. The great hoardings and the publicity neons of the cities of capitalism are the immediate visible sign of 'The Free World'.

For many in Eastern Europe such images in the West sum up what they in the East lack. Publicity, it is thought, offers a free choice.

It is true that in publicity one brand of manufacture, one firm, competes with another; but it is also true that every publicity image confirms and enhances every other. Publicity is not merely an assembly of competing messages: it is a language in itself which is always being used to make the same general proposal. Within publicity, choices are offered between this cream and that cream, that car and this car, but publicity as a system only makes a single proposal.

It proposes to each of us that we transform ourselves, or our lives, by buying something more.

This more, it proposes, will make us in some way richer—even though we will be poorer by having spent our money.

10 Publicity persuades us of such a transformation by showing us people who have apparently been transformed and are, as a result, enviable. The state of being envied is what constitutes glamour. And publicity is the process of manufacturing glamour.

It is important here not to confuse publicity with the pleasure or benefits to be enjoyed from the things it advertises. Publicity is effective precisely because it feeds upon the real. Clothes, food, cars, cosmetics, baths, sunshine are real things to be enjoyed in themselves. Publicity begins by working on a natural appetite for pleasure. But it cannot offer the real object of pleasure and there is no convincing substitute for a pleasure in that pleasure's own terms. The more convincingly publicity conveys the pleasure of bathing in a warm, distant sea, the more the spectator-buyer will become aware that he is hundreds of miles away from that sea and the more remote the chance of bathing in it will seem to him. This is why publicity can never really afford to be about the product or opportunity it is proposing to the buyer who is not yet enjoying it. Publicity is never a celebration of a pleasure-in-itself. Publicity is always about the future buyer. It offers him an image of himself made glamorous by the product or opportunity it is trying to sell. The image then makes him envious of himself as he might be. Yet what makes this self-which-he-might-be enviable? The envy of others. Publicity is about social relations, not objects. Its promise is not of pleasure, but of happiness: happiness as judged from the outside by others. The happiness of being envied is glamour.

Being envied is a solitary form of reassurance. It depends precisely upon not sharing your experience with those who envy you. You are observed with interest but you do not observe with interest—if you do, you will become less enviable. In this respect the envied are like bureaucrats; the more impersonal they are, the greater the illusion (for themselves and for others) of their power. The power of the glamorous resides in their supposed happiness: the power of the bureaucrat in his supposed authority. It is this which explains the absent, unfocused look of so many glamour images. They look out *over* the looks of envy which sustain them.

The spectator-buyer is meant to envy herself as she will become if she buys the product. She is meant to imagine herself transformed by the product into an object of envy for others, an envy which will then justify her loving herself. One could put this another way: the publicity image steals her love of herself as she is, and offers it back to her for the price of the product.

Does the language of publicity have anything in common with that of oil painting which, until the invention of the camera, dominated the European way of seeing during four centuries?

It is one of those questions which simply needs to be asked for the answer to become clear. There is a direct continuity. Only interests of cultural prestige have obscured it. At the same time, despite the continuity, there is a profound difference which it is no less important to examine.   15

There are many direct references in publicity to works of art from the past. Sometimes a whole image is a frank pastiche of a well-known painting.

Publicity images often use sculptures or paintings to lend allure or authority to their own message. Framed oil paintings often hang in shop windows as part of their display.

Any work of art 'quoted' by publicity serves two purposes. Art is a sign of affluence; it belongs to the good life; it is part of the furnishing which the world gives to the rich and the beautiful.

But a work of art also suggests a cultural authority, a form of dignity, even of wisdom, which is superior to any vulgar material interest; an oil painting belongs to the cultural heritage; it is a reminder of what it means to be a cultivated European. And so the quoted work of art (and this is why it is so useful to publicity) says two almost contradictory things at the same time: it denotes wealth and spirituality: it implies that the purchase being proposed is both a luxury and a cultural value. Publicity has in fact understood the tradition of the oil painting more thoroughly than most art historians. It has grasped the implications of the relationship between the work of art and its spectator-owner and with these it tries to persuade and flatter the spectator-buyer.

The continuity, however, between oil painting and publicity goes far deeper than the 'quoting' of specific paintings. Publicity relies to a very large extent on the language of oil painting. It speaks in the same voice about the same things. Sometimes the visual correspondences are so close that it is possible to play a game of 'Snap'—putting almost identical images or details of images side by side. It is not, however, just at the level of exact pictorial correspondence that the continuity is important: it is at the level of the sets of signs used.   20

Compare the images of publicity and paintings in this book, or take a picture magazine, or walk down a smart shopping street looking at the window displays, and then turn over the pages of an illustrated museum catalogue, and notice how similarly messages are conveyed by the two media. A systematic study needs to be made of this. Here we can do no more than indicate a few areas where the similarity of the devices and aims is particularly striking.

The gestures of models (mannequins) and mythological figures.

The romantic use of nature (leaves, trees, water) to create a place where innocence can be refound.

The exotic and nostalgic attraction of the Mediterranean.

The poses taken up to denote stereotypes of women: serene mother (madonna), free-wheeling secretary (actress, king's mistress), perfect hostess (spectator-owner's wife), sex-object (Venus, nymph surprised), etc.

The special sexual emphasis given to women's legs.

The materials particularly used to indicate luxury: engraved metal, furs, polished leather, etc.

The gestures and embraces of lovers, arranged frontally for the benefit of the spectator.

The sea, offering a new life.

The physical stance of men conveying wealth and virility.

The treatment of distance by perspective-offering mystery.

The equation of drinking and success.

The man as knight (horseman) become motorist.

Why does publicity depend so heavily upon the visual language of oil painting?

Publicity is the culture of the consumer society. It propagates through images that society's belief in itself. There are several reasons why these images use the language of oil painting.

Oil painting, before it was anything else was a celebration of private property. As an art-form it derived from the principle that *you are what you have.*

It is a mistake to think of publicity supplanting the visual art of post- 25
Renaissance Europe; it is the last moribund form of that art.

Is it Italian tile? Or a real Armstrong floor?

Come and play footsy with Armstrong

Publicity is, in essence, nostalgic. It has to sell the past to the future.
It cannot itself supply the standards of its own claims. And so all its references to quality are bound to be retrospective and traditional. It would
lack both confidence and credibility if it used a strictly contemporary
language.

Publicity needs to turn to its own advantage the traditional education
of the average spectator-buyer. What he has learnt at school of history,
mythology, poetry can be used in the manufacturing of glamour. Cigars
can be sold in the name of a King, underwear in connection with the
Sphinx, a new car by reference to the status of a country house.

In the language of oil painting these vague historical or poetic or
moral references are always present. The fact that they are imprecise and
ultimately meaningless is an advantage: they should not be understandable, they should merely be reminiscent of cultural lessons half-learnt.
Publicity makes all history mythical, but to do so effectively it needs a visual language with historical dimensions.

Lastly, a technical development made it easy to translate the language
of oil painting into publicity clichés. This was the invention, about fifteen
years ago, of cheap colour photography. Such photography can reproduce
the colour and texture and tangibility of objects as only oil paint had been
able to do before. Colour photography is to the spectator-buyer what oil
paint was to the spectator-owner. Both media use similar, highly tactile

means to play upon the spectator's sense of acquiring the *real* thing which the image shows. In both cases his feeling that he can almost touch what is in the image reminds him how he might or does possess the real thing.

30　　　Yet, despite this continuity of language, the function of publicity is very different from that of the oil painting. The spectator-buyer stands in a very different relation to the world from the spectator-owner.

The oil painting showed what its owner was already enjoying among his possessions and his way of life. It consolidated his own sense of his own value. It enhanced his view of himself as he already was. It began with facts, the facts of his life. The paintings embellished the interior in which he actually lived.

The purpose of publicity is to make the spectator marginally dissatisfied with his present way of life. Not with the way of life of society, but with his own within it. It suggests that if he buys what it is offering, his life will become better. It offers him an improved alternative to what he is.

The oil painting was addressed to those who made money out of the market. Publicity is addressed to those who constitute the market, to the spectator-buyer who is also the consumer-producer from whom profits are made twice over as worker and then as buyer. The only places relatively free of publicity are the quarters of the very rich; their money is theirs to keep.

All publicity works upon anxiety. The sum of everything is money, to get money is to overcome anxiety. Alternatively the anxiety on which publicity plays is the fear that having nothing you will be nothing.

35　　　Money is life. Not in the sense that without money you starve. Not in the sense that capital gives one class power over the entire lives of another class. But in the sense that money is the token of, and the key to, every human capacity. The power to spend money is the power to live. According to the legends of publicity, those who lack the power to spend money become literally faceless. Those who have the power become lovable.

Publicity increasingly uses sexuality to sell any product or service. But this sexuality is never free in itself; it is a symbol for something presumed to be larger than it: the good life in which you can buy whatever you want. To be able to buy is the same thing as being sexually desirable; occasionally this is the explicit message of publicity as in the Barclaycard advertisement above [not shown]. Usually it is the implicit message, i.e. If you are able to buy this product you will be lovable. If you cannot buy it, you will be less lovable.

For publicity the present is by definition insufficient. The oil painting was thought of as a permanent record. One of the pleasures a painting gave to its owner was the thought that it would convey the image of his present to the future of his descendants. Thus the oil painting was naturally painted in the present tense. The painter painted what was before him, either in reality or in imagination. The publicity image which is ephemeral uses only the future tense. With this you *will* become desirable. In these surroundings all your relationships *will* become happy and radiant.

Publicity principally addressed to the working class tends to promise a personal transformation through the function of the particular product it is selling (Cinderella); middle-class publicity promises a transformation of relationships through a general atmosphere created by an ensemble of products (The Enchanted Palace).

Publicity speaks in the future tense and yet the achievement of this future is endlessly deferred. How then does publicity remain credible—or credible enough to exert the influence it does? It remains credible because the truthfulness of publicity is judged, not by the real fulfilment of its promises, but by the relevance of its fantasies to those of the spectator-buyer. Its essential application is not to reality but to day-dreams.

To understand this better we must go back to the notion of *glamour.* 40 Glamour is a modern invention. In the heyday of the oil painting it did not exist. Ideas of grace, elegance, authority amounted to something apparently similar but fundamentally different.

Mrs. Siddons as seen by Gainsborough[1] is not glamorous, because she is not presented as enviable and therefore happy. She may be seen as wealthy, beautiful, talented, lucky. But her qualities are her own and have been recognized as such. What she is does not entirely depend upon others wanting to be like her. She is not purely the creature of others' envy— which is how, for example, Andy Warhol presents Marilyn Monroe.[2]

Glamour cannot exist without personal social envy being a common and widespread emotion. The industrial society which has moved towards democracy and then stopped half way is the ideal society for generating such an emotion. The pursuit of individual happiness has been acknowledged as a universal right. Yet the existing social conditions make the individual feel powerless. He lives in the contradiction between what he is and what he would like to be. Either he then becomes fully conscious of the contradiction and its causes, and so joins the political struggle for a full democracy which entails, amongst other things, the overthrow of capitalism; or else he lives, continually subject to an envy which, compounded with his sense of powerlessness, dissolves into recurrent day-dreams.

It is this which makes it possible to understand why publicity remains credible. The gap between what publicity actually offers and the future it promises, corresponds with the gap between what the spectator-buyer feels himself to be and what he would like to be. The two gaps become one; and instead of the single gap being bridged by action or lived experience, it is filled with glamorous day-dreams.

The process is often reinforced by working conditions. The interminable present of meaningless working hours is 'balanced' by a dreamt future in which imaginary activity replaces the passivity of the moment. In his or her day-dreams the passive worker becomes the active consumer. The working self envies the consuming self.

No two dreams are the same. Some are instantaneous, others 45 prolonged. The dream is always personal to the dreamer. Publicity does not manufacture the dream. All that it does is to propose to each one of us that we are not yet enviable—yet could be.

[1]*Mrs. Siddons* by Thomas Gainsborough, 1727–88, National Gallery, London.
[2]*Marilyn Monroe* by Andy Warhol.

Publicity has another important social function. The fact that this function has not been planned as a purpose by those who make and use publicity in no way lessens its significance. Publicity turns consumption into a substitute for democracy. The choice of what one eats (or wears or drives) takes the place of significant political choice. Publicity helps to mask and compensate for all that is undemocratic within society. And it also masks what is happening in the rest of the world.

Publicity adds up to a kind of philosophical system. It explains everything in its own terms. It interprets the world.

The entire world becomes a setting for the fulfilment of publicity's promise of the good life. The world smiles at us. It offers itself to us. And because *everywhere* is imagined as offering itself to us, *everywhere* is more or less the same.

Publicity, situated in a future continually deferred, excludes the present and so eliminates all becoming, all development. Experience is impossible within it. All that happens, happens outside it.

50   The fact that publicity is eventless would be immediately obvious if it did not use a language which makes of tangibility an event in itself. Everything publicity shows is there awaiting acquisition. The act of acquiring has taken the place of all other actions, the sense of having has obliterated all other senses.

Publicity exerts an enormous influence and is a political phenomenon of great importance. But its offer is as narrow as its references are wide. It recognizes nothing except the power to acquire. All other human faculties or needs are made subsidiary to this power. All hopes are gathered together, made homogeneous, simplified, so that they become the intense yet vague, magical yet repeatable promise offered in every purchase. No other kind of hope or satisfaction or pleasure can any longer be envisaged within the culture of capitalism.

Publicity is the life of this culture—in so far as without publicity capitalism could not survive—and at the same time publicity is its dream.

Capitalism survives by forcing the majority, whom it exploits, to define their own interests as narrowly as possible. This was once achieved by extensive deprivation. Today in the developed countries it is being achieved by imposing a false standard of what is and what is not desirable.

READING CRITICALLY FOR IDEAS, STRUCTURE, AND STYLE

1. How does advertising use the motifs and themes found in traditional oil paintings that display wealth and belong to a cultural

heritage to sell modern products? What are people really buying along with the product (floor tile, etc.)? How would you answer Berger's question "Why does publicity [advertising] depend so heavily on the visual language of oil painting?"

2. What are some of the different forms in today's advertising that represent themes from the past? Why would these themes be appealing to today's audiences?

3. Implicit in Berger's Marxist critique of capitalism is the belief that advertising "helps to mask and compensate for all that is undemocratic within society." Do you agree with him that "the choice of what one eats (or wears or drives) takes the place of significant political choice"? Why or why not?

EXTENDING INSIGHTS THROUGH WRITING

1. To what advertising images are you most responsive? Analyze a few of these ads as Berger might see them. For example, what function does glamour (as Berger uses the term) serve in making people dissatisfied with themselves and their lives?

2. Advertisers spend a considerable amount of time, money, and effort in formulating brand names for their products. Discuss the connotations of one or several of these names. For example, in the category of brand names for cars and SUVS, what emotional needs are designed to be met by Regal, Grand Marquis, Riviera, Monte Carlo, Mustang, Firebird, Thunderbird, Explorer, Cherokee, or any other names?

CONNECTING PERSPECTIVES
ON THE ARTS OF CIVILIZATION

1. Berger says that art suggests cultural authority, spirituality, and dignity because it is supposedly superior to "vulgar material interest" and "a reminder of what it means to be a cultured European." In your opinion, is nineteenth-century music, as discussed by Edward Rothstein, popular with modern audiences for the same reasons? Why or why not?

2. Why wouldn't the modern shopping mall, as an extension of Berger's argument, serve the same function in our consumer culture as cathedrals did in medieval times, as discussed by John Ruskin, in "The Stones of St. Mark's"?

BOOK CONNECTIONS FOR CHAPTER 7

1. Compare the dramatist's method for exploring the meaning of events, described by Aristotle, with the historians' method, described by R. G. Collingwood in "What Is History?" in Chapter 3.

2. Was Leonardo da Vinci, as described by Giorgio Vasari, a hero in Carlyle's sense of the term (see "On Heroes and Hero-Worship" in Chapter 3)? Why or why not?

3. In what respects does Michelangelo as described by Henry Moore (in David Sylvester's interview) embody the spirit of the Renaissance as Bill Gates (see "The Road Ahead" in Chapter 5) embodies the spirit of our information age?

4. How do the accounts of Joseph Addison (see "Reflections in Westminster Abbey" in Chapter 1) and John Ruskin deepen our understanding of the meaning cathedrals have in European culture?

5. Discuss the different attitudes towards the meaning of Tutankhamen's tomb (see Howard Carter's "Finding the Tomb" in Chapter 3) with the Taj Mahal as described by P. D. Ouspensky as memorials in terms of what they reveal about Egyptian and Indian civilizations.

6. How are many of the different sources and strengths of the English language, as described by Paul Roberts, displayed in John F. Kennedy's "Inaugural Address 1961" in Chapter 3?

7. James Baldwin, in his "Letter to My Nephew" (in Chapter 2), advises his nephew to purge himself of personal bitterness. In what way does this correspond to Gustav Flaubert's artistic credo?

8. Contrast the different motives for returning to the past described by Edward Rothstein regarding nineteenth-century music and Neil Postman on eighteenth-century thinkers (see "Information" in Chapter 5).

9. In what sense is the re-creation of the meaning of events within the mind of the historian, advocated by R. G. Collingwood in "What Is History?" (Chapter 3), similar to the perception created in the mind of the audience through *montage* described by Sergei Eisenstein?

10. Although Pavlova is Agnes De Mille's personal hero, would she qualify as a hero from Thomas Carlyle's (see "On Heroes and Hero-Worship" in Chapter 3) perspective? Why or why not?

11. Discuss how both John Berger and Neil Postman in "Information" (in Chapter 5) offer radical critiques of modern culture from different perspectives.

Writing About Great Ideas

Writing About Great Ideas

Much of the writing you are expected to do at your college or university involves responding to material you have read, lectures you have heard, events you have observed, and your conversations with others inside and outside of the classroom. Being able to write effectively is important since it is the principal means by which you demonstrate your mastery of the course material. Your ability to communicate your understanding depends on using language precisely.

WRITING AN ANALYTICAL ESSAY

An analytical essay in which you argue for an interpretation is one of the basic forms of writing you will most often be expected to produce in college level courses. In it, you build on previously developed critical thinking and reading skills in understanding a text and evaluating its effectiveness. Writing an analytical essay offers you the opportunity to convert your critical reading of an essay into a fully considered assessment of the author's ideas, assumptions, and skill in using evidence. The simplest way to do this is to find a question about any aspect of an essay you read that you want to answer (the "Reading Critically for Ideas, Structure, and Style" assignments are designed to stimulate these kinds of questions). The question you formulate can become the topic or subject of your paper. When you write an analytical essay, you examine your own beliefs about an issue and explain how you arrived at them.

The idea that expresses your opinion is called the thesis and contains a specific claim that your essay will propose and defend. For example, after reading Matt Ridley's "Genome" (Chapter 4) on the genetic basis of language, you might question whether genes, rather than culture, are responsible for our ability to acquire language. Based on your analysis of Ridley's argument, you conclude that the case for genetic influence on language acquisition is not as clear-cut as Ridley claims. In turn, your thesis (or the claim your essay will try to prove) could read:

> Matt Ridley's mishandling of rhetorical strategies in his essay, "Genome," undermines his credibility in proving that genetics are more important than culture in determining language acquisition.

The thesis or claim is an asssertion that must be genuinely debatable; that is, there should be some alternative, or opposing opinion. Because others might disagree with your assessment or interpretation you must present evidence (most often, in the form of relevant quotations drawn from the text) and explain your interpretation of these quotations and the ideas in the essay in a way that will persuade your readers. In essence, you create an argument that answers a question, makes a claim, provides supporting evidence, and explains your reasons as well as any assumptions as to why you have reached this conclusion.

When you write an analytical essay, you move beyond your personal reactions to what you have read, and evaluate some aspect of the article—the author's claims, use of evidence, chain of reasoning, organization, or style. You also need to understand the author's values, beliefs, and purpose in writing the essay.

You make use of specific skills in carefully reading and annotating the text, and identifying the thesis and key supporting points. You must also be able to evaluate the different kinds of evidence the author uses (including, quotations, expert opinion, personal observations, statistics, empirical data, case histories, analogies, and precedents) and assess how well the evidence supports the author's assertions.

PRE-WRITING TECHNIQUES

Discovering how best to approach your topic is easier if you try one or several of the pre-writing, or invention strategies, many writers have found helpful. Pre-writing techniques allow you to explore ideas in an informal way before putting in time and effort in writing a rough draft. The basic strategies we will discuss include free-writing, the five W's, and mapping (or clustering).

Free-Writing

Free-writing is a technique for setting down whatever occurs to you on the topic within a few minutes. You will find you are more creative when you simply free-associate without stopping to censor, evaluate, or edit your thoughts. Free-writing is meant to be casual, informal, and tentative. You write to define the issue. Your goal is to get a clear perception of key aspects of the issue in order to discover how to focus your argument. You need not worry about spelling, punctuation, or grammar. For example, free-writing based on Matt Ridley's essay ("Genome" in Chapter 4) might read:

Ridley seems to be pushing the theory that genes control language. Little attempts to present opposing viewpoints, and this weakens his argument. Seems to be emotionally attached to this theory which may be correct although the way he defends it raises doubts.

The Five W's

Next you might wish to ask, and answer, the questions that journalists often use to determine what can be known about the topic [in this case, applied to Ridley's essay]:

- **Who** is involved in the situation? [geneticists, linguists, learning specialists, biologists]
- **What** is at stake? [the influence of genes as opposed to culture in the acquisition of language]
- **Where** did the action take place? [MIT, Oxford University, culminating in the decoding of the human Genome in laboratories and research institutions in Canada, England and Hawaii]
- **When** did the action take place? [starting with Noam Chomsky's theoretical work in the 1960s, Derek Bickerton's research in 1990 and most recently, studies by Myrna Gopnick and Steven Pinker, and in the present, the Human Genome Project]
- **Why** is what happened important? [this theory, if proved, would refute fundamental assumptions of social scientists who assume that culture, rather than biology and genetics, are responsible for much of human behavior]

By answering some or all of these questions, you can get a clearer picture of the different aspects of the whole situation. You can then decide which of these elements to focus on to produce an effective essay.

Mapping

This technique allows you to visually perceive the relationship between important ideas. Begin by writing down the word that contains a key idea or represents the starting point, draw a circle around it and when you think of related ideas, topics, or details that are connected to it, jot them down nearby and draw lines as a way of representing the connections between related ideas. The key to making mapping useful is to define the nature of the relationships indicated by the lines of connection between the circles. If you skip this step, you will generate a simplistic thesis. For example, notice how the following "map" helps the student see that the "flaws in Ridley's argument" raise basic questions as to whether "genes [are] more important than culture."

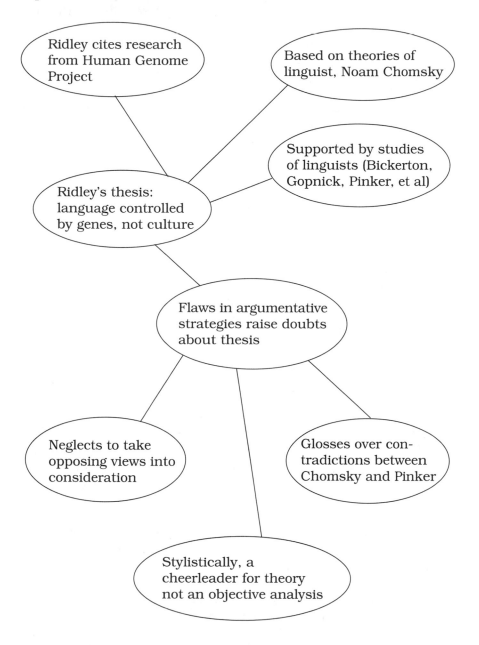

IDENTIFYING YOUR THESIS

It is useful to think of the thesis as a type of contract that obligates you to analyze and interpret specific aspects of the article in order to clarify, illustrate, and support your opinion. An effective thesis is created from the material generated through such pre-writing strategies as mapping and freewriting and should contain an assertion that you feel you can reasonably prove. For example, after reading Neil Postman's "Information" in Chapter 5 asserting the contemporary relevance of eighteenth-century thinkers, a student might formulate a trial thesis that questioned whether Postman had proved his case. In this student's view, at least, Postman failed to show how simply reading eighteenth-century texts could provide insight into modern problems, thus:

> Neil Postman presents the texts written by eighteenth-century thinkers as talismans whose virtue will rub off on the modern world rather than demonstrating how this would work in any practical sense.

The trial thesis should contain your assertion or claim stated as a single sentence. The way in which the thesis statement is phrased can suggest the kind of analysis that will best illustrate and support your claim. For example, the thesis above might suggest that Postman's essay might best be analyzed as a faulty causal argument (see the discussion of causation in the introduction) and cite instances where Postman fails to demonstrate that studying the works by eighteenth-century thinkers will have tangible consequences for today's world.

Formulating a Thesis for an Essay Based on Two or More Sources

Since *Past to Present* is organized around the historical changes in conversations that define the history of a set of primary ideas, there are many opportunities for writing essays based on two or more sources after each selection ("Connecting Perspectives ...") and at the end of each chapter ("Book Connections"). For example, in Chapter 2 ("The Collective Experience") selections by Simone de Beauvoir ("The Married Woman") and Marilyn Yalom ("The Wife Today") could be analyzed in relationship to each other for what they show about the evolution of the wife's role over the last fifty years and encourage an inquiry into the reasons for these changes.

Your paper would focus specifically on what each selection had to say on some aspect of this topic. Does one source reinforce or contradict another? Do they represent entirely different points of view without opposing each other? What additional insights might outside sources (from the library and the Internet) add to your analysis? The thesis you formulate will refer to both sources and express your own position on the issue. For example, a trial thesis based on both selections might read as follows:

> Simone de Beauvoir provides the underlying rationale for feminism that has resulted in women today no longer needing to marry for the sake of economic survival.

An example of the potential for a conversation on the history of a primary idea across chapters would be a comparative analysis between Thomas Paine's "Rights of Man" in Chapter 2 ("The Collective Experience") and John F. Kennedy's "Inaugural Address 1961" in Chapter 3 ("The Historical Dimension"). After reading, annotating and evaluating each reading you might decide that Kennedy's concept of liberty and the role of the government is quite different from Paine's and you might wish to explore why this is so. A trial thesis might read as follows:

> Kennedy's rhetoric encouraging citizen activism superficially might appear to echo the self-sufficiency proposed by Thomas Paine, but is actually a response to the perceived threats during the Cold War.

Using Your Thesis To Organize Your Essay

As we have seen a thesis may be written in response to a single reading or to several sources. You might consider your trial thesis as a blueprint of a building that shows what the building will look like before money, time, and effort is spent on its construction. It makes sense to invest time into drafting your thesis rather than continually rewriting your paper, hoping that some central idea will emerge. The thesis statement may be explicitly stated or remain implicit in your analysis.

To help you get a clearer idea of the shape of your paper, you might create an informal outline (of words and phrases arranged in a list according to the ideas you propose to discuss). An informal outline can help you explore the insights expressed in your thesis and help you identify the key ideas each section will develop. Keep in mind that your analyses may very well turn up evidence that does not support your initial thesis and you must be prepared to revise it to account for this divergent evidence.

An analytical essay does not have to address every aspect of the original selection, but only those elements that you wish to draw into your discussion. After formulating (and reformulating) a thesis that expresses a claim (see "Purposes for Writing" in the Introduction for a discussion of different kinds of claims), begin to assemble evidence by summarizing (described in "Keeping a Reading Journal"), paraphrasing, and quoting from particular passages that will develop, illustrate and support your assertion.

CREATING A ROUGH DRAFT

Creating a rough draft offers the best way in which to explore the ideas you developed during the pre-writing stage and serves as a precursor to your final paper.

A rough draft helps you see the relationships implicit in the materials you generated in your pre-writing activities, and in your reading journal, annotations, and informal outline (if you used one) that served as a focus of your thesis. Plan to write one section of the paper at a time. This allows you to concentrate on the details within that section to determine if they really support your thesis. You can try out different organizational arrangements (for example, causal argument, comparison and contrast, or problem solving) and see which sections need additional supporting evidence.

The objective of a rough draft is to get your ideas down on paper without worrying about diction or spelling (which you can correct later). You also don't have to write paragraphs in any set sequence. Would a change in the order of presentation make your ideas clearer and hence, more persuasive? It can also be helpful to review each paragraph or section of the draft to see whether it supports your thesis.

Writing the Introduction

Some writers find it helpful to compose the introduction first, informing readers in a straightforward way of the issue, topic or idea the paper will cover. At other times, the introduction is not self-evident, so it is better to proceed to subsequent paragraphs and return to the introduction later when you have a clearer idea of the focus of the paper. Introductions, if possible, should capture the readers' attention and can include:

- a provocative question that challenges your readers to reexamine their beliefs on the subject

- a dramatic or amusing story, anecdote, or an attention-getting quotation

- a brief overview of the issue in its historical context

- a striking statistic

- a brief description of both sides of a debate, or

- A description of a central person, place or event

You may wish to include the central idea your paper will develop and/or suggest the kind of analysis you intend to pursue in arguing for your interpretation.

Writing the Middle of the Essay

The choices open to you when you write the middle portion, or body, of your essay depend on the relationships and inferences implied in your thesis.

Each paragraph in the middle section should contain a topic sentence that elaborates on some aspect of the thesis. Just as the thesis serves as the controlling idea for the entire essay, the topic sentence serves as the focus for all the sentences within that paragraph. Each paragraph should contain supporting material (in the form of summaries, paraphrases or quotes) that illustrates, amplifies or clarifies the idea in the topic sentence.

Although the rhetorical methods you use (we cover these in "Using Rhetorical Patterns for Developing Ideas" in the Introduction) depend on the nature of your claim, a few general points should be made:

1. If your thesis makes a factual claim that defines a phenomenon or characterizes it in a way that is arguable, you will need to defend your particular interpretation or definition. For example:

    Buddhism as expressed in the Buddhacarita differs from most other religions in that it is less concerned with establishing the existence of a God or gods than in teaching a method by which human beings can be released from the condition of suffering that defines human existence.

    To develop a factual claim, you need to add several "because" clauses that express your reasons for holding this view. To argue for this claim, you would have to show that Buddhism as exemplified in "The Enlightenment of the

Buddha: Buddhacarita" (in Chapter 6) does not take as its starting point metaphysical questions such as who made the world and what is the meaning of life and what, if anything, happens to us after death. Support for your claim might take the form of a comparison between Buddhism and other religions.

2. If your thesis makes a value judgment (that something is good or bad according to a specified standard) you must support your analysis with clearly defined ethical or moral criteria. For example:

> It is doubtful whether eighteenth-century writers such as Rousseau, Diderot and Voltaire can provide guidance sorely lacking in modern culture as Neil Postman suggests in "Information" (in Chapter 5).

To develop this thesis, the student must explain and defend the value judgment that writers' works evolve within very specific historic and cultural circumstances that cannot be generalized into future eras.

3. If your thesis identifies the likely causes or probable consequences of something, be sure to consider alternative explanations. For example:

> The circumstances described in "I Have Nothing More to Say" (Chapter 1) suggest that without the inspired and courageous role Joan of Arc played, it is doubtful whether the English would have been expelled from Burgundy and France unifed as a nation.

This claim would require some research into Joan of Arc's role in the 1400s, and an assessment of interpretations by historians on both sides of the issue.

4. If your thesis statement proposes a course of action, you must consider alternative solutions to the problem, and give good reasons for accepting yours. For example:

> Although the Human Genome Project discussed by Matt Ridley in "Genome" (in Chapter 4) has made it possible to discover genetic predispositions for disease, insurance companies should not be allowed to use genetic screening to set rate structures.

Someone who held this view would have to demonstrate that the use of genetic screening constituted an invasion of privacy, and answer the objection that insurance companies have a right to be aware of any potential liability from future costly claims. Arguments are more persuasive when readers feel that the writer has not dodged any significant objections that might be made to his or her claims. You should anticipate opposing viewpoints and summarize them fairly and point out their inadequacies.

As you are drafting this middle section, pay particular attention to the relationships or connections that can be demonstrated with transitional words or phrases such as "because" or "therefore" to signal causal relationships; "moreover" or "furthermore" to signal additional information; or "however" or "although" to signal a qualification.

Writing the Conclusion

The most traditional conclusion simply sums up points made in the paper and relates them back to the thesis. The conclusion should bring together the important lines of reasoning developed in the body of the essay. After reading your essay, the reader must feel that you fulfilled the obligation stated in your thesis. You can achieve this sense of closure by: (1) referring to points already presented in the opening paragraph or introduction, (2) summarizing points made in the body of the paper as they relate to the thesis, (3) challenging the reader to think further about the issue.

REVISING THE ROUGH DRAFT

Revision is part of the editing process and occurs as you transform your rough draft into a final draft. Your thesis plays an important role in this process since it provides a way of testing every aspect of your essay to see whether it actually develops the point you wish to communicate. In the process of revising, you re-evaluate the original thesis in light of the evidence you discovered and may revise it to take into account divergent evidence you have uncovered. Revising can be thought of as a way to bring the key idea into sharper focus and to delete whatever does not develop, illustrate, clarify or substantiate it. The ultimate goal when revising is to clearly demonstrate the relationship between your claim, the supporting evidence you cite, and the arguments, reasons, and analysis you present to make your point. You must also make explicit any assumptions you rely on to reach your conclusions.

You will probably write several drafts before your essay says exactly what you want it to say. You might try reading it aloud in order to notice mistakes in grammar, syntax, or style, that otherwise would have escaped your attention. You may also wish to show your paper to others to get their reactions; many campuses have writing centers or tutoring services that can help you.

Revising for Organization

When you begin to revise, first look at your essay's overall structure. Does the introduction capture your reader's attention, and clearly present your thesis? Is there any section that would be better placed elsewhere? You may want to rearrange paragraphs or sections, if you discover that a change in the order of presentation would make your ideas clearer.

Try to see your paper as a reader would, that is, as someone who did not know in advance the ideas you wanted to present. At what points might the reader need more examples or better evidence to clarify an idea? Where might more effective transitions be required to signal relationships between different parts of your paper? Are the issues raised in the same order as implied by your thesis? Would some other arrangement more effectively communicate these relationships? Which of your assumptions need to be articulated and defended? Have you unintentionally contradicted yourself in different parts of your essay? Have you taken into account what someone who holds an opposing view might have to say about your analysis? What new information could you add to make your argument more persuasive?

Revising for Style

If you are satisfied with the overall organization, and the sequence in which ideas are presented, you can improve your essay's grammar, usage, punctuation, and style. Just as every paragraph must support the development of the paper's thesis, and just as every sentence within a paragraph must support, illustrate or clarify that paragraph's idea, so every word in a sentence must contribute to the thought expressed in that sentence. Look for sentences where a verb in the passive voice might be recast in the active voice and follow the subject-verb-object structure.

Consider how you might improve your choice of words to express your ideas simply, clearly and concretely. Eliminate mixed metaphors (such as "don't pull the wool out from under me") jargon, or specialized terms (unless you define them when you first use them), and clichés (such as "cool as a cucumber"). Substitute single words for roundabout phrases, such as **although** for "in spite of the fact that," **because** for "due to the fact that," **if** for "in the event that," **after** for "at the conclusion of," or **now** for "at this point in time." Lastly, consider your working title. Titles are a concise means of focusing the reader's attention on the main idea of your essay. You may wish to revise it to more accurately reflect your claim.

Proofreading

Proofread your paper for inconsistencies in syntax, grammatical structure, usage, or for repeated words or phrases. If you habitually misspell certain words keep a list of these and consult it when you proofread. Be sure you have correctly documented the source of every quote, paraphrase, and summary (we describe the method of in-text citation and correct documention in the next section, "Drawing on Sources for Evidence.") Compare your in-text citations with the list of works cited and check them against the record of your sources to make sure you did not change any words or punctuation.

Revising with a Computer

If you revise with a computer, you can create multiple drafts and try out different configurations by cutting and pasting sentences and paragraphs. Some computer programs also provide outline tools and spell-checkers that can help you edit your paper. Keep in mind that spell-checking programs cannot tell if a word is incorrectly used if that word is spelled correctly (for example, "too" for "to" or "two", "their" for "there," or "peace" for "piece"). Remember to keep a printed version on hand and create a backup file at the end of each session. Keep in mind that computer-generated printouts look like finished products, but are really only works in progress.

Formatting

Most English instructors require papers to be formatted in the Modern Language Association style described in the *MLA Handbook for Writers of Research Papers,* 5th ed. (New York: Modern Language Association of America, 1999) and on the MLA website <www.mla.org>. The MLA system of documentation is divided into two parts that complement each other. First you document any source in the body of the paper that you quote, paraphrase or summarize. These in-text citations are accompanied by a separate list of works ("Works Cited") that appears at the end of your paper. Students in the social sciences (such as psychology and sociology) use the style manual of the American Psychological Association (APA) while those in the life sciences follow the style recommended by the Council of Biology Editors (CBE).

Unless your instructor specifies otherwise, the following format is standard:

- Provide one inch margins on the top, bottom and sides of each page.
- Number each page (and any running heads)
- Indent the first line of each paragraph 1/2 inch
- Double space the text in standard 12-point font
- Provide a separate list of works cited at the end of the paper
- Put your name, title of the essay, name of the course and date on the first page (title page)

DRAWING ON SOURCES FOR EVIDENCE

After formulating a thesis, you must support it with reasons, arguments, and analysis based on relevant passages in the text. For some papers, you may do additional research, using books and journals from your library, or information found on the Internet. Whatever sources you use (whether print or electronic), you must evaluate the quality of the information, and be careful to select only that material which genuinely illuminates your argument.

When you use sources from the Internet, you have to be especially careful to evaluate the web pages you intend to use in terms of the reliability of the source, timeliness, (when was the content posted?), and relevance. The domain name can provide a clue about the nature of the source. Common abbreviations include *.com* for companies; *.edu* for colleges and universities; *.gov* for government agencies; *.mil* for the military; *.net* for some Internet service providers and *.org* for nonprofit organizations. Keep in mind that the information available on the Internet, although seemingly plentiful, excludes many scholarly journals, which are often the most authoritative source for some subjects. The Internet excludes them because many of these journals have not been converted to digital format yet.

Paraphrases

A good portion of your analysis will rely on paraphrasing information from your sources. This process involves re-presenting the meaning of a passage in your own words, and clearly demonstrates that you have understood what you read. Unlike summaries (which compress entire articles down to single paragraphs), paraphrases attempt to convey the complexity and richness of the original passage—the ideas, the tone, and the pattern of reasoning. Sometimes a paraphrase can be the same length as the original passage, sometimes a bit shorter. Remember that your ideas should take center stage and only be illustrated by paraphrased source material.

Clearly introduce source material (in this case, a paraphrase) by providing the author's name and the title of the work from which the material is drawn. A parenthetical citation at the end of a paraphrased passage contains information that a reader would need to locate the original source. For example, what follows is a paraphrase of a section drawn from an essay in Chapter 4:

> Konrad Lorenz in "The Dove and the Wolf" discovered that wolves, contrary to popular belief, do not fight each other to the death. Instead, the weaker of the two combatants will offer his jugular vein in a submission gesture to the stronger, an action which paradoxically inhibits the victor from killing his defeated rival. (32)

Quotations

Quotations are an indispensable form of evidence you use to support, illustrate, or document your assertions. Direct quotation involves copying the author's words **exactly** as they appear in the original. Quotation marks placed at the beginning and end remind readers that this is a word-for-word copy, including the original punctuation. Quotations should be carefully chosen so that they genuinely illuminate your ideas, and contribute to the persuasiveness of your argument. Your essay should not represent a patchwork of stitched-together quoted sources. Only use quotes when the author's wording is so unique or authoritative that a paraphrase would not do it justice.

Brief Quotations (of fewer than four lines) are normally run into the text, and enclosed in double quotation marks (""). Be sure you reproduce all punctuation and capitalization exactly as it appears in the original. Include the author's name with the quotation either in your lead-in to the quote or in the parenthetical reference. Parenthetical citation of page numbers follow the closing quotation marks, but precede the punctuation mark at the end of the sentence. For example:

> In his essay, "How to Kill an Ocean," Thor Heyerdahl says "The ocean is in fact remarkably shallow for its size." (447)

After you have introduced material from a source including the author and title you can refer back to that source by repeating the author's name in subsequent references. For example:

In explaining this seeming paradox, Heyerdahl goes on to state that "It is the vast extent of ocean surface that has made man of all generations imagine a correspondingly unfathomable depth" (447).

Longer Quotations (of more than four lines) are separated from the text, indented one inch from the left margin, double spaced like the rest of the manuscript, and reproduced without quotation marks. These block quotations are introduced with a colon (:) following a grammatically complete lead-in. Parenthetical citation of page numbers follows the quotation's final punctuation. For example:

Simone de Beauvoir uses an intriguing analogy to characterize the everyday life of the housewife:

> Few tasks are more like the torture of Sisyphus than housework, with its endless repetition: the clean becomes soiled, the soiled is made clean, over and over, day after day. The housewife wears herself out marking time, she makes nothing, simply perpetuates the present. ("The Married Woman" 335).

If you omit a part of the original sentence you quote, in order to more easily integrate it into your own text, you must place an ellipsis or three spaced periods inside brackets [...] where the omitted phrase occurred. Ellipses are useful for condensing lengthy quotes and can focus your readers' attention on the point you want to emphasize from your source material. For example:

Simone de Beauvoir observes that "Few tasks are more like the torture of Sisyphus than housework [...] The housewife [...] simply perpetuates the present. ("The Married Woman" 335).

If you add words to a quotation to clarify it, use squared brackets ([]) around the words you have added. For example:

> Alan Watts defines square zen as the "Zen of established tradition in Japan with its clearly defined hierarchy, its rigid discipline, and its specific tests of *satori* [sudden enlightenment]" ("Beat Zen, Square Zen, and Zen" 863).

If you wish to emphasize a word or phrase in a quotation, you may italicize or underline it, but should indicate you have done so by adding the phrase "emphasis added" in parentheses after the closing quotation mark. For example:

Diane Ackerman reminds us that "the ancient Egyptians *swore oaths* on an onion as we might on a Bible" (emphasis added "The Social Sense" 127).

If you are quoting someone else who has been quoted by the author (and you don't have have access to the original material), you cite the writer of the quote in your introduction to it and the author of the work in which the quote appeared in the parenthetical citation. For example:

According to John Paul II, "the biological nature of every person is untouchable" (qtd. in Kolata 630).

If you are quoting a quote by someone else, the inside quotation is enclosed in single quotation marks and the surrounding quote appears in double quotation marks. For example:

Maurizio Chierici quotes Colonel Paul Tibbets, the pilot of the *Enola Gay*, the plane that carried the atomic bomb, " 'I did my duty; I would do it again.' " ("The Man from Hiroshima" 645).

Documenting Sources

You must document any evidence you cite whether in the form of quotes, paraphrases or summaries from a source. Not to do so, is to commit plagiarism, that is, appropriating the language, ideas, and thoughts of someone else and presenting them as if they were your own. In addition to in-text citations of sources you quote, paraphrase or summarize, you should also provide a "Works Cited" page at the end of your essay (alphabetized by author's last name) that gives all publishing information that will enable the reader to locate the original source (the page number in the parenthetical reference directs the reader to the exact place in the article where the information appears). Begin the first line of each entry at the left margin and indent subsequent lines 1/2 inch from the left margin. Double space the entire list both between and within entries.

TYPICAL ENTRIES
IN MLA STYLE

Examples of Works Cited Documentation

Book by One Author:
Ackerman, Diane. *A Natural History of the Senses.* New York: Random House, 1991.

Book by Two or More Authors:
Ward, Peter D., and Donald Brownlee. *Rare Earth.* New York: Copernicus, 2000.
(Note that only the first author's name is reversed.)

Work in an Anthology:
"The Enlightenment of the Buddha: Buddhacarita" *Buddhist Texts Through the Ages.* Ed. E. Conze. London: Faber and Faber, 1954.

Article in a Weekly Magazine:
Sylvester, David. "Genius of Michelangelo by Moore" *The New York Times Magazine,* 8 March 1964: 24–29.

Article in a Monthly Magazine:
Hasler, Arthur D. and James A. Larsen. "The Homing Salmon." *Scientific American* Aug. 1955: 70–73 + (A plus sign shows that the article is not printed on consecutive pages; if it were, a page range would be given: 70–75 for example.)

Article in a Journal:
Holden, Constance. "Identical Twins Reared Apart." *Science* 207 (1980): 28–34.

Film or Videotape:
The Messenger: The Story of Joan of Arc. Dir. Luc Bresson. Perf. Milla Jovovich., Columbia, 2000.

Television Program:
The Mahabharata. Perf. Bruce Myers. PBS, New York. 28 Feb. 1989.

Personal Interview:
Ruesch, Hans. Personal Interview. 17 Mar. 2001.

Documenting Electronic Sources:
Web sources are documented in the same way as are traditional print sources. You should provide the title of the site, the name of the institution or organization associated with the site, the date of access, and the URL enclosed in angle brackets < >. You must check your citation of electronic sources carefully since every letter, number, symbol, and space must appear exactly as it does on the screen. Otherwise, it is impossible to retrieve your source. If you run into any difficulty, check the MLA website, <www.mla.org>.

E-Mail:
Rothstein, Edward. "Concerts." E-mail to the author. 2 Dec. 2000.

Article in an Online Reference Book:
"Shaw, George Bernard." *Encyclopaedia Britannica Online.* Vers. 99.2. 1994–2001. Encyclopaedia Britannica. 23 July 2001 <http://search.eb.com/bol/topic?eu=68917&sctn=1>.

Article in an Online Journal:
Imholtz, August A. "Plato in Wonderland." *Classics Ireland* 7 (2000): 6 pars. 23 July 2001 <http://www.ucd.ie/~classics/2000/ imholtz.html>.

Article in an Online Magazine:
Rosenberg, Scott. "Why Bill Gates Still Doesn't Get the Net." *Salon* Mar. 1999. 23 July 2001 <http://www.salon.com/21st/books/ 1999/03/ cov_30books.html>.

Professional Web Site:
EyeWire Studios. Grand Prairie, TX. April 1999. 19 Aug. 1999 <http://www.eyewire.com>.

A Sample Comparative Essay

The following sample essay is based on the selections by Alan Watts ("Beat Zen, Square Zen, and Zen") and Sigmund Freud ("Typical Dreams") reprinted in Chapter 6 ("The Mind and the Spirit: Understanding the Unknown"). The essay was developed as a result of the discussion of critical reading and rhetorical patterns in the Introduction and the guidelines for "Writing About Great Ideas" in the Appendix. The sample essay is organized as a comparison of the primary ideas presented by Alan Watts and Sigmund Freud and analyzes each in relationship to the other in order to demonstrate the striking similarities between these two methodologies. This essay can serve as an example of the kinds of conversations between the great ideas from past to the present that this anthology is designed to encourage. The rhetorical techniques and primary methods of development are noted in the margin.

East Meets West:
Zen Buddhism and Psychotherapy

Although Zen and psychotherapy are each a characteristic expression of Eastern and Western thought, respectively, the similarities between the two greatly outweigh the differences. In general, psychotherapy and Zen are concerned with methods of helping us to fulfill our capacities and to adjust to our environments. In order to appreciate these deep similarities, we must become familiar with their basic precepts, tenets, and concepts.

Thesis: A Factual claim of resemblance

Zen, a sect of Mahayana Buddhism that originated in China in the thirteenth century, claims to transmit the spirit or essence of Buddha (which consists in experiencing the enlightenment [*satori*] that Buddha possessed). All sects of Zen believe in mind-to-mind instruction from master to disciple, for the purpose of finding spiritual realization in daily work. In Zen, the teacher is not a teacher in the Western sense nor is there rote learning, memorizing, or the shaping of behavior.

Description

Zen is actually a way of life that involves a resolution of the struggle between the individual and the environment through an experience called enlightenment (*satori*) where the self becomes identified with the world.

Definition of key term

Alan Watts believes that "in Zen the *satori* experience of awakening to our 'original inseparability' with the universe seems, however elusive, always just round the corner" (837). From this and similar descriptions

Quotation

742

one can infer that *satori* brings a joy, a feeling of one-ness with all things, and a heightened sense of reality which cannot be adequately translated into the language of the everyday world.

When we turn to psychotherapy we discover a program designed to treat all forms of suffering in which emotional factors play a part. Sigmund Freud was one of the first to observe the relationship between emotionally-charged, damaging experiences in childhood and later mental illness. Often the most significant clue was provided by the patient's dreams, as Freud observed in "Typical Dreams': "The connection in which such dreams [of nakedness] appear during my analyses of neurotics proves beyond a doubt that a memory of the dreamer's earliest childhood lies at the foundation of the dream" (753). The theory and practice of psychoanalysis grew out of these discoveries and greatly influenced the subsequent development of psychotherapy. Psychotherapy is essentially a process of re-education, both emotionally and intellectually, through which the patient develops better patterns of adjusting to life. The therapist tries to bring about a reconciliation between the individual's feelings and the existing social norms and helps the individual to be self-sufficient without being in conflict with the environment.

Transition

Example

Definition

From Freud's essay, we can infer that the basic method used in psychotherapy is to "train" the conscious mind to perceive distortions embedded in the unconscious and to relinquish these fictions. For example, Freud led his patients to see that their dreams in which their siblings died did not reflect their present feelings but rather were surviving wishes from childhood ("the wishes represented as fulfilled in dreams are not always current wishes" [755]).

Process Analysis

Example

This realization (or insight) released patients from their feelings of guilt. Effective insight is not thinking, but is rather the experience of seeing something as being new and yet as if one had always known it. Authentic therapeutic insight is sudden, like *satori*. It arrives without being premediated or being forced and cannot be adequately translated into words.

Comparison/contrast

As with psychotherapy, the practice of Zen not only leads to seeing into the nature of one's own being, but also liberates energies that are in ordinary circumstances distorted. It is the object of Zen, therefore, to prevent us from becoming mentally ill.

According to Watts, "Zen is above all the liberation of the mind from conventional thought, and this is something utterly different from rebellion against convention, on the one hand, or adapting foreign conventions, on the other" (840).

In summary, Zen and psychoanalysis strive to eliminate unreal perceptions in order to lead the follower to experience a form of enlightenment (or "insight"). Both emphasize the aim of well-being, rather than just freedom from illness. Freud's aim, like that of the Zen masters, was to free man from himself.   *Conclusion*

Psychotherapy as Freud envisaged it is a method to help us fulfill our capacities and adjust ourselves to the environment in the most natural and comfortable manner possible. Its goal is to free the individual from the pain and torture suffered as a result of inner conflicts and guilt. Zen, on the other hand, is a technique designed to achieve enlightenment and spiritual freedom. Thus, these two methods of gaining insight into one's own nature are actually quite close despite the many differences in the language, time, history and culture of those who articulated the original concepts of these great ideas.   *Re-statement of thesis*

CREDITS

Diane Ackerman, "The Social Sense" from *A Natural History of the Senses*. Copyright © 1990 by Diane Ackerman. Reprinted with the permission of Random House, Inc.

James Baldwin, excerpt from "My Dungeon Shook: Letter to My Nephew on the One Hundredth Anniversary of the Emancipation" from *The Fire Next Time* (New York: The Dial Press, 1963). Copyright © 1963, 1962 by James Baldwin, copyright renewed. Reprinted with the permission of The James Baldwin Estate.

Simone de Beauvoir, "The Married Woman" from *The Second Sex*, translated by H.M. Parshley. Copyright 1952 and renewed © 1980 by Alfred A. Knopf, Inc. Reprinted with the permission of Alfred A. Knopf, a division of Random House, Inc.

John Berger, Chapter 7 from *Ways of Seeing*. Copyright © 1972 by John Berger. Reprinted with the permission of Viking Penguin, a division of Viking Penguin, a division of Penguin Putnam Inc.

The Bhagavad Gita, excerpts from *The Bhagavad Gita: A New Translation* by K. W. Bolle. Copyright © 1979 by The Regents of the University of California. Reprinted with the permission of the University of California Press.

Buddha, "The Enlightenment of the Buddha" from *Buddhist Texts Through the Ages*, edited by Edward Conze. Copyright © 1995 by Muriel Conze. Reprinted with the permission of Oneworld Publications.

Maurizio Chierici, "The Man from Hiroshima" from *Granta* 22 (Autumn 1987). Reprinted with the permission of the author.

R. G. Collingwood, "What Is History?" from *The Idea of History*. Reprinted with the permission of Oxford University Press, Ltd.

Clarence Darrow, "The Myth of the Soul" from *The Forum* (October 1928). Reprinted with the permission of the Clarence Darrow Estate.

Agnes De Mille, "Pavlova" from *Dance to the Piper: Memoirs of the Ballet* (Boston: Little, Brown and Company, 1952). Copyright 1952, 1953 and renewed © 1979, 1980 by Agnes De Mille. Reprinted with the permission of Harold Ober Associates, Inc.

Gayatari Devi and Santha Rama Rau, "A Visit to Baroda" from *A Princess Remembers: The Memories of the Maharani of Jaipur*. Copyright © 1992. Reprinted with the permission of Rupa & Company, New Delhi.

Sergei Eisenstein, "The Cinematographic Principle and the Ideogram" (including figures) from *Film Form*, edited and translated by Jay Leyda. Copyright 1949 by Harcourt, Inc. and renewed © 1977 by Jay Leyda. Reprinted with the permission of Harcourt, Inc.

Christopher Evans, "The Revolution Begins" from *The Micro Millennium*. Copyright © 1979 by Christopher Evans. Reprinted with the permission of Viking Penguin, a division of Penguin Putnam Inc. and Victor Gollancz, Ltd.

Gustav Flaubert, "Letters to Louise Colete" from *The Selected Letters of Gustav Flaubert*, translated and edited by Francis Steegmuller (New York: Farrar, Straus and Giroux, 1953). Copyright 1953 and renewed © 1981 by Francis Steegmuller. Reprinted with the permission of McIntosh & Otis.

Anne Frank, excerpt from *Anne Frank: The Diary of a Young Girl, The Definitive Edition*, edited by Otto H. Frank and Mirjam Pressler, translated by Susan Massotty. Copyright © 1995 by Doubleday, a division of Random House, Inc. Reprinted with the permission of the publishers.

Bill Gates, excerpt from *The Road Ahead*. Originally published in *Newsweek* (November 27, 1995). Copyright © 1995 by William H. Gates III. Reprinted with the permission of Viking Penguin, a division of Penguin Putnam Inc.

Oscar Handlin, excerpt from "The Crossing" in *The Uprooted*, Second Enlarged Edition. Copyright © 1951, 1973 by Oscar Handlin. Reprinted with the permission of Little, Brown and Company (Inc.).

Arthur D. Hasler and James A. Larsen, "The Homing Salmon" from *Scientific American* (August 1955). Copyright © 1955 by Scientific American, Inc. All rights reserved. Reprinted with the permission of the publishers.

Constance Holden, "Identical Twins Reared Apart" from *Science* 207, no. 4437 (March 21, 1980). Copyright © 1980 by American Association for the Advancement of Science.

INDEX